COMING TO GRIPS WITH

GENESIS

BIBLICAL AUTHORITY AND THE AGE OF THE EARTH

Terry Mortenson, Ph.D.

Thane H. Ury, Ph.D.

Editors

First printing: October 2008
Second printing: April 2009

ISBN-13: 978-0-89051-548-8
ISBN-10: 0-89051-548-4
Library of Congress Number: 2008935776

Cover by Farewell Communications

Printed in the United States of America

Please visit our website for other great titles:
www.masterbooks.net

For information regarding author interviews,
please contact the publicity department at (870) 438-5288.

Master
Books
A Division of New Leaf Publishing Group

Contents

Foreword — *Henry M. Morris* 5

Foreword — *John MacArthur* 9

Prologue 15

1. The Church Fathers on Genesis, the Flood, and the
   Age of the Earth — *James R. Mook* 23

2. A Brief Overview of the Exegesis of Genesis 1–11:
   Luther to Lyell — *David W. Hall* 53

3. "Deep Time" and the Church's Compromise:
   Historical Background — *Terry Mortenson* 79

4. Is Nature the 67th Book of the Bible? — *Richard L. Mayhue* 105

5. Contemporary Hermeneutical Approaches to Genesis 1–11
   — *Todd S. Beall* 131

6. The Genre of Genesis 1:1–2:3: What Means This Text?
   — *Steven W. Boyd* 163

7. Can Deep Time Be Embedded in Genesis?
   — *Trevor Craigen* 193

8. A Critique of the Framework Interpretation of the
   Creation Week — *Robert V. McCabe* 211

9. Noah's Flood and Its Geological Implications
   — *William D. Barrick* 251

10. Do the Genesis 5 and 11 Genealogies Contain Gaps?
    — *Travis R. Freeman* 283

11. Jesus' View of the Age of the Earth — *Terry Mortenson* 315

12. Apostolic Witness to Genesis Creation and the Flood
    — *Ron Minton* 347

13. Whence Cometh Death? A Biblical Theology of Physical
Death and Natural Evil — *James Stambaugh* 373

14. Luther, Calvin, and Wesley on the Genesis of Natural Evil:
Recovering Lost Rubrics for Defending a *Very Good* Creation
— *Thane H. Ury*..399

Epilogue 425

Appendices

A Biographical Tribute to Dr. John C. Whitcomb Jr.
— *Paul J. Scharf*..437

Affirmations and Denials Essential to a Consistent
(Biblical) Worldview 453

Recommended Resources 459

Contributors to the Book 465

Subject Index 469

Name Index 475

Scripture Index..479

Foreword

Dr. Henry M. Morris

A volume such as this is long overdue and very much needed in the world of evangelical theology. And it is singularly appropriate that it be dedicated to my long-time friend and associate, Dr. John Whitcomb. I consider it a privilege to write a foreword endorsing the book and encouraging Christians everywhere to read it and use it in their own ministries and witness for the Lord. It is especially recommended that evangelical pastors and Bible professors in seminaries and Bible colleges carefully consider its evidences and arguments. Compromise on issues related to creation and primeval history has been much too common among Christian leaders. John Whitcomb, for nearly 50 years, has seemed almost like a voice crying in the wilderness, seeking to call his theological brethren back to the clear biblical teachings on these great themes. But now they *are* coming back, and the authors of the chapters in this book give good reasons why.

It has long seemed anomalous to me, as a professional scientist and non-professional Bible reader, that the modern revival of literal biblical creationism (the term I prefer to "young-earth creationism") has been led mostly by scientists rather than theologians. The book *The Genesis Flood* published in 1961, for example, contained more scientific discussion than biblical. The Creation Research Society was formed in 1963 as an organization of creationist scientists, and there has been a great proliferation of creationist organizations and ministries since that time; these have all been mainly staffed by scientists. Many other books on "creation-science" have followed, again written mostly by scientists.

It is true that there are many good scientific evidences pointing to special creation, a young earth, and the global Flood, and these have been persuasively advanced by creationist scientists in debates, seminars, and conferences for many years and with great results. But the *compelling* and *definitive* evidences are biblical, not scientific. Science and the scientific method do support creation, but can never either prove creation or disprove evolution. Nor can it determine the age of the earth or prove that there was a worldwide deluge in the prehistoric past.

The Bible is explicitly clear on these issues, however. There is not even a hint of evolution or the long ages implied by evolution in the Bible. Neither is there any biblical intimation that the Genesis Flood was a local Flood or a tranquil Flood, as theological theories that compromise with evolution would require. One does not have to be a theologian or Bible scholar to see this. It becomes quite evident to anyone who simply reads the Bible and believes it to be the inerrant Word of God.

But why don't most theologians see this? Especially evangelical theologians and pastors trained in evangelical seminaries? That has been the anomaly. They all profess to believe the Bible as the inspired Word of God, and that is clearly what the Bible records.

Yet for a long time even orthodox, conservative, evangelical seminaries have been teaching their students to accommodate evolution — or at least the long ages of evolution — in their worldviews. They have used the gap theory or the day/age theory or even the highly ambiguous framework theory to try to do this.

But these don't work biblically and are unnecessary scientifically. I realize that the underlying motive in these compromise views has been to defend the gospel and win people to Christ in spite of the predominance of secularism in our society. But they certainly are not necessary. Seminaries do not usually include much science in their curricula, but the general feeling has been that since "science" has proved evolution and the geological ages to have occurred, these concepts *must* be incorporated somehow in our theologies, no matter how much we have to distort or "spiritualize" Genesis to do so.

I realize that the scientific establishment is still strongly committed to evolutionism, even though there are now literally thousands of what they call "young-earth creationists" who are fully credentialed scientists. The leading scientific journals and even most newspapers refuse to publish creationist articles and the scientific societies are all dominated by evolutionists. Their leaders vigorously oppose including creationism (or even the mention of any anti-evolution evidences) in the public schools. They repeat the mantra, "Creation is religion, evolution is science" over and over whenever the question comes up.

All this seems to intimidate most theologians to such an extent that true literal biblical creationism has long been taught almost as rarely in Christian seminaries as it has in state universities.

But evangelical theology ought to be governed by the Word of God rather than the pronouncements of scientists. That is why this volume is so timely and so necessary. The authors of these chapters are fully qualified to write on this subject from a biblical and theological perspective, and they have shown unequivocally that God's Word teaches special creation, a young earth, a worldwide Flood, and the God-centered worldview in general. For all who really believe in biblical inerrancy and perspicuity, these studies should settle the matter once and for all.

They won't do so, however, for secular evolutionists. The evolutionary worldview will almost certainly continue to dominate the world as a whole; in fact, biblical prophecy would indicate that this will be the case. But that does not justify evangelical compromise. We should "*let God be true, but every man a liar*" if it comes to that (Rom. 3:4; KJV). It is His Word that will govern at the judgment seat of Christ, not that of "science."

As a matter of fact, there is no real scientific evidence for evolution anyhow. This has been amply demonstrated in the writings of many creationist scientists. No one has ever observed any genuine evolution taking place (macro-evolution, that is) in the thousands of years of recorded history — so it is certainly not a part of *observational* science (and real science should involve observation and repetition).

Furthermore, despite certain disputable claims, no one has ever demonstrated an authentic evolutionary transitional series among all the billions of fossils preserved in the sedimentary rocks of the earth's crust. So evolution did not occur in the past either, as far as the evidence shows.

In fact, evolution on any significant scale seems impossible scientifically. The law of entropy expresses the universal principle of decrease in organized complexity — certainly not molecules-to-man increase in complexity!

These truths are abundantly documented in the books and articles of many qualified scientists who are creationists. Theologians who think otherwise have not really studied these writings as they should.

In reality, evolutionism is a religion — not science at all. It is a belief system, attempting to explain the existence of all things without God. It might as well be called the religion of atheistic humanism, or the religion of the coming Antichrist. There is certainly no good reason for theologians or pastors or Bible teachers in general to defer to it or compromise with it any longer. "*Preach the word*" was Paul's closing admonition to young pastor Timothy (2 Tim. 4:2; KJV). The Word as it truly is, not some compromise with modern "*science falsely so called*" (1 Tim. 6:20; KJV).

That is also true with respect to the age of the earth and the global Flood. Creationist sciences have pointed out literally scores of worldwide natural processes that intimate that the earth is much too young for real evolution to have taken place. The recent RATE Project, carried out by scientists from the Institute for Creation Research and the Creation Research Society, have even shown that radioisotope time measurements (based on such processes as uranium decay and radiocarbon decay) indicate a young earth. Until now, these radiometric systems have been offered as clinching "proofs" for "deep time" and an old earth operating according to naturalistic, uniformitarian processes. But that "proof" cannot justifiably be used any longer.

The biblical record (especially 2 Pet. 3:3–6) makes it clear that uniformitarianism is a completely invalid premise when applied to events before or during the Genesis Flood. This premise, however, is exactly the basis on which the vast structure of the geologic column and the assumed geological ages has been erected.

Now, however, a growing number of geologists — though still committed to evolutionary naturalism — are abandoning uniformitarianism. They recognize the fact that practically every geologic formation of any size and significance was formed in at least some kind of local "catastrophe" — not slowly and gradually over a long period of time. That is, uniformitarianism as a guiding principle in geological interpretation ("the present is the key to the past," they used to say) is being replaced by "neo-catastrophism."

Since it is generally recognized that there is no worldwide "time gap" in the geologic column, and since every significant unit in the column must have been formed rapidly and catastrophically, the necessary scientific conclusion ought to be that the entire column must have been formed rapidly and catastrophically, without any significant interruption. There are many other scientific indications that the global deluge did indeed occur.

None of this is real proof, of course. As Christians, we should not be looking to geology for our ultimate answers anyway. The only firm proof is that which has been recorded in the Word of God. For those who really believe the Bible to be the inspired and inerrant Word of God, that should be sufficient. But apparently it has not been sufficient for many evangelical theologians, who have labored mightily to explain the Bible records in some way that can accommodate the geological ages and a multi-billion-year age for the earth.

That stratagem will not work anymore, at least not for anyone who reads this book. The chapters of this book show convincingly that the biblical record is founded on recent creation and a worldwide Flood. Creationist scientists are increasingly demonstrating that true science supports this revelation. Like it or not, that's how it is!

John Whitcomb has been stressing this great truth for many years. It is wonderfully fitting that so many other outstanding Bible scholars are now convinced of this too and have dedicated this splendid symposium to him and his time-tested, Bible-honoring teaching ministry.

— Henry M. Morris
June 2005

Editors' Note

After a short series of strokes, on February 25, 2006, at the age of 87, Dr. Henry Morris (1918–2006) went to be with the Lord he loved and served so faithfully for so many decades. Ask any scholar who has delved into the central issues of literal biblical creationism, and the names John Whitcomb and Henry Morris immediately spring to mind as icons in the movement. Both editors were greatly influenced by many of Morris's more than 60 books (including *The Genesis Flood*, co-authored with Dr. John Whitcomb in 1961) and his other writings. He was a godly, gracious scholar and scientist who carefully expounded and tenaciously defended the truth of God's Word from the very first verse. All modern young-earth creationists stand on the shoulders of this giant of the faith. Although some of the chapters of this book were not done at the time of his death, he was confident from his knowledge of many of the authors that he could recommend the book to readers. We are honored to have his preface for this volume.

Foreword

John MacArthur

The apostle Paul closed his first epistle to Timothy by urging the young pastor to guard the deposit of truth that had been entrusted to him, "avoiding the profane and idle babblings and contradictions of what is falsely called knowledge" (1 Tim. 6:20–21). In the King James Version, the text famously speaks of "*science* falsely so called."

Over the course of human history, all kinds of speculative ideas have been falsely labeled "science" and mistakenly accepted as true and reliable knowledge by otherwise brilliant people. The now-discredited dogmas of older scientific theories are numerous — and in some cases laughable. They include *alchemy* (the medieval belief that other base metals could be transmuted into gold); *phrenology* (the Victorian belief that the shape of one's skull reflects character traits and mental capacity); *astrology* (the pagan belief that human destiny is determined by the motions of celestial bodies); and *abiogenesis* (the long-standing belief that living organisms are spontaneously generated by decaying organic substances). All those false beliefs were deemed credible as "science" by the leading minds of their times.

Consider just one of those — abiogenesis. Popularly known as "spontaneous generation," this idea has long been, and continues to be, one of the archetypal expressions of "science falsely so called." It is also one of the most persistent of all demonstrably pseudoscientific fictions. The notion that aphids arise naturally from dew on plant leaves, mold is generated automatically by aging bread, and maggots are spontaneously begotten by rotting meat was more or less deemed self-evident by most of humanity's brightest intellects[1] from the time of Aristotle until 1861, when Louis Pasteur conclusively proved that non-living matter cannot spawn life on its own.

Unless otherwise noted, all Scripture in this chapter is from the NKJV of the Bible.

1. Alexander Ross, an early 17th-century Scottish writer and intellectual, harshly criticized Sir Thomas Browne for questioning the dogma of spontaneous generation. Under the heading "Mice and other vermin bred of putrefaction, even in men's bodies," he wrote: "He doubts whether mice can be procreated of putrefaction. So he may doubt whether in cheese and timber worms are generated; Or if Betels and wasps in cowes dung; Or if

It is one of the great ironies of scientific history that the first edition of Charles Darwin's *On the Origin of Species* was published exactly two years before Pasteur's famous experiments proved that life cannot arise spontaneously from non-living matter. The publication of Darwin's book marked the apotheosis of evolutionary theory, and it was rooted in the basic presupposition that under the right circumstances, life can spring on its own from non-living matter. In other words, two years before abiogenesis was scientifically debunked, it was in effect canonized as the central dogma of modern secular belief about the origins of life. The discovery that fleas don't magically form out of decomposing dander on the backs of dirty dogs did not dissuade most in the scientific world from embracing the theory that all life in the universe arose by itself out of nothing. The belief that life spontaneously came from non-life remains to this day the great unexplained (albeit easily disprovable) assumption underlying the dogma of evolution.

The irony of that is utterly lost on many in the scientific community today, where evolution has become an article of faith — *unshakable* faith, it turns out.

Evolutionists have conveniently "solved" the problem of abiogenesis by repeatedly moving their estimates of the earth's age backward toward infinity. Given enough time, it seems, *anything* is possible. Trying desperately to keep the biblical concept of eternity at bay, evolutionists have thus devised an alternative kind of infinitude. Every time a challenge to current evolutionary theory arises, geologists and astronomers dutifully tack billions and billions of eons onto their theories about the earth's age, adding however many ancient epochs are deemed necessary for some new impossibility to be explained.

In 2001, I wrote a book dealing with Genesis 1–3. I began that book's introduction by suggesting that naturalism has become the dominant religion of contemporary secular society. "*Religion* is exactly the right word to describe naturalism," I wrote. "The entire philosophy is built on a faith-based premise. Its basic presupposition — a rejection of everything supernatural — requires a giant leap of faith. And nearly all its supporting theories must be taken by faith as well."[2] Here, then, is a classic example of what I was talking about: the typical evolutionist's *starting* point is this notion that life arose spontaneously from inanimate matter sometime in eternity past. That requires not merely the willful suspension of what we know for certain about the origins of life and the impossibility of abiogenesis — but also enough deliberate gullibility to believe that moving-target estimates of the earth's antiquity can sufficiently answer all the problems and contradictions sheer naturalism poses.

---

butterflies, locusts, grasshoppers, shel-fish, snails, eeles, and such like, be procreated of putrefied matter, which is apt to receive the form of that creature to which it is by the formative power disposed. *To question this, is to question Reason, Sense, and Experience:* If he doubts of this, let him go to *Egypt,* and there he will finde the fields swarming with mice begot of the mud of [the Nile]." *Arcana Microcosmi,* (London: Newcomb, 1652), book 2, chapter 10, p. 156.

2. John MacArthur, *The Battle for the Beginning* (Nashville, TN: W Publishing Group, 2001), p. 11.

Meanwhile, in the popular media, evolutionary doctrine and ever-expanding notions of prehistory are being promoted with all the pious zeal of the latest religious sect. Watch the Internet forums, programs on the Discovery Channel, interviews and articles published in the mass media, school textbooks, and books aimed at lay readers — and what you will usually see is raw assertions, demagoguery, intimidation, and ridicule (especially when the subjects of biblical theism and the Genesis account of creation are raised). But question the dogma that all life evolved from a single spontaneously generated cell, point out that the universe is full of evidence for intelligent design, or demand the kind of proof for evolutionary origins that would ordinarily pass scientific muster, and the ardent evolutionist will simply dismiss you as a heretic or a bigot of the worst stripe. What they are tacitly acknowledging is that as far as they are concerned, evolution is a doctrine that must be received with implicit faith, not something that can be scientifically demonstrated. After all, the claims of true *science* can always be investigated, observed, reproduced, tested, and proved in the laboratory. So to insist that evolution and so-called "deep time" doctrines must be accepted without question is really just a tacit admission that these are not scientific ideas at all.

Consider these quotations from typical evolutionist writers:

- No biologist today would think of submitting a paper entitled "New evidence for evolution"; it simply has not been an issue for a century.[3]

- It is time for students of the evolutionary process, especially those who have been misquoted and used by the creationists, to state clearly that evolution is a *fact,* not theory. . . . All present forms of life arose from ancestral forms that were different. Birds arose from nonbirds and humans from nonhumans. No person who pretends to any understanding of the natural world can deny these facts.[4]

- Here is what separates real scientists from the pseudoscientists of the school of intelligent design. . . . One thing all real scientists agree upon is the fact of evolution itself. It is a fact that we are cousins of gorillas, kangaroos, starfish, and bacteria. Evolution is as much a fact as the heat of the sun. It is not a theory, and for pity's sake, let's stop confusing the philosophically naive by calling it so. Evolution is a fact.[5]

But as those statements themselves show, evolution is a dogma, not a demonstrable "fact." I stand by the position I took in *The Battle for the Beginning*: "Belief in evolutionary theory is a matter of sheer faith. [It is] as much a religion as any theistic worldview."[6]

3. Douglas J. Futuyma, *Evolutionary Biology,* 2nd ed., (Boston, MA: Sinauer Associates, 1986), p. 15.
4. R.C. Lewontin, "Evolution/Creation Debate: A Time for Truth," *Bioscience* (1981): 31: p. 559.
5. Richard Dawkins, "The Illusion of Design," *Natural History* (November 2005): p. 53.
6. MacArthur, *The Battle for the Beginning*, p. 12.

I'll go even further: *science* cannot speak with any authority about when the universe began, how it came into being, or how life originated on earth. Science by definition deals with what can be observed, tested, measured, and investigated by empirical means. Scientific data by definition are facts that can be demonstrated by controlled, repeatable experiments that always yield consistent results. The beginning of the universe by its very nature falls outside the realm of scientific investigation.

To state the case plainly: there is no scientific way to explain creation. *No one* but God actually observed creation. It did not happen by any uniform, predictable, observable, repeatable, fixed, or natural laws. It was not a natural event or a series of natural events. The initial creation of matter was an instantaneous, monumental, inexplicable miracle — the exact opposite of a "natural" phenomenon. And the formation of the universe was a brief series of supernatural events that simply cannot be studied or explained by science. There are no natural processes involved in creation; the act of creation cannot be repeated; it cannot be tested; and therefore naturalistic theories purporting to explain the origin and age of the universe are unverifiable.

In other words, creation is a theological issue, not a scientific one. Scripture is our only credible source of information about creation, because God Himself was the only eyewitness to the event. We can either believe what He says or reject it. But no Christian should ever imagine that what we believe about the origin of the universe is merely a secondary, nonessential, or incidental matter. It is, after all, the very starting point of God's self-revelation.

In fact, in its profound brevity, Genesis 1:1 is a very simple, clear, and unequivocal account of how the universe, the earth, and everything on the earth came to be: "In the beginning God created the heavens and the earth." That is not an ambiguous statement. Until Darwinian evolution undertook a campaign to co-opt the story of creation and bring it into the realm of naturalistic "science" — and especially before modernist skepticism began to seep into the Church — no one who claimed to be a Christian was the least bit confused by the Genesis account.

Christians should not be intimidated by dogmatic naturalism. We do not need to invent a new interpretation of Genesis every time some geologist or astronomer declares that the universe must be older than he previously thought. Nor should we imagine that legitimate science poses any threat to the truth of Scripture. Above all, we must not seek ways to circumvent the clear meaning of God's Word, compromise our trust in the Creator, or continually yield ground to every new theory of falsely so-called science. That is precisely what Paul was warning Timothy about.

Sadly, it seems evolutionary thinking and qualms about the Genesis account of creation have reached epidemic levels among professing Christians in recent decades. Too many Christian leaders, evangelical schools, and Bible commentators have been willing to set aside the biblical account of a relatively young earth in order to accommodate the ever-changing estimates of naturalistic geologists and astronomers. They have thrown away sound hermeneutical principles — at least in the early chapters of Genesis — to accommodate the latest theories of evolution. When I encounter people who think evolutionary doctrine trumps the biblical account of creation, I like to ask them where their belief in the Bible kicks in. Is it in chapter 3, where the Fall of Adam and original sin are accounted for? In chapters 4–5, where early human history is chronicled? In chapters 6–8, with the record of the Flood? In chapter 11, with the Tower of Babel? Because if you bring naturalism and its presuppositions to the early chapters of Genesis, it is just a short step to denying *all* the miracles of Scripture — including the Resurrection of Christ. If we want to make science the test of biblical truth rather than vice versa, why would it not make just as much sense to question the biblical record of the resurrection as it does to reject the Genesis account? But "if Christ is not risen, your faith is futile; you are still in your sins! . . . If in this life only we have hope in Christ, we are of all men the most pitiable" (1 Cor. 15:17–19).

The contributors to this volume all take Genesis seriously and accept its account of a relatively young earth. Together they have given us a profoundly helpful resource on the subject. Whether you are a lay person seeking to understand how Scripture dovetails with true science, a seasoned pastor studying Genesis and grappling with conflicting opinions about the timing and duration of creation, or a scholar looking for credible resources explaining the young-earth view, you will be greatly edified by these essays.

It is a distinct and special privilege to commend this volume in honor of Dr. John C. Whitcomb's teaching ministry. He is a pioneer and hero in the field of biblical creationism who fully understands that the origin of the universe is a theological question which is settled for us by *Scripture*. We salute him for his substantial preaching, teaching, and writing labors over the past six decades. He has faithfully upheld the truth about Jesus Christ, that "All things were made through Him, and without Him nothing was made that was made" (John 1:3) and "by Him all things were created that are in heaven and that are on earth, visible and invisible. . . . All things were created through Him and for Him. And He is before all things, and in Him all things consist" (Col. 1:16–17) and "For in six days the LORD made the heavens and the earth, the sea, and all that is in them" (Exod. 20:11).

I am delighted to participate with many of Dr. Whitcomb's former students and friends who joined together for this tribute because of their common commitment to understanding that the Bible clearly and confidently teaches creation *ex nihilo* in such a way as to make the idea of a "young earth" not only reasonable, but certain.

— John MacArthur
President
The Master's College and Seminary

Prologue

Having lectured collectively in 23 different countries on the subject of creation, the editors can attest to the robust international interest in this vital topic. Origins-related concerns have enjoyed a healthy resurgence in recent years. This is partly due to the growth of the creationist and Intelligent Design movements. But another key factor has been news items touting the latest missing link, some newly "evolved" strain of bird flu, traces of water on Mars, or any number of alleged confirmations of Darwinism. Add to this steady media barrage the not-so-subtle hegemony of science taken for granted in academia, and believers are constantly wrestling to balance faith and science.

More and more evangelicals are realizing that the creation-evolution controversy is every bit as much about philosophical assumptions as it is about empirical evidence. Even more importantly, despite the frequently heard assertion that the age of the earth is a non-issue, there has been an awakening to the idea that it has serious theological implications. The age of the earth controversy has been brewing for some time, and believers across the globe are searching for answers like never before.[1]

A number of leading evangelical authors have quite appropriately urged Christians to fortify the philosophical foundations undergirding their Christian worldview. Yet many of these same writers seldom address the age of the earth. For example, David Noebel examines various worldviews in relation to theology, philosophy, ethics, biology, psychology, sociology, law, politics, economics, and history. But he leaves geology and cosmology unvetted, despite the significant role of these disciplines in undermining a biblical worldview.[2] In *Worldviews in*

---

1. For example, Joseph A. Pipa and David W. Hall, *Did God Create in Six Days?* (Taylors, SC: Southern Presbyterian Press, 1999); J.P. Moreland and John Mark Reynolds, eds., *Three Views on Creation and Evolution* (Grand Rapids, MI: Zondervan, 1999); David G. Hagiopian, ed., *The Genesis Debate: Three Views on the Days of Creation* (Mission Viejo, CA: Crux Press, 2001); John Ankerberg TV debates (Hugh Ross v. Kent Hovind debate in October 2000, and the 8-part "The Great Debate" series of Ken Ham and Jason Lisle v. Hugh Ross and Walter Kaiser aired in January–February 2006.

2. David A. Noebel, *The Battle for Truth* (Eugene, OR: Harvest House, 2001).

Conflict, Ronald Nash tackles naturalism and the problem of evil, but surprisingly uses little Scripture and totally ignores the Fall.[3] Nash correctly asserts that naturalism is "the major competition" for Christianity in the West, but he says nothing about evolution or deep time, the two dominant pillars propping up naturalist philosophy. James Sire's *The Universe Next Door* helpfully compares Christianity to the other major worldviews. But in the first three editions he had almost no discussion of God's curse on the creation and no mention of the Flood, both of which are critically important for the question of the age of the earth.[4]

Other theologians and apologists contend that the age of the earth is a non-issue, with the usual claim being that it is too divisive (the implied charge is that young-earthers are the polemical culprits), or that it is an impediment to those considering the truth claims of Christianity. In a paper delivered at the International Council on Biblical Inerrancy (ICBI), Gleason Archer even made the claim that young-earth creationists are "undermining the inerrancy of Scripture."[5] But creationist signers of ICBI's Articles of Affirmation and Denial wonder why this is the case, since they seem to be in the distinct minority when firmly adhering to Article XII, which states that inerrantists "deny that scientific hypotheses about earth history may properly be used to overturn the teaching of Scripture on creation and the flood."[6]

A more serious accusation against young-earth creationists is that we are in some manner denying reality. Gleason Archer and Hugh Ross go so far as to say that young-earth creationism "forces a gnostic-like theology — a belief that the physical realm is illusory and that only the spiritual realm is real," and that "ultimately this [young-earth] view denies the Bible itself."[7] The readers of this volume will have to decide if that assessment itself matches reality.

In their apologetics text, Norman Geisler and Peter Bocchino urge young-earthers to "stop the infighting over the question of age" because "many sincerely honest and intellectually gifted scholars" argue for an old earth.[8] While sincerity,

---

3. Ronald H. Nash, *Worldviews in Conflict* (Grand Rapids, MI: Zondervan, 1992).

4. James W. Sire, *The Universe Next Door* (Downers Grove, IL: IVPress, 1997, 3rd ed.).

5. Gleason Archer, "A Response to The Trustworthiness of Scripture in Areas Relating to Natural Science," in Earl Radmacher and Robert Preus, eds., *Hermeneutics, Inerrancy and the Bible* (Grand Rapids, MI: Zondervan, 1984), p. 325.

6. "The Chicago Statement on Biblical Inerrancy," in Norman L. Geisler, ed., *Inerrancy* (Grand Rapids, MI: Zondervan, 1980), p. 496.

7. Gleason L. Archer and Hugh Ross, "The Day-Age View," in Hagopioan, ed., *The Genesis Debate*, p. 128–131. See also, Andy Butcher, "He Sees God in the Stars," *Charisma* (June 2003), p. 38–44; and Hugh Ross, *Creation and Time* (Colorado Springs, CO: NavPress, 1994), p. 118.

8. Norman Geisler and Peter Bocchino, *Unshakeable Foundations* (Bloomington, MN: Bethany House, 2001), p. 175, fn. 6. It could well be asked why the same sense of tolerance was not extended to Murray Harris, Clark Pinnock, John Sanders, or various annihilationists whom Geisler has harshly criticized over the years; men who may be

honesty, and intellectual giftedness are crucial qualities for an apologist to have, they are certainly no guarantor of scientific truth, much less of correct biblical thinking.

In 1982, the editors of *Christianity Today* expressed their concerns about the age of the earth controversy by contending:

> The creation scientists who defend a recent earth may well be carrying on the battle at too broad a front. It is not essential to firm commitment to an infallible or inerrant Bible that one must also deny the validity of the entire geological timetable. Or insist that the universe is of recent origin.[9]

But inerrantists who want to guard against carrying on the battle on too *narrow* a front would ask: "If God's Word is sufficiently clear on the age of the earth and universe, can a devoted follower of Christ really be expected to adopt the evolutionary time scale created by unbelieving scientists?" In uncritically referring to "*the* geological timetable" as though it enjoyed the same empirical status as the periodic table, we cannot help but think that these editors of *Christianity Today* have already unconsciously elevated the authority of geological theory over Scripture. As will be shown, the deep-time geological timetable is actually an interpretive philosophical construct.

There are two other problems with this *CT* claim. The first is the apparent assumption that creationists do not have a sufficient understanding of geology. This reflects an ignorance of the vast amount of research done by creationist geologists.[10] But second, and far more serious, is the door to further compromise that this kind of thinking opens. Will those who think that homosexuality and adultery are condemned in Scripture, be muzzled by the mere rhetorical

---

mistaken, but nonetheless personify "sincerely honest and intellectually gifted scholars." We wish Geisler would subject the case put forth by old-earth creationists to the rigorous philosophical and exegetical scrutiny for which he is known and appreciated by so many. In his 2003 explanation for why he resigned from the Evangelical Theological Society, Geisler said he still loved the "organization and that for which it once firmly stood — the total factual inerrancy of the written Word of God." It is interesting that his resignation was due to ETS allowing open theists to retain membership in the society. What makes this ironic is that the exegetical methods of open theists, annihilationists, and deep-time theists are so similar. More importantly, Geisler and Wayne House have said that open theism is a frontal assault on the nature of God, and therefore mandates vigorous confrontation; which is exactly the same motive prompting this present work.

9. Editors, "Of Evolution and Creation and the Space Between," *Christianity Today* 26 (May 7, 1982): p. 13, quoted in J. Kenneth Eakins, "The Relationship of the Bible to Natural Science," *The Proceedings of the Conference on Biblical Inerrancy 1987* (Nashville, TN: Broadman Press, 1987), p. 360.

10. See the recommended resources at the end of this book for geological evidence of a young earth and global Flood.

device that such judgments reject the validity of the entire corpus of modern psychological research? May we still follow our exegetical conscience and maintain that the exodus of Israel happened just as Moses records, or will we be chided for not fully embracing the research of secular and theologically liberal Egyptologists? The word inerrancy as defined by ICBI, and affirmed by most evangelicals, has historic content and limits, and becomes vacuous if it is made to accommodate extrabiblical influences, which upon close examination prove to be anti-biblical. Creationists are saying that a firm commitment to an infallible and innerant Bible should be just that; *firm*, and not tossed to and fro by the latest in a long series of ever-evolving edicts from scientism.

Another manner in which the age of the earth is downplayed is found with Wayne Grudem, who sees the matter as subordinate to weightier doctrines. In his excellent and widely used systematic theology text, Grudem writes that the Bible's teaching on the age of the earth "is really much less important" than the following doctrines: (1) God created the universe out of nothing; (2) creation is distinct from God, yet always dependent on God; (3) God created the universe to show his glory; (4) the universe God created was very good; (5) there will be no final conflict between Scripture and science; and (6) secular theories that deny God as Creator, including Darwinian evolution, are clearly incompatible with belief in the Bible. Grudem then says that earth's age is far less important than two other subjects to be treated later in his text: (7) the creation of the angelic world, and (8) the creation of man in the image of God. [11]

But these statements by Grudem are mere assertions, supported neither by argument nor by biblical evidence. Note that his first point on *creatio ex nihilo* is a sound theological inference based on Scripture rather than an explicit teaching culled from Genesis. Contrast this with the numerous explicit statements about the days of creation (in Genesis and other Bible passages) and the time elapsed since creation in the genealogies of Genesis 5 and 11. Consider also that answers to the question of the age of the earth have a direct bearing to points 3 and 4, both of which fit more naturally within a young-earth view. Furthermore, judging from how much less the Word of God says about most of the matters which Grudem deems more important, compared to the space Scripture gives to time elements in creation, the age of the earth hardly deserves the "lesser status" he suggests.

Grudem is correct to argue that theories that deny God as Creator (including Darwinian evolution) are incompatible with Scripture. But we contend that this claim of incompatibility must assume a literal reading of Genesis 1–2. When God created the first plants, animals, and people, He emphasized ten times that He made these creatures as distinct "kinds," in mature form ready to reproduce "after their kind" (rather than to change from one kind into a different kind). If God's Word is true, then microbe-to-microbiologist evolution is false. But if the Bible is right about this, then is it not creating a double standard when we don't believe

---

11. Wayne Grudem, *Systematic Theology* (Grand Rapids, MI: Zondervan, 1994), p. 289.

what God says about the age of the earth? Why not take the date and duration of creation week just as literally and the order of creation events (the order of which rules out the big bang and the evolutionary geological ages)? And why not assume that the global, world-destroying Flood would have produced a massive amount of lasting geological evidence (e.g., sediment layers, erosional features, lava deposits, and fossils), instead of following Davis Young in adopting a "geologically insignificant" view of the Flood, as Grudem does?[12] This present work suggests compelling exegetical, theological, and historical reasons to take Genesis 1–11 literally; that is, as early Hebrews would have understood Moses' words.

Furthermore, the dominant cosmological theories for the origin of the universe and the earth over millions of years have little need of the "God hypothesis," and thus are just as incompatible with belief in the Bible. When scientific theories stem from anti-biblical philosophical presuppositions (as will be shown later in the case of old-earth geology), should they be given any credence in adjudicating our interpretation of Scripture? Old-earth proponents show little discernable hesitation in asking the Church to tether its exegesis to the assured convictions of conventional geology, inferring that we need to concede what the majority of geologists claim as absolute fact.

But history indicates that nearly all scientific breakthroughs have come from the minority who have been willing to challenge convention. Scientists should be the last to forget that the scientific majority has time and again been proven wrong. And evangelicals should never disregard this important reminder from history, nor doubt that the Semmelweis-reflex is alive and well.[13] Dr. Jeremiah Ostriker, distinguished professor of astrophysical science and former director of the Princeton University Observatory, seems to think a little more humility is needed in the scientific community: "If you look historically, almost all of the models at any given time that people have are wrong. So there's no particular reason why they shouldn't be at this time, and why should scientists be so stupid as to not realize this?"[14]

---

12. Ibid., p. 306–307. Grudem says the Flood was worldwide and "did have a significant impact on the face of the earth." But he does not specify what the geological significance was and clearly indicates that he thinks the vast majority of the sedimentary rocks were formed over millions of years, not by the Flood.

13. For example, the five-time exiled Athanasius almost single-handedly convinced the majority that Arius' view of Christ's nature was wrong; in Luther's day most of the Church was wrong on indulgences and the doctrine of salvation; Galileo's telescope was called a tool of the devil; most 18th-century physicians wrongly thought bleeding cured illness; Wegener's theory of continental drift was at first mocked; and most modern scholars accept Darwinism as fact (though most old-earth creationists do not). Claiming that hand washing would save lives, Ignaz Semmelweis faced ridicule and strong opposition from medical colleagues. As a result, the label "Semmelweis-reflex" was coined to describe the automatic rejection of ideas without giving the slightest thought, inspection, or experiment, simply because it challenges entrenched paradigms.

14. Alan Lightman and Roberta Brawer, eds., *Origins: The Lives and Worlds of Modern*

Whatever happened to the key Reformation principle of *analogia fidei*, by which believers strove for doctrinal truths by comparing Scripture with Scripture? Dare we argue that inspiration extends to jots and tittles, paying meticulous attention to tiny exegetical details in the New Testament, only to suspend this same rigorous analysis when we come to the creation and Flood accounts? Why is the rule of context drilled into the minds of seminary students, only to be arbitrarily suspended when dealing with these two biblical topics? We will contend that that the real smoking pistols behind the debate over the age of the earth are the undermining of biblical authority and renuancing of God's goodness.

But how we approach this conflict speaks to more than just our understanding of the nature of revelation. As will be shown, it goes straight to the heart of how we see the nature of the Creator himself. In warning about dangerous trends within evangelical circles, Geisler makes a point that certainly applies here: "Christians should not tamper with the nature of the eternal God."[15] We could not agree more.

It has been our personal experience that professors at evangelical colleges and seminaries are usually not conversant with the best young-earth creationist arguments. There are a number of scholarly works dealing with specific aspects of the creation versus evolution issue. Sometimes the best treatments are found only in difficult-to-obtain journals or books, which most libraries do not carry. Thus, the editors of this work felt the strong need for a single volume that would present evangelicals with key historical, exegetical, and theological arguments demonstrating that the Bible teaches a recent and literal six-day creation and global catastrophic Flood.

The even larger controlling thesis for this book is that the age of the creation is foundationally and critically important for Christian doctrine. It really does matter what we believe on this issue. To be sure, we are not insisting that a person must be a young-earth creationist to be saved and in a right relationship with God. Faith in Christ alone is sufficient for that. But what we believe on this topic does relate critically to inerrancy, hermeneutics, and Scripture as the final authority in all matters that it addresses. At stake also are our views of death and the character of God, which carry implications for our faith in the eschatological hope of the gospel. The history of the Church's beliefs about Genesis 1–11 should also be of interest to all believers.

No matter where you are in the world, you will find that evolution and deep time are taught as undisputed fact in the schools (at least the universities, if not also in primary and secondary schools), in natural history museums, in science programs on TV, and through national parks, the media, and Hollywood. Christians must have a firm trust in the Word of God and a clear understanding that

---

Cosmologists (Cambridge, MA: Harvard University Press, 1990), p. 262–263.

15. Norman Geisler, *Creating God in the Image of Man?* (Minneapolis, MN: Bethany House, 1997), p. 11. The same apt warning has cogent application throughout the entirety of this present volume.

Satan is extremely clever in sowing seeds of doubt which later lead to a denial of God's Word. "Has God said . . . ?" was quite effective in deceiving Eve, and we must guard against the same tactic today. Only in this way can we stand strong and witness in this world that is so thoroughly indoctrinated with evolutionary thinking. God has spoken — that's not the question; the important question is, are we listening?

In the face of the worldwide challenge of the secular dogmas of evolution and millions of years, and a spirit of appeasement within the Church, may this text help to convince many to believe, proclaim, and defend the truth of Genesis 1–11. This is no arcane debate over trivial matters. Instead, it is all about glorifying the Creator's name and nature, upholding the authority and clarity of His Word, and strengthening His Church for the purpose of bringing to salvation many sinners from every tribe and tongue and people and nation. That is our prayer as you read the following essays.

A word must be said regarding the target readership for this book. Our primary audience is professors and students at Christian colleges and seminaries, hoping that this text will serve as a primary or supplementary text for appropriate courses. However, we constantly had the lay reader in mind in the choice of chapter topics and the editorial process. To that end, we have transliterated and translated the Hebrew and Greek words used in the chapters and in other ways sought to make the writing style amenable to non-scholars. Keeping a high level of scholarly engagement while also remaining lay-friendly was a delicate dual objective, and we leave it to your judgment whether we have struck this happy medium.

Finally, we want our readers to know that we have dedicated this book first to the honor of our Creator, Lord, and Savior, the triune God of the Bible. But we are also dedicating it to the honor of one of His faithful servants, Dr. John C. Whitcomb Jr. Many of the contributing authors to this volume were once Dr. Whitcomb's students. All of the authors are personally indebted to his contributions on this subject.

Dr. Whitcomb's biography at the end of the volume explains that he has not always been a young-earth creationist. His change from old-earth to young-earth came about under the influence of the late Dr. Henry Morris, founder and long-time president of the Institute for Creation Research. This relationship later led to co-authoring the monumental work, *The Genesis Flood* (1961), which launched the modern young-earth creationist movement. Subsequently, Dr. Whitcomb has written several other books defending the literal truth of Genesis.

It has aptly been said that a trailblazer is recognized by the arrows in his back! We are deeply indebted to you, Dr. Whitcomb, for holding firm to your convictions for half a century; especially in light of the accommodationist storms you've had to weather. Few theologians have done as much in expounding and defending young-earth creationism. By teaching these truths to countless students in your seminary courses, lecturing internationally, and authoring engaging texts, you continue to inspire, and your legacy will be rich and lasting. This book is a very modest effort by the contributing authors and editors to say, "Thank you, Dr. Whitcomb, for your winsome and courageous spirit, and your faithful teaching, especially with respect to this great question of origins. You set the gold standard for what godly scholarship should be, and these essays aspire to follow your lead."

— Terry Mortenson,
— Thane Hutcherson Ury
August 26, 2008

Chapter 1

The Church Fathers on Genesis, the Flood, and the Age of the Earth

James R. Mook[1]

Personal Note on Dr. Whitcomb

My first exposure to Dr. Whitcomb came in my Bible college studies and my first church youth ministry when I read The Genesis Flood *(co-authored with Dr. Henry M. Morris). I had been educated in public schools, so I had been taught evolutionary theory — without being exposed to creation science. When I became involved in a church youth program in the 1970s, I wanted high school teens to read and learn about creation science, so they could see its validity and have an intelligent response to science teachers who advocated evolution in their high schools and later, in their colleges and universities. Those teens found Dr. Whitcomb's books especially enlightening. Later, in the 1990s, in my teaching as a seminary professor, my students also found these works illuminating and liberating as they noted Darwinism's unscientific and philosophical presuppositions, and discovered that the geological data are scientifically compatible with the biblical creation and Flood accounts. When I finally met Dr. Whitcomb in recent years, I found him a godly, affable, kind, and precise theologian and apologist, and I was able to personally express to him what I reaffirm here — my deep appreciation for his diligent and courageous work in confronting and refuting evolutionary concepts of the origin and history of the earth, both inside and outside the Church.*

---

1. I am indebted to Thane Ury for his considerable help in getting this chapter into final form.

The Importance of the Church Fathers to the Age Controversy

The opening chapters of Genesis are the most foundational in all of Scripture. Indeed, for the Christian faith, nothing makes lasting sense if these chapters are undermined. Here the foundation of nearly every major Christian theme can be found. This explains in part why the early Church writers dealt so much with these chapters, reminding us in the process that the history of theological development is essentially the history of exegesis.

From the early days of the Church, appeals to patristic exegesis have always played a key role in theological debate and helped to clarify the parameters of orthodoxy. The controversies over Christological, Trinitarian, and canonizing matters were intense, and sometimes took centuries to resolve. But what God-fearing Christian today is not profoundly grateful for those like Athanasius in the early community of faith, who risked even their lives to "contend earnestly for the faith which was once for all delivered to the saints" (Jude 1:3; NKJV).

Fast-forward to our day, where the controversy over the age of the earth continues. There has been a renewal of interests in the Church fathers, and how they handled matters such as the length of the creation days, the age of the earth, and the Genesis Flood. [2] Since their voice on theological matters has always been coveted, it would be expected that, along with a cautious use of their wisdom, there is also a tendency with some to misread the patristic literature. The teachings of the fathers can be just as surely taken out of context, eisegeted, or muffled altogether, as the Scriptures can be.

It is not insignificant that notable authors have recruited some fathers as accepting the idea of deep time. Scholars like William G.T. Shedd believe some in the patristic era taught the day-age theory. Henri Blocher claims Augustine held to a framework type view. Arthur Custance finds a champion of the gap theory in Origen. Such diversity of opinion can be highly confusing to the layperson, and leads us to ask four important questions. First, which specific ancient treatises were these modern scholars using to class the ancients into such post-Darwinian-sounding categories? Second, were there any treatises or resources these modern writers overlooked? Third, if there were overlooked resources, was this innocent oversight due to perhaps consulting only secondary sources? And fourth, if these men were presented with sufficient patrological counter-evidence, would they acknowledge this in subsequent writings? This chapter aims to counter some

---

2. Useful resources on the fathers have been scarce. One bright spot recently has been the massive undertaking, by InterVarsity Press, *The Ancient Christian Commentary on Scripture Project*, general editor, Thomas Oden. This 28-volume series highlights the patristic commentators up to A.D. 749, and really should be on the shelves of every evangelical scholar or Christian who desires to understand the fullness of their heritage. Here we sample what reverence for the Revealer and His revelation looks like, unfettered by the constraints of modernity (cf. note 12 below). The demarcation of A.D. 749 is not arbitrary, but marks the death of John Damascene, which closed the era of the Eastern fathers. The Western fathers are dated by Isidore's death in A.D. 636.

of the misreadings of the fathers, and provide clarity by analyzing the original sources to see if their writings aid and abet modern deep-time theories.

Contemporary Misreadings of the Fathers

Proponents of the day-age view and framework hypothesis claim six-day creationism is of fairly recent vintage, and a reactionary movement against uniformitarian or proto-Darwinian ideas. They propose that prominent early Church exegetes pursued *theological* meaning as of the highest priority (rather than historical meaning), and would not identify with modern young-earth theses. While some may wonder whether their views have any relevance in the current debate, others, such as Hugh Ross, know the value that a theological position has if it can claim the imprimatur of the Church fathers.

Thus, like Shedd, Blocher, and Custance, Ross makes an attempt to buttress his old-earth position with some patristic clout. And four common lines of reasoning seem to link all their proposals. First, these modern old-earth advocates think that at the time when the Church was clarifying and fortifying its creeds, the age of the earth was less vital to the fundamentals of Christianity. Second, it is implied (if not stated), if these God-fearing men from the past (the fathers) felt comfortable with a wide spectrum of exegetical method and hermeneutical conclusions on the age of the cosmos, we should emulate them. Third, they say, we have sufficient patristic confirmation that young-earth creationism was not the position of the Early Church, and definitely not compulsory to classic orthodoxy. And, fourth, when modern scholars invoke Augustine and others as comfortable with deep time, the pivotal premise seems to be that belief in millions of years is not a fallback concession brought on by uniformitarianism, but has always been a position compatible with orthodoxy.

Christians should be aware of the great cloud of witnesses in Church history, and a judicious use of the fathers can be both relevant and edifying.[3] And even though the Christian's highest and final authority should always be Scripture, the more knowledge of Church history one has, the better. In being tutored by the fathers, we will be better armed to discern and respond to the novel theological heterodoxies in their day and ours.

Ross's use of the fathers can be found in *Creation and Time*, and then later, in concert with Gleason Archer, in *The Genesis Debate*.[4] But his strongest appeal to the fathers can be found in his book *A Matter of Days*. There his chapter, "Wisdom of the Ages," is devoted to showing that the early churchmen paid comparatively little attention to the length of the creation days. Those who did address the matter, says Ross, would not take the creation days as 24 hours in

---

3. *Ad fontes*, or *back to the sources* (literally, "to the fountains, springs"), is as appropriate now for Christians, as ever.

4. Hugh Ross and Gleason L. Archer, "The Day-Age View" (and responses to the 24-hour view and the framework view), in David G. Hagopian, ed., *The Genesis Debate: Three Views on the Days of Creation* (Mission Viejo, CA: Crux Press, 2001).

length. He further asserts that the extant writings indicate that the fathers "acknowledged" that the length of the days of creation "presented a challenge to their understanding and interpretation," so, except for Augustine, they "expressed their views tentatively" and "charitably tolerated a diversity of views." rather than dogmatically insisting on only one interpretation.[5]

Earlier, Ross contended that: "Many of the early Church Fathers and other biblical scholars interpreted the creation days of Genesis 1 as long periods of time." He suggests that Irenaeus, Origen, Basil, Augustine, and Aquinas were all day-age proponents.[6] Even though Ross is somewhat more nuanced than his earlier views in his *Creation and Time* chapter, "Interpretations of Early Church Leaders,"[7] his portrayal is still substantially the same, and thus, as we will demonstrate below, still very inaccurate. A natural reading of the Church fathers shows that though they held diverse views on the days of creation, and correctly gave priority to the *theological* meaning of the creation, they definitely asserted that the earth was created suddenly and in less than 6,000 years before their time. They left no room for the "old earth" views promoted by Ross and other moderns.

The Naturalistic Milieu of the Fathers

Common sense would have us agree with Ross's view that the fathers were not influenced by Darwinism or modern geological interpretations for an old earth.[8] This seeming truism misses the deeper picture that Greek thought included kinds of evolutionary and uniformitarian concepts even before the time of Christ.[9] The early apologists opposed Greek cosmogonies by asserting the biblical revelation of creation. For example, Hippolytus (c. A.D. 170–225 or 235), a presbyter in Rome, was familiar with and rejected many Greek naturalistic teachings. In Book

5. Hugh Ross, *A Matter of Days: Resolving a Creation Controversy* (Colorado Springs, CO: Navpress, 2004) p. 48–49. See also *Creation and Time* (Colorado Springs, CO: Navpress, 1994), p. 24.

6. Hugh Ross, *The Fingerprint of God* (Orange, CA: Promise Publishers, 1991, 2nd ed.), p. 141.

7. Ross, *Creation and Time*, p. 24.

8. Ross, *Matter of Days*, p. 49.

9. In a search for precursors to evolutionary theory, Henry Osborn was astonished to find that many Darwinian-like notions could be detected as far back as the 7th century B.C. See Henry F. Osborn, *From the Greeks to Darwin*, 2nd ed. (New York: Charles Scribner's Sons, 1929), p. xi; cf. 41–60 and 91–97). Osborn relied heavily on Edward Zeller, *A History of Greek Philosophy*, trans. S.F. Alleyne (New York: Longmans, Green, and Co., 1881). Anaximander (611–547 B.C.) believed man descended from fishes; and Empedocles (490–435 B.C.) has been called "the father of evolution." See Richard Lull, *Organic Evolution* (New York: Macmillan, 1947]), p. 6. On the furor over Darwinism, Matthew Arnold remarked to John Judd: "Why, it's all in Lucretius (99–55 B.C.)." See John Judd, *The Coming of Evolution* (Cambridge: Cambridge University Press, 1910), p. 3. I am indebted to Thane Ury for these references.

I of *The Refutation of All Heresies*, he defined the various views of Greek "natural philosophers," summarizing them as follows:

> From a body devoid of quality and endued with unity, the Stoics, then, accounted for the generation of the universe. For, according to them, matter devoid of quality, and in all its parts susceptible of change, constitutes an originating principle of the universe. For, when an alteration of this ensues, there is generated fire, air, water, earth. The followers, however, of Hippasus, and Anaximander, and Thales the Milesian, are disposed to think that all things have been generated from one (an entity), endued with quality. Hippasus of Metapontum and Heraclitus the Ephesian declared the origin of things to be from fire, whereas Anaximander from air, but Thales from water, and Xenophanes from earth. "For from earth," says he, "are all things, and all things terminate in the earth."[10]

Basil of Caesarea (A.D. 329–379), Bishop of Caesarea, frequently alludes to the views of the philosophers and their cosmologies. He opposed Greek error with the observation that each of these theories has been overturned by succeeding views, and none of them really held to an intelligent first cause, but ascribed everything to "chance." He wrote:

> "In the beginning God created the heaven and the earth." I stop struck with admiration at this thought. . . . The philosophers of Greece have made much ado to explain nature, and not one of their systems has remained firm and unshaken, each being overturned by its successor. It is vain to refute them; they are sufficient in themselves to destroy one another. Those who were too ignorant to rise to a knowledge of a God, could not allow that an intelligent cause presided at the birth of the Universe; a primary error that involved them in sad consequences. Some had recourse to material principles and attributed the origin of the Universe to the elements of the world. Others imagined that atoms, and indivisible bodies, molecules and ducts, form, by their union, the nature of the visible world. Atoms reuniting or separating, produce births and deaths and the most durable bodies only owe their consistency to the strength of their mutual adhesion: a true spider's web woven by these writers who give to heaven, to earth, and to sea so weak an origin and so little consistency! It is because they knew not how to say "In the beginning God created the heaven and the earth." Deceived by their inherent atheism it appeared to them that nothing governed or ruled the universe, and that all was given up to chance. To guard us

---

10. Hippolytus, *Refutation of all Heresies* 10.2, in Alexander Roberts, James Donaldson, Philip Schaff, Henry Wace, eds., *The Ante-Nicene Fathers*, 10 vols (Peabody, MA: Hendrickson, 1994 reprint ed.), vol. 5. Hereafter cited as *ANF*. See also 10.3, which further specifies names and theories of Greek natural philosophers.

against this error the writer on the creation, from the very first words, enlightens our understanding with the name of God; "In the beginning God created."[11]

Consider also Lactantius (c. A.D. 250–325), who strongly opposed the old-earth views of Plato and other Greek philosophers:

> Plato and many others of the philosophers, since they were ignorant of the origin of all things, and of that primal period at which the world was made, said that many thousands of ages had passed since this beautiful arrangement of the world was completed; and in this they perhaps followed the Chaldeans, who, as Cicero has related in his first book respecting divination, foolishly say that they possess comprised in their memorials four hundred and seventy thousand years; in which matter, because they thought that they could not be convicted, they believed that they were at liberty to speak falsely. But we, whom the Holy Scriptures instruct to the knowledge of the truth, know the beginning and the end of the world, respecting which we will now speak in the end of our work, since we have explained respecting the beginning in the second book. Therefore let the philosophers, who enumerate thousands of ages from the beginning of the world, know that the six thousandth year is not yet completed, and that when this number is completed the consummation must take place, and the condition of human affairs be remodeled for the better, the proof of which must first be related, that the matter itself may be plain. God completed the world and this admirable work of nature in the space of six days, as is contained in the secrets of Holy Scripture, and consecrated the seventh day, on which He had rested from His works. But this is the Sabbath-day, which in the language of the Hebrews received its name from the number, whence the seventh is the legitimate and complete number. For there are seven days, by the revolutions of which in order the circles of years are made up. . . .[12]

It simply will not do to claim that the fathers' concept of the creation was formed in a vacuum (i.e., without the pressure of modern evolutionary and uniformitarian concepts). The fathers asserted their views in large part to refute Greek philosophy's naturalistic theories of origins, which were very similar to modern ideas.[13]

---

11. Basil of Caesarea, *Hexaemeron* 1.2 in Alexander Roberts, James Donaldson, Philip Schaff, Henry Wace, eds., *The Nicene and Post-Nicene Fathers, Series 2* (Peabody, MA: Hendrickson, 1994) vol. 8. Hereafter cited as *NPNF2*. Basil's words about the temporary life of naturalistic theories should be considered when we use current scientific theories of origins as epistemic foundations for interpreting Scripture.

12. Lactantius, *Institutes* 7.14, in *ANF*, vol. 7

13. Though the fathers did not deal with the same challenges we face today, theirs were just as challenging, and they were just as prone as anyone to being products of their

The Length of the Days of Creation

The fathers favored a sudden, not a gradual, creation. Literalists specified that the six days of creation were each 24 hours long. Allegorists, like Clement,[14] Origen, and Augustine, did not consider the days of creation as 24-hour days, but, even as old-earth advocate Davis Young states, neither did they see non-literal days conflicting with their young-earth view.[15]

The Literalists

In the ancient Church there was a tension between allegorists and literal interpreters. One prominent literalist, Lactantius, a rhetorician who became the tutor of Constantine's son, viewed the creation days as 24-hour days.[16] He invoked the biblical account of creation against the old-earth views of Plato and other Greek philosophers, contending that less than 6,000 years ago God had created in six days. He believed that the "seven days" make up one week, "by the revolutions of which in order the circles of years are made up."[17] It seems clear that for Lactantius the creation days were the same kind of days that make up every week of a year.

Victorinus, bishop of Pettau (d. A.D. 304) affirmed that the first day of creation was divided into 12 hours for day and 12 hours for night. He said, "Even such is the rapidity of that creation; as is contained in the book of Moses, which he wrote about its creation, and which is called Genesis. God produced that entire mass for the adornment of His majesty in six days; on the seventh to which He consecrated it. . . . In the beginning God made the light, and divided

---

environment. A variety of strong philosophical and cultural pressures were always in the air. The impact of these factors on the theologizing of each father is sometimes easy to detect, and other times can only be inferred. Suffice it to say, none of their thoughts were forged in a hermetically sealed milieu. In addition to the influences from their own upbringing and training, threats like NeoPlatonism, Stoicism, Gnosticism, Manichaeism, Graeco-Roman mystery religions, polytheism, and a wide variety of philosophies, cults, and Christological heresies were always in the background.

14. Thinkers like Tertullian, Origen, and Eusebius are better classed as Ecclesiastical writers. We use "fathers" in this chapter with slightly wider semantic latitude than might patrological purists. It is only for convenience.

15. Davis A. Young, *Christianity and the Age of the Earth* (Grand Rapids, MI: Zondervan, 1982), p. 19 and 22.

16. Many who do not specify a 24-hour length nevertheless seem naturally read as understanding each day to be a normal solar day, since they are giving literal meaning to the other terms of Genesis 1. See Theophilus of Antioch (c. A.D. 115–168–181), *To Autolycus* 2.11–12); Methodius (A.D. 260–312), *The Banquet of the Ten Virgins* 8.11; 9.1; Epiphanius of Salamis (A.D. 315–403), *Panarion* 1.1.1.; Cyril of Jerusalem (c. A.D. 315–386), *Catechetical Lectures* 12.5. For more discussion, see Robert Bradshaw, "Creation and the Early Church," chapter 3, n.p. [cited March 31, 2005], www.robibrad.demon.co.uk/Chapter3.htm.

17. Lactantius, *Institutes* 7.14, in *ANF*, vol. 7. See the full quote above.

it in the exact measure of twelve hours by day and by night. . . . The day, as I have above related, is divided into two parts by the number twelve — by the twelve hours of day and night."[18]

Ephrem the Syrian (c. A.D. 306–373) (deacon, hymnwriter, and influential theologian and Bible commentator) was one of the few fathers who knew Hebrew. He was very literal in his concept of the length of the Genesis 1 days: "Although the light and the clouds were created in the twinkling of an eye, still both the day and the night of the First Day were each completed in twelve hours."[19] Ephraim opposed an allegorical interpretation of Genesis 1:

> So let no one think that there is anything allegorical in the works of the six days. No one can rightly say that the things pertaining to these days were symbolic, nor can one say that they were meaningless names or that other things were symbolized for us by their names. Rather, let us know in just what manner heaven and earth were created in the beginning. They were truly heaven and earth. There was no other thing signified by the names "heaven" and "earth." The rest of the works and things made that followed were not meaningless significations either, for the substances of their natures correspond to what their names signify.[20]

In his *Hexaemeron* ("six days"), a group of Lenten homilies on the days of creation,[21] Basil of Caesarea specifically also opposed the "distorted meaning of allegory," accusing allegorists of serving "their own ends" and giving "a majesty of their own invention to Scripture"; advocating instead a humble acceptance of the "common sense," the "literal sense" of Scripture "as it has been written."[22] Basil was specific that creation happened quickly, and in 24-hour days. Referring

18. Victorinus, *On the Creation of the World*, in *ANF*, vol. 7. p. 341

19. Ephrem the Syrian, *Commentary on Genesis* 1, quoted by Seraphim Rose, *Genesis, Creation and Early Man: The Orthodox Christian Vision* (Platina, CA: Saint Herman of Alaska Brotherhood, 2000), p. 101.

20. Ephrem the Syrian, *Commentary on Genesis* 1.1, in Kathleen E. McVey, ed., *Ephrem the Syrian: Selected Prose Works*, trans. Edward G. Mathews and Jospeh P. Amar, in *The Fathers of the Church* (*FC* hereafter) (Washington, D.C., 1961), 91:74.

21. Hexaemera is the body of treatises, sermons, and commentaries ordering all knowledge in terms of the six days of creation: some more exegetical and others more allegorical. Hexaemeral literature is the whole corpus of writings dealing with the subject, whether formal, secondary, or poetic renderings of the Genesis creation account. This genre became a special focus of some Church fathers, especially for Lent, remaining quite popular into the 1600s. Many authors followed Basil's pattern of nine homilies. Basil's brother, Gregory of Nyssa, and Ambrose wrote a *Hexaemeron*. For Jewish and Christian hexaemeral authors before Basil, like Chalcidius, Philo Judaeus, Hippolytus, Papias, Pantaenus, and numerous other later hexaemerists, see Frank Egleston Robbins, *The Hexaemeral Literature: A Study of the Greek and Latin Commentaries on Genesis* (Chicago, IL: University of Chicago Press, 1912).

22. Basil, *Hexaemeron* 9.1, in *NPNF2*, vol. 8.

to the creation of light on the first day, he says, "So, with a single word and in one instant, the Creator of all things gave the boon of light to the world."[23] Note Basil's clarity with respect to the length of the days:

> *And the evening and the morning were one day.* Why does Scripture say "one day the first day"? Before speaking to us of the second, the third, and the fourth days, would it not have been more natural to call that one the first which began the series? If it therefore says "one day," it is from a wish to determine the measure of day and night, and to combine the time that they contain. Now twenty-four hours fill up the space of one day — we mean of a day and of a night; and if, at the time of the solstices, they have not both an equal length, the time marked by Scripture does not the less circumscribe their duration. It is as though it said: twenty-four hours measure the space of a day, or that, in reality a day is the time that the heavens starting from one point take to return there. Thus, every time that, in the revolution of the sun, evening and morning occupy the world, their periodical succession never exceeds the space of one day. . . . God who made the nature of time measured it out and determined it by intervals of days; and, wishing to give it a week as a measure, he ordered the week to revolve from period to period upon itself, to count the movement of time, forming the week of one day revolving seven times upon itself: a proper circle begins and ends with itself.[24]

---

23. Ibid., 2.8, in *NPNF2*, vol. 8.

24. Ibid. Ross and Archer are incorrect when they assert that in the very next paragraph one can find proof that Basil allowed for the possibility that the creation days could be longer than 24 hours. The point that Basil was making is that day "one" is *not* the rest of eternity ("age of age, and ages of ages"). Basil's previous comments still control the meaning of "day" as a 24-hour period. Here is the section in question: "But must we believe in a mysterious reason for this? God who made the nature of time measured it out and determined it by intervals of days; and, wishing to give it a week as a measure, he ordered the week to revolve from period to period upon itself, to count the movement of time, forming the week of one day revolving seven times upon itself: a proper circle begins and ends with itself. Such is also the character of eternity, to revolve upon itself and to end nowhere. If then the beginning of time is called 'one day' rather than 'the first day,' it is because Scripture wishes to establish its relationship with eternity. It was, in reality, fit and natural to call 'one' the day whose character is to be one wholly separated and isolated from all the others. If Scripture speaks to us of many ages, saying everywhere, 'age of age, and ages of ages,' we do not see it enumerate them as first, second, and third. It follows that we are hereby shown not so much limits, ends and succession of ages, as distinctions between various states and modes of action." See Ross and Archer, "The Day-Age Reply," p. 205.

Robert Letham seems to think that there is a tension between Basil's concept of 24-hour days and his saying that everything was created "in less than an instant" in the "rapid and imperceptible moment of creation" (1.6). The tension is resolved by observing that Basil held a view that everything was created by God foundationally, and then

"Basil the Great" was one of the most important Church leaders and theologians of the fourth century, strongly defending Nicene Trinitarianism against the Arian and Sabellian heresies.[25] He also is noted for famine relief; establishing a poorhouse, a hospital, and a hospice; and writing monastic guidelines. History has judged Basil's *Hexaemeron* the most substantial; it inspired many others to also write commentary on the six days. In his own *Hexaemeron*, Gregory said, "What the saintly Basil wrote about the creation of the world . . . should suffice and alone take second place to the divinely inspired Testament." Gregory said that in his own writing he would not "fall in line with common opinion." He wished only "to understand . . . what the text means which follows a certain defined order regarding creation. 'In the beginning God created the heavens and the earth' [Gen. 1.1], and the rest which pertains to the cosmogenesis which the six days encompass."[26]

The Allegorists

Allegorical interpreters among the fathers were especially remarkable in resisting the old-earth theories of their day, even though they did differ on whether the days of creation were real days of 24-hours each, or simply symbolic representations of the order of creation.

Clement of Alexandria (c. A.D. 150–211 or 216), head of the Catechetical School of Alexandria, claimed that the six days were not literal but rather symbolic expressions of the sequential order of creation in an instant before time began:

> God's resting is not, then, as some conceive, that God ceased from doing. For, being good, if He should ever cease from doing good, then would He cease from being God, which it is sacrilege even to say. The resting is, therefore, the ordering that the order of created things should be preserved inviolate, and that each of the creatures should cease from the ancient disorder. For the creations on the different days followed in a most important succession; so that all things brought into

---

formed through the seven days of creation. "The beginning, in effect, is indivisible and instantaneous." See Robert Letham, " 'In the Space of Six Days': The Days of Creation from Origen to the Westminster Assembly," *WTJ* 61 (1999): p. 152–153.

25. Thomas Torrance nicely sums up Basil's historical significance: "Essential to [Basil's] cosmological outlook lies the Christian concept of the radical contingence of the universe and its rational order. And central to all that is the conception, so impossible for the ancient Greeks, of the contingent nature of the human mind created by God out of nothing but given a unique relation to his own transcendent Mind through grace. The incorporation of those ideas in Basil's Hexameron played a very important role, not only in challenging the intellectual foundations of the classical outlook upon the world of visible and invisible reality, but in helping to transform the Greek mind in a way that has left its mark upon the very basis of western culture." Thomas F. Torrance, *The Christian Frame of Mind: Reason, Order and Openness in Theology and Natural Science* (Colorado Springs, CO: Helmers and Howard, 1989), p. 5.

26. Gregory of Nyssa, *Hexaemeron*, trans. Richard McCambly, in J.P. Migne, ed., *Patrologia Graeca* (Paris: Migne, 1863), 44:68–69.

existence might have honor from priority, created together in thought, but not being of equal worth. Nor was the creation of each signified by the voice, inasmuch as the creative work is said to have made them at once. For something must needs have been named first. Wherefore those things were announced first, from which came those that were second, all things being originated together from one essence by one power. For the will of God was one, in one identity. And how could creation take place in time, seeing time was born along with things which exist.[27]

This view, that God created everything "at once" and "together," would be espoused later by Origen and Augustine of Hippo.

Origen (c. 185–254) was also a head of the Catechetical School of Alexandria. Even though his teachings are now recognized as aberrant in significant ways, he was one of the greatest minds in Christian antiquity. Unfortunately, despite the fact that he was one of the most prolific authors of his time, most of his works have perished. He was one of the most controversial scholars between Paul and Augustine, and is referred to as the "father of biblical criticism." His *On First Principles* was the first attempt at a systematic theology in the East. But he is chiefly remembered as one of the main formulators of the allegorical hermeneutic in the ancient Church. As a result, he viewed the six days as only "apparent" in signifying literal days.[28] Indeed, Origen held that no one with "understanding" will interpret Genesis 1 as a "pure history of events." These things should not be taken as having actually occurred, but rather should be taken in a spiritual

---

27. Clement of Alexandria, *Stromata* 6.16, in *ANF*, vol. 2.

28. Origen, *Contra Celsus* 6.60, in *ANF*, vol. 4: "We answered to the best of our ability this objection to God's 'commanding this first, second, and third thing to be created,' when we quoted the words, 'He said, and it was done; He commanded, and all things stood fast;' remarking that the immediate Creator, and, as it were, very Maker of the world was the Word, the Son of God; while the Father of the Word, by commanding His own Son — the Word — to create the world, is *primarily* Creator. And with regard to the creation of the light upon the first day, and of the firmament upon the second, and of the gathering together of the waters that are under the heaven into their several reservoirs on the third (the earth thus causing to sprout forth those (fruits) which are under the control of nature alone, and of the (great) lights and stars upon the fourth, and of aquatic animals upon the fifth, and of land animals and man upon the sixth, we have treated to the best of our ability in our notes upon Genesis, as well as in the foregoing pages, when we found fault with those who, taking the words in their *apparent* signification, said that the time of six days was occupied in the creation of the world, and quoted the words: 'These are the generations of the heavens and of the earth when they were created, in the day that the Lord God made the earth and the heavens.' " See also 4.11–13 on Origen's trichotomous "threefold" hermeneutic. See also Bernard Ramm, *Protestant Biblical Interpretation*, (3rd ed.; Grand Rapids, MI: Baker, 1970), p. 31–33, for Jean Daniélou's caution that Origen's practice was more allegorical than his theory. Cf. Louis Berkhof, *Principles of Biblical Interpretation* (Grand Rapids, MI: Baker, 1950), p. 20.

sense.[29] Origen also maintained that the seventh day of Genesis 1 continues until the end of the world.[30]

In the same paragraph, Origen asserts: "And the attentive reader may notice in the Gospels innumerable other passages like these, so that he will be convinced that in the histories that are literally recorded, circumstances that did not occur are inserted."[31] Since evangelicals cannot hold to biblical inerrancy while also embracing Origen's concept of Genesis and the Gospels, the perceptive reader will ask for clarification. If Ross can be faulted for cherry picking the fathers for statements lending themselves to a deep-time conclusion, what exempts creationists from the similar charges here? How can we affirm some of Origen's handling of Genesis, and not the rest, especially later when he writes that the Gospels are literal history? These are valid questions, and we offer seven caveats.

First, we include Origen here in response to deep-time advocates who invoke him in their argument against literal days to show that Origen is no real help to them. Second, creationists seldom refer to Origen, and when they do, it is usually to highlight his occasional "young-earth" type statements, but only for their historical value, and never using his ideas as any type of endorsement. Third, while Origen's allegorizations may have devotional, historical, or some other value, we would warn that they should be handled responsibly and very cautiously. Fourth, an important element to keep in mind is that even though Origen did not take Genesis 1 as literal history, he does affirm some things that Ross and Letham curiously disregard. For example, in rebuking Celsus, Origen clearly states that "the Mosaic account of creation . . . teaches that the world is not yet ten thousand years old, but very much under that."[32] Elsewhere he asserted this view specifically against views held by Greeks and Egyptians that the "the world is uncreated" and eternal.[33] So Letham's or Ross's appeals to Origen as an ancient precedent for "a non-literal view of Genesis 1" are mitigated by (as Letham admits) Origen's Neoplatonic allegorism and his young-earth assertions (which Letham does not mention).[34] Fifth, granting that Origen did not take the days literally, it is a huge leap of eisegetical faith to say he held a day-age view or a framework hypothesis. Nowhere does he enunciate such a thesis. Sixth, Origen's handling of Scripture is usually showcased in evangelical seminaries today as a

29. Origen, *De Principiis* 4.1.16 (Greek translation), in *ANF*, vol. 4; Ross, *Matter of Days*, p. 44.

30. Origen, *Contra Celsus* 6.61 in *ANF*, vol. 4: ". . . the day of the Sabbath and rest of God, which follows the completion of the world's creation, and which lasts during the duration of the world, and in which all those will keep festival with God who have done all *their* works in *their* six days, and who, because they have omitted none of their duties, will ascend to the contemplation (of celestial things), and to the assembly of righteous and blessed beings."

31. Origen, *De Principiis* 4.1.16 (Greek translation), in *ANF*, vol. 4.

32. Ibid., 1.19.

33. Ibid., 1.20.

34. Letham, "'Space of Six Days,'" p. 151–152.

primer on how *not* to handle the Bible. And such suspect method leads to our seventh and final point: many of Origen's beliefs are so clearly unorthodox that he seems hardly the type of figure with which modern-day accommodationists would want to be aligned. Any advantages he might offer are totally eclipsed by the disadvantages he brings to the hermeneutical table. The suggestion by Letham and Ross that creationists are not acknowledging or respecting Origen's authority is misleading. Given Origen's break with orthodoxy in so many areas, the more interesting question should be posed to Letham and Ross as to why the use of Origen is seen as helpful in buttressing an apology for deep time.

Ambrose (c. A.D. 338–397), bishop of Milan, and spiritual and exegetical mentor of Augustine, used his understanding of Greek to study Philo, Origen, and Athanasius, and to correspond with Basil. Though a Neoplatonist and an Alexandrian type of allegorist in general,[35] Ambrose had a literal concept of the length of the six days in his commentary on Basil's *Hexaemeron*:

> Scripture established a law that twenty-four hours, including both day and night, should be given the name of day only, as if one were to say the length of one day is twenty-four hours in extent. . . . The nights in this reckoning are considered to be component parts of the days that are counted. Therefore, just as there is a single revolution of time, so there is but one day. Thus were created the evening and the morning. Scripture means the space of a day and a night, and afterwards no more says day and night, but calls them both under the name of the more important: a custom which you will find throughout Scripture.[36]

So Ambrose held that each "day" of creation was 24 hours in length, and the term "day" also included the night, because the day is the more important of each 24 hours.

Augustine of Hippo (A.D. 354–430) is the most commonly cited authority who, it is claimed, allowed for the days of creation to be longer than 24 hours. Jack Lewis says that Augustine believed that Genesis 1 was an allegory about the future.[37] But he further asserts that Augustine also wanted to set forth what the author was "trying to say about God and the world."[38] Augustine took Genesis 2:4 to indicate that everything was created simultaneously — not in six days.[39]

35. Peter Brown, *Augustine of Hippo: A Biography* (Berkeley, CA: University of California Press, 1967), p. 85, 153–154.

36. Ambrose, *Hexaemeron* 1.10.3–7, in Ambrose, *Hexameron, Paradise, and Cain and Abel*, trans. John J. Savage, in FC (Washington, D.C., 1961), 42:42–43.

37. Jack P. Lewis, "The Days of Creation: An Historical Survey of Interpretation," *JETS* 32 (1989): p. 440–444. Lewis's synthesis of Augustine's view is the major basis of my summary. See also Letham, " 'Space of Six Days,' " p. 154–157; Bradshaw, "Creation and the Early Church," chapter 3, www.robibrad.demon.co.uk/Chapter3.htm.

38. Lewis, "Days of Creation," p. 440.

39. Louis Lavallee noted the source of Augustine's instantaneous creation view as being a mistranslation of the LXX of Sir 18:1: "According to translator J.H. Taylor (*The Literal*

His view was that God created matter and souls as they are inherently; He created everything else in invisible forms (seminal principles) that would develop from these "seminal principles" in the ongoing providential, post-creation working of God. The initial creation was made without "any interval of time."[40] Lewis notes that this concept of providential progressive development was appealed to as precedent for later evolutionary systems. But this appeal is highly ironic, since on closer examination it is apparent that Augustine believed in instantaneous completion of the distinct kinds of plants and animals. As Lewis sees it, according to Augustine, God finished creating after His work symbolized by the portrayal of the "sixth day" and creates no new creatures in the ages of providential post-creation work.[41]

But Sarfati well observes that Augustine relied almost exclusively on the Latin Bible, because he did not know Hebrew and only came to have a basic facility in Greek in later life, long after his Genesis commentary was done. As Sarfati notes, because he did not know Hebrew, he perhaps did not know of the Hebrew word for "instant" (רֶגַע, used in Exod. 33:5; Num. 16:21, 45; Ezra 9:8). Perhaps if Augustine had known Hebrew, he would not have espoused his view of the total creation occurring in an instant. But such it was and, as Sarfati points out, Augustine's interpretation "is *diametrically opposite* to what long-agers claim!"[42]

Augustine asserts that the six days are difficult for people to conceive, but that they were not literal days, because there was only one day of creation.[43]

Meaning, 1. 254), 'The word *simul* ("at one time," "all together") in the Latin version seems to be a mistranslation of the Greek *koine* ("commonly," "without exception").' Jerome, not accepting the Apocrypha as Scripture, did not retranslate Sirach, so the Vg today contains this OL reading." (Louis Lavallee, "Augustine on the Creation Days," *JETS* 32 (1989): p. 469-61, n. 20) Since Clement and Basil held a similar view (based on Gen. 2:4), it is unlikely that Augustine invented this view.

40. Augustine, *Confessions* 13.33.48, in Alexander Roberts, James Donaldson, Philip Schaff, Henry Wace, eds., *The Nicene and Post-Nicene Fathers, Series 1* (*NPNF1* hereafter) (reprint ed.; 14 vols; Hendrickson, 1994), vol. 1: "They have therefore their successions of morning and evening, partly hidden, partly apparent; for they were made from nothing by Thee, not of Thee, nor of any matter not Thine, or which was created before, but of concreted matter (that is, matter at the same time created by Thee), because without any interval of time Thou didst form its formlessness. For since the matter of heaven and earth is one thing, and the form of heaven and earth another, Thou hast made the matter indeed of almost nothing, but the form of the world Thou hast formed of formless matter; both, however, at the same time, so that the form should follow the matter with no interval of delay."

41. Lewis, "Days of Creation," p. 441–442.

42. Jonathan Sarfati, *Refuting Compromise* (Green Forest, AR: Master Books, 2004), p. 118. On the distinction between יוֹם (*yôm*) and רֶגַע (*rega*) in the Hebrew Bible, see also Jim Stambaugh, "The Days of Creation: A Semantic Approach," *Journal of Ministry and Theology* 7 (Fall 2003): p. 61–68.

43. Augustine, *City of God* 11.6, in NPNF1, vol. 2: "And if the sacred and infallible Scriptures say that in the beginning God created the heavens and the earth, in order that it may

Lewis accurately observes that Augustine believed that the six days of Genesis 1 are the progressive revelation of the creative activity to the angels and to those humans who cannot understand that He created everything at once. The days of Genesis 1 are the manifestation of the sequence in the one moment of creation. And yet what they portray happened in one instant. The days are not solar days, and they are not long ages of time, but revelatory symbols of the progression in the one creation moment.[44]

Lewis is correct in noting that Augustine did not believe that creation occurred within the span of six literal days. But what appears at first glance to be a point against a recent creation dissipates on closer reflection. First, it is a *non sequitur* to infer that a non-literal interpretation implies an old-earth interpretation. Second, there is no evidence to suggest that Augustine (or any of the fathers) would entertain the idea that creation took place millions of years ago. On the contrary, thirdly, it seems clear that Augustine believed creation happened in an instant. Indeed, fourthly, he explicitly argued that scriptural history contradicted those who held that the world was "many thousand years" old. He believed that the Scriptures taught that the earth was not even 6,000 years old.[45]

> They are deceived, too, by those highly mendacious documents which profess to give the history of many thousand years, though, reckoning by the sacred writings, we find that not 6,000 years have yet passed.[46]

> As to those who are always asking why man was not created during these countless ages of the infinitely extended past, and came into being

---

be understood that He had made nothing previously — for if He had made anything before the rest, this thing would rather be said to have been made 'in the beginning' — then assuredly the world was made, not in time, but simultaneously with time. For that which is made in time is made both after and before some time — after that which is past, before that which is future. But none could then be past, for there was no creature by whose movements its duration could be measured. But simultaneously with time the world was made, if in the world's creation change and motion were created, as seems evident from the order of the first six or seven days. For in these days the morning and evening are counted, until, on the sixth day, all things which God then made were finished, and on the seventh the rest of God was mysteriously and sublimely signalized. What kind of days these were it is extremely difficult, or perhaps impossible, for us to conceive, and how much more to say!"

44. Lewis, "Days of Creation," p. 441–442; Augustine, *City of God* 11.33, in *NPNF1*, vol. 2: ". . . first of all, the creation is presented in sum, and then its parts are enumerated according to the mystic number of the days."

45. In general, most of the early fathers relied on the Septuagint or Latin translations, did not know Hebrew or Aramaic (Origen and Eusebius were notable exceptions), and were not particularly well-versed in Semitic patterns of thought.

46. Augustine, *The City of God* 12.10, in *NPNF1*, vol. 2.

so lately that, according to Scripture, less than 6,000 years have elapsed since (h)e began to be. . . .[47]

Lest it be argued on the basis of Augustine's statements that Adam was created less than 6,000 years ago but the rest of creation is much older than that, it should be remembered that Augustine believed that God created everything, at least seminally, in an instant. And attention should be paid to Augustine's comments that those who believe that the earth is much older are in opposition to the history set forth in Scripture (see below). Furthermore, as will be demonstrated shortly, Augustine believed that the "six days" of creation typologically predicted that the entire history of the earth would last six millennia.

In summary, we would ask those who invoke Augustine's authority in defense of deep time and against literal 24-hour days, to bear the following six points in mind. First, his *Interpretation of Genesis* was based on Jerome's Latin translation, not the original language. Second, he had to use the Latin because he did not know Hebrew, so he never personally grappled with the original text of Genesis. Third, he is identified with the Alexandrian school, which is well known more for its heavy allegorizing than any rigorous systematic philological method. Fourth, he did not believe there was human death before the Fall. Fifth, he believed in a literal global Flood. And sixth, modern readings of his work do not inspire confidence that he ever distanced himself far enough from his early Neoplatonic leanings. Given these facts, old-earth proponents are not justified when they invoke Augustine's convictions on the length of the creation days as an argument in support of the acceptance of millions of years and against the young-earth perspective.[48]

The Eschatological Typology of the Six Days

Contrary to the impression left by Hugh Ross and others, consideration of the fathers' views of the length of the days of creation leads to the conclusion that the Church fathers were young-earth creationists. First, most treated the days as 24 hours in length, some even specifying the number of hours. Second, those who maintained that the days of Genesis 1 were only symbolic still believed that creation occurred over a relatively short period of time, even in one instant.

---

47. Ibid., 12.12.

48. Old-earth and young-earth creationists must resolve to be consistent in their use and trust of Augustine or any patristic authority. Obviously we are not saying the fathers cannot be invoked, trusted, and emulated at times.

   Quite the contrary, since a strong thesis of this volume is *ad fontes* ("back to the sources"). We are aware that some of the limitations above also apply to those fathers whom young-earth creationists showcase. We are just putting forth the modest proposal that we appeal responsibly to icons of the past, and not engage in proof-texting or special pleading. While the fathers' authority is a precious commodity, integrity demands that we also acknowledge any areas in these luminaries which offset or even nullify our argument.

Third, no father's writing leaves room for current old-earth creationists to appeal to them for support for their interpretation of the creation days as being long ages of millions of years each.

Another strong proof of the young-earth creationism of the Church fathers is their sex/septa-millennial view that the earth was less than 6,000 years old — and would not remain in its current state after the end of 6,000 years. In the first two centuries of Church history, the Church fathers had a premillennial eschatology in which the seventh age of 1,000 years would be the Millennium. Later the predominant eschatology became amillennialism as Christianity became not only a legal religion, but also the official religion of the Roman Empire. But even after the eschatological shift, the fathers continued to espouse the 6,000-year schema of world history.

Background

The basis of the sex/septa-millenary view was a typological interpretation of the six days of creation. Based on Psalm 90:4 and 2 Peter 3:8 ("with the Lord one day *is* as a thousand years, and a thousand years as one day" NKJV), the fathers believed that each day of creation typified a period of one thousand years in the future history of the earth.[49] This typology had a pre-Christian history. In the 19th century, D.T. Taylor summarized much of the literature on the sex/septa-millenary concept.[50] He noted that according to 18th century astronomer David Gregory, the ancient Cabalists[51] derived the 6,000 years from the six occurrences of the Hebrew letter *aleph* (the notation for 1,000 in Jewish arithmetic) in Genesis 1:1 and from the six days of creation, since 1,000 years are as one day. Taylor notes that Plutarch said that the Chaldeans, Zoroaster, and the Persians held that human history would last 6,000 years. According to Arnold Ehlert, the Tuscans, Persians, and Etruscans believed that there were six ages of

---

49. This section contradicts Ross and Archer, who state: "Justin Martyr, Irenaeus, Lactantius, Victorinus of Pettau, and Methodius of Olympus all explicitly endorse six consecutive thousand-year periods for the Genesis creation days." (Ross and Archer, "The Day-Age Response," p. 69; see also Ross, *Matter of Days*, p. 45). This statement is quite inaccurate as Duncan and Hall demonstrate in response (J. Ligon Duncan III and David W. Hall, "The 24-Hour Reply," *The Genesis Debate*, p. 99–102). The fathers considered in this section were not stating that the days of creation were each 1,000 years long, but that the days typologically predicted subsequent ages of world history, each of which would be 1,000 years long. See also Sarfati, *Refuting Compromise*, p. 114–122.

50. D.T. Taylor, *The Voice of the Church on the Coming and Kingdom of the Redeemer: or, a History of the Doctrine of the Reign of Christ on Earth* (8th ed.; Albany, OR: Ages Software, 1997), p. 32–36. The eighth edition was published in 1866 by the Scriptural Tract Repository.

51. Cabal (Hebrew קבל "to receive") basically refers to a corpus of ancient mystical teachings with rabbinic origins, based on an esoteric interpretation of the Hebrew Old Testament, and containing strong elements of pantheism. The esoteric teachings of Cabalism are still seen in the ultra-Orthodox Hasidic and Lubavitch sects.

1,000 years each in the creation, and humanity would exist for another 6,000 years.[52] Jewish rabbis especially held the typological eschatology of the six days. Edersheim's summary of the Talmud (Sanhedrin) includes this opinion of Rabbi Kattina based on Psalm 90:4:

> The world is to last 6,000 years, and during one millennium it is to lie desolate, according to Is. 2:17. R. Abayi held that this state would last 2,000 years, according to Hosea 6:2. The opinion of R. Kattian was however, regarded as supported by this, that in each period of seven there is a Sabbatic year, the day here = 1,000 years of desolateness and rest — the appeal being to Is. 2:17; Ps. 92:1, and 90:4.[53]

Ante-Nicene Premillennialists

Justin Martyr (c. A.D. 100–165) asserted to the Jew, Trypho, that "right-minded Christians" believe that after a resurrection of the death, there will be "a thousand years in Jerusalem. The city will then be built, adorned, and enlarged, [as] the prophets Ezekiel and Isaiah and others declare."[54] Justin's concept that a "day" can be a typological prediction of 1,000 years is seen in his view that Adam died in less than 1,000 years — so he died "in the day" he ate of the tree, just as God had warned. Justin associated this predictive nature of a day with the "the expression, 'The day of the Lord is as a thousand years.' " And then he linked this expression to the apostle John's prediction that "those who believed in our Christ would dwell a thousand years in Jerusalem; and that thereafter the general, and, in short, the eternal resurrection and judgment of all men would likewise take place."[55]

---

52. Arnold D. Ehlert, "*A Bibliography of Dispensationalism, Part 1*," *BSac* 101 (January 1944): p. 99.

53. Alfred Edersheim, *The Life and Times of Jesus the Messiah* (2 vols.; reprint ed.; Grand Rapids, MI: Eerdmans, 1977), 2:738.

54. Justin Martyr, *Dialogue with Trypho,* p. 80, in *ANF,* vol. 1.

55. Ibid., p. 81. The full quote reads: "For as Adam was told that in the day he ate of the tree he would die, we know that he did not complete a thousand years. We have perceived, moreover, that the expression, 'The day of the Lord is as a thousand years,' is connected with this subject. And further, there was a certain man with us, whose name was John, one of the apostles of Christ, who prophesied, by a revelation that was made to him, that those who believed in our Christ would dwell a thousand years in Jerusalem; and that thereafter the general, and, in short, the eternal resurrection and judgment of all men would likewise take place." Justin does not say that the sixth day of creation was meant to last 1,000 years — but that within the time limit of the day (1,000 years) in which Adam lived, he would die, if he ate of the tree. Justin cannot be justifiably used (contra Ross and Archer, "Day-Age Reply," p. 204; Ross, *Matter of Days*, p. 43) as precedent for allowing for the days of creation to be long ages. (A similar argument against Ross and Archer can be made about Irenaeus' words in *Against Heresies* 5:23.2. Irenaeus did not mean that the sixth day of creation was 1,000 years, but that in the sixth day, the day in which Adam was created, he began his own day (of 1,000

The *Epistle of Barnabas* (c. A.D. 130–131) is an early indication of the acceptance of this six-day typology. Built on the Sabbath command in the Decalogue, the six days are said to point to God's working in the present world to end in 6,000 years, with the return of Christ at the beginning of the "seventh day" to commence His Sabbath, and the "eighth day," the day of Jesus' Resurrection, being the final Sabbath for the resurrected in a new world.[56]

Crutchfield notes that Barnabas viewed days 1–5 as foreshadowing the first 5,000 years of history (the past). He saw day 6 as looking toward his own age, the 1,000 years of the sixth age (the present). Day 7 was a prediction of the millennium, the seventh era of 1,000 years. And day 8 anticipated the eternal state. Barnabas' use of this typology would be echoed by many later fathers, even those who disagreed with his premillennialism (e.g., Origen and Augustine). They would equate the seventh day with the eternal state.[57]

Irenaeus (c. A.D. 130–202 or 212), Bishop of Lyon, was the first great systematic theologian of the early Church. A strong opponent of Gnosticism, Irenaeus felt that the number 666 in Revelation sums up "the whole of that

---

years), became a debtor to death in that day, and did not live until the end of *his* day (his 1,000 years). Cf. Bradshaw, "Creationism and the Early Church," www.robibrad. demon.co.uk/chapter3_pf.htm. Justin is also reported to have held that because the seventh day of Genesis 1 was not described as having "evening" and "morning," it "is a distinct indication of the consummation which is to take place in it before it is finished." — *Fragments from the Lost Writings of Justin* 15 (*ANF*, vol. 1) — from the writings of Anastasius.

56. *Epistle of Barnabas*, p. 15, in *ANF*, vol. 1: "Further, also, it is written concerning the Sabbath in the Decalogue which [the Lord] spoke, face to face, to Moses on Mount Sinai, 'And sanctify ye the Sabbath of the Lord with clean hands and a pure heart.' And He says in another place, 'If my sons keep the Sabbath, then will I cause my mercy to rest upon them.' The Sabbath is mentioned at the beginning of the creation [thus]: 'And God made in six days the works of His hands, and made an end on the seventh day, and rested on it, and sanctified it.' Attend, my children, to the meaning of this expression, 'He finished in six days.' This implieth that the Lord will finish all things in six thousand years, for a day is with Him a thousand years. And He Himself testifieth, saying, 'Behold, to-day will be as a thousand years.' Therefore, my children, in six days, that is, in six thousand years, all things will be finished. 'And He rested on the seventh day.' This meaneth: when His Son, coming [again], shall destroy the time of the wicked man, and judge the ungodly, and change the sun, and the moon, and the stars, then shall He truly rest on the seventh day. . . . 'Your new moons and your Sabbath I cannot endure.' Ye perceive how He speaks: Your present Sabbaths are not acceptable to Me, but that is which I have made, [namely this] when, giving rest to all things, I shall make a beginning of the eighth day, that is, a beginning of another world. Wherefore, also, we keep the eighth day with joyfulness, the day also on which Jesus rose again from the dead. . . ."

57. Larry V. Crutchfield, "The Early Church Fathers and the Foundations of Dispensationalism: Dispensational Concepts in the Apostolic Fathers," *Conservative Theological Journal* 2 (1998): p. 258–259.

apostasy which has taken place during six thousand years." And then he affirmed that the world will be "concluded" in the same number of thousands of years as the number of days in which it was made. The six days of creation followed by the seventh day of God's rest was "an account of the things formerly created, as also it is a prophecy of what is to come." The basis of this eschatological linkage was that "the day of the Lord is as a thousand years; and in six days created things were completed: it is evident, therefore, that they will come to an end at the sixth thousand year."[58] Irenaeus went on to provide a premillennial picture of the Second Advent. After the "Antichrist" will have reigned "in the temple at Jerusalem" for "three years and six months," the Lord will return, send the Antichrist and his followers "into the lake of fire," and bring in "the times of the kingdom . . . the rest . . . that is, the rest, the hallowed seventh day; and restoring to Abraham the promised inheritance, in which kingdom the Lord declared, that 'many coming from the east and from the west should sit down with Abraham, Isaac, and Jacob.' "[59]

Hippolytus, commenting on the image of Daniel 2, identified the toes of clay and iron as the "ten horns," the "antichrist" being "the little horn springing up in their midst." The "stone" that will break the image and fill "the whole earth" is Christ, "who comes from heaven and brings judgment on the world." Christ's "first appearance . . . in the flesh . . . in Bethlehem, under Augustus" occurred "in the year 5500." (The dating was confirmed by John's words, "Now it was the sixth hour," indicating that it was the middle of "the day," since one day with the Lord "is 1,000 years," and half of that is 500) For the next 500 years the gospel would be preached to the whole world, and then "the 6,000 must needs be accomplished, in order that the Sabbath may come, the rest, the holy day 'on which God rested from all His works.' " The Sabbath is the symbol of the "kingdom of the saints," which will fulfill the typological prophecy of the six days of creation:[60]

> . . . for "a day with the Lord is as a thousand years." Since, then, in six days God made all things, it follows that 6, 000 years must be

---

58. Irenaeus, *Against Heresies* 5.28.2-3, in *ANF*, vol. 1.

59. Ibid., 5.30.4. See also 5.33.2; 5.29.2.

60. Hippolytus, *On Daniel* 2.3-6, in *ANF*, vol. 3. Other fathers also gave specific dates for the age of the earth: Theophilus of Antioch (c. A.D. 180) — 5,698 years (*To Autolycus* 3.28); Cyprian of Carthage (c. A.D. 205–258) — "six thousand years are now nearly completed since the devil first attacked man" (*Exhortation To Martyrdom* 11); Julius Africanus (c. A.D. 200–232–245) lists both 5500 and 5531 as the date of the First Advent (*The Extant Fragments Of The Five Books Of The Chronography Of Julius Africanus* 1; 18.4). Three who were not premillennialists, but did specify the age of the earth, were Clement of Alexandria (5,592 years — *Stromata* 1.21); Eusebius of Caesarea (c. 270–340) (5,228 years — *Chronicle*); and Augustine of Hippo (*City of God* 12:11). See Bradshaw, "Creationism and the Early Church," chapter 3, Table 3.4, www.robibrad. demon.co.uk/Chapter3.htm.

fulfilled. And they are not yet fulfilled, as John says: "five are fallen; one is," that is, the sixth; "the other is not yet come."[61]

Victorinus of Pettau also looked forward to the "seventh millenary of years, when Christ with His elect shall reign." He called this future kingdom "that true and just Sabbath." And he also based his time construct on the typological prophecy of the days of creation in keeping with the biblical association of a thousand years with one day: "Wherefore to those seven days the Lord attributed to each a thousand years; for thus went the warning: 'In Thine eyes, O Lord, a thousand years are as one day.' Therefore in the eyes of the Lord each thousand of years is ordained, for I find that the Lord's eyes are seven. Wherefore, as I have narrated, that true Sabbath will be in the seventh millenary of years, when Christ with His elect shall reign."[62]

Methodius (A.D. 260–312), Bishop of Olympus, was a literalist opponent of Origen's allegorism. Methodius posited that the six days of creation were followed by the seventh day of God's resting from His works of creation, and the ingathering of fruits in the seventh month for "the feast of the Lord," signify "that, when this world shall be terminated at the seventh thousand years, when God shall have completed the world, He shall rejoice in us."[63] This "feast" appears to be the OT feast of tabernacles, which, to Methodius, pointed to the believer's resurrection, the departure from the "Egypt of this life," the setting up of "my tabernacle, adorned with the fruits of virtue, on the first day of resurrection" to "celebrate with Christ the millennium of rest, which is called the seventh day, even the true Sabbath." After this, even as the Israelites "after the rest of the Feast of Tabernacles came in to the land of promise," "after the space of a thousand years" believers will have their bodies changed "from a human and corruptible form into angelic size and beauty" to ascend "into the very house of God above the heavens."[64]

Lactantius addressed his *Institutes* to Constantine, and made extensive use of the typological eschatology of the days of creation in setting forth his premillennial scheme:

> Therefore, since all the works of God were completed in six days, the world must continue in its present state through six ages, that is, six thousand years. For the great day of God is limited by a circle of a thousand years, as the prophet shows, who says "In Thy sight, O Lord, a thousand years are as one day." And as God labored during those six days in creating such great works, so His religion and truth must labor during these six thousand years, while wickedness prevails and bears rule. And again, since God, having finished His works, rested the seventh

---

61. Hippolytus, *On Daniel* 2.4, in *ANF*, vol. 3.
62. Victorinus of Pettau, *On the Creation of the World*, in *ANF*, vol. 7.
63. Methodius, *The Banquet of the Ten Virgins (or Concerning Chastity)* 9.1, in *ANF*, vol. 6.
64. Ibid., 9.5.

day and blessed it, at the end of the six thousandth year all wickedness must be abolished from the earth, and righteousness reign for a thousand years; and there must be tranquility and rest from the labors which the world now has long endured.[65]

Lactantius believed that the making of "the earthly man" on the sixth day and placing him "into a home now carefully prepared," so in the present "sixth day," "the heavenly people," "the true man," "a holy people" is being "formed by the word of God," "fashioned for righteousness by the doctrine and precepts of God." The first man was "mortal and imperfect" and was "formed from the earth" to "live a thousand years in this world." Even so, "a perfect man" is being formed "from this earthly age" to be "quickened by God" and "bear rule in this same world through a thousand years."[66] When will this happen? When "the six thousand years shall be completed," and "the last day of the extreme conclusion is now drawing near." In fact, based on the "foretold signs" of this "consummation," everyone who has written on "how great is the number of years from the beginning of the world," though varying greatly among themselves on the amount of these years that have passed, at most allow that the remaining time would be no more than 200 years ("all expectation does not exceed the limit of two hundred years").[67]

We know that Lactantius was thinking about a literal "thousand years of the kingdom" by examining his treatment of the beginning and ending of the "seven thousand of the world." He said that at the outset of the "sacred reign" that Satan "will be bound by God." And when this era begins to end, Satan will be "loosed afresh" and will "assemble all nations" to "make war against the holy city." When this "innumerable company of the nations" shall "besiege and surround the city," "the last anger of God shall come upon the nations, and shall utterly destroy them."[68]

It is especially pertinent to note that Lactantius wrote these things based on his confidence in Scripture — and in opposition to old-earth philosophers of his day:

> If any one wishes for them, or does not place full confidence in us, let him approach to the very shrine of the heavenly letters, and being more fully instructed through their trustworthiness, let him perceive

---

65. Lactantius, *The Divine Institutes* 7.14, in *ANF*, vol. 7.

66. Ibid.

67. Ibid., 7.25. Lactantius believed that this will not happen until the city of Rome falls, so God should be implored to delay, if possible, "that detestable tyrant should come who will trader-take so great a deed, and dig out that eye, by the destruction of which the world itself is about to fall." (Remember that Lactantius was in the service of the emperor. How different is the attitude about Rome since the earlier days of persecution!) Lactantius was not anticipating the continuation of Rome for a long time.

68. Ibid., 7.26.

that the philosophers have erred, who thought either that this world was eternal, or that there would be numberless thousands of years from the time when it was prepared. For six thousand years have not yet been completed, and when this number shall be made up, then at length all evil will be taken away, that justice alone may reign.[69]

Post-Nicene Anti-Chiliasts

With the eschatological shift away from premillennialism beginning in the third century, it is not surprising that not as many extant writings seem to appeal to the sex/septa-millenary construct. Yet the view did survive — but in an altered eschatology. Taylor noted that Jerome (c. A.D. 340–420) and Hilary of Poitiers (c. A.D. 291–371) asserted that at the end of the 6,000 years, the Second Advent would occur, followed by the eternal, heavenly (i.e., non-earthly) kingdom.[70]

Augustine rejected premillennialism as a "carnal" doctrine after having espoused it earlier in his life,[71] but he did not reject the sex/septa millennial

---

69. Lactantius, *Epitome of the Divine Institutes* 70, in *ANF*, vol. 7.

70. Taylor, *Voice of the Church*, p. 82–84.

71. Augustine, *City of God* 20.7ff., in *NPNF1*, vol. 2. Note his change from his earlier "chiliasm": "The evangelist John has spoken of these two resurrections in the book which is called the Apocalypse, but in such a way that some Christians do not understand the first of the two, and so construe the passage into ridiculous fancies. For the Apostle John says in the foresaid book, 'And I saw an angel come down from heaven. . . . Blessed and holy is he that hath part in the first resurrection: on such the second death hath no power; but they shall be priests of God and of Christ, and shall reign with Him a thousand years.' Those who, on the strength of this passage, have suspected that the first resurrection is future and bodily, have been moved, among other things, specially by the number of a thousand years, as if it were a fit thing that the saints should thus enjoy a kind of Sabbath-rest during that period, a holy leisure after the labors of the six thousand years since man was created, and was on account of his great sin dismissed from the blessedness of paradise into the woes of this mortal life, so that thus, as it is written, 'One day is with the Lord as a thousand years, and a thousand years as one day,' there should follow on the completion of six thousand years, as of six days, a kind of seventh-day Sabbath in the succeeding thousand years; and that it is for this purpose the saints rise, viz., to celebrate this Sabbath. And. this opinion would not be objectionable, if it were believed that the joys of the saints in that Sabbath shall be spiritual and consequent on the presence of God; for I myself, too, once held this opinion. But, as they assert that those who then rise again shall enjoy the leisure of immoderate carnal banquets, furnished with an amount of meat and drink such as not only to shock the feeling of the temperate, but even to surpass the measure of credulity itself, such assertions can be believed only by the carnal. They who do believe them are called by the spiritual Chiliasts, which we may literally reproduce by the name Millenarians. It were a tedious process to refute these opinions point by point: we prefer proceeding to show how that passage of Scripture should be understood." See also *Psalms* 6.1 for Augustine's change of the normal structure of 7,000 years before the Second Advent.

construct of earth's history. As was noted earlier, he believed that not even 6,000 years had passed since the beginning of creation.[72]

It needs to be emphasized again that Augustine held this 6,000-year view because he believed that Scripture taught it, and he maintained the view against old-earth views of his day. For example, he opposed the Egyptian claim that it had had knowledge of the stars for more than 100,000 years — because their claim contradicted the history given by God. He also rejected other historians on this point, because they contradict each other:

> In vain, then, do some babble with most empty presumption, say-ing that Egypt has understood the reckoning of the stars for more than a hundred thousand years. For in what books have they collected that number who learned letters from Isis their mistress, not much more than two thousand years ago? Varro, who has declared this, is no small authority in history, and it does not disagree with the truth of the divine books. For as it is not yet six thousand years since the first man, who is called Adam, are not those to be ridiculed rather than refuted who try to persuade us of anything regarding a space of time so different from, and contrary to, the ascertained truth? For what historian of the past should we credit more than him who has also predicted things to come which we now see fulfilled? And the very disagreement of the historians among themselves furnishes a good reason why we ought rather to believe him who does not contradict the divine history which we hold. . . . But we, being sustained by divine authority in the history of our religion, have no doubt that whatever is opposed to it is most false. . . .[73]

Augustine's eschatology changed the "seventh day" from being the seventh period of 1,000 years to being the eternal state following the Second Advent. He said that the "seventh day" looked to the "Sabbath of eternal life."[74] Like Pseudo-Barnabas, Tertullian, and Victorinus, Augustine did refer to an "eighth day" and built his argument for Sunday being the worship day of the Church as the "eighth day." He did not hold to an earthly millennium for the seventh day, but he emphasized the "eighth day" (the first day of the week) as symbolizing resurrection and the rest of the "seventh day," which was eternal:

> If, in reading Genesis, you search the record of the seven days, you will find that there was no evening of the seventh day, which signified that the rest of which it was a type was eternal. The life originally bestowed was not eternal, because man sinned; but the final rest, of which the seventh day was an emblem, is eternal, and hence the eighth day also will have eternal blessedness, because that rest, being eternal, is taken

---

72. See quotes at footnotes 44 and 45.
73. Ibid., 18.40.
74. Augustine, *Confessions* 13.36.51, in *NPNF1*, vol. 1.

up by the eighth day, not destroyed by it; for if it were thus destroyed, it would not be eternal. Accordingly the eighth day, which is the first day of the week, represents to us that original life, not taken away, but made eternal.[75]

Based on this quote, note carefully that Augustine explicitly appealed to "the seven days" of Genesis 1 as a typological pattern for the ages of earth's history, so he definitely considered the creation of the earth (including the creation of man) to have occurred less than 6,000 years ago. Augustine closed his *City of God* with the "eighth day" symbolizing the eternal heavenly life of the "seventh day" — after a history of six ages on earth:

This Sabbath shall appear still more clearly if we count the ages as days, in accordance with the periods of time defined in Scripture, for that period will be found to be the seventh. The first age, as the first day, extends from Adam to the deluge; the second from the deluge to Abraham, equaling the first, not in length of time, but in the number of generations, there being ten in each. From Abraham to the advent of Christ there are, as the evangelist Matthew calculates, three periods, in each of which are fourteen generations, — one period from Abraham to David, a second from David to the captivity, a third from the captivity to the birth of Christ in the flesh. There are thus five ages in all. The sixth is now passing, and cannot be measured by any number of generations, as it has been said, "It is not for you to know the times, which the Father hath put in His own power." After this period, God shall rest as on the seventh day, when He shall give us (who shall be the seventh day) rest in Himself. But there is not now space to treat of these ages; suffice it to say that the seventh shall be our Sabbath, which shall be brought to a close, not by an evening, but by the Lord's day, as an eighth and eternal day, consecrated by the resurrection of Christ, and prefiguring the eternal repose not only of the spirit, but also of the body. There we shall rest and see, see and love, love and praise. This is what shall be in the end without end. For what other end do we propose to ourselves than to attain to the kingdom of which there is no end?[76]

Thus, Augustine saw the first five ages/days of world history to have been complete, and the sixth age/day was, in his day, "passing." It is not clear that he believed that each age of earth's history would be exactly 1,000 years, as previous writers believed. In fact, it appears that he believed that one could not determine the length of the sixth age. But it would be ended by the seventh. Augustine saw the "seventh age" to be not "of this world":

75. Augustine, *Letter 55: Part 2 of Replies to Questions of Januarius* 9.17, in *NPNF1*, vol. 1.
76. Augustine, *City of God* 22.30, in *NPNF1*, vol. 2.

. . . at the beginning of the world, and at the time when God made heaven and earth and all things which are in them, He worked during six days, and rested on the seventh day. For it was in the power of the Almighty to make all things even in one moment of time. For He had not labored in the view that He might enjoy (a needful) rest, since indeed "He spake, and they were made; He commanded, and they were created;" but that He might signify how, after six ages of this world, in a seventh age, as on the seventh day, He will rest in His saints; inasmuch as these same saints shall rest also in Him after all the good works in which they have served Him — which He Himself, indeed, works in them, who calls them, and instructs them, and puts away the offenses that are past, and justifies the man who previously was ungodly.[77]

Note again that Augustine held that God "made heaven and earth and all things which are in them . . . even in one moment of time." The "seventh day" in the Genesis account signified "a seventh age," which would be "after six ages of this world." Augustine was explicit that the seventh age would not be on earth, but in heaven:

In the creation God finished His works in six days, and rested on the seventh. The history of the world contains six periods marked by the dealings of God with men. . . . the sixth is now in progress, and will end in the coming of the exalted Savior to judgment. What answers to the seventh day is the rest of the saints — not in this life, but in another, where the rich man saw Lazarus at rest while he was tormented in hell; where there is no evening, because there is no decay.[78]

Later in life, Augustine may not have been totally committed to his concept that the six days were not literal days. Indeed, in his *Retractions (Revisions)*, he indicated that in his *The Literal Meaning of Genesis*, he had asked more questions than "answers found," and of these answers found "only a few were assured."[79] Since he did not specify the "answers," it cannot be concluded that he was referring to the nature of six days. But the even more relevant point to note here is that even in his most allegorical moments in studying Genesis, Augustine held that the earth was less than 6,000 years old in his day, and to believe that the earth was considerably older was to oppose God's history given in Scripture. Augustine was the climax of the mainstream majority young-earth creationist patristic tradition.

77. Augustine, *The Catechising of the Uninstructed* 17.28, in *NPNF1*, vol. 3.
78. Augustine, *Reply to Faustus the Manichaean* 12.12, in *NPNF1*, vol. 4. For this period, see also *Sermon 75.4* (vol. 6); *Tractates on John* 15.6, 9 (vol. 7).
79. Augustine, *Revisions* 2.24, in John E. Rotelle, ed., *On Genesis*, trans. Edmund Hill (Hyde Park, NY: New City Press, 2002), p. 167.

The Fathers on the Flood

The fathers do not seem to have based their concept of the age of the earth on Noah's Flood, obviously because geological concerns were not then at issue in judging the age of the earth. Later in post-Reformation Europe, geology, the Flood, and the age of the earth would be linked together. For the moment it is sufficient to note that most of the fathers treated the Flood as a real and worldwide event — condemning pagan flood stories as not referring to the biblical Flood, since these stories concerned only localized floods.

Justin Martyr did not have much to say on this subject. But he did remark that "the whole earth, as the Scripture says, was inundated, and the water rose in height fifteen cubits above all the mountains."[80]

With even more specifics, Theophilus (c. 115–185), Patriarch of Antioch, contradicted Plato, who had said that the deluge "extended not over the whole earth, but only over the plains, and that those who fled to the highest hills saved themselves." Theophilus also rejected other Greek views that Deucalion and Pyrrha were preserved through the deluge in a "chest," and that a certain Clymenus lived in a second flood. He referred to these Greeks as "miserable, and very profane and senseless persons," countering them by noting that "Moses, our prophet and the servant of God, in giving an account of the genesis of the world," described the details of how the Flood "came upon the earth" — "relating no fable of Pyrrha nor of Deucalion or Clymenus; nor, forsooth, that only the plains were submerged, and that those only who escaped to the mountains were saved." Theophilus went on to argue that Moses never taught that there was a second flood, but "that never again would there be a flood of water on the world; as neither indeed has there been, nor ever shall be." According to Theophilus, Moses recounted that "the flood lasted forty days and forty nights," that "the water overtopped every high hill 15 cubits," and that "the race of all the men" was "destroyed" except for the eight people in the ark. Theophilus further comments on the Flood by noting that "of the ark, the remains are to this day to be seen in the Arabian mountains," and closes his section by referring to Moses' account as "the history of the deluge."[81]

The important early North African Trinitarian theologian Tertullian (A.D. 115–222) asserted that the "whole orb" was "overrun by all waters." His proof was that "To this day marine conchs and tritons' horns sojourn as foreigners on the mountains, eager to prove to Plato that even the heights have undulated."[82] Tertullian also referred to the deluge as "that world-wide calamity, the abolisher of all things."[83]

Gregory of Nazianzus (A.D. 329–389) was a Bishop of Constantinople (380–381) and one of the anti-Arian "Three Great Cappadocian" theologians.

---

80. Justin Martyr, *Dialog* 138, in *ANF*, vol. 1.
81. Theophilus of Antioch, *To Autolycus* 3.18-19, in *ANF*, vol. 2.
82. Tertullian, *On the Pallium* 2, in *ANF*, vol. 4.
83. Tertulliam, *On the Apparel of Women* 1.3, in *ANF*, vol. 4.

Gregory pointed to Noah as having been "entrusted with the saving of the whole world from the waters" and as having "escaped the Deluge in a small Ark."[84] And the great western theologian Augustine climaxed the fathers' affirmation that the Noachian Flood was worldwide. Augustine argued against an exclusively allegorical interpretation by asserting that the Flood was "so great" that its waters rose "fifteen cubits above the highest mountains."[85]

Further evidence of the fathers' consistency of the worldwide Flood view is given by Young, who relates that Procopius of Gaza (c. A.D. 465–528) in his *Commentary on Genesis* and Pseudo-Eustathius (n.d.) in his *Commentary on Hexaemeron* argue for the worldwide extent of the Flood by recalling that marine remains (e.g., shells, various types of fish) had been found on high mountains. Pseudo-Eustathius claimed that the fish must have been "gathered together in the caves of the mountains when they were caught in the mud." Young notes that Pseudo-Justin (probably Theodoret of Cyrus — c. 393–466) was the only extant father to suggest the possibility of a local Flood.[86]

Conclusion

The Church fathers had much to say about the creation. Indeed, for them, the chronological framework in Genesis foreshadowed the entire eschatological unfolding of world history. They saw that the present and the future were implicitly anticipated by the beginning of the created order. And, in opposition to the naturalism of their day with respect to the age of the earth, the fathers were clear:

1. The fathers wrote in an intellectual milieu that was filled with naturalistic cosmogonies, most of which held the earth to be either very old or even eternal. The fathers considered these thinkers to be atheistic, even if the philosophers posited an intelligent cause, because they did not believe in the God of the Bible.

2. Most of the fathers countered the naturalistic theories of origins of their day with the authoritative scriptural account of creation. The Alexandrians allowed for more use of scientific studies, but they still saw Scripture as having the final say on their view of the divine act of creation.

3. We have shown that most of the fathers held to the six days as being literal 24-hour days. At the very minimum, they all believed that creation was sudden. In strong contrast to the claims of Hugh Ross, we have demonstrated that no father proposed anything that could be taken as affirming deep time. It does not follow logically that if a father did not specify the exact

84. Gregory of Nazianzus, *Second Theological Oration* 18, in *NPNF2*, vol. 7.

85. Augustine, *City of God* 15.27 in *NPNF1*, vol. 2. For more on the fathers and the Flood, see Bradshaw, "Creationism and the Early Church," chapter 6, table 6.1. Online: www. robibrad.demon.co.uk/Chapter6.htm

86. Davis A. Young, *The Biblical Flood* (Grand Rapids, MI: Eerdmans, 1995), p. 26–27.

length of each creation day, or even treated them as purely symbolic, then he would not see the time frame of creation as being important, or that deep time was a viable option. The oft-used counter examples of Clement, Origen, and Augustine, best understood through the lens of Alexandrian allegorical hermeneutics, all held that the creation had been fully completed in an instant.

4. Regardless of their differing hermeneutical approaches to Genesis 1, the fathers held to the sex/septa-millenary typological eschatology of the six days. The tradition among the fathers was that the creation occurred less than 6,000 years in the past, and the world would end or dramatically change at the Second Advent, which would occur at the end of the 6,000 years.

5. The fathers asserted that the Flood in Genesis 6–8 was worldwide in extent, and some held that the existence of fossils was evidence of this cataclysm.

6. The fathers were young-earth creationists.

7. The fathers were not striving for novelty. They merely saw their task as culling from, accentuating, and preserving ancient apostolic orthodoxy.

The writings of the Church fathers can give understanding to Christians today. The fathers were not perfect, but they sought to reverentially interact with the Bible as the authoritative Word of God, and they articulated the great foundational orthodox doctrines of the Trinity and the person of Christ. Their doctrinal work still beneficially influences the evangelical Church today through their creeds, which we hear resonating with Scripture. It ought not be assumed, therefore, that the fathers' thoughts on the age of the earth, the days of creation, and the worldwide Flood should be considered inferior to and be replaced by Enlightenment science. This is especially the case, when, as seen above, the fathers had such unanimity in their belief that the Bible truthfully teaches that the earth was created in six literal days and only several thousand years ago, and that the Flood was a worldwide cataclysm. The fathers held fast to this Bible-based cosmogony in the face of the naturalistic evolutionary theories of their time, because the fathers believed that the latter concepts were rooted in paganism, not in Scripture. We believe it would please the Lord for the Church to heed and affirm what John Chrysostom wrote 1,600 years ago:

> Not to believe what is contained in the Divine Scripture, but to introduce something else from one's own mind — this, I believe, subjects those who hazard such a thing to great danger (*Homilies on Genesis*, XIII, p. 3).

Chapter 2

A Brief Overview of the Exegesis of Genesis 1–11: Luther to Lyell

David W. Hall

George Santayana once wrote that "Those who cannot remember the past are condemned to repeat it." Some scholars seem no less immune to this proclivity to repeat errors or mis-statements from the past. One area of study where this is clearly evident is in the assessment of history by Christian scholars; particularly when it comes to *who* affirmed *what*, and *when*, regarding creation and related matters. One of the many examples is Walter Kaiser, who states that the "day-age view has been the majority view of the church since the fourth century."[1]

Since there are so many unchecked citations, urban legends, and outright misappropriations of key historical thinkers, this catalogue of the history of the exegesis of Genesis 1–11 prior to the mid-19th century when the Church abandoned its traditional view may be useful as a resource to scholars or anyone interested in proper biblical interpretation.

One such urban legend suggests that it was at the height of the Fundamentalist/Modernist controversy when reactionary young-earth evangelicals hatched the idea of a literal six-day creation *ex nihilo*. John McIntyre, professor of physics at Texas A&M University, has warned against what he calls "Christian amnesia," which allegedly forgets the earlier commentators on creation: "[Some] Christians have introduced a modern, naïve 24-hour interpretation for days in Genesis, disagreeing with the classical, sophisticated analysis of these days by Augustine, Aquinas, and Calvin. . . . How can Christian scholars today ignore so completely

---

1. Walter Kaiser et al, *Hard Sayings of the Bible* (Downers Grove, IL: IVPress, 1996), p. 104. See also Walter Kaiser, *Toward an Old Testament Theology* (Grand Rapids, MI: Zondervan, 1978), p. 75.

the great Christian scholars of the past?"[2] This essay challenges McIntyre's assessment from the Reformation onward, as Mook's previous chapter has done regarding the pre-Reformation period.

Accordingly, what follows is a summary of the most noteworthy theologians from 1500 to roughly 1830 (about the time of Charles Lyell, the figurehead leader of the geological theory of deep time). As will be demonstrated, virtually all of them adopted an essentially uniform view of creation and the age of the earth.[3] We contend that it is a very difficult task to reproduce pre-1800 Christian literature that both employs rigorous exegetical methodology and that defends something other than a literal interpretation of Genesis 1–11.

The colorful phrase of C.S. Lewis, "chronological snobbery," may reverberate in our minds at this point. For often it seems that many are all too ready to disqualify earlier Christians from the discussion simply *because* they are earlier (or "pre-scientific"). Notwithstanding, we would be wise to heed the challenge of some "rediscoverers" of older orthodoxy, especially if they contend against history's quite compelling interpretations of Scripture, which can be found in the consensual exegesis of earlier writers. Thus we would argue that a thoroughly evangelical interpretation of Genesis today does not only demand a commitment to inerrancy, but also a more serious regard for the history of exegesis of Genesis 1–11.

One can only speculate why it is often unbelievers, rather than Christian theologians and historians, whose objectivity seems much less jaded in acknowledging this. In spite of his strong anti-Christian bias, Andrew Dickson White traces a long historical thread of interpretation spanning from Aquinas to Calvin who adhered to a rather literal scheme of biblical interpretation.[4] In the late 19th century, White grudgingly admitted that Calvin had a "strict" interpretation of Genesis, and that "down to a period almost within living memory [1896], it was held, virtually 'always, everywhere, and by all,' that the universe, as we now see it, was created literally and directly by the voice or hands of the Almighty, or by both — out of nothing — in an instant or in six days. . . ."[5] With many testimonies like this beyond reasonable dispute, why some modern evangelicals continue to misrepresent matters is another question to be pursued by other studies.

When one considers the totality of primary sources, rather than the unsubstantiated claims of modern proponents of old-earth creationism, we will

---

2. John A. McIntyre, *The Misuse of Science* (unpublished manuscript, 1993), p. 24.

3. Some of this material appeared earlier in David W. Hall, *Holding Fast to Creation* (Powder Springs, GA: The Covenant Foundation, 2001, 2nd ed.). See also David W. Hall, "The Evolution of Mythology: Classic Creation Survives as the Fittest Among Its Critics and Revisers," in Joseph A. Pipa Jr. and David W. Hall, eds., *Did God Create in Six Days?* (White Hall, WV: Tolle Lege Press, 2005), p. 265–301.

4. Andrew Dickson White, *A History of the Warfare of Science with Theology in Christendom* (New York: D. Appleton and Co., 1896), p. 49.

5. Ibid., p. 60.

see that Martin Luther, John Calvin, the Westminster Divines, John Wesley, and the like are no friends of deep time or gradual creation. Their voices were virtually unanimous, clear in their exegesis, and quite distinct from geologically constrained eisegesis that has followed in the wake of uniformitarian geology of the last 200 years. To say that most Bible interpreters from Luther to Lyell held beliefs compatible with a 14-billion-year-old cosmos constitutes revisionist history to an embarrassing extreme.

The Protestant Reformers

Martin Luther's view is so explicit as to largely go uncontested.[6] Numerous citations could be assembled, showing that he clearly and firmly held to literal days, no death or natural evil before the Fall, and a global Flood.[7] But it bears mentioning that Luther (1483–1546) is not so much misappropriated as he is often completely ignored. Omitting Luther (and others) as a reference point strongly illustrates the selective biases of the researcher. In a recent article, Robert Letham confirms that Luther "without ambiguity adopts the interpretation that the days of creation are of twenty-four hours duration, at the same time arguing that the earth is only six thousand years old."[8]

Just prior to Calvin, we can find the testimony of Anglican bishop Hugh Latimer (1485–1555), who expressed what he believed was the representative view held by the Christian world of his time. His comments take for granted a literal view of Genesis 1. In a sermon in 1552, he admonished his hearers with these sobering words: "How can we be so foolish to set so much by this world, knowing that it shall endure but a little while? For we know by scripture, and all learned men affirm the same, that the world was made to endure *six thousand years*. Now, of these six thousand be passed already *five thousand five hundred and fifty-two*, and yet this time which is left shall be shortened for the elect's sake, as Christ himself witnesseth."[9] A week later he again admonished his hearers to consider their ways because "the world was ordained of God to endure, as scripture and all learned men agree, six thousand years: now of this number are gone *five thousand five hundred fifty-two*, so that there is left only four hundred and fifty lacking two: and this but a little time. . . ."[10] Together with the helpful mathematical subtraction, we must also hear something else he was saying: Latimer obviously believed in a literal chronological computation of the creation account. The ease with which he moved on from his premise (the age of the earth)

---

6. Cf. e.g., Martin Luther, *Luther's Works*, vol. 17 (St. Louis, MO: Concordia, 1972), p. 29, 118.
7. See Thane Ury's chapter in the present work.
8. Robert Letham, " 'In the Space of Six Days': The Days of Creation from Origen to the Westminster Assembly," *Westminster Theological Journal*, vol. 61:2 (Fall 1999): p. 149–174. Cf. also footnote 28 on Luther in Pipa and Hall, *Did God Create in Six Days?*, p. 280.
9. *The Works of Hugh Latimer*, I:20; italics added.
10. Ibid., I:52.

to admonishment is startling. But there is another observation that cannot be overlooked. He claimed that all "learned men agree." Of his contemporaries' views on creation, he would know better than most of us.

Thus, claims that late-Medieval and Reformation-era Christians held to anything less than a strong view of special creation are akin to other revisionist efforts. Upon scrutiny, that claim is found to be indefensible, relatively recent, and more a function of accommodating ideology than historical accuracy. Prior to Lyell, it was unthinkable for faithful Christians to suggest that creation could occur apart from God's directive Word, and much less that this would happen over the course of several undefined and long epochs of time. Robert Bishop concurs: "Neither the original audience of that book [Genesis] nor anyone else until about two hundred years ago would have understood a 'geological era' to be a meaningful concept."[11] There is scant evidence, if any, that prior to the 19th century any view of creation that accorded with macro-evolution was anything but aberrant.

Howard Van Till, among others, has claimed that John Calvin (1509–1564) held ideas that were quite compatible with the discoveries of modern science.[12] Upon scrutiny, however, that is as equally untrue as the distorted handling of the patristic literature by old-earth advocates. Calvin had a consistent view of creation, affirming, for example, that "God, *by speaking*, was Creator of the universe."[13] Moreover, Calvin affirmed: "Indeed, the testimony of Moses in the history of creation is very clear" that God created out of "formless matter."[14]

Rather than advocating continuous creation as a reconciling motif, Calvin noted that, "We are drawn away from all fictions to the one God who distributed his work into six days that we might not find it irksome to occupy our whole life in contemplating it."[15] He repeatedly and consistently referred to Moses as "a sure witness and herald of the one God, the Creator."[16] Calvin also wrote: "[C]reation is not inpouring, but the beginning of essence out of nothing."[17]

In his major exposition of creation, Calvin began by stating agreement with earlier treatments of this subject by Basil and Ambrose. Summarizing the "first history of the creation of the universe, as it has been set forth briefly by Moses," Calvin noted:

> From this history we shall learn that God by the power of his Word
> and Spirit created heaven and earth out of nothing; that thereupon he

---

11. Robert C. Bishop, "Science and Theology: A Methodological Comparison" in *Journal of Interdisciplinary Studies*, vol. v, no. 1/2 (1993): p. 155.

12. Howard Van Till, *The Fourth Day* (Grand Rapids, MI, MI: Eerdmans, 1986).

13. John Calvin, *The Institutes of the Christian Religion*, J. T. McNeill, ed. (Philadelphia, PA: Westminster Press, 1960), 1.13.7. Italics added.

14. Ibid., 1.13.14.

15. Ibid., 1.14.2.

16. Ibid.

17. Ibid., 1.15.5.

brought forth living beings and inanimate things of every kind, that in a wonderful series he distinguished an innumerable variety of things, that he endowed each kind with its own nature, assigned functions, appointed places and stations.[18]

His discussion aimed at practical knowledge, that is, that believers would not merely know the truths about creation, but also to be led to praise the Creator. God is so powerful that, far from six days being too short a span of time to create all the beauty around us, Calvin averred: "For it is not without significance that he divided the making of the universe into six days, even though it would have been no more difficult for him to have completed in one moment the whole work together in all its details than to arrive at its completion gradually by a progression of this sort."[19] Calvin's *Institutes* do not aid and abet the doctrines of progressive or theistic evolution, nor a creation from already existing matter.

Calvin's view may further be confirmed from a perusal of key verses from his *Commentaries*. In his treatment of Genesis 1:1, he expounded:

> When God in the beginning created the heaven and the earth, the earth was empty and waste. He moreover teaches by the word "created," that what before did not exist was not made. . . . Therefore his meaning is that the world was made out of nothing. Hence the folly of those is refuted who imagine that unformed matter existed from eternity; and who gather nothing else from the narration of Moses than that the world was furnished with new ornaments, and received a form of which it was before destitute.[20]

Commenting on the fifth day of creation, Calvin observed that even God's shaping of new life from that which does exist is praiseworthy: "Therefore, there is in this respect a miracle as great as if God had begun to create out of nothing those things which he commanded to proceed from the earth. And he does not take his material from the earth, because he needed it, but that he might the better combine the separate parts of the world with the universe itself."[21]

Calvin commented on Hebrews 11:3: "For they who have faith do not entertain a slight opinion as to God being the Creator of the world, but they have a deep conviction fixed in their minds and behold the true God. And further, they understand the power of his word, not only as manifested instantaneously in creating the world, but also as put forth continually in its preservation."[22] On

---

18. Ibid., 1.14.20.
19. Ibid., 1.14.22.
20. John Calvin, *Commentary on Genesis* (Grand Rapids, MI: Baker, 1979), 1:70.
21. Ibid., p. 90.
22. John Calvin, *Commentary on the Epistle to the Hebrews* (Grand Rapids, MI: Baker, 1979), p. 264–265.

this passage, he had noted earlier that "even infidels acknowledge" creation.[23] On Isaiah 40:22, Calvin observed: "Formerly he spoke of the creation of the world, but now he comes to the continual government of it; for God did not only for a single moment exert his power for creating the world, but he manifests his power not less efficaciously in preserving it. And this is worthy of observation; for our minds would be little impressed by knowing that God is the creator of the world, if his hand were not continually stretched out for upholding it in existence." In context, Calvin — far from minimizing momentary creation — extolled it; but he also urged upon the sanctified mind the importance of continually knowing God and His governance.

Interestingly, had Calvin wanted to advocate "long days," two verses often used today by day-age proponents could have been useful: Psalm 90:4 and 2 Peter 3:8. Calvin, nevertheless, refrained from injecting the idea that the first days of creation could be as long as millennia, and he interpreted these passages to mean simply that God is above time.

In his 1554 commentary's discussion of Genesis 1:5, Calvin makes his well-known statement about divine accommodation, which has led some to imagine that if Calvin was alive today he would be an non-literalist regarding Genesis 1. But careful attention to his text indicates otherwise. He wrote:

> Here the error of those is manifestly refuted, who maintain that the world was made in a moment. For it is too violent a cavil to contend that Moses distributes the work which God perfected at once into six days, for the mere purpose of conveying instruction. Let us rather conclude that God himself took the space of six days, for the purpose of accommodating his works to the capacity of men.[24]

He consciously rejects Augustine's view,[25] and shows that in his mind Genesis is not simply a literary framework for teaching theology, but records the "works" of God on those days. Furthermore, elsewhere in the commentary he affirms (1) that light was created before the sun and moon, (2) that the gathering of the waters on day 2 was a miracle, (3) that He created the stars on the fourth day, (4) that Adam was made literally from the dust of the earth, (5) that the Flood was

23. Ibid.
24. John Calvin, *Genesis,* translated by John King (Edinburgh: Banner of Truth, 1992 reprint), p. 78. He makes similar comments on 1:16 (pages p. 86–87).
25. It is a popular myth that Augustine provides some sort of preemptive imprimatur for uniformitarianism. As Mook points out in his chapter in this volume, Augustine was confused about the length of the days of creation because of his faulty Latin translation and his ignorance of Hebrew. But, while it is true that Augustine did not hold to 24-hour days, he actually went in the opposite direction and took all six days of creation as happening in a singular instant. There is thus great irony when Hugh Ross and other old-earther proponents genuflect at Augustine's feet. In their misunderstanding of Augustine's view, they completely overlook the fact that the post-Reformation "debate" was not deep time vs. literal days, but instead nano-seconds vs. literal days.

global, and (6) that the genealogies in Genesis 5 and 11 were strict chronologies (with no gaps).[26] Thus we conclude that Calvin presents a consistent view on this subject, and it stands in strong contrast to modern attempts to fit millions of years into the Genesis account.

Calvin's lieutenant, Theodore Beza (1519–1605), stated his views clearly and succinctly as well. He affirmed that Hebrews 11:3 taught creation *ex nihilo*.[27]

After consulting the writings of the early Protestant leaders, Calvin, Beza, and Luther, we can summarize their views as follows:

- Genesis 1–11 is intended to be understood as literal history
- These men employed a normal hermeneutic
- They concluded that the universe was less than 6,000 years old
- They held to literal days

From Calvin to Ussher

During the century after Calvin's death (1564), various Reformed theologians[28] addressed questions that are often presented today as if they are insuperable barriers to embracing the traditional interpretation of Genesis 1–11. This apparent insuperability is most likely attributable to contemporary theologians being unacquainted with how well our exegetical forefathers already dealt with objections that became more pertinent after modern scientific revolutions. The following questions to be examined underscore alleged difficulties which, many feel, necessitate exegetical revision:

1. Did the Reformers address the issue of light being created on the first day with the sun not created until the 4th day?

2. Did they posit ordinary providence or mediate agencies as the primary means of creation?

3. Did they define what they meant by "day"?

4. Did they allow for long periods of creation?

5. Did they uniformly commit themselves to a particular chronology?

6. Did their writings reflect merely personal views about creation or was there an orthodox interpretation on Genesis for this period?

---

26. Calvin, *Genesis*, p. 76 (point 1 above), 81, (point 2), 83 (point 3), 111 (point 4), 250, 272, and 281 (point 5), and 231 and 313 (point 6)..

27. Theodore de Beze, *Cours Sur les Epitres aux Romains et aux Hebreaux (1564-1566)* in *Travaux d'Humanism et Renaissance* (Geneva: Librarie Droz, 1988), vol. 226, p. 311. Puritan leader William Perkins taught similarly on 11:3 in his lengthy *Commentary on Hebrews 11* (Boston, MA: Pilgrim Press, 1992 reprint).

28. Portions of this section are taken from my "History Answering Present Objections: Exegesis of the Days of Creation a Century Before and After Westminster, 1540–1740," with Mark Herzer and Wesley Baker in my *Holding Fast to Creation* (Powder Springs, GA: The Covenant Foundation, Second edition © 2001).

In several studies, the massive, uniform, and clear testimony (both explicit and implicit) by Westminster Divines has been assembled on related issues.[29] Meeting in 1643–1648, of course, it is hardly conceivable that those interpreters created an exegetical consensus *ex nihilo*. Informed historians realize that the Westminster Divines floated in the middle of a stream of interpretation; they certainly did not live in a hermeneutical vacuum. Exegetes, including Calvin and other major Reformers, preceded the Westminster Divines by a century; meanwhile, other Reformed interpreters persisted in offering classical interpretations of Genesis 1 for at least a century after the Westminster Assembly concluded. Since earlier studies have focused mainly on what the Divines themselves wrote in other essays, this discussion will provide some of the broader context for this and other studies. We shall continue to test our hypothesis and see if those 17th-century Divines foisted new interpretations on the Church. Compared with exegetes in the prior century and the next, do we discover unity or a kaleidoscope of opinions? Accordingly, below the reader will find commentary by representative Reformed theologians from 1540–1740.

Subsequent to Calvin, moreover, an impressive train of Genevan scholars left answers to many of the questions posed above. The fact that answers are recorded should, as much as anything else, convince modern participants in these debates that these objections are neither unanswerable nor novel. Similar challenges persist to the present, and are often touted as the death knell to traditional, young-earth creationist views. But upon examination, the student of history will discover that these alleged impasses have already long ago been weighed and found wanting.

The 1562 *Annotations from the Geneva Bible* provided authoritative commentary on related issues, and was penned while Calvin was still alive and at the height of his fame. On Genesis 1:3, Genevan annotators — certainly representative of many others associated with the "Protestant Rome" — provide one of the earliest English interpretations of the creation narratives: "The light was made before either sunne or moone was created; therefore we must not attribute that to the creatures that are God's instruments which only appertaineth to God."

The question of light preceding the sun is still surprisingly perceived by some to be an insurmountable difficulty for creationists. But these earlier Reformed commentators recognized the issue and saw no problem whatsoever. They simply drew a distinction between the light coming from a undesignated luminary source on ordinary days 1–3, and the sunlight and moonlight which shined from the 4th ordinary day onward. The days were not considered different in degree; only the light source was different from what man has observed since the fourth day of creation. The miraculous was embraced by earlier Genevans, who also commented on Genesis 1:8: "So that we see it is the only [exclusively] power of God's Worde that maketh the earth fruteful, which is naturally barren."[30] The onus is

---

29. Cf. David W. Hall, "What Was the View of the Westminster Assembly Divines on Creation Days?" in Pipa and Hall, *Did God Create in Six Days?*, p. 41–52.
30. *Annotations from the Geneva Bible* (1562), p. 4.

upon modern old-earth accommodationists to prove that these annotations in the Genevan Bible were anything but the accepted position of the day.

Calvin's esteem for Wolfgang Musculus (1497–1563) is evident in the preface to his *Commentary on the Psalms*, where Calvin singled out Martin Luther and Wolfgang Musculus for praise. Musculus' writings continued to influence exegetes a century later. In 1554, Musculus composed a very influential treatise on Genesis, *In Genesim Moses Commentarii Plenissimi*. While commenting on the fourth day of creation, he interpreted:

> There were days before the sun, just as also there was night before the moon and stars. . . . At that time the days had an inexplicable light, with no observable sign of their stage, or even of their midpoint, which are governed (with regard to our experience) by the sun's course, as it is ordered and noted [by us]. Therefore it is rightly attributed to the sun because I do not say that it constitutes, but rather that it orders and arranges the day. However, I have not been inconsistent with the point in this place, understanding the work not as artificial but as *natural days*: and not only of the sun, but also of the moon and the stars. . . . In the space of a year there are twelve revolutions of the moon: i. e., twelve months are completed. And a solar year is when the sun returns to the end of its own circuit whence it began.

On Genesis 1:1, Musculus notes that God created "on the first day." On Genesis 1:3, answering the query why the phrase "morning and evening" is employed, Musculus writes that the evening is not the end, but the beginning of the "the natural day." Shortly thereafter, he would clarify that the evening is the "ordinary part of the day in which evening precedes and morning follows."[31] He also argued that in Leviticus 23, Moses linked an evening to the Sabbath, as one day of seven. For that reason, he explained, the Jews reckoned their time with evening being the beginning of the natural day. Musculus agreed with Basil who numbered the hours not as counting the mode *a termino ad que*, but as *a termini a quo*.[32] Concurring with Basil (and other Church fathers), Musculus commented that the reckoning of time for the Hebrews was from the beginning hour, not the end but the beginning of the first hour. He also referred to Chrysostom who agreed in his *Fourth Homily on Genesis*: "Morning, however, is the end of the night and the completion of the day." Musculus apparently saw the Orthodox Church as holding the same opinion, with no dissenting voice, adding that Lombard also confirmed that "morning" is not the first of the day. Musculus consistently interpreted the days as natural days: "For natural days

---

31. Wolfgang Musculus, *In Genesim Moses Commentarii Plenissimi* (Geneva, 1554), p. 9.

32. Musculus' Latin phrasing literally means "not as counting the mode from the point to which time was begun but as from which time was marked." Thus, he reinforced the Hebrew way of reckoning time by interpreting the days as beginning (not ending) with the evening.

are comprised of these parts — evening and morning — in order that we may rightly [understand] the three-day period as having ceased in the space of three nights and days."

He further added that the whole world was created by the sixth day: "Thus the days are numbered as time is." The days were, he wrote, "in time" and "Just as the entire world was constituted in the revolution of 6 days, so it continues." Musculus' massive commentary, certainly a theological paradigm of its day, did not seem to distinguish between the length and quality of the days, as if the fourth day began a new or different chronology.

Each day, he thought, was "reduced to diurnal (evening) which began to be morning." "Evening and morning" should be understood just as in Psalm 55:17: "Evening and morning . . . I will . . . cry aloud" (NKJV). Musculus saw no reason to interpose an artificially long period in the creation days, commenting: "Just as a natural day, not night, is called a day," so evening and morning shall flow as long as light fills this space of night and day.[33]

Long before modern theories, Musculus was aware of light prior to solar light; he also admitted that the quality of time before the creation is not comprehended simplistically. Still, he and most of his contemporaries logically inferred that creation was autumnal, and that the first year of creation was comprised of "12 months time," just as years and days were interpreted as "in time."[34] He knew that any difficulty presented by observation was ultimately resolvable by this simple proposition: "the sun is not the origin of light."[35]

Peter Martyr (1499–1562) was one of the most powerful Reformers both on the continent and in Great Britain. In a 1543 article, Martyr wrote, "The evening and morning were made the first days of the gathering together and spreading forth of light before the bringing forth of the sunne."[36] He also testified, "When we speak of the creation of things, we bring not forth one thing out of another after Aristotle's manner, but we affirm all natures, as well as bodies without bodie [angels, demons], to be created of nothing by the word of God."[37] Of value to the modern interpreter, Martyr dismissed two recent notions: (1) He affirmed that the first days, complete with evening and morning, were ordinary days, prior to the creation of the sun; and (2) He rejected creation as necessarily employing either Aristotle's specific forces or using any force other than "the word of God." His perspicuity leaves little room for speculation as to where he stood.

Martyr's view is substantially the same as Archbishop Ussher's later comment on fiat creation: "How and in what manner did God create all things? By no

33. Ibid., p. 13.
34. Ibid., p. 26.
35. Ibid., p. 29.
36. Peter Martyr, "The Propositions of D. Peter Martyr, disputed openlie in the Common Schooles at Strasbourgh," contained in Peter Martyr's *Works* (London, 1558, trans. by Anthony Marten, reprint of 1543 original), p. 144.
37. Ibid., p. 144.

means or instruments, (which he needeth not as man doth) but by his powerfull word, that is, by his only will, calling those things that are not as though they were, Heb. 11.3. Rom. 4.17. Ps. 148.5."[38]

Martyr, far from lacking enlightenment, proceeded to speak to concerns centuries ahead of rival theories. He noted: "For God, to the intent he would manifest both his power and his mercy, created of nothing an *infinit* sort of man in the whole nature of things." Rather than depending on ordinary providence alone or primarily, earlier orthodox theologians like Martyr believed the following: "The keeping back of waters from joining the earth, we attribute not to the stars, but to the word of God, as also the power whereby plants and herbs are brought out of the earth. . . . Albeit it is said, 'Let the waters or earth bring forth this or that,' yet the creation of all things must be attributed to God alone."[39]

Another Genevan contemporary of Calvin, the great jurist Francois Hotman, offered his opinion in a 1569 work, *Consolatio Sacris Litteris*. Showing that the language of the Irish Articles and the Westminster Confession merely reflected the view received for some time by the orthodox, he opens with this: "The world was created by God in the space of six days."[40] Following that bold and clear affirmation is this:

> [On the first day God created matter in general — the chaos:] then finally the light. And it was therefore numbered as the first day. However, in the following five days He separated the parts of that mass [and] thus arranged them. Now the second day he divided the heap of waters. . . . The third day followed in which God [created] the earth's mass. . . . Then on the fourth day he created the heavenly sphere in which He arranged the sun, moon and the remainder of the starry host, from one of whose fixed direction He communicated the measure of its light, which He created on the first day, in order that from the running of their courses, the reckoning of years, months, and even days may be established. On the fifth day merely. . . . But now on the sixth day, for the first time [we have] the beasts walking [on the earth].[41]

It is clear from this that Hotman — hardly to be imagined as differing from Calvin, Martyr, Musculus, and others — thought the days were sequential, ordinary, and calculated as we count normal days today.

Among the first-generation Reformed theologians, these classical interpretations prevailed at least until the time of the Westminster Assembly. Far from this survey being only selective in its testimony, one is hard pressed indeed to find any exception to this rule, either in Geneva, the Palatinate [Germany], Zurich, Holland, or England. One certainly has difficulty finding exponents of day-age,

---

38. Ussher, *Summe and Substance* (London, 1647), p. 94.
39. Martyr, "The Propositions of D. Peter Martyr . . . ," p. 144.
40. Francois Hotman, *Consolatio Sacris Litteris* (Geneva, 1569), p. 1.
41. Ibid.

analogical days, or the framework theory from 1540 to 1740. This is highly peculiar — not to mention worthy of explanation — given the common refrain today that the Reformers and the Divines were so varied, if not progressive, on this complex of issues.

Continental Reformed Theologians, 1590–1690

In his commentary on the Heidelberg Catechism, Zacharias Ursinus concluded that "According to the common reckoning, it is now, counting from this 1616 of Christ, 5534 years since the creation of the world."[42] He adds that Melancthon estimated the age at 5,579 years, Luther estimated 5,576, and those of Geneva estimated 5,559 years. Ursinus, in 1616 — not to mention the other Reformers — would have to be totally repudiated in 30 years, if the Westminster Assembly held to a long or undefined period of creation. Ursinus continues: "These calculations harmonize sufficiently with each other in the larger numbers, although some years are either added or wanting in the smaller numbers. According to these four calculations, *made by the most learned men of our time,* it will appear by comparing them together, that the world was created by God at least not much over 5559 or 5579 years. The world, therefore, was not created from everlasting, but had a beginning."[43] William Perkins adopted the same chronology and age of the universe, signaling his position.[44]

Later, Ursinus commented on the fourth commandment: "That by the example of himself resting on the seventh day, he might exhort men, as by a most effectual and constraining argument, to imitate him and so abstain on the seventh day, from the labors to which they were accustomed *during the other six days* of the week."[45]

The most luminous Westminster Divine from Calvin's Geneva was John Diodati. In his *Pious Annotations Upon the Holy Bible* (1643), he articulated several times the same view as Calvin, and the perspective espoused long after the Westminster Assembly. Commenting on Genesis 1:3, Diodati wrote, "It is likely that the light was at first imprinted in some part of the heaven, whose turning made the first three days, and the fourth it was restrained into the body of the Sun, or of all the other stars; but in a different degree."[46] On verse 4, he remarks that, according to the prevailing Genevan view at the time of the Westminster Assembly, God "ordained the heaven to turn continually about; and that when the Hemisphere [ed., Lightfoot also computed the hemispheric effect to buttress his literalism], wherein the light was imprinted was above the earth, it should

---

42. Zacharias Ursinus, *Commentary to the Heidelberg Confession*, (Columbus: Scott and Bascom Printers, 1852, reprint of 1616 original).

43. Ibid., p. 1450, emphasis added.

44. William Perkins, *Works*, I:143–4.

45. Ursinus, *Commentary to the Heidelberg Confession*, p. 531, emphasis added to show the basis of comparison.

46. John Diodati. *Pious Annotations Upon the Holy Bible* (London, 1643).

then be day; and when it was under the earth, it should be night, which was the beginning of the vicissitude or the succession of day and night."[47]

Diodati's *Annotations* — one of the most authoritative works for a century — also explained the meaning of "evening" in Genesis 1 as "that is night" when the Jews begin their scheme of chronology by reckoning days to begin at sundown, contrary to the Western time conventions. Diodati continued to speak of the meaning of evening as "that in this first turning of the heaven, none but the aforesaid things were created."[48] On Genesis 2:2, Diodati— the successor to Calvin and Beza — commented: "He ceased to shew his vertue and power in creating of new kindes of creatures, yet ceased not in working of their preservation, sustenance, and increase by order of nature and in guiding them with his providence."[49] Further, Diodati noted that God "ended the worke of Creation on the seventh day . . . by this rest God would not proceed *in infinitum* in creating, so would he not leave anything imperfect which he intended to make."[50]

On Hebrews 11:3, Diodati wrote, "That is to say the world [see Heb. 1:2, where he defined the world as 'all temporal things subject to the course, divisions, and successions of time'] [was created by the Word] of nothing, by the onely omnipotency and will of God."[51] And on Romans 4:17, Diodati explained, "That is to say, by his Worde hee makes them to be . . . as he did in the creation of all things, and in the miraculous resurrections wrought by Christ — let there be light, Lazarus come forth, etc."[52] So, by attributing all of creation to the omnipotence and will of God and His Word, he rules out creation by ordinary providence alone or primarily.

The 1619 Dutch *Annotations upon the Whole Bible ordered by the Synod of Dordt* was a commentary admired by the Westminster Divines and other Puritans. Here we find the following comment on Genesis 1:5: "The meaning of these words [day/night] is that night and day had made up one natural day together, which with the Hebrews began with the evening and ended with the approach of the next evening, comprehending twenty four houres." Can objective research uncover similar precedence to support post-Lyellian views on Genesis 1? And what are we to conclude when moderns ignore such strong testimony?

Johannes Polyander, writing between Dordt and Westminster, made clear that these views continued to dominate the landscape of his time. In 1624, Polyander defended this thesis: "We know the creation of the world was produced from nothing except the virtue and omni-power of God as confirmed by the Scriptures and the Apostles Creed."[53] Polyander thought that both the Scriptures and the

---

47. Ibid.
48. Ibid.
49. Ibid.
50. Ibid.
51. Ibid.
52. Ibid.
53. Cited in Herman Bavinck, ed., *Synopsis Purioris Theologiae* (1624, reprint 1881), p. 83.

creed called for creation to be understood as by divine fiat, without other natural processes. He continued to aver that the world was created *ex nihilo* and that God disposed all of creation "in the space of six days to show forth his immense glory and wisdom."[54] It should be noted that Polyander's Latin wording here (*sex dierum spatio disposuit*, "in the space of six days") is semantically very similar to both Calvin's and Westminster's phraseology, showing the near universal approbation of that phrasing at this time.

Other post-Reformation giants affirmed this same consensus. Johan Osiander affirmed that the creation of all plants, animals, and man occurred during six days.[55] Another Dutch contemporary of the Westminster Divines, Johann Henrici Heideggeri, affirmed similar conclusions. In his "Chronologia Sacra Patriarchum," his first entry was this: "Adam was created on the 6th day of the world around autumn, the day corresponding to our last day of October." That time is dated as year 1 in his "chronology," with others following in sequence.[56]

Heideggeri also iterated that the creation of the world began in autumn and stated elsewhere that Moses intended to refer to Year One. Heideggeri was so serious about the chronology that he also discussed whether October 26th could have been the first day of creation, if October 31st was the creation of Adam on the morning of the sixth sequential and normal day.[57] Moreover, the Reformation consensus did not shy away from dating this creation to 3,983 years before Christ's birth — as Perkins and many others did. Heideggeri even suggests that Adam was created "in our third hour."[58] While Heideggeri understood that such chronology may have been little more than an illuminating tradition, what is important for our study is to note that he and others viewed the hours of the sixth day as real-time like ours — not a fictitious or misleading literary device. Later, Heideggeri affirmed that this sixth day was distributed into 12 hours of light and darkness.[59] He always treated the time markers as real time, beginning with the question, "In what time of year was Adam created?"[60]

No reputable Reformed theologian from Calvin through 50 years after Westminster provides any theological latitude for what are now known as the gap theory, the day-age theory, the analogical days theory, or the framework hypothesis. Further, these exemplary defenders themselves addressed most of the queries that modern Christians think are so insoluble. They were well versed in the responses already given by Basil, Ambrose, Chrysostom, Lombard, and others. They were united in maintaining that "the power of God's Word" was the "only" power that animated

---

54. Ibid.

55. Johan Osiander, *Orthodox Animadversions* (Tubingen, 1693), p. 301 (Locus V, xiii).

56. ohann Henrici Heideggeri, *Historia Sacra Patriarchum, Exercitationes Selectae* (1668; reprint Tigurinie, 1729), Part III, p. 547.

57. Johann Henrici Heideggeri, *Exercitu Quarta*, p. xv, 84.

58. Ibid.

59. Ibid.

60. Ibid.

all of creation. They saw no need to posit forces, processes, or length of days longer than "natural days" to provide for God's miraculous creation. They rested their exegesis on miracle, not on post-creational providence. Many of these theologians used the phrase "*in tempora*" (in time), or specified that days and nights had 12 hours, or frequently used the Latin dative of time to signify that they meant real, not figurative, hours. They were not as ambiguous as some modern old-earth proponents wish to represent them. None of them advocated long periods of creation or non-sequential days. Most of these adopted a common chronology and provided dates of years since creation that can only comport with a literal view.

The study below answers another important question that is frequently asked: Can the likes of British Puritans such as Ames, Perkins, Lightfoot, and others be understood as ambiguous or latitudinarian on this issue, especially in light of the massive textual evidence now available? History answers that query in the negative, once again disproving the hypothesis of modernity.

British Puritan Exegetes

The Puritan giant William Ames (1576–1633) by all accounts would be considered standard-bearer for Reformed orthodoxy. He lived a short time before the Westminster Assembly, denied the Augustinian scheme, was a dominant influence on the Divines, and helped pave the way for the Westminster consensus. But due to the biased modern scholarship of John Macpherson, for over a century Ames was thought to lend credence to cosmological constructions that were compatible with evolutionary schemes. In an apparent attempt to manufacture support where none existed, Macpherson erroneously claimed that Ames held to long intervening ages between the creation days.[61] Unfortunately, as is often the case, such misstatements are widely circulated and uncritically accepted, before actually consulting the author's own words.

Close scrutiny of Ames exposes Macpherson's historical revisionism. What Ames asserted was that — contrary to Augustine — the entire cosmos was not created *simul & uno momento* (simultaneously and in one moment); rather, the various *parts* were created "each in turn, succeeding in six days, with [normal] intervention [between each day]."[62] If Ames is understood as opposing the Augustinian/Alexandrian view that all six days of creation occurred in a singular instant, then Ames' claim is little more than a reaffirmation of Ambrose's (traditional) view. His words themselves align with the Westminster Divines on this subject, rather than opposing them. Furthermore, insofar as Ames was not commonly understood as holding to long periods of creation (nor was that the view of the

61. For a fuller treatment of this, see David W. Hall, "The Evolution of Mythology: Classic Creation Survives as the Fittest Among its Critics and Revisers," in Pipa and Hall, *Did God Create in Six Days?* p. 285–287.

62. William Ames, *The Marrow of Theology* (Boston, MA: Pilgrim Press, 1968), p. 102. See also my web-posted version for more references at: http://home.comcast. net/~webpages54/ap/hallcreation.html.

other testimonies above), something more than Macpherson's revisionism is needed to suggest that Ames would side with deep time.

Cambridge Fellow, William Perkins (1558–1602), was a puritan, polemicist, and preacher *par excellence*. His works at the height of British Puritanism became as popular as Calvin's, and he was a literalist cut from the same cloth as Ussher, Lightfoot, the Westminster Divines, and his famous convert, William Ames.

On the creation days, Perkins commented, "The sixth shall be touching the time of the beginning of the world, which is between five thousand and six thousand yeares a goe. For Moses hath set downe exactly the computation of time from the making of the world to his owne daies: and the Prophets after him haue with diligence set down the continuance of the same to the very birth of Christ. . . . Some say there bee 3929 from the creation to Christs birth as Beroaldus: some 3952 as Hierome and Bede: some 3960 as Luther and Io. Lucidus: some 3963 as Melancton in his *Chronicle*, and Functius: some 3970. As Bullinger and Tremelius: some towardes 4000. as Buntingus. . . ."[63]

Arguing against Augustine's proposed instantaneous creation, Perkins maintained: "Seventhly, some may aske in what space of time did God make the world? I answer, God could haue made the world, and all things in it in one moment: but hee began and finished the whole worke in six distinct daies."[64] As to why God took this many days to make the creation, Perkins argued: "in six distinct daies, to teach us, what wonderfull power & liberty he had ouer al his creatures: for he made the light when there was neither Sun nor Moone, nor Stars; to shew, that in giuing light to the world, he is not bound to the Sun, to any creature, or to any means: for the light was made the first day: but the Sunne, the Moone, and the Stars were not created before the fourth day."[65] Perkins, in his context, along with his chronology and the way his disciples understood him, assuredly provides no support for modern views of deep time, but confirms the orthodoxy of the young-earth creationist view.

Henry Ainsworth, a close predecessor to the Divines, shared the consensual view of the day. In his *Annotations on the Pentateuch and Psalms*, in reference to Genesis 1, he wrote, "Both large days, of 24 hours, from sun-setting to sun-setting; and strict, of 12 hours, from sun-rising to sun-setting, as is observed before on ver. 5, a special use whereof is shown in Psal. civ. 19–23."[66] On Genesis 1:5 he argues, "Which is with us the space of twenty-four hours."[67]

Prior to Ussher, most others defined the creation days in similar fashion. Gervase Babington (1550–1610), Bishop of Worchester, commented on Genesis 1:7

---

63. William Perkins, *An Exposition of the Creede*, I:143. This confirms that all the cited authors took the days of creation literally.

64. Ibid., I:143.

65. Ibid., I:143.

66. Henry Ainsworth, *Annotations on the Pentateuch and Psalms* (Soli Deo Gloria, 1997 reprint), p. 6.

67. Ibid.

that God created "not in one moment, but in six dayes space," thereby exhibiting an early use of "in the space of six days" to refer to actual days.[68] Later, Babington noted that God rested on the seventh day, following "six daies creating."[69] There was certainly no hint of an expansive period of creation at that time.

Another precursor to the Westminster Assembly was Andrew Willet (1562–1621). In his *Hexapla in Genesis*, Willet discussed whether the world was made in six days or instantaneously. Believing that the Mosaic account "must be taken plainly," he argued, "For if the world was made at once, how can it be true, that it was made in six days? Augustine other-where holdeth the contrary, that the world was not made in one day, but in order. . . ."[70] This text indicates that the generation prior to the Westminster Assembly consistently denied Augustine's view of instantaneous creation.

Another contemporary of the Westminster Assembly, John Richardson (1580–1654), Bishop of Ardagh, had a hand in these *Annotations*. His later (1655) supplement to those additions was endorsed by Ussher and Westminster Divine Thomas Gataker. With the blessings of at least one leading Divine (Gataker), Richardson wrote in his *Annotations on Genesis* that the creation days were "natural days consisting of 24 hours."[71] Furthermore, he commented, "The Evening, which is the beginning of the Night, and the Morning, which is the beginning of the Day, called the first day, largely taken, the Day natural of 24 houres." Later, on Genesis 1:5, Richardson wrote that the day's time was one of normal Jewish reckoning, "as the beginning of the natural day of twenty four hours was reckoned from the Creation . . . the Point Material is, That it must comprehend twenty four houres."

Lancelot Andrewes, Bishop of Winchester, asserted that the creation days should be measured as follows: "from Sunne to Sunne is counted a day."[72] Later, Andrews would affirm: "[T]herefore we say a day hath twenty four hours . . . this was a day by itself, as the other six days were by themselves."[73] Citing Basil, Andrews commented that the word *yôm* ("day" in Gen. 1:5) "had a meaning for our natural use that we should esteem twenty four hours one day. . . . The first day is an example to the days after."[74]

Later theologians who repudiated Augustine's misguided position continued this and *only this* tradition until the mid-18th century. The only debate about the pervasiveness of this classic creation view is *when* it began to be challenged or when its eclipse started. It seems indisputable that Reformed exegetes rather uniformly rejected Augustinian's thinking on this point, following instead Peter Lombard

68. *The Workes of Gervase Babington* (London: 1622), p. 6.
69. Ibid., p. 9.
70. Andrew Wilett, *Hexapla in Genesis* (London: 1632)
71. John Richardson, *Annotations on Genesis* (London: 1655).
72. Lancelot Andrewes, *Lectures Preached in St. Paul's Church* (London: 1657), p. 661.
73. Ibid., p. 662.
74. Ibid., p. 663.

and Aquinas. They definitely maintained a consensus of interpreting the Genesis creation "day" as a normal day, before, during, and after the Reformation. Some contemporary old-earth proponents have suggested that there is ambiguity regarding whether the key players immediately preceding Westminster "spoke as one man." But such claims are groundless, at least among orthodox Reformed scholars.

Summary on Westminster Assembly

Surprisingly, there are some who contend that the Westminster Divines left a legacy of agnosticism, indifferentism, or pluralism on the length of days and related matters. But in order to take these charges seriously, critics will have to supply hard documentation from the Divines themselves that they presaged the broadmindedness and tolerance characteristic of modern old-earth proponents.[75] We have demonstrated that the Divines *did* have a fixed view on the length of creation days in the mid-1600s; a tradition which continued with rare exception at least until the late 1700s.

The Westminster standards consciously asserted a truth claim by their words: "in the space of six days." That language had specific meaning when it was asserted, and its meaning still is verifiable and unambiguous. Accordingly, those over the past 150 years who have claimed that the confessional words "in the space of six days" really could mean up to 14 billion years demonstrate that they simply have not done their homework in the relevant primary sources.

After considerable research on the matter, no credible evidence has surfaced that the Divines allowed for non-literal days or a framework-type hypothesis.[76] To the contrary, at least 23 Westminster Divines (who were either present, commissioned to serve, or recorded the actual proceedings of the Assembly) testified — explicitly or implicitly — to their belief in six 24-hour days of creation (contrary to Augustine's position) and that creation week was only a few thousand years ago. Not all the Divines left testimony on this point, but my research has uncovered none who contradicted the normal-day view. The onus is on old-earth proponents to provide the documentary evidence that the Church at this time was vague about her understanding of Genesis 1–11.

Reformed Theologians a Century after Westminster, 1640–1740

Shortly after the Westminster Assembly, John Owen, Thomas Vincent, Thomas Manton, Thomas Watson, Francis Turretin, and many others confirmed

---

75. For more documentary evidence on the Westminster Divines' original intent, see David W. Hall, "What Was the View of the Westminster Assembly Divines on Creation Days?" in Pipa & Hall, *Did God Create in Six Days?* p. 41–52.

76. Many of the Westminster Divines did not leave written commentary on the subject, but I have found none who contradicted the normal-day view. My initial research unearthed 11 Westminster divines who clarified what they meant by "in the space of six days," the phrase employed in their confession (ch. 4) and catechisms. Responding to challenges to my findings, subsequent research has expanded the list to 25. See also my *Holding Fast to Creation*, and Pipa and Hall, *Did God Create in Six Days?*, p. 41–52.

the view of their predecessors, as well as repudiating the Augustinian view. Thomas Wylie's *Catechism* (ca. 1640) also counters Augustine with this affirmation: "Q: How many dayes was the Lord in the work of creation? A: Though all might have been ended at one instant, yet it cost the Lord six dayes for our capacitie."[77]

Writing in 1679, Francis Turretin noted, but then rejected, the Augustinian view and sided with Ussher: "Nor does the sacred history written by Moses cover any more than six thousand years. . . . Greek history scarcely contains the history of two thousand years."[78] Turretin went so far as to commend Ussher and others for specifying that creation happened in autumn, not spring.[79]

Publishing slightly later than Turretin, Thomas Boston continued the Reformed repudiation of Augustinianism on this point (again using the "in the space of six days" phrase). Boston wrote:

> Our next business is to shew in what space of time the world was created. It was not done in a moment [as Augustine], but in the space of six days, as is clear from the narrative of Moses. It was as easy for God to have done it in one moment as in six days. But this method he took, that we might have that wisdom, goodness, and power that appeared in the work, distinctly before our eyes, and be stirred up to a particular and distinct consideration of these works, for commemoration of which a seventh day [24 hours] is appointed a sabbath of rest.[80]

Later, Boston reiterates *contra* Augustine and John Colet that "although God did not make all things in one moment," still "in the space of these six days the angels were created."[81] He then proceeds to enumerate what was done on each day, assuredly not envisioning more than 24 hours for those days. Agreeing with Ussher, Boston echoes the consensus of his day: "It is probable that the world was created in autumn, that season of the year in which generally things are brought to perfection. . . ."[82] On such chronological matters, Ussher, not Augustine, dominated the 17th-century Divines, both before and after the Westminster Assembly.

William Beveridge (1637–1708) was a Calvinistic Bishop and a pious High Churchman. Living shortly after the Westminster Assembly, he was a noted preacher who revived Calvinist piety in the Anglican Church. He authored the popular work *Private Thoughts on Religion*. Regarding the first day, he said,

---

77. Thomas Wylie, *Catechism* (London, 1644), p. 244.
78. Francis Turretin, *Institutes of Elenctic Theology*, 3 vol. (Phillipsburg, NJ: Presbyterian and Reformed, 1992, reprint of 1679–1685 original and edited by James T. Dennison), I:438.
79. Ibid., p. 442.
80. *The Complete Works of Thomas Boston* (Wheaton, IL: Richard Owen Roberts, 1980 reprint), p. 173.
81. bid.
82. Ibid., p. 174.

"So the light which was first made had the same motions, making day where it shone, and night in all other places till it rose upon them: and this it did as the sun now doth in twenty-four hours; so that the evening, when this light sat in any place, and the morning, when it rose again, was the first natural day, of the same length as ours now are."[83]

Thomas Ridgeley (1667–1734), the author of the most comprehensive commentary on the Westminster Larger Catechism, made several important points. He addressed *how* God created (by the Word of God's Power) and *why* (for His glory) in a section entitled "The Work of the Six Days of Creation."[84] Here he explained what was created on each day and how the angels and light were created on the first day, though not "collected into the sun and fixed stars" until the fourth.[85]

Ridgeley discussed the Augustinian theory of instant creation, and clearly voiced his disagreement. There is even a section entitled, "Creation not Eternal," wherein he said, "We have in scripture of the time that the world has continued, which is no more than between five or six thousand years."[86] Like Scottish member of the Westminster Assembly, Robert Baillie, Ridgeley also inquired into "what time or season of the year all things were created?" and concluded that it was at autumn.[87]

Ezekiel Hopkins (1633–1689), Bishop of Derry, addressed the question of when the Sabbath was instituted. He wrote:

> . . . he rested precisely on the Seventh Day after the creation; therefore, that very Seventh Day did God sanctify, and made it the beginning of all ensuing Sabbaths. So that you see the Sabbath is but one day younger than man; ordained for him, in the state of his uprightness and innocence. . . . And, although we find no more mention of the Sabbath, until Moses had conducted the Children of Israel into the Wilderness, which was about *two thousand four hundred and fifty years* after the creation. . . .[88]

Previously, Hopkins dated the actual time of the delivery of the Ten Commandments: "The TIME, according to the best computation of chronology, was *about two thousand four hundred and sixty* years after the Creation of the World. . . ."[89] Not only does he argue for the age of the earth, but expressly says that the

---

83. *The Works of the Right Rev. William Beveridge, D.D.*, 9 Vols. (James Duncan and G. & W.B. Whittaker, 1824), III: 482.

84. Thomas Ridgeley, *Commentary on the Larger Catechism*, 2 vols. (Edmonton, AB Canada: Still Waters Revival Books, [1855] 1993), 1:331–336.

85. Ibid., 1:333.

86. Ibid., 1:328. Ridgeley even disagreed with Augustine's slightly older age of the creation, which Ridgeley attributed to Augustine's dependence on the Septuagint.

87. Ibid., 1:336.

88. *The Works of Ezekiel Hopkins*, 3 vols (Soli Deo Gloria: 1995), 1:366–367.

89. Ibid., 1:237.

Sabbath was "one day younger than man," making it clear that he viewed each creation day as twenty-four hours.[90]

Francis Roberts (1609–1675) was a close friend of Robert Baillie, and labored on Baillie's behalf whenever need arose to rouse public support for his policies. Roberts himself wrote something regarding the creation account. "The world's creation is described here . . . according to Gods orderly proceedings in six distinct daies-work"[91] Also, like all the other Divines of his times, he firmly dates the entire history recorded in Genesis from the date of creation: "This History of Genesis is evidently an History of 2368 years continuance."[92]

In his commentary on Genesis, George Hughes (1603–1667) wrote, "The issue of all in the constitution of the first Day, one Day, to the letter. But read first: Evening and Morning are taken synecdochically[93] for all the darkness and all the light, which maketh a natural Day. . . . The Time of light, or that which is said to consist of twelve houres is the civil Day."[94]

John Trapp (1601–1669) was a popular and learned Bible commentator who received the rectory of Welfrod in Gloucestershire and Warwickshire from the Assembly of Divines in 1646. In his commentary on the Pentateuch (in reference to Gen. 1:2), Trapp stated, "The Lord afterward did form it . . . in three days laying the parts of the world, and in other three days adorning them."[95] In his *Theologia Theologiae: The True Treasure*, he indicated when those creation days were, when he dated Ezra "about three thousand and six hundred years after the creation, and before any chronicles of the world now extant in the world,"[96] which is similar to the way people were dated by scholars in the 1540–1640 period.

Wesley and Early 19th Century Commentaries

The men previously discussed were Reformed bible scholars. Nonetheless, Arminian leader John Wesley (1701–1791) had the same view of Genesis as his Reformed brethren.[97] He clearly appreciated the practical benefits of science and wrote two books to popularize useful knowledge in medicine and electricity. But he was wary of theoretical science because of its potential for leading people toward deism or atheism. In his two-volume *Survey of the Wisdom of God in the*

---

90. Ibid.
91. Francis Roberts, *Clavis Bibliorum* (London: George Calvert, 1665), p. 7.
92. Ibid., p. 6.
93. A *synecdoche* is a literary term where a part represents the whole, or conversely the whole stands for the part. Psalm 24:4 states the need for clean hands and a pure heart, which are representative of the whole person.
94. George Hughes, *An Analytical Exposition of the Whole First Book of Moses, called Genesis* (London: 1672), in loc.
95. John Trapp, *A Commentary or Exposition Upon the Books of the Old and New Testaments*, 5 Vols. (London: Thomas Newberry, 1657), I:3.
96. John Trapp, *Theologia Theologiae: The True Treasure*, vol. 4:683.
97. I am grateful for Dr. Terry Mortenson's research and assistance in this section.

Creation (1763) he presented the traditional arguments from design for God's existence, which were so popular in 18th and early 19th century Britain.[98]

Wesley never wrote extensively on creation or the Flood, but in this work he stated his belief that the various rock strata were "doubtless formed by the general Deluge" of Noah's day. He believed that the creation account was, along with the rest of the Scriptures, "void of any material error."[99] About the age of the earth, he wrote, "The Scripture being the only Book in the world that gives us any account of the whole series of God's Dispensations toward man from the Creation for four thousand years."[100] In several published sermons he repeatedly emphasized that the original creation was perfect, without any moral or physical evil (such as earthquakes, volcanoes, weeds, and animal death), both of which came into the world after man sinned.[101]

At the beginning of the 19th century, when the idea of millions of years took deep root in geology, the literal interpretation of Genesis continued to dominate the Church. Extremely important in this regard is the work of Thomas H. Horne (1780–1862), who was an Anglican clergyman, although for much of his working life he also served as assistant librarian in the department of printed books at the British Museum. He did not write a commentary on the Bible, but he was one of the great biblical scholars of his time.

Among his numerous literary productions, his greatest work was the massive *Introduction to the Critical Study of the Holy Scriptures*, first published in 1818 in three volumes (1,700 pages) after 17 years of research. Not finding an adequate resource for his own study of the Bible, Horne had read, and in many cases bought, the writings of the most eminent biblical critics, both British and foreign.[102] Continually revised and expanded, Horne's work grew to five volumes by the ninth edition in 1846, with two more editions after that in the UK and also many editions in America during these years. In spite of its size and cost, those editions sold over 15,000 copies in the UK and many thousands in the USA.[103] From the outset it received high reviews from magazines representing all the denominations (including both high church and evangelical Anglican)

98. John Dillenberger, *Protestant Thought and Natural Science* (New York: Doubleday, 1960), p. 156–58.

99. John Wesley, *Survey of the Wisdom of God in the Creation*, 2 vol. (Bristol, 1763), II:22, p. 227. On the global Flood, see also his sermon on original sin in *The Works of the Rev. John Wesley*, 14 vol. (London, 1829-31), IV:54–65.

100. Wesley, *Survey of the Wisdom of God in the Creation*, II:227.

101. John Wesley, *Works of John Wesley*, IV:206–215 ("God's Approbation of His Works), IV:215–224 ("On the Fall of Man"), VII:386–399 ("The Cause and Cure of Earthquakes"), IX:191–464 ("The Doctrine of Original Sin, according to Scripture, Reason and Experience", especially pages 196–197).

102. T.H. Horne, *Introduction to the Critical Study and Knowledge of the Holy Scriptures* (London, 1818), I:3.

103. S. Austin Allibone, *A Critical Dictionary of English Literature*, 3 Vol. (London, 1877), I:890.

and was one of the primary textbooks for the study of the Scriptures in all English-speaking Protestant colleges and universities in the British Empire.[104] A one-volume abridged version, designed for the common man, was *A Compendious Introduction to the Study of the Bible*, which was first published in 1827 and eventually reached a tenth edition in 1862.

Like most British Christians at this time, Horne was firmly committed to the verbal, plenary, infallible inspiration of Scripture. Referring to the arguments of continental biblical critics, Horne vigorously contended for the Mosaic authorship of the Pentateuch and the literal historicity of Genesis, especially the first three chapters, stating that Genesis "narrates the true origin and history of all created things, in opposition to the erroneous notions entertained by the heathen nations."[105] Horne also responded to objections against belief in a global Noachian Flood. He believed that it was confirmed by the fossils, the size of the human population, the late inventions and progress of the arts and science, and the Flood traditions among other people groups from around the world.[106] Not until the 1856 edition of his *Introduction* (and because of the influence of old-earth geological theory) did Horne abandon this position in favor of the gap theory and local Flood theory.[107]

Many commentaries were available in the English-speaking world in the early decades of the 19th century and the vast majority held to the traditional view, even advocating Ussher's date of 4004 B.C. for creation.[108] The most popular commentaries are worthy of a brief comment. All of them held firmly to the young-earth creation view.

Thomas Scott (1747–1821) was an Anglican clergyman, who befriended and eventually succeeded John Newton as pastor of Olney, Buckinghamshire. His Bible commentary was first written between 1788 and 1792. In the UK it went through four editions in Scott's lifetime and at least two after that, with another eight editions in America, all together totaling more than 37,000 copies (a handsome sales record in those days). It was also translated into Welsh

---

104. Ibid., I:889; "Horne, Thomas H.," *Dictionary of National Biography*, 22 Vol. (Oxford: Oxford University Press, 1917), vol. 9, 1257–1258. Sample reviews are quoted in the preface to T.H. Horne, *A Compendious Introduction to the Study of the Bible* (1827, second edition) and included *Christian Remembrancer* (high church Anglican), *Evangelical Magazine* (non-conformist), *Congregational Magazine, Home Missionary Magazine, Wesleyan Methodist Magazine,* and *Gentlemen's Magazine*.

105. T.H. Horne, *Introduction to the Critical Study and Knowledge of the Holy Scriptures* (1818), II:18–38.

106. Ibid., I:485–490, II:37.

107. Ibid. (1856), I:583–590. He indicated that William Buckland and John Pye Smith were the two primary influences in his change of thinking.

108. For a more detailed discussion of Horne's work and the commentaries in use in the early 19th century, see Terry Mortenson, *The Great Turning Point: The Church's Catastrophic Mistake on Geology — Before Darwin* (Green Forest, AR: Master Books, 2004), p. 40–47.

and Swedish. According to Sir James Stephens, it was "the greatest theological performance of our age and country."[109]

George D'Oyly (1778–1846), a notable Anglican theologian and principal promoter of the establishment of King's College in London, and Richard Mant (1776–1848), an Anglican rector and later bishop, were two high churchmen. They published a commentary in 1817 for middle-class people as an alternative to the most popular evangelical works by Thomas Scott and Matthew Henry. They consulted 160 authors for their notes. A second edition came out in 1823 and the small paper copies made it the cheapest of all extant commentaries in 1818.[110]

Adam Clarke (1762?–1832) was a Methodist preacher, a close friend of John Wesley, and his denomination's greatest scholar at the time. In addition to preaching 6,615 different sermons during the years 1782–1808 (and walking over 7,000 miles to the various preaching points in and around London), he mastered the classics, early Christian fathers and oriental writers, learning Hebrew, Syriac, Arabic, Persian, Sanskrit and other eastern languages to do so. Natural science was also a favorite subject. Over the years he became a fellow of the Antiquarian Society (1813), the Royal Irish Academy (1821), the Geological Society (1823), the Royal Asiatic Society (1823) and other societies. His greatest work was his commentary, which was produced from 1810 to 1826 and saw several revised editions through 1874.[111]

Dr. John Gill (1697–1771) was a Baptist pastor and Bible scholar. His magnum opus, *Exposition of the Holy Scriptures*, was produced between 1746 and 1766. According to T.H. Horne, he had no equal in rabbinical literature, but he often excessively spiritualized the biblical text,[112] which makes his literal interpretation of Genesis all the more significant. Another Baptist theologian was Andrew Fuller (1754–1815), who as a pastor influenced William Carey to become the first missionary with the Baptist Missionary Society, which Fuller helped found and directed. Fuller's two-volume *Expository Discourses on the Book of Genesis* appeared in 1806.[113] Matthew Henry (1662–1714) was

109. "Scott, Thomas," *Dictionary of National Biography*, vol. 17, 1011–1013; William Symington, "Introduction," in Thomas Scott, *The Holy Bible with explanatory notes by T. Scott* (1841), p. xx.

110. T.H. Horne, *Introduction to the Critical Study and Knowledge of the Holy Scriptures* (1818), II: Appendix, p. 31; John Overton, *The English Church in the Nineteenth Century: 1800–1833* (London, 1894), p. 178.

111. "Clarke, Adam," *Dictionary of National Biography*, vol. 4, 413–414; J.B.B. Clarke, *An Account of the Infancy, Religious and Literary Life of Adam Clarke* (London, 1833), II:313, 350, 402; III:35–36, 213, 472.

112. "Gill, John," *Dictionary of National Biography*, vol. 7, 1234; T.H. Horne, *Introduction to the Critical Study and Knowledge of the Holy Scriptures* (1818), II: Appendix, p. 27. Adam Clarke said much the same about Gill in his *The Holy Bible with Commentary* (London, 1836), I:9.

113. "Fuller, Andrew," *Dictionary of National Biography*, vol. 7, p. 749–750.

a non-conformist divine and his commentary was well-known and valued throughout the 18th and 19th centuries.[114]

All these commentators held to a literal six-day creation about 4000 B.C. and a global Flood at the time of Noah. English commentaries did not abandon this view until about 1845, by which time Lyell's uniformitarian framework for interpreting the rocks was in complete control of geology.[115] Due to the influence of higher critics of the Bible on the European continent, the young-earth view was abandoned there much earlier.

Although the commentaries in widespread use in the 1820s and 1830s defended the young-earth view, this did not reflect the views of all evangelicals and high churchmen, as Mortenson will discuss next in his chapter on the origin of old-earth geology. In addition to the prominent old-earth proponents discussed there, the editors of the high church magazines *British Critic* and *Christian Remembrancer*, and the evangelical magazine, *Christian Observer*, also generally accepted the old-earth geological theory, though they did not firmly commit themselves on how it should be harmonized with Scripture (i.e., day-age or gap theory on Genesis 1, and local or tranquil Noachian Flood). All these Christians adopted their old-earth interpretations of Genesis because of the influence of the new geological theories, but they all professed to believe that the Scriptures were divinely inspired, infallible, and historically reliable. So for these evangelical and high church old-earth proponents the issue was not the nature of Scripture, but rather its correct interpretation and the role of science in determining that interpretation.

Conclusion

We have provided substantial documentation that key Christian thinkers during the years from Luther to the triumph of Lyellian uniformitarianism (just like Christian thinkers from the Apostles to Luther) took Genesis 1–11 as straightforward literal history. Where is the evidence of sound biblical interpreters defending the day-age or gap or analogical days or framework views of the modern old-earth proponents in the Church?

As Mortenson explains in the next chapter, the Church did not change her views on creation, the Flood, and the age of the earth in the early 19th century because more careful exegesis demanded it, but because old-earth geological theories were taken as proven fact and imposed on the text of Genesis.

By the late 19th century, the theological landscape had thus shifted, allowing Warfield, Shedd, and others to pretend that Calvin and the ancients had actually anticipated much of modern evolutionary thought. With such stalwarts boarding the modernist train in this area — oddity though it was, in view of their persistent rejection of certain areas of progressive thought — cover was provided

---

114. "Henry, Matthew," *Dictionary of National Biography*, vol. 9.
115. Nigel M. de S. Cameron, *Evolution and the Authority of the Bible* (Exeter, UK: Paternoster Press, 1983), p. 72–83.

for the weakening evangelical tradition of the 20th century. Rather quickly that tradition moved toward a hermeneutic siding with the claims of the skeptical scientific establishment. The result was that several newer paradigms of interpretation became approved, and many fine evangelicals seldom heard the classic view, finding themselves instructed only by one side of the argument.

Ben Stiller starred in a 2004 box-office success, *Dodgeball*. In that movie, as in the game of dodgeball, all kinds of contortions are needed to avoid disqualification. Sometimes, the contortions are close to perversions. In this sport, one may attempt so strenuously to dodge the ball that he may step over another line, hit another player, or fall in some other respect. It now appears that the history of post-1800 exegesis is much like that: it has dodged one theoretical toss or thrust after another. In the process, these evolving-to-fit-current-theory views have become so contorted or mutated that the historic view is no longer recognizable. However, once realized, that should be a methodology to avoid.[116]

The doctrine of creation may also provide a mirror for modern Christians. It may be used to reflect our image, which we often cannot see unless we have such a reflecting glass. We like to tell ourselves that we are not tainted by worldly theories, but the history of this question, particularly among evangelicals, seems to tell the opposite story: one of increasing conformity to the world's philosophy.

Moreover, this topic is a good test for exegetical, theological, and historical method. As one differs with the ancient consensus on this issue, one is called on to defend that aberration. As we do so, we discover that we are forced to adopt or embrace methodological principles that we would quickly jettison on other biblical teachings. We certainly would not sit back and wait upon science to give us permission to believe in Jesus' incarnation or Resurrection, would we? Then why do we do so with the doctrine of creation? Just where would we stop if we started to subject our theology and creeds to modernity's seal of approval?

But why is Jerusalem so eager to relinquish its rich grammatical-historical heritage to gain the respect of Athens? Is it not the wiser course of action simply to retain a consistent theological method and continue to abide by the time-tested exegesis of our predecessors?

Abraham Lincoln was surely correct when he recommended: "When you are lost in life, do as you would if lost in a forest. Retrace your steps." It might help many Christians to exit this morass if we re-set our minds with this short review. Could it be that our godly forefathers, who were not biased by evolutionary concerns, interpreted Genesis better than most modern Christian scholars?

---

116. Rather than calling Darwin to task, some theologians have even recently said that the Church needs to apologize to Charles Darwin for its rejection of his theory. See Rev. Dr. Malcolm Brown (Director of Mission and Public Affairs for the Church of England), "Good Religion Needs Good Science," www.cofe.anglican.org/darwin/malcolmbrown. html, accessed Sept. 16, 2008.

Chapter 3

"Deep Time" and the Church's Compromise: Historical Background

Terry Mortenson[1]

The writings of Dr. John Whitcomb on creation in The Genesis Flood, The World That Perished, and The Early Earth, were very helpful to me as a young Christian in college, as I thought through the challenge of evolution and millions of years. I was also edified by his wonderful analysis of the Book of Esther (Esther: Triumph of God's Sovereignty). While I studied at Trinity Evangelical Divinity School, I became personally acquainted with him by phone and have crossed paths with him many times since then. A couple of years ago I had the privilege of being a co-speaker with him at a creation seminar in Wisconsin. In all my interactions with him, he has always impressed me as a godly man with a great heart for God, His glory, and His Word, and a burden for the lost. As one of a few theologians in the last half century who has taken a strong stand for truth of Genesis 1–11, he has been a constant encouragement to me. It is a joy for me to contribute to this volume in honor of this faithful servant of Christ.

Introduction

That the earth and the universe are millions (even billions) of years old is accepted as scientific fact today, not only by non-Christians but also by most

---

Unless otherwise noted, all Scripture in this chapter is from the NASB version of the Bible.

1. This essay is adapted from material previously published in two book chapters. See Terry Mortenson "The Historical Development of the Old-Earth Geological Timescale" in John K. Reed and Michael J Oard, eds., *The Geologic Column* (Chino Valley, AZ: Creation Research Society Books, 2006), p. 7–30, and Terry Mortenson, "Where Did the Idea of 'Millions of Years' Come From?" in Ken Ham, ed., *The New Answers Book 2* (Green Forest, AR: Master Books, 2008), p. 63–73. This material is used here with kind permission from the publishers.

Christians, including most Christian leaders and scholars. But this widespread belief in "deep time" is a relatively new phenomenon and it is vitally important to understand how it arose and became so accepted by Christians.

Before examining this history, we need to remember the words of the apostle Paul. To the Corinthian church he wrote:

> For though we walk in the flesh, we do not war according to the flesh, for the weapons of our warfare are not of the flesh, but divinely powerful for the destruction of fortresses. We are destroying speculations and every lofty thing raised up against the knowledge of God, and we are taking every thought captive to the obedience of Christ (2 Cor. 10:3–5).

Paul says we are involved in a great battle — a war of ideas. Speculations (or imaginations, as the KJV renders the Greek here) and lofty ideas are raised up against the knowledge of God, which therefore means against the truth He has revealed in His Word. Paul tells us more about these anti-biblical ideas when he warns the Colossian Christians: "See to it that no one takes you captive through philosophy and empty deception, according to the tradition of men, according to the elementary principles of the world, rather than according to Christ" (Col. 2:8). Paul did not give warnings in vain. He knew it was a very real possibility that Christians could be led astray by false ideas. He warned Timothy about this when he said, "O Timothy, guard what has been entrusted to you, avoiding worldly and empty chatter and the opposing arguments of what is falsely called 'knowledge' — which some have professed and thus gone astray from the faith" (1 Tim. 6:20–21). There is also the danger of cultural peer pressure. In Galatians 2:11–14, Paul describes Peter succumbing to it as he fell into hypocrisy and subtle gospel-subverting behavior because of the fear of man.

As we trace the history of this idea of millions of years, we will see that it is the product of speculation and imagination rooted in anti-biblical philosophical assumptions. And we will see that many good, sincere Christian leaders and scholars were taken captive by this idea, which in turn led to its widespread acceptance in the church over the past 200 years. Consequently, this led many to go astray from the faith, even into spiritual shipwreck.

The Origins of "Deep Time"

Geology, as a separate field of science with systematic field studies, collection and classification of rocks and fossils, and development of theoretical reconstructions of the historical events that formed those rock layers and fossils of rock, is only about 200 years old.

Prior to this, back to ancient Greek times, people had noticed fossils in the rocks. Many believed that the fossils were the remains of former living things turned to stone, and many early Christians (including Tertullian, Chrysostom, and Augustine) attributed them to Noah's Flood. But others rejected these ideas and regarded fossils as either jokes of nature, the products of rocks endowed with life in some sense, the creative works of God, or perhaps even the deceptions of Satan. The debate was finally settled when Robert Hooke (1635–1703), a British naturalist, confirmed by microscopic analysis of fossil wood that fossils were the mineralized remains of former living creatures.

Before 1750, one of the most important geological thinkers was Niels Steensen (1638–1686), or Steno, a Dutch anatomist and geologist. In his geological book *The Prodromus to a Dissertation Concerning Solids Naturally Contained within Solids* (1669) he proposed the now widely accepted principle of superposition. This states that sedimentary layers were deposited in a successive, essentially horizontal fashion, so that a lower stratum was deposited before (and is therefore older than) the one above it. He expressed belief in a roughly 6,000-year-old earth[2] and that the global Noachian Flood deposited most of the fossil-bearing sedimentary rock layers.

Over the next century, several authors, including the English geologists John Woodward (1665–1722) and Alexander Catcott (1725–1779) and the German geologist Johann Lehmann (1719–1767), wrote books reinforcing this young-earth, global-Flood view. This was consistent with what the church believed for the first 18 centuries, as other chapters in this book document.[3]

In the latter decades of the 18th century, some English and European geologists attributed the rock record to geological processes over a long period of time rather than to the Flood. Several prominent French scientists also contributed to the idea of millions of years. The widely respected scientist Comte de Buffon (1707–1788) believed that the history of the earth was governed by the laws of nature. He therefore resolutely rejected a biblical Flood of Noah's day. He imagined in his book *Epochs of Nature* (1779) that the earth was once like a hot molten ball (having been torn from the mass of the sun), which had cooled passing through seven epochs to reach its present state over about 75,000 years (though his unpublished manuscript says about 3,000,000 years). He also believed that through the influence of heat on "aqueous, oily, and ductile" substances the first living matter was spontaneously generated.[4]

The astronomer Pierre Laplace (1749–1827) proposed the "nebular hypothesis" in his *Exposition of the System of the Universe* (1796). This theory said that the

---

2. He held to Ussher's date of 4004 B.C. for creation.

3. See also Terry Mortenson, *The Great Turning Point: The Church's Catastrophic Mistake on Geology — Before Darwin* (Green Forest, AR: Master Books, 2004), p. 40–47, for a discussion of the views of the commentaries used in the early 19th century, almost all of which followed Archbishop Ussher's date for creation of 4004 B.C. For a discussion of the Eastern Orthodox view in church history, see Terry Mortenson, "Orthodoxy and Genesis: What the Fathers Really Taught" (a review of Fr. Seraphim Rose's book *Genesis, Creation and Early Man* [St. Herman of Alaska Brotherhood, 2000]), www.answersingenesis.org/tj/v16/i3/orthodoxy.asp.

4. Charles C. Gillispie, ed., *Dictionary of Scientific Biography*, "Buffon, Georges-Louis Leclerc, Comte de" (New York: Scribner, 1970–1980, 16 vol.), 2:578–579. *Dictionary of Scientific Biography* is hereafter cited as *DSB*.

solar system was once a hot, spinning gas cloud, which over long ages gradually cooled and condensed to form the planets. Though this speculative hypothesis (with no observational or experimental support) was rejected by most scientists at the time, it is the dominant view now as part of the big-bang cosmology. In 1809, Jean Lamarck, a specialist in shell creatures, advocated in his *Philosophy of Zoology* a hypothesis of biological evolution over long ages. Most scientists (including non-Christian ones) rejected the idea of evolution at this time, but this theory helped prepare the way for Darwin's famous book *Origin of Species* in 1859. Lamarck's imagined mechanism for such evolution (the inheritance of acquired characteristics) has long been shown to be false.

New theories in geology were also being advocated at the turn of the 19th century, as geology began to develop into a disciplined field of scientific study. Abraham Werner (1749–1817) was a popular mineralogy professor in Germany. Unfortunately, as one evolutionist historian of geology put it, "Werner was disposed to teach dogmatic theory and speculation with little regard for facts and apparently little, if any, regard for demonstrable principles. . . . He proposed his own ideas based primarily upon assumptions."[5] His 28-page book on mineralogy, *Short Classification and Description of the Various Rocks* (1786), included a short section laying out his theory of earth history based on his study of sedimentary rocks near his home. He speculated that most of the crust of the earth had been precipitated chemically or mechanically by a slowly receding global ocean over the course of about a million years. It was an elegantly simple theory, but Werner failed to give careful attention to the fossils in the rocks. This was a serious mistake, since the fossils tell us much about when and how quickly the sediments were deposited and transformed into stone. Werner was a dynamic and popular teacher and many of the 19th century's greatest geologists were his students. Although his simplistic theory was quickly discarded, his idea of a very long history for the earth stuck with his students.[6]

In Scotland, James Hutton (1726–1797) was developing a different theory of earth history. He studied medicine at the university. After his studies, he took over the family farm for a time. But his real love was the study of the earth. In 1785, he published a journal article and in 1795 a book, both with the title *Theory of the Earth*. He imagined that over long ages the continents were being slowly eroded into the oceans. Those sediments were gradually hardened by the internal heat of the earth and then raised by convulsions to become new land masses, which would eventually be eroded into the oceans, hardened and elevated. So in his view, earth history was cyclical, and in a famous statement which brought the charge of atheism from many of his contemporaries he said that he could find no evidence of a beginning in the rock record, which made earth history indefinitely long. He too paid little attention to the fossils in the rocks.

---

5. William B.N. Berry, *Growth of a Prehistoric Time Scale* (San Francisco, CA: W.H. Freeman, 1968), p. 36 and 38.

6. Gillispie, *DSB*, "Werner, Abraham Gottlob," 14:260–261.

Catastrophist — Uniformitarian debate

One who did pay much attention to the fossils was Georges Cuvier (1768–1832), the famous French comparative anatomist and vertebrate palaeontologist. In the late 18th and early 19th centuries he developed what became known as the *catastrophist* theory of earth history. It was expressed clearly in his book *Theory of the Earth* (1813).[7] Cuvier believed that over the course of long, untold ages of earth history many catastrophic floods of regional or nearly global extent had destroyed and buried creatures in sediments, with some of them being preserved as fossils. All but one of these catastrophes occurred before the creation of man, according to Cuvier. He strongly rejected Lamarck's theory of evolution, believing that God supernaturally created different creatures at different times in earth history.

William Smith (1769–1839) was a drainage engineer and surveyor, who in the course of his work around Great Britain became fascinated with the strata and fossils. Like Cuvier, he rejected biological evolution and had an old-earth catastrophist view of earth history. In three works published from 1815 to 1817, he presented the first geological map of England and Wales and explained an order and relative chronology of the rock formations as defined by certain characteristic (index) fossils.[8] He became known as the "Father of English Stratigraphy" because he developed the method of giving relative dates to the rock layers on the basis of the fossils found in them, a method still used today by evolutionary geologists.[9]

Two other catastrophists need to be mentioned because of their great influence on the church. One was William Buckland (1784–1856), professor of geology at Oxford and the leading geologist in England in the 1820s. Initially, he followed the catastrophist views of Cuvier and Smith. Like a number of scientists of his day, Buckland was an Anglican clergyman. Two of his students, Charles Lyell and Roderick Murchison, went on to become very influential uniformitarian geologists in the 1830s and beyond.   In his *Vindiciae Geologicae* (1820), Buckland argued that geology was consistent with Genesis, confirmed natural religion by providing evidence of creation and God's continued providence, and proved virtually beyond refutation that the global, catastrophic Noachian Flood had occurred. However, the geological evidence for the Flood was, in Buckland's view, only in the superficial formations of sands and gravel and the topographical features of the continents. He believed that the thousands of feet

---

7. The French original appeared in 1812.
8. William Smith, *A Memoir to the Map and Delineation of the Strata of England and Wales, with part of Scotland* (London, 1815); William Smith, *Strata Identified by Organized Fossils* (London, 1816); William Smith, *Stratigraphical System of Organized Fossils* (London, 1817).
9. Michael Foote and Arnold I. Miller, *Principles of Paleontology* (New York: W.H. Freeman, 2007), p. 150–151; and Charles C. Plummer and David McGeary, *Physical Geology* (Dubuque, IA: Wm. C. Brown, 1993), p. 167.

of sedimentary rock layers (like we see in the Grand Canyon) were antediluvian by untold thousands of years. To harmonize his view with Genesis he considered the possibility of the day-age theory, but favored the gap theory, both of which were developed in the early 1800s. In so doing, he gave absolutely no analysis of the text of Genesis to show how old-earth theory could be harmonized with the Bible. He simply quoted other geologists or theologians as his authority. And like Cuvier, he believed in multiple supernatural creations and that the creation of man was only a few thousand years ago.

Three years later, Buckland published his widely read *Reliquiae Diluvianae* (1823), providing what he thought was a further defense of the Flood (albeit limited in its geological effects). While he discussed superficial geological features as further support for his views, he again failed to deal with the biblical text regarding the Flood. It is clear from Buckland's personal correspondence in the 1820s that, in his mind, geological evidence had a superior quality and reliability over textual evidence in reconstructing the earth's history, because written records were susceptible to deception or error, whereas the rocks were truthful and could not be altered by man. [10] He did not assert that the biblical text had errors, but he certainly implied it with this line of reasoning.

Adam Sedgwick (1785–1873) was Buckland's counterpart at Cambridge, receiving the chair of geology in 1818, at a time when by his own admission he knew next to nothing about geology. He was a quick learner, however. He too was an ordained Anglican clergyman and insisted all his life that old-earth theories did not contradict the Bible. But neither in his initial years as a catastrophist nor later during most of his life as a uniformitarian did he ever once even attempt to show how geological theory and the text of Genesis 1–11 could be harmonized. [11] It is not even clear if he held to the gap theory or the local Flood or tranquil Flood views of Noah's Flood. It should also be noted that Sedgwick helped train Charles Darwin in old-earth thinking while the latter was a student at Cambridge. Darwin then simply applied those anti-biblical ways of thinking to develop his theory of slow gradual biological evolution. When Robert Chambers published a theory of evolution in 1845, Sedgwick vociferously opposed it in an 85-page review article, calling it a "strange delusion" under the influence of "the serpent coils of false philosophy." [12] In 1865, in the wake of the publication of Darwin's *Origin of the Species* (1859), Sedgwick joined 616 other signatories of a declaration presented at the annual meeting of the British Association for the Advancement

---

10. Nicolaas A. Rupke, *The Great Chain of History: William Buckland and the English School of Geology 1814–1849* (Oxford: Clarendon Press, 1983), p. 60–61.

11. V. Paul Marston, "Science and Meta-science in the World of Adam Sedgwick" (England: Open University, Ph.D. Thesis, 1984), p. 528–543. Marston carefully studied all of the writings of Sedgwick related to science.

12. Adam Sedgwick, review of *Vestiges of the Natural History of Creation* (London, 1845), *The Edinburgh Review*, vol. LXXXII, no. 65 (July 1845). Quotes from pages 3 and 85.

of Science. These signatories expressed their concerns that Darwin's theory was "casting doubt upon the Truth and Authenticity of the Holy Scriptures."[13] So, by undermining Scripture through his advocacy of old-earth geology, this Anglican clergyman and Cambridge professor (Sedgwick) paved the way for Darwin to undermine Scripture further through biology, much to Sedgwick's dismay.

Through the influence of Buckland and Sedgwick and others, old-earth catastrophist (or "diluvial," as it was sometimes called) geology was widely accepted in the 1820s by most geologists, and by many clergy and theologians in Britain and North America.

A fatal blow to catastrophism came during the years 1830 to 1833, when Charles Lyell (1797–1875), a lawyer and former student of Buckland, published his influential three-volume work, *Principles of Geology*. Reviving and augmenting the ideas of Hutton, Lyell's *Principles* set forth the principles by which he thought geological interpretations should be made. His theory was a radical *uniformitarianism* in which he insisted that only present-day processes of geological change at *present-day rates of intensity and magnitude* should be used to interpret the rock record of past geological activity. In other words, geological processes of change have been uniform throughout earth history. No continental or global catastrophic floods have ever occurred, insisted Lyell.

Lyell's work led Buckland in the early 1830s to abandon this diluvial, catastrophist interpretation of the geological evidence. He publicized this change of mind in his famous two-volume *Bridgewater Treatise* on geology in 1836, where in a mere paragraph in one place and a short footnote in another place he described the Flood as tranquil and geologically insignificant.[14] Sedgwick publicly recanted his catastrophist view in 1831, as he also embraced Lyell's uniformitarianism.

Lyell is often given too much credit (or blame) for destroying faith in the Genesis Flood and the biblical time scale. But many professing Christians (geologists and theologians) contributed to this undermining of biblical teaching before Lyell's book appeared. The catastrophist theory had greatly reduced the geological significance of Noah's Flood and expanded earth history well beyond the traditional biblical view. Lyell's work was simply the final blow for belief in the Flood. By explaining the whole rock record by slow gradual processes, he thereby reduced the Flood to a geological non-event. Catastrophism did not die out immediately, although by the late 1830s only a few catastrophists remained, and they believed Noah's Flood was geologically quite insignificant.

By the end of the 19th century, the age of the earth was considered by all geologists to be in the hundreds of millions of years. Radiometric dating methods

13. *The Declaration of Students of the Natural and Physical Sciences* (London, 1865).

14. William Buckland, *On the Power, Wisdom and Goodness of God as Manifested in the Creation: Geology and Mineralogy Considered with Reference to Natural Theology* (London: John Murray, 1836, 2 vol.), I:16 and I:94–95. This was one of eight "Bridgewater Treatises" published in the 1830s, which presented design arguments for the existence of God.

began to be developed in 1903, and over the course of the 20th century the age of the earth expanded to 4.5 billion years.

Assumptions, Observations, and Interpretations

What most people do not realize is that the old-earth theories (like Darwin's evolution theory and the later big-bang theory of cosmology) were not developed by "just letting the facts speak for themselves." It is critically important to understand the difference between observations and interpretations and the highly influential role that philosophical/religious assumptions play in making the observations, deciding what data to collect and report to the scientific community, and how the data is interpreted.

The architects of "deep time" were not unbiased, objective pursers of truth. There is no such person who has ever existed, and scientists are, by their academic training, often blind to the philosophical, non-scientific assumptions that affect what they see and how they interpret what they see, as well as what kinds of experiments they will do, what kinds of questions they will explore, and what kinds of conclusions they will consider as possible answers to those questions. Regarding early 19th century geology, a respected historian of science has noted:

> Most significantly, recent work in cultural anthropology and the sociology of knowledge has shown that the conceptual framework that brings the natural world into a comprehensible form becomes especially evident when a scientist constructs a classification [of rock strata]. Previous experience, early training, institutional loyalties, personal temperament, and theoretical outlook are all brought to bear in defining particular boundaries as "natural."[15]

We must also add other factors that can distort a scientist's thinking or the published results thereof: peer pressure, greed, envy, love of money or reputation, etc., can lead to deception and fraud that can go undetected by the scientific community for a very long time.[16] Now, it would be misleading and mistaken to think that all these factors influence all scientists to the same degree. Furthermore, a major component of anyone's theoretical outlook is his religious worldview (which could include atheism or agnosticism). Worldview had a far more significant influence on the origin of old-earth geology than has often been perceived or acknowledged. A person's worldview not only affects the interpretation of the facts but also the observation of the facts. Another prominent historian of science rightly comments about scientists, and non-scientists: "Men often perceive what they expect, and overlook

---

15. James A. Secord, *Controversy in Victorian Geology: The Cambrian-Silurian Dispute* (Princeton, NJ: Princeton Univ. Press, 1986), 6.

16. William Broad and Nicholas Wade, *Betrayers of the Truth: Fraud and Deceit in the Halls of Science* (London: Century Publishing, 1982). Both authors are highly regarded secular scientific journalists.

what they do not wish to see."[17] A leading historian of geology, Martin Rudwick, provides an enlightening description of the controversy in the late 1830s over the identification of the Devonian formation in the geology of Britain. He wrote:

> Furthermore, most of their recorded field observations that related to the Devonian controversy were not only more or less "theory laden," in the straightforward sense that most scientists as well as historians and philosophers of science now accept as a matter of course, but also "controversy laden." The particular observations made, and their immediate ordering in the field, were often manifestly directed toward finding empirical evidence that would be not merely relevant to the controversy but also *persuasive*. Many of the most innocently "factual" observations can be seen from their context to have been sought, selected, and recorded in order to reinforce the observer's interpretation and to undermine the plausibility of that of his opponents.[18]

In Lyell's covert promotion of Scrope's uniformitarian interpretations of the geology of central France, Lyell had similarly said in 1827, "It is almost superfluous to remind the reader that they who have a theory to establish, may easily overlook facts which bear against them, and, unconscious of their own partiality, dwell exclusively on what tends to support their opinions."[19] However, many geologists, then and now, would say that Lyell was blind to this fact in his own geological interpretations.

So the influence of worldview on the observation, selection, and interpretation of the geological facts was (and still is) significant, especially given the limited knowledge of people individually and collectively in the still infant stage of early 19th century geology. As the philosopher of science Thomas Kuhn has noted:

> Philosophers of science have repeatedly demonstrated that more than one theoretical construction can always be placed upon a given collection of data. History of science indicates that, particularly in the early developmental stages of a new paradigm, it is not even very difficult to invent such alternatives.[20]

Philosophical assumptions drove the development of the old-earth theories in the early 1800s. Two key assumptions were: (1) everything in the physical

---

17. Colin A. Russell, "The Conflict Metaphor and Its Social Origins," *Science and Christian Belief*, 1:1 (1989): p. 25.
18. Martin J.S. Rudwick, *The Great Devonian Controversy: The Shaping of Scientific Knowledge among Gentlemanly Specialists* (Chicago, IL: University of Chicago Press, 1985), p. 431–432.
19. Charles Lyell, "Review of Scrope's *Memoir on the Geology of Central France*," *Quarterly Review*, 36:72 (1827): p. 480.
20. Thomas S. Kuhn, *The Structure of Scientific Revolutions* (Chicago, IL: University of Chicago Press, 1970), p. 76.

universe can and indeed must be explained by time, chance, and the laws of nature working on matter; and (2) natural physical processes have always acted in the same manner, rate, and intensity as we see operating today. These assumptions form the basis of uniformitarian naturalism, which took control of modern science in the early 19th century, decades before Darwin published *Origin of Species* in 1859. Although many scientists today allow for occasional large-scale catastrophes in their models of earth history, uniformitarian thinking is still endemic and naturalism is king. So the heart of the debate about the age of the earth and about how to correctly interpret the geological record is a massive worldview conflict.

Many 18th and 19th century old-earth proponents clearly expressed their naturalistic uniformitarian worldview. For example, Buffon wrote:

> In order to judge what has happened, or even what will happen, one need only examine what is happening. . . . Events which occur every day, movements which succeed each other and repeat themselves without interruption, constant and constantly reiterated operations, these are our causes and our reasons.[21]

Elsewhere Buffon argued:

> . . . we must take the earth as it is, examine its different parts with minuteness, and, by induction, judge of the future, from what at present exists. We ought not to be affected by causes which seldom act, and whose action is always sudden and violent. These have no place in the ordinary course of nature. But operations uniformly repeated, motions which succeed one another without interruption, are the causes which alone ought to be the foundation of our reasoning.[22]

Hutton similarly wrote, "The past history of our globe must be explained by what can be seen to be happening now. . . . No powers are to be employed that are not natural to the globe, no action to be admitted except those of which we know the principle."[23] Elsewhere he rejected the idea of a global Flood on the basis of reasoning the present to the past: "But surely, general deluges form no part of the theory of the earth; for, the purpose of this earth is evidently to maintain vegetable and animal life, and not to destroy them."[24] Of course the

---

21. Quoted in "Buffon," *DSB*, p. 2, 578.
22. Comte de Buffon, *Natural History* (London: Strahan & Cadell, 1781, William Smellie, transl., 8 vol.), 1:34.
23. Quoted in Arthur Holmes, *Principles of Physical Geology* (New York: Ronald Press, 1965), p. 43–44. Holmes does not cite his source. The second half of his quote is found in Hutton's *Theory of the Earth* (Edinburgh: William Creech, 1795, 2 vol.), 2:547. I could not find the first half of the quote in vol. 1 or 2 or in Hutton's 1788 journal article with the same title.
24. Hutton, *Theory of the Earth*, 1: 273.

present earth does support plants and animals, and there are no global floods today. But that doesn't mean a global Flood didn't happen in the past.

Obviously, by insisting that geologists must reason only from known, present-day, natural processes, these men ruled out *a priori* (i.e., before ever looking at the rocks and fossils) God's supernatural creation of the world in six days and the supernaturally induced, global, year-long, catastrophic Noachian Flood, as described in Genesis. Werner, Laplace, Smith, Lyell, and other leading developers of old-earth thinking followed this same naturalistic uniformitarian reasoning. Sadly, many Christian geologists (e.g., Britain's Buckland and Sedgwick, America's Benjamin Silliman and Edward Hitchcock) were infected to varying degrees with this kind of thinking, apparently without realizing it.

It is no wonder that these old-earth proponents could not see the overwhelming geological evidence confirming the biblical teaching about creation, the Flood, and the age of the earth. It is equally unremarkable that all the geology students who have been educated with the same presuppositions for the last 200 years also have not been able to see the abundant evidence confirming Genesis. The rest of the public (blind to the presuppositions) is then easily led by the geologists (through the media, museums, national park signage, school textbooks, and science programs on TV) to accept millions of years.

Anti-biblical Attitudes among Geologists

Not only were the developers of old-earth theory biased by the above-mentioned various influences. Their naturalistic (deistic or atheistic) way of thinking also developed in the social context of an overtly Christian culture in Europe and it was in most cases the result of a conscious rejection of Scripture (or at least Genesis). This anti-biblical worldview was often deliberately hidden from view in published works that played lip service to God's existence. But unpublished writings from the same men are more straightforward. Buffon correctly perceived that his old-earth theory would not be acceptable to the Catholic Church. So although his unpublished manuscript estimates three million years for the age of the earth, his published book gives an age of 75,000 years (which was equally unpalatable to Catholic theologians). Jacques Roger, a leading 20th-century French historian of science, says that "Buffon was among the first to create an autonomous science, free of any theological influence."[25] Of course, the discerning Christian will realize that Buffon did no such thing. Rather, he wanted to enslave science to his own unbiblical theology and to "free" science from the Christian framework that was the womb for modern science and makes sense of the world.

Cuvier's opposition to biblical truth was more subtle. In his *Theory of the Earth*, he briefly mentioned Genesis, the creation, the Deluge, and God, but dismissed all earlier efforts to make sense of the geological record in light of those

---

25. Quoted in J.J. O'Connor and E.F. Robertson, "Georges Louis Leclerc Comte de Buffon," June 2004, www-history.mcs.st-andrews.ac.uk/Biographies/Buffon.html, accessed October 8, 2008.

two events. He himself made no attempt to correlate his theory with biblical history, except to allude to the post-Flood biblical chronology as giving a reasonable date for the Flood. But he did not specifically refer to any passage, and he ignored Genesis 1–9 and Exodus 20:8–11.

The uniformitarian geologist Charles Lyell explained in a lecture at King's College London in 1832:

> I have always been strongly impressed with the weight of an observation of an excellent writer and skillful geologist who said that "for the sake of revelation as well as of science — of truth in every form — the physical part of Geological inquiry ought to be conducted as if the Scriptures were not in existence."[26]

Such reasoning might be permissible if the Bible did not describe any events relevant to the formation of the rocks of the earth (such as the creation week and the Flood). But since the Bible does speak of such events, Lyell's approach is like trying to write a history of ancient Rome by studying the surviving monuments, buildings, artwork, and coins, while intentionally ignoring the writings of reliable Roman historians. The results would not be very accurate.

A few years earlier, Lyell had privately revealed his animosity toward the Bible and his devious plan to undermine its teachings. Writing to his friend Roderick Murchison (a fellow old-earth, uniformitarian geologist), in a private letter dated August 11, 1829, just months before the publication of the first volume of his *Principles of Geology* (1830), Lyell revealed:

> I trust I shall make my sketch of the progress of geology popular. Old [Rev. John] Fleming is frightened and thinks the age will not stand my anti-Mosaical conclusions and at least that the subject will for a time become unpopular and awkward for the clergy, but I am not afraid. I shall out with the whole but in as conciliatory a manner as possible.[27]

About the same time Lyell corresponded with his friend, George P. Scrope (another old-earth geologist and MP of British Parliament), saying, "If ever the Mosaic geology could be set down without giving offense, it would be in an historical sketch."[28] Why would Lyell want to rid geology of the historically accurate (inspired) record of the Flood? Because as a Unitarian (or deist) he was

---

26. Quoted in Martin J.S. Rudwick, "Charles Lyell Speaks in the Lecture Theatre," *The British Journal of the History of Science*, 9:32 (1976),: p. 150.

27. Quoted by John Hedley Brooke, "The Natural Theology of the Geologists: Some Theological Strata," in L.J. Jordanova and Roy S. Porter, eds., *Images of the Earth* (British Society for the History of Science, Monograph 1, 1979), p. 45, bracketed words added. Fleming was a Presbyterian minister and zoologist and a proponent of the old-earth, tranquil Flood view of Noah's Flood.

28. Quoted in Roy Porter, "Charles Lyell and the Principles of the History of Geology," *The British Journal for the History of Science*, 9:2:32 (July 1976): p. 93.

living in rebellion against his Creator, Jesus Christ, and he wanted geology to function with naturalistic presuppositions. Lyell revealed more of his thinking when he wrote Scrope again on June 14, 1830:

> I am sure you may get into Q.R. [*Quarterly Review*] what will free the science [of geology] from Moses, for if treated seriously, the [church] party are [sic] quite prepared for it. A bishop, Buckland ascertained (we suppose [John] Sumner), gave Ure[29] a dressing in the *British Critic and Theological Review*. They see at last the mischief and scandal brought on them by Mosaic systems. . . . Probably there was a beginning — it is a metaphysical question, worthy of a theologian — probably there will be an end. Species, as you say, have begun and ended — but the analogy is faint and distant. Perhaps it is an analogy, but all I say is, there are, as Hutton said, "no signs of a beginning, no prospect of an end" . . . . All I ask is, that at any given period of the past, don't stop inquiry when puzzled by refuge to a "beginning," which is all one with "another state of nature," as it appears to me. But there is no harm in your attacking me, provided you point out that it is the proof I deny, not the probability of a beginning. . . . I was afraid to point the moral, as much as you can do in the Q.R. about Moses. Perhaps I should have been tenderer about the Koran. Don't meddle much with that, if at all. If we don't irritate, which I fear that we may (though mere history), we shall carry all with us. If you don't triumph over them, but compliment the liberality and candour of the present age, the bishops and enlightened saints will join us in despising both the ancient and modern physico-theologians. It is just the time to strike, so rejoice that, sinner as you are, the Q.R. is open to you.
>
> P.S. . . . I conceived the idea five or six years ago [1824–25], that if ever the Mosaic geology could be set down without giving offence, it would be in an historical sketch, and you must abstract mine, in order to have as little to say as possible yourself. Let them feel it, and point the moral.[30]

From a study of Lyell's writings, Porter concludes that Lyell saw himself as "the spiritual saviour of geology, freeing the science from the old dispensation of Moses."[31] So, behind the scenes, many early geologists were strategizing about how to undermine faith in the Scriptures, especially the history of Genesis 1–11

29. Andrew Ure was a renowned chemist and one of the scriptural geologists who opposed the old-earth geological theories. For a discussion of his life and writings (especially his 1829 *New System of Geology*), see Mortenson, *Great Turning Point*, p. 99–113. The life and writings of six other scriptural geologists are discussed in that book also.
30. Katherine M. Lyell, *Life, Letters and Journals of Sir Charles Lyell, Bart.* (London: John Murry, 1881), 2 vol.), I:268–271; bracketed words added
31. Roy S. Porter, "Charles Lyell and the Principles," p. 91.

and to convince the Church that the Bible has nothing relevant to say to the question of the age and history of the earth. Those geologists were extremely successful in accomplishing their objective.

But none of this is surprising when we consider the theological orientation of the men who were most influential in the development of the old-earth theory. Buffon was a deist or atheist, disguising the fact with occasional references to God.[32] Laplace was an open atheist.[33] Lamarck straddled the fence between deism and atheism.[34] Werner was a deist[35] or possibly an atheist,[36] and hence "felt no need to harmonize his theory with the Bible."[37] Historians have concluded the same about Hutton.[38] William Smith was a vague sort of theist, but according to his nephew (a fellow geologist) he was most definitely not a Christian.[39] Cuvier was a nominal Lutheran, but recent research has shown that in practice he was an irreverent deist.[40] Lyell was probably a deist (or a Unitarian, which is essentially the same).[41] Many of the other leading geologists of the 1820s and 1830s were likewise anti-Christian. So these men were hardly unbiased, objective pursuers of truth, as they would have wanted their contemporaries to believe and as modern evolutionists and many historians of science want us to view them. The evolutionary paleontologist Philip Gingerich candidly admits, "Science emerged from a *philosophically motivated* enquiry into the nature of our world, and it has usurped some of the mystery formerly included in religion."[42]

Theologians and Bible scholars need to grasp this point. Collins is wide of the mark when he states the following at the end of his brief discussion on geology in partial defense of his old-earth views:

32. "Buffon," *DSB*, 2:577–578.

33. John H. Brooke, *Science and Religion: Some Historical Perspectives* (Cambridge: Cambridge University Press,1991), p. 238–240.

34. Ibid., p. 243.

35. Leroy E. Page, "Diluvialism and Its Critics in Great Britain in the Early Nineteenth Century," in C.J. Schneer, ed., *Toward a History of Geology* (Cambridge, MA: M.I.T. Press, 1969), p. 257.

36. A. Hallam, *Great Geological Controversies* (Oxford: Oxford University Press, 1989), p. 23.

37. "Werner," *DSB*, 14:259–260.

38. Dennis R. Dean, "James Hutton on Religion and Geology: The Unpublished Preface to his *Theory of the Earth* (1788)," *Annals of Science*, 32 (1975): p. 187–193.

39. Smith's own writings reveal this vague theism, as do comments by geologist John Phillips, Smith's nephew and geology student. See John Phillips, *Memoirs of William Smith*, (London: John Murray, 1844), p. 25.

40. Brooke, *Science and Religion*, p. 247–248.

41. Colin A. Russell, *Cross-currents: Interactions between Science and Faith*. (Leicester, UK: IVPress, 1985), p. 136.

42. Philip Gingerich, *Journal of Geological Education*, 31 (1983), p. 144 (italics added). Gingerich is a leading expert on whale fossils and a professor of paleontology at the University of Michigan.

First, it is true that modern geology does not depend on Scripture (it isn't true that it ignores it, though: many works cite James Ussher's chronology for the world). But this is a far cry from saying that it sets itself in opposition to the Bible. In fact, most of the pioneering geologists in early nineteenth-century England were pious Anglicans — some were clergy. It would only be right to say that geology opposes Scripture if we were sure that Scripture requires us to believe that the world is young — and the early geologists thought the Bible gave room for other possible interpretations.[43]

This statement is quite misleading. Those few modern geology books that mention the Bible or Ussher do so with subtle or blatant scoffing. They certainly never take the Bible's teaching or Ussher's scholarly work on chronology seriously. Furthermore, the early 19th century clergy-geologists (such as the Anglicans William Buckland, Adam Sedgwick, and William Conybeare) who advocated millions of years never showed from the biblical text *how* their views of earth history were consistent with Scripture. They simply asserted on their own authority that there was no conflict between the old-earth theories and Scripture.[44] So, they may have been pious in the sense of a moral life, faithful church attendance, and faith in Christ as Savior, but not pious in how they handled (or rather ignored) the Word of God given in Genesis.

After discussing briefly the work of Steve Austin (PhD young-earth creationist geologist) and G. Brent Dalrymple (leading evolutionary geologist) on radiometric dating, Collins concludes his short section on geology with this statement:

> There are plenty of technical details on both sides [of radiometric dating and the question of the age of the earth], and I don't pretend to know how to assess them. However, I am confident in saying that Dalrymple[45] has played fair with people he disagrees deeply with — he has read Austin's material and measured it against reasonable criteria for a technical work. He found it wanting because it did not meet the criteria. It therefore doesn't look to me like Austin's claim to call into question radiometric dating should carry much weight with us. I conclude, then that I have no reason to disbelieve the standard theories of the geologists, including their estimate for the age of the earth. They may be wrong, for

43. C. John Collins, *Science and Faith: Friends or Foes?* (Wheaton, IL: Crossways, 2003), p. 247.

44. I document this failure of these ordained geologists to deal with Scripture in Mortenson, *Great Turning Point*, p. 200–203.

45. Collins indicates in the notes to this section of his book that he read a 24-page article by Dalrymple on radiometric dating and consulted five secular geological textbooks. But he apparently read only five 4-page articles by Austin (only two of which dealt with radiometric dating).

all I know; but if they are wrong, it's not because they have improperly smuggled philosophical assumptions into their work.[46]

As we have seen, Collins is badly mistaken about the influential role of philosophical assumptions in geology. Is it not puzzling that Collins admits that the geologists may be wrong about the age of the earth, for all he knows, and yet he is willing to let those old-earth geological theories (which he admittedly is not qualified to evaluate technically) influence his interpretation of Scripture; and he rejects the arguments of Bible-believing creationist geologists who show both *that* and *why* those geological theories are wrong? It is sad to see an excellent Old Testament theologian with admittedly no training in geology or the history of geology telling Christians that the arguments of young-earth creationist PhD geologists should not carry much weight with Christians.

Christian Responses to Old-earth Geology

During the first half of the 19th century, the Church responded in various ways to these old-earth theories of the catastrophists and uniformitarians. A number of writers in Great Britain (and a few in America) who became known as "scriptural geologists" raised biblical, geological, and philosophical arguments against the old-earth theories. Some of them were scientists, some were clergy. Some were both ordained and scientifically well informed, as was common in those days. Many of them were very geologically competent by the standards of their day, both by reading and by their own careful observations out among the rocks and fossils. They believed that the biblical account of creation and Noah's Flood explained the rock record far better than the old-earth theories.[47] Other Christians in the early 1800s quickly accepted the idea of millions of years and tried to fit all this time into Genesis somewhere, even though the uniformitarians and catastrophists were still debating and geology was in its infancy as a science.

In 1804, Thomas Chalmers (1780–1847), a young Presbyterian pastor, began to preach that Christians should accept the millions of years. He asserted that "the writings of Moses do not fix the antiquity of the globe. If they fix anything at all, it is only the antiquity of the [human] species."[48] In an 1814 review of Cuvier's catastrophist *Theory of the Earth*, he proposed that all the time could fit between Genesis 1:1 and 1:2.[49] By that time, Chalmers was becoming a highly influential evangelical leader and consequently this "gap theory" became very popular. It is noteworthy that although Chalmers was a pastor, he was not truly born again through

---

46. Collins, *Science and Faith*, p. 250.

47. See Mortenson, *Great Turning Point* (2004), for a full discussion of seven of the most prominent scriptural geologists and their arguments against these developing old-earth theories and various Christian compromises with the idea of millions of years.

48. William Hanna, *Memoirs of the Life and Writings of Thomas Chalmers, D.D., LLD.* (New York: Harper & Brothers, 1853, 3 vol.), 1:390.

49. Francis C. Haber, *The Age of the World: Moses to Darwin* (Baltimore, MD: The Johns Hopkins Press, 1959), p. 202–202.

faith in Christ until 1811, which was seven years after he had compromised with millions of years.[50] He never questioned that old-earth belief after his conversion.

In 1823, a respected evangelical Anglican theologian, George Stanley Faber (1773–1854), became one of the early advocates of the day-age view, namely that the days of creation were not literal but figurative of long ages.[51] Following out-of-date geological writings, he mistakenly thought that the order of the fossils (as the old-earth geologists presented them) "confirmed in a most curious manner the strict accuracy" of the order of creation events in Genesis 1.[52] His argument shows that his interpretations of Scripture are heavily controlled by old-earth geology. He admits that the Church historically believed in a global Flood, but he rejected that idea because of geology and accepted Cuvier's catastrophist view of earth history.[53] He illogically argued that since God is still resting from His creation work, the seventh day of creation week has not ended and "is in truth a period commensurate with the duration of the created Universe."[54]

To accept these geological ages, Christians also had to reinterpret the Flood account in Genesis 6–9. We have already noted catastrophists such as Buckland and Sedgwick. In an 1826 article, John Fleming (1785–1857), a Presbyterian minister, took issue with Buckland and others by contending that Noah's Flood was so peaceful it left no lasting geological evidence.[55] In rejecting the catastrophic nature of the Flood, Fleming made no specific reference to the details of the Genesis narrative. This "tranquil Flood view" was not as popular at the time as the local Flood view of John Pye Smith (1774–1851), a Congregational theologian. He argued that the Flood was a localized inundation in the Mesopotamian valley (modern-day Iraq).[56] After the victory of Lyell's uniformitarian view in the late 1830s, those who still believed the Flood was catastrophic embraced the local Flood view. All these views had one thing in common — they agreed that the Flood had no relevance in explaining the origin of the thousands of feet of sedimentary rock strata.

---

50. Hanna, *Memoirs*, 1:193–197.

51. George Stanley Faber, *A Treatise on the Genius and Object of the Patriarchal, Levitical and Christian Dispensations* (London, 1823, 2 vol.), 1:111–166. In one place, he says that at least 6,000 years elapsed before Adam (p. 141), but elsewhere he says the days of creation were "each of immense length" (p. 156).

52. Ibid., 1:126. At that time (1823), as today, the order of Genesis and the order of the fossils contradicted each other at many points. Knowledge of the fossil record was increasing rapidly at this time and Faber was relying on geological writings that were over ten years old.

53. Ibid., 1:121.

54. Ibid., 1:115–116.

55. John Fleming, "The Geological Deluge, as Interpreted by Baron Cuvier and Professor Buckland, Inconsistent with the Testimony of Moses and the Phenomena of Nature," *Edinburgh Philosophical Journal*, XIV:28 (April 1826): p. 205–239.

56. John Pye Smith, *On the Relation Between the Holy Scriptures and Geological Science* (London: Jackson and Walford, 1839), p. 154–159 and 299–304.

Liberal theology, which by the early 1800s was dominating the church in Europe, was beginning to make inroads in Britain and North America in the 1820s. The liberals considered Genesis 1–11 to be as historically unreliable and unscientific as the creation and flood myths of the ancient Babylonians, Sumerians, and Egyptians. So, obviously, it was useless in understanding the geology of the earth.

In spite of the efforts of the scriptural geologists, these various old-earth reinterpretations of Genesis prevailed so that by about 1845 all the commentaries on Genesis had abandoned the biblical chronology and the global Flood.[57] By the time of Darwin's *Origin of Species* (1859), the young-earth view had essentially disappeared within the Church. From that time onward, most conservative Christian leaders and scholars of the Church accepted the millions of years as scientifically proven fact, and insisted that the age of the earth was not important because, in their minds, the Scriptures were silent on the subject. Many otherwise godly men also soon accepted evolution. Space allows me to mention only a few examples.

The Baptist "prince of preachers," Charles Spurgeon (1834–1892), uncritically accepted the old-earth geological theory (though he apparently did not realize that the geologists were thinking in terms of millions of years). In an 1855 sermon he said:

> Can any man tell me when the beginning was? Years ago we thought the beginning of this world was when Adam came upon it; but we have discovered that thousands of years before that God was preparing chaotic matter to make it a fit abode for man, putting races of creatures upon it, who might die and leave behind the marks of his handiwork and marvelous skill, before he tried his hand on man.[58]

During his life, Spurgeon never gave any sustained attention in his preaching to the subject of evolution and the age of the earth, and he never explained how the Scriptures could be interpreted to fit the long ages into the Bible. His few brief statements show that he was opposed to Darwinian evolution, calling it a lie.[59] However, in 1876, he was reasoning on the basis of the assumed fact of millions of years of history before man was created.[60]

The Presbyterian theologian at Princeton Seminary, Charles Hodge (1797–1878), strongly opposed evolution in his excellent book *What is Darwinism?*

57. Nigel M. de S. Cameron, *Evolution and the Authority of Scripture* (Exeter, UK: Paternoster Press, 1983), p. 72–83.

58. C.H. Spurgeon, "Election" (1855), *The New Park Street Pulpit* (Pasadena, TX: Pilgrim Publ. 1990), vol. 1, p. 318.

59. C.H. Spurgeon, "Hideous Discovery," *Metropolitan Tabernacle Pulpit* (Pasadena, TX: Pilgrim Publ., 1986), Vol. 32 (Sermon 1911, given on 2July 25, 1886), p. 403.

60. Charles Spurgeon, *Jesus Rose for You* (New Kensington, PA: Whitaker House, 1998), p. 45–47. This is from his sermon "Christ, the Destroyer of Death," preached on Dec. 17, 1876. His comments on geology are under point 1, "Death an Enemy."

(1874), which he judged to be an atheistic theory. However, he made his peace with millions of years. Early in his life he favored the gap theory, but after 1860 he advocated the day-age view. He asserted, with very little supporting argumentation, that the Bible does not teach us about the age of the earth or the age of humanity.[61] Like his father, A.A. Hodge (1823–1886) accepted deep time, but went a little further in toying with the idea that perhaps God used the evolutionary process to create.[62] He also concluded that history in the Bible only goes back to the time of Abraham.[63]

B.B. Warfield (1851–1921) followed Hodge as the lead theologian at Princeton. He was an ardent evolutionist during his student years but vacillated in his confusing views on evolution over the course of his career. The editors of his works on the subject call him a "conservative evolutionist."[64] Given that he thought Adam and Eve's bodies could have arisen by natural processes (under God's providence, of course),[65] "theistic evolutionist" is the label others have given him.[66] As for deep time, he did not accept the greatest estimates of the geologists, but did believe in millions of years and favored the day-age view. He argued that the Genesis genealogies had no chronological value and so thought that the time from Adam to Abraham was closer to 200,000 years than 2,000. He said that the genealogies in Scripture "are, in a word, so elastic that they may be commodiously stretched to fit any reasonable demand on time."[67] The compromise of Hodge, Hodge, and Warfield, in spite of their good intentions and sincere evangelical faith, contributed to the eventual victory of liberal theology at Princeton after the latter's death.[68]

---

61. Charles Hodge, *Systematic Theology* (Grand Rapids, MI: Eerdmans, 1997, 3 vol., reprint of 1872–73 original), 1:570–71 and 2:40–41. The only verses from Genesis that Hodge references in his chapter on creation (in vol. 1) are: 1:2, 1:3, 1:14, 1:27, 2:4, and 2:7. But in no instance does he exegete the text. In his chapter on the origin of man (in vol. 2) he quotes only Genesis 1:26–27 and 2:7 in the first paragraph. Regarding the age of mankind, he believed that the genealogies in Genesis 5 and 11 had missing names and therefore were not chronological. He was following the arguments of his OT colleague at Princeton, William Henry Green.

62. Archibald Alexander Hodge, *Outlines of Theology* (Grand Rapids, MI: Eerdmans, 1991, reprint of 1879 revised edition), p. 245–246.

63. Morton H. Smith, "The History of the Creation Doctrine in the American Presbyterian Churches," in Joseph A. Pipa Jr. and David W. Hall, eds., *Did God Create in Six Days?* (Whitehall, WV: Tolle Lege Press, 2005), p. 7–16.

64. Mark A. Noll and David N. Livingstone, *Evolution, Science and Scripture: B.B. Warfield, Selected Writings* (Grand Rapids, MI: Baker, 2000).

65. Ibid., p. 213.

66. For example, J.I. Packer concludes this. Ibid., p. 38.

67. Ibid., p. 222.

68. On the influence of these three men in the debate about evolution within Presbyterian circles, see Smith, "History of the Creation Doctrine," p. 7–16. For an enlightening discussion of the secularization of once Christian universities in America, a demise in which old-earth evolutionism played a prominent role, see Jon H. Roberts and James

The tragic spiritual demise of evangelist Charles Templeton (discussed later) was one of the consequences.

C.I. Scofield put the gap theory in his notes on Genesis 1:2 in his *Scofield Reference Bible*, which had an impact on the thinking of millions of Christians around the world in the 20th century. It was a simple assertion with no argumentation in defense of it. The 12 volumes of *The Fundamentals* were published in 1909 to defend orthodox Christianity in the face of the challenge of liberal theology engulfing the Church at that time. Most of the 68 articles in those volumes are still well worth reading.[69] But four of them were written on the subject of science and they all were compromised with millions of years, accepting what the geologists said and giving very little attention to the details of the text of Genesis.

In 1945, Wilber Smith, respected Bible professor at Moody Bible Institute and later at Fuller Theological Seminary, wrote a massive book in defense of the Christian faith, *Therefore, Stand*. He warned in the preface that Christians should not "compromise with these agnostic and skeptical tendencies" in our culture.[70] But in his 86-page chapter on creation, he did precisely that, as he completely ignored the Noachian Flood, accepted what the leading geologists said about millions of years of earth history, and then argued for the day-age view of creation. He also insisted that the age of the earth is not taught in Scripture (though he ignored the Genesis genealogies, the numbering of the days along with the repetitive refrain about evening and morning, and God's commentary on creation in Exodus 20:8–11). He did reject Darwinian evolution because of the scientific evidence for the fixity of species[71] and because God completed His creative work at the end of the creation week after He made Adam and Eve. But in spite of his great learning and wide reading, he mistakenly told his readers that belief in a 6,000-year-old creation was a "medieval affirmation, which had no biblical foundation."[72] More recently, the late Gleason Archer reasoned:

> From a superficial reading of Genesis 1, the impression would seem to be that the entire creative process took place in six twenty-four-hour days. If this was the true intent of the Hebrew author . . . this seems to run counter to modern scientific research, which indicates that the planet Earth was created several billion years ago. . . .[73]

Turner, *The Sacred and the Secular University* (Princeton, NJ: Princeton University Press, 2000).

69. See R.A. Torrey, ed., *The Fundamentals* (Grand Rapids, MI: Kregel, 1990, reprint of 1958 edition).

70. Wilbur M. Smith, *Therefore, Stand* (Grand Rapids, MI: Baker, 1945), p. xiii.

71. Ibid., p. 325-327. Sadly, he only quotes leading scientists, but makes no mention of the fact that Genesis clearly teaches that God created different and distinct kinds of plants and animals to reproduce after their kind.

72. Ibid., p. 312.

73. Gleason Archer, *A Survey Of Old Testament Introduction* (Chicago, IL: Moody Press, 1985), p. 187.

Similarly, Bruce Waltke has asserted:

> The days of creation may also pose difficulties for a strict historical account. Contemporary scientists almost unanimously discount the possibility of creation in one week, and we cannot summarily discount the evidence of the earth sciences.[74]

But it is not the geological evidence or modern scientific research that makes the literal interpretation of Genesis 1 unacceptable, as these otherwise excellent Old Testament professors believe. Numerous similar statements from Christian scholars and leaders in the last few decades could be quoted to show that their interpretation of Genesis, like that of their predecessors over the past 200 years, is controlled or influenced by the fact that they assume that the geologists have proven millions of years. As a result, most Christian colleges, universities, seminaries, and mission organizations around the world are compromised with the millions of years. But, as their writings clearly reveal, these respected scholars and leaders over the past two centuries clearly have not adequately considered the theological implications of millions of years (e.g., death before the Fall) nor have they understood the non-scientific, philosophical (uniformitarian and naturalistic) assumptions that have controlled geology.[75] Contrary to their sincere intentions, they have accepted ideas that implicitly and seriously undermine the authority of Scripture.

The historiography of old-earth proponents on this point also needs to be corrected. Davis Young, former geology professor at Calvin College who has influenced many theologians to accept millions of years, remarked about old-earth proponents in the early 19th century:

> The contemporary church would benefit immensely from a rediscovery of the compelling writing of Smith, Hitchcock, and Miller. The specific exegeses of Genesis espoused by these individuals may be open to criticism, but it is to their credit that they viewed the growing body of extra-biblical evidence devastatingly opposed to the traditional ideas of the deluge not as a threat to faith but as an occasion for reaching a better understanding of Genesis.[76]

In reply, it should be noted that the minimal exegesis of Rev. John Pye Smith was refuted biblically and geologically by the scriptural geologist, Rev. George Young, who by both reading and geological fieldwork knew far more

---

74. Bruce K. Waltke, *Genesis* (Grand Rapids, MI: Zondervan, 2001), p. 77.
75. See, for example, my analysis of the old-earth arguments of three leading theologians: "Systematic Theology Texts and the Age of the Earth: A Response to the Views of Erickson, Grudem, and Lewis & Demarest," a paper presented at the 2006 annual meeting of the Evangelical Theological Society, available from me in electronic form.
76. Davis Young, *The Biblical Flood* (Grand Rapids, MI: Eerdmans, 1995), p. 152.

about geology than Smith did.[77] Edward Hitchcock and Hugh Miller also did very little exegesis either. But if their exegesis of God's Word was open to much criticism (as it was and still is), why should Christians trust their interpretations of the geological record (which is much more difficult to interpret than the propositional truth statements of Scripture), especially since those interpretations relied heavily on the interpretations of other geologists at the time whose presuppositions for interpreting the geology were hostile to Scripture? Davis Young is advocating, as he has for decades, that secular, anti-biblical *interpretations* of geological evidence be accepted as *fact* and used to reinterpret the text of Scripture. Furthermore, the decades following the deaths of Smith, Hitchcock, and Miller show that these old-earth theories were indeed a threat to the faith, as many once orthodox churches, seminaries, and denominations have now become liberal and apostate.

Young himself is moving slowly down that slippery slide. Early in the course of his academic career, at the time of his 1977 book *Creation and the Flood* (which greatly influenced many theologians), he believed in a global, tranquil Flood that left no lasting geological evidence, an illogical view that essentially turns the Flood into a myth.[78] By 1995, Young had abandoned this view and began to argue that the Flood was localized in the Middle East.[79] Also, for years he advocated the day-age view. In 1990, he acknowledged that he had repented of that view a few years earlier, because of all the "textual mutilation" and "exegetical gymnastics" involved. But that so-called repentance did not lead Young to believe Genesis is literal history, as the Church did for 18 centuries. Rather, Young advocated the utterly illogical view that Genesis 1–11 "may be expressing history in non-factual terms."[80] He said this because "[d]ickering with the biblical text doesn't seem to

77. See the chapter on George Young in Mortenson, *Great Turning Point*, p. 157–178.

78. How could a mere 4,500 years erase the evidence of the year-long global Flood that was designed to destroy not only all land animals, people, and birds, but the surface of the earth itself (Gen. 6:7, 13) and involved global torrential rain (24 hours/day for at least 40 days and probably 150 days) and tectonic movements of the earth (fountains of the great deep bursting open) for 150 days? That is illogical. And yet Young believes (*Creation and the Flood* [Grand Rapids, MI: Baker, 1977], p. 172–174) that far more geographically and temporally limited floods or gradual processes of geological change have left thousands of feet of stratigraphic evidence that has endured for millions of years and even survived the Flood with no noticeable change! This is another illogical belief.

79. Davis A. Young, *The Biblical Flood* (Grand Rapids, MI: Eerdmans, 1995), p. 242.

80. Leading up to that conclusion and describing his "repentance," Young explained, "The Day-Age hypothesis insisted with at least a semblance of textual plausibility that the days of creation were long periods of indeterminate length, although the immediate context implies that the term, *yôm*, for 'day' really means 'day.' . . . There were some textual obstacles the Day-Agers developed an amazing agility in surmounting. . . ."

After discussing some examples of contradiction in order of events between Genesis 1 and evolution history, he continues, "This obvious point of conflict, however, failed to dissuade well-intentioned Christians, my earlier self included, from nudging the

make it fit the scientific data." So, like most geologists and non-geologists, he has labeled as "data" what are actually *interpretations* of some of the data, based on anti-biblical presuppositions. Should any Bible-believing Christian trust a geologist (even if he professes to be an evangelical) who reasons and "repents" like that?

Compromise unnecessary

The sad irony of all this Christian compromise over the past 200 years is that in the last half century, the truth of Genesis 1–11 has been increasingly vindicated, often by the work of evolutionists who scoffingly reject God's Word. Lyell's uniformitarian *Principles* dominated geology until about the 1970s, when Derek Ager (1923–1993), a prominent British geologist, and other evolutionary geologists increasingly challenged Lyell's assumptions.[81] They have argued that much of the rock record shows evidence of rapid catastrophic erosion or sedimentation, drastically reducing the time involved in the formation of many geological deposits. Ager explained the influence of Lyell on geology this way:

> My excuse for this lengthy and amateur digression into history is that I have been trying to show how I think geology got into the hands of the theoreticians [in context Ager has in mind the uniformitarians] who were conditioned by the social and political history of their day more than by observations in the field. So it was — as Steve Gould put it — that Charles Lyell "managed to convince future generations of geologists that their

---

text to mean something different from what it says. In my case, I suggested that the events of the days overlapped. Having publicly repented of that textual mutilation a few years ago, I will move on without further embarrassing myself. . . ."

Following an examination of other unsuccessful techniques for harmonizing Genesis with old-earth geology, Young confesses "Genius as all these schemes may be, one is struck by the forced nature of them all. While the exegetical gymnastic maneuvers have displayed remarkable flexibility, I suspect that they have resulted in temporary damage to the theological musculature. Interpretation of Genesis 1 through 11 as factual history does not mesh with the emerging picture of the early history of the universe and of humanity that has been deciphered by scientific investigation. Dickering with the biblical text doesn't seem to make it fit the scientific data. . . ." His conclusion follows: "The Bible may be expressing history in nonfactual terms." Davis Young, "The Harmonization of Scripture and Science" (1990 Wheaton symposium), quoted in Marvin Lubenow, *Bones of Contention* (Grand Rapids, MI: Baker, 1992), p. 232–234. I have an audio tape of the entire lecture on file.

81. Besides Ager's writings, other recent works (all by non-creationists) exposing the fallacy of uniformitarianism include Edgar B. Heylmun, "Should We Teach Uniformitarianism?" *Journal of Geological Education*, vol. 19 (Jan. 1971):p. 35–37; Stephen J. Gould "Catastrophes and Steady State Earth," *Natural History*, vol. 84, no. 2 (Feb. 1975): p. 14–18; Stephen J. Gould, "The Great Scablands Debate," *Natural History* (Aug./Sept. 1978): p. 12–18; James H. Shea, "Twelve Fallacies of Uniformitarianism," *Geology*, vol. 10 (Sept. 1982): p. 455–460; Erle Kauffman, "The Uniformitarian Albatross," *Palaios*, vol. 2, no. 6 (1987): p. 531.

science had begun with him." In other words, we have allowed ourselves to be brain-washed into avoiding any interpretation of the past that involves extreme and what might be termed "catastrophic" processes.[82]

Now, it should be obvious that if Lyellian, uniformitarian brainwashing blinded men from seeing the evidence of any catastrophic processes, it would have surely kept them from seeing any evidence for the year-long worldwide Flood described in Genesis. So, as one who rejected the inspired, inerrant, historical account of Noah's Flood, the neo-catastrophist Ager continued to insist that geology offers no confirmation of the Flood. He could not see it because he did not want to see it. As Paul says, men "suppress the truth in unrighteousness" (Rom. 1:18–20).

These "neo-catastrophist" reinterpretations of the rocks have developed contemporaneously with a resurgence of "Flood geology," an interpretation of the rock record very similar to that of the 19th century scriptural geologists and a key ingredient to young-earth creationism, which was essentially launched into the world by the publication of *The Genesis Flood* (1961) by Drs. John Whitcomb and Henry Morris. This movement is now worldwide in scope[83] and the scientific sophistication of the scientific model is rapidly increasing with time.[84] It is

---

82. Derek Ager, *The Nature of the Stratigraphical Record* (London: Macmillan, 1981), p. 46–47. Ager's last book, published posthumously, was *The New Catastrophism* (Cambridge: Cambridge University Press, 1993), which documented some of the geological evidence for catastrophic deposition and erosion of sediments that he observed around the world. In the latter book Ager says, "I should, perhaps, say something about the title of this book. Just as politicians rewrite human history, so geologists rewrite earth history. For a century and a half the geological world has been dominated, one might even say brainwashed, by the gradualistic uniformitarianism of Charles Lyell. Any suggestion of 'catastrophic' events has been rejected as old-fashioned, unscientific and even laughable. This is partly due to the extremism of some of Cuvier's followers, though not of Cuvier himself. On that side too were the obviously untenable views of Bible-oriented fanatics, obsessed with myths such as Noah's Flood, and of classicists thinking of Nemesis [Greek goddess of divine retribution]. That is why I think it necessary to include the following 'disclaimer': *in view of the misuse that my words have been put to in the past, I wish to say that nothing in this book should be taken out of context and thought in any way to support the views of the 'creationists' (who I refuse to call 'scientific')*" (p. xi, emphasis in the original).

83. Even the evolutionists have noted that there are over 30 countries (including Russia, Korea, Australia, and Germany) that have creationist organizations. Korea's organization has about 2,000 scientist members. See Debora MacKensie, "Unnatural Selection," *New Scientist*, no. 2235 (April 22, 2000): p. 38.

84. Peer-reviewed geology papers by practicing MS-degree and PhD young-earth geologists based on literature and field research regularly appear in the *Creation Research Society Quarterly*, the *Journal of Creation*, the online *Answers Research Journal*, and at the "International Conference on Creationism" which has been held in Pittsburgh about every four years since 1986.

incumbent on Christian scholars and other leaders to become informed about the growing body of scientific evidence that confirms the literal truth of Genesis. To say that creationists are not real scientists doing real science is a statement of ignorance or misrepresentation. Resources explaining some of that scientific evidence verifying Genesis are recommended in the appendix. I would especially draw attention to John Morris's *The Young Earth* and Don DeYoung's *Thousands, not Billions* (with the documentary DVD by the same title).

Disastrous consequences of compromise

The scriptural geologists of the early 19th century opposed old-earth geological theories not only because the theories reflected erroneous scientific reasoning and were contrary to Scripture, but also because the scriptural geologists believed that the Christian compromise with such theories would eventually have a catastrophic effect on the health of the Church and her witness to a lost world. Henry Cole, an Anglican minister, wrote:

> Many reverend Geologists, however, would evince their reverence for the divine Revelation by making a distinction between its *historical* and its *moral* portions; and maintaining, that the latter only is inspired and absolute Truth; but that the former is not so; and therefore is open to any latitude of philosophic and scientific interpretation, modification or denial! According to these impious and infidel modifiers and separators, there is not one third of the Word of God that *is* inspired; for not more, nor perhaps so much, of that Word, is occupied in abstract moral revelation, instruction, and precept. The other two thirds, therefore, are open to any scientific modification and interpretation; or, (if scientifically required,) to a total denial! It may however be safely asserted, that whoever professedly, before men, disbelieves the inspiration of any part of Revelation, disbelieves, in the sight of God, its inspiration altogether. . . . What the consequences of such things must be to a revelation-possessing land, time will rapidly and awfully unfold in its opening pages of national skepticism, infidelity, and apostasy, and of God's righteous vengeance on the same![85]

Cole and other opponents of the old-earth theories rightly understood and warned that the historical portions of the Bible (including Genesis 1–11) are foundational to the theological and moral teachings of Scripture. Destroy the credibility of the Bible's history and sooner or later (it might take decades) we will see the rejection of the Bible's theology and morality both inside and outside the Church. The subsequent history of the once-Christian nations of Europe and North America has confirmed the scriptural geologists' worst fears about the church and society.

---

85. Henry Cole, *Popular Geology Subversive of Divine Revelation* (London: Hatchard and Son, 1834), p. ix–x, 44–45 (footnote).

One of the innumerable tragic examples of the consequences of this compromise with millions of years (and in many cases evolution also) is Charles Templeton (1915–2001). As a contemporary and friend of Billy Graham, many considered him to be an even more gifted young evangelist than Billy. He led many to Christ as he preached to thousands in North America and Britain. But he had questions about evolution. He went to Princeton Seminary in the late 1940s looking for answers. But by that time this seminary, where the orthodox Hodge, Hodge, and Warfield had once taught, was immersed in liberal theology. Templeton's professors convinced him that he must accept evolution and millions of years, thereby destroying his faith in the foundational book of the Bible and undermining his faith in the gospel. After seminary, he preached for a few more years. But finally his shattered faith forced him to leave the ministry and go into journalism. He died in 2001 as a miserable atheist. But in 1996 he published *Farewell to God: My Reasons for Rejecting the Christian Faith*. At the conclusion of that book he wrote, "I believe that there is no supreme being with human attributes — no God in the biblical sense — but that life is the result of timeless evolutionary forces, having reached its present transient state over millions of years."[86]

False ideas have terrible consequences. It is time for the Church, especially her leaders and scholars, to stop ignoring the age of the earth and the scientific evidence that increasingly vindicates the Word of God. The Church must repent of her compromise with millions of years (with the attendant ignoring or rejection of the global Noachian Flood) and once again believe and preach the literal truth of Genesis 1–11.

---

86. Charles Templeton, *Farewell to God* (Toronto: McClelland & Stewart, 1996), p. 232. His sad story is recounted in Ken Ham and Stacia Byers, "The Slippery Slide to Unbelief," *Creation ex nihilo* 22:3 (June 2000), p. 8–13, www.answersingenesis. org/creation/v22/i3/unbelief.asp.

Chapter 4

Is Nature the
67th Book of the Bible?

Richard Mayhue

*D*r. *John Clement Whitcomb Jr. first crossed my path in January 1971 when I, as a freshly saved naval officer, attended lectures jointly given with Dr. Henry Morris on creationism at Scott Memorial Baptist Church in San Diego, California. By August 1971, having resigned my commission in the United States Navy, I sat in Dr. Whitcomb's class on Job at Grace Theological Seminary in Winona Lake, Indiana. Subsequently, he participated as a member of my Th.M. thesis committee and my Th.D. dissertation committee, all at Grace. This stalwart of the faith not only taught me throughout my student days, but he also then became a senior colleague in my junior teaching days (Greek and New Testament) at Grace where he always sought to be a personal encouragement. Some of my most treasured memories come from the times when he was a faculty prayer partner. Over the ensuing years, I have been immeasurably enriched by knowing "Jack" Whitcomb as a theological mentor and friend.*

Throughout his Christian life, Dr. Whitcomb has taken 2 Timothy 4:7–8 and Jude 3 seriously in his teaching and writing ministries. While indefatigably contending for the once-for-all-delivered faith, passionately fighting the good fight, and relentlessly holding high the Holy Scriptures, he has been running the race non-stop as a brilliant and articulate spokesman for the cause of his Lord and Savior, Jesus Christ, especially in the matters of creation,[1] the Genesis Flood,[2] and the historicity of the Old Testament.[3]

Unless otherwise noted, all Scripture in this chapter is from the NAS95 version of the Bible.

1. John C. Whitcomb, *The Early Earth*, rev. ed. (Grand Rapids, MI: Baker, 1986).
2. Henry M. Morris and John C. Whitcomb Jr., *The Genesis Flood* (Grand Rapids, MI: Baker, 1967); John C. Whitcomb, *The World that Perished* (Grand Rapids, MI: Baker, 1988).
3. John C. Whitcomb Jr., *Darius the Mede* (Philadelphia, PA: Presbyterian and Reformed,

As a tribute to this special man who has contributed so much to my life over the past four decades, I gladly take pen in hand to write affirmingly on a theme for which he has expended much of his energies — the validation and defense of a young earth. With this chapter, I salute you, Dr. Whitcomb, because you have selflessly devoted your ministry to the glory of God as recited in His absolutely inerrant and wholly sufficient Word — the Bible — which provides the whole counsel of God (Acts 20:27).

The Question

Is nature the 67th book of the Bible? Providing the answer to this provocative query demands much more time and effort than might be realized at first hearing. It involves matters of: (1) canonicity; (2) the correct interpretation of Psalm 19, Acts 14, Acts 17, Romans 1, and Romans 10; (3) the unique authority of Scripture; (4) the character similarities and differences between general and special revelation; (5) man's fallen mind and the empirical approach to science; (6) proper hermeneutical principles of biblical interpretation; and (7) a biblical worldview.

This significant question should not be taken lightly nor answered quickly. Yet, this appears to be the manner in which Dr. Hugh Ross[4] has treated this matter. In a discussion whose length falls short of three full pages, this popular author, uncritically and without reservation, writes what appears to be intended as a self-evident axiom, "The facts of nature may be likened to a sixty-seventh book of the Bible."[5] What is the reader to make of Ross's assertion? Is he right? Or, is he wrong?

1963); John C. Whitcomb, *Esther: The Triumph of God's Sovereignty* (Chicago, IL: Moody, 1979); John C. Whitcomb, *Daniel* (Chicago, IL: Moody, 1985); John J. Davis and John C. Whitcomb, *A History of Israel from Conquest to Exile* (Grand Rapids, MI: Baker, 1980).

4. Hugh Ross earned a Ph.D. in astronomy at the University of Toronto (1973) and is president of Reasons to Believe (www.reasons.org), an organization devoted to promoting a progressive view of origins (over exceedingly long spans of time) in support of an old-earth theory based primarily on allegedly unassailable scientific research. His writings include: *The Fingerprint of God: Recent Scientific Discoveries Reveal the Unmistakable Identity of the Creator* (Orange, CA: Promise Press, 1991); *Creation and Time: A Biblical and Scientific Perspective on the Creation-Date Controversy* (Colorado Springs, CO: NavPress, 1994); *Beyond the Cosmos: What Recent Discoveries in Astronomy and Physics Reveal about the Nature of God* (Colorado Springs, CO: NavPress, 1999); *The Genesis Question: Scientific Advances and the Accuracy of Genesis* (Colorado Springs, CO: NavPress, 2001); *The Creator and the Cosmos: How the Greatest Scientific Discoveries of the Century Reveal God*, 2nd ed. (Colorado Springs, CO: NavPress, 2001); *A Matter of Days: Resolving a Creation Controversy* (Colorado Springs, CO: NavPress, 2004).

5. Ross, *Creation and Time*, p. 56. His volume, especially the section in which the quoted sentence appears (p. 53–72), has received mixed reviews. Positive reviews include, for

Ross's Affirmation — Reliable or Suspect?

In six brief paragraphs and a small chart,[6] Ross swiftly breezes through this profound question without any apparent caveats or hesitations regarding his "Absolutely!" answer. He cites no authority other than himself in support of his rather dogmatic answer. While on the surface his own affirmation might appear sufficient to certify the point, to someone reasonably familiar with Scripture and/or to one trained in critical theological thinking, Ross's answer proves unsatisfactory for at least five major reasons.

First, Ross's chart[7] comprised of 23 biblical texts which supposedly authenticate his answer, upon further reflection, disappointingly turns out to be a result of proof-texting (i.e., citing a scriptural text in support of one's conclusion when upon closer inspection the text is either not directly related or actually contradicts the point being made). The following observations warrant this conclusion.

1. Ecclesiastes 3:11 and Romans 2:14–15 deal with general revelation in the human conscience, but not general revelation in nature, as Ross asserts.

2. Romans 10:16–17 and Colossians 1:23 refer to the preaching of the gospel by humans, not the general revelation of nature, as Ross says.

3. Psalms 50:6 (heavens refers to angels); 85:11 (attributes of King Jesus); 97:6 (heavens refers to angels); 98:2–3 (God's dealings with Israel) have alternative interpretations that are as likely or more likely than that of general revelation in nature, as Ross suggests.

4. Proverbs 8:22–31 is a speech delivered by "lady wisdom" personified, not about general revelation in nature, as indicated by Ross.

5. Job 10:8–14; 12:7; 34:14–15; 35:10–12; 37:5–7; 38–41; Psalms 8; 104; 139; and Habakkuk 3:3 deal with what one can learn about nature from the special revelation of Scripture, not what one can learn from general revelation in nature alone, as Ross teaches.

example, Paul Copan, *JETS* 39 (1996): p. 307–08; Guillermo Gonzalez, *PSCF* 46 (1994): p. 270. Others have been somewhat neutral, such as John A. Witmer, *BibSac* 153 (1996): p. 493. Many who have been critical, especially of Ross's handling of Scripture, are represented by Mark van Bebber and Paul S. Taylor, *Creation and Time: A Report on the Progressive Creationist Hugh Ross*, 2nd ed. (Gilbert, AZ: Eden, 1996); John MacArthur, *The Battle for the Beginning* (Nashville, TN: W Group, 2001), p. 60–62; Jonathan Sarfati, *Refuting Compromise: A Biblical and Scientific Refutation of "Progressive Creationism" (Billions of Years), as Popularized by Astronomer Hugh Ross* (Green Forest, AR: Master Books, 2004). Additional articles can be located at the websites of Answers in Genesis (www.answersingenesis.org) and Institute for Creation Research (www.icr.org).

6. Ross, *Creation and Time*, p. 55–58.

7. Ibid., p. 57.

6. Only Psalm 19:1–6; Acts 14:17; 17:23–31; and Romans 1:18–25; 10:18 do, in fact, refer to general revelation in nature, which is the singular subject Ross addresses.

So, in Ross's answer to the question, "Is nature the 67th book of the Bible?" only five (22 percent) of the 23 passages he cites actually appear to support his basic point and then not to the depth or breadth that Ross intimates. Seventy-eight percent of the Scripture citations were misunderstood by him and thus mistakenly utilized. One's confidence in Ross's ability to objectively and skillfully handle the Bible quickly erodes in this torrent of error.

Second, Ross claims that Romans 10:16–17[8] and Colossians 1:23[9] refer to preaching the gospel to all the world through the general revelation of nature. However, even a cursory reading of Romans 10:16–17 makes it plainly evident that Paul is talking about the gospel in Scripture (i.e., "the word of Christ," being proclaimed by human preachers). While the interpretation of Colossians 1:23 is not so immediately obvious, the consensus of conservative, evangelical commentators confirms that Paul is referring to the human preaching of the gospel, either using hyperbole in referring to the then known world or proleptically in anticipation of the gospel being preached throughout the world.[10]

Third, Ross is mistaken in his understanding and application of general revelation. As demonstrated above in points one and two, this astronomer-by-training has badly interpreted Scripture in arriving at his proposed broad, philosophical approach to general revelation. He goes so far as to imply that all which is discoverable in the realm of "science" is general revelation and, as such, is equal in value and quality to the special revelation of Scripture. Ross asserts, without any reasonable or factual proof, that "the Bible teaches a dual, reliably consistent revelation."[11] By this, he intends to imply that general revelation is not only equal in its quality of revelation, but also its authority. Thus, general revelation, considered by him as any discoverable fact of science, would actually have the apparent authority to interpret Scripture, not the reverse.

The subject of general revelation will be examined in more detail later in this chapter. However, a few preliminary observations sufficiently prove Ross's view deficient.

1. Psalm 19 does compare general revelation (19:1–6) with scriptural revelation (19:7–11). But in fact, it actually contrasts them; thus, they are not

---

8. Ibid.

9. Ibid., p. 56–57.

10. This writer surveyed over 25 evangelical commentaries and not even one suggested that this text might refer to the preaching of the gospel through general revelation in nature. See Van Bebber's expanded discussion in *Creation and Time: A Report*, p. 37–39. Douglas F. Kelly, *Creation and Change* (Ross-shire, Great Britain: Christian Focus, 1997), p. 230–31, in notes 49 and 50, comments on Ross's tortured efforts in handling Scripture elsewhere.

11. Ross, *Creation and Time*, p. 56.

compared as absolute equals, like Ross teaches, but rather Psalm 19 exalts Scripture as the greater and most valued of God's revelation.

2. Ross places science on the same level as Scripture. He fails to distinguish between science as the alleged facts of nature explained by man and Scripture as the certain facts of God given and explained by God. Since science does not carry the inerrant quality of Scripture, one can conclude that Ross greatly overestimates nature/science and woefully undervalues Scripture.

3. He expands the concept of general revelation to include all discoverable/knowable information outside of Scripture. However, a careful analysis of the very few biblical passages that speak to this subject (i.e., Psalm 19:1–6; Acts 14:17; 17:23–31; Romans 1:18–25 and 10:18) severely limit the scope and purpose of this legitimate source of divine revelation.

Let the writer simply ask two questions about general revelation in nature to demonstrate that God intended it to serve more narrow purposes in contrast to the broad informative and authoritative scope of Scripture. First, if only general revelation was available, would we know about God like a person knows God from the Bible?[12] Second, could a person be redeemed based on general revelation alone?[13] The answer to both questions is a resounding "no!" Since this is so, why would anyone exalt the lesser to the same, if not greater, status as the actual greater?

Morris and Whitcomb anticipated Ross' claim[14] three decades earlier when observing:

> It has often been maintained that God has given us two revelations, one in nature and one in the Bible and that they cannot contradict each other. This is certainly correct; but when one subconsciously identifies with natural revelation his own interpretations of nature and then denounces theologians who are unwilling to mold biblical revelation into conformity with his interpretation of nature, he is guilty of serious error. After all, special revelation supersedes natural revelation, for it is only by means of special revelation that we can interpret aright the world about us.[15]

---

12. From nature, we would not know that God is portrayed as a person, as a male, as a Trinity, as the only true God, and as possessing incommunicable attributes (e.g., his glory and omniscience) and communicable attributes (e.g., his love and grace) to name just a few essential features of God as revealed in Scripture, but not by general revelation in nature. Our knowledge of God would be impoverished by comparison, if limited to what general revelation in nature provides.

13. A brief glance at Romans 10:9–13 alone settles the issue.

14. See Ross, *Creation and Time*, p. 56, 58 where he uses the word "dual" to express the equality of general and special revelation.

15. Morris and Whitcomb, *Genesis Flood*, p. 458, n. l.

Fourth, Hugh Ross asserts that general revelation in nature has the "inspired" quality of Scripture[16] and he applies 2 Timothy 3:16 to it. While all of God's revelation is true and unassailable because the source is God himself,[17] only Scripture is "inspired" in the biblical sense that the Holy Spirit guided men to inerrantly record in written form this God-breathed Word (2 Pet. 1:21). Further, Scripture affirms about itself alone that, because it is "inspired," it is therefore "profitable for teaching, for reproof, for correction, for training in righteousness" (2 Tim. 3:16). Verse 17 continues as a "purpose" explanation of verse 16. Certainly, not even Ross believes that general revelation in nature was given "that the man of God may be adequate, equipped for every good work" (2 Tim. 3:17).

Fifth, adding any additional revelation to Scripture makes the so-called "facts of nature" canonical.[18] So, when Ross considers nature the 67th book of the Bible, he is in effect calling the Scriptures incomplete and thus reopening the canon for additional revelation.

Do we know for certain that God will or will not amend our current Bible with a 67th book? Or in other words, "Is the canon forever closed?" Several significant observations, when taken together, have convinced the Church over the centuries that the canon of Scripture is actually closed, never to be reopened.

1. The Book of Revelation is unique to the Scripture in that it describes with unparalleled detail the end-time events which precede eternity future. As Genesis began Scripture by bridging the gap from eternity past into a time/space existence with the only detailed creation account (Gen. 1–2), so Revelation transitions out of time/space back into eternity future (Rev. 20–22). Genesis and Revelation, by virtue of their contents, are the perfectly matched bookends of Scripture (i.e., the "alpha and omega" of the canon, the beginning and the end).

2. Just as there was prophetic silence after Malachi completed the Old Testament canon, so there was a parallel silence (even to this very day) after John delivered Revelation. This leads to the conclusion that the New Testament canon was then closed also.

3. Since there have not been nor now are any authorized prophets or apostles in the Old Testament or New Testament sense, then there are no potential providers of future inspired, canonical revelation.

---

16. Ross, *Creation and Time*, p. 56.

17. Richard L. Mayhue, "The Authority of Scripture," *TMSJ* 15 (Fall 2004): p. 227–236.

18. F.F. Bruce, *The Canon of Scripture* (Downers Grove, IL: IVP, 1988); R. Laird Harris, *Inspiration and Canonicity of the Bible*, rev.ed. (Grand Rapids, MI: Zondervan, 1969), p. 129–294; Bruce Metzger, *The Canon of the New Testament* (Oxford: Oxford Press, 1987).

4. Of the four exhortations not to tamper with Scripture (Deut. 4:2; 12:32; Prov. 30:6), only the one in Revelation 22:18–19 contains warnings of severe divine judgment for disobedience. Further, Revelation is the only book of the New Testament to end with this kind of admonition. Therefore, these facts strongly suggest that Revelation was the last book of the canon and now that the book is complete, to either add or delete would bring God's severe displeasure.

5. Finally, the early church (i.e., those closest in time to the Apostles) believed that Revelation concluded God's inspired writings, the Scriptures. Therefore, the 21st century Church should also believe that the canon is and will remain closed because, according to Scripture, there will be no future 67th book of the Bible, not even nature itself.

In concluding this section, the reader should consider that if Ross handles science as imprecisely as he does theology, then his science is also highly suspect. For example, he writes, "Some readers might fear that I am implying God's revelation through nature is somehow on an equal footing with His revelation through the words of the Bible."[19] Some might defend him at this point by responding that the reason one does not need to fear is because Ross is not equating the two and has been misunderstood. However, in the context that follows, this scientist is actually saying in effect, "Don't fear that I am putting both on an equal footing because human reasoning leads one to fearlessly do just that." He is actually attempting to reassure those whom he would persuade to his thinking that to equate general revelation in nature with special revelation is perfectly permissible and harmless, and even the correct thing to do. His conclusions are based on faulty human reason without the proper assistance and authority of divine revelation and, thus, in error and in opposition to what the Bible actually teaches, as will be demonstrated in the discussion that follows.

Exploring the Issue

Demonstrating that Hugh Ross's positive answer to the question is wrong does not automatically make one correct when responding, "No, nature is not the 67th book of the Bible!" One must also establish that the "no!" reply proceeds factually, fairly, and logically from a serious investigation of at least six important factors. These issues need to be carefully considered when formulating and stating a confident reply. The following discussion will follow these lines of thought: 1) biblical texts, 2) the authority of Scripture, 3) the character of revelation, 4) man's fallen mind and empiricism, 5) proper hermeneutics, and 6) a biblical worldview.

Biblical Texts

Many theologians' understanding of general revelation is that there are just seven explicit biblical passages which deal with this subject (Ps. 19:1–6;

---

19. Ross, *Creation and Time*, p. 57.

Eccles. 3:11; Acts 14:17; 17:23–31; Rom. 1:18–25; 2:14–15; 10:18).[20] These are texts that, with few exceptions, have no hotly disputed textual variants or really attractive alternative interpretations. Thus, these selections provide desirably unarguable evidence for developing an exegetical basis on which to build a theology of general revelation.

These few passages develop all that the special revelation of Scripture teaches about general revelation.[21] Thus, whatever comprises our theology of general revelation as taught in Scripture must come from these sources. This demands that God's special revelation define God's natural revelation without contaminating the subject with man's philosophical reasoning. A brief discussion of each biblical passage follows.

Psalm 19:1–6[22]

This grand psalm provides six major insights into general revelation. First, as to its *source*, the heavens comprise a significant element of general revelation (19:1). Second, in regard to its *message*, God's glory as the Creator of the heavens is unmistakable (19:1). Third, the never-ceasing cycle of day and night testify to its *permanency* so long as the created order exists (19:2). Fourth, as to *character*, it is a silent witness comprised of phenomenalogical evidence (19:3). Fifth, its *extent* has no geographical limitations since the evidence can be observed everywhere (19:4a, b). Sixth, as to its *order* or *regulation*, the predictability of sunrise and sunset points to the precise order of the creation and thus the orderliness of the Creator (19:4c–6).

---

20. None of these seven biblical texts teach that history is one of the sources of general revelation. In contrast, these theology texts do include history as part of general revelation: Millard J. Erickson, *Christian Theology* (Grand Rapids, MI: Baker, 1986), p. 154–55; Norman Geisler, *Systematic Theology*, vol. 1 (Minneapolis, MN: Bethany, 2002), p. 70–71; and Renald Showers, "General Revelation," part 1, *Israel My Glory* (August/September 1995): p. 22. To say that history is not part of general revelation is not to deny that Scripture speaks of God's providential hand in human history (cf. Job 12:23; Dan 2:21, 4:17). However, what we know for certain about God's activities in history comes from the special revelation of Scripture, not from any human account of history itself treated as a distinct source of general revelation.

21. Robert L. Thomas, *Evangelical Hermeneutics: The New Versus the Old* (Grand Rapids, MI: Kregel, 2003) develops this thesis in chapter 5, "General Revelation and Biblical Hermeneutics," p. 113–40. "Any efforts to widen the scope of general revelation to include information or theories about aspects of creation, man, or anything else besides God do not have support from the Bible, which limits the scope of general revelation to information about God" (p. 117).

22. See James B. Jordan, *Creation in Six Days: A Defense of the Traditional Reading of Genesis One* (Moscow, ID: Canon, 1999), p. 113–115, who compares the teaching of Psalm 19 with those who want to extend the psalm's meaning into the realm of scientific inquiry. John Street, "Why Biblical Counseling and Not Psychology?" in John MacArthur, gen. ed., *Think Biblically!* (Wheaton, IL: Crossway, 2003), p. 214–219 looks at Psalm 19 in light of recent writings concerning psychology.

Then in verses 7–11 the expansive nature of special revelation in Scripture is contrasted with the severe limitations (in scope of and intent of the message) of general revelation in the heavens. First, the *source* is the Word of God (19:7–8). Second, the *message* is of salvation (19:9–14). Third, in regard to *permanency*, it will outlast the created order (Isa. 40:8; Matt. 24:35; Mark 13:31). Fourth, the *nature* of Scripture is propositional (i.e., words, sentences, paragraphs, etc.) (Ps. 19:7–8; 2 Tim. 3:16). Fifth, the *extent* of special revelation reaches to both earth and heaven (Ps. 19:7–8; 119:89). Sixth, regarding the Bible's *regulation*, it is conducted flawlessly by God the Spirit (Ps. 19:7–14; 2 Tim. 3:16–17; 2 Pet. 1:20–21).

It is no exaggeration to say that Psalm 19 is the classic text when establishing the superiority of special revelation in Scripture over general revelation in nature. So it is no surprise then, that in the progress of God's special revelation in Scripture explaining general revelation, that this text appears first. Psalm 19 concludes that throughout all time, all languages, and all cultures the message of general revelation has been delivered non-verbally in such a manner that every human could comprehend that the God of power and order exists and thus all glory should be rendered unto Him.

Ecclesiastes 3:11

Solomon pens a short, pregnant truth that eternity is set in the heart of every person. It undoubtedly resulted from man being created in the image of God (Gen. 1:27) which subsequently was severely distorted in the fall (Gen. 3:1–21), thus needing to be restored by God's gracious salvation (Rom. 3:21–26). This hints at what Paul later makes clearer regarding general revelation through man's conscience (cf. Rom. 2:14–15). There is a limited intuitive sense of God's existence in every person that points to the fact that humans are immortal, not temporal. It must be further noted that this text does not directly answer the question at hand since it does not deal with nature but rather human conscience.

Acts 14:17[23]

Here, Paul is rejecting man's worship of him which should have been rightly rendered to God alone, who created the heavens and earth (14:15). He goes on to make a statement about God's general revelation in reference to "rains from heaven" (cf. Job 5:10; Matt. 5:45) and "fruitful seasons" (cf. Gen. 1:14, 29). These two features served as an ongoing witness, in effect a continuous revelation of God's goodness (in spite of their evil) by satisfying their hearts with food and gladness (14:17).

Several characteristics of general revelation can be observed in this text. First, it is available throughout history, from beginning to end. Second, it is provided for all humans. Third, it can be observed by the most scientifically unsophisticated. Fourth, it reveals something about God's nature.

---

23. See Stephen R. Spencer, "Is Natural Theology Biblical?" *GTJ* 9 (1988): p. 59–72.

Acts 17:23–31[24]

Paul is in Athens, one of the great centers of intellectualism in that day. In spite of their great learning, the Apostle indicts the Athenians as the spiritually ignorant (17:23, 30). He then confronts them with the truth of God as Creator (17:24), sustainer (17:25), sovereign (17:26), Savior (17:27), and source of life (17:28–29).

The major and explicit emphasis of this passage is God's special revelation through Paul's preaching (cf. 17:23, "I proclaim to you" and 17:30, God is now "declaring to men") and Christ's resurrection (17:31). The minor and implicit emphasis is upon the most general of general revelation, which points to God as the source of the people's origin to which Paul alludes in his preaching. Of the seven hallmark texts on general revelation, this one makes the least contribution, since its main point concerns that which can be known through special revelation, i.e., the miraculous resurrection of Christ and the apostolic witness of Paul, here included as Scripture.

Romans 1:18–25

Paul here contrasts this revelation (*apokaluptō*) of God's righteousness to be embraced by faith (1:15–17) with the revelation of God's wrath which falls upon people for rejecting what can be known by sight (i.e., God's eternal power and deity, 1:18–3:20). That which is known (*gnōstos*) about God among them vividly pointed to God himself as the source of their knowledge (1:19), which came about by viewing God's creation (1:20). The invisible omnipotence and deity of the Creator can unmistakably be seen in His observable creation, thus leaving all people without excuse (1:20) for not honoring God (1:21), for exchanging the truth for a lie (1:25), and for serving the creation rather than the Creator (1:23, 25). Because of this rejection and reversal, God's wrath comes upon man.

It should be noted that the three conclusions drawn from Acts 14:17 are also found here. God has revealed himself from the time of creation to the present in His created order. This revelation has been available to all of mankind. No special scientific knowledge or equipment was necessary to understand God's message about himself.

Romans 2:14–15

In a rather vague way, Paul seems to allude here to an inner sense (cf. "conscience" in 2:15) which contrasts with the external general revelation of the created order. He argues that even though unbelieving Gentiles do not have the Law (i.e., Old Testament Law), they nonetheless have a moral standard of sorts by which they strive to live. This would seem to parallel the thought of Ecclesiastes 3:11 that with the fall of Adam, the image of God was severely damaged but not eliminated. God still has an inner witness in all men that generally points them

---

24. Ibid.

to the God of righteousness. However, it must be noted that this text does not address the subject of general revelation in nature, but rather general revelation in human conscience — that revelation in man's soul is about God and His moral standards.

Romans 10:18

Paul quotes Psalm 19:4 in affirming that, even without a preacher, humans are not ignorant of God. They have known about God through general revelation (cf. Ps. 19:1–6). The general revelation of 10:18 is contrasted with the preaching of special revelation in 10:14–17.

This last biblical text on general revelation returns to the first text in Psalm 19. In context, the order is reversed (Ps. 19:1–6 on general revelation and Ps. 19:7–11 on special revelation; Rom. 10:14 – 17 on special revelation and Rom. 10:18 on general revelation).

Summary

The following observations can be made from the Bible about general revelation:

1. The breadth of content is limited to the knowledge of God, not all knowledge.

2. The time span is all of time, not just more recent times.

3. The witness is to all people, not just to some with scientific training.

4. The acquisition is made by human sight and sense, not with scientific equipment or technique.

5. The whole corpus of general revelation was available immediately after creation. It did not accumulate with the passing of time and the progressive collection of knowledge.

Therefore, the concept of general revelation in nature as defined by Scripture should not be broadened or expanded any further than the special revelation of Scripture allows in its only five texts (Ps. 19:1–6; Acts 14:17; 17:23–31; Rom. 1:18–25; 10:18). To do so, would be to do the unthinkable — add to the Scripture without divine authorization.[25] Thus, Scripture itself rejects the notion that nature is the 67th book of the Bible, as Ross wrongly asserts.[26]

---

25. John D. Hannah, "*Bibliotheca Sacra* and Darwinism: An Analysis of the Nineteenth-Century Conflict Between Science and Theology," *GTJ* 4 (1983): p. 37–58. "It behooves us to remember to be cautious not to neglect the exegesis of Scripture and the qualitative gulf between special and general revelation" (p. 58).

26. Ross, *Creation and Time*, p. 55–58.

The Authority of Scripture[27]

The concept of *authority* is thoroughly woven into the fabric of Scripture. It is unmistakably obvious from Genesis 1:1 ("In the beginning God created . . .") to Revelation 22:20 ("Yes, I am coming quickly") and everywhere between. This idea of "ultimate right" is inextricably linked with God's sovereignty (Rom. 11:36).

What is truly known about authority did not originate outside of Scripture, but rather within. Thus, it is not a secular concept that has been co-opted by religion. On the contrary, it is a sacred element of the very person of God. What Scripture properly teaches about authority has actually been shamefully distorted by this world's system and wrongfully employed by all world religions.

The rightful idea of authority has fallen on hard times at the start of the 21st century. Illegitimate forms and expressions of authority range from the illegal and abusive exercise of political totalitarianism to individual authority emerging from a postmodern mindset of selfishness.

The appropriate approach to this discussion commences with a working definition of authority in general, especially legitimate authority exercised in a proper fashion. A representative dictionary definition records that authority is the "power or right to enforce obedience; moral or legal supremacy; right to command or give a final decision."[28]

Bernard Ramm suggests:

> Authority itself means *that right or power to command action or compliance, or to determine belief or custom, expecting obedience from those under authority, and in turn giving responsible account for the claim to right or power.*[29]

The New Testament noun (appearing 102 times) most commonly translated "authority" is ἐξουσία *(exousia)*. A representative lexical definition reads, "The power exercised by rulers or others in high position by virtue of their office."[30]

However, with a biblical worldview, original authority and ultimate authority reside with God and God alone. God did not inherit His authority — there was no one to bequeath it to Him. God did not receive His authority — there was no one to bestow it on Him. God's authority did not come by way of an election — there was no one to vote for Him. God did not seize His authority — there was no one to steal it from. God did not earn His authority — it was already His. God inherently embodies authority because He is the great "I AM" (Exod. 3:14; John 8:58).

---

27. This section has been adapted from Richard L. Mayhue, "The Authority of Scripture," *TMSJ* 15 (Fall 2004): p. 227–236.

28. *The New Shorter Oxford English Dictionary*, s.v., "authority."

29. Bernard Ramm, *The Pattern of Religious Authority* (Grand Rapids, MI: Eerdmans, 1959), p. 10, emphasis in the original.

30. *BDAG*, 3rd ed. rev., s.v., "ἐξουσία." Cf. *TDNT*, s.v., "ἐξουσία."

God's authority becomes obvious and unquestionable when one considers three facts. First, God created the heavens and earth and that which is therein (Gen. 1–2). Second, God owns the earth, all that it contains, and those who dwell in it (Ps. 24:1). Third, in the end God consumes it all in that He declared, "Behold, I am making all things new" (Rev. 21:5).

To understand and accept the fact of God's authority is as simple as accepting the fact of God Himself. Romans says this best: "For there is no authority except from God, and those which exist are established by God" (Rom. 13:1). This classic text lays out clearly the source of all authority and articulates the principle of "Divine delegation" (cf. Job 34:13; John 19:11).

There are numerous statements in the OT which explicitly testify to God's authority. For example, "That power belongs to God" (Ps. 62:11) and "Power and might are in Your hand so that no one can stand against You" (2 Chron. 20:6).

Jesus declared, "All authority has been given to Me in heaven and on earth" (Matt. 28:18). Jude wrote, "[T]o the only God our Savior, through Jesus Christ our Lord, be glory, majesty, dominion and authority, before all time and now and forever. Amen" (Jude 25).

This truth fleshes out in syllogistic fashion thusly:

1. Scripture is the Word of God.

2. The words of God are authoritative.

Conclusion: Scripture is authoritative.

Both the ontological basis (God is) and the epistemological basis (God speaks only truth) are established in Scripture (Gen. 1:1; Ps. 119:142, 151, 160). John Frame succinctly asserts, "There is no higher authority, no greater ground of certainty. . . . The truth of Scripture is a presupposition for God's people."[31] Thus, the very nature of God and God's Word is not determined inductively by human reason but deductively from the testimony of Scripture (cf. Ps. 119:89; Isa. 40:8).

The outworking of God's authority in Scripture can be summarized in a series of negative (what it is not) and positive (what it is) statements.

1. The authority of Scripture is *not* a derived authority bestowed by humans; rather it is the *original* authority of God.

2. It *does not* change with the times, the culture, the nation, or the ethnic background; rather it is the *unalterable* authority of God.

3. It is *not* one authority among many possible spiritual authorities; rather it is the *exclusive* spiritual authority of God.

---

31. John M. Frame, *Apologetics to the Glory of God* (Phillipsburg, NJ: Presbyterian and Reformed, 1994), p. 127. See also Greg L. Bahnsen, "Inductivism, Inerrancy, and Presuppositionalism," *JETS* 20 (December 1977): p. 289–305; John M. Frame, "Van Til and the Ligonier Apologetic," *WTJ* 47 (1985): p. 279–299; Tim McConnel, "The Old Princeton Apologetics: Common Sense or Reformed?" *JETS* 46 (December 2003): p. 647–672.

4. It is *not* an authority that can be successfully challenged or rightfully over-thrown; rather it is the *permanent* authority of God.

5. It is *not* a relativistic or subordinate authority; rather it is the *ultimate* authority of God.

6. It is *not* merely a suggestive authority; rather it is the *obligatory* authority of God.

7. It is *not* a benign authority in its outcomes; rather it is the *consequential* authority of God.

While general revelation in nature is as authoritative as Scripture since both come from the same authority-source (i.e., God, general revelation is not self-authenticating). Only what special revelation authenticates about the scope of general revelation's authority should be accepted. What one allows as authoritative from general revelation in nature should not exceed or go beyond what the Bible has specified.

If Ross would subscribe to this biblical truth, he would therefore have to withdraw his assertion that "nature is . . . on an equal footing with His revelation through the words of the Bible."[32] He would also have to admit that his thesis, ". . . the Bible teaches a dual, reliably consistent revelation," is in error.[33]

The Character of Revelation

To fully grasp the qualitative and functional differences between general revelation[34] and special revelation, one need only consider the following three contrasts between the two. First, the world of general revelation in nature will perish (Isa. 40:8; Matt. 24:35; Mark 13:31; Luke 21:33; 1 Pet. 1:24; 2 Pet. 3:10), but the Word of special revelation will not pass away because it is forever (Ps. 119:89; Isa. 40:8; Matt. 24:35; Mark 13:31; Luke 21:33; 1 Pet. 1:25). Second, the world of general revelation in nature was cursed and in bondage to corruption (Gen. 3:1–24; Rom. 8:19–23) and is therefore not the perfect world God

---

32. Ross, *Creation and Time*, p. 57.
33. Ibid., p. 56.
34. While much has been written on general revelation, the following materials are the more helpful. G.C. Berkouwer, *General Revelation* (Grand Rapids, MI: Eerdmans, 1955); G.C. Berkouwer, "General and Special Divine Revelation," *Revelation and the Bible*, ed. by Carl F.H. Henry (Grand Rapids, MI: Baker, 1958), p. 13–24; Bruce A. Demarest, *General Revelation: Historical Views and Contemporary Issues* (Grand Rapids, MI: Zondervan, 1982); Gordon R. Lewis and Bruce A. Demarest, *Integrative Theology*, vol. 1 (Grand Rapids, MI: Zondervan, 1987), p. 61–82; James Leo Garrett Jr., *Systematic Theology*, vol. 1 (Grand Rapids, MI: Eerdmans, 1990), p. 43–91; N.H. Gootjes, "General Revelation in Its Relation to Special Revelation," *WTJ* 51 (1989): p. 359–368; Wayne Grudem, *Systematic Theology* (Grand Rapids, MI: Zondervan, 1994), p. 121–124; Spencer, "Natural Theology," p. 59–72; Thomas, *Evangelical Hermeneutics*, p. 113–140.

originally created (Gen. 1:31), while the word of special revelation is inspired of God and thus always perfect and holy (Ps. 19:7–9; 119:140; 2 Tim. 3:16; Rom. 7:12). Third, the scope of general revelation in nature is severely limited compared to the multi-dimensional expanse of special revelation in Scripture.

To enlarge this line of thinking, consider these additional differences.

	General Revelation in Scripture	*Special Revelation in Scripture*
1.	Condemns only.	Condemns and redeems.
2.	Harmonizes with special revelation, but does not provide new material.	Enhances and explains in detail the content of general revelation, but goes significantly beyond.
3.	Its perceived message needs to be confirmed by Scripture.	Scripture is self-authenticating and self-confirming in its claim to be God's Word.
4.	Needs to be interpreted in light of special revelation.	Needs no other revelation to interpret — it interprets itself.
5.	Never equated with Scripture by Scripture.	Has no peer.

With this in mind, consider Hugh Ross's demand that nature be considered as "His Word written on the heavens and earth."[35] First, the world of natural revelation is not revealed in "words," as is Scripture alone. Second, the general revelation of nature is never spoken of in Scripture as the Word of God, but frequently Scripture is referred to by this term (Acts 7:38; Heb. 4:12; 1 Pet. 1:23).

Therefore to reason (as does Ross) that both nature and Scripture are revelations of God and thus equal in all respects is like arguing in the physical realm that both an infant and a 21-year-old athlete are humans created by God and thus fully capable of competing in the Olympics. This would be absurd, for while both are human, they each possess drastically differing athletic capabilities.

Man's Fallen Mind and Empiricism

Revelation does not include what man discovers on his own (i.e., knowledge) but rather what God discloses that otherwise man could not find on his own. General revelation in nature, as defined by special revelation, discloses the existence of God, the glory of God, the power and intelligence of God, the benevolence of God, and the fallenness (evil) of humanity.

When the human race fell in Genesis 3, one of the terrible consequences included the spiritual debilitation of the mind. The New Testament uses 12

---

35. Ross, *Creation and Time*, p. 55.

different negative Greek words to describe the ruin of man's intellectual capacity.

1. Debased — Romans 1:28	7. Deluded — Colossians 2:4
2. Hardened — 2 Corinthians 3:14	8. Deceived — Colossians 2:8
3. Blinded — 2 Corinthians 4:4	9. Sensuous — Colossians 2:18
4. Futile — Ephesians 4:17	10. Depraved — 1 Timothy 6:5
5. Darkened — Ephesians 4:18	11. Corrupted — 2 Timothy 3:8
6. Hostile — Colossians 1:21	12. Defiled — Titus 1:15

As a result of this mental mayhem, people are "always learning and never able to come to the knowledge of the truth" (2 Tim. 3:7), and some even "have a zeal for God, but not in accordance with knowledge" (Rom. 10:2). The cause of this universal trauma on the mind was Eve's efforts to question and edit God's special revelation in Genesis 2:17. She did this by employing an erroneous view of general revelation, manifest by human empiricism (the foundation of scientific inquiry), in order to validate or invalidate God's special revelation which did not then nor ever will need human authentication.

At the completion of creation, "God saw all that He had made, and behold, it was very good" (Gen. 1:31). Adam and Eve were in righteous fellowship with God and had been given dominion over all of God's creation (Gen. 1:26–30). A life of earthly bliss described their potential future and that of their offspring before sin entered the picture. Genesis 3:1–7 describes the far-reaching and devastating blow to the human mind which would affect every human being who ever lived thereafter. Without question, Satan waged war against God and the human race in this monumental passage where the battlefield turns out to be Eve's mind. In the end, Eve exchanged the truth of God (Gen. 2:17) for the lie of Satan (Gen. 3:4–5) and the human mind has never been the same since.

The empirical method in primitive form actually originated in Genesis 3 when Eve concluded that the only way by which she could decide whether God was right or wrong (after Satan had planted seeds of doubt about God's truthfulness in her mind — Gen. 3:4) involved testing Him with her own mind and senses. Paul explained it this way in Romans 1:25, speaking of those who would follow on the spiritually perilous path of Eve and then Adam: ". . . they exchanged the truth of God for a lie, and worshiped and served the creature rather than the Creator."

In short order, Eve had basically bought into the lie of Satan and faced a momentous choice. Either she could disobediently choose to eat or she could obediently choose to refrain. Eve believed that she alone could determine the best option with her own mind; God's command was apparently no longer authoritative. God's verbal revelation was perceived to no longer dictate what was right and what was wrong in her life. God's authoritative instruction appeared now to be optional because, all of a sudden due to Satan's influence, there were other alternatives.

"When the woman saw that the tree was good for food, and that it was a delight to the eyes, and the tree was desirable to make one wise, she took from its fruit and ate; and she gave also to her husband with her, and he ate" (Gen. 3:6). Here, one finds the first historical practice of empirical research and inductive reasoning in its infancy. In the initial act of human rebellion, Eve decided to conduct three tests on the tree in order to see whether God or Satan was right.

So, she subjected the tree to these tests, the first being that of physical value. She observed the tree, and in examining it she saw that its fruit was "good for food." It had nutritional value. These might have been Eve's thoughts. *Maybe Satan is right. Maybe God was over-restrictive in preventing me from having all the joy of life and all the fruit in the garden.*

Based on this seemingly positive response, she ran a second test. Eve realized that the fruit was "a delight to the eyes." Not only would it benefit her body nutritionally, but she also discovered that it had emotional or aesthetic value. Putting this into postmodern language, she felt good about looking at the tree.

Eve wasn't satisfied yet. She wanted to be thorough. Perhaps she thought, *I'll take it one step further.* Then came a final test. She looked and saw that the tree was desirable "to make one wise." It had intellectual value that would make her wise like God.

In the midst of Eve's deliberation, she saw and thought that the tree really was good. It met her needs physically, aesthetically, and intellectually. Her mind drew the inference that either God was wrong or God had lied; Satan's deceit had successfully lured her away from God's absolute and unfailing truth. The human mind was about to be wasted forever. Being deceived, Eve was then led to disobey; she rejected God's instructions and took from the tree's fruit and ate. Adam quickly did the same (Gen. 3:6).

Paul summarizes Eve's disastrous act this way. "But I am afraid that, as the serpent deceived Eve by his craftiness, your minds will be led astray from the simplicity and purity of devotion to Christ" (2 Cor. 11:3; cf. 1 Tim. 2:14). The seduction of Eve's mind by Satan's deceit and Adam's blatant disobedience resulted in the corruption of their souls and, as a result, the souls of all humans who would follow (Rom. 5:12). Thus, the human mind was wasted by sin. Man's mind was so debilitated that fellowship with God was no longer humanly possible and the ability to see and understand life from God's perspective vanished. The human race was now estranged from its God and Creator.

As a result, God's original two created human beings and every one of their offspring experienced a brutal reversal in their relationship with Him and His world.

1. They no longer would concern themselves with thoughts of God, but only with the thinking of men (Ps. 53:1; Rom. 1:25).

2. They no longer would have spiritual sight, but were blinded by Satan to the glory of God (2 Cor. 4:4).

3. They would no longer be wise, but foolish (Ps. 14:1; Titus 3:3).

4. They would no longer be alive to God, but rather dead in their sins (Rom. 8:5–11).

5. They no longer would set their affections on the things above, but on the things of earth (Col. 3:2).

6. They would no longer walk in light, but rather in darkness (John 12:35–36, 46).

7. They no longer would possess eternal life, but rather faced eternal death — i.e., eternal separation from God (2 Thess. 1:9).

8. They would no longer live in the realm of the Spirit, but rather the flesh (Rom. 8:1–5).

The subsequent consequences of this catastrophe seem to be lost on Ross who insists that knowledge (not revelation) gained by human observation in nature should be equal to or even superior to God's special revelation in Scripture. He attempts to make the humanly discoverable or understandable equal to revelation which by definition can only be known accurately by divine disclosure.[36]

The truth is that general revelation as defined by Scripture does not uncover anything that one could not find in the special revelation of Scripture. Both Eve and Dr. Ross engaged in the confused substitution of knowledge acquired by human acquisition for revelation received by God's gracious provision in both general and special revelation.

Proper Hermeneutics

The consensus of the evangelical community in the late 20th century on proper hermeneutics was expressed by the writings which resulted from the multiple meetings of the International Council on Biblical Inerrancy (ICBI).[37] The following excerpts express their conclusions regarding special and general revelation.[38]

---

36. Ibid., p. 55–58.

37. Over a ten-year period (1977–1987), the International Council on Biblical Inerrancy (ICBI) held three summits for scholars (1978, 1983, 1986) and two congresses for the Christian community at large (1982, 1987) to formulate and disseminate the biblical truth about inerrancy.

38. Norman L. Geisler and J.I. Packer, *Explaining Hermeneutics: A Commentary* (Oakland, CA: ICBI, 1983), p. 15–16.

Article XX. WE AFFIRM that since God is the author of all truth, all truths, biblical and extrabiblical, are consistent and cohere, and that the Bible speaks truths when it touches on matters pertaining to nature, history, or anything else. We further affirm that in some cases extrabiblical data have value for clarifying what Scripture teaches, and for prompting correction of faulty interpretations.

WE DENY that extrabiblical views ever disprove the teaching of Scripture or hold priority over it.

What is in view here is not so much the nature of truth (which is treated in Article VI), but the consistency and coherence of truth. This is directed at those views which consider truth paradoxical or contradictory. This article declares that a proper hermeneutic avoids contradictions, since God never affirms as true two propositions, one of which is logically the opposite of the other.

However, whatever prompting and clarifying of Scripture that extrabiblical studies may provide, the final authority for what the Bible teaches rests in the text of Scripture itself and not in anything outside it (except in God himself). The denial makes clear this priority of the teaching of God's scriptural revelation over anything outside it.

Article XXI. WE AFFIRM the harmony of special with general revelation and therefore of biblical teaching with the facts of nature.

WE DENY that any genuine scientific facts are inconsistent with the true meaning of any passage of Scripture.

This article continues the discussion of the previous article by noting the harmony of God's general revelation (outside Scripture) and His special revelation in Scripture. It is acknowledged by all that certain **interpretations** of Scripture and some **opinions** of scientists will contradict each other. However, it is insisted here that the **truth** of Scripture and the **facts** of science never contradict each other.

"Genuine" science will always be in accord with Scripture. Science, however, based on naturalistic presuppositions will inevitably come in conflict with the supernatural truths of Scripture....

While these brief but weighty statements do not explore the subjects in great detail, nor necessarily agree with every conclusion of this chapter, they do establish several very crucial principles.

1. God's special revelation in Scripture takes priority over God's general revelation in nature.

2. God's special revelation in Scripture interprets God's general revelation in nature, not the opposite.

The basis for the ICBI conclusions is the traditional, time-tested, grammatical-historical hermeneutical approach to interpreting the Bible.[39] However, when one is committed to harmonizing fallible, sinful men's interpretations of their limited observations of the cursed and corrupted creation with the inerrant propositional truth statements of Scripture by deviating from the historical-grammatical method, then in effect a new hermeneutic has been substituted as a means that allegedly justifies the end of bringing Scripture into harmony with the perceptions of fallen, darkened minds.

Another aspect of proper hermeneutics that is almost always absent in the discussion of general and special revelation is divine illumination, whereby Scripture promises divine aid from the Holy Spirit to true believers in Christ to help them correctly interpret the Bible.

> Now we have received, not the spirit of the world, but the Spirit who is from God, so that we may know the things freely given to us by God, which things we also speak, not in words taught by human wisdom, but in those taught by the Spirit, combining spiritual thoughts with spiritual words (1 Cor. 2:12–13).

People commonly use the expressions, "It just dawned on me," or "The light just came on" to describe dim thoughts which later take on new understanding. God's Spirit does that for believers with Scripture.

A great prayer to offer as we study Scripture is, "Open my eyes, that I may behold wonderful things from Your law" (Ps. 119:18). It acknowledges a colossal need for God's light in understanding Scripture. So do verses like, "Teach me, O Lord, the way of Your statutes, and I shall observe it to the end. Give me understanding, that I may observe Your law and keep it with all my heart" (Ps. 119:33–34; see also v. 102).

God not only wants Christians to know but to understand and obey. So He gives them the help that they need through His Holy Spirit. Believers, like the two to whom Jesus spoke on the road to Emmaus, require God's assistance: "Then He opened their minds to understand the Scriptures" (Luke 24:45). God's ministry of illumination by which He gives light on the meaning of Scripture is affirmed by the Psalmist (Ps. 119:130).

Paul and John also comment on this in the New Testament.

> I pray that the eyes of your heart may be enlightened, so that you may know what is the hope of His calling, what are the riches of the glory of His inheritance in the saints, and what is the surpassing greatness of His power toward us who believe. These are in accordance with the working of the strength of His might (Eph. 1:18–19).

---

39. Milton S. Terry, *Biblical Hermeneutics*, 2nd ed. 1890 (Grand Rapids, MI: Zondervan, rpt. 1950), p. 173, 203–210.

... the anointing which you received from Him abides in you, and you have no need for any one to teach you; but as His anointing teaches you about all things, and is true and is not a lie, and just as it has taught you, you abide in Him (1 John 2:27).

While the truth of divine illumination does not eliminate the need for gifted men to teach (Eph. 4:11–12; 2 Tim. 4:2) or the hard labor of serious Bible study (2 Tim. 2:15), it does promise that there is no need to be enslaved to Church dogma or to be led astray by false teachers. Our primary dependence for learning Scripture should be upon the author of Scripture — God himself.

It needs to be noted that:

1. There is no promise of divine illumination for scientific observation or interpretation of those observations.

2. There is no promise of divine illumination for general revelation.

3. However, there is a promise of divine illumination only for the special revelation of Scripture.

Hugh Ross gives lip service to "sound biblical exegesis," but contradicts what he says by what he does in adopting a new hermeneutic at the neglect of the historical-grammatical approach.[40] By equating the value and priority of general revelation with that of special revelation, he either denies the unique promise of divine illumination for special revelation or erroneously assumes that divine illumination applies also to general revelation.

A Biblical Worldview

What is a worldview? A worldview comprises a person's collection of presuppositions, convictions, and values from which he tries to understand and make sense out of the world and life. "A worldview is a conceptual scheme by which we consciously or unconsciously place or fit everything we believe and by which we interpret and judge reality."[41] "A worldview is, first of all, *an explanation and interpretation of the world and second, an application of this view to life.*"[42]

How does one form a worldview? Where does one begin? Every worldview starts with presuppositions (i.e., beliefs that one presumes to be true without supporting independent evidence from other sources or systems). Interpreting reality, in part or in whole, requires that one adopt an interpretive stance since there is no "neutral" thought in the universe. This becomes the foundation upon which one builds.

What are the presuppositions of a Christian worldview that is solidly rooted and grounded in Scripture? Carl F.H. Henry, an important Christian thinker in

40. Ross, *Creation and Time*, p. 58.
41. Ronald H. Nash, *Faith and Reason* (Grand Rapids, MI: Zondervan, 1988), p. 24.
42. W. Gary Phillips and William E. Brown, *Making Sense of Your World from a Biblical Viewpoint* (Chicago, IL: Moody, 1991), p. 29.

the last half of the 20th century, answers the question very simply: ". . . evangelical theology dares harbor one and only one presupposition: the living and personal God intelligibly known in his revelation."[43] Without equivocation, Dr. Henry forthrightly and clearly believes that "Our theological systems are not infallible, but God's propositional revelation is."[44] Henry earlier had elaborated on this theme: "In its ontological and epistemological predictions Christianity begins with the biblically attested self-disclosing God, and not with creative speculation free to modify theism as an interpreter wishes."[45] Ronald Nash approaches the question in a similar manner: "Human beings and the universe in which they reside are the creation of God who has revealed himself in Scripture."[46]

For the sake of this chapter, let it be stated that two major presuppositions underlie the thoughts included. The first is the eternal existence of the personal, transcendent, triune, Creator God. Second, the God of Scripture has revealed His character, purposes, and will in the infallible and inerrant pages of His special revelation, the Bible, which is superior to any other source of revelation or human reason alone.

It would be worth mentioning here that one's approach to Christian apologetics will influence one's approach to a worldview.[47] The appropriate question to be asked is "should one develop the content of an apologetic system evidentially by human reasoning and then move *to* special revelation or presuppositionally starting *from* special revelation?"[48] Evidentialists, like Ross, start with data outside of Scripture in order to supposedly prove or better understand Scripture,[49] while presuppositionalists begin with Scripture in order to understand the world.[50]

---

43. Carl F.H. Henry, *God, Revelation and Authority*, vol. 1, *God Who Speaks and Shows* (Waco, TX: Word, 1976), p. 212.

44. Carl F.H. Henry, "Fortunes of the Christian World View," *Trinity Journal* 19 (1998): p. 168.

45. Ibid., p. 166.

46. Nash, *Faith and Reason*, p. 47. He gives the same answer in *Worldviews in Conflict* (Grand Rapids, MI: Zondervan, 1992), p. 52.

47. Portions of this section have been excerpted from the Introduction (written by this author) to MacArthur, gen. ed, *Think Biblically!*, p. 13–16.

48. Robert L. Reymond, *The Justification of Knowledge* (Philadelphia, PA: Presbyterian and Reformed, 1976), p. 7–8. Also see Steven B. Cowan, ed., *Five Views on Apologetics* (Grand Rapids, MI: Zondervan, 2000).

49. A recent volume espousing this approach has been provided by R.C. Sproul, John Gerstner, and Arthur Lindsley, *Classical Apologetics: A Rational Defense of the Christian Faith and A Critique of Presuppositional Apologetics*. For a thorough critique see George J. Zemek, "Classical Apologetics: A Rational Defense: A Review Article," *GTJ* 7 (Spring 1986): p. 111–123.

50. See Cornelius Van Til, *Christian Apologetics*, 2nd ed, William Edgar, ed. (Phillipsburg, NJ: P&R, 2003) and Stephen R. Spencer, "Fideism and Presuppositionalism," *GTJ* 8 (Spring 1987): p. 89–99. Also consider John C. Whitcomb Jr., "Contemporary Apologetics and the Christian Faith," part 1, *BibSac* 134 (April–June 1977): p. 99–106 and *The World that Perished*, p. 95–139.

Generally speaking, one's view of general revelation will greatly influence one's apologetic system. The conclusions drawn earlier in this chapter concerning the limitations of general revelation in nature as defined by special revelation in Scripture will direct one toward a presuppositional apologetic.[51]

What is the Christian worldview?[52] This author offers the following as a working definition:

> The Christian worldview sees and understands God the Creator and His creation (i.e., man and the world) primarily through the lens of God's special revelation, the Holy Scriptures, and secondarily through God's natural revelation in creation as interpreted by human reason and reconciled by and with Scripture, for the purpose of believing and behaving in accord with God's will and, thereby, glorifying God with one's mind and life, both now and in eternity.

What essentially distinguishes the Christian worldview from other worldviews? At the heart of the matter, a Christian worldview contrasts with competing worldviews in that it 1) recognizes that God is the unique source of all truth, and 2) relates all truth back to an understanding of God and His purposes for this life and the next. Arthur Holmes superbly summarizes the unique implications of a Christian worldview when relating absolute truth to God.

1. To say that truth is absolute rather than relative means that it is unchanging and universally the same.

2. Truth is absolute not in or of itself but because it derives ultimately from the one, eternal God. It is grounded in His "metaphysical objectivity," and that of His creation.

3. Absolute propositional truth, therefore, depends on the absolute personal truth (or fidelity) of God, who can be trusted in all He does and says.[53]

Are there any common misperceptions about the Christian worldview, especially by Christians? There are at least two mistaken notions. The first error is that a Christian view of the world and life will differ on all points from other worldviews. While this is not true (e.g., all worldviews accept the law

---

51. The classic historical illustration of the importance of one's apologetic methodology revolves around the "Galileo affair." See Terry Mortenson, "Philosophical Naturalism and the Age of the Earth: Are They Related?", *TMSJ* 15 (Spring 2004): p. 73–74.

52. For a brief history of the Christian worldview in general and the recent spiritual climate in America, see Henry, "Fortunes," p. 163–176 and Carl F.H. Henry, "The Vagrancy of the American Spirit" *Faculty Dialogue* 22 (Fall 1994): p. 5–18. Historically speaking, James Orr is generally credited as the first modern theologian to organize Christian thought around the core idea of "worldview," in *The Christian View of God and the World* (Edinburgh: A. Elliot, 1893; reprint, Grand Rapids, MI: Eerdmans, 1948).

53. Arthur F. Holmes, *All Truth is God's Truth* (Grand Rapids, MI: Eerdmans, 1977), p. 37.

of gravity), the Christian worldview will differ and be unique on the most important points, especially as they relate to the character of God, the nature and value of Scripture, and the exclusivity of Jesus Christ as Savior and Lord. The second error is that the Bible contains all that we need to know. Common sense should put this misdirected thought out of business. However, it is true that the Bible alone contains all that Christians need to know about their spiritual life and godliness through a knowledge of the one true God, which is the highest and most important level of knowledge (2 Pet. 1:2–4). Also, while it does not exhaustively address every field, when Scripture speaks in any subject area, it speaks authoritatively. One's approach to Christian apologetics and to worldview will ultimately influence one's approach to integration, i.e., the combining and understanding of special revelation, general revelation, and knowledge obtained by human learning.[54] Three important principles should guide us as we consider the integration of sources of knowledge.

1. While all truth is God's truth, not all truth is revealed truth and not all statements that claim to be truth are actually true.

2. Revealed truth is certain, while non-revealed truth claims can often be wrong and are subject to change. For example, the content of Genesis 1–2 is absolutely certain by virtue of it being divinely revealed truth, while scientific theories of origins are tentative at best.

3. Revealed truth should help to interpret non-revealed truth/knowledge. For example, the certain content of Genesis 1–2 should be used to validate or invalidate the tentative scientific theories on origins.

This is not intended to make theologians into scientists, but rather to use revealed truth as a benchmark by which to judge non-revealed truth claims.

However, this should prevent scientists from unwarrantedly usurping the role of the theologian, as Ross has. By elevating non-revelatory truth claims based on study of the creation to the level of general revelation, he has tried to establish a "dual, reliably consistent revelation,"[55] which puts human interpretations of the cursed and corrupted creation on an equal footing with God's blessed and inerrant revelation through Holy Scripture.[56] In so doing, he has then made it appear that non-revelatory knowledge, falsely classified as general revelation in nature, is equal to and at times superior to special revelation in Scripture. Thus, he has used supposed science to interpret Scripture, and wrongly claimed that he had biblical authority to do so.

Unfortunately, Ross's worldview is not consistently biblical in its construction. His apologetic approach is evidential not presuppositional, and he integrates

---

54. See Thomas, *Evangelical Hermeneutics*, p. 121–131 for an excellent discussion and summation of the issues. Also consult Spencer, "Natural Theology."

55. Ross, *Creation and Time*, p. 56.

56. Ibid., p. 57.

non-revelatory, tentative knowledge with the certainty of revealed truth as though they were equals. In so doing, his thinking and conclusions are severely called into question and his progressive creationist views should be rejected.

J. Robertson McQuilken warned about this mistake over three decades ago. While he made the following statement with regard to the behavioral sciences, it is equally true and applicable to the natural sciences.

> My thesis is that in the next two decades the greatest threat to biblical authority is the behavioral scientist who would in all good conscience man the barricades to defend the front door against any theologian who would attack the inspiration and authority of Scripture while all the while himself smuggling the content of Scripture out the back door through cultural or psychological interpretation.[57]

The Answer

No — nature is not the 67th book of the Bible! To equate acquisition of general knowledge with divine revelation (general or special) is a faulty exaggeration that results in untruth. To expand general revelation beyond the limits set by special revelation is unbiblical and leads to theological error.

Nature is not the 67th book of the Bible for the following seven reasons.

1. It violates Scripture's warning not to add to the scriptural canon.

2. It dramatically overstates what Scripture says about general revelation.

3. It falsely elevates general revelation to the same authority level as special revelation.

4. It wrongly equates the character of general and special revelation.

5. It fails to take into account the Fall and man's diminished intellectual capacity to think in the realm of general knowledge.

6. It deviates from the norm of historical-grammatical hermeneutics.

7. It is derived from a flawed worldview, apologetics, and approach to integration.

Thus, Dr. Hugh Ross needs to rethink and abandon his answer to the question of nature being the 67th book of the Bible and bring his response into conformity with Scripture. In so doing, he would ultimately correct his tragic error in promoting a progressive view of origins in support of an old-earth theory which is contrary to the Genesis record. Christian scholars, leaders, laypeople, and students who have accepted Dr. Ross's progressive creationist views should also abandon this position as unbiblical, and instead believe Genesis.

---

57. J. Robertson McQuilken, "The Behavioral Sciences Under the Authority of Scripture," *JETS* 20 (March 1977): p. 37.

Chapter 5

Contemporary Hermeneutical Approaches to Genesis 1–11

Todd S. Beall

I first met Dr. John Whitcomb over 37 years ago when I was a sophomore at Princeton University. Dr. Whitcomb gave a special series of lectures at Princeton on May 15, 1971. Though I was a believer who viewed Genesis literally (and did not accept evolution), I had never before heard such an intelligent defense of the Genesis account. I still have my notes of Dr. Whitcomb's lectures on that day. In particular, I remember being struck by his discussion on 2 Peter 3:1–6 and its implications for the theory of uniformitarianism. Three years later I visited Dr. Whitcomb at his home in Indiana and asked his advice on seminaries. He is the one who told me about Capital Bible Seminary in Maryland, just 30 minutes away from my home! I enrolled there in the fall, graduated in 1977, and began teaching at Capital the same year. Over the years, Dr. Whitcomb has taught the Pentateuch at our seminary, and students love him just as much as I did years ago. Dr. Whitcomb is a wonderful, gracious, humble man (with a marvelous sense of humor!) who demonstrates the essence of Christianity in his family life and his love for people, and yet has remained a steadfast and energetic defender of the truth of God's Word without compromise. He is a model for each of us to follow. I consider it a great privilege to be a part of this volume in his honor.

When originally given this chapter topic, I thought that the concept would be fairly easy to research. Surely there were three to five (or even five to ten) hermeneutical approaches to Genesis 1–11 that could be easily discerned and discussed. Now, after surveying over 200 sources and spending countless hours, I realize that, in fact, categorization of hermeneutical approaches is far from easy. The problem is at least three-fold. First, there is a vast amount of literature on Genesis 1–11 (from all sorts of perspectives).[1] I venture to say that it may be the most-discussed section of Scripture. Second, most scholars are not clear on their hermeneutical method at all. Third, while some scholars do use a particular hermeneutical approach to Genesis 1, that approach is not applied consistently to the rest of Genesis 1–11 nor to the rest of the book as a whole (to be fair, some scholars are only concerned with Genesis 1, and do not deal with the issue in the later chapters). This presents a problem when one wishes to discuss a hermeneutical approach to the entire section.

It seems to this writer that the proper hermeneutical approach to Genesis 1–11 should satisfy two conditions: first, allowing for differences in genre, it should be able to be applied uniformly throughout these 11 chapters, and indeed through the rest of the Book of Genesis. In other words, the hermeneutical approach should only diverge in different sections of the book if it can be demonstrated that those chapters are a different genre. Second, the hermeneutical approach should arise from a study of the Scriptures themselves, not an external set of rules imposed on the Scriptures. Of course, this is easier said than done, because each interpreter comes to the Scriptures with preset opinions that often shape his or her interpretation rather than allowing the Scriptures to speak for themselves.

For sake of discussion, we will break the hermeneutical approaches into four basic groups: (1) Genesis 1–11 is basically myth, with little or no historicity; (2) Genesis 1–11 is not myth, but is largely figurative; (3) Genesis 1–11 is neither myth nor entirely literal, but partly figurative; and (4) Genesis 1–11 should be taken literally (i.e., at face value). The first view is held largely by critical scholars, who deny the inerrancy of Scripture. The second and third views are held by a variety of liberal and evangelical scholars. Those views both deny that Genesis 1–11 is myth, and yet have an uneasiness with the literal approach, especially as it relates to the creation account in Genesis 1. The fourth view is held largely by conservative evangelical or Jewish scholars.

Genesis 1–11 as Myth

Interestingly, the two hermeneutical approaches that seem most consistent in their interpretation of Genesis 1–11 are the first and the fourth: either the accounts are basically myth or they are to be taken literally. The first view, that Genesis 1–11 is myth, has been held in various forms by many critical scholars over the past two hundred years. While the term *myth* is notoriously difficult to define, the basic understanding is that a myth is a traditional pre-scientific story normally revolving around gods and heroes, which explains the origin of

---

Unless otherwise noted, all Scripture in this chapter is from the NKJV of the Bible.

1. In his survey of recent literature on Genesis 1–11, J.W. Rogerson speaks of the three main hermeneutical approaches to Genesis 1–11 in recent years: feminist, literary, and liberation readings. He actually expresses great regret (and views it as a failure of proper education on the subject) that there are still more articles published on the "Genesis versus science" debate than on any other topic in Genesis 1–11. Rogerson, "Genesis 1–11," *Currents in Research* 5 (1997): p. 68.

something.[2] A classic statement of the critical position is given by Hermann Gunkel, who regarded Genesis 1 as "a faded myth."[3]

Essentially, Gunkel saw Genesis 1 as a late prose recension of the ancient Babylonian myths of creation.[4] John Skinner likewise perceived a strong foreign influence (especially Babylonian) "in the primaeval traditions of chapters 1–11, where a mythical origin can be proved by direct comparison with oriental parallels, and is confirmed by slight touches of mythological thinking which survive in the biblical records."[5] Similarly, E.A. Speiser viewed the primeval history (Genesis 1–11) as "imported for the most part" from a single place, namely Mesopotamia, and that it represented "the best that was available in contemporary scientific thinking."[6] A more recent example of the same line of thinking comes from Thomas Thompson, who states that "Genesis 1–11 is a composition that epitomizes biblical mythology. The long historiographic narrative which follows Genesis 1–11 is but an expansive and ephemeral illustration of this mythical world."[7]

The hermeneutical advantage of the mythical approach is its consistency, especially in its early advocates. Scholars such as Wellhausen and Gunkel not only viewed Genesis 1–11 as mythical, they saw Genesis 12–50 (the Patriarchs) in

2. John Skinner differentiates between a legend and a myth in that the legend starts with a historical fact, but the myth does not. John Skinner, *A Critical and Exegetical Commentary on Genesis*, ICC (Edinburgh: T & T Clark, 1930, 2nd ed.), p. ix. For four different definitions of *myth*, see J.W. Rogerson, "Slippery Words V: Myth," *Expository Times* 90 (1978): p. 10–14. Rogerson states that "Gen. 1 is myth, i.e., it contains truths about God the creator; although the truths are expressed in terms of obsolete science" (p. 12). See also George J. Brooke, "Creation in the Biblical Tradition," *Zygon* 22 (1987): p. 233–234.

3. Hermann Gunkel, *Creation and Chaos in the Primeval Era and the Eschaton* (Grand Rapids, MI: Eerdmans, 2006 [orig. published in German in 1895]), p. 80. See also his *The Legends of Genesis* (Eugene, OR: Wipf and Stock, 2003, reprint [orig. pub. 1901]).

4. Ibid. Interestingly, Gunkel noted the vast difference between the "totally wild and grotesquely titanic barbaric poetry" of the Babylonian account and the "solemn, elevated tranquility" of the "temperate prose" of Genesis (p. 80). Gunkel believed that Genesis is late, because all of the other recensions of the myth are poetic, while Genesis 1 is prose (p. 81).

5. Skinner, *Genesis*, x. Later Skinner stated that the Israelites "purified the crude ideas of pagan mythology and made them the vehicle of the highest religious teaching" (p. xi).

6. E.A. Speiser, *Genesis* (Anchor Bible; New York: Doubleday, 1964), p. liv-lv.

7. Thomas Thompson, "Historiography in the Pentateuch: Twenty-five Years after Historicity," *Scandinavian Journal of the Old Testament* 13 (1999), p. 280. See R. Davidson, *Genesis 1–11* (The Cambridge Bible Commentary; Cambridge: Cambridge University Press, 1973), p. 8–12: "It is only when we come to the story of Abraham in chapter 12 that we can claim with any certainty to be in touch with traditions which reflect something of the historical memory of the Hebrew people" (p. 8).

largely the same non-historical light.[8] And since they traced much of Genesis 1–11 back to Babylonian sources that were simply imported and refined by the biblical writers, the entire section (not simply Genesis 1) was regarded as non-historical.

Denial of Inspiration of Scripture

But there are two major problems with this hermeneutical approach. First, for evangelical scholars, the view that Genesis 1–11 is mythological, based on the (untrue) legends from Mesopotamia or elsewhere, is not consistent with the divine authority and inspiration of Scripture. Since there are numerous references to these chapters in the NT, it is not merely a question of the veracity of the OT — if untrue, then Jesus, Peter, and Paul are in error as well.[9] Indeed, if there was no actual fall of man, then there would be no need for a Savior.[10] While it is possible that there may have been some influence from other ancient Near Eastern (ANE) writings or traditions on Genesis 1–11, complete denial of the history of Genesis 1–11 is simply not an option. As Bruce Waltke well states, "The word *myth* misrepresents the Genesis account and does an injustice to the integrity of the narrator and undermines sound theology."[11]

A Babylonian Origin?

Second, even if the inspiration and integrity of the biblical text were not an issue, the mythological approach fails on another level as well. And that is simply that there is no evidence of literary "borrowing" in Genesis, from Mesopotamia or elsewhere. The early fascination by Gunkel and others with comparisons to the then newly translated Babylonian composition *Enuma Elish* is understandable. But his view that the similarities between the two accounts indicates that Genesis borrowed from *Enuma Elish*, though still repeated, is now widely disputed. In fact, one of Gunkel's main contentions was that the Hebrew *tehom* ("deep") in Genesis 1:2 was borrowed from the name of the Babylonian goddess Tiamat, the sea dragon who fought with Marduk before the cosmos was created.[12] But such a view is now discredited, since David Tsumura and others have shown that the

---

8. Wellhausen especially held that all the patriarchs were non-historical. Gunkel thought that there was greater authenticity to the patriarchal narratives. See Albright's introduction to Gunkel's *The Legend of Genesis*, p. viii-ix.

9. See, for example, Jesus' reference to creation (Gen. 1:27 and 2:24) in Matthew 19:4–6; his mention of Noah and the Flood (Gen. 6:1–8) in Matthew 24:37–39; Peter's reference to the Flood in 2 Peter 3:5–6; and Paul's reference to Adam, Eve, and the Fall in 1 Timothy 2:13–14. These passages and others are discussed later in this chapter.

10. See especially Romans 5:12–21.

11. Bruce Waltke, *Genesis: A Commentary* (Grand Rapids, MI: Zondervan, 2001), p. 74. See also Victor Hamilton's excellent discussion of the treatment of Genesis 1–11 as myth in Victor P. Hamilton, *The Book of Genesis: Chapters 1–17*, New International Commentary on the Old Testament (Grand Rapids, MI: Eerdmans, 1990), p. 56–59.

12. Gunkel, *Creation and Chaos*, p. 74–79. See also Bernhard Anderson, *Creation Versus Chaos: The Reinterpretation of Mythical Symbolism in the Bible* (Philadelphia, PA: Fortress, 1987), p. 15–40.

derivation of Hebrew *tehom* from *Tiamat* is phonologically impossible.[13] The actual similarities of *Enuma Elish* and Genesis 1 are few: Marduk splitting Tiamat into two spheres of water (similar to the waters of the firmament on day 2) is probably the most notable. The rest of the parallels (creation of light, dry land, the luminaries, and man) are of the most general type. James Atwell's conclusion is that these correspondences "are not striking," and the order of events "does no more than witness to a general ancient Near Eastern background to both accounts."[14] Similarly, W.G. Lambert's conclusion after close analysis of *Enuma Elish* and Genesis 1 is that there is "no evidence of Hebrew borrowing from Babylon."[15]

A classic mistake made by Gunkel and others is to emphasize the parallels without considering the immense differences in the accounts.[16] For example, the purpose of *Enuma Elish* was to exalt Marduk in the pantheon of Babylon, with creation being a minor part of the account, whereas in Genesis, God's work of creation is the central theme.[17] Second, *Enuma Elish* confuses spirit and matter (reflecting the Babylonian concept of the eternality of matter). Third, as Westermann notes, the creation account of Genesis is devoid of either conflict or struggle in the formation of the earth, all of which are common features in the Egyptian, Babylonian, and other ANE creation accounts.[18] In *Enuma Elish*

---

13. David Tsumura, *Creation and Destruction: A Reappraisal of the Chaoskampf Theory in the Old Testament* (Winona Lake, IN: Eisenbrauns, 2005), p. 36–53; Gerhard F. Hasel, "The Polemic Nature of the Genesis Cosmology," *The Evangelical Quarterly* 46 (1974): p. 82–83; R. Laird Harris, "The Bible and Cosmology," *Journal of the Evangelical Theological Society* 5 (1962): p. 11–17; James E. Atwell, "An Egyptian Source for Genesis 1," *Journal of Theological Studies* 51 (2000): p. 446. The two words share a common etymology ("deep waters"), but *tehom* cannot be derived from *Tiamat*. See also Walter Kaiser's helpful discussion in *The Old Testament Documents: Are They Reliable and Relevant?* (Downers Grove, IL: InterVarsity, 2001), p. 60–63.

14. Atwell, "Egyptian Source," p. 449.

15. W.G. Lambert, "A New Look at the Babylonian Background of Genesis," in *I Studied Inscriptions Before the Flood: Ancient Near Eastern, Literary, and Linguistic Approaches to Genesis 1–11*, eds. Richard Hess and David Tsumura (Winona Lake, IN: Eisenbrauns, 1994), p. 105.

16. As N.M. Sarna notes, to ignore the differences between Genesis and ANE parallels "is to present an unbalanced and untrue perspective and to pervert the scientific method" (*Understanding Genesis* [New York: Schocken, 1970] p. xxvii). So also Gerhard Hasel, "The Significance of the Cosmology in Genesis in Relation to Ancient Near Eastern Parallels," *Andrews University Seminary Studies* 10 (1972): p. 4; Gordon Wenham, *Genesis 1–15* (Word Biblical Commentary; Waco, TX: Word, 1987), p. xlviii-l. See also Peter Enns, *Inspiration and Incarnation* (Grand Rapids, MI: Baker, 2005) p. 26: while scholars initially exaggerated the influence of *Enuma Elish*, "as time went on, scholars generally began to develop a more sober appreciation for the relevance of the Babylonian material, mainly the recognition of these dissimilarities."

17. Wenham, *Genesis 1–15*, p. 8.

18. Claus Westermann, *Genesis 1–11: A Commentary* (Minneapolis, MN: Augsburg, 1984), p. 80–81.

the universe came into being as a consequence of an epic battle between the gods.[19] Marduk's acts require much physical effort, while God's only required the spoken word. Fourth, there is no creation of light (as the first act of creation), nor is there a detailed creation account of vegetation, animals, birds, or fish. Fifth, the capriciousness of the gods in *Enuma Elish* is contrasted by God's determined purpose in Genesis. There is no female deity involved in creation in the Genesis account, as there are in the other ANE creation stories.[20] Finally, in *Enuma Elish*, man was created to be a servant, but in Genesis 1 man was created to rule the earth.[21]

A Canaanite Origin?

Some scholars have posited a Canaanite background for Genesis 1, seeing in Genesis 1:2 a demythologization of a Canaanite sea dragon myth.[22] But the conflict of the storm-god Baal with the sea-god Yam mentioned in the Ugaritic texts has nothing at all to do with the creation of the cosmos. In Ugaritic texts, Baal is not treated as a creator-god at all.[23] Furthermore, as Tsumura points out, in the Ugaritic texts, the Canaanite sea-dragon is Yam, not Taham — but the term *yam* ("sea") does not appear in Genesis 1 until verse 10, where the plural form *yammim* is used as the antithesis of *erets* ("land").[24]

An Egyptian Origin?

Other scholars have seen a strong Egyptian background to the creation stories in Genesis 1 and 2. This concept was first proposed in the late 1800s by the Egyptologist A.H. Sayce, who lamented the excessive interest in Babylonian creation texts.[25] It has been revived in recent years by James Hoffmeier,

---

19. John Currid, *Ancient Egypt and the Old Testament* (Grand Rapids, MI: Baker, 1997), p. 63.

20. David Tsumura, "Genesis and Ancient Near Eastern Stories of Creation and Flood," in *I Studied Inscriptions Before the Flood: Ancient Near Eastern, Literary, and Linguistic Approaches to Genesis 1–11*, eds. Richard Hess and David Tsumura (Winona Lake, IN: Eisenbrauns, 1994), p. 31–32.

21. John Davis, *Paradise to Prison: Studies in Genesis* (Grand Rapids, MI: Baker, 1975), p. 71. See also George Klein, "Reading Genesis 1," *Southwestern Journal of Theology* 44 (2001): p. 25–30.

22. J. Day, *God's Conflict with the Dragon and the Sea: Echoes of a Canaanite Myth in the Old Thestament* (Cambridge: Cambridge University Press, 1985), p. 50–53.

23. Tsumura, "Genesis and Ancient Near Eastern Stories of Creation and Flood," p. 32. The creator-god in Ugaritic mythology is El. See further Tsumura, *Creation and Destruction*, p. 55. As Marvin Pope notes, "There is hardly anything that could be called a creation story or any clear allusion to cosmic creativity in the Ugaritic texts." Marvin Pope, *El in the Ugaritic Texts* (Leiden: Brill, 1955), p. 49.

24. Tsumura, *Creation and Destruction*, p. 54–56.

25. James K. Hoffmeier, "Some Thoughts on Genesis 1 and 2 and Egyptian Cosmology," *Journal of the Ancient Near Eastern Society* 15 (1983): p. 41.

John Currid, and James Atwell, among others.[26] One difficulty in analyzing the Egyptian cosmogony is that there is a multiplicity of texts with quite different accounts of creation.[27] Nonetheless, concepts such as creation stemming from a single god (though different sources name different gods as the creator — Re, Ptah, Khnum, Atum, and others); creation by divine fiat; creation of primordial matter; creation of the firmament; and making man from clay are all found in Egyptian sources.[28]

Once again, however, the differences between the Egyptian accounts and Genesis 1 are far more striking. First, the primary Egyptian creation accounts (Heliopolis, Memphis, and Hermopolis) deal with the creation of the gods and the cosmos (heaven, earth, and sun), but do not mention creation of man or animals. These are covered in different Egyptian texts.[29] Second, the Egyptian creation accounts are concerned primarily with the creation of the gods themselves, not the universe. And, depending on the source, these gods are created in various ways: by command (Ptah spoke them into being);[30] by the god Atum's semen and fingers;[31] by spitting ("Atum spit me out in the spit of his mouth");[32] and

---

26. Ibid., p. 39-49; Currid, *Ancient Egypt*, p. 53–72; Atwell, "Egyptian Source," p. 449–77. See also Gordon Johnston, "Genesis 1–2:3 in the Light of Ancient Egyptian Creation Myths," (paper delivered at the Annual Meeting of the Evangelical Theological Society, Nov 15, 2006), p. 1–24. The first portion of Johnston's paper (p. 1–8) has now been published under the title "Genesis 1 and Ancient Egyptian Creation Myths," *Bibliotheca Sacra* 165 (2008): p. 178–194.

27. These include Pyramid Texts, Coffin Texts, The Book of the Dead, and The Memphite Theology. Hoffmeier, "Egyptian Cosmology," p. 41–42; Currid, *Ancient Egypt*, p. 55. Currid cites John Wilson on the matter: "We cannot settle down to a single codified account of beginnings. The Egyptians accepted various myths and discarded none of them" (Ibid.).

28. Hoffmeier, "Egyptian Cosmology," p. 44–48; Currid, *Ancient Egypt*, p. 55–73.

29. There is a brief reference to man's creation in the "Instruction of Merikare" and another in the "Great Hymn to Knhum." Currid, *Ancient Egypt*, p. 53–73. Tony Shetter ("Genesis 1–2 in Light of Ancient Egyptian Creation Myths" [paper delivered at the Annual Meeting of the Evangelical Theological Society, Nov 15, 2006], p. 10) sees the creation traditions of Heliopolis, Memphis, and Hermopolis as paralleling the first creation account in Genesis (focusing on creation of the world in general), and the creation tradition of Khnum paralleling the second creation acount of Genesis (creation of humans). He even suggests that the presence of two creation stories in Genesis results from the need of the Hebrews "to refute the two Egyptian creation traditions" (p. 14). But this is unlikely, especially since the climax and culmination of Genesis 1 is the creation of man, which is entirely omitted in the first Egyptian creation tradition.

30. Memphis "Shabaka Stone," in James B. Pritchard, ed., *Ancient Near Eastern Texts Relating to the Old Testament* (Princeton, NJ: Princeton University Press, 1969), p. 4–6. Hereafter this work will be referred to as *ANET*.

31. Ibid.

32. Coffin Text, Spell 76.3-4.

even by an act of masturbation by Atum.[33] The contrast between these texts and Genesis, where there is only one God, whose presence is assumed throughout, and who simply speaks everything else into existence, could hardly be greater.

Third, in Egyptian cosmogony the creative events are cyclical, with the sun being reborn each day and the Nile receding each year. By contrast, the creation of Genesis 1 occurs in a strict linear succession of days and is completed by the seventh day. There is no parallel to this concept either in Egyptian or Babylonian cosmogony.[34] Finally, in the Egyptian cosmogony (as in the Babylonian) there is an intermingling of the gods with creation: indeed, as Currid notes, "each of the gods fashioned was a personification of an element of nature."[35] In Genesis, God is utterly separate from and precedes His created universe.[36]

Summary of Differences between ANE Cosmologies and the Genesis Creation Account

Bill Arnold summarizes well the differences between the various ANE cosmologies and the worldview of Genesis 1–2. First, the Genesis account is monotheistic, contrasting with the polytheism of the ANE. Second, God is transcendent, "not continuous with the world he has created."[37] Third, Israel is totally disinterested in the origins of God, whereas the ANE was preoccupied with this concern. Fourth, God is a nonsexual being (without physical progeny). And fifth, the ANE devalued history, whereas Israel "elevated history to an entirely new level in the ancient world," attaching importance to the beginning of time and space (creation) and the beginning of the nation Israel. The result is that while the ANE cultures expressed their theology in the form of myths and legends, Israel was primarily interested in the writing of history. As Arnold observes, "such a role for historical narrative was radically new in the ancient Near East.[38]

Borrowing from ANE Flood Stories?

Though space will not permit a detailed treatment, we should also mention the similarities between ANE flood myths (most notably, the Gilgamesh Epic and the Atrahasis Epic) and the biblical Flood account. As in the case of the creation account, some scholars have used the similarities of these ancient flood stories to demonstrate the secondary and inferior nature of the biblical Flood account in Genesis 6–9. For example, Skinner states that the dependence of

33. Pyramid Text, Utterance 527. See Currid, *Ancient Egypt*, p. 56–62. Note that while much is made of Ptah's speaking lesser gods into existence (supposedly paralleling God's divine fiat in Genesis 1), in the same text Atum creates the lesser gods "from his semen and fingers." Ibid., p. 61.

34. Hasel, "Polemic Nature," p. 84–85; Currid, *Ancient Egypt*, p. 73.

35. Currid, *Ancient Egypt*, p. 60.

36. See also George Klein, "Reading Genesis 1," p. 31.

37. Bill Arnold, *Encountering the Book of Genesis* (Grand Rapids, MI: Baker, 1998), p. 49.

38. Ibid., p. 51. Arnold's whole discussion is found on p. 48–51.

the biblical narrative of the Flood on the Babylonian legends "hardly requires detailed proof."[39]

To be sure, as with the creation accounts, there are similarities between the ANE flood myths and Genesis: the impending flood is revealed to the hero; he is delivered from the flood with his family; a large boat is built; birds are sent out to determine how far the waters have receded; and the hero worships at the end of the flood. But once again, there are major differences: monotheism in Genesis versus the polytheism of the ANE myths; the reason for the flood (sin in Genesis; the people making too much noise in the Atrahasis Epic, disturbing the sleep of the gods![40]); the holiness of God in Genesis versus the capriciousness of the gods in the Gilgamesh Epic (they swarm "like flies" around the sacrifice given by Utnapishtim); and the godliness of Noah versus the questionable ethics of Utnapishtim (the hero of Gilgamesh).[41] After extensive analysis, Alexander Heidel concludes that there is insufficient evidence that Genesis borrowed from the ANE myths: "The arguments which have been advanced in support of the contention that the biblical account rests on Babylonian material are quite indecisive."[42] He observes that while the "skeleton" has some similarities, "the flesh and blood and, above all, the animating spirit are different."[43]

It should also be mentioned here that there are no real parallels in ANE literature either to the Table of Nations in Genesis 10 or to the Tower of Babel in Genesis 11. As Albright writes, the Table of Nations "stands absolutely alone in ancient literature without a remote parallel even among the Greeks. . . . The Table of Nations remains an astonishingly accurate document."[44] As for the Tower of Babel, as Wenham notes, "no good Near Eastern parallel to the tower of Babel

---

39. Skinner, *Genesis*, p. 177.

40. No real reason is given for the flood in the Gilgamesh Epic. Even Speiser, who holds to strong Mesopotamian influence on Genesis, acknowledges the strong moral emphasis in Genesis versus the lack of a plausible cause for the flood in the Gilgamesh Epic (*Genesis*, p. 54–55).

41. While Noah's godliness is stressed, he is hardly an active "hero" as Utnapishtim is. In fact, Noah does not speak until the aftermath of the Flood, while Utnapishtim speaks throughout the story, and is given immortality at the end.

42. Alexander Heidel, *The Gilgamesh Epic and Old Testament Parallels* (Chicago, IL: University of Chicago Press, 1946), p. 267. See further the detailed comparison by Nozomi Osanai, "A Comparative Study of the Flood Accounts in the Gilgamesh Epic and Genesis" (unpublished master's thesis, Wesley Biblical Seminary, 2004), as well as Wenham's excellent summary of the differences between the accounts in his *Genesis 1–15*, p. 164–66.

43. Heidel, *Gilgamesh Epic*, p. 268.

44. William F. Albright, *Recent Discoveries in Bible Lands* (New York: Funk & Wagnalls, 1955), p. 70–71. Similarly, D.J. Wiseman states, "The origin of this material is unknown. It is impossible to be dogmatic as this chapter remains unique in ancient literatures" (D.J. Wiseman, ed., *Peoples of Old Testament Times* [Oxford: Oxford University Press, 1973], p. xviii).

story is known."[45] There is a Sumerian text which mentions that the whole world spoke the same language, but it is unclear whether the text is speaking of the past or looking forward to the future. In any case, there is no mention of judgment in the Sumerian text.[46]

Conclusion on the Matter of Genesis 1–11 "Borrowing" from ANE Texts

What, then, should we make of the similarities between various ANE texts and Genesis? Far from Genesis "borrowing" from these various creation and flood myths, what seems clear is that Genesis stands apart in theme, purpose, and grandeur from these other texts. The reason is readily apparent: Genesis is truth as given by the Creator himself. The other ANE texts, in cultures marred by centuries of sin and rebellion against God, have preserved a vestige of the truth here and there from what their ancestors knew. If indeed we accept Genesis as truth, then all peoples came from Adam and Eve (and from Noah and his family), and all had the same history in the beginning. These ANE texts preserve elements of the truth taken from their collective memory.

Genesis 1–11 as Largely Figurative

The second major hermeneutical approach to Genesis 1–11 is that this section is not myth (i.e., untrue), but it is to be taken almost entirely figuratively, not literally. Those who take this approach believe that Genesis 1–11 is a genuine revelation from God (thus differing from the first approach presented above), but it is more like a story or parable, intending to convey theological truth and nothing more.[47]

Many scholars who hold this position state that we must understand Genesis 1–11 through the framework of the ANE milieu, not through our own modern framework. For example, Peter Enns states that the Bible should be understood in light of the ANE cultural context in which it was given, rather than our own.[48] Enns even calls this section "myth," defined as "an ancient, premodern, prescientific way of addressing questions of ultimate origins and meaning in the form of stories: Who are we? Where do we come from?"[49] Since Abraham came from Mesopotamia, Enns argues, he

---

45. Wenham, *Genesis 1–15*, p. 236.
46. See Samuel N. Kramer, "The 'Babel of Tongues': A Sumerian Version," *Journal of the American Oriental Society* 88 (1968): p. 108–111.
47. Richard Bube calls this view the "essentially nonliteral view." Bube, "Final Reflections on the Dialogue: Reflection 1," in *Three Views on Creation and Evolution*, eds. J.P. Moreland and John Mark Reynolds (Grand Rapids, MI: Zondervan, 1999), p. 252.
48. Peter Enns, *Inspiration and Incarnation* (Grand Rapids, MI: Baker, 2005), p. 41.
49. Ibid., p. 50. Though Enns calls Genesis 1–11 "myth," he differs from scholars holding the first view since he believes that it is a genuine revelation from God. That is why, despite his use of the term "myth," it seems best to classify his approach in this section.

. . . shared the worldview of those whose world he shared and not a modern, scientific one. The reason the opening chapters of Genesis look so much like the literature of ancient Mesopotamia is that the worldview categories of the ancient Near East were ubiquitous and normative at the time. . . . God adopted Abraham as the forefather of a new people, and in doing so he also adopted the mythic categories within which Abraham — and everyone else — thought.[50]

Enns concludes that it is a

. . . fundamental misunderstanding of Genesis to expect it to answer questions generated by a modern worldview, such as whether the days were literal or figurative, or whether the days of creation can be lined up with modern science, or whether the flood was local or universal. The question that Genesis is prepared to answer is whether Yahweh, the God of Israel, is worthy of worship. . . . It is wholly incomprehensible to think that thousands of years ago God would have felt constrained to speak in a way that would be meaningful only to Westerners several thousand years later. To do so borders on modern, Western arrogance.[51]

Enns is not alone in this approach. In his article on "Creation" John Walton spends most of the article discussing the ANE documents rather than the biblical text. He states:

. . . the theological message of the Bible was communicated to people who lived in the ancient Near Eastern world. If we desire to understand the theological message of the text, we will benefit by positioning it within the worldview of the ancient world rather than simply applying our own cultural perspectives.[52]

Later Walton states:

. . . nowhere in the ancient Near East did people think of creation primarily in terms of *making* things. It is only our post-Enlightenment, Western way of thinking that focuses so steadfastly and exclusively on physical structure and formational history. . . . The origin of matter is what our society has taught us is important (indeed that matter is all there is), but we cannot afford to be so distracted by our cultural ideas. Matter was not the concern of the author of Genesis[53]

---

50. Ibid., p. 53.
51. Ibid., p. 55.
52. John Walton, "Creation," *Dictionary of the Old Testament: Pentateuch*, eds. T. Desmond Alexander and David W. Baker (Downers Grove, IL: InterVarsity, 2003), p. 156.
53. Ibid., p. 161–62.

In his commentary on Genesis, Walton adds, "It is fruitless to ask what *things* God created on day one, for the text is not concerned about *things* and therefore will not address itself to that question."[54]

Similarly, Howard Van Till holds that Genesis 1 should be read as an "artistic portrait," as a form of "storied theology," an "example of something written in the form of Ancient Near Eastern artistic literature. . . . It is a piece of Ancient Near Eastern *primeval history* literature."[55] Elsewhere Van Till makes a large distinction in Genesis between primeval history (Genesis 1–11) and patriarchal history (Genesis 12–50). Whereas patriarchal history is drawn from remembered historical oral tradition, primeval history is "Hebrew literature written in the literary tradition of ancient Near Eastern cultures."[56] The stories of primeval history "serve as 'packaging' that contains the message content," rather than the content itself.[57] Whether those stories are true or not

> . . . is a Western question, not an ancient Eastern or Hebrew question. It shifts the emphasis away from the heart of the matter and directs attention to peripheral matters, to matters beyond the scope of the narrative. . . . The truth of a concrete story in ancient Hebrew literature does not necessarily lie in its specific details but rather in the eternal verities it illustrates.[58]

Thus, according to this view, those who expect to find truth in the details of Genesis 1–11 are naive and perhaps even arrogant. Recognizing that Genesis 1–11 is not intended to be taken literally frees us from a host of knotty problems — problems that (according to this view) the text does not even address.

An ANE Worldview?

But this view, while it may at first sound appealing, fails miserably when one actually considers the arguments in a bit more detail. First, and foremost, the

---

54. John H. Walton, *Genesis* (The NIV Application Commentary; Grand Rapids, MI: Zondervan, 2001), p. 84.

55. Howard J. Van Till, "The Fully Gifted Creation," in *Three Views on Creation and Evolution*, eds. J.P. Moreland and John Mark Reynolds (Grand Rapids, MI: Zondervan, 1999), p. 209–211. Though I disagree completely with Van Till's conclusion, I agree with his analysis that old earth special creationists are "in the exceedingly awkward position of attempting to interpret some of the Genesis narrative's pictorial elements (interpreted as episodes of special creation) as historical particulars but treating the narrative's seven-day timetable as being figurative. I see no convincing basis for this dual interpretive strategy" (p. 211). Earlier, Van Till commends the young earth special creationist position of at least having "the merit of attempting to follow a consistent interpretive strategy in the early chapters of Genesis" (Ibid.).

56. Howard J. Van Till, *The Fourth Day* (Grand Rapids, MI: Eerdmans, 1986), p. 79–82.

57. Ibid., p. 82.

58. Ibid., p. 82–83. Van Till concludes that they are most similar to parables. "Though it is not to be taken literally, it is to be taken seriously" (Ibid.).

Bible claims to be the authoritative Word of God. This means that God super-intended and directed what was to be written. To argue that Moses or whoever wrote Genesis 1–11 was so immersed in the ANE world that it caused him to write in the way of other ANE literature is to deny the uniqueness of the biblical record. Certainly God *could* have directed Moses to write in this way, but He was under no *obligation* to do so! In fact, ironically it is the creation account that would have had to be supernaturally revealed (whether passed on orally or directly given) to Moses, since no human was alive to witness the acts of the first five days! Why would God have used ANE myths to reveal His truth to Moses concerning this unique event?

The discussion of ANE literature under the previous view showed that while there are some similarities between the biblical record in Genesis and ANE myths, there are far more significant differences. Even those who wish to see a great deal of ANE influence in the biblical text admit that the biblical record is unique.[59] And the Lord continually tells the children of Israel in the OT *not* to be like all the other nations in their worship of other gods, in their worldview, and so forth: they are unique as a people, and they serve a God who alone is worthy of worship, trust, and obedience. Far from following the thinking of the ANE, Israel was told to reject it categorically.[60] In fact, the biblical account in Genesis is so unlike other ANE literature that many scholars hold that the creation account is actually a polemic against the ANE creation myths.[61] If the perspective of Genesis 1–11 is so contrary to the ANE worldview, then why should we assume that it was written according to that same worldview? Actually, it stands apart from the ANE worldview in every respect, beginning with the most obvious difference: there is only one God, not many; He is eternal, not a created being; and He created the rest of the world in an orderly, purposeful way.[62]

---

59. See Gunkel's comments in note 4 above.

60. See for example the warnings against following after the religious practices of Israel's neighbors in Deut 18:9–14.

61. For example, see Conrad Hyers, *The Meaning of Creation: Genesis and Modern Science* (Atlanta: John Knox, 1984), p. 42–46; John H. Stek, "What Says the Scripture?" in *Portraits of Creation*, ed. Howard J. Van Till (Grand Rapids, MI: Eerdmans, 1990), p. 229–231; Waltke, *Genesis*, p. 76; Hasel, "Polemic Nature," p. 81–91; Johnston, "Genesis 1–2:3," p. 10–14; Shetter, "Genesis 1–2," p. 30–33; and Wenham, *Genesis 1–15*, p. xlv, 9.

62. These major differences have been discussed more fully in the previous section. Van Groningen points out that the attempt to draw out theological "facts" from Genesis 1–11 from a non-factually historical text is "a type of inverted allegorical exegesis." While allegorical exegesis drew spiritual truths from historic events, "contemporary exegetes attempt to draw historical facts from symbolic, mythical, religious stories which have been drawn from various deeply religious pagan sources." G. Van Groningen, "Interpretation of Genesis," *Journal of the Evangelical Theological Society* 13 (1970): p. 217.

As noted earlier, it is not surprising at all that ANE myths contain vestiges of the (correct) biblical account, since the Bible states that all civilizations came from Adam (and later, Noah). As Noel Weeks states simply, "It would be rather ridiculous to argue that God chose to convey certain theological truths in terms of the flood concepts already possessed by the Mesopotamians. Obviously both Bible and Sumerian traditions mention a flood because there was a flood."[63]

Is Genesis 1–11 to be Interpreted Differently from Genesis 12–50?

A major argument of Van Till and others is that since Genesis 1–11 is primeval history, it is to be interpreted differently from the rest of Genesis and the rest of the OT.[64] In other words, a unique hermeneutic should be used for these chapters, since they are not "history."[65] This permits scholars to treat Genesis 1–11 figuratively (or, as Van Till states, like a parable), but the remainder of Genesis (the accounts of Abraham, Isaac, Jacob, and Joseph) as historical.

Unfortunately for this interpretation, such a distinction between Genesis 1–11 and 12–50 will not hold up under scrutiny. Genesis 12 would make little sense by itself, without the preparatory genealogy given in chapter 11 (where Abram, Sarai, and Lot are first introduced). But since Genesis 11 gives the genealogy of Shem, this connects it back to the genealogy of chapter 10, to the Flood account in chapters 6–9, and to the genealogy of chapter 5, where Noah, Shem, Ham, and Japeth are first mentioned. But since Genesis 5 is a genealogy that begins with Adam himself, this takes us back to the creation account in Genesis 1–2 where Adam is first mentioned! What kind of hermeneutical gymnastics will allow us to take Abraham, Isaac, and Jacob as historical people, but not Adam, Noah, Shem, Ham, and Japeth?[66] As Charles Mabee observes, the "modern theological distinction between primordial history and history as we know it" is "grounded in a false metaphysics of spatialized time. . . . What this distinction really implies is that the primordial history conceives of a different understanding of time than the contemporary sequential view: a distinction that

---

63. Noel Weeks, "The Hermeneutical Problem of Genesis 1–11," *Themelios* 4 (1978): p. 14.

64. See also Westermann, *Genesis 1–11*, p. 1–5.

65. Sadly, even Bruce Waltke succumbs to this argument, though only for the creation account. He writes, "The creation account is unlike any other history. History is generally humanity recounting its experiences. The Genesis creation account is not a record of human history, since no humans are present for these acts" (*Genesis*, p. 76). That argument strikes me as one of the silliest I have heard. The Genesis account is "history," not simply human history. Why define "history" simply in terms of human history, and then claim that the creation account is not "history," since humans were not present?

66. Westermann recognizes the importance of the genealogies in Genesis 1–11. He states that too much attention has been paid to creation and the Fall as the "themes" of Genesis 1–11, and the genealogies have been ignored (*Genesis 1–11*, 2–5). He concludes, "The genealogies are an essential constituitive part of the primeval story and form the framework of everything that is narrated in Gen. 1–11" (p. 6).

does not exist in the text."[67] Mabee notes that "as far as the Hebrew narrative is concerned, Adam and Noah are not any less authentic personages than Abraham and Jacob. The effect of placing the former in an earlier chronological frame of reference (which we may term *mythological*) is to domesticate this material under a preconceived framework and render it theologically impotent."[68]

Similarly, D.J.A. Clines notes that "there is no clear-cut break at the end of the Pentateuch. . . . The precise beginning of the Abraham material — and therewith the conclusion of the pre-Abrahamic material — cannot be determined. . . . There is at no point a break between primeval and patriarchal history — 11:10 (descendants of Shem) resumes from 10:21–31 (family of Shem) and is directed toward 11:27–30 (Abram and Sarai)."[69]

There are two other structural indicators that Genesis 1–11 is to be understood in a similar way to Genesis 12–50. First, Genesis 12 begins with a *waw* consecutive verb, *wayomer* ("and he said"), indicating that what follows is a continuation of chapter 11, not a major break in the narrative. Second, it is widely agreed that the structure of the entire book is based on the phrase *eleh toledoth* ("these are the generations of . . ." or "this is the history of . . .") that occurs ten times in Genesis.[70] Each time this phrase occurs, it narrows the focus to something that has already been discussed: the heavens and the earth (2:4), Adam (5:1), Noah (6:9), the sons of Noah (10:1), Shem (11:10), Terah (11:27), Ishmael (25:12), Isaac (25:19), Esau (36:1), and Jacob (37:2).[71] Since six of these occurrences are in Genesis 1–11 and four occurrences are in Genesis 12–50, it seems clear that the author intended both sections to be understood in the same way, as a consecutive history.[72] Therefore, hermeneutically there is no warrant for treating Genesis 1–11 differently from the rest of the book.

---

67. Charles Mabee, *Reading Sacred Texts Through American Eyes* (Macon, GA: Mercer University Press, 1991), p. 87–88.

68. Ibid., p. 88.

69. D.J.A. Clines, "Theme in Genesis 1–11," in *I Studied Inscriptions Before the Flood: Ancient Near Eastern, Literary, and Linguistic Approaches to Genesis 1–11*, eds. Richard Hess and David Tsumura (Winona Lake, IN: Eisenbrauns, 1994), p. 305.

70. Eleven times, if the second mention of Esau in 36:9 is included.

71. Hamilton, *Genesis*, p. 2–8; Wenham, *Genesis 1–15*, p. xxii. Walter Kaiser observes that "The real key to the literary genus of this difficult section of Scripture is found in the author's recurring formula 'the generations of' which demonstrates *his* organization and *his* understanding of the materials." Kaiser, "The Literary Form of Genesis 1–11," in *New Perspectives on the Old Testament*, ed. J. Barton Payne (Waco, TX: Word, 1970), p. 61.

72. So also Walter C. Kaiser Jr., "Legitimate Hermeneutics," in *Inerrancy*, ed. Norman L. Geisler (Grand Rapids, MI: Zondervan, 1979), p. 145. Elsewhere, Kaiser makes the point that this linear view of history is quite different from the cyclical view of time found in ANE cosmologies: "It is this linear view of events and happenings [found in Genesis 1–11] that actually inaugurates the very discipline of history." Kaiser, *Old Testament Documents*, p. 83. See also G.C. Aalders, *Genesis, vol. 1* (The Bible Student's Commentary; Grand Rapids, MI: Zondervan, 1981), p. 45: "The entire design of the book [of Genesis] indicates that the positive intent was to present actual history."

Furthermore, if Genesis 1–11 is to be taken as a parable and not as history, there should be indications in the text to this effect. For instance, in the NT parables, either the word "parable" is used or a formula such as "a certain man . . ." or some other literary device.[73] But there are no such devices used in Genesis 1–11. While Walton's statement that "it is fruitless to ask what *things* God created on day one, for the text is not concerned about *things*" may sound good, in fact, the text of Genesis 1 is quite concerned about *things*: there are 22 *things* created in Genesis 1 alone! Kaiser notes that Genesis 1–11 contains 66 geographical names, 88 personal names, 48 generic names, and 21 identifiable cultural items such as gold, bdellium, onyx, brass, iron, harp, pipe, and so forth.[74] He observes that Genesis 10 alone has five times more geographical data than that of the entire Koran.[75] To suggest that Genesis 1–11 is simply a parable or story and is not concerned with things or history has no support whatsoever in the text of these chapters.

How Did New Testament Writers Understand Genesis 1–11?

Another difficulty for those who hold a figurative/allegorical understanding of Genesis 1–11 is the New Testament understanding of these chapters. In other words, if Genesis 1–11 is to be taken non-literally, then the New Testament writers should provide important evidence for this hermeneutical approach. In fact, the opposite is the case. There are at least 25 New Testament passages that refer to Genesis 1–11, and all take the account literally. Mortenson and Minton discuss this point in detail in their chapters in this volume. But a brief summary is helpful for the argument here.

The creation account is referenced by Jesus in Matthew 19:4–6 (and the parallel account in Mark 10:6–8). This passage is especially significant since Jesus cites both Genesis 1:27 and Genesis 2:24 as Scripture that is authoritative in settling the question of divorce. There is no indication that He takes either the creation of man in Genesis 1 or the account of the creation of Eve in Genesis 2 as an allegory or a figure. Paul cites Genesis 2:24 ("and they shall become one flesh") as authoritative in his section on marriage in Ephesians 5:31 and his argument against sexual immorality in 1 Corinthians 6:16.[76] In a similar way, Hebrews 4:4 cites Genesis 2:2 (God resting on the seventh day) as authoritative Scripture.[77]

---

73. See the helpful introduction to parables by Robert H. Stein, "The Genre of the Parables," in *The Challenge of Jesus' Parables*, ed. Richard N. Longenecker (Grand Rapids, MI: Eerdmans, 2000), p. 30–50.

74. Kaiser, *Old Testament Documents*, p. 82. See also his excellent discussion in "The Literary Form of Genesis 1–11," p. 59–61.

75. Ibid.

76. Also in 1 Corinthians 11:8–9 Paul explains that the woman was created from the man.

77. Likewise 2 Corinthians 4:6 says that God said "light shall shine out of darkness," a possible allusion to Genesis 1:2–5.

The account of the Fall is also regarded literally by New Testament writers. In 2 Corinthians 11:3, Paul refers to the serpent tempting Eve by his craftiness. Even more telling is Paul's discussion of the role of women and men in 1 Timothy 2:11–14. In this passage, Paul gives two reasons why a woman should not have authority over a man: first, "Adam was formed first, then Eve" (referring to Genesis 2:20–23, which states clearly that Eve was created after Adam); and second, because "Adam was not deceived, but the woman being deceived fell into transgression" (referring to the account of Satan tempting Eve in Genesis 3:1–13 — Eve specifically mentions being deceived by the serpent in Genesis 3:13).[78] Another important passage is Romans 5:12–14, which traces the beginning of sin specifically to Adam, explaining that "death reigned from Adam to Moses." Here, both Adam and his sin are mentioned, in the same phrase as Moses. If Adam was not historical, then what about Moses?[79]

Cain's murder of Abel in Genesis 4 is also mentioned in the New Testament. First John 3:12 mentions Cain, "who was of the wicked one and murdered his brother."[80] Jesus himself mentions "the blood of Abel" in Luke 11:51 and Matthew 23:35 when speaking of the prophets who had been killed. This is a clear reference to Genesis 4:10–11 in which the Lord tells Cain that his brother's blood cries out to Him from the ground.[81]

What about the account of the Flood? Again, the New Testament writers have no doubt of the historicity of Noah or the Flood. Jesus says that His second coming will be similar to the days of Noah, when "they were eating and drinking, marrying and giving in marriage, until the day that Noah entered the ark" (Matt. 24:37–38). What is noteworthy here is not simply the reference to Noah and the ark, but the details about marrying — the precise context of the Flood according to Genesis 6:2–4. Time and again the New Testament writers refer to the details (not just the "concepts") of Genesis 1–11. In Luke 17:26–27, Jesus speaks similarly about Noah, the ark, and the Flood, and then continues with the example of Lot and Sodom and the Lord's judgment on Sodom and even on Lot's wife (Luke 17:28–29, 32). Again, Noah and the ark are treated as history in the same manner as Lot and Sodom.[82] There is no hermeneutical distinction to be made between Genesis 6–8 and Genesis 19 in Jesus' thinking.

---

78. See also the reference in Revelation 12:9 to the serpent deceiving the whole world (cf. Rev. 20:2–3).
79. So also 1 Corinthians 15:22: "As in Adam all die, so in Christ will all be made alive." The effect of the Fall on creation is expressed clearly in Romans 8:19–22.
80. See also Jude 11: "They have gone in the way of Cain, run greedily in the error of Balaam for profit, and perished in the rebellion of Korah." Cain is regarded as historical, just like Balaam and Korah.
81. See also Hebrews 12:24.
82. So also John W. Wenham, "Christ's View of Scripture," in *Inerrancy*, ed. Norman Geisler (Grand Rapids, MI: Zondervan, 1980), p. 9. Wenham's entire essay is excellent, as is the following essay in the same book: Edwin A. Blum, "The Apostles' View of Scripture," p. 39–53.

Peter similarly speaks of Noah and the Flood in 1 Peter 3:20, 2 Peter 2:5, and 2 Peter 3:5–6.

In the great chapter on faith, the writer to the Hebrews begins by speaking of God creating the world (Gen. 1), then mentions Abel's better sacrifice than Cain's (another "detail" from Gen. 4:3–7), Enoch being taken by God and not seeing death (specifically quoting Gen. 5:24), and Noah's faith in building the ark (Heb. 11:3–7). In the following verses he praises the faith of Abraham, Sarah, Isaac, Jacob, Joseph, Moses, Rahab, the judges, David, Samuel, and the prophets (Heb. 11:8–32). How can we take the people and events in verses 8–32 as historical, but not those mentioned in verses 3–7? The writer to the Hebrews sees the entire Old Testament as historically accurate.

Finally, as mentioned earlier, it is important to remember that Genesis 1–11 is not simply about the creation, the Fall, and the Flood: it includes extensive genealogies.[83] And the genealogy of Jesus in Luke 3:23–38 ends with 20 names taken from Genesis 1–11 (Terah to Adam), taken as historical persons along with the first 55 names mentioned in the genealogy.[84] How can one decide that these final 20 names were part of "primeval history" and not historical, but the other 55 names are historical? Such an approach simply does not make sense. It is more consistent (with Wellhausen and some critical scholars) to view *all* of the Pentateuch as non-historical than to see only Genesis 1–11 as non-historical. They must be taken together, since there is absolutely no indication that the New Testament writers saw it any other way.[85]

In an attempt to get around the clear evidence that the New Testament writers view Genesis 1–11 as historical, some scholars believe that Jesus, Paul, Peter, and other New Testament writers simply accommodated their teachings to the views of the people of the day.[86] But that position is untenable. First, in every case mentioned above, Jesus, Paul, Peter, and the writer of the Hebrews brought up the passages in Genesis to validate their point. There was no need for Jesus to cite Genesis 1 and 2 in His discussion about divorce, but He did. There was no need for Jesus to speak of Noah and the Flood in discussing His second coming, but He did. There was no need for Paul to speak of the creation of Eve from Adam to verify his position on headship, but he did. Such alleged

---

83. See Westermann's comment about the importance of the genealogies in Genesis 1–11 (cited in note 66 above).

84. Enoch is also mentioned as "the seventh from Adam" in Jude 14, thus verifying the genealogy of Genesis 5:1–18.

85. Van Groningen rightly emphasizes the importance of the New Testament witness in the interpretation of Genesis: "If the New Testament writers are properly considered as inspired writers, as they indeed are, their consideration of Genesis as revelation of historical events as well as facts, must be accepted and followed" ("Interpretation of Genesis," p. 215).

86. For example, H.R. Boer, *Above the Battle? The Bible and Its Critics* (Grand Rapids, MI: Eerdmans, 1975), p. 95. Boer writes: "Jesus again and again accommodated himself to existing beliefs which we no longer accept."

accommodation on the part of New Testament writers is not consistent with the doctrine of inerrancy. And accommodation on the part of Jesus is doubly problematic — not only in terms of inerrancy but also in terms of Jesus' integrity and sinlessness. Furthermore, Jesus did not hesitate to correct the wrong views of the day.[87] In fact, five times in the Sermon on the Mount, Jesus draws a contrast between what the religious leaders of the day were saying ("You have heard that it was said") and what He taught ("but I say").[88] As one writer states concerning Jesus' statements about the Old Testament, "They form together a great avalanche of cumulative evidence that cannot honestly be evaded."[89] Clearly, Jesus and the Apostles saw Genesis 1–11 as historical fact, not incorrect "packaging" of theological truth.[90]

Genesis 1–11 as Partly Figurative

The third hermeneutical approach to Genesis 1–11 is that it is not entirely mythical or figurative, but not entirely literal either. Select portions are to be taken figuratively.[91] The approaches taken here vary widely, but as we shall see, they share a common thread. A few sample opinions follow.

John Stek sees basic conceptual affinities with ANE cosmologies, and views Genesis 1–2 as a polemic against ANE mythic theologies.[92] Genesis 1:1–2:3 serves as the prologue to the rest of the Pentateuch. The manner and form of the creation account in Genesis 1:1–2:3 belong to "the metaphorical character of the presentation."[93] The days are regular days, but they are not to be taken literally:

> In his storying of God's creative acts, the author was "moved" to sequence them after the manner of human acts and "time" them after the pattern of created time in humanity's arena of experience. Such sequencing and dating belonged integrally to the whole fabric of his account (the heavenly King commanding his realm into existence and ordering its internal affairs), whereby he made imaginable the unimaginable.[94]

---

87. As John Wenham wryly observes, "He did not show Himself unduly sensitive about undermining current beliefs" ("Christ's View of Scripture," p. 14).
88. Matthew 5:21–22, 27–28, 33–34, 38–39, 43–44.
89. Wenham, "Christ's View of Scripture," p. 29.
90. It is sad that some evangelical authors pay so little attention to Jesus' view of Genesis 1–11. For example, not one of the passages cited above is discussed in Peter Enns' book *Inspiration and Incarnation*. (Jude 14 is mentioned, but in an entirely different context.)
91. This view is called by Richard Bube the "essentially literal view": though Genesis 1–3 is essentially historical, it "allows for figurative nonliteral descriptions to occur in the text. The emphasis is on *harmonizing* the literal biblical text with scientific descriptions" ("Final Reflections," p. 251–52).
92. Stek, "What Says the Scripture?" p. 226–231.
93. Ibid., p. 234–237.
94. Ibid., p. 237–238.

The author used a seven-day period because "throughout the ancient Near East the number seven had long served as the primary numerical symbol of fullness/completeness/perfection, and the seven-day cycle was an old and well-established convention."[95] Thus, Stek's approach is similar to Van Till's (discussed above), but Stek limits this hermeneutical approach to Genesis 1:1–2:3.

John Collins holds that the genre of Genesis 1:1–2:3 is "exalted prose narrative": "by calling it exalted, we are recognizing that . . . we must not impose a 'literalistic' hermeneutic on the text."[96] So the days of Genesis 1 are not to be taken literally, but rather analogically: "the days are God's workdays, their length is neither specified nor important, and not everything in the account needs to be taken as historically sequential."[97]

Gordon Wenham holds that the days of Genesis are literal, 24-hour periods, but because of the "literary nature of Genesis 1," chronological sequence is not the narrator's concern.[98] Wenham gives four reasons for his non-literal view. First, there are various literary devices used in the chapter the "six-day schema," "repeating formulae, the tendency to group words and phrases into tens and sevens, literary techniques such as chiasm and inclusio, the arrangement of creative acts into matching groups, and so on."[99] Second, evening and morning appear three days before the sun and moon. Third, Genesis 1 "stands outside the main historical outline of Genesis" (the *toledoths*). So it is "an overture to the rest of the story and therefore does not stand foursquare with the rest of Genesis, to be interpreted according to precisely the same criteria."[100] Finally, "all language about God is analogical," so we need not assume that "his week's work was necessarily accomplished in 144 hours."[101]

Victor Hamilton similarly holds that *yôm* ("day") in Genesis 1 should be taken literally as a 24-hour day. However, a "literary reading" places the creation story in its historical context, as an alternative to the ANE worldview. So the term "day" should not be understood as "a chronological account of how many hours God invested in his creating project, but as an analogy of God's creative activity."[102] Similarly, W. Robert Godfrey agrees that the days of Genesis 1 "are ordinary, twenty-four hour days," but they are to be regarded as "a model for our working, not as a time schedule that God followed. . . . The days are actual for us but figurative for God."[103] Derek Kidner likewise seems to take the days as

---

95. Ibid., p. 239.

96. C. John Collins, *Genesis 1–4: A Linguistic, Literary, and Theological Commentary* (Phillipsburg, NJ: P&R, 2006), p. 44.

97. Ibid., p. 124.

98. Wenham, *Genesis 1–15*, p. 19.

99. Ibid., p. 39.

100. Ibid., p. 40.

101. Ibid.

102. Hamilton, *Genesis*, p. 53–56.

103. W. Robert Godfrey, *God's Pattern for Creation: A Covenantal Reading of Genesis 1* (Phillipsburg, NJ: P&R, 2003), p. 90.

literal days of a week, but it is "phenomenological language" (like our own talk of "sunrise") which "turns ages into days." God thus makes concessions to us in language that we may understand. Kidner concludes that "it is only pedantry that would quarrel with terms that simplify in order to clarify."[104]

Finally, Bruce Waltke also views the six days of Genesis 1 as "our twenty-four hour days," but then he adds that they are "metaphorical representations of a reality beyond human comprehension and imitation."[105] Waltke believes that a non-literal view is "consistent with the text's emphasis on theological, rather than scientific, issues."[106] Waltke gives six reasons for not viewing the creation account as "straightforward, sequential history."[107] First, reading it this way creates an irreconcilable contradiction between "the prologue of Genesis and the supplemental creation account in Genesis 2:4–25," since according to Genesis 2 God planted a garden, caused trees to grow, and formed the birds and animals in between creating the man and the woman. Second, a straightforward reading of Genesis 1:4 and 14 "leads to the incompatible notions that the sun was created on the first day and again on the fourth day."[108] Third, Waltke explains that the author's concern is "not scientific or historical but theological and indirectly polemical against pagan mythologies."[109] Fourth, Waltke observes that the "symmetrical nature of the account" indicates its non-literal nature.[110] Waltke sees the days neatly divided into two triads of three days: the things created in the second three days rule over the corresponding resources created in the first three days.[111] Fifth, Waltke notes that the use of the "widely attested seven-day

104. Derek Kidner, *Genesis: An Introduction and Commentary* (Tyndale Old Testament Commentaries; Downers Grove, IL: InterVarsity, 1967), p. 56–58.

105. Waltke, "The Literary Genre of Genesis, Chapter One," *Crux* 27 (1991): p. 8.

106. Waltke, *Genesis*, p. 61.

107. Indeed, Waltke informs us that the text is "begging us not to read it in this way" ("Literary Genre," p. 6). Waltke gives three reasons in "Literary Genre" and another three reasons in *Genesis*. I have combined them here.

108. Waltke, "Literary Genre," p. 7.

109. Waltke, *Genesis*, p. 76.

110. Ibid., p. 76–77.

111. Ibid., p. 57. This is in essence the framework hypothesis, first proposed by the Dutch theologian Arie Noordtzij in his work *Gods Woord en der Eeuwen Getuigenis*, published in 1924. An English translation of much of his work is given in N.H. Ridderbos, *Is There a Conflict Between Genesis 1 and Natural Science?* (Grand Rapids, MI: Eerdmans, 1957). The framework hypothesis has many advocates, including: Meredith Kline "Because It Had Not Rained," *WTJ* 20 (1958): p. 146–57; Mark D. Futato, "Because It Had Rained: A Study of Gen. 2:5–7 with Implications for Gen 2:4–25 and Gen 1:1–2:3," *WTJ* 60 (1998): p. 1–21; Lee Irons with Meredith Kline, "The Framework View," in David Hagopian, ed., *The Genesis Debate: Three Views on the Days of Creation* (Mission Viejo, CA: Crux, 2001), p. 217–253); Henri Blocher, *In the Beginning: The Opening Chapters of Genesis* (Downers Grove, IL: InterVarsity, 1984); Waltke, *Genesis*, p. 58–59, 73–78; Hamilton, *Genesis*, p. 54–56; Wenham, *Genesis 1-15*, p. 39–40; Mark Throntveit, "Are the Events in the Genesis Creation Account Set Forth in Chronological

typology" of the ANE shows that the narrator is using a stereotypical formula that is not intended to be taken literally.[112] Finally, Waltke states that "the language of our creation narrative is figurative, anthropomorphic, not plain: God lisped so that Israel could mime him, working six days and resting the seventh."[113] "The writer's vantage point is with God in His heavenly court."[114]

A Special Hermeneutic for Genesis 1?

It should be noted that all of the scholars mentioned above would hold to the essential historicity of Genesis 3–11. In fact, most would argue that all of Genesis 3–11 be taken literally. Thus their viewpoint is not the same as those who view all of Genesis 1–11 as a story or parable (view 2 mentioned above). Their problems are primarily with Genesis 1. So the first question to be asked is, hermeneutically should Genesis 1 (or, more precisely, Genesis 1:1–2:3) be separated from the rest of Genesis? That is what Stek holds (and thus justifies his non-literal reading of Genesis 1:1–2:3), calling it a "prologue" to the rest of Genesis.[115] Wenham likewise holds that since Genesis 1 is outside the *toledoth* outline, it is an "overture" to the rest of the story, and thus doesn't need to be interpreted the same way.[116]

Yet there is no basis for separating Genesis 1:1–2:3 from the rest of the book. Even Waltke, while also calling Genesis 1:1–2:3 a prologue, acknowledges that it is clearly linked to the remaining sections: "The author of Genesis links this prologue to the rest of his book structured about ten historical accounts by clearly linking it with his first two accounts. The first account . . . (2:4–4:26) is unmistakably coupled with the prologue by the addition, 'when the Lord God made the earth and the heavens.' "[117] Indeed, each of the *toledoths* carries on the story of a subject mentioned in the preceding account[118] So, contrary to Wenham, the first *toledoth* in Genesis 2:4 is linked to Genesis 1 in the same way that the second *toledoth* in Genesis 5:1 is linked to the account of Adam in Genesis 1–4. The same pattern is seen in the other *toledoths*. Those who seek to separate Genesis 1:1–2:3 from the rest of Genesis fail as miserably as those who seek to separate Genesis 1–11 from the rest of the book. To give just one example mentioned earlier, Jesus did not distinguish between Genesis 1 and 2

Order? No," in *The Genesis Debate: Persistent Questions about Creation and the Flood*, ed. Ronald F. Youngblood (Grand Rapids, MI: Baker, 1990) p. 36–55; and Godfrey, *God's Pattern*, p. 85–90.

112. Ibid., p. 76–77.

113. Waltke, "Literary Genre," p. 8.

114. Waltke, "Literary Genre," p. 7. "The language is anthropomorphic, representing God in human dress." (Ibid., p. 5).

115. Stek, "What Says the Scripture?" p. 241.

116. Wenham, *Genesis 1–15*, p. 40.

117. Waltke, "Literary Genre," p. 6.

118. Andrew Kulikovsky, "A Critique of the Literary Framework View of the Days of Creation," (unpublished paper for Louisiana Baptist University, July 28, 2001), p. 15.

when he quoted from both chapters in answering the question about divorce (Matt. 19:4–6; Mark 10:6–8).

Is Genesis 1 a Separate Genre?

Many would argue that Genesis 1 should be viewed non-literally because it is a separate genre from the rest of the book. This argument is at once seemingly more sophisticated (what layman would dispute this claim, not being as aware of various genres, etc.?) and more elusive, since in fact a separate genre for Genesis 1 is difficult to demonstrate. Indeed, among those who view Genesis 1 as a separate genre, there is little unanimity as to its precise classification.[119]

Some see Genesis 1 as poetic.[120] Wenham calls it a "hymn."[121] If Genesis 1 was poetic, then one would expect to observe many figurative expressions in the text. But even Waltke rejects the classification of Genesis 1 as a poem or a hymn: "Is it a hymn? Hardly, for the poetic mode, the linguistic conventions, and doxological tone of known ancient Near Eastern hymns are notably absent in Genesis 1."[122] Gunkel, who viewed the genre of Genesis as "legend," states that apart from Genesis 49, "all that the book contains is prose in form."[123] It is not written using Hebrew parallelism, but rather the normal prose structure. The contrast between it and a genuinely poetic passage that celebrates God's creation, such as Psalm 104, is striking. Psalm 104 is a poetic description of the creation; Genesis 1 is not.[124]

The inescapable conclusion is that Genesis 1 is narrative prose. Even Westermann agrees that Genesis 1:1–2:4 "is a narrative."[125] Collins calls it "exalted prose narrative," acknowledging that it is not poetry, and that "we are dealing with prose narrative," yet trying still to maintain the possibility of a non-literal hermeneutic.[126] Though acknowledging that Genesis 1 is narrative, Waltke then concludes that the genre is "a literary-artistic representation of the creation"

---

119. See John S. Feinberg's excellent summary of the various views on the literary genre of Genesis 1 in his *No One Like Him: The Doctrine of God* (Wheaton, IL: Crossway, 2001), p. 574–578.

120. For example, Walter Brueggemann, *Genesis: A Bible Commentary for Teaching and Preaching* (Atlanta, GA: John Knox, 1982), p. 26–28. See also Arnold, *Encountering the Book of Genesis*, 23: "Its elevated style is more like poetry."

121. Wenham, *Genesis 1–15*, p. 10. But Wenham points out that Genesis 1 differs from the ANE creation stories, which are poetic: "Gen. 1 is not typical Hebrew poetry." He ends up calling it "elevated prose, not pure poetry," since "most of the material is prose" (Ibid.).

122. Waltke, "Literary Genre," p. 6.

123. Gunkel, *Legends of Genesis*, p. 37–38.

124. See the further discussion of this point by Boyd in his chapter.

125. Westermann, *Genesis 1–11*, p. 80. See also Gerhard Hasel's helpful summary of the genre of Genesis 1 in "The 'Days' of Creation in Genesis 1: Literal 'Days' or Figurative 'Periods/Epochs' of Time?" *Origins* 21 (1994): p. 15-21.

126. Collins, *Genesis 1-4*, p. 44.

— which, in fact, is not a genre type at all.[127] The best that Stek can do is to call it *sui generis* (its own genre), which emphasizes the uniqueness of Genesis 1. Surely we would agree with Stek that in theme Genesis 1 is unique; but it is hardly unique in form.[128]

Indeed, Genesis 1 is presented in a normal narrative form. The standard form in Hebrew for consecutive, sequential narrative prose is the *waw* consecutive imperfect.[129] Genesis 1 contains 50 *waw* consecutive imperfect forms in its 31 verses, an average of 1.6 per verse. This represents more *waw* consecutive forms than all but 3 of the first 20 chapters in Genesis.[130] By contrast, in the poetic section of Genesis 49:1b–27 (Jacob's blessing of his sons), there are only a total of eight *waw* consecutive forms, or 0.30 per verse.[131] To put it another way, Genesis 1 has five times more narrative sequential markers than a comparably long poetic section. There seems to be no doubt that the author of Genesis 1 intended that the narrative be understood as normal sequential action. The genre is clearly narrative, not poetry.[132]

Are There Irreconcilable Contradictions between Genesis 1 and 2?

Scholars give various other reasons for taking Genesis 1 non-literally. As mentioned above, Waltke gives six reasons for a non-literal approach, many of which are shared by others who hold a similar non-literal view. These six objections to the literal view will be briefly discussed in turn.[133]

---

127. Waltke, "Literary Genre," p. 9. Waltke has adopted this phrase from Henri Blocher. It is fascinating that in an article entitled "The Literary Genre of Genesis, Chapter One," Waltke ultimately refuses to choose a normal genre category, and finds the need to make up a phrase that describes the content, not really the genre, of Genesis 1.

128. So also Hasel, "'Days' of Creation," p. 20: "It is hardly *sui generis* in an exclusive literary sense which will remove it from communication on a factual, accurate and historical level."

129. Bruce K. Waltke and Michael O'Connor, *An Introduction to Biblical Hebrew Syntax* (Winona Lake, IN: Eisenbrauns, 1990), p. 543.

130. The three chapters in Genesis 1–20 with more *waw* consecutive imperfect forms are chapters 5 (60), 11 (51) and 19 (64).

131. Todd S. Beall, William A. Banks, and Colin Smith, *Old Testament Parsing Guide* (Nashville, TN: Broadman and Holman, 2000), p. 1–15, 46.

132. See also Hasel, "'Days' of Creation," p. 20: "The creation account of Genesis 1 is a historical prose-record." Likewise Kaiser states, "Basically, there are two broad categories for arranging the material: poetry or prose. The decision is easy: Genesis 1–11 is prose and not poetry. The use of the *waw* consecutive with the verb to describe sequential acts, the frequent use of the direct object sign and the so-called relative pronoun, the stress on definitions, and the spreading out of these events in a sequential order indicates that we are in prose and not in poetry. Say what *we* will, the author plainly intends to be doing the same thing in these chapters that he is doing in chapters 12–50." Kaiser, "Literary Form of Genesis 1–11," p. 59–60.

133. I am simply using Waltke's objections as the basis of discussion because they are the most complete. The objections of Wenham and others mentioned above are also

First, there is supposedly an irreconcilable contradiction between Genesis 1 and 2, since in chapter 2 God apparently creates the man and then plants a garden and creates birds and animals before creating the woman, whereas in chapter 1 the man and the woman are created after all the rest. But Genesis 2 is not a second, chronological creation account; instead, it is topical, preparing the way for Genesis 3. Waltke is concerned that the trees God planted in Eden would not have had time to grow and bear fruit,[134] but since God can cause water to turn into wine in an instant, and can cause Aaron's rod to sprout and bud (Num. 17:8), somehow a fast-growing tree does not seem like such a great problem![135] Whether God created special birds and cattle (Gen. 2:19–20) on day 6 specifically for Eden, or whether Genesis 2:19 simply refers to the birds and cattle already created on previous days, is of little consequence: either way, there is no contradiction with Genesis 1. Each element mentioned in Genesis 2 is necessary for a proper understanding of Genesis 3; there is no contradiction between the two accounts.[136]

Was the Sun Created Twice?

Waltke says that "a straightforward reading of Genesis 1:4 and 14 leads to *the incompatible notions that the sun was created on the first day and again on the fourth day.*"[137] This objection is raised by many other scholars as well.[138] But the text does not speak of the sun being created on day one; only light was created then. We are not told what the light source is, but it clearly was not the sun. The light of day 1 is a special creation of God, distinct from the sun. If some have a problem with understanding light without the sun, then they should recognize that something similar will be true in the eternal state. According to Revelation 21:23 and 22:5, the sun will not be needed at all, since the Lord himself is the

addressed within the course of the discussion here.

134. Waltke, "Literary Genre," p. 7.

135. See also James B. Jordan, *Creation in Six Days: A Defense of the Traditional Reading of Genesis One* (Moscow, ID: Canon, 1999), p. 45–46. Interestingly, Waltke himself mentions Jesus turning water into wine, but rejects the instantaneous growth view since the text of Genesis 2 doesn't specifically state it (Ibid., p. 7).

136. See also Robert V. McCabe, "A Defense of Literal Days in the Creation Week," *Detroit Baptist Seminary Journal* 5 (2000): p. 120–122; and Wayne Grudem, *Systematic Theology* (Grand Rapids, MI: Zondervan, 1994), p. 303, where he notes, "Genesis 2 implies no description of sequence in the original creation of the animals or plants, but simply recapitulates some of the details of Genesis 1 as important for the specific account of the creation of Adam and Eve in Genesis 2."

137. Waltke, "Literary Genre," p. 7 (italics his).

138. For example, see Van Til, *The Fourth Day*, p. 88–92; Meredith Kline, "Space and Time in the Genesis Cosmogony," *Perspectives on Science and Christian Faith* 48 (1996), p. 6–8; Wenham, *Genesis 1-15*, p. 40; Irons and Kline, "The Framework View," 220.21; Throntveit, "Events in the Genesis Creation Account," 37-40; Godfrey, *God's Pattern for Creation*, p. 41–45; and Ronald F. Youngblood, *The Book of Genesis: An Introductory Commentary* (Grand Rapids, MI: Baker, 1991, 2nd ed.), p. 26–27.

light. So just as in the first three days of the creation week, in the eternal state there will once again be light without the sun. Though we cannot conceive of "evening and morning" apart from the sun, surely God can.[139]

A Polemic against ANE Mythologies?

Next, Waltke asserts that the author's concern was not "scientific or histori-cal," but was instead "polemical against pagan mythologies."[140] Stek, Hamilton, Wenham, and Futato make similar observations.[141] In response, despite the assertions of these scholars, it is not clear from the text of Genesis that this is the author's purpose.[142] In fact, scholars who hold this view do not even agree on whether Genesis 1 is a polemic against Babylonian, Canaanite, or Egyptian mythologies.[143] Regardless, even if Genesis 1 is a polemic against one or more of these ANE mythologies, why would this conclusion lead to the idea that Genesis 1 is not to be taken literally? The two concepts are simply not related. For example, John J. Davis argues that the ten plagues in Moses' day were each directed against Egyptian gods, a supposition directly supported by the text (see Exod. 12:12; Num. 33:4), unlike the supposition made about Genesis 1.[144] But that polemical purpose for the plagues in no way causes Davis to view them as anything but literally fulfilled. The same holds true for Genesis 1.

Does a Symmetrical Structure Indicate Non-literalness?

Waltke, Wenham, and others also contend that the structure of the days of Genesis 1 is symmetrical, with days 4–6 paralleling days 1–3, and that this sym-metry demonstrates its non-literal nature. Often the following pattern is noted:

Creation kingdoms	Creature kings
Day 1: light; day and night	Day 4: light-bearers: sun, moon, stars
Day 2: sea and sky	Day 5: sea creatures; birds
Day 3: land and vegetation	Day 6: land creatures; man[145]

---

139. See further Jordan, *Creation in Six Days*, p. 48–49.

140. Waltke, *Genesis*, p. 76.

141. Stek, "What Says the Scripture?" p. 229–231; Hamilton, *Genesis*, p. 55; Wenham, *Genesis 1-15*, p. xlv, 9; Futato, "Because It Had Rained," p. 1–21. Others view Genesis 1 as a polemic, but do not necessarily reject a literal approach to the text. So Hasel, "Polemic Nature," p. 81–91; Johnston, "Genesis 1-2:3," p. 10–14; and Shetter, "Genesis 1-2," p. 30–33.

142. See Jordan, *Creation in Six Days*, p. 235: "Nothing in these texts so much as hints that they were written as polemics against anything."

143. Futato says Canaanite Baalism ("Because It Had Rained," p. 1–21); Johnston ("Genesis 1–2:3," p. 10–14) and Shetter ("Genesis 1-2," p. 30–33) say Egyptian; Wenham says Babylonian and Egyptian (*Genesis 1–15*, p. 9); and Hasel says Babylonian, Egyptian, and Canaanite ("Polemic Nature," p. 81–91).

144. John J. Davis, *Moses and the Gods of Egypt* (Grand Rapids, MI: Baker, 1971), p. 86–96.

145. Waltke, *Genesis*, p. 57–58, 76–77; Kline, "Space and Time," p. 2–15; Irons and Kline,

This view is called the framework hypothesis, and seems to be increasingly popular among evangelicals.[146] A full critique of the framework hypothesis is given elsewhere in this book, so only a few comments will be made here. First, the light of day 1 is not dependent on the sun, so the sun is hardly the "ruler" of it. Second, the waters existed on day 1, not just day 2. Third, in verse 14 the "lights" of day 4 are set in the "expanse" created on day 2 (not day 1). Fourth, the sea creatures of day 5 were to fill the "water in the seas" which were created on day 3, not day 2, contrary to the chart above (see Gen. 1:10); and none of the sea creatures or birds or land creatures other than man were to "rule" anything anyway. Finally, man was created on day 6 not to rule over the land and vegetation (created on day 3), but over the land animals created on day 6 and the sea creatures and birds created on day 5. In other words, despite the nice chart, the patterns simply do not hold up.[147]

Furthermore, even if the pattern held true completely (which it assuredly does not), it would hardly be an argument for a non-literal approach to the chapter, especially since the chapter has so many sequential markers. Just because something is presented according to a pattern does not mean that the pattern is non-literal.[148] After all, as was previously discussed, the entire Book of Genesis is patterned according to the *toledoths* ("this is the account of . . .): does that mean that the accounts of Noah, Shem, Terah, Ishmael, Isaac, Esau, and Jacob are not literal or chronological?[149] As E.J. Young states, "Why, then, must we

---

"Framework View," p. 224; Wenham, *Genesis 1–15*, p. 6–7; Arnold, *Encountering the Book of Genesis*, p. 24; Youngblood, *Genesis*, p. 25–27.

146. See note 111 above.

147. See further, Edward J. Young, *Studies in Genesis One* (Philadelphia, PA: Presbyterian and Reformed, 1964), p. 68–73; Grudem, *Systematic Theology*, p. 302; Todd S. Beall, "Christians in the Public Square: How Far Should Evangelicals Go in the Creation-Evolution Debate?" (paper delivered at the Annual Meeting of the Evangelical Theological Society, Nov. 15, 2006), p. 6–10; and Joseph A. Pipa, Jr., "From Chaos to Cosmos: A Critique of the Non-Literal Interpretations of Genesis 1:2–2:3," in *Did God Create in 6 Days?*, eds. Joseph Pipa, Jr. and David Hall (White Hall, WV: Tolle Lege, 2005, 2nd ed.), p. 170–74.

148. The same observation holds true for other literary devices seen by Wenham (*Genesis 1–15*, p. 39) and others. Structure does not necessitate or even suggest non-literalness. And many of these so-called "literary devices" are questionable. For example, Wenham says that the number of Hebrew words in Gen. 1:1–2 and 2:1–3 are all multiples of seven (p. 6). But in order to arrive at this conclusion, Wenham needs to *add* the number of words in 2:1–3 together: separately they are 5, 14, and 16 words respectively. Are we to believe that the author of Genesis went through this exercise in mental gymnastics of adding the words in three verses simply to arrive at 35, a multiple of seven? Wenham mentions other phrases that occur seven times, but since creation occurred in seven days, it is simply the repetition of these phrases at the beginning or end of each day that create the "7." See also my discussion on the use of seven in the immediately following paragraphs.

149. So also Weeks, "Hermeneutical Problem," p. 17. See further Pipa, "From Chaos to Cosmos," p. 184–85.

conclude that, merely because of a schematic arrangement, Moses has disposed of chronology?"[150]

Does the Use of Seven Days Indicate Non-literalness?

Waltke, Stek, and Walton believe that since the seven days of Genesis 1 reflects a "widely attested seven-day typology of the ancient world," it suggests that the author is using a stereotypical formula rather than a literal period of seven days.[151] Waltke notes that "within ancient Near Eastern material, the pattern of six as incompleteness and seven as resolution is quite common."[152]

There are indeed some interesting uses of seven days in ANE literature: the construction of Baal's palace in seven days (*ANET*, p. 134); the attack of King Keret upon the city of Udum (*ANET*, p. 144–45); Danel's seven days of offerings to the gods followed by seven days of feasting (*ANET*, p. 150); and in the Gilgamesh Epic, seven days for Utnapishtim's boat to be built, and seven days of the flood raging followed by seven days of waiting for the waters to subside (*ANET*, p. 93–94).[153]

But there are a number of problems with Waltke and Stek's analysis. First, none of the cited texts have anything to do with creation, and none of the ANE creation texts mention a seven-day period of creation. Second, the only texts that have something to do with building *anything* are Baal's palace construction and the construction of Utnapishtim's boat. But these have nothing to do with the creation of the world. Third, even these two acts of construction from ANE texts indicate that the building was done in seven days. But Genesis 1 states that the world was created in six days, not seven. The seventh day was merely for God to rest. Fourth, just because there are some parallel ANE texts that mention seven days has nothing to do with the literalness of the days of Genesis 1. In fact, in all the ANE texts cited, the days were regarded as literal days, not symbolic: it took seven actual days to build Baal's palace, and so forth. In other words, the

---

150. Young, *Studies in Genesis One*, p. 66.

151. Waltke, *Genesis*, p. 77; Stek, "What Says the Scripture?" p. 239; Walton, *Genesis*, p. 155. See also Youngblood, *Genesis*, p. 26, 31. Walton sees in the ANE texts a liturgical significance "connected to the construction of sanctuaries." He concludes that the seven-day creation cycle in Genesis "put the creation narrative in the context of an enthronement/temple dedication-type of setting" (*Genesis*, p. 157). That conclusion is a stretch, to say the least, since the Genesis text mentions nothing of a temple or a building/throne dedication.

152. Waltke, *Genesis*, p. 77. See also U. Cassuto, *A Commentary on the Book of Genesis, Part One* (Jerusalem: Magnes Press, 1961), p. 12–13: "Akkadian and Ugaritic literature . . . prove that a series of *seven consecutive days* was considered a perfect *period* in which to develop an important work" (italics his).

153. Stek, "What Says the Scripture," p. 239. Note that in the case of the Gilgamesh Epic, the sevens could well be patterned after the actual Flood account, since Noah waited two periods of seven days before sending the birds out (Gen. 8:10, 12). In the Gilgamesh Epic, a dove, a swallow, and a raven were sent out on the seventh day.

days were still 24-hour measures of time, not some symbolic figure without any actual time value or with a value of thousands or millions of years.

We wonder if it has ever occurred to these scholars that the reason the number seven was regarded as the number of completeness might be traced back to a distant memory of the actual literal creation week as described in Genesis. The reason that "seven" was so prominent in the ANE may very well have been that they knew (having descended from Adam and Noah) that God created the world in a period of seven days — a period that then became the measurement of time for mankind's activity. Why must we assume that the author of Genesis "borrowed" his idea of seven from the ANE, rather than that he received it by special revelation from God and that the ANE pagans developed their idea from truth handed down about the Creator's actual acts?[154]

Did God Lisp so that We Could Understand?

Finally, Waltke, Kidner, Wenham, and others explain that God is simply using anthropomorphic, rather than literal, language in Genesis 1. Waltke states that "God lisped so that Israel could mime him, working six days and resting the seventh."[155] Kidner likewise views God as making "concessions to us in language that we may understand," but which apparently is not to be taken literally.[156]

Certainly the Bible has anthropomorphic language. But in point of fact, Genesis 2 and 3 contain more anthropomorphic language than Genesis 1: God "breathing" into man's nostrils (Gen. 2:7), His "walking in the garden" (Gen. 3:8), and so forth. Yet even understanding the occasional use of anthropomorphic language, how does that relate to our understanding of the days of Genesis 1? Anthropomorphisms usually take the form of a body part or organ or movement to describe God's actions, but they never take the form of a unit of time such as a day. As Young states, the word anthropomorphic "can be applied to God alone and cannot properly be used of the six days."[157] Pipa notes that "God is eternal, but once he created time and space his operations within time and space are in time as we understand it. . . . Are there any examples in Scripture in which the time markers of God's work are anthropomorphic?"[158] In fact, Exodus 20:8–11 says that our week was patterned after God's creation week: the same term for "days" is used both for His creation week and for our week.

---

154. By this statement I am not implying that other cultures were innocent in what they did. They rebelled against God and His revelation through their own sin, and made up competing cosmologies to substitute for the truth of God's revelation. Satan is a master at using partial truth as a substitute for God's truth (2 Cor. 11:14).

155. Waltke, "Literary Genre," p. 5, 7.

156. Kidner, *Genesis*, p. 56–58. See also Wenham, *Genesis 1–15*, p. 40: "All language about God is analogical," so there is no need to think that He finished His work in 144 hours. See also Collins, *Genesis 1–4*, p. 124, who advocates the "analogical days" position: "The days are God's work-days, their length is neither specified nor important."

157. Young, *Studies in Genesis One*, p. 58.

158. Pipa, "From Chaos to Cosmos," p. 163.

Does God really have to "lisp," as Waltke says, in order to communicate with us? Does this not imply that God did a poor job in creating man in the first place? Did He not design our human capacity to speak and communicate? Are we not made in His image? Of course He is infinite and we are finite, and He is the Creator and we are the creatures; but isn't man's main problem of communicating with God due to our sin, not our finiteness?[159] Contrary to Waltke, Wenham, and Kidner, all of Genesis 1 begs that we read it as historical sequential narrative prose, not as some figurative or analogical or anthropomorphic account. Furthermore, if God could speak literally about the creation of Adam and Eve and their sin and about Noah, Abraham, Isaac, Jacob, Joseph, Moses, and the Exodus, which most, if not all, of these scholars accept as literal history, then why can't God speak of literal events on literal days of creation in a way that we can readily understand? The logic of this "lisp" argument does not make sense. If God created over millions of years and in the order that evolutionary scientists say, then He is a very incompetent communicator in Genesis 1.

Once again, hermeneutically it is important to be consistent in our treatment of Genesis 1. As Pipa notes, the style of Genesis 2 and 3 is more figurative (with more anthropomorphisms) than Genesis 1, so why not regard these chapters as non-literal?[160] The same is true for the Flood account, Babel, and so forth. Such an arbitrary method of interpreting Scripture has no exegetical brakes: it is only one step away from denying miracles and the bodily resurrection of Christ.[161] How do we determine what is literal and what is not, if we ignore the plain markings of genre in the text itself?[162]

Accommodation to Scientific Thinking?

There is actually a seventh reason that Waltke gives for rejecting a literal understanding of Genesis 1, while accepting a literal understanding of the rest of the chapters of Genesis. Waltke notes that there are three basic interpretations for the "days": "literal twenty-four hour periods, extended ages or epochs, and structures of a literary framework designed to illustrate the orderly nature of God's creation." Then Waltke states that the first two interpretations

---

159. See further Jordan, *Creation in Six Days*, p. 105–111, concerning anthropomorphisms in Genesis 1.
160. Pipa, "From Chaos to Cosmos," p. 194.
161. Ibid., p. 194–96.
162. Feinberg gives a similar warning: "If the days may be figurative, then why not God, etc., as figures to represent something else? What is the hermeneutic that tells us that some elements in this story are figures of speech and literary devices and others are not? . . . If this account is just a literary device, what does that tell us about other stories Moses recounts? Are the ten plagues at the time of the Exodus another literary device, not to be taken literally? . . . Once you treat a piece whose literary genre seems to involve history as though it does not, that also raises serious questions about other texts that appear to be history" (*No One Like Him*, p. 613–615).

"pose scientific and textual difficulties," which he explains in his footnote as follows: "In the case of the first suggestion, most scientists reject a literal twenty-four-hour period. In the case of the second, the pattern in the text of morning-evening seems inconsistent with the epoch theory."[163] In other words, Waltke rejects a literal 24-hour "day" because "most scientists" reject it! This, we suspect, is the main reason for those who adopt an inconsistent hermeneutic for Genesis 1–11 and especially for Genesis 1: a straightforward reading of Genesis 1 conflicts with the current scientific theory of origins. Indeed, when presenting the three basic views on Genesis 1, Bube notes that the emphasis of "the essentially literal view" is "on *harmonizing* the literal biblical text with scientific descriptions."[164] What is especially sad is that Waltke, a wonderful Hebrew scholar, rejects the normal meaning of the text in Genesis 1 not on exegetical grounds, but on scientific grounds! As I have written elsewhere, I believe that many evangelicals take an inconsistent hermeneutical approach to Genesis 1 because they are embarrassed by the six 24-hour day approach and wish to distance themselves from it.[165]

Confirmation of my suspicions comes from an unlikely source. In his work entitled *Fundamentalism*, James Barr takes conservative evangelicals to task for insisting on a literal interpretation of Scripture but then abandoning it when it comes to the creation story in Genesis. Barr explains that "as the scientific approach came to have more and more assent from fundamentalists themselves, they shifted their interpretation of the Bible passage from literal to non-literal in order to save . . . the inerrancy of the Bible." In order to avoid the consequence of an errant Bible, the fundamentalist "has tried every possible direction of interpretation other than the literal." Yet, Barr rightly continues, "in fact the only natural exegesis is a literal one, in the sense that this is what the author meant."[166]

Conclusion

Barr is right on target. As this chapter has shown, there is no justification for applying a different hermeneutic to Genesis 1–11 or to Genesis 1 than to the rest of Genesis. As Weeks has observed, "The basic question is whether our interpretation of the Bible is to be determined by the Bible itself or by some other authority. Once science has been set up as an autonomous authority it inevitably

---

163. Waltke, *Genesis*, p. 61.
164. Bube, "Final Reflections," p. 251–252. This view is equivalent to my "Genesis 1–11 as partly figurative" category (view 3, above).
165. Beall, "Christians in the Public Square," p. 6. So also Feinberg: "What I find particularly troublesome in too many presentations on the doctrine of creation is that a primary goal (if not *the* primary goal) in interpreting the biblical text is to harmonize it with the prevailing scientific understanding of our world. For me, that is not the way to do evangelical systematic theology. . . . Scripture must be allowed to speak for itself on its own terms" (*No One Like Him*, p. 579).
166. James Barr, *Fundamentalism* (Philadelphia, PA: Westminster, 1977), p. 42.

tends to determine the way in which we interpret the Bible."[167] Our conclusion is that the only proper hermeneutical approach to Genesis 1–11 (including Genesis 1) is to regard it as historical narrative that is meant to be taken literally. To use some other hermeneutical approach and apply it in a piecemeal fashion is to ignore the plain evidence given by our Lord, the New Testament writers, and the text of Genesis itself.

---

167. Weeks, "Hermeneutical Problem," p. 16.

Chapter 6

The Genre of Genesis 1:1–2:3: What Means This Text?

Steven W. Boyd

Portions of this chapter were originally published in my chapter, Steven W. Boyd, "Statistical Determination of Genre in Biblical Hebrew: Evidence for an Historical Reading of Genesis 1:1–2:3," in RATE II (Radioisotopes and the Age of the Earth: Results of a Young-Earth Creationist Research Initiative, edited by Larry Vardiman, Andrew A. Snelling, and Eugene F. Chaffin [El Cajon, CA: Institute for Creation Research and Chino Valley, AZ: Creation Research Society, 2005]), p. 631–734. This revised material is used with permission from the Institute for Creation Research. Below, I refer to my RATE II chapter as RATE chapter.

1. Introduction

The starting point for understanding any text is to read it according to its *genre*.[1] The original readers (or listeners) an author had in mind when he wrote[2] would have recognized intuitively what type of text they were reading (or

---

1. *Genre* is the category of literature into which a particular text falls, which was clearly recognized by its original readers. For surveys of genre theory written by literary theorists, see *The New Princeton Encyclopedia of Poetry and Poetics* (*NPEPP*), s.v. "genre"; *The Harper Handbook of Literature*, 2nd ed., s.v. "genre criticism"; *A Handbook of Critical Approaches to Literature*, 4th ed., s.v. "genre criticism"; and Paul A. Bové, "Discourse," in F. Lentricchia and T. McLaughlin, eds., *Critical Terms for Literary Study* (Chicago, IL: The University of Chicago Press, 1995, 2nd ed.), p. 50–51, hereafter cited as *CTLS*. See further Grant R. Osborne, "Historical Narrative and Truth in the Bible," *JETS* 48/4 (December 2005): p. 679–683 and the references he cites for the concept of genre applied to biblical texts. Also see *RATE* chapter, p. 631–639.

2. There are sound reasons for assuming the Mosaic authorship of this text and an Exodus date of 1446 B.C. Thus, the *latest date* for this text is the death of Moses in

hearing), because they would have been familiar with the literary conventions of their day.[3] In fact, the author — aware that his readers had this knowledge — worked it into his text.[4] On the other hand, we modern readers must deduce what would have been obvious to the original readers: perforce we must marshal the data to determine the genre of a text.[5]

For Genesis 1:1–2:3, three characteristics stand out: it is a magisterial literary composition; it is a foundational theological treatise; and it is a literal[6] historical account.[7] I will touch on the first and second of these below, but

---

approximately 1406 B.C. The original readers therefore would have been 15th century B.C. Israelites, who were about to enter and conquer the Promised Land.

3. This would have been part of the *conceptual representation* of the original readers, which is *the particular historical, cultural, linguistic, and ideological context an author shared with his original readers*. For discussion, see Nicolai Winther-Nielsen, "Fact, Fiction and Language Use: Can Modern Pragmatics Improve on Halpern's Case for History in Judges?" in V. Philips Long, David W. Baker, and Gordon J. Wenham, eds., *Windows into Old Testament History: Evidence, Argument, and the Crisis of "Biblical Israel,"* p. 44–81 (Grand Rapids, MI: Wm. B. Eerdmans Publishing Co., 2002), p. 53–69; and *RATE* chapter, p. 639–641.

4. Winther-Nielsen memorably says, "Words are anchored in worlds by the will of the writer" (Winther-Nielsen, "Fact, Fiction, and Language Use," p. 67) and citing Thomlin, Forrest, Pu and Kim: "Instead the speaker [or author] becomes the architect of his text who guides his listener [or reader] in construing a *conceptual representation* of events and ideas. The speaker [author] as the architect and the hearer [reader] as constructor must both construe a coherent text through their integration of knowledge and management of information. The hearer [reader] makes pragmatic implicatures from the contextual situation and builds cognitive inferences from the text and the world knowledge he shares with the speaker [author]" (Ibid., p. 69) [emphasis mine]. For additional discussion see *RATE* chapter, p. 639–641.

5. See my elaboration of these ideas in *RATE* chapter, p. 640–641, and the references cited there.

6. "Literal" denotes both corresponding to reality and exact or, as Westermann says about this text, straightforward: "The average reader who opens his Bible to Genesis 1 and 2 receives the impression that he is reading a sober account of creation, which relates facts in much the same manner as does the story of the rise of the Israelite monarchy, that is, as straightforward history" (Claus Westermann, *The Genesis Accounts of Creation*, trans. Norman E. Wagner [Philadelphia, PA: Fortress, 1964], p. 5). For further discussion on "real" see *RATE* chapter, p. 690–691, in particular, Sailhamer's quote explaining what a realistic portrayal of events means.

7. Meir Sternberg discusses three issues in his marvelous introduction to his magnum opus, *The Poetics of Biblical Narrative: Ideological Literature and the Drama of Reading* (Bloomington, IN: Indiana University Press, 1985), which are germane to this study: (1) in the Bible there is a *non-contradictory balance* between its three characteristics: it is a literary masterpiece, it purports to be reporting historical events, and it is giving a clear ideological message; (2) it is easy to under-read the Bible but almost impossible to counter-read the Bible (in other words, many times readers do not pick up all the subtleties of the text, but the theological message is clear); (3) the biblical authors

will concentrate on the third, because it is at the center of a maelstrom of controversy.

The first characteristic is that it is a *magisterial literary composition*. Hardly any thinking person would deny that this chapter is one of the greatest in literature. Words can at best only inadequately describe the extraordinary first text of the Bible and quickly spend the repertoire of superlatives of the English language: profound, majestic, full of grandeur, foundational, fundamental, vast, sweeping, towering, incomparable, unplumbable, and inexhaustible. At the same time it has been described as austere,[8] tranquil,[9] patient,[10] reticent[11] and forgiving.[12]

---

believed that they were writing real history. Sternberg's main thesis is that the genius of Old Testament narrative is that the historiographical, literary and theological (what he calls "ideological") aspects of the text are not only in balance but dependent on one another in a non-mutually exclusive nexus. On the three-fold character of biblical texts, Winther-Nielsen echoes Sternberg: ". . . historical narrative in the Hebrew Bible is an intricately woven material or 'texture' of historical, literary, and ideological threads" (Nielsen, p. 45). On the non-contradictory balance of the literary and historical, Osborne asserts, "While biblical history is presented in narrative form, this by no means obviates its status as history. There is no theoretical reason why literary and historical interests cannot coincide, and why the stories cannot be trustworthy representations of what really happened" (Osborne, p. 683). Merrill emphasizes the relationship of the historical and the theological and exposes the false dichotomy that a text cannot be both theological and historical, when he writes that the narrative's ". . . character as sacred history — a notion that must never be ignored — does not in any way diminish its value as a source of 'ordinary' historical information" (Eugene H. Merrill, "Archaeology and Biblical History: Its Uses and Abuses," in *Giving the Sense: Understanding and Using Old Testament Historical Text,* ed. David M. Howard and Michael A. Grisanti, p. 74–96 [Grand Rapids, MI: Kregel Publications, 2003], p. 78).

8. E.A. Speiser, *Genesis: Introduction, Translation and Notes* (Garden City, NY: Doubleday and Company, Inc., 1964), p. 8.

9. U. Cassuto, *A Commentary on the Book of Genesis: Part I: From Adam to Noah* (Jerusalem: The Magnes Press, 1998), p. 7.

10. "Patient" in the context of literary theory means a text's "ability to endure and survive rigorous criticism." I owe this description of Genesis 1:1–2:3 to John Hotchkiss (chairman of the English department at The Master's College), which he offered in a private communication about the qualities of a magisterial literary composition.

11. This term, also used by Hotchkiss, means that a text does not say everything; thus, it allows room for interpretation.

12. "Forgiving" means that a text can survive incorrect interpretation, such as has been applied to Genesis 1:1–2:3. It must be said that in light of this avalanche of adulation, which has been heaped upon this text, the words "incoherent" (Bruce K. Waltke, *Literary form of Genesis 1:1–2:4a,* p. 1–20 [unpublished paper presented at Dallas Theological Seminary, 2004], p. 11) or "messy," (Peter Enns, *Inspiration and Incarnation: Evangelicals and the Problem of the Old Testament* [Grand Rapids, MI: Baker, 2005], p. 109), which also have been used to describe it, seem oddly out of step. See further, Beale's blistering review article of Enns's book, G.K. Beale, "Myth, History, and Inspiration: A Review Article" of *Inspiration and Incarnation* by Peter Enns," *JETS* 49/2 (2006): p. 287–312.

By any standard, Genesis 1:1–2:3 is a great literary classic. Sainte-Beuve defines a "classic" as literature that enriches the human mind, increases its treasure, advances it a step, is broad and great, refined, sensible, sane, beautiful in itself, which has spoken to all in a unique way, easily contemporary with all time, a text with uniformity, wisdom, moderation and reason, a text which is elegant, clear, noble and has an airily veiled strength.[13]

But perhaps it is the word "sublime," which best apprehends these 34 verses. In his essay, "On the Sublime," Longinus characterizes sublime literature as literature that transports the reader. It has a spark that leaps from the soul of the author to the soul of the reader. There is an echo of greatness of spirit (of the author). It contains great thoughts and stirs noble feelings.[14]

So, in every sense, it is a *magisterial* text in that one never tires of reading it, it invites a closer reading, it inspires awe and wonder and deep respect, and it lies at the foundation of worldviews. The literary aspects of the text will be explored in **Section 2.2** below.

The second characteristic of Genesis 1:1–2:3 is that it is a *foundational theological treatise*. It is the foundation of Christian theology: our God, our Savior, is both Creator and Redeemer. In addition, it presents a powerful polemic against the prevalent polytheism of the Ancient Near East. These ideas will be further developed in **Section 2.3** below.

The third characteristic goes to the heart of the matter: Genesis 1:1–2:3 is also a *literal historical account*. Whereas, few would disagree with the first two characteristics mentioned above, the stumbling block for many is to accept this text as historical narrative, which therefore speaks authoritatively about the origin of the universe, life, and man and about the age of the earth.

It should be obvious to modern readers (just as it was to its original readers) that this text should be approached mindful of this third characteristic. But unfortunately, to many it is not. Hence, the bulk of this chapter (**Section 2.1** below) will be devoted to proving — by means of statistical, literary, and theological arguments — what would have been axiomatic to its original readers: this text is a literal historical account. In addition, there is a need to demonstrate that reading this text as a literal historical account leads to the conclusion that the earth is thousands . . . not billions of years old.

1.1 The Implications of Genre

Two principal genres have been proposed for this text: extended poetic metaphor and narrative. If this text is poetic metaphor, what are the implications for determining the age of the earth? On the other hand, what are they if it is narrative?

---

13. From Saint-Beuve's essay, "What is a Classic?" (translated by Elizabeth Lee) in J. Smith and E. Parks, *The Great Critics: An Anthology of Literary Criticism* (New York: Norton, 1967), p. 596–599.
14. Longinus's essay "On the Sublime," is discussed in J. Smith and E. Parks, *The Great Critics*, p. 62–63.

Let us consider first the implications if the text is poetic metaphor. A metaphor has two parts: the *vehicle,* the actual words of the metaphor, and the *tenor,* the meaning of the words.[15] The *tenor* is derived by exploring the similarities and differences between the words of the metaphor. For example, consider Exodus 15:8a: "By the breath of your nostrils the waters heaped up."[16] The reference to God's nose is anthropomorphic language — God does *not* have a nose, for, as the Scriptures teach, He is a spiritual being, not a material being (John 4:24). The presence of such clearly figurative language signals metaphor. So, "nose" does not refer to a literal nose in this verse. Similarly, the phrase "the LORD is my rock" prompts the question: in what sense is the Lord like a rock?[17] And, conversely, in what sense is He not?

In metaphor, words do not have their normal range of meaning; instead, the meaning of individual words is controlled by the metaphor. The individual words of the *vehicle* do not have a one-to-one correspondence to people, things, states, and actions in the world. So if the text is poetic metaphor, the real life referents of the words in the text and the sequence of events portrayed by them is not the meaning of the text. That is to say the words do not tell us what really happened. But scientists can only work with observable, measurable reality. So if the text is poetic metaphor, it has nothing to say about scientific theories of origins and therefore nothing about the age of the earth.

On the other hand, if the text is narrative, it could have much to say about origins and the age of the earth. It depends on the *intent* of the author.[18] Did

---

15. *NPEPP,* s.v. "metaphor."

16. Unless indicated otherwise, Scripture quotes are my translations.

17. Below, I will follow the usual convention, translating *YHWH* (the covenant name of God, which testifies to His self-existence) as "LORD," but *Adonai* (meaning "master") as "Lord." Outside of translation, I will use "Lord."

18. Wimsatt and Beardsley stated in their classic essay "The Intentional Fallacy": "The design or intention of the author is neither available nor desirable as a standard for judging the success of a work of literary art" (W.K. Wimsatt and M.C. Beardsley, "The Intentional Fallacy," in ed. D. Newton-De Molina, *On Literary Intention: Critical Essays,* p. 1–13 [Edinburgh: Edinburgh University Press, 1976], p. 1). In their essay (originally published in *Sewanee Review* 54 [summer 1946]) they argued that we cannot know an author's intent, because it was in the mind of the author, a place inaccessible to us. Wimsatt emended this quote to "The design or intention of the author is neither available nor desirable as a standard for judging *either the meaning or* the success of a work of literary art" in his essay "Genesis: A Fallacy Revisited," in Newton-De Molina, p. 136 [emphasis mine]. The original essay, Wimsatt's second essay, *Hirsch's* rejoinders and clarifications on both sides during the heat of the debate are in Newton-De Molina's anthology. More recently, Patterson traces the issues in the debate among literary theorists, starting with Wimsatt and Beardsley's seminal essay, continuing with Hirsch's insistence on authorial intention and determinancy of meaning, interacting with the deconstructional hermeneutics of Derrida and Foucault and concluding with the admission of de Man that the deconstructive impulse is dependent on the preexistence of a certain kind of reading (Annabel Patterson, "Intention," in *CTLS,* p. 140–146).

he want his narrative to be read as a historical account or not? If he did not, we are at an impasse again. But if he did, this text speaks directly to the age of the earth. Because if the text is a literal historical account, there is a one-to-one correspondence between words and reality and a careful philological study of them, comprising morphology, syntax, and lexicography, will allow the reconstruction of the events reported in the text, in particular their sequence and duration.

To answer the question about the author's intention, it is necessary to expand the question to biblical narratives in general. How did authors of biblical narratives understand the events about which they wrote? Did authors of biblical narratives believe that they were referring to real events? If they did not, we are at a dead end yet again. But if they did — it can and will be argued — so does this text at the beginning of Genesis.

Why is it necessary to prove what would have been intuitive to the original readers of this text, namely, that Genesis 1:1–2:3 is a literal historical account? Because, if we get this wrong, we *will* misinterpret the text. But why is it so important that *this* text be correctly interpreted? Its location. And what is at stake? The truth.

Genesis 1:1–2:3 is the foundation of theology and is at the interface of Scripture and scientific interpretation of empirical evidence. The battle for truth has escalated to a full-scale war. The battlefields where opponents fight over this interface used to be limited to the arcane world of academic journals, books, and conferences, but it is confined to them no longer. The field of combat has expanded to the forum of popular culture, primetime TV, newspapers, popular magazines, and the courts.

Why has this happened? The first reason is that postmodern man has come to realize that one's view of origins — inextricably linked to the understanding of this text — defines one's worldview. Determining the genre of this text therefore is not merely an academic exercise, of interest only to specialists, but is the essential

---

Graff contributes significantly to the discussion on intention by cogently arguing that we infer other peoples' intent in speech and writing from the *context* of the utterance: "At first thought, it may seem that because an intention is a private experience that happens in one's own head, nobody but the person harboring the intention could know what it is. But a little further reflection and observation should suggest that we come to conclusions all the time about the intentions of other people. . . . we infer the intentions of speakers and writers from situational clues of various kinds — the form and features of the utterance itself, the circumstances in which the utterance is made, the information we already may possess about the speaker or writer. Such inferences about the circumstances of an utterance that help us infer a picture of the probable kind of utterance it is are what we call the 'context' of the utterance" (Gerald Graff, "Determinacy/Indeterminacy," in *CTLS*, p. 166). Vanhoozer shows how the post-Hirschian hermeneutics of Fish and Derrida have taken away the author, the text, and the reader (Kevin Vanhoozer, *Is there a Meaning in this Text?: The Bible, the Reader, and The Morality of Literary Knowledge* [Grand Rapids, MI: Zondervan, 1998]). Finally, see the discussion of authorial intent and how to discern it in *RATE* chapter, p. 639–641.

first step for anyone wanting to correctly interpret this text.

Were it not for the unproven and unprovable theories of evolutionary biology, geology, and cosmology, and the faulty but rarely challenged assumptions of radioisotope dating, no one would be questioning what kind of text this is or the age of the earth.[19]

This is a needless tragedy among evangelicals, "needless" because evangelicals do not have to adjust Scripture to accommodate to science and a "tragedy" because by taking this stand, they unwittingly ally themselves with those who are trying to destroy the Bible.

The second reason the age of the earth has become such a cultural issue is that any statement to the effect that the earth is thousands — not billions — of years old, assaults "fortress uniformitarian-geology," an edifice built since the 18th century, and thereby provokes its defenders to demand evidence supporting such a claim.

Creationists have been presenting this evidence for years. The man we honor through this publication has been a pioneer in this effort and has labored tirelessly to convince the Church of the importance of the early chapters of the Bible. The warning to the Church is clear. A largely immoral and godless society is stark testimony to the effect that embracing evolution has on a people.

Others have picked up the gauntlet — most recently, the RATE Group.[20]

And the third reason for this issue's prominent currency is that the philosophical idea that the text is not admissible as evidence in the creation-evolution debate is being challenged as arbitrary and presumptuous. The biblical evidence has been barred or belittled based on two unproven suppositions connected with the relationship between text and empirical evidence. The first is that the textual evidence is inferior to physical evidence. And the second supposition is

19. The history of the Church's thinking on this issue, discussed in chapters 1, 2, and 3 of this volume, shows this to be the case.

20. The RATE Group engaged in the following pioneering research on radioisotope dating. Austin and Snelling applied all four long-age radioisotope dating methods to the same rock unit. Snelling also exhaustively studied polonium radiohalos in biotite in granodiorite and fission tracks in volcanic tuff. Humphreys developed an alternative geochronometer from a previously ignored by-product of radioactive decay, helium, by measuring the helium "leak rate" as a function of temperature. Baumgardner applied carbon-14 dating techniques to diamonds. Chaffin developed new nuclear decay models to account for accelerated decay. The results of their experimental, field, and theoretical research are dumbfounding. They found that a previously unknown phenomenon, accelerated decay of radioactive isotopes, occurred in the past. This means that the age of a rock cannot be derived from radioisotope dating methods. Moreover, the presence of helium in zircon crystals, radiohalos from short-half-lived polonium in biotite, and carbon-14 in diamonds prove that the earth is thousands, not billions, of years old. For the technical discussions of the RATE scientists' projects and findings see their chapters in *RATE II*. For a technical summary of the RATE Group's findings, see Vardiman's concluding chapter in *RATE II*, p. 735–772. For a less technical layman's summary, see Donald DeYoung, *Thousands, not Billions: Challenging an Icon of Evolution, Questioning the Age of the Earth* (Green Forest, AR: Master Books, 2005).

that an anti-supernatural bias allows for an objective evaluation of the evidence, which will lead us to the truth. Belief in the supernatural, it is claimed, distorts a person's ability to ascertain the truth.

Let us consider the validity of the first of these. The idea that Scripture is not a reliable source of scientific and historical information is an elaborate super-structure built on the most arbitrary, flimsiest and — on the face of it — most fatuous and contumacious of philosophical presuppositions: God's statements are not admissible in the question of origins!

This ephemeral foundation was laid even before the Enlightenment. In 1615, Galileo wrote to the Grand Duchess Christina that the intention of the Bible is "to teach how one goes to heaven not how heaven goes."[21] The implication of this audacious assertion is that the Bible, God's revealed message to man, whom He created in His image so that he could rule over His creation, offers no contribu-tion to man's understanding of His creation! He argued in a different context that not only should the Bible not be used to judge scientific theories but also that those theories should be used to judge the Bible:

> Nothing physical which sense experience sets before our eyes, or which necessary demonstrations prove to us, ought to be called in ques-tion . . . upon the testimony of biblical passages which may have some different meaning beneath their words. . . . On the contrary, having ar-rived at any certainties in physics, we ought to utilize these as the most appropriate aids in the true exposition of the Bible.[22]

Francis Bacon expressed similar ideas:

> For our Saviour sayeth, "You err, not knowing the Scriptures, nor the power of God;" laying before us two books or volumes to study, if we will be secured from error; first the Scriptures, revealing the will of God and then the creatures expressing his power; whereof *the latter is the key unto the former* [emphasis mine].[23]

But the 18th-century philosopher Emanuel Kant (who offered "the most

---

21. Cited by Terry Mortenson, *The Great Turning Point: the Church's Catastrophic Mistake on Geology — Before Darwin* (Green Forest, AR: Master Books, 2004), p. 20.

22. Ibid., p. 20–21. Contrast this statement of Galileo and those of Bacon and Kant below with Article XII of the Affirmations and Denials of the Chicago Statement on Bibli-cal Inerrancy, which clearly states: "We **affirm** that Scripture in its *entirety* is inerrant, being free from all falsehood, fraud, or deceit. We **deny** that biblical infallibility and inerrancy are limited to spiritual, religious, or redemptive themes, exclusive of asser-tions in the fields of history and science. *We further **deny** that scientific hypotheses about earth history may properly be used to overturn the teaching of Scripture on creation and the flood*" [italics mine] (from R.C. Sproul, *Explaining Inerrancy* [Orlando, FL: Ligonier Ministries, 1996], p. 36). Interestingly, many of the participants at the Chicago summit on inerrancy at which this article was crafted were old-earth creationists.

23. Mortenson, *The Great Turning Point*, p. 21.

clear-cut descriptions of the entire century to be found anywhere"[24]) went much further than Galileo and Bacon by asserting that if the Bible was not brought to the bar of human reason and passed its judicial review, then it could not lay claim to sincere respect:

> Our age is the age of criticism, to which everything must be sub-jected. The sacredness of religion, and the authority of legislation, are by many regarded as grounds of exemption from the examination of this tribunal. But if they are exempted, they become the subjects of just suspi-cion, and cannot lay claim to sincere respect, which reason accords only to that which has stood the test of a free and public examination.[25]

But these men were wrong! It is arrogant to suggest that the plain statements of the Word of God should stand at the bar of man's transient scientific theories or that the incomprehensible profundities of God's revelation should have to stand up to a way of human reasoning which *a priori* is forbidden to appeal to the supernatural and is therefore made incapable of plumbing Scripture's depths! The Bible does not just teach us how to go to heaven but also how the heavens go!

There is real content in the biblical texts that deal with matters commonly considered to be the exclusive jurisdiction of scientists and historians. These biblical texts are not vacuous, ripe to be filled with whatever meaning their reader chooses. Their words are not bereft of meaning; they correspond to reality. In matters of history, they do more than say *that* something happened; they actually tell us *what* happened, in what order, and when. And when *properly* read they yield a treasure trove — largely untapped by scientists — of God's perspective on His creation. In particular, for the geologists, physicists and geophysicist on the RATE team, the assumption that the biblical chronology is correct led them to postulate a ground-breaking theory in physics and geology, accelerated radioisotope decay. They then designed experiments to test for its existence, and consequently discovered that it did indeed happen in the past.

But I will go even further than to contradict the statements of Galileo, Ba-con, and Kant. I maintain that we cannot rightly understand how the heavens go *unless* we see them through God's perspective and, conversely, that *a priori* exclusion of this biblical evidence will actually mislead scientists into drawing the wrong conclusions. In other words, the physical evidence cannot be prop-erly understood unless it is coupled with and interpreted through the divine perspective. This is the meaning of Proverbs 1:7a, "The fear of the LORD is the beginning of *knowledge*" (emphasis mine). But it is two additional texts which decisively quash the two suppositions concerning the relationship between text

---

24. J. Hayes and F. Prussner, *Old Testament Theology: Its History and Development* (Atlanta, GA: John Knox Press, 1985), p. 53.
25. From Emanuel Kant, *Critique of Pure Reason*, p. 15 (as cited by Hayes and Prussner, *Old Testament Theology*, p. 53).

and empirical evidence: Joshua 4:1–9 and 2 Kings 6:8–12.

1.2 Joshua 4:1–9. The Indispensable Role of Text as an Interpretive Grid

This text illustrates how the Lord views physical evidence that He caused to be put in place and thereby demonstrates that divine revelation is necessary to correctly interpret empirical evidence. Consequently, this invalidates the first supposition.

This account of the relocation of 24 stones is noteworthy. After the nation had crossed the dry riverbed of what had been the roiling Jordan at flood-stage and while the priests were still standing in the middle of it, carrying the ark of the covenant, Joshua ordered at God's behest that stones be placed as memorials to the miraculous parting of the river, which reprised the crossing of the Red Sea a generation before. Twelve men, one from each tribe, were to take stones from the midst of the Jordan riverbed and place them on its western bank. In addition, they were to carry stones from the western bank and pile them in the riverbed at the very spot where the priests were standing. And finally, in a frame-break (an author's direct address to his contemporary readers) Joshua told his readers that the stones were still there — a claim they easily could confirm or confute.

What was the purpose for these two piles of stones? Apart from the divine signifying of their meaning, the Israelites who were there and particularly their descendants who would follow — let alone our generation — could only have guessed. But we are not left bewildered, nor were they. The answer is given in the text:

> . . . in order that this might be a sign in your midst. When your sons ask tomorrow, 'What are these stones to you?' Then you will say to them that the waters of the Jordan were cut off from before the ark of the covenant of the LORD when it passed through the Jordan. So the waters of the Jordan were cut off. And these stones will become a memorial to the Israelites in perpetuity" (Josh. 4:6–7).

This brings out the point alluded to above: the divine interpretation is necessary to understand the meaning of the physical evidence.

The stones provided a durable memorial, which theoretically could have lasted forever, provided they were not moved. Yet, the Lord commanded that the significance of the memorials was to be conveyed to subsequent generations when (not if) they asked the question, "What do these stones mean?" In fact, they would be perpetual signs and memorials. Although the stones are long gone from both the bank and center of the river, the record of their placement is their lasting memorial.

We are now in the position to extract a principle applicable to our study. God has given us two witnesses to everything He has done: tangible physical evidence and His Word. As far as the former is concerned, men must convert evidence into words for it to be accessible and coherent, and then added to the body of knowledge. But the latter is already in words, positioned to test the conclusions men draw from the physical evidence. The witnesses are innately unequal in value: the Bible trumps science, not the other way around, as is customarily thought.

1.3 Second Kings 6:8–12. The Inevitable Result of Anti-Supernatural Presuppositions

The second supposition is that an anti-supernatural bias allows for an objective evaluation of the evidence, which will lead us to the truth. But 2 Kings 6:8–12 shows us that just the opposite is the case: such a bias will mislead the seeker of truth!

According to the text, Ben Hadad, the king of Aram, held secret strategy meetings with his generals to set ambushes against the army of Israel. Likely, he was attempting to kill or capture Joram, the king of Israel at that time. But his every attempt at ambushing the army of Israel was thwarted by Elisha, who having been informed by the Lord about the location of the ambush, warned Joram. The latter sent scouts each time to confirm that an ambush had been set at the location told to him by the prophet. The king of Aram was completely frustrated and drew the conclusion that anyone would draw *if the possibility of supernatural intervention is not even entertained*: one of his men was a spy for the king of Israel! How else could the king of Israel know the location of his camp? Gathering his highest officials together and not knowing the identity of the putative traitor and assuming that he could not have acted alone or at least not without the knowledge of the others, he effectively and collectively accused them all of treason, hoping no doubt that one of his officials would break and divulge the identity of the turncoat in order to mitigate his own punishment. One of his officials did speak up, but not to unmask a betrayer. Rather, he wanted to quickly disabuse the king of his line of reasoning, to correct the king, a thing normally not done. But the situation was not normal. This was no time for the usual sycophantic prattle to the king. The king was looking for a scapegoat to assuage his fury. So the man blurted out to the king, to which he immediately appended, "My lord, the king," to lessen the audacity of his outburst. He was saying in essence, "Your assessment of this situation is wrong, O my lord, the king. There is something going on here that you have not considered: a prophet of Israel can tell the king of Israel what you say in your most private moments!" Ben Hadad's blind rage then turned toward Elisha, whom God protected in an extraordinary way, dispatching a heavenly army to surround the army of Aram.

Consequently, Ben Hadad's initial interpretation of the evidence, as he saw it, was completely wrong, because *a priori* he had excluded any supernatural explanation for what he was observing. And so it is with all anti-supernatural bias: it leads to faulty, rather than accurate, interpretation of the evidence.

Having employed the Scriptures to dispense with these suppositions, we now turn to examine the genre of the creation account.

2. Characteristics of the Text

2.1 Literal Historical Account

The proof that Genesis 1:1–2:3 is a literal historical account has three parts. Part one is a statistically rigorous, irrefutable proof that it is narrative. Part two is a literary argument, in which a ponderous weight of evidence is adduced, which shows that authors of biblical narratives believed that they were referring to real events. Part three is an argument from the doctrine of inspiration.

2.1.1 Statistical Determination of the Genre of Genesis 1:1–2:3.

Elsewhere I have surveyed Hebraists' descriptions of biblical Hebrew poetry and narrative and concluded that their qualitative approach has failed to precisely distinguish these two genres.[26] I developed a quantitative alternative therefore to distinguish the genres, a statistical method applied to Hebrew finite verbs,[27] which can determine the genre of Hebrew texts to a high degree of accuracy. This statistical study consisted of seven steps.[28] [Editor's note: This section outlines the procedure of the statistical study detailed in *RATE* chapter and concludes with its findings (the last two paragraphs of this section 2.1.1)].

The first step was to use the descriptions of narrative and poetry, which are found in the literature, to identify all narrative and poetic texts in the Hebrew Bible. This population of 522 texts consists of 295 narrative texts and 227 poetic texts.

The second step was to generate a stratified, random joint-sample of 48

---

26. *RATE* chapter, p. 642–648.

27. The biblical Hebrew verb forms marked for person (1st person [I, we], 2nd person [you] and 3rd person [he, she, it, they]) as well as gender and number are *qatal* (perfect), *w³qatal* (waw-perfect), *yiqtol* (imperfect) and *wayyiqtol* (preterite). The translation possibilities for the verbal root שׁמע *šmᶜ* ("hear") in past tense narrative are as follows: for *qatal,* "he heard" or "he had heard" ("tense" determined by context; this form is usually not at the beginning of a clause or sentence); for *w³qatal,* "he would hear" (must be at the beginning of a clause or sentence); for *yiqtol* (usually not at the beginning of a clause or sentence), "he would hear"; and for *wayyiqtol,* "he heard" (must be at the beginning of the clause or sentence). For a discussion of the suitability of finite verbs for this analysis see *RATE* chapter, p. 650–651; 720–721 n. 39.

28. What follows in this section is a simplified explanation of my statistical study. The details along with very helpful graphs and tables can be found in *RATE* chapter, p. 650–676, and 693–704, appendices A, B, and C. All of the following are from *RATE* chapter: the details of the mathematical analysis of the classification accuracy, p. 669–674; the most dramatic visualization of the contrast between narrative and poetry, p. 658–659 figure 4 and 660–661 figure 5, respectively; the distribution of the relative frequency of *wayyiqtols* varying with genre (p. 662 figure 8); the logistic regression curve used to predict the genre of texts from the joint-sample of known genres (p. 667 figure 9); the prediction accuracy (p. 668 table 1); and, finally, the band of possible logistic regression curves for the entire population of texts at a 99.5% confidence level and where Genesis 1:1–2:3 falls on this curve (p. 674, figure 10). I will cite further specific sections of *RATE* chapter in the abbreviated discussion below.

narrative texts and 49 poetic texts.[29]

The third step was to calculate the different ratios among the finite verbs for each text and test to see if the distribution of these ratios were significantly different enough to use them to predict whether a given text within the sample was narrative or poetry.

The fourth step was to develop a logistic regression (LR)[30] classification model for different ratios in order to test the null hypothesis against the alternative hypothesis.[31] My null hypothesis was that there is no logistic regression model derived from these ratios that classifies texts any better than random classification. Conversely, my alternative hypothesis was that there is a logistic regression model derived from these ratios that classifies texts better than random classification. Subsequent analysis showed that the ratio of *wayyiqtol*s to the total number of finite verbs yielded the best classification model.[32] So the null hypothesis was refined, accordingly.

The fifth step was to classify all the texts in the joint sample using the model logistic curve, which was generated from the ratios of *wayyiqtol*s to finite verbs for these texts.[33]

The sixth step was to compare the classifications by the model to the actual classifications. The results were astonishing. The model classified 95 of the 97 texts correctly (either as narrative or poetry), which is an extraordinary level of accuracy, and allowed us to reject the null hypothesis at a highly significant statistical level. It was also determined that the model reduced classification errors at an extremely high level. All in all, the model is a superb classifier of texts within the sample.[34] But the sample, by design, did not include Genesis

---

29. This is a random sample of narrative and poetic texts, generated by a statistical program, which ensured that the texts to be analyzed represented all portions of the Hebrew Scriptures: the Torah, the Prophets (both former and latter) and the Writings. For further explanation and the raw data, see *RATE* chapter, p. 657 and 698–702, appendix B.

30. A type of statistical analysis suited for two-value data. More precisely, a non-linear regression model, based on the log of the odds $(P/(1-P))$, where P is the probability of the occurrence of an event. LR is ideal for categorical data — when there are only limited values for the dependent variable (in our case, two: narrative vs. poetry). For further details, see *RATE* chapter, p. 663–665 and references and discussions in *RATE* chapter, p. 721–722, endnotes 43–51; and *The Oxford Dictionary of Statistical Terms* (*ODST*), s.v. "logistic regression."

31. A *null hypothesis* is a testable hypothesis formulated in a statistical analysis, which "determines the probability of the type I error" (*ODST*, s.v. "null hypothesis"). A *type I error* is the rejection of a hypothesis when in fact it is true (*ODST*, s.v. "type I error"). Rejection of the null hypothesis means acceptance of the alternative hypothesis. For the full statements of the null hypothesis and alternative hypothesis that I employed, see *RATE* chapter, p. 657.

32. For a description of the models see *RATE* chapter, p. 665-666.

33. The logistic curve derived from the raw data was used to classify the texts of the joint-sample (see *RATE* chapter, p. 667, figure 9).

34. See further *RATE* chapter, p. 667–669. This conclusion arises from a statistical analysis

1:1–2:3.

A seventh step was necessary therefore to extend the results from the level of the sample to the level of the population, which included Genesis 1:1–2:3. My findings in this step were that the probability that Genesis 1:1–2:3 is narrative is between .999942 and .999987 at a 99.5 percent confidence level. I conclude therefore that *it is statistically indefensible to argue that this text is poetry.*[35]

Having proven that the Genesis text is certainly narrative, we now turn to examine the implications of that finding. And in order to understand the intention of the author of this text with regards to his narrative, we will look at the perspective biblical authors at large had toward the events to which they refer in their narratives.

2.1.2 Literary Argument

In *RATE* chapter I adduce 15 proofs that authors of biblical narratives considered that their narratives referred to real events.[36] But below I will sketch only ten: (1) customs are elucidated, (2) ancient names and current sayings are traced back to their origins, (3) monuments and pronouncements are assigned a concrete reason as well as a slot in history, (4) historical footnotes are sprinkled throughout the text, (5) written records used as sources are cited, (6) precise chronological reference points are supplied, (7) genealogies are given, (8) prophetic utterances are recalled and related to events in the narrative, (9) "time words" invite ancient readers to validate historical claims made in the text, and (10) historical "trajectories" link different portions of the text and widely separate historical periods.[37]

(1) Customs are elucidated.[38] Authors would have had little reason to

---

of the classification accuracy (*RATE* chapter, p. 669–674).

35. See the conclusions of the statistical study in *RATE* chapter, p. 675–676.

36. The complete list in *RATE* chapter is: (1) God's people are defined in terms of their past; (2) God's people are commanded to keep the memory of their past alive; (2) God's people engage in retrospection on their past; (4) the remembrance of the past devolves on the present and determines the future; (5) customs are elucidated; (6) ancient names and current sayings are traced back to their origins; (7) monuments and pronouncements are assigned a concrete reason as well as a slot in history; (8) historical footnotes are sprinkled throughout the text; (9) written records used as sources are cited; (10) precise chronological reference points are supplied; (11) genealogies are given; (12) observations of cultic days and seasons are called acts of commemoration; (13) prophetic utterances are recalled and related to events in the narrative; (14) "time words" challenge ancient readers to validate historical claims made in the text; and (15) historical "trajectories" link different portions of the text and widely separate historical periods. The details are found in *RATE* chapter, p. 676–690 and 705–712 (Appendix D, Tables D1–D8).

37. The discussions below are based on the originals in *RATE* chapter, the locations of which will be given in the notes.

38. Details and more examples of narrative texts exhibiting this characteristic are in *RATE* chapter, p. 677–678.

elucidate customs if they were not convinced of their historicity. As a first example, consider the explanation given for a dietary exclusion: it was originated to memorialize when God dislocated Jacob's hip with a touch while they wrestled (Gen. 32:26, 32–33).

A second elucidated custom involved the removal of a sandal, which signified that a kinsman redeemer had refused to engage in levirate marriage, that is, a brother's duty to raise up children for his heirless, deceased brother, by marrying his widow (Deut. 25:5–10). In Ruth 4:7, the author explains this custom, which the author thought might not have been familiar to the reader. The custom is introduced with the phrase, "This was (the way) formerly in Israel concerning redemption and exchange, to confirm any word: a man would draw off his sandal." The word "formerly" suggests that the custom was not practiced in the author's day — a fact that the author deemed important for his readers to know (Ruth 4:8).[39]

The third custom is discussed in 1 Samuel 30. Upon returning to Ziklag, David discovered that a band of Amalekites had raided and kidnapped his family. He and his six hundred men immediately set off after the criminals. Arriving at the Wadi Besor, two hundred of his men were too exhausted to continue on. Four hundred continued with David. After slaughtering all but four hundred of the Amalekites (who had escaped on camels) and rescuing his family, David returned to the two hundred who had remained behind and shared the booty with them against the protests of some of the four hundred. The author of the text offered this account in part to explain that the custom, that those who stayed with the supplies would receive the same portion of the booty as those who fought in the battle, originated in an order from David, issued at that time (1 Sam. 30:24–25).

(2) Ancient names and current sayings are traced back to their origins. A biblical author frequently explained how a place received its name by appealing to the historical context in which the naming occurred. Often this name persisted in the author's day. It is clear that the author expected his readers would be interested in the explanation of the origin of names current in their day. Also, historical tracings of the origins of sayings are attested in many passages.[40]

(3) Monuments and pronouncements are assigned a concrete reason as well as a slot in history.[41] Biblical authors frequently explained the purposes for the placement of monuments, which often involved the naming of these monuments. Four of these stand out. First, there is the dual naming of Gilead. Laban gave it an Aramaic name; Jacob, its Hebrew name (Gen. 31:44–54). Second,

---

39. See proof (9) below for further discussion on authorial claims of discontinuity, such as this.

40. A few passages proving this point are Genesis 4:17; Numbers 11:4–34; Deuteronomy 3:14; Joshua 7:26; Judges 1:26; 2 Samuel 6:8; 1 Kings 9:13; 2 Kings 14:7; and 1 Chronicles 13:11. For many more examples and a thorough discussion of this point see *RATE* chapter, p. 682 and 705–706 (Table D2).

41. An expansion on the following discussion and more examples of narrative texts exhibiting this characteristic are in *RATE* chapter, p. 682–684.

monuments were created to mark the crossing of the Jordan (Josh. 4:1–9). Third, a cairn was erected over the corpses of Achan and his family (Josh. 7:25–26). And fourth, in Joshua 14:6–14 we are given the explanation of how Caleb obtained his inheritance.

Biblical authors also explained why things were the way they were in their day. Three examples of this will suffice. The first concerns Israel; the other two do not, and, in fact, take place outside of the land of Israel. All three accounts move us to ask the question how did the author know this? The first, although it involves Israel, is about a non-Israelite, Rahab. The author anticipated and supplied the answer to the question: how did a non-Israelite former prostitute end up living in their midst (Josh. 6:25)?

The second story explains why the lands and crops of the Egyptian people and the people themselves belonged to Pharaoh in the author's day, but the priests were not so subjected (Gen. 47:13–22).

The third story recounts how the Lord degraded, defeated, and destroyed Dagon after the Philistines defeated Israel at the Battle of Aphek. They captured the ark of the covenant, brought it to Ashdod, and inferring that Israel's humiliation implied that Dagon had defeated the Lord, positioned the ark next to the statue of Dagon to proclaim his victory. But it was the Lord who was victorious and the fallen trunk of the idol, headless and handless on his dais, precluded his priests from treading on his dais even in the author's day.[42]

(4) Historical footnotes are sprinkled throughout the text. In most cases, details of the narrative, which at first appear to be tangential to the narrative turn out not to be so.[43] Our concern here is those instances in which we cannot ascertain how a detail impinges on the development of the narrative. This historical information — supplied apparently for the benefit of the interested reader — can be divided into three categories: details concerning persons, details about places, and miscellaneous details. One example from the first category is the information recorded in Deuteronomy 2:10–11: the name which the Moabites called the former inhabitants of their land. An example from the second category is that Hebron was *formerly* called *Qiryat Arba* (Josh. 14:15; Judg. 1:10). And an example from the third category is that we are informed of the lyrics of Heshbon's previous victory chant over the Moabites (Num. 21:26–30).[44]

(5) Written records used as sources are cited. Not surprisingly, there are references made to the Book of the Law of Moses (Josh. 8:31; 23:6; 2 Kings 14:6; Neh. 8:1), the Book of Moses (2 Chron. 35:12; Ezra 6:18), the Book of the Law

---

42. See proof (9) below for a discussion on testable authorial claims of continuity, such as this.

43. Narrative studies argue — and for the most part, correctly — that inclusion of details in the text is driven by the plot of the narrative (*RATE* chapter, p. 724 endnotes 59 and 60).

44. For many more examples and a thorough discussion of this point, see *RATE* chapter, p. 684 and 706 (Table D3).

of God (Josh. 24:26), the Book of the Law (Josh. 8:34), the Book of the Law of the Lord (2 Chron. 17:9) and the Book of the Covenant (2 Kings 23:21).[45]

(6) Precise chronological reference points are supplied. The Bible begins with an account locked into time. A prominent feature of the creation account in Genesis 1:1–2:3 is the steady sequence of six days (explicitly marked off by the phrase "evening was; morning was: Xth day" after God's creative acts on each of the first six days). Consider four of the many examples like this. First, the five fixed dates pertaining to the Flood are referenced to the years of Noah's life (Gen. 7:6, 11; 8:4–5, 13–14). A second example (and there are many of this type) is Sarah's age given at her death (Gen. 23:1–2). A third, well-known example is the year of the Exodus given with reference to the year Solomon began to build the Temple (1 Kings 6:1). A fourth is that "in the fourteenth year of king Hezekiah, Sennacherib the king of Assyria came up against all the fortified cities of Judah and seized them" (Isa. 36:1).[46]

(7) Genealogies are given. This preoccupation with the progenitors of the past is not gratuitous; rather, it serves at least three historiographic purposes. Alone or often intertwined with narrative,[47] these genealogies serve to *structure* history, *survey* history, and *support* history. Taking these in turn and offering one example of each, genealogies (such as Gen. 4) furnish a type of historical record for a given a historical period. Sometimes no events are recorded. In these cases they therefore provide the actual *structure* of history. Moreover, when long periods of time are to be covered (such as in 1 Chron. 1–9), genealogies can *survey* history. And finally, they can *support* history, such as in linking David to Judah through Perez; thus, legitimizing his reign (Gen. 49:10; Ruth 4:18).[48]

(8) Past prophetic utterances are recalled.[49] With this rubric and the two that follow, the bi-directionality of the biblical time-line is established and aligned with a largely continuous narrative from Genesis 1:1 through Nehemiah 13:31. We begin by looking at the time-line in two directions. The first direction is an orientation toward the prophet's future. When reporting declarations about the future, the biblical authors often explicitly linked prophetic statements to particular contexts. But by the nature of things, verification of a prophet's authenticity by this measure was only possible after the fact. Mentions of such verifications are rare in the text and are significant therefore when they occur. When an author from a later time and further along in the development of the canon of Scripture mentioned a fulfillment of a prophetic pronouncement, he makes us focus on the second direction, an orientation toward the past (both his

---

45. For a thorough discussion of this point see *RATE* chapter, p. 684 and 707 (Table D4).
46. For many more examples and a thorough discussion of this point see *RATE* chapter, p.684–685 and 708–709 (Table D5).
47. I.e., with narrative imbedded in genealogies or genealogies imbedded in narrative.
48. For more examples and discussion see *RATE* chapter, p. 685 and 710 (Table D6).
49. The following discussion is an expansion of *RATE* chapter, p. 685–686.

and that of his characters), in particular the context, which provoked the initial utterance. We will look at four: three cursorily; one in detail.

The first three are these. Joshua had cursed anyone who would rebuild Jericho (Josh. 6:26) and the fulfillment was announced after the death of the sons of Hiel, who rebuilt Jericho (1 Kings 16:34). The second is a prophet's decree that Eli's line would be removed from the priesthood (1 Sam. 2:31) with the fulfillment announced after the banishment of Abiathar (1 Kings 2:27). Third, Daniel prayed that the Lord would repatriate the nation (Dan. 9:2–19), because he recalled that Jeremiah had prophesied that the duration of the captivity would be 70 years (Jer. 25:11–12).

The fourth example is the link between the prophecy concerning Josiah and its fulfillment. This was fully developed by the author in 1 Kings. Not only did the narrator point out the connection between prophecy and fulfillment, as in the first two examples above, but also one of the characters in the story makes the observation. So an unnamed man of God cursed the altar at Bethel, which Jeroboam, the first king of the northern kingdom of Israel, was consecrating. He said: "O Altar, O Altar, thus the Lord says, 'Indeed a son will be born to the House of David — Josiah, his name — and he will offer upon you the priests of the high places, who burn sacrifices on you, and human bones will be burned on you'" (1 Kings 13:2). Three hundred years later Josiah was not only zealously removing the pagan altars and high places from his kingdom, but also desecrating them (2 Kings 23). At Bethel, he ordered that bones from the tombs be burned on the altar. The author of 2 Kings comments: "So he defiled it according to the word of the Lord which the man of God, who had proclaimed these words, had proclaimed" (2 Kings 23:16). Subsequently, when Josiah inquired about the identity of a monument, the inhabitants of that city answered, "It is the tomb of the man of God, who came from Judah. He proclaimed these things which you have done against the altar at Bethel (verse 17)." Josiah, out of respect, ordered that the bones of the man of God not be disturbed.

(9) The use of "time words" to explicitly indicate testable temporal continuity or discontinuity. Biblical authors could have told their stories without making any connections to their present. And thus their texts would only have been unverifiable tales — riveting, to be sure — but of little historical interest.[50] But they did just the opposite, anchoring their stories to testable and therefore falsifiable claims. Indeed, their express statements linking the past to their present or severing the present from the past was a risky business if they did not

---

50. This rubric militates against those biblical historians who maintain, as Ian Provan states, that biblical narratives depict a "'fictive world,' entire in itself and referring only to itself. Its integrity must not be compromised by seeking to relate it to anything outside itself." On the contrary, it is obvious that the author went out of his way to relate his history to his readers' time by breaking away from his narrative and addressing his readers directly (called "breaking frame"). Provan's quote is cited by Michael Grisanti, *BibSac* 161 (April–June 2004): p. 167.

know their facts! In essence, they were challenging their contemporary readers to disprove their claims.[51]

Two classes of temporal markers are attested which link at least two separate times, the author's present and his past. The first group of time words indicates temporal continuity with the past. The most common of these is עַד הַיּוֹם הַזֶּה , "until this day." A special case of this class are those accounts which also include the phrase לְמִיּוֹם, "since the day," or its equivalent, because it suggests an uninterrupted continuity. The more common "until this day," on the other hand, allows for a break in continuity as long as it was reestablished by the author's time. As a result, the special case would be "easier" for a reader, who was a contemporary of the author, to falsify. The second group of time words marks discontinuity with the past. The most important word in this class is לְפָנִים, "formerly." We will look at these in turn below.

Our first examples from the continuity class are remarkable statements in which Moses claimed knowledge of Egyptian history. Commenting on the unprecedented phenomenon of the fiery hail to come, Moses said, "There has not been like it in Egypt since it was founded until now" (Exod. 9:18). And in describing the severity of the locust plague to come, Moses said, ". . . which neither your fathers nor your fathers' fathers have seen since they were upon the land (of Egypt) until this day" (10:6).

The following are three more from the Book of Joshua, in which he noted situations that obtained during his time, the truth of which could have been easily tested: Ai was still in ruins after Joshua destroyed it (Josh. 8:28); the corpse of its king was still buried under the same pile of rocks, which Joshua had heaped on him (8:29); and the Hivites who lived in Gibeon, who through a clever (and desperate) ruse, had duped Joshua into making a covenant with them, were still a servant class of "hewers of wood" and "drawers of water" in Israel (9:27).

The author(s) of the Books of Samuel also made additional historically verifiable statements about his (their) day: the deposition of the ark of the covenant (1 Sam. 6:18) and Ziklag still belonged to the kings of Judah (27:6).

Turning to the Book of Kings we discover more of the same type of claims — some of them quite interesting. The ark was placed in the temple, with its long axis in line with that of the temple's long axis (1 Kings 8:8). Solomon had incorporated all foreign enclaves into a greater Israel (9:20–21). Israel had seceded from Judah, forming the northern kingdom of Israel (12:19). Water, which had been miraculously purified by Elisha, was still potable (2 Kings 2:22). Moab had

---

51. Sternberg comments: "Whatever the truth value of the references and explanations made, their very making strengthens the truth claim by anchoring the discourse in public and accessible features of reality. 'You see how the traces of time within our observation make perfect sense within our account of time,' the narrator seems to be saying to his audience. . . . the present witnesses lend an air of truth to the evocation of the past from which they issued" (Sternberg, *The Poetics of Biblical Narrative*, p. 31–32).

broken away from Judah (8:22). Rezin, the king of Aram had forcibly removed the Judahites from Eilat and subsequently, the city had been occupied by the Edomites (16:6).[52]

Now we turn to the discontinuity class. By using the term "formerly," a biblical author was stating that the present names, customs, sayings, and situations, which were familiar to his readers, were different in the past. Although not verifiable, the very mention of these differences enforces the historical nature of the account. As I mentioned above, why would the author go to the trouble of concocting an elaborate past, which would only tangentially engage his readers. If there were only a few of these it would be one thing. But in fact, there are many.[53]

(10) Historical trajectories. This is perhaps the most interesting characteristic of the Old Testament's historiographic presentation. I call this category *historical trajectories*, because certain people, statements, and ideas were projected with such great force in the first five books of the Bible that their trace is found through large expanses of text and time. Outside of the obvious promises made to the patriarchs are the not so obvious — but very important — trajectory of Joseph's bones, the enigma of Balaam, the Lord's dogged pursuit of the Amalekites,[54] and the checkered history of Moab and Ammon. We will only look at the first and last of these, beginning at the deathbed of Joseph.

Recognizing that he was to die soon, Joseph asserted that God would intervene on their behalf and bring them up from Egypt and into the land, which He swore to Abraham, to Isaac, and to Jacob (Gen. 50:24). Moreover, repeating his assertion and even strengthening it ("God will surely intervene") in an act of faith reminiscent of his father's, Joseph charged his family to not leave his bones in Egypt (Gen. 50:25). But Genesis ends with Joseph embalmed in a sarcophagus in Egypt.

We do not hear again the slightest rattle of these bones until suddenly they are clanking quite loudly at the Exodus: "Moses took the bones of Joseph with

---

52. The only difference of the Hebrew names for the Arameans and the Edomites is ד (*daleth*) versus ר (*resh*). In the history of the Hebrew language — and evidenced in the preceding sentence in this note — the shape of *daleth* has closely resembled (and in some cases been identical to) the shape of *resh* in all periods (cf. Ada Yardeni, *The Book of Hebrew Script: History, Paleography, Script Styles, Caligraphy and Design* [London: The British Library and New Castle, DE: Oak Knoll Press, 2002], p. 2, figure 1). Paleographical considerations cannot resolve the textual problem. Nevertheless, "Edomites" — rather than "Arameans" — is the preferred reading based upon the context, since the author described Tiglath Pileser III's destruction of Aram in the next paragraph in the text.

53. Examples of the second class are Deuteronomy 2:10, 12, 20; Joshua 11:10, 14:15, 15:15; Judges 1:10–11, 23, 3:2; Ruth 4:7; 1 Samuel 9:9; 1 Chronicles 4:40, 9:20; 2 Chronicles 9:11; and Nehemiah 13:5. For more examples of the first class and a thorough discussion of this point see *RATE* chapter, p. 686 and 712 (Table D8).

54. An expansion on the following discussion and a tracing of Balaam and the Amalekites through the Scripture are in *RATE* chapter, p. 686–690.

him, because he had clearly made the children of Israel take an oath, 'God will surely intervene for you, then you will bring out my bones from this place with you'" (Exod. 13:19).

Again there was silence, and the skeleton quietly hung in the closet until the children of Israel buried it back in the land: "And the bones of Joseph, which the children of Israel had brought up from the land of Egypt, they buried in the portion of the field, which Jacob had purchased from Hamor, the father of Shechem for one hundred pieces of silver" (Josh. 24:32). The burial of Joseph's bones, a historical closure, completed an *inclusio*[55] in the narrative. That is, Joseph was the first son of Jacob to leave the land and with his burial he was the final son to return.

For a second example, we will trace back to the patriarchal period the checkered history of Moab and Ammon. What is most significant about this trajectory is the way in which later texts refer to incidents reported in earlier texts, forming the links of a chain that goes back to the origin of these peoples. The author of Chronicles has the latest mention of Moab and the sons of Ammon. He looks back to the time in which Jehoshaphat — pleading for the Lord to deliver Judah from an invading horde which included Moabites and Ammonites, made the following biting observation: "So now as far as the sons of Ammon, Moab and Mount Seir are concerned, among whom you would not allow Israel to enter, when they came from Egypt, with the result that they turned aside from them and did not destroy them, they would recompense us by coming and driving us from your possession, which you caused us to possess" (2 Chron. 20:10–12). The original records of these divine prohibitions are found in Deuteronomy 2:9 and 19. Concerning Moab, the Lord said, "Do not harm Moab and do not stir up strife for battle against them, because I have not given you any of his land as a possession; because to the sons of Lot I have given Ar as a possession (2:9)." The Lord's prohibition regarding Ammon is almost identical (2:19). These texts look back to the time just before the children of Israel arrived at the plains of Moab. They had just defeated the Canaanites and Amalekites at Hormah. Fresh from this victory and perhaps wanting more, Israel was eager to fight the Moabites and Ammonites, but the Lord forbad it. In explaining to them His reasons for this prohibition, He affirmed that they were sons of Lot. This of course takes us back to the story about Lot and his daughters told in Genesis 19. His daughters made Lot drunk on two successive nights. In his inebriated state he impregnated each of his daughters. Their sons by their father were the progenitors of the Moabites and the Ammonites.

The chain is complete. It extends back from the days of the author of Chronicles to the time of Jehoshaphat; from his time to the days before the Conquest; from the days before the Conquest to the patriarchal period.

The statistical study described above (section 2.1.1) established by mathematical rigor that Genesis 1:1–2:3 is narrative, not poetry. The just-concluded

---

55. *Inclusio* is a literary device whereby a section of Scripture (whether a few verses or many chapters) is framed by placing similar material at the beginning and end of a section.

literary arguments adduce a weight of evidence that makes it clear that the authors of these narratives believed that they were referring to real events. That is, narratives are historical narratives. As I have stated elsewhere, "Since Genesis 1:1–2:3 has the same genre as historical narrative texts and is linked lexically and thematically to these texts it *should* be read as these texts are read: as a realistic portrayal of the events."[56]

2.1.3 Doctrinal Argument

As modern readers, we are faced with a choice: to believe or not to believe that it happened the way the author described. *Should* we as readers believe what the authors wrote? If we are faithful to their presentation, we should. These historians do not allow us to be dispassionate observers of the past as we read their texts. They *compel us* to believe the past they portray. But *will* we believe what Genesis 1:1–2:3 then is clearly saying?

Sternberg forcefully argues:

> Were the narrative written or read as fiction, then God would turn from the lord of history into a creature of the imagination, with the most disastrous results. The shape of time, the rationale of monotheism, the foundations of conduct, the national sense of identity, the very right to the land of Israel, and the hope of deliverance to come: all hang in the generic balance. Hence, the Bible's determination to sanctify and compel literal belief in the past. It claims not just the status of history but . . . of *the* history, the one and only truth that, like God himself, brooks no rival . . . .*if as seekers for the truth, professional or amateur, we can take or leave the truth claim of inspiration, then as readers we must simply take it* — just like any other biblical premise or convention, from the existence of God to the sense borne by specific words — ***or else invent our own text***.[57]

Will we believe this text? Sternberg's words should challenge us as Christians to see that this text is meant to be read as a historical narrative. That was the intent of its human author, who carried out the intent of its divine Author. To read it any other way is to read it against His intent. So, to return to the question, will we believe this text? If we are faithful followers of Christ, we must.[58]

2.2 Magisterial Literary Composition

How does the text's magisterial literary composition interact with its proven historical literalness to inform our understanding of the text? It does so in at least two ways. First, our understanding must be informed by the realization that the author also wrote from a divine perspective, writing about

---

56. *RATE* chapter,*p.* 690–691. An expanded discussion is in *RATE* chapter, p. 690–692.
57. Sternberg, *The Poetics of Biblical Narrative,* p. 32–34. Italics are Sternberg's emphasis. The bold is my emphasis.
58. This is an abridgment of the conclusion of the *RATE* chapter, p. 690–692.

events absent of man or inaccessible to man, such as men's thoughts, events happening at a distance or hidden from men, and, of course, all the creation events of Genesis 1.

Secondly, our understanding must be tempered by the fact that we must read this text as its first readers would have read it.[59] The human author certainly wrote his text with his first readers in mind, but the timelessness of the text is testimony that the divine Author had a wider readership in mind. Nevertheless, our starting point must be the understanding of the first readers.

The procedure an author followed to write his text can be pictured as in figure 1. The author looked first at an event (1) and then at his original readers (2) in order to produce his text (3).[60]

Obviously, texts mean what words mean, but words mean what the original readers would have thought them to mean.[61] This is particularly the case with historical narratives.[62] Our consideration of these readers constrains us to approach the text cognizant of two caveats. The first is that the original readers were not scientists. The author therefore did not write a science textbook. And we should not approach it as a science textbook. What this means is that we should not expect it to have the wording of a so-called "precise" scientific description.

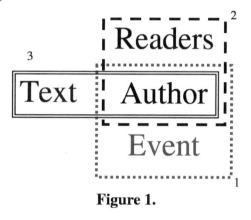

Figure 1.

The second caveat is that it was originally written to a 15th-century B.C. audience, whose perception of the world was limited to their five senses. They could not see microscopic organisms and structures with their naked eyes any more than we can. Only observations accessible to the unaided senses are discussed. The author employed therefore a phenomenological perspective in his writing,

---

59. See **Section 1** above and notes 3, 4, and 5.
60. For more discussion on the hermeneutical significance of the relationship of author to readers, see *RATE* chapter, p. 639–641 figure 1.
61. Although it is possible that we would understand the text better than the original readers, it is improbable, because unless later Old Testament texts or New Testament texts elucidate the text in question — all other things being equal — they knew the language and culture of their day better than we. And in light of this they should be our guide.
62. In historical narrative there is much less linguistic latitude than in poetic prophetic passages, which are frequently metaphorical, and thus more difficult to understand. I believe that in 1 Peter 1:10–12, Peter is referring to texts of the latter type.

consistent with the narrow linguistic constraints of historical narrative.[63] He described the world as it appears to the naked eye, heard by the ear, touched by the hand, smelled by the nose, and even tasted. Moreover, ideas utterly unknown to them because they are based in modern thought would have been utterly foreign to the readers' approach to the text.

Let us consider two examples in light of these caveats: the terminology used for sunset and the descriptions of the rock hyrax.[64]

2.2.1 Terminology for Sunset

The Hebrew expression for sunset, מְבוֹא הַשֶּׁמֶשׁ (mᵊḇôᵓ haššemeš) literally means "the entering place of the sun" (it is also one of the ways to indicate the direction west). Are we to infer from this that the ancient Hebrews erroneously understood that the sun orbited the earth? No! No more than our English expression *sunset* implies that the sun moves around the earth. Both of these are phenomenological language.

2.2.2 Descriptions of the Rock Hyrax

For a second example, we turn from astrophysics to zoology. According to Leviticus 11:5–6 and Deuteronomy 14:7, hyraxes were excluded from the ancient Israelite diet because they chew the cud[65] but do not have split hooves. But as a matter of fact, they are not true ruminants.[66] They do not regularly bring up partially digested food and re-chew it. Nevertheless, zoologists have observed them chewing some distance away from their browsing area.[67] But these scientists are equivocal on the reason for this chewing. Rahm says the animals ruminate.[68] What he means by this is unclear, since they do not have multiple stomachs.

---

63. Thus, for example, in Genesis 1:16–17 the Hebrew verbs עשׂה ("make, do, perform") and נתן ("give, place, allow") mean "make" and "place," respectively, in context.

64. Translated "cony" by the ASV, KJV, NIV and NJB; "badger" by the NAS and TNK; and "rock badger" by the ESV and NKJ, the שָׁפָן (šāpān), is the *Procavia capensis* of the family *Procaviidae,* order *Hyracoidea.* Immortalized by Agur in Proverbs 30:26 for their prowess among the crags (also in Psalm 104:18), these small mammals still today frequent rocky areas and can be seen gamboling about the boulder strewn ruins of the synagogue at Chorazin by the Sea of Galilee. For a defense of the identification of the *šāpān* as the rock hyrax, see Nosson Slifkin, *The Camel, the Hare and the Hyrax: A Study of The Laws of Animals with One Kosher Sign in Light of Modern Zoology* (Nanuet, NY: Targum Press, 2004), 99–105. Slifkin also definitively argues that the *šāpān* is not a rabbit, hare or jerboa (Slifkin, *The Camel, the Hare and the Hyrax,* p. 120–125).

65. Literally, "one which brings up" in Hebrew.

66. A *ruminant* is a mammal with four stomachs (sometimes only three), which allows it to digest cellulose in stages.

67. As Cansdale remarks: "The hyrax never seems to stop chewing as it sits outside of its hole and it could be easily said to ruminate" (George Cansdale, *All the Animals of Bible Lands* [Grand Rapids, MI: Zondervan, 1970], p. 130–131).

68. *Grzimek's Animal Life Encyclopedia*, Vol. 12, s.v. "hyraxes" (by Urs Rahm) [1975], p. 513–522, esp. 514.

Heock (from a later edition of the same encyclopedia) disagrees.[69]

Slifkin discusses three possible reasons why Scripture says hyraxes chew the cud in ruminant-like fashion: (1) they produce chewing motions unrelated to eating,[70] (2) they have a highly complex digestive system[71] and (3) they are engaging in *myrecism*.[72] What is significant is that it *appears* to be chewing the cud.

In any case, visual inspection is sufficient to show that they do not have split hooves.[73] They have four stubby digits on their front feet with hoof-like nails and three on the rear with the center toe having a claw. In short, because they appear to ruminate (or might actually ruminate) and do not have split hooves they were considered ceremonially impure.

2.3 Foundational Theological Treatise

And finally, we must understand that Genesis 1:1–2:3 is a *foundational theological treatise*.[74] Commonly, scholars compare Genesis 1:1–2:3 with ancient

69. *Grzimek's Animal Life Encyclopedia*, 2nd ed, Vol. 15: *Mammals IV*, s.v. "Hyracoidea" (by Hendrik Hoeck), *Gale Virtual Reference Library*, Thomson Gale, Trial Site Database, http://find.galegroup.com/gvrl/infomark.do?&contentSet=EBKS&type=r etrieve&tabID=T001&prodId=GVRL&docId=CX3406700925&eisbn=0-7876-7750-7&source=gale&userGroupName=special_gvrlonly&version=1.0 (accessed January 18, 2007).

70. Slifkin, *The Camel, the Hare and the Hyrax,* p. 107–110 (where he cites conflicting authorities!).

71. The digestive system of the hyrax is complex and almost unique among mammals, having three separate areas for food fermentation: the fore-stomach, the caecum, and the paired colonic appendages (Ibid., p. 115–117, in particular the drawing on page 116; and Hoeck). The additional chambers slow down the digestive process and culture bacteria, both necessary to digest cellulose (Dennis Englin [Professor of Biological Sciences at The Master's College], personal communication). Recent studies have concluded that the hyrax digests cellulose as well as a ruminant (Johan J.C. Sauer, "The Efficiency of Crude Fiber Digestion in the Hyrax Procavia Capensis" [Ph.D. diss., University of Pretoria (South Africa), 1987], Abstract in proquest.umi.com; J.R. Paul-Murphy, C.J. Murphy *et al*, "Comparison of Transit Time of Digesta and Digestive Efficiency of the Rock Hyrax, the Barbados Sheep and the Domestic Rabbit," *Comparative Biology and Physiology A* 72/3 [1982]: p. 611–613, [cited by Slifkin, *The Camel, the Hare and the Hyrax,* p. 117]).

72. A behavior in which the animal regurgitates a little food and re-chews it, but it does not play as significant a role in digestion as it does with ruminants (Slifkin, *The Camel, the Hare and the Hyrax,* p. 110–111).

73. Photographs of their feet are in Slifkin, *The Camel, the Hare and the Hyrax,* p. 106. Zoologists originally classified them as *Ungulata*, "hooved," but since have changed their taxonomy to superorder *Paenungulata*, "near ungulates" (Rahm, *Grzimek's Animal Life Encyclopedia*, Vol. 12, s.v. "hyraxes" p. 513).

74. This is one of the most profoundly theological texts in the Bible, in that the Hebrew word for God, אֱלֹהִים, occurs 35 times. In biblical Hebrew, normally, when a sentence continues the topic of the previous sentence, the topic is not relexicalized (repeated as the subject) but carried by the pronominal clitics in the verb inflection. Redundant

Near Eastern (ANE) creation accounts, emphasize the similarities, and draw conclusions based on them.[75] But this is a flawed approach, because it ignores the fact that it would be the atypical nature of the Genesis account that would attract the attention of the original readers.[76] We will consider briefly therefore three radical contrasts between this text and ANE creation myths, which makes the Genesis account into a polemic against such ANE texts.[77]

The first comprises five ways the Lord essentially differs from ANE "deities." First, the Lord is self-existent and eternal; the ANE gods are born from eternal matter. Second, the Lord is uncreated; the ANE gods are created in some way. Third, the existence of the Lord is neither proved nor asserted but rather assumed; in the ANE texts the focus is on theogony (the origin of the gods). Fourth, the Lord is separate from His creation; the ANE gods are deified natural forces. And fifth, the Lord is an unopposed sovereign Creator; the ANE texts feature battles among the gods, after which the victor creates.[78]

relexicalization emphasizes the topic (its uniqueness, contrast with other possible topics, etc.). But here we have a 35-fold relexicalization, an unprecedented and unmatched level of redundant relexicalization, to drive home the point that *God* is the *Creator*.

75. Most often the Babylonian accounts (both *Enūma Elish* and *Atra-ʿasīs*) are examined for parallels. But John Currid looks at the Egyptian (John D. Currid, *Ancient Egypt and the Old Testament* [Grand Rapids, MI: Baker Books, 1997], p. 53–73). So does Gordon Johnston. He argues that Genesis 1 is an anti-Egyptian-cosmogony polemic, noting both "striking similarities" and "dramatic differences" between Genesis 1 and the Egyptian creation myths (Gordon H. Johnston, "Genesis 1 and Ancient Egyptian Creation Myths," *Bibliotheca Sacra* 165 [April–June 2008]: p. 178–194, esp, 182–194). I will be mostly discussing the Babylonian material below, but the same arguments apply to the Egyptian.

76. When the ANE creation and flood texts were unearthed, scholars noted the similarities between them and the biblical account. And so they began to read the Bible in light of these "so-called" parallels. But an ancient reader would not have reacted this way to the biblical texts in light of the ANE texts. The latter were familiar to them. Thus, what would have stood out for them would have been the differences between the biblical account and the ANE account. The author meant for the similarities to be an impetus to the reader to note the contrasts.

77. Also because of the wider purposes of the divine Author, the text functions as a polemic against all erroneous views, of our time as well as those of when it was written. Gordon Wenham comments forcefully on the latter, "Gen. 1 is a deliberate statement of [the] Hebrew view of creation over against rival views. It is not merely a demythologization of oriental creation myths, whether Babylonian or Egyptian; rather it is polemical repudiation of such myths" (Gordon J. Wenham, *Genesis 1–15*, Word Biblical Commentary, vol. 1 [Waco, TX: Word Books, Publisher, 1987], p. 9).

78. For further details see Gerhard F. Hasel, "The Significance of the Cosmology in Gen. 1 in Relation to Ancient Near Eastern Parallels," *AUSS* 10 (1972): p. 19–20; idem., "The Polemical Nature of the Genesis Cosmology," *EvQ* 46 (1974): p. 81–102; Nahum M. Sarna, *Genesis: The Traditional Hebrew Text with New JPS Translation / Commentary by Nahum M. Sarna* (Philadelphia, PA: The Jewish Publication Society, 1989), p. 3–4; and Wenham, *Genesis 1–15*, p. 9–10.

The second contrast is six-fold, pertaining to the nature of creation. (1) The Lord created by fiat and unopposed actions; the ANE gods, by birth, battle, magic and opposed action. (2) The Lord created from no preexistent matter; the gods, from eternal matter or vanquished foes.[79] (3) The Lord created in a sequence of days; the gods — there is no analogy. (4) The Lord purposefully progressed in His creation toward the creation of man; the gods created man as an afterthought. (5) The Lord created man deliberately and personally; the gods created man from the entrails of a vanquished foe,[80] because they needed someone to feed them (as in *Enūma Elish*) or created him from one of the lower hierarchy of gods,[81] because they needed someone to dig the canals (as in *Atra-ḫasīs*). (6) The Lord blessed man and placed him as vice-regent over the natural realm; the ANE texts have man subservient to the nature gods and terrified of them.

The third contrast is between the mythical ANE accounts and the patently anti-mythical character of Genesis 1:1–2:3. The latter is evidenced by its lack of struggle or competing deities, the preexistence of the Creator rather than matter, the distribution of בָּרָא (*bārāʾ*, "create") the mention of תְּהוֹם (*tᵊhôm*, "world ocean") and the account of the fourth day.[82] I will explain the last three in order below.

In biblical Hebrew, the verb בָּרָא (create) always has God for its subject and never mentions the material from which He created. Its presence in a verse therefore underscores that *God* is the *Creator*. With this emphasis, its occurrence in verses 1, 21, 27(3x) and 2:3 (elsewhere in Genesis 1, עָשָׂה [*ʿāśāh*, "make"] is used) is decidedly anti-mythical. In verse 1 it proves that *God* is the creator of matter. This is in stark contrast to the pre-existence of *matter* in all the ANE texts. The three-fold usage of בָּרָא which makes verse 27 a poetic tricolon, drives home the points that 1) God deliberately and purposeful created man to be His representative, 2) he was the pinnacle of creation and 3) God created him to rule over the natural world. This differs altogether from the ANE myths, in which man is created as an afterthought and serves the nature deities. The occurrence of בָּרָא in verse 21 shows that *God created* the gigantic sea creatures; they are *not* gods and goddesses, as they are portrayed in the ANE myths.[83] Finally, in 2:3 in an *inclusio* with 1:1 the presence of בָּרָא confirms that *God is the Creator* of everything. Only He was pre-existent.

79. In *Enūma Elish* (a Babylonian creation myth) the victorious *Marduk* fashioned the universe by arching the exploded carcass of his nemesis, the monstrous serpent goddess *Tiamat*.

80. *Kingu*, the monstrous serpent god, who was *Tiamat's* henchman.

81. *Ilu-wer*

82. Sarna states, "The outstanding peculiarity of the biblical account is the complete absence of mythology in the classic pagan sense of the term" and "Nowhere is the non-mythological outlook better illustrated than in the Genesis narrative. The Hebrew account is matchless in its solemn and majestic simplicity" (Nahum M. Sarna, *Understanding Genesis* [New York: Schocken Books, 1966], p. 9–10).

83. For example, *Kingu* and *Tiamat* in *Enūma Elish*.

Second, the significance of the word תְּהוֹם (*t°hôm*, "world ocean") in the text arises from its unmistakable phonetic similarity to *Tiamat* (the Babylonian goddess).[84] But according to verse 2, תְּהוֹם (*t°hôm*) is the result of God's creation; it is not an ANE goddess.

Lastly, four aspects of the amazing account of the fourth day of creation week prove it to be blatantly anti-mythical, in that it relentlessly strips the sun, moon, and stars of the divine status vested in them in Egypt and Mesopotamia and relegates them to serve man as navigational aids and time-markers rather than to determine his future. First, the sun and moon are not named to show that they are not even sentient, let alone gods. The lack of both naming and blessing in these verses is striking, in that in the other days of creation week, the Lord either named or blessed.[85] Second, this lack is almost awkward as the author carefully avoids mentioning the common Hebrew (and Semitic) names for the sun and the moon, שֶׁמֶשׁ (*šemeš*, cf. its obvious phonetic equivalent to the Babylonian name for the sun god, *Šamšu*) and יָרֵחַ (*Yārēaḥ*), respectively. Yet, elsewhere there is no such reluctance (e.g., Ps. 121:6). Third, the complex palistrophic structure of the passage delimits their "rule" to *serving man*, by linking verse 16b ("the great light for the ruling of the day and the small light for the ruling of the night") with verse 14b ("let them be for signs, for appointed times and for days and years").[86] This is diametrically opposed to the ANE concept of

---

84. See note 79 above.

85. On the first three days of creation week He named light, darkness, firmament, dry land, and the gathering of water, "day," "night," "heaven," "earth" and "seas," respectively. On the last three days He blessed the sea creatures and flying animals, man, and the seventh day.

86. The palistrophic structure (corresponding clauses form an ABCDD´C´B´A´ or similar pattern) in Genesis 1:14–19 comprises eleven purposes clauses *a–k*. Six (*a, f* and *i–k*) are construed by ל + infinitive construct of three different verbal roots: 1) להבדיל "to divide," 2) להאיר "to shine light" and 3) למשל "to rule." Three (*b, c,* and *d*) are in verse 14b, "for signs, for appointed times, for days and years." Two (*g* and *h*) are imbedded in verse 16, "the big light source for the *ruling* of the day and the small light source for the *ruling* of the night." "For ruling" in this verse is לממשלת, which is ל plus a noun from the verbal root of clause *j* (root 3). Finally, clause *e*, "for light sources," is connected to clause *f*, "to shine light on the earth," and thus, corresponds semantically to the latter.

    The clauses are arranged as follows: the last clause *(k)* clearly corresponds to the first *(a)*, because both have root 1 and they have semantically equivalent objects. We will call them therefore *a* and *a'*. Furthermore, the third *(f)* is identical to the third from last *(i)*. So they are *f* and *f'*. In addition, *g* and *h* are the same, enabling us to assign *g* to both. This leaves us *b, c* and *d* and *j*. The schema, then, is as follows: *a* [*b, c* and *d*] *f g–g f* [*j*] *a'*. That is, among the clauses corresponding to one another because they have identical roots, the *b, c* and *d* grouping is between the first and second and *j* is between the last and second to last. The result is that the precision of the author's meticulously crafted structure directs the reader to semantically equate *b, c* and *d* with *j*. And since g and *j* have the same root, we can thus understand the meaning of "the

their role as capricious, merciless, implacable, divine judges, unmoved by their supplicants' servile appeasements to avert being smitten. And, fourth and finally, the creation of the stars, not of man (as in the ANE texts), is described almost as an afterthought, commonly translated, "He made the stars also."[87]

3. Conclusion; or, Why the Earth Must Be Young

Three major implications arise from this study. First, it is not statistically defensible to read Genesis 1:1–2:3 as poetry. Second, since Genesis 1:1–2:3 is narrative, it should be read as other Hebrew narratives are intended to be read — as a concise report of actual events in time-space history, which also conveys an unmistakable theological message. Third, when this text is read as narrative, there is only one tenable view of its plain sense: these were six literal days of creation. The words mean what a 15th century B.C. Israelite would have understood them to mean in any other historical narrative, with the referents and events corresponding to the words. So, יוֹם (*yôm* "day") in this text, just as in any historical narrative, refers to a normal day. This text's original readers would never have thought it meant "age."

Other modern readings[88] are as much counter-readings[89] as the ANE creation accounts are. The following thrust by Sternberg silences such:

> Suppose the Creation narrative elicited from the audience the challenge "But the Babylonians tell a different story." . . . Would the biblical narrator shrug his shoulders as any self-respecting novelist would do? *One inclined to answer in the affirmative would have to make fictional sense of all the overwhelming evidence to the contrary; and I do not see how even a confirmed anachronist would go about it with any show of reason. This way madness lies — and I mean interpretive, teleological as well as*

---

    big light source for the *ruling* of the day and the small light source for the *ruling* of the night."

87. The creation of the stars is presented as an afterthought, because the verb "make" (at the beginning of the verse) is separated from its third direct object "the stars" by the interposition of the description of the role of the great light and the small light. The verb is not repeated in spite of the length of the intervening phrase. An interpretive translation would be "He made (the great light with a certain role and the small light with a certain role) and the stars."

88. For a discussion of objections to an historical reading of this text and answers to these, see *RATE* chapter, p. 635–639.

89. In a narrow sense, a "counter-reading" is any incorrect interpretation of a text, and is a reading therefore against the author's intent. Such a reading will be assured by not reading a text according to its genre. Reading Genesis 1:1–2:3 incorrectly as poetry rather than as narrative is an example. But, in a wider sense, a counter-reading is also a counter-reading of reality. Asserting the big-bang theory or macro-evolution against the literal historical account of this great text is as much a counter-reading as the bizarre "reality" portrayed in the ANE texts. For additional thoughts see note 7 above.

theological madness.[90]

When the biblical creation account in Genesis 1:1–2:3 is read as an ordinary narrative text, albeit, with extraordinary theological content, it is clear what the author is asserting: eternal God created space, time, matter, the stars, the earth, vegetation, animals, and man in one week. Furthermore, if the Flood account (Gen. 6:5–9:29) is read in the same way (and it should be for it also is clearly historical narrative), we must conclude that that same author is asserting that the originally created earth was inundated with a global catastrophic deluge. Based on this approach to these texts, the only tenable view for the age of the earth is that it is young — only thousands of years old, not billions of years old.

---

90. Sternberg, *The Poetics of Biblical Narrative*, p. 32, emphasis mine.

Chapter 7

Can Deep Time Be Embedded in Genesis?

Trevor Craigen

A set of audio tapes on creation by Dr. John Whitcomb given to me in 1973 by an American missionary serving at that time in Johannesburg, South Africa, were unlike anything I had heard up to that day on the subject. From then on, a keen interest in the biblical teaching on creation grew ever stronger in my mind. January 1976 marked the beginning of five or so memorable years on the campus of Grace Theological Seminary, when my life and thoughts were deeply influenced and impacted by Dr. Whitcomb, as well as by his colleagues.

This short essay, then, is submitted in honor of one who first taught me and then granted me the privilege of teaching alongside of him at Grace Seminary Extension in Europe, 1983–1988. His lectures have stood the test of time, and frankly, although academia may call for courteous attention to another's views on the meaning and significance of the Genesis account of creation, the answer to the question which heads this essay, is an immediate negative. It seems to be old ground being plowed afresh, with the terms used having changed somewhat but with the hermeneutics continuing to be shaped and influenced to one degree or another by prevailing scientific opinions, theories, and hypotheses, none of which, it must be pointed out, are immune from amendment or replacement.

Now, the term *embedded* is instantly understood to be describing how something is fixed firmly in surrounding matter, being so enclosed that it becomes an integral part of the whole, as it were. Given the specific mention of deep time in the initial inquiry, then obviously the response required, in this instance, is that time of unlimited duration, stretching far backward into antiquity and beyond has become an integral part of the text, if not its ambience.

It would appear, then, (1) that some element of grammar, syntax, context, literary genre, science, or tradition immediately triggers the understanding that deep time is being expressed or portrayed, (2) that the span of time normally associated with time terms in Scripture — day, week, month, year — are disregarded or re-interpreted to contribute to this idea of unlimited duration of time, (3) that the only passage which brings such discussions forcibly to the fore is the Genesis creation account, and thus (4) that the critical issue here in the interpretation of the passage is time and more time for the events recorded in the biblical account to have occurred in the past.

Before making any final comment on embedded meaning and time, a reminder of important and pertinent information on the use of *day* (Hebrew: *yôm*) and the meaning of this main time term in Genesis is unfortunately necessary. More information on deep time and on the conflict between the biblical and evolutionary order of creative events is also needed.

Analyses and Arguments Acknowledged

Repackaging the lexical, grammatical, and syntactical analyses from the increasing number of good books and many journal articles on this subject of origins is not the design of this essay.[1] Cross-referencing to certain, selected resources is quite in order. Given the nature of the other essays in this volume, every effort has been made to avoid unnecessary repetition of information.

Arguments in support of a literal seven-day creation week were introduced into Dr. Whitcomb's lectures and appeared in his writings. In his book *The Early Earth*, for example, four main observations[2] were made: (1) when *yôm* is used with a numerical adjective it always restricts the meaning to a literal 24-hour day in the OT, (2) the accompanying, qualifying phrase "the evening and morning" in Genesis 1 also indicates a normal 24-hour cycle of the earth rotating on its axis in reference to a fixed astronomical light source, (3) the analogy for the cycle of human work and rest in Exodus 20:8–11 would be meaningless, if the creation "week" were made up of long, indefinite periods of time, and (4) two well-known units of time, "days" and "years," are linked in Genesis 1:14, their duration being determined "by the fixed movements of the earth in reference to the sun."[3] Former students of Dr. Whitcomb have written on the meaning

---

1. Apart from various books referenced or mentioned in this essay, a number of others are definitely worthy of mention; Kurt P. Wise, *Faith, Form and Time: What the Bible Teaches and Science Confirms about Creation and the Age of the Universe* (Nashville, TN: Broadman & Holman Publishers, 2002); John MacArthur, *The Battle for the Beginning* (Nashville, TN: Word Publishing, 2001); Stuart Burgess, *Hallmarks of Design: Evidence of Design in the Natural World* (Epsom, Surrey, UK: Day One Publishers, 2000); John Morris, *The Young Earth* (Green Forest, AR: Master Books, 1994).

2. Dr. Whitcomb's own wording in these observations has been retained in order that the reader today might see just how he expressed his arguments, which certainly are not above refinement and restatement.

3. John Whitcomb, *The Early Earth* (Grand Rapids, MI: Baker, 1986, rev. ed.), p. 28–32, adds that the first three days were the same length as the other days because the same descriptive phrases are used for all six days. God created that localized light source on

of *yôm*, adding to the multiple studies already done.[4] Readers of these articles quickly realize that this term's semantic range does not easily promote indefiniteness to the days in Genesis.

Order in Conflict

A point often overlooked by those attempting to add millions of years to Genesis 1 is the sharp contradiction between the order of creative events in Genesis and the order of events in the evolutionary proposals. We would first note that according to Genesis both earth and light were created before the sun, moon and the stars, contrary to evolutionary cosmology. The simple two-column table below brings out in the 12 line-items,[5] which were selected because their opposite sides fitted around the "before" used like a pivot — swing the words from one side to the other, and the exact opposite is asserted. Terry Mortenson has produced a chart showing some 26 discrepancies in the order (see following page).[6]

Richard Niessen puts forward 33 significant discrepancies between creation and evolution in order to establish just how much "the Evolutionary Scenario" and "the Biblical Record" are totally at variance with one another.[7] These discrepancies cover a wide range of material from the first moment of creation until post-Flood activities and events. Only 7 of the 33 contrasts were placed in the two-column table. The left column introduces an important item for the evolutionary scheme of things. The right column responds with a fact taken from the biblical record — the contrast is quite apparent!

---

day 1 so that the earth passed through the same kind of day/night cycles as it has since day 4 and the creation of the sun.

4. James Stambaugh, "The Days of Creation: A Semantic Approach," *The Journal of Ministry & Theology*, 7:2 (Fall 2003): p. 42–68, and first published under the same title in *Creation Ex Nihilo Technical Journal* 5/1 (1991): p. 70–78, and Robert V. McCabe, "A Defense of Literal Days in the Creation Week," *Detroit Baptist Seminary Journal* 5 (Fall 2000): p. 97–123. Weston Fields, *Unformed and Unfilled* (Nutley, NJ: Presbyterian and Reformed Publ., 1976), p. 165–179, bluntly concludes at the end of a chapter entitled "The Day-Age Theory," "The Day-Age theory is impossible. It is grammatically and exegetically preposterous. Its only reason for existence is its allowance for the *time* needed by evolutionary geology and biology."

5. Specifically documenting the order of what preceded what in evolutionary development is hardly necessary since it is not exactly an unknown subject.

6. See Terry Mortenson, "Evolution vs. Creation: The Order of Events Matters," http://www.answersingenesis.org/docs2006/0404order.asp, accessed March 8, 2008, for a good display of 29 differences between the orders, which was taken as a base for this table.

7. Richard Niessen, "Significant Discrepancies Between Theistic Evolution and the Bible," *Education for Eternity*., 1:10 (August 1979): p. 1–4. This article was also published as "Several Significant Discrepancies between Theistic Evolution and the Biblical Account," *Creation Research Society Quarterly* 16 (March 1980): p. 220–221, and cited also by Carl F.H. Henry, *God, Revelation, and Authority* (Waco, TX: Word Books, 1983), p. 147–148.

The Evolutionary Scenario "Genesis 1:1–2:3 reversed"	The Biblical Record in Genesis 1:1–2:3
1. Sun, moon, and stars before the earth	1. Earth before the sun, moon, and stars
2. Sun before light on the earth	2. Light on the earth before the sun
3. Dry land before seas	3. Seas before dry land
4. Sun before plants	4. Plants before the sun
5. Plants before fruit trees	5. Fruit trees before other plants
6. Land animals before trees.	6. Trees before land animals
7. Insects before flowering plants	7. Flowering plants before insects
8. Marine creatures before land plants	8. Land plants before marine creatures
9. Land reptile or dinosaurs before birds	9. Birds before dinosaurs or any reptile
10. Land animals before sea monsters	10. Sea monsters before land animals
11. Thorns and thistles before man	11. Man before thorns and thistles
12. Death before man	12. Man before death

John Whitcomb mentioned just five discrepancies noticeable in the order of creation events, but they sufficed to make the point of substantial variance. These are:

- land plants and fruit trees preceded marine creatures
- birds preceded reptiles
- whales preceded land mammals
- insects coming in after plants
- the sun only being created *after* the earth and plants had already been made.[8]

Hugh Ross, whose theories and explanations are not being critiqued here, nevertheless draws up a single listing which reveals his amendments to the order of events in Genesis 1. His proposal has made changes to allow for day-ages of millions of years each, and for a universe he calculates to be approximately 16

8. Whitcomb, *The Early Earth*, p. 75–76.

billion years old.[9] Audaciously, he then declares his amended reading to be in perfect accord with the findings of modern science. The unavoidable has occurred: "day 4 does not say what it says," is the silent declaration behind the one being openly made. The first two lines of his Table 14.2 read:

1. Creation of the physical universe (space, time, matter, energy, galaxies, stars, planets, etc.)
2. Transformation of earth's atmosphere from opaque to translucent.

On the line which would cover day 4, Ross says:

> Transformation of the atmosphere from translucent to transparent (Sun, Moon, and stars became visible for the first time).[10]

But a careful reader of Genesis 1 will readily see that almost none of this is mentioned in the text, and the time when the heavenly bodies were made is quite contrary to what the text says. Eisegesis, not exegesis, is at work here.

With the creation week being a tightly knit sequence of the Lord God's creative working,[11] then the age of man is calculable from one perspective in relation to that of the universe and all other creatures. Quite simply put: Adam and Eve are exactly five days younger than the heavens and the earth, three days younger than earth's vegetation, two days younger than the sun, moon, and stars, and one day younger than fish and bird life, and only part of a day younger than the rest of created life. This exercise requires affirming that the creation week be kept intact just as per the words of Moses. However, it is easy to see how even a minimal acceptance of the evolutionary order, immediately carries with it (1) questions about the obvious differences with the order in the Genesis account and (2) questions about the lack of time in the biblical record, which in turn gives rise to questions about the meaning of "day," "evening and morning," and "without form and void," and perhaps "in the beginning."

Inserting billions of years into the biblical account is understood to be part of harmonizing the Bible and science and, in so doing, to render an "informed interpretation" of the creation account. It doesn't matter where all these years slip in; made as part of each day, or placed between the days, constituting the

---

9. Hugh Ross, *The Fingerprint of God: Recent Scientific Discoveries Reveal the Unmistakable Identity of the Creator* (Orange, CA: Promise Publishing Co., 1989), p. 158–159, and refer to "Table 13.2: Measurements of the age of the universe," which shows a mean age of 16±3 billion years.
10. See also Table 16.1, "Order of the Creation Events," in his *Creation and Time: A Biblical and Scientific Perspective on the Creation-Date Controversy* (Colorado Springs, CO: NavPress, 1994), p. 153, where he adds a few extra bits of information, such as the clearing away of the solar system's interplanetary debris which prevented light from reaching the surface of the oceans. He also exchanged the description of the atmosphere as translucent with "occasionally transparent" (i.e., on what would be day 4).
11. See below under "*Inclusio* and Sequence."

gap between Genesis 1:1 and 1:2, or even occurring before verse 1. Certainly, this subject has spawned many books and journal articles of both a popular and academic nature. Tracking down all that has been written and classifying that in terms of how they handled the inspired text would be a formidable task. Compiling such a complete annotated bibliography is beyond the confines of this essay. Any interaction with the technical aspects of geology, biology,[12] astronomy, and other disciplines pertinent to dealing with theories on the origins of man, the world, and the universe have been left to those who are far more qualified to offer an informed critique.[13] This insertion of much more time into the six days of the creation week falls under the rubric of *deep time*.[14]

Deep Time: New Concept, Old Proposal

Time can be described in a number of different ways and fitted into a number of different categories.[15] Indeed, the subject of time has intrigued philosophers, historians, theologians, and scholars of the past and present.[16] Researchers continue to wrestle with the question of the nature and origin of time, its passage and flow, direction and measurement; whether absolute or relative, static or dynamic. And then there is the hypothesis on time dilation.[17] Only time will tell where all this will end up!

---

12. *Deep time* also features outside of geology in the study of species under the rubric of cladistics, or phylogenetic systematics. Cladograms are line diagrams similar to genealogies and replace the "trees" of descent from a single ancestor as per the drawings seen often in textbooks on evolution. See Henry Gee's book *In Search of Deep Time: Cladistics, the Revolution in Evolution* (London: Fourth Estate, 2001), for both an explanation of and examples of cladograms.

13. See the list of recommended resources at the end of this book.

14. Don DeYoung, *Thousands Not Billions: Challenging an Icon of Evolution, Questioning the Age of the Earth* (Green Forest, AR: Master Books, 2007), p. 13, notes that deep time is a major icon or symbol of evolution, but he also assigns it as a label for the multi-billion-year time spans when talking about the age of the earth and that of the universe, and deep space too.

15. For a thorough introduction to and instruction on time see William Lane Craig, *Time and Eternity: Exploring God's Relationship to Time* (Wheaton, IL: Crossway Books, 2001). See also the well-known classic, Oscar Cullmann's *Christ and Time* (London, UK: SCM Press, 1951) p. 53, where he speaks of the Bible's linear understanding of time, and about ten lines later, further remarks that "the New Testament knows only the linear time concept of today, yesterday, and tomorrow."

16. Alan G.Padgett, *Science and the Study of God: A Mutuality Model for Theology and Science* (Grand Rapids, MI: Eerdmans, 2003), p. 122, reminds the reader that one of the oldest philosophical conundrums is the simple question: "What is time?" It seems so everyday, so ordinary, yet at the same time so enigmatic. See also Hendrikus Berkhof, *Christ the Meaning of History* (London, U.K.: SCM, 1966), p. 21, who observes that the Christian view of time is that it has a direction and a purpose.

17. John Byl, "On Time Dilation in Cosmology," *Creation Research Society Quarterly*, 34 (June 1997), p. 26–34.

In coining the phrase *deep time*, John McPhee, a writer in the field of geology, sought "to distinguish geological time from the scale of time that governs our everyday lives."[18]

An understanding of cosmological and geological history and the concomitant history of life requires a comprehension of time which initially may be more than disconcerting.[19]

Geology's Time Scale

By means of the phrase *deep time,* geology's immense intervals measured in millions of years supposedly was brought within reach of minds which were used to thinking in substantially far lesser terms of measurement than are found in geology and paleontology. All the zeroes belonging to those very lengthy epochs are somewhat incomprehensible to the ordinary person (and to be honest, to the geologists and paleontologists, too). *Deep time* ameliorates the sense of being overwhelmed by such large numbers.

Henry Gee's introduction to the concept of *deep time* describes it as other than "ordinary time" or "everyday time."[20] He opines that knowledge of past history is "determined by the density, connectedness, and context of events."[21] The further back one goes in time, however, the more loosely connected become the events occurring within that time span. When centuries become millions of years and more, then these vast intervals totally dwarf the events within them. When such great drafts of time are also disconnected by great gulfs of space (with the distances measured in light-years and not in ordinary linear terms), it signals something far different, something other than normal time. "This is geological time, far beyond everyday human experience. This is Deep Time. Deep Time is like an endless, dark corridor, with no landmarks to give it scale."[22]

Deep time has been taught for almost two centuries as proven fact. The education system is designed to indoctrinate students. For example, an ENSI website (acronym for Evolution & the Nature of Science Institutes), posted a lesson plan entitled "Deep Time: Finding the Ages of Rocks and Fossils." The lesson was to make certain that students were informed about the high level of confidence which they should have in the geological ages of an old earth. At the same time, it should reveal an example of pseudoscience (which is unidentified) and in so doing improve science literacy and critical thinking.[23] Furthermore,

---

18. John McPhee, *Basin and Range* (Farrar, Straus, & Giroux, 1981) as cited by Henry Gee, *In Search of Deep Time: Beyond the Fossil Record to a New History of Life* (New York: The Free Press, 1999), p. 2.

19. See http://en.wiki.pedia.org/wiki/Deep_time#Scientific_concept, accessed May 8, 2008, which also reports that deep time may have been first recognized in 11th century China by Shen Kuo, the polymath.

20. Henry Gee, *In Search of Deep Time*, p. 26.

21. Ibid,, p. 25–26.

22. Ibid.

23. Larry Flammer, "Deep Time: Finding the Ages of Rocks and Fossils." Two of the

lesson procedure called for the teacher to try to get a class consensus that "the studies of Deep Time are very reliable and well-established, based upon compelling scientific work, with few minor discrepancies."[24]

The qualitative difference of deep time from ordinary time supposedly allows for species to transmute, whereas such changes over the millions of needed years cannot be put within the confines of ordinary, everyday time. In ordinary time (i.e., time since man first appeared) organisms breed true to their kind, and no tracing backward in ordinary time will find any evidence of evolutionary changes (i.e., changes that transform one kind of creature into a distinctly different kind, say, a reptile to a bird). In fact, "Deep Time is the key to the origin of species because intervals of time of geological extent were required for Darwin's mechanism — natural selection — to do its work and change one species into another. Evolution is a consequence of Deep Time."[25]

Furthermore, the perception of the passing of time and the measurement thereof within ordinary time is that all events are connected, a chain of cause and effect prevailing. Everyday life thus appears continuous. At a certain point in looking back, the events become less clearly connected. All deep time can do is indicate the point of ancestral convergence, or the node from which a divergence occurred, but finding any more information from the fossil record is impossible.[26] Common ancestry is an accepted item for the evolutionist, but the identity of that common ancestor is lost in the dark of deep time's vast intervals.

Creation's Time Term

The primary time word in Genesis 1:1–2:3, *yôm* (here translated "day"), quickly becomes the point of debate in contexts treating origins. This watershed term divides students, even language scholars, into two major categories: those who cannot accept it to mean in Genesis 1 a normal, straightforward day, and those who can. The words of one who does not accept the literal-day view are instructive: "It is straightforward to see as well that these days are presented to us as six separate periods of time, that took place one after the other — after all, they're the first day . . . second day, and so on to the seventh day."[27] So, a very important decision has to be made by the exegete on whether this necessarily means that everything narrated on a given day is supposed to have taken place on that day. The debate over the meaning of that Hebrew word for day in the

---

      materials available for teachers to download are labeled, "DEEP TIME Instructional
      narrative" and "DEEP TIME Worksheet," the latter dealing with half-lives, and further,
      to see how geochronology works, one must take a peek at DEEP TIME (author's use
      of upper case). All the information here was extracted from or based upon http://www.
      indiana.edu/~ensiweb/lessons/deep.les.html, accessed July 31, 2007.

24. Ibid., Lesson procedure, point 12 .
25. Ibid., p. 34.
26. Ibid.
27. C.J. Collins, *Science and Faith: Friends or Foes?* (Wheaton, IL: Crossway Books, 2003),
      p. 69.

creation account in Genesis 1:1–2:3 will not be easily dismissed. Several points should be considered in coming to a conclusion on this matter.

Grammatical Considerations

In both the Hebrew and Greek languages of the Bible the word "day" may refer to the complete 24-hour day, or it may designate the period of daylight as distinguished from nighttime, the period of darkness. The day (i.e., daytime) is divided into three periods, namely "morning," "noonday," and "evening."[28]

An extended, non-literal meaning is permissible for *yôm* when it is *not* used as an unadorned noun (i.e., one without prefix or suffix). Grammatically, *yôm* can stand in an indefinite temporal clause or in a definite temporal clause.[29] Combining with a preposition, as in *bᵉyom*, it is an indefinite temporal clause and is translated as "in the day" or simply "when." Here, "in the day" indicates the time when something was done, for example, "in the day the Lord made the heavens and the earth" (Gen. 2:4), or "in the day that you eat from it" (Gen. 2:17; 3:5). Since in the case of Genesis 2:4 the immediate context focuses on the creation of the heavens and the earth and everything in them, then "in the day"[30] here covers the whole six days of creation. This construction, however, may be more definite and specific, for example, in Genesis 2:17 and 3:5 (Adam's sin and God's judgment were on a particular day) and in Genesis 2:2 "on the seventh day God completed His work," or literally "on the day, the seventh one,"[31] which tells us precisely when God's creative acts were completed.

True, *yôm* is sometimes used in the Old Testament in an indefinite way to refer to more time than a standard day. Some argue from this fact that therefore all or some of the creation week's days could possibly be indeterminately long spans of time. But this overlooks the cluster of terms used with *yôm* in Genesis 1.

As Hasel persuasively argued, "This triple interlocking connection of singular usage, joined by a numeral, and the temporal definition of 'evening and morning,' keeps the creation 'day' *the same throughout* the creation account."[32] His closing observation is worth repeating in full.

---

28. Any good lexicon will supply the references for these periods of the day. That noonday could be a period of time as well and not just always a certain moment, is indicated in Isa. 16:3, "In the midst of the noonday." Within that period the actual point at which noon is reached would be indicated by the position of the sun and the shadow on the sundial.

29. The noun is singular and anarthrous, with a *beth* preposition prefixed and in construct with an infinitive construct — a well-attested construction of the indefinite. But when the singular noun occurs with the prefixed preposition (either *bᵉ* or *cᵉ*), and with the definite article, it is a temporal clause with specificity.

30. The Hebrew text has no definite article with the noun, thus literally reading as "in day" (*beyôm*).

31. The Hebrew text has the definite article, thus reading as "in the day" (*bayôm*).

32. Gerhard Hasel, "The 'Days' of Creation in Genesis 1: Literal 'Days' or Figurative 'Periods/Epochs' of Time?" *Origins* 21/1 (1994): p. 26 (emphasis added).

The author of Genesis 1 could not have produced more comprehensive and all-inclusive ways to express the idea of a literal "day" than the ones that were chosen. There is a complete lack of indicators from prepositions, qualifying expressions, construct phrases, semantic-syntactical connections, and so on, on the basis of which the designation "day" in the creation week could be taken to be anything different than a regular 24-hour day. The combinations of the factors of articular usage, singular gender, semantic-syntactical constructions, time boundaries, and so on, corroborated by the divine promulgations in such Pentateuchal passages as Exodus 20:8–11 and Exodus 31:12–17, suggest uniquely and consistently that the creation "day" is meant to be *literal, sequential, and chronological* in nature.[33]

This conclusion was reached after thorough consideration of various figurative interpretations of the creation "days" (which Hasel rejected) and of the literary genre of Genesis 1 (he argued for an accurate historical prose record). In contending for the clarity of the term *yôm* in Genesis 1, Hasel looked at commentaries, dictionaries, and lexicons, at semantics and at usage in the singular, with the article, and with a numeral. He had also considered the "evening-morning" temporal boundary, the Pentateuchal Sabbath passages, and finally the clear sequence of events in the record.

In a well-researched book, *Yesterday, Today and Tomorrow*, Simon J. DeVries gave full attention to an inductive study of certain key adverbial expressions connected to the primary word for the basic unit of time in Hebrew, i.e., day, *yôm*. The Hebrews spoke about the day, from the point of view of the writer or hearer, as being in the past (*bayyôm hahû'*), as being in the present (*hayyôm, hayyôm hazzeh, bayyôm hazzeh*) and as being in the future (*bayyôm hahû'*).[34] The basic meaning is the period of light, that is, from dawn until sunset, which means that it often occurs in contrast to the night (e.g., Gen. 8:22; Num. 11:32). The whole period from sunrise to sunrise, or sunset to sunset, is also covered by that basic unit of time, for example, 40 days and 40 nights (Exod. 24:18, with both nouns in the singular), whereas the same time span elsewhere is just "40 days" (Gen. 50:3, with the noun in the singular), obviously , the latter incorporating the nights as well. His opening chapter introduced how essential a clue the term *day* is in understanding the Hebraic concept of time, and what vocabulary in association with *yôm* allowed for expression of both definite and indefinite periods including of boundless or immeasurable duration.[35] In other words, the meaning of *yôm* was quite

---

33. Hasel, "The 'Days' of Creation," p. 31 (emphasis added).

34. Ibid., p. 38., translation of the transliterations shown in the three parentheses for the past, the present, and the future, are as follows: ("in that day"), ("the day or today," "this day," "in this day"), and finally, ("in that day").

35. Ibid., p. 43, and DeVries noted at this point the striking contrast between singular and plural uses of *yôm*, which come into play with this type of vocabulary.

normative, straightforward, and plain, that is, a day means a literal 24-hour day, or part of the day as opposed to the night.

Scholarly Affirmations of the Literal Day View

Affirmation and confirmation on *yôm* (day) meaning a literal day come from the pens of a number of authors, all noted by Hasel and all concurring in their judgment that "day"in Genesis 1 should be taken literally and normatively. Not one of the six selected by Hasel would be classified as a recent-creationist or young-earth proponent. They had other reasons for rejecting what they themselves, each one, declared to be true of the text. These writers' acknowledgments are worth naming and noting.[36]

> Gerhard von Rad: "The seven days are unquestionably to be understood as actual days and as a unique, unrepeatable lapse of time in the world."[37]

> Gordon Wenham: "There can be little doubt that here 'day' has its basic sense of a 24-hour period."[38]

> Victor Hamilton: "Whoever wrote Gen. 1 believed he was talking about literal days."[39]

> Hermann Gunkel, form critic though he was, yet he concluded, "Naturally, the 'days' are days and nothing else."[40]

> John Stek: "Surely there is no sign or hint within the narrative itself that the author thought his 'days' to be irregular designations — first a series of undefined periods, then a series of solar days — or that the 'days' he bounded with 'evening and morning' could possibly be understood as long eons of time. His language is plain and simple. . . . and he speaks in plain and simple terms of one of the most common elements in humanity's experience of the world. . . . In his storying of God's creative acts, the author was 'moved' to sequence them after the

36. Each source cited by Hasel was checked, to avoid citing as a secondary source.
37. Gerhard von Rad, *Genesis: A Commentary*, (Philadelphia, PA: Westminster Press, 1972), p. 65.
38. Gordon Wenham, *Genesis 1–15*, in Word Biblical Commentary, vol. 1, ed. by David Hubbard, et. al. (Waco, TX: Word Books, 1987), p. 19.
39. Victor Hamilton, *The Book of Genesis: Chapters 1–17*, in The New International Commentary of the Old Testament (Grand Rapids, MI: Eerdmans, 1990), p. 53.
40. Hermann Gunkel, *Genesis,* translated and interpreted by Hermann Gunkel, translated by Mark Biddle (Macon, GA: Mercer University Press, 1997), p. 108, who significantly remarks in the same paragraph that "the application of the days of creation to 1,000-year periods or the like is, thus, a very capricious corruption from entirely allogenous circles of thought."

manner of human acts and 'time' them after the pattern of created time in humanity's arena of experience."[41]

James Barr: Against figurative interpreters, he stated that the "creation" days were six literal days of a 144-hour period.[42]

Uses of *Yôm* in Genesis, Outside Chapter 1

In the rest of the chapters of Genesis there are no unusual uses of *yôm* in either singular or plural. None of the contexts of those uses leads the reader to interpret the terms "day" or "days" in an indefinite way that could be equivalent to *deep time*. It might be argued that these uses are outside the creation account. However, elsewhere in the Pentateuch mention of creation does not mandate an immediate response, "*Deep time* is being revealed here!" Instead, very quickly the reader grasps how "day," "month," "week," and "year" are being used in their usual literal sense. They are words which cover a certain, definite span of time.

The plural form, *yamim*, occurs 846 times in the Old Testament, and in the plural, the unadorned noun means "a span of time" but always a span of literal days. Terms in the immediate context and/or the use of the definite article ("the") give specificity to that span of time, such as a number/numerical adjective with days (e.g., Gen. 7:4, 11, 24), or days used with years and months and modified with a numerical adjective, pinpointing the exact date of an event (e.g., Gen. 7:11). "Days" are used alongside "years" to indicate clearly the length of a person's life. It is expressed with some variation as: "so all the days of PN[43] were *x* years" (e.g., ten times in Gen. 5, and also in Gen. 9:29; 11:32), or "the days of PN were x years" (e.g., Gen. 35:28), or even the more grandiose, "the days of the years of the life of PN which he lived, *x* years" (e.g., Gen. 25:7; KJV). Prior to the Flood the Lord himself declared that as for man "his days shall be *x* years" (e.g., Gen. 6:3, 11). In honor of an old man, the statement could be "an old man of ripe age," which literally reads as "being old and satisfied with days" or "full of days" (e.g., Gen. 35:29).

Pharaoh's inquiry about Jacob's age was verbose. He asked, literally, "How many are the days of the years of your life?" to which Jacob responded in kind, "the days of the years of my sojourning," then added in the next clause "the days of the years of my life," (Gen. 47:8–9). Jacob also noted for Pharaoh that his age had not reached that of his forebears, whose life span was expressed as "the days of the years of the life of my fathers in the days of their sojourning. "In the days of PN" would indicate the time during which that person lived (e.g., Gen. 14:1; 26:1, 15, 18), or in general terms the time of an event: "in his days (Peleg's) the

41. John Stek, "What Says Scripture?" in Howard Van Til et al., *Portraits of Creation: Biblical and Scientific Perspectives on the World's Formation* (Grand Rapids, MI: Eerdmans, 1990), p. 237–238.

42. Ibid., p. 41–43.

43. PN = personal name

earth was divided" (Gen. 10:25), and "Reuben went out in the days of the wheat harvest and found mandrakes" (Gen. 30:14). In these last two instances, the construct plural noun with its prefixed preposition (*bîmê*, in the days of) might not specify an exact date but the span of time during which the event occurred is quite clearly delineated, given the information in the immediate context. Also, the basic formula, "PN lived *x* years," can occur without mention of days in a genealogy which indicates the length of life before and after a particular event such as the birth of certain descendant. For example, the pattern "PN lived *x* years and begot PN$_1$ after he begot PN$_1$, PN lived *y* years" occurs nine times in Gen. 11). In an earlier genealogy, the same chiastic-like formula is followed by the patriarch's age at death, but with the sum of *x* and *y* years referred to as days. So, the formula "PN lived *x* years and begot PN$_1$ after he begot PN$_1$, PN lived *y* years . . . so all the days of PN were *z* years" appears nine times in Genesis 5.

The point to note from these cases is that these time terms are not used without regard to the time measurement inherently belonging to the word *yôm*, and the meaning is immediately recognizable by the reader. "Plural 'Days' and Long Periods of Time" and "Singular 'Day' and Short Periods of Time" are two headings in Stambaugh's thorough treatment of *yôm*. In the plural, it communicates specific length of time, but also when joined with "long ago" (*qerem*) and with "of old" (*'olām*) it could cover hundreds of years.[44] He adds: "the maximum time allowed by the historical reference [e.g., Gen. 6:4] could only be on the order of thousands of years and not orders of a higher magnitude." In these cases, Moses had available for his use a substantial stock of time words to clearly indicate long periods of time, when he wanted to do so.[45]

Creation's Time-Frame in an Old-Earth View

The meaning accorded to *yôm* has an immediate impact on how the week of creation is to be defined and measured. If *yôm* does not signify a normal day of 24 hours, then a tightly knit sequence of a week of six working days and one resting day is consequently rejected or modified. Inevitably, in this case, the biblical account is granted elasticity. Thus, speaking of a "creation week" is acceptable, so long as it remains undefined and open-ended in duration. Defining that week in terms of human existence, history, and life, so that a precise calculation of 168 hours is made (7 days x 24 hours/day) is far more difficult to accept and to openly affirm, it would seem, in the present intellectual environment, in which the Scriptures are generally looked upon with amusement or outright hostility, and every reactionary attitude in between.

In regards to the non-literal interpretations, the time frame adopted by the interpreter appears not to have arisen from the biblical text but from some other kind of criteria or influence being brought to bear upon the text. That is, because it is assumed that vast amounts of deep time are necessary for everything

---

44. See Stambaugh, "Days of Creation," p. 58–59, for pertinent references and examples.
45. Ibid., p. 60.

to have come into being, the biblical account of one literal week of creation is deemed, frankly, just too short. But is this not eisegesis being put into practice, rather than exegesis?

"Elastic" Days

How *yôm* is understood with regards to time in Genesis 1 might be put into these various rudimentary formulae: [1] days = literal days, or [2] days = ages, or [3] days = literal days + ages, or [4] divine days for days 1–3 + literal days for days 4–6, or [5] days = anthropomorphic/analogical days, or [6] days = days of revelation, or [7] certain days are longer than literal ones.

All but the first formula allows for flexing the narrative so as to invest it with all the extra time needed for correlating the biblical account with the demands of current scientific consensus and its view of origins. All but the first are accompanied by an unquestioning acceptance of the scientific evidence for the antiquity of the earth.[46] Those views are commonly known as Theistic Evolution, Progressive Creationism, Ruin-Reconstructionism, and the Pre-Creation Chaos Theory. All but the first view of the days of Genesis 1 (the young-earth creationist view) would also include undefined and indefinite periods of time, that is, the time words used are granted no specificity. Gibson has written an informative article on these and other models of origins, which he calls "intermediate."[47] He concludes that all the models discussed "suffer from serious scientific problems or are entirely ad hoc and conjectural." He adds: "It may be that there really is no way to find harmony between the biblical view of origins and current scientific thinking."[48]

Collins sees the refrain, "there was evening and there was morning," not as specifying the divisions of a whole day but as an indicator of the night time which falls between them, and apparently suggests that he is doing more work on this proposal. Noting the absence of this refrain to close off the seventh day leads him to suggest the distinct possibility that life continues on in God's open-ended seventh day.[49] He argues that the weekly pattern is established, six days working and one day resting, but that it is wrong to think of this as in any way being identical to God's working and resting. Thus, it is better to speak of it as an analogical copying.[50] But in this case, the use of an anthropomorphism for

46. Resources recommended at the end of this book present strong scientific evidences that challenge the consensus view.

47. Jim Gibson, "Issues in 'Intermediate' Models of Origins," *Journal of the Adventist Theological Society* 15/1 (Autumn 2004): p. 71–92. Here the term "intermediate" signifies that elements of the biblical story of creation are mixed with elements of the scientific story of origins. He notes that "all these models share the biblical idea that nature is the result of divine purpose and the 'scientific' idea of long ages of time" (p. 71).

48. Gibson, "Models of Origins," p. 91.

49. C John. Collins, *Science & Faith: Friends or Foes?* (Wheaton, IL,: Crossway Books, 2003), p. 84.

50. Ibid., p. 6.

the benefits of the Sabbath day devoted to the honor of God subtly slips over into a description of the day *itself*. Apparently, we are supposed to understand that here is a "day" without any inherent time limit to it! Furthermore, Collins argues, were the sixth day to be understood according to its normal time span, then there is simply too much to do on that day. With a gap of some time supposedly implied between the creation of Adam and Eve,[51] any normal, straightforward understanding of this day is not possible, he contends.[52] The other days of creation week would then be non-literal as well.

Collins openly acknowledges, "My own reading of Genesis means that I have no problem with the amount of time the theory [the big bang] calls for."[53] What is more troubling about this statement is that he also admits that "Since I am not a cosmologist, I have no way of knowing whether the technical details of the Big Bang theory are sound or not."[54] A few pages later he admits that "There are plenty of technical details on both sides [of the creationist versus evolutionist debate about the validity of radiometric dating methods], and I don't pretend to know how to assess them. . . . I conclude then, that I have no reason to disbelieve the standard theories of the geologists, including their estimate for the age of the earth."[55] It is hard not to conclude that his admitted cosmological and geological ignorance is influencing his reading of Genesis 1.

Inclusio and Sequence

In Genesis 1:1–2:3, the definite article occurs with days 1, 6, and 7, but is lacking with days 2 through 5. Some have quickly assumed that this lack allows for indefinite days and a non-fixed order. But this approach overlooks the significance of the opening and closing definite articles. The indefinite noun, *yôm*, joined with an indefinite cardinal numeral, *'echad*, has an emphatic counting force, a definite sense, and still retains the force of an ordinal number, that is, "the first day."[56] Employment of an enveloping, or *inclusio* technique suggests a tightly knit sequence is in place, and forbids random order or open-ended chronology in the creation account. The definite articles, one by syntactical function (1:5) and one by actual articular usage (2:2–3), provides a clear boundary setting the days within an uninterrupted tightly knit frame; the days being thus chronological

---

51. Ibid., p. 88.
52. Ibid., p. 6–87.
53. Ibid., p. 233
54. Ibid.
55. Ibid., p. 250.
56. Hasel, "The 'Days' of Creation," p. 27. See also Andrew E. Steinmann, "'*echad* [transliteration] as an Ordinal Number and the Meaning of Genesis 1:5," *JETS* 45/4 (December 2002): p. 577–584, whose final conclusion states that the word "day" in and of itself does not mean a 24-hour day, but the use of '*echad* in Genesis 1:5 "and the following unique uses of the ordinal numbers on the other days demonstrates that the text itself indicates that these are regular solar days" (p. 84).

and sequential.[57] The joining of the definite article to the noun and the numeral (2:2–3, in contrast to the definite article joined only the numeral on the sixth day — 1:31) perhaps sets the account within the larger frame of six days work plus one day rest; a schema which the Lord had set up as the weekly rhythm for mankind in His world.

The reader cannot but be aware that the record points to orderly sequence within such a specific time frame. Indeed, as Bruce Waltke points out, Genesis does not follow the ancient Near Eastern (ANE) mythopoetic idea of cyclical time, in which time really has no significance and equally history has no meaning. Time in Genesis is linear with events occurring successively within time.[58]

Scientifico-Concept Exegesis[59]

Despite Hasel's seminal article, others will undoubtedly continue to disagree, though most old-earth proponents seem to have overlooked Hasel's work. The question is whether or not their disagreement will be based on grammatical considerations or on what Carl Henry forthrightly and perceptively labeled "scientifico-concept exegesis." He observed that accommodating historical-grammatical exegesis to scientific perspectives brought about this type of exegesis which gradually replaced the historical-grammatical.[60] Insightfully, he noted that clergymen, reluctant to abandon the "biblical importance of cosmic and human beginnings" and equally reluctant to enter into dispute with scientific views of the origins of man and the world, began increasingly to speak of an evolutionary hypothesis discernible in the biblical text. The tension created over the validity of creation changed the hermeneutics. All the information and evidence given in the wealth of resources — books, DVD's, magazines, and technical journals, and multiple websites — made available by Answers in Genesis, the Institute for Creation Research, the Creation Research Society, and other creationist organizations has not resolved the debate nor eased the tension. But it does not appear that most exegetes have seriously considered the arguments and evidences presented in these young-earth resources related to the history and age of the creation. Henry also well remarked:

> But if God can convey authoritative information about himself and his relations to man, it is unclear why he cannot also convey — as the creation account on the surface implies — reliable knowledge, however limited, about man, nature, and their interrelationships. If God can

---

57. Ibid., p. 27–28.
58. Bruce Waltke, "יוֹם (yôm)" in R. Laird Harris, Gleason L. Archer, and Bruce K. Waltke, eds., *Theological Wordbook of the Old Testament* (Chicago, IL: Moody Press, 1980), 1:371.
59. Carl F.H. Henry, *God, Revelation and Authority* (Waco, TX: Word Books, Publishers, 1983), 6:139.
60 Ibid., 6:113

commend truths about himself, why must he tell falsehoods about the universe and his relationship to it?[61]

One prominent opponent of young-earth creationism acknowledged that a straightforward understanding of the Genesis record:

> . . . without regard to all the hermeneutical considerations suggested by science, is that God created heaven and earth in six solar days, that man was created on the sixth day, that death and chaos entered the world after the fall of Adam and Eve, and that all of the fossils were the result of the catastrophic universal deluge which spared only Noah's family and the animals therewith.[62]

He then summarily dismisses all these biblically accurate propositions by noting that this biblical teaching denies and belittles the vast amount of scientific evidence amassed to support the theory of the antiquity of the earth. But, in response, surely if the biblical record by virtue of what it says belittles any theory invented by men, then that theory is worthy of belittlement and of searching re-examination. Wilder-Smith appropriately and pointedly asked: "Why are so many evangelical Christians so eager to harmonize their beliefs with a 'working hypothesis' that is so deficient in scientific evidence of an experimental nature?"[63] Why indeed?

If science is accorded a primary place in exegesis then having more time becomes mandatory, otherwise there is an uncomfortable disjuncture between Genesis and the scientific community's theories on origins and the length of time needed to bring about all that Moses spoke of in his first book.

A Slate of Closing Questions

Carl Henry, who introduced the descriptive phrase "scientifico-concept exegesis," identifies the three very influential referents which will intersect with each other when one is deciding on the importance of a six-day creation in his worldview. These referents are authoritative Scripture, philosophical reasoning, and scientific empiricism.[64]

The following pointed questions still stand behind the initial negative response to the inquiry voiced as the title of this essay. Can deep time be embedded in Genesis? The elasticizing which takes place when *yôm* is not taken as a normal day in Genesis 1 and when harmony with the dominant theory about the age and history of creation is demanded instead gives rise to questions regarding the place and importance of man in relation to the history of the world:

---

61. Ibid.

62. Pattle T. Pun, "A Theory of Progressive Creationism," *Journal of the American Scientific Affiliation* 39 (Mar 1987): p. 14.

63. A. E. Wilder-Smith, *Man's Origin, Man's Destiny: A Critical Survey of the Principles of Evolution and Christianity* (Minneapolis, MN: Bethany House, 1968), p. 307.

64. Henry, *God, Revelation and Authority*, 6:138.

(1) In the history of the earth as conceived by the various old-earth reinterpretations of the text, man, who is the only creature made in the image of God and who was commanded to rule as vice-regent over the rest of creation, only occupies a very tiny part of that history. Isn't it problematical that most of the creatures, over which he was to rule, lived and died (with many species supposedly becoming extinct) millions of years before the vice-regent was created?

(2) In such a deep-time scenario, can man be given any significance in relation to the universe in God's program? This is especially so, if time is the arena of Yahweh's purposeful acts. After all, is not man the crowning piece of God's creative activity?[65]

(3) Does not the elasticizing of the biblical record on origins allow for prevailing, but changing, hypotheses to be accepted as "truthful" aids to interpretation? Could that not also be a tacit expression of a willingness to jettison the clear meaning of the text, if the exegete deems it necessary to do so?

(4) Finally, what of this question of embedded meaning? Significantly, nothing in the context or in the grammar or syntax or vocabulary suddenly and immediately dictated spans of time of unknown duration, or spans of known time interspersed by unknown ages-long eras. Deep time, indeed, did not arise automatically from the text itself. As Mortenson has shown in his chapter on the historical roots of this debate about the age of the creation, no author spotlighted this or that element as necessarily and forcibly overriding all specificity of a span of time, in favor of vagueness of time.

Hopefully, evangelical studies of creation will not take the path leading down to the following scenario:

> The task of relating science and theology at some point will involve the need to re-articulate the idea of God and its surrounding network of symbols in the light of the framework of an incredibly vast, unimaginably old, expanding universe, and of biological evolution through a process that seems to be deeply characterized by the polarity of necessity and chance.[66]

Were this to happen, Genesis 1 would rise up in righteous indignation.

---

65. At hearing these words, former students of Dr. Whitcomb's may remember his "only man" refrain which followed right after pointing out that though the physical differences between man and ape are quite great, the spiritual/mental/linguistic/cultural differences are only a little short of infinite. Eleven times *only man* rang out as the opening words to identifying yet another difference: "*only man* is self-conscious as a person, *only man* is . . . etc." See also Whitcomb, *Early Earth*, p. 120, 130–131.

66. Zachary Hayes, "God and Theology in an Age of Scientific Culture" *New Theology Review* 8:3 (August 1995): p. 17.

Chapter 8

A Critique of the Framework Interpretation of the Creation Week

Robert V. McCabe

In the fall semester of 1974, I was a student at Grace Theological Seminary and enrolled in a class on Genesis taught by Dr. John C. Whitcomb, Jr. Over the course of that semester, I was impressed with his theological depth and his ability to articulate the theological content of the early chapters of Genesis. What I remember most was his defense of recent creationism, the global nature of Noah's Flood, and his refutation of those views that compromise watershed biblical truths. Since that class on Genesis and the completion of my academic work at Grace, I have developed an increasing concern over a growing apathy and skepticism toward the theological substance in the early chapters of Genesis. In response to this type of erosion in doctrine, I have attempted over the last ten plus years to develop a course on biblical creationism. In producing this class, I have immersed myself in Dr. Whitcomb's many articles and books that have an impact on this subject. I have used books such as The Genesis Flood,[1] The Early Earth,[2] The World That Perished,[3] and The Moon,[4] not to mention collateral reading from his many other articles. His ministry has profoundly affected my understanding of young-earth creationism. On pages 78–82 of The Early Earth, Whitcomb provides a brief assessment of the framework interpretation. With admiration and thankfulness for my former professor, I presently take up the same task of providing a critique of the framework

---

Unless otherwise noted, all Scripture in this chapter is from the NASB version of the Bible.

1. John C. Whitcomb Jr. and Henry M. Morris, *The Genesis Flood* (Philadelphia PA: Presbyterian & Reformed, 1961).
2. John C. Whitcomb Jr., *The Early Earth,* rev. ed. (Grand Rapids, MI: Baker, 1986).
3. John C. Whitcomb Jr., *The World That Perished* (Grand Rapids, MI: Baker, 1973).
4. John C. Whitcomb Jr. and Donald B. DeYoung, *The Moon* (Grand Rapids, MI: Baker, 1978).

view of the creation week.[5]

In contrast to the traditional interpretation of Genesis 1 as a sequential account of God's creative activity in six literal days, the framework view affirms that the creation "week" itself is a figurative structure. According to the framework theory, Genesis 1, therefore, does not address and provide any information to establish the age of the earth with the result that this position capitulates to the demands of modern science for an earth that is 4 to 5 billion years old. This understanding of the creation account was initially set forth in 1924 by Professor Arie Noordzij of the University of Utrecht.[6] While Noordzij's framework view did not initially gather many adherents, it acquired more prominence through N.H. Ridderbos's book, Is There a Conflict Between Genesis 1 and Natural Science?[7] *However, the current popularity of this interpretation is largely a result of the work of Reformed scholar Meredith G. Kline.[8] His initial entry was an article in 1958, "Because It Had Not Rained."[9] Since Kline's initial article, some other reputable Christian scholars have attempted to provide defenses of the framework interpretation.*

In essence, the framework view asserts that the creation "week" of Genesis 1:1–2:3 is a literary framework intended to present God's creative activity in a topical, non-sequential manner, rather than a literal, sequential one. The framework theory is supported by three major arguments. First, the figurative nature of the creation account demonstrates that it is arranged topically rather than chronologically. Second, ordinary providence governed the creation account. Third, the unending nature of the seventh day indicates that the six days of the creation week are not normal days.[10] These three theses provide an appropriate structure

---

5. This chapter is a condensation of two previous articles that I have written: "A Critique of the Framework Interpretation of the Creation Account (Part 1 of 2)," *Detroit Baptist Seminary Journal* 10 (2005): p. 19–67; and "A Critique of the Framework Interpretation of the Creation Account (Part 2 of 2)," *Detroit Baptist Seminary Journal* 11 (2006): p. 63–133.

6. For a summary and critique of Noordzij's 1924 work, *God's Word en der Eeuwen Getuigenis,* see Edward J. Young, *Studies in Genesis One* (Phillipsburg, NJ: Presbyterian & Reformed, 1964), p. 43–105.

7. N.H. Ridderbos, *Is There a Conflict Between Genesis 1 and Natural Science?* trans. John Vriend (Grand Rapids, MI: Eerdmans, 1957).

8. Meredith G. Kline, "Space and Time in the Genesis Cosmogony," *Perspectives on Science and Christian Faith* 48 (March 1996): p. 2.

9. Meredith G. Kline, "Because It Had Not Rained," *Westminster Theological Journal* 20 (May 1958): p. 145–157. See also Kline's subsequent article, "Space and Time," 2–15.

10. A wide range of scholars who argue that the days of the creation week are figurative and that the actual "week" itself is a metaphor that pictures a topical arrangement of these figurative "days" espouses the framework position. It should be noted that not all framework advocates would use all three of these major arguments I have outlined above. More precisely, some framework advocates use Gen. 2:5 to support the creation week being controlled by ordinary providence, while others do not. The chief advocate using Gen. 2:5 to support the framework has been Meredith G. Kline, "Because It Had

to evaluate the biblical legitimacy of the framework view.

The Figurative Nature of the Creation Account

The framework interpretation argues that God used the imagery of an ordinary week to serve as a figurative framework for God's acts of creation.[11] I will initially provide an explanation of this argument followed by an evaluation of it.

Explanation

According to Kline, "Exegesis indicates that the scheme of the creation week itself is a poetic figure and that the several pictures of creation history are set within the six work-day frames not chronologically but topically."[12] To gain a more complete picture of this argument, the "six work-day frames," the creation account's topical arrangement, and its arrangement as a "poetic figure" require a more detailed analysis.

Not Rained," p. 145–157. Others who follow Kline include: Henri Blocher, *In the Beginning,* trans. David G. Preston (Downers Grove, IL: InterVarsity Press, 1984), p. 53, 56; Mark D. Futato, "Because It Had Rained: A Study of Gen. 2:5–7 with Implications for Gen. 2:4–25 and Gen. 1:1–2:3," *Westminster Theological Journal* 60 (Spring 1998): p. 2–10, 13–17; Mark Ross, "The Framework Hypothesis: An Interpretation of Genesis 1:1–2:3," in *Did God Create in Six Days?* ed. Joseph A. Pipa Jr. and David W. Hall (Taylors, SC: Southern Presbyterian Press, 1999), p. 122–128; Lee Irons with Meredith G. Kline, "The Framework View," in *The Genesis Debate: Three Views on the Days of Creation,* ed. David G. Hagopian (Mission Viejo, CA: Crux Press, 2001), p. 230; W. Robert Godfrey, *God's Pattern for Creation* (Phillipsburg, NJ: Presbyterian & Reformed, 2003), p. 52–53.

However, a number of framework interpreters do not use Gen. 2:5 to support their interpretation of the literary framework in Gen. 1:1–2:3. See Mark A. Throntveit, "Are the Events in the Genesis Creation Account Set Forth in Chronological Order? No," in *The Genesis Debate: Persistent Questions About Creation and the Flood,* ed. Ronald Youngblood (Nashville, TN: Nelson, 1986), p. 36–55; Gordon J. Wenham, *Genesis 1–15,* Word Biblical Commentary (Waco, TX: Word, 1987), p. 19, 39–40; Victor P. Hamilton, *The Book of Genesis: Chapters 1–17,* New International Commentary on the Old Testament (Grand Rapids, MI: Eerdmans, 1990), p. 53–56; Ronald F. Youngblood, *The Book of Genesis,* 2nd ed. (Grand Rapids, MI: Baker, 1991), p. 24–33; Bruce K. Waltke with Cathi J. Fredricks, *Genesis: A Commentary* (Grand Rapids, MI: Zondervan, 2001), p. 56–58, 73–78; and R. Kent Hughes, *Genesis: Beginning and Blessing,* Preach the Word (Wheaton, IL: Crossway, 2004), p. 24–27.

11. Kline, "Because It Had Not Rained," p. 157.

12. Meredith G. Kline, "Genesis," in *New Bible Commentary,* ed. D. Guthrie and J.A. Motyer, 3rd ed. (Grand Rapids, MI: Eerdmans, 1970), p. 82; see also Ross, "Framework Hypothesis," p. 114.

Six Workday Frames

The overall literary structure used in the creation account is a scheme of "six work-day frames," with each day of work in Genesis 1 serving as a picture frame. Each day of the creation "week" is introduced by a divine announcement, *wayyōmer 'ĕlōhîm* ("and God said," Gen. 1:3, 6, 9, 14, 20, 24). In addition, *wayyōmer 'ĕlōhîm* is used twice on two different days: the third day (Gen. 1:9, 11) and the sixth (1:24, 26). According to the framework position, these eight uses of *wayyōmer 'ĕlōhîm* provide a frame for each day of the creation account,[13] and it is from these eight uses that framework supporters assert that there are eight creative events.[14] Within each frame, the author of Genesis either gives one snapshot of God's creative work, such as is reflected by the fiat-fulfillment expressions (e.g., Gen. 1:3, fiat: "Let there be light"; fulfillment: "and there was light"), on the first, second, fourth, and fifth days, or he gives two snapshots on each of the remaining days, the third and the sixth. When the six workday frames are viewed as a whole, the eight creation events are symmetrically divided into two parallel units of three days, with day 1 corresponding to day 4, day 2 to 5, and day 3 to 6. Thus, the first three days form a unit of four creative activities that are paralleled by the last three days with the same number of creative events, with the concluding day in each triad, days 3 and 6, presenting two snapshots of creation. The first triad has been classified as "creation kingdoms" (the creation of empty and undeveloped mass and space) and the second as "creature kings" (things created to develop and fill what was created in the first triad).[15] The intent of both triads is for literary and theological purposes, rather than chronological. As such, the literary parallels of the two triads are subordinate to the seventh day that is set up as a Sabbath rest of the "Creator King."[16] The following chart reflects the framework's view of the symmetrical design of the creation "week."

Creation Kingdoms		Creature Kings	
Day 1	Light	Day 4	Luminaries
Day 2	Firmament: sky & seas	Day 5	Inhabitants: sea & winged creatures
Day 3	Dry land, Vegetation	Day 6	Land animals, Man
The Creator King			
	Day 7	Sabbath	

As this chart shows, the structural arrangement of both triads indicates that the literary arrangement of the creation account was not to establish a

---

13. Waltke, *Genesis*, p. 56.
14. Irons and Kline, "Framework View," p. 227–28; Hamilton, *Genesis*, p. 119; Waltke, *Genesis*, p. 56; Wenham, *Genesis 1–15*, p. 6–7.
15. Irons and Kline, "Framework View," p. 224.
16. Ibid., p. 224–225.

chronological sequence, but to have a literary structure of creative activities that "culminates in the Sabbath."[17]

A Topical Arrangement

This structure reflects the framework interpretation's contention that the creation account was written topically. To demonstrate that the creation week is a topical account, the author of Genesis has supposedly placed some obvious inconsistencies into the early chapters of Genesis. Framework advocates note that an obvious example of an intentional inconsistency relates to God's creation of light. On the first day of creation, God created light, yet the source of light is not created until the fourth day.[18] This suggests that day 1 and day 4 describe the same creative activity. On day 1, the creation of light is briefly described; however, on day 4, the creation of light is described in detail. According to the framework view, the creation of light on day 4 serves as an example of temporal recapitulation.[19] This type of inconsistency, labeled as dischronologization, indicates, it is said, that the creation week is topically arranged.

An Artistic Narrative

The symmetrical structure and topical arrangement of the creation narrative allegedly implies that it is not a normal historical narrative, but one that involves a highly artistic style,[20] or a "semi-poetic style."[21] In keeping with its supposed semi-poetic texture, framework defenders interpret the temporal markers, the days and the "evening and morning" expressions, as metaphors to describe heavenly time, and not earthly literal time.[22] Framework advocates agree that this type of rhetorical feature is supportive of a topical account of creation, rather than a chronological one. In addition, the symmetrical nature of the creation "week" is reflected by its arrangement into six units of days, or "panels,"[23] with each panel following a typical progression, such as "God saw," "there was," and God's evaluation of the cited creative activity as "good." Each panel is concluded with a chronological refrain: "And there was evening and there was morning, one day," etc.[24] The precise use of numbers, rather than showing a sequence of days, "attests to God's logical and timely shaping of cre-

---

17. Ridderbos, *Genesis 1 and Natural Science,* p. 32.
18. Ross, "Framework Hypothesis," p. 120; and Godfrey, *God's Pattern,* p. 40–41.
19. Irons and Kline, "Framework View," p. 229–230.
20. Blocher, *In the Beginning,* p. 50.
21. Kline, "Because It Had Not Rained," p. 156.
22. Some framework advocates refer to the time markers of the creation narrative as metaphors (so Irons and Kline ["Framework View," p. 240]; and Ross ["Framework Hypothesis," p. 120]). Others refer to them as anthropomorphic expressions (so Ridderbos [*Genesis 1 and Natural Science,* p. 30]; Blocher [*In the Beginning,* p. 57]; and Waltke [*Genesis,* p. 77]).
23. Waltke, *Genesis,* p. 56.
24. Ibid., p. 57; Kline, "Space and Time," p. 10.

ation."[25] When the creation account's topical arrangement and its symmetrical nature are linked with the use of metaphors or anthropomorphisms for heavenly time, framework proponents conclude that the creation narrative is not normal historical narrative, but reflects a highly stylized use of narrative.[26] The framework view's interpretation of the symmetrical nature and topical arrangement of the creation account results in undermining the substance of this account as genuine history. In sum, this thesis of the framework view argues that an inherent fabric of Genesis 1:1–2:3 is something of a hymnic use of narrative, a semi-poetic account, that, in its design of presenting a theology of the Sabbath, uses the figurative framework of a "week" to topically arrange certain creation motifs.[27]

Evaluation

To refute these three features of the framework that reputedly support interpreting the creation account figuratively, my critique will start by demonstrating that the creation account is genuine historical narrative and not an artistic account that undermines the historical substance of Genesis 1:1–2:3.

Genuine Sequential Narrative

While there may be some debate about the extent of the creation account's artistic nature, it is an incontrovertible fact that it is not a poetic text.[28] In addition to Genesis 1:1–2:3 not exhibiting linear parallelism as would be the case in a poetic text, it is demonstrably permeated with a grammatical device that sets it apart as an unambiguous narrative account: the *waw* consecutive. By way of supplementing Steven Boyd's excellent chapter in this book, I offer these further considerations.

Though the *waw* consecutive may appear in poetic literature, it is not a defining characteristic of Hebrew poetry.[29] However, it is a significant component of Hebrew historical narrative and generally provides an element of sequence to past time narrative.[30] *Waw* consecutives, according to Pratico and Van Pelt, "are used primarily in narrative sequence to denote consecutive actions, that is, actions occurring in sequence."[31] For example, in the Book of Genesis the *waw* consecutive

25. Waltke, *Genesis*, p. 57.

26. Blocher, *In the Beginning*, p. 52.

27. Ibid., p. 50.

28. Walter C. Kaiser, Jr., "The Literary Form in Genesis 1–11," in *New Perspectives on the Old Testament*, ed. J. Barton Payne (Waco, TX: Word, 1970), p. 59–60; and Gerhard F. Hasel, "The 'Days' of Creation in Genesis 1," *Origins* 21 (1994): p. 19–21. Framework advocates also recognize this point. For example, see Blocher, *In the Beginning*, p. 32, and Hughes, *Genesis*, p. 26.

29. Paul Joüon, *A Grammar of Biblical Hebrew*, 2 vols., trans. and rev. T. Muraoka (Rome: Pontifical Biblical Institute, 1993), 2:390, sec. 118c.

30. Bill T. Arnold and John H. Choi, *A Guide to Biblical Hebrew Syntax* (Cambridge, UK: Cambridge University Press, 2003), p. 84, sec. 3.5.1.

31. Gary D. Pratico and Miles V. Van Pelt, *Basics of Biblical Hebrew* (Grand Rapids, MI:

is used 2,107 times, with an average distribution of approximately 42 uses per chapter. In Genesis 2:4–25 the *waw* consecutive is used 21 times in 22 verses; and in 3:1–24 it is used 34 times. However, in a chapter that is poetic, Genesis 49:2–33, the *waw* consecutive appears only 15 times in 31 verses. But in the chapter preceding Genesis 49, 48:1–18, the *waw* consecutive is used 36 times and, in the chapter that follows it, 50:1–23, the *waw* consecutive appears 41 times.[32]

The use of *waw* consecutive to communicate sequential, past tense material is the expected style for a historical book like Genesis. If the author of Genesis wanted to preserve past tense, sequential material, we would expect his literary style to include a consistent use of the *waw* consecutive. What is germane to this argument is that the *waw* consecutive appears 55 times in the 34 verses found in Genesis 1:1–2:3. Thus, the use of the *waw* consecutive in the prologue to the historical narrative of Genesis, Genesis 1:1–2:3, is consistent with the narrative material found in the remainder of Genesis. If Moses did not intend the creation account to be taken sequentially, then why did he so frequently use a grammatical form that is regularly used for sequence?[33] My argument is not that *waw* consecutive always denotes sequence, for, within a narrative sequence, it may occasionally represent non-sequential action, such as a pluperfect (action that is anterior to the mainline narrative) or a consequence;[34] however, it is quite certain that *waw* consecutive is predominantly used sequentially with a preterite[35] in narrative literature.[36] Such is the case in Genesis 1:1–2:3. After verses 1–2,[37] the mainline

Zondervan, 2001), p. 192. In this paper I use the expression *waw* consecutive as a simplified expression to refer to a specialized form of the Hebrew conjunction *waw* that is prefixed to an imperfect form, a derivative of the archaic preterite. As far as actual biblical Hebrew grammar is concerned, there are actually two types of *waw* consecutives: *waw* consecutive prefixed to an imperfect/preterite form and *waw* consecutive prefixed to a perfect form. The most common of these two forms is the first kind, *waw* consecutive plus the imperfect/preterite (this is also referred to as *waw* conversive, *waw* inversive, relative *waw*). This type of *waw* consecutive is generally used in narration connected with past time. The second type of *waw* consecutive is joined to the perfect aspect. This may be used in reference to future time (for a brief discussion of these two forms, see Thomas O. Lambdin, *Introduction to Biblical Hebrew* [New York: Charles Scribner's Sons, 1971], p. 107–9). In addition, *waw* consecutive plus the perfect also commonly carries over a temporal situation presented in a preceding verb (see Bruce K. Waltke and M. O'Connor, *An Introduction to Biblical Hebrew Syntax* [Winona Lake, IN: Eisenbrauns, 1990], p. 502–504).

32. I have derived these statistics about the uses of *waw* consecutive from Accordance 7.03 (OakTree Software, 2006), available at www.oaksoft.com.
33. John D. Currid, *A Study Commentary on Genesis, Volume 1: Genesis 1:1–25:18* (Darlington, England: Evangelical Press, 2003), p. 39.
34. In this context, a consequence is an action or state that it is a result of a preceding *waw* consecutive.
35. This is an action or state in the past tense.
36. See Arnold and Choi, *Biblical Hebrew Syntax,* p. 84–85, sec. 3.5.1.
37. When Gen. 1:1 states that God created "the heavens and the earth," this refers to God's

narrative of the creation account is carried along by the *waw* consecutive, just as the *waw* consecutive is consistently used in the Book of Genesis.

However, if the *waw* consecutive may also be translated as a pluperfect, does this not imply that a few of the 55 *waw* consecutives in Genesis 1:1–2:3 may involve temporal recapitulation, just as framework supporters contend occurred on the fourth day (Gen. 1:14–19)?[38] Though the *waw* consecutive in some contexts may allow for temporal recapitulation, its use as the mainline sequence advances the divine creative activities of Genesis 1:1–2:3, and more specifically, this sequential advancement in verses 14–15 excludes any interpretation that takes day 4 as an example of temporal recapitulation.[39] To demonstrate that the mainline narrative is advanced by the sequential use of the majority of the 55 *waw* consecutives, I have provided the following chart to illustrate the sequential nature of Genesis 1:1–2:3. To portray this point, I have taken the liberty of modifying the NASB's translation of the *waw* consecutives.[40] While the *waw* consecutive is unmistakably identifiable in a Hebrew text, the same is not true in an English version. Rather than providing a functional translation, the purpose of my chart is to illustrate some basic information about the *waw* consecutive and how each of the 55 uses fits into three subcategories. In identifying the 55 uses of *waw* consecutive, I have supplied an italicized "then" with the 46 constructions containing a sequentially arranged *waw* consecutive (abbreviated in the chart as Sequential WC), an italicized "and" for the eight epexegetical uses (abbreviated Epexegetical WC) and an italicized "thus" for the only example of a consequential use (abbreviated Consequential WC). See the chart on the following two pages.

Observations about *Waw* Consecutive in Genesis 1:1–2:3

As related to Genesis 1:1–2:3, some observations about the various uses of *waw* consecutive are necessary. First, the mainline narrative does not begin until verse 3. This indicates that the first creative activity of verse 1 initiating the space and time continuum provides an informing background for the development of the narrative line in Genesis 1:3–2:3. What this further suggests for an exegetical treatment of this text is that the historical narrative in the remainder of the account explains how an unformed and empty earth and empty heavens in verse 1

---

first creative act that initiates the space and time continuum in the created realm. Both the heavens and earth were created in totality, but incomplete. The heavens were dark and void of any heavenly objects and the earth was an unformed and empty, water-covered sphere surrounded by the darkness of the heavens (v. 2). The narrative sequence of Gen. 1:3–31 describes how God formed and filled the heavens and earth of verses 1–2.

38. Irons and Kline, "Framework View," p. 221–24, 228–230.

39. See Charles V. Taylor, "Syntax and Semantics in Genesis One," *Creation Ex Nihilo Technical Journal* 11 (1997): p. 183–186.

40. As the various English translations show, the *waw* can be translated as "and," "so," "then," "thus," "now," etc., depending on context and to provide acceptable English style.

were purposefully and progressively formed and filled.[41] Second, since the seventh day does not advance the sequence of creative activities, the *waw* consecutive that begins 2:1 summarizes and draws a consequence from Genesis 1. Third, we should not be surprised that there is only one sequential use of *waw* consecutive on the seventh day. After the text's announcement that God ceased from His creative work, the sequence that follows is the pronouncement of God's blessing on the seventh day. Fourth, the mainline narrative of the creation account is advanced by the 46 sequential uses of *waw* consecutive. Whatever else the many uses of this type of *waw* consecutive may reflect, we are dealing with historical narrative that is sequentially advanced. Thus, *waw* consecutive advances the mainline narrative of this account. Fifth, while the eight epexegetical uses of *waw* consecutive may seemingly create a problem for the traditional understanding of the creation account, a proper understanding of the epexegetical use shows how this kind of *waw* consecutive is in harmony with a literal interpretation. This less commonly used subcategory of *waw* consecutive does not follow a preceding *waw* consecutive in either temporal or logical sequence; rather it provides an explanation of the preceding *waw* consecutive. With the epexegetical use of *waw* consecutive, "the major fact or situation is stated first, and then the particulars or details, component, or concomitant situations are filled in."[42] For example, the first epexegetical use of *waw* consecutive is found on day 3 in verse 12: "And the earth brought forth vegetation, plants yielding seed after their kind, and trees bearing fruit, with seed in them, after their kind." What should be noted is that the preceding verse contains two *waw* consecutives used sequentially: "Then God said, 'Let the earth sprout vegetation, plants yielding seed, and fruit trees bearing fruit after their kind, with seed in them, on the earth'; and it was so." Initially we see in verse 11 the divine speech ("then God said"). This is followed by a divine fiat ("Let the earth sprout vegetation") and the fulfillment of that fiat ("and it was so"). Verse 12 gives the particulars of that fulfillment, "then it was so," and in so doing reiterates, with slight variation, what was indicated in the fiat of verse 11. The epexegetical *waw* consecutives follow this pattern throughout the creation week. Because framework advocates use the *waw* consecutives in verses 16–17 and other *waw* consecutives on day 4 to undermine a literal interpretation of the creation week, we will look at these in greater detail.

The Use of *Waw* Consecutive on Day 4

Seven *waw* consecutives are used to describe the activities of day 4 in Genesis 1:14–19. More specifically, Irons and Kline use the two *waw* consecutives in

---

41. See Joseph A. Pipa Jr., "From Chaos to Cosmos: A Critique of the Non-Literal Interpretations of Genesis 1:1–2:3," in *Did God Create in Six Days?* ed. Joseph A. Pipa, Jr., and David W. Hall (Taylors, SC: Southern Presbyterian Press, 1999), p. 188–189; and J. Ligon Duncan III and David W. Hall, "The 24-Hour View," in *The Genesis Debate: Three Views on the Days of Creation*, ed. David G. Hagopian (Mission Viejo, CA: Crux Press, 2001), p. 28.

42. Waltke and O'Connor, *Biblical Hebrew Syntax*, 551, sec. 32.2.2a.

Day	Verse	Sequential WC	Epexegetical WC	Consequential WC
1	1:3	*then* God said		
		then there was light		
	4	*then* God saw		
		then God separated		
	5	*then* God called		
		then there was evening		
		then there was morning, the first day		
2	6	*then* God said		
	7	*then* God made		
		then [God] separated the waters		
		then it was so		
	8	*then* God called		
		then there was evening		
		then there was morning, the second day		
3	9	*then* God said		
		then it was so		
	10	*then* God called		
		then God saw		
	11	*then* God said		
		then it was so		
	12		*and* the earth brought forth	
		then God saw		
	13	*then* there was evening		
		then there was morning, the third day		
4	14	*then* God said		
	15	*then* it was so		
	16		*and* God made	
	17		*and* God placed	

verses 16–17 to undermine a sequential understanding of any *waw* consecutive in Genesis 1:1–2:3.[43] Using these two epexegetical *waw* consecutives in Genesis 1 to bolster the framework position, Irons and Kline argue that the activities of day 4, represented by the seven uses of *waw* consecutive in verses 14–19, are an example of dischronologization.[44] This implies that the first use of *waw* consecutive on day 4, "*then* God said" (v. 14), is an example of temporal recapitulation, a pluperfect that describes the same events as day 1 but from a

43. Lee Irons with Meredith G. Kline, "The Framework Reply," in *The Genesis Debate: Three Views on the Days of Creation*, ed. David G. Hagopian (Mission Viejo, CA: Crux Press, 2001), p. 283.

44. Irons and Kline, "Framework View," p. 222; see also Futato, "Because It Had Rained," p. 14.

Day	Verse	Sequential WC	Epexegetical WC	Consequential WC
	18	*then* God saw		
	19	*then* there was evening		
		then there was morning, the fourth day		
5	20	*then* God said		
	21	*then* God created		
		then God saw		
	22	*then* God blessed		
	23	*then* there was evening		
		then there was morning, the fifth day		
6	24	*then* God said		
		then it was so		
	25		*and* God made	
		then God saw		
	26	*then* God said		
	27	*then* God created		
	28	*then* God blessed		
			and God said	
	29	*then* God said		
	30	*then* it was so		
	31	*then* God saw		
		then there was evening		
		then there was morning, the sixth day		
7	2:1			*thus* the heavens & the earth were completed
	2		*and* God completed	
			and He rested	
	3	*then* God blessed		
			and God sanctified	

different perspective, as we have previously observed. This would also be true for the second use of *waw* consecutive on day 4, "*then* it was so" (v. 15).[45] In answer to the framework, however else verse 14, as well as verse 15, may be understood, the *waw* consecutive that begins this verse, *wayyō'mer* ("*then* God said"), cannot be an example of temporal recapitulation of day 1.[46] If there is any consistency to the mainline narrative sequence, as reflected by *waw* consecutive, and especially with the number of consistent uses of *wayyō'mer 'ĕlōhîm* ("then God said"), a pluperfect understanding of *wayyō'mer 'ĕlōhîm* in verse 14 (i.e., "God had said" — in recapitulation of the first day's activity in v. 3) has absolutely no warrant

---

45. See Irons and Kline, "Framework View," p. 221.

46. For a more complete discussion of the textual differences between days 1 and 4, see my "Critique of the Framework Interpretation (Part 1)," p. 37–47.

in the mainline narrative sequence of this account. Verses 14–15 are part of the general structure that Moses uses for each day of creative activity: divine speech ("*then* God said," v. 14), fiat ("Let there be lights in the expanse . . . and let them be for signs . . . and let them be for lights in the expanse. . . ." v. 14–15), and fulfillment ("*then* it was so," v. 15). Therefore, the *waw* consecutive in verse 14 is not an example of temporal recapitulation but is a normal, sequential use of *waw* consecutive.

In actuality, the two epexegetical uses of *waw* consecutive in verses 16–17 appear after two sequential *waw* consecutives in verses 14–15 and make the most exegetical sense when taken as having a supportive role for the preceding sequential *waw* consecutives in verses 14–15. In reference to the first *waw* consecutive used at the beginning of verse 16 ("and God made the two great lights"), Irons and Kline insist that this *waw* consecutive cannot be used chronologically: "The *waw*-consecutive occurs in the very next verse: 'And God made the two great lights' (v. 16). If the *waw*-consecutive always denotes sequence, this statement would have to refer to an event chronologically subsequent to verses 14–15."[47] On the one hand, I can agree with Irons and Kline's point that *waw* consecutive is not always used sequentially and that there are several examples in the creation narrative that are clearly nonsequential. As reflected by the preceding chart, not all the *waw* consecutives in the creation account are used sequentially. My chart indicates that 46 of the 55 *waw* consecutives are used sequentially, eight epexegetically, and one consequentially.

On the other hand, I totally disagree with Irons and Kline's conclusion: "Therefore, students of the Bible cannot appeal to the presence of the *waw*-consecutive in Genesis 1 as evidence for a strictly sequential reading."[48] Their conclusion is overstated. Why cannot students of the Bible appeal to the *waw* consecutive to defend a sequential reading? The 46 sequential uses of *waw* consecutive in Genesis 1:1–2:3 indicate that the mainline narrative is advanced by this sequential construction. While there are nine exceptions (easily recognizable in the context) to the general sequential pattern of *waw* consecutive, these exceptions do not negate the general function of this grammatical construction. In fact, the predominant sequential use of the *waw* consecutive in 46 examples undoubtedly suggests a chronological reading of the text.

Because the two *waw* consecutives in verses 16–17 are epexegetical, verses 16–17 give detail to the fulfillment in verse 15 ("*then* it was so") by providing more specific data and suggesting the immediacy of the fulfillment of the fiat. In keeping with the fiat of verses 14–15, the epexegetical uses of *waw* consecutive at the beginning of verse 16 ("God said") and the beginning of verse 17 ("God placed them") specify the content of verses 14–15. Verse 16 identifies the "lights" of verse 14 as the sun, moon, and stars, and verses 17–18 specify that these luminaries are placed in "the expanse of the heaven" and reiterates

---

47. Irons and Kline, "Framework Reply," p. 283.
48. Ibid.

their threefold function stated in verses 14–15.[49] Rather than interpreting verses 14–19 as a temporal recapitulation of day 1, the general structural pattern of this creation day and the uses of *waw* consecutive reflect that day 4 is a progression after day 3, including two epexegetical uses of *waw* consecutive in verses 16–17 that provide greater detail to the fiat and fulfillment sequence of verses 14–15. While the *waw* consecutive demonstrates that the creation week is a literal account, do the repetitive elements work against a literal interpretation of Genesis 1:1–2:3, as the framework position argues?

Repetitive Elements and Narrative

The consistent use of 55 *waw* consecutives in Genesis 1:1–2:3 reflects that the content of this pericope is genuine history sequentially presented to summarize God's creative activity, including the first Sabbath, in the space of seven, consecutive literal days. The very substance of the creation account indicates that the framework's supposed parallelism between the "creation kingdoms" of days 1–3 and the "creature kings" of days 4–6 is not as lucid and symmetrical as framework proponents have maintained. Though the framework's two triads of days do not convincingly treat the exegetical details of the creation account, this does not mean that the creation narrative is not a stylized use of narrative. The author of Genesis used repetitive elements, such as "God said" (verses 3, 6, 9, 11, 14, 20, 24, 26, 28, 29), "let there be" or an equivalent jussive (verses 3, 6, 9, 11, 14, 20, 24, 26), "and there was" or "and it was so" (verses 3, 7, 9, 11, 15, 24, 30) "and there was evening and there was morning" (verses 5, 8, 13, 19, 23, 31),[50] to reflect a stylized use of Hebrew narrative. Framework supporters and recent creationists have some level of agreement that the text has a number of repetitive elements that demonstrate a stylized narrative.

Where framework proponents and their opponents diverge is how they interpret this stylized use of narrative. Kline qualifies his description of the creation account's literary style with this: "The semi-poetic style, however, should lead the exegete to anticipate the figurative strand in this genuinely historical record of the origins of the universe."[51] While calling the account a "genuinely historical record," Kline uses a "semi-poetic style" to find more "figurative" elements in this account than are normally found in narrative material. In contrast, Duncan and Hall, while also recognizing that the creation account has a stylized nature, resolutely claim that it "is written with many other markers typical of literal historical accounts. Moreover, it is consistently taken as historical throughout Scripture."[52] Pipa qualifies his use of "exalted prose" by his insistence that Genesis 1 is written in the same historical style

---

49. The threefold function attributed to the luminaries appears to reflect a chiastic arrangement between verses 14–15 and verses 17–18 (Currid, *Genesis,* p. 76).
50. See Wenham, *Genesis 1–15,* p. 6.
51. Kline, "Because It Had Not Rained," p. 156.
52. Duncan and Hall, "24-Hour View," p. 35.

as the remainder of the Book of Genesis.[53] From a hermeneutical perspective, the framework's "semi-poetic style," or whatever similar descriptive category one of its proponents uses, wishfully provides framework interpreters a license to interpret key aspects of the text figuratively. This approach by framework proponents, consequently, allows for an accommodation to an old-earth model. From an opposite hermeneutical standpoint, young-earth creationists interpret the text literally, just as they do the remainder of the historical material in the Book of Genesis, while they recognize that this passage, by the use of repetitive textual details, is stylized. They think it makes perfect sense that the infinite Creator of the heavens and the earth as well as language would give us an accurate historical narrative of His unique creative acts written in a coherent and exquisite style.

More expressly, it seems clear that the attempt by framework advocates to find more elements that are "figurative" in the creation account provides their justification for jettisoning a literal interpretation of the temporal markers in favor of a figurative understanding. The framework view argues that if one takes a literal interpretation of the creation account, meaning there is no sun for the first three days of creation, then each "day," along with its subordinate parts of "evening" and "morning," cannot be literal.[54] Against a non-literal interpretation of the creation week, God himself, on the first day of creation after creating light and darkness, "separated the light from the darkness" (Gen. 1:4). From verse 5 a definition for *day* may be gleaned: "God called the light day, and the darkness He called night. And there was evening and there was morning, one day." In short, each day of the creation week is defined as "the period of light-separated-from-darkness,"[55] and not a "solar" day as framework advocates caricaturize the traditional literal interpretation of the creation week.[56]

Nevertheless, we must still explain how the repetitive elements of the creation account can legitimately be harmonized with the traditional literal interpretation of Genesis 1:1–2:3. As Moses sought to represent in written form the events from the creation account, the literary shape of his material was controlled by two necessary elements: the actual events that took place during the creation week and His divinely given interpretation of the material. In the case of the creation account, God obviously gave direct revelation concerning the details of Genesis 1:1–2:3 to someone as early as Adam but no later than Moses, and Moses accurately preserved this in written form. That which actually happened during the creation week placed certain limitations on Moses' use of this material, and his theological message controlled how he selected and arranged this material. Repetition was part of his style of writing the creation narrative; however, he

53. Pipa, "Genesis 1:1–2:3," p. 166.

54. Kline, "Because It Had Not Rained," p. 156.

55. Robert E. Grossmann, "The Light He Called 'Day,' " *Mid-America Journal of Theology* 3 (1987): p. 9.

56. See Irons and Kline, "Framework View," p. 247.

did not use repetitious elements either in a rigid manner or to undermine the historical substance of the creation week.[57] The repetitious elements of the text relate to a general pattern that provides an outline for each day of divine creative activity.

This structural pattern has a few common elements. For each day, God's creative activity and its cessation are summarized by a fivefold structure: divine speech ("God said"), fiat ("let there be," or an equivalent, such as "let the waters teem," v. 20),[58] fulfillment ("there was," "it was so," "God created," etc.), evaluation ("God saw that it was good"),[59] and twofold conclusion ("there was evening and there was morning," the first day, etc.).[60] With this structural arrangement, excluding verses 1–2 where God describes His first creative activity in verse 1 along with a description of the earth's initial state in verse 2, each day of creative activity is begun with a *waw* consecutive, "then God said" (*wayyō'mer 'ĕlōhîm*), and is concluded with two *waw* consecutives, "and there was evening [*wayʻhî 'ereb*] and there was morning [*wayʻhî bōqer*]," followed by a sequentially numbered day.

While this structural scheme highlights key activities for each day, the *waw* consecutive advances the events of each day sequentially, and, after a concluding appositional phrase for each day containing a sequentially numbered day, it advances to the next day by introducing it with another *waw* consecutive, "then God said" (*wayyō'mer 'ĕlōhîm*). With a literal interpretation of the creation narrative, the fivefold structural scheme is integrated with the use of *waw* consecutive. As we have previously noted, the mainline narrative in Genesis 1:1–2:3 is advanced by *waw* consecutive. Though 16 percent of the *waw* consecutives are not sequential, the 84 percent that are sequential provide solid evidence for a literal interpretation as opposed to a topical interpretation of the creation week.

A Chronological Account

Not only is the creation account sequentially arranged, but it is also a chronological account. The chronological nature of Genesis 1:1–2:3 is tied to the historic literal day interpretation of the "days" of the creation week. Because

---

57. Inerrancy allows for literary shaping but never at the expense of the historical accuracy of the actual events, and it requires that the historical account sets parameters on literary shaping.

58. The verbs used in the fiat segment of this fivefold structure are usually jussives, with the exception of v. 26, where a cohortative is found, "let us."

59. For an explanation of the omission of the divine evaluation on day 2, see Pipa, "Genesis 1:1–2:3," p. 176. Whatever the reason for this omission by Moses, this fivefold structure was intended only as a general arrangement.

60. With some qualification, Young follows this fivefold pattern (*Studies in Genesis One*, p. 84). This fivefold pattern can also be adequately explained as a sixfold structural pattern (so Duncan and Hall, "24-Hour View," p. 32) or sevenfold (so Wenham, *Genesis 1–15*, p. 17–19).

a number of authors have provided defenses for a literal interpretation of "day" in this account,[61] we will briefly summarize this evidence.

Initially, we should note that the noun *yôm* ("day") always refers to a normal literal day when it is used as a singular noun and is not found in a compound grammatical construction.[62] *Yôm* is used in the Hebrew Old Testament 2,304 times. Of these, it is used in the singular 1,452 times.[63] In Genesis 1:1–2:3 *yôm* is used 14 times, 13 times in the singular and once in the plural (v. 14).[64] The lone plural use of "days" does not contradict our understanding of "day" as a normal day. Its use in 1:14 is consistent with our argument. While the use of the plural "days" is clearly not a reference to any of the specific days of the creation week, its use in 1:14 has specific reference to the movement of the heavenly bodies, which do enable people to measure the passage of literal days and literal years and recognize literal signs and seasons, according to their God-declared purpose. These are regular 24-hour days! Returning to our point about the 13 uses of "day" in Genesis 1, this type of singular use of "day" with a non-extended meaning is used consistently in this manner throughout Genesis, the Pentateuch, and the entire Old Testament to denote literal 24-hour days.[65]

Additionally, because the word "day" in the creation account is qualified by "evening" and "morning," each day is to be taken literally. The clauses in which these two nouns are found, "and there was evening and there was morning," stand in juxtaposition with each enumerated day of the creation week (1:5, 8, 13, 19, 23, 31). Whether "evening" and "morning" are used together in a context with "day" (19 times beyond the six uses in Genesis 1) or they are used without "day"

---

61. For a few examples, see Whitcomb, *Early Earth*, p. 28–37; Duncan and Hall, "24-Hour View," p. 21–119; Kenneth L. Gentry, Jr., "The Traditional Interpretation of Genesis 1," in *Yea, Hath God Said: The Framework Hypothesis/Six-Day Creation Debate*, by Kenneth L. Gentry, Jr., and Michael R. Butler (Eugene, OR: Wipf and Stock Publishers, 2002), p. 33–66; Hasel, " 'Days' of Creation in Genesis 1," p. 5–38; James B. Jordan, *Creation in Six Days* (Moscow, ID: Canon Press, 1999); Douglas F. Kelly, *Creation and Change* (Ross-shire, Great Britain: Mentor, 1997), p. 107–135; Pipa, "Genesis 1:1–2:3," p. 153–198; James Stambaugh, "The Days of Creation: A Semantic Approach." *Creation Ex Nihilo Technical Journal* 5 (1991): p. 70–78; and my "Defense of Literal Days in the Creation Week," *Detroit Baptist Seminary Journal* 5 (Fall 2000): p. 97–123.

62. By compound grammatical construction, I am referring to the following types of items: the noun *yôm* being used with a preposition immediately attached to it, *yôm* being a part of a longer prepositional construction which has a verbal immediately following it, *yôm* being a part of the multi-word construction known as the construct-genitive relationship, *yôm* being used in a compound construction (*yôm yôm*). See Hasel, " 'Days' of Creation in Genesis 1," p. 23–24.

63. *Theological Lexicon of the Old Testament*, s.v. "יוֹם," by J. E. Jenni, 2:526–272. *Yôm* is used in the Pentateuch 668 times. Of these, the singular form is used 425 times. It is used in Genesis 152 times, with 83 of these in the singular.

64. *Yôm* is used in Genesis 1:5 (twice), 8, 13, 14 (twice), 16, 18, 19, 23, 31; 2:2 (twice) and 2:3.

65. Hasel, " 'Days' of Creation in Genesis 1," p. 23–26.

(38 times), they are used consistently in reference to literal days. "Evening" and "morning" are best understood as references to the beginning and conclusion of the nighttime period that concludes each of the creation days, after God had ceased from that day's creative activity. The night cycle of evening to morning is reflected in the description of the Passover ritual in Deuteronomy 16:4: "For seven days no leaven shall be seen with you in all your territory, and none of the flesh which you sacrifice on the *evening* of the first day shall remain overnight until *morning*." With this interpretation, each day of the creation week has an "evening-morning" conclusion. The use of *waw* consecutive with each clause containing evening ("and there was evening") and morning ("and there was morning") indicates that at the conclusion of a creation day, the next sequence was evening and this was followed by the next significant sequence, morning.[66]

Furthermore, Exodus 20:8–11 and 31:14–17 support the historic, literal-day interpretation. For example, the context of Exodus 20:8–11 is that of God giving Israel the Decalogue and, in particular, the fourth commandment about Israel keeping the Sabbath holy. God's motive for this command (v. 11) was based on the pattern that He had set in the creation week, "For in six days the LORD made the heavens and the earth, the sea and all that is in them, and rested on the seventh day; therefore the LORD blessed the Sabbath day and made it holy." If we follow the figurative use of day, this verse could be translated: "For in six geological ages of six million years the LORD made heaven and earth, the sea, and all that in them is, and rested the seventh geological age lasting millions of years: wherefore the LORD blessed the Sabbath geological age of millions of years and hallowed it." Obviously, Moses had six literal days in mind with the seventh day also being a 24-hour period.

Finally, since *yôm* (day) is often modified in Genesis 1:1–2:3 by a numerical qualifier, each day must be a literal day. In each case where Moses summarizes God's creative work for that day, the word *yôm* is qualified by a number — "first day" (v. 5),[67] "second day" (v. 8), etc. When *yôm* is used with a numerical qualifier

---

66. For support of this interpretation of "evening" and "morning," see Pipa, "Genesis 1:1–2:3," p, 168; and Gentry, "Traditional Interpretation of Genesis 1," p. 36–39.

67. The phrase *yôm 'ekhad* accurately translated as either "one day" or "the first day." The use of the cardinal number *'ekhad* ("one"), rather than the ordinal *ri'shon* ("first") as in Num. 7:12 (*yôm ri'shon*, "the first day"), allows for a complexity in that a cardinal number is used in a clear numbering context. It may be that Moses used the cardinal *'ekhad* because, with day 1 of the creation week, he is defining a day as a "period of light-separated-from-darkness" (Grossmann, "Light He Called 'Day,'" p. 9). However, the semantic range of *'ekhad* is broad enough to allow for it to be used in a sequential context like Genesis 1. On the sequential use of *'ekhad*, see Waltke and O'Connor, *Biblical Hebrew Syntax*, p. 274; Ludwig Koehler and Walter Baumgartner, *The Hebrew and Aramaic Lexicon of the Old Testament*, 2 vols., rev. W. Baumgartner and J.J. Stamm, study ed. (Leiden: Brill, 2001), 1:30, hereafter cited as *HALOT*; and Francis Brown, Samuel R. Driver, and Charles A. Briggs, eds., *A Hebrew and English Lexicon of the Old Testament* (Oxford: Clarendon, 1972, reprint ed.), p. 25, hereafter cited as BDB.

in the Old Testament, it is never used in a figurative sense. This use of a numeral to qualify *yôm* is clearly demonstrated in Numbers 7. In this context, leaders from each tribe of Israel brought various gifts to the Lord for the dedication of the altar on 12, sequential, literal days, even though this section begins and ends with the non-literal use of *b^eyôm* ("when" or "in the day that") in 7:10 and 7:84 (as in Gen. 2:4). Thus, the use of "day" with a numerical adjective is a clear reference to a literal day.[68] What should not be missed with this point is that the use of sequential numbers with days unambiguously communicates that the first week in the space and time continuum was a week of seven literal, sequentially numbered days.

In reviewing this evaluation of the first major thesis of the framework, the creation week should be interpreted literally because it is permeated with a sequential use of *waw* consecutive. I have also stated that a stylized use of narrative is compatible with a literal view of the creation week. In contrast to the framework's figurative six workday frames, it was finally argued that a consistent interpretation of the theological and exegetical details associated with the creation account supports taking this pericope as a sequential and chronological account. In short, these three arguments indicate that the first premise of the framework is not supported by consistent exegesis. How substantive are the other arguments used to support the framework?

The Creation Account Controlled by Ordinary Providence

Although a number of framework interpreters do not use this as an essential thesis, those who follow Kline promote this as such. With this second major argument, some framework interpreters present the case that God used ordinary providence[69] to create during the creation "week."

Explanation

God's exclusive use of ordinary providence during the creation period is based on an argument that Genesis 2:5 presupposes this thesis. The chief advocate of this position is Kline, who argues:

> The Creator did not originate plant life on earth before he had pre-pared an environment in which he might preserve it without by-passing secondary means and without having recourse to extraordinary means such as marvelous methods of fertilization. The unargued presupposition

---

68. Hasel has made this same point, "When the word *yôm*, 'day,' is employed together with a numeral, which happens 150 times in the Old Testament, it refers in the Old Testament invariably to a literal day of 24 hours" " 'Days' of Creation in Genesis 1," p. 26.

69. Ordinary providence, which is normally referred to as providence, is God's non-miraculous operations in sustaining and directing all of His creation. For a discussion of providence, see John M. Frame, *The Doctrine of God* (Phillipsburg, NJ: Presbyterian & Reformed, 2002), p. 274–288.

of Gen. 2:5 is clearly that the divine providence was operating during the creation period through processes which any reader would recognize as normal in the natural world of his day.[70]

This means that there was "a principle of continuity between the mode of providence during and after the creation period."[71] Since a literal interpretation of Genesis 1 requires God's use of extraordinary providence[72] in the creation week, the literal interpretation is in conflict with the "because it had not rained" argument. If this argument is correct, "Genesis 2:5 forbids the conclusion that the order of narration [in Genesis 1] is exclusively chronological."[73]

Evaluation

Rather than presupposing that the "unargued presupposition" of Genesis 2:5 is that normal providence governed the creation period, the context of this verse is not intended to describe how the entire creation week was controlled but what the state of the created order actually was on day 6 of the creation week when God formed His image bearer to rule on earth as His vice-regent. Kline's presupposition about Genesis 2:5 is unacceptable because of the incompatibility of this interpretation of Genesis 2:5 with two contexts: its immediate context and the surrounding context of Genesis 2:4–25.

The Immediate Context of Genesis 2:5

After providing a summarized overview of the seven days of the creation week in Genesis 1:1–2:3, Moses' use of the first of 11 *tôlᵉdôt* headings in the Book of Genesis returns the reader to day 6 in order to provide a more detailed explanation of man's formation and placement in the Garden of Eden. The first of 35 uses of the compound divine names, *'Elōhîm Yahweh*, "the LORD God," in 2:4–3:23 demonstrate the tight contextual unity of Genesis 2–3. Both the *tôlᵉdôt* heading

---

70. Kline, "Because It Had Not Rained," p. 149–50. Because Futato's article is predicated upon Kline's 1958 article, his article is intended to complement Kline's. After providing more exegetical details to Gen. 2:5–7, Futato uses these details to show their implications for reading Gen. 2:4–25 and 1:1–2:3 and for their theological implications in Gen. 1–2 ("Because It Had Rained," p. 10–21). While a full discussion of Futato's article is not necessary for the argument of this paper, a fuller interaction with this article may be found in the following: Michael R. Butler, "The Question of Genesis 2:5," in *Yea, Hath God Said: The Framework Hypothesis/Six-Day Creation Debate*, by Kenneth L. Gentry Jr. and Michael R. Butler (Eugene, OR: Wipf and Stock Publishers, 2002), p. 102–122; Jordan, *Creation in Six Days*, p. 235–245; Pipa, "Genesis 1:1–2:3," p. 154–160; and McCabe, "Critique of the Framework Interpretation (Part 2)," p. 65–66, 79–81.

71. Irons and Kline, "Framework View," p. 230.

72. Extraordinary providence, generally referred to as miracle, is God's miraculous intervention in the created order. For a discussion of miracle, see Frame, *The Doctrine of God*, p. 241–273.

73. Kline, "Because It Had Not Rained," p. 154; so also Godfrey, *God's Pattern*, p. 52–53.

and *'Elōhîm Yahweh* reflect a clear change of contextual emphasis that focuses on what became of God's perfect creation.[74] What clearly works against Kline's assertion about 2:5 is the context of this verse, as Butler has incisively noted: "The most compelling reason to reject Kline's understanding of Genesis 2:5 is that his interpretation is out of accord with the context of Genesis 2:4–3:24 — the context which the *toledoth* formula of Genesis 2:4 places it. Genesis 2:5 does not have reference to the creation-in-process described in Genesis 1 (Kline's reading), but to the completed creation ready for man to inhabit and subdue."[75]

Interpreters have seen a number of difficulties in Genesis 2:5–6.[76] While the purpose of this paper does not allow for an examination of all the difficulties in these verses, it is necessary to demonstrate that the syntactic nature of verses 5–6 provides a setting for the primary proposition in verse 7: the formation of man.[77]

Genesis 2:5–6 contains six clauses. Four of them are circumstantial clauses, one in verse 5 is an explicit causal clause,[78] and the final one in verse 6 is a clause introduced by *waw* consecutive plus a perfective verb form.[79] The circumstantial clauses are readily identified since each is introduced by a simple conjunctive *waw* attached to a non-verbal form.[80] To illustrate the circumstantial use of *waw*, I have inserted *waw* in brackets in this arrangement:

> [5]Now [*waw*] no shrub of the field was yet in the earth,
> and [*waw*] no plant of the field had yet sprouted,
> for the LORD God had not sent rain upon the earth;
> and [*waw*] there was no man to cultivate the ground.
> [6]But [*waw*] a mist used to rise from the earth
> and water the whole surface of the ground.

Not all commentators view the four circumstantial clauses as being equally coordinate. The specific issue relates to the last clause in verse 5, "and [*waw*] there was no man to cultivate the ground." Is this last clause outside of the preceding

---

74. For a fuller development of Gen. 2:4 and its significance for the traditional, literal interpretation of Genesis 2, see my "Critique of the Framework Interpretation (Part 2)," p. 69–76.

75. Butler, "Question of Genesis 2:5," p. 101.

76. See Wenham, *Genesis 1–15*, p. 57.

77. For discussions of the actual interpretation of Gen. 2:5, see Butler, "Question of Genesis 2:5," p. 101–131.

78. This clause is introduced by the causal conjunction *kî*.

79. As noted above, n. 33, *waw* consecutive plus the perfect may carry over a temporal nuance from a preceding verb. The last clause in Gen. 2:6 is an example of this. In this case, the *waw* consecutive plus the perfect (*wᵉhišqah*, "and [used to] water") carries over an iterative sense from the preceding imperfect form (*ya'āleh*, "[a mist] used to rise") (see Waltke and O'Connor, *Biblical Hebrew Syntax*, p. 502–504).

80. For a description of a simple conjunctive *waw* used circumstantially, see Arnold and Choi, *Biblical Hebrew Syntax*, p. 147.

causal clause and is it coordinate with the other three circumstantial clauses, as our preceding textual arrangement reflects? Or, is this clause coordinate with the previous causal clause, "for the LORD God had not sent rain upon the earth"?[81] Because the *waw* conjunction at the head of the fourth clause implies a close syntactic relationship with the preceding causal clause, my preference is to follow this latter understanding and take the fourth clause as coordinate with the causal third clause. This would indicate that the last two clauses provide two reasons for the vegetation deficiencies specified in the first half of verse 5: no rain and no man to cultivate. Verses 6–7, then, explain how the two shortages were corrected: God provided a water supply (v. 6) and created man (v. 7), who becomes the focus of the narrative sequence in verses 7–25. God's taking care of both deficiencies indicates that He had not finished His week of creation. Nevertheless, I recognize that commentators are divided about the clausal arrangement and that a reasonable case may be marshaled to support either view.[82]

What is unmistakable in this text is that whichever view a commentator follows about the arrangement of the clauses in verse 5, most maintain that verses 5–6 provide a setting for verse 7 and not a statement about God's mode of operation in the creation week. For example, Westermann states, "The structure of this first part is quite clear and easy to explain: verses 4b–6 comprise the antecedent, verse 7 is the main statement."[83] Hamilton explains: "Verses 4b–7 are one long sentence in Hebrew, containing a protasis (v. 4b), a series of circumstantial clauses (v. 5–6), and an apodosis."[84] While both explanations about the relationship between verses 4–7 are nuanced differently, each has the formation of man in verse 7 as the primary proposition in verses 5–7. To state this another way, the six clauses of verses 5–6, which, in contrast to the 21 *waw* consecutives initiated in verse 7, are grammatically nonsequential and provide certain conditions associated with the occurrence of the action in the main clause of verse 7 ("Then the LORD God formed [*wayyîtser*] man of the

---

81. For example, Allen P. Ross sees three circumstantial clauses, with the last clause of v. 5 serving as an addition to the preceding causal clause (*Creation and Blessing* [Grand Rapids, MI: Baker, 1988], p. 119), as does Kenneth A. Mathews (*Genesis 1–11:26*, New American Commentary [Nashville, TN: Broadman, 1996], p. 193).

82. David Tsumura presents some of the difficulties with Gen. 2:5–6, while supporting the option that there are four coordinate circumstantial clauses (*Creation and Chaos* [Winona Lake, IN: Eisenbrauns, 2005], p. 78–80).

83. Claus Westermann, *Genesis 1–11: A Commentary*, trans. John J. Scullion (Minneapolis: Augsburg, 1984), p. 197. So also Gerhard Von Rad, *Genesis*, vol. 1 (Philadelphia, PA: Westminster, 1961), p. 74–75.

84. Hamilton, *Genesis: Chapters 1–17*, p. 156. Other interpreters who essentially follow this view include C. John Collins, *Genesis 1–4: A Linguistic, Literary, and Theological Commentary* (Phillipsburg, NJ: Presbyterian & Reformed, 2006), p. 133; Mathews, *Genesis 1–11:26*, p. 193; Pipa, "Genesis 1:1–2:3," p. 157; William D. Reyburn and Euan McG. Fry, *A Handbook on Genesis* (New York: United Bible Societies, 1997), p. 60; and Ross, *Creation and Blessing*, p. 119.

dust from the ground").[85] As the case is in biblical Hebrew, the *waw* consecutive stands at the head of the clause it governs. Not only does *wayyîtser* begin the first clause in verse 7, but it also initiates the mainline narrative sequence followed by a series of *waw* consecutives in verses 7–9.[86] The relationship that the six nonsequential clauses in verses 5–6 have with the introductory clause in verse 7, which begins with the *waw* consecutive, can be viewed in this manner:

> [5]Now [*waw*] no shrub of the field was yet in the earth,
> and [*waw*] no plant of the field had yet sprouted,
> for the LORD God had not sent rain upon the earth;
> and [*waw*] there was no man to cultivate the ground.
> [6]But [*waw*] a mist used to rise from the earth,
> and water the whole surface of the ground.
> [7]Then the LORD God formed [*wayyîtser*] man of dust
> from the ground.

While the formation of man from dust of the ground in verse 7 undoubtedly provides a semantic link with verses 5–6, *wayyîtser* initiates the mainline narrative thread that is sequentially followed by 5 *waw* consecutives in verses 7b–9. The paragraph in verses 10–14 interrupts the string of *waw* consecutives with a series of circumstantial clauses that explain the resplendent nature of the eastern area of Eden where God had planted the garden and placed man in verse 8. This paragraph, focusing on the four rivers that flowed from Eden, is anticipatory of the next *waw* consecutive in verse 15[87] which resumes the narrative sequence with a series of 15 *waw* consecutives in verses 15–25. Unmistakably, verses 5–6 provide the setting for the continuation of the narrative rather than supporting Kline's "unargued presupposition."

The Surrounding Context of Genesis 2:4–25

Genesis 2:5 is part of a series of six nonsequential clauses in verses 5–6 that provide circumstances associated with the formation of man in verse 7: "Then the LORD God formed man of dust from the ground, and breathed into his nostrils the breath of life; and man became a living being." This creative activity in verse 7 is summarized by a series of three *waw* consecutive verbs ("formed [*wayyîtser*]," "breathed" [*wayyippakh*], "became" [*wayhî*]). In the Hebrew text, each of these *waw* consecutives, as previously noted, advances a narrative sequence. In this verse, we should note the logic of the sequential verbs: the Lord

---

85. So also Francis I. Andersen, *The Sentence in Biblical Hebrew* (New York: Mouton Publishers, 1974), p. 86; Tsumura, *Creation and Chaos,* p. 80; and Wenham, *Genesis 1–15,* p. 57.

86. So also Alviero Niccacci, "Analysis of Biblical Narrative," in *Biblical Hebrew and Discourse Linguistics,* ed. Robert D. Bergen (Dallas, TX: Summer Institute of Linguistics, 1994), p. 187.

87. Ibid., p. 187–188.

God first formed the man from "the dust of the ground," he next breathed into man's "nostrils the breath of life," and finally "man became a living being." While this grammatical device has uses other than a strict sequence of actions, that nevertheless is a primary function of the verb form. Minimizing the sequential force of the *waw* consecutives in Genesis 2:4–25 would support the argument of some framework advocates that this pericope is a topical account. Though a few *waw* consecutives in this passage are not strictly sequential, the majority of them are used sequentially and they establish a sequence of activities that took place on day 6 of the creation week.

As was previously noted in reference to the use of *waw* consecutive in Genesis 1:1–2:3, this verbal form provides the basic framework that advances the narrative sequence. Although *waw* consecutive has different uses in Genesis 2:4–25, the sequential use of 17 of the 21 *waw* consecutives is the backbone of this narrative section. To communicate this, I have again taken the liberty of adapting the NASB's translation of the 21 *waw* consecutives. These *waw* consecutives are used in four ways: 17 are sequential, 2 are resumptive, 1 is a pluperfect, and 1 is consequential. In the chart on the following page, I have supplied an italicized "*then*" with the 17 examples of sequentially arranged *waw* consecutives (listed in the chart as Sequential WC), an italicized *and* for the two resumptive uses (Resumptive WC), an italicized "*now*" for the lone pluperfect (Pluperfect WC), and an italicized "*thus*" for the final example of a consequential use (Consequential WC).

Observations about *Waw* Consecutive in Genesis 2:4–25

A few items should be observed. First, as previously mentioned, the main-line narrative is started in verse 7a, continued by a tight sequence of five *waw* consecutives in verses 7b–9, briefly interrupted by five verses (10–14), resumed with two *waw* consecutives in verse 15, and advanced to completion with 13 *waw* consecutives in verses 16–25. Second, since the mainline narrative sequence begins in verse 7, this suggests that verses 4–6, as we have noted, constitute an informing background for verse 7 with its inception of the narrative unit that continues through verse 25. Third, the mainline sequence of events is advanced by 17 sequential uses of *waw* consecutive, which show that this passage is a historical narrative that is incrementally moved along. Fourth, the two *waw* consecutives in verse 15 have a resumptive function. While they form a sequence with the event represented by the fifth *waw* consecutive in verse 8 ("placed," *wayyitta*'), they do not form a strict sequence with the sixth *waw* consecutive in verse 9 ("caused to grow," *wayyasmakh*). Fifth, the final *waw* consecutive in verse 25 ("Thus [the man and his wife] were," *wayyihyû*) brings this unit to a conclusion.[88] The preceding *waw* consecutive in verse 23a ("*then* [the man] said," *wayyō'mer*) communicates Adam's delighted response to the formation of the woman from his "rib." In contrast to the animals that Adam had just named, the woman was made from

---

88. Ibid., p. 189.

Verse	Sequential WC	Resumptive WC	Pluperfect WC	Consequential WC
7	*then* the Lord God formed man *then* breathed *then* man became			
8	*then* the Lord God planted a garden *then* there he placed			
9	*then* the Lord God caused to grow			
15		*and* the Lord God took the man *and* put him into the Garden of Eden		
16	*then* the Lord God commanded			
18	*then* the Lord God			
19			*now* the Lord God had formed	
	then brought them			
20	*then* the man gave names			
21	*then* the Lord God caused a deep sleep *then* he slept *then* he took one of of his ribs *then* he closed up the flesh			
22	*then* the Lord God fashioned *then* he brought her			
23	*then* the man said			
25				*thus* the man and his wife were both naked

man and was a genuine complement for him.[89] The storyline is advanced to verse 23 with the 20th example of a *waw* consecutive; however, the editorial interruption in verse 24 applies the creation ordinance of marriage to Adam and Eve's posterity. As an outgrowth of the whole narrative, especially verses 23a–24, the account is completed with the final *waw* consecutive in verse 25, which in its consequential use concludes the pericope.[90] Sixth, while the two resumptive uses of *waw* consecutive in verse 15 and the one use of a pluperfect in verse 19 may

89. See Mathews, *Genesis 1–11:26*, p. 218–219.
90. Arnold and Choi, *Biblical Hebrew Syntax*, p. 85–86.

seemingly create a problem for my interpretation of the creation account, they are readily harmonized with the sequential material. Since the reputed difficulty with the *waw* consecutive revolves around these three uses of *waw* consecutive, these need more explanation.

Resumptive Uses of *Waw* Consecutive in Genesis 2:15

Most commentators recognize that the two *waw* consecutives in Genesis 2:15 resume the narrative thread of verse 8.[91] However, framework advocates try to demonstrate the presence of nonsequential *waw* consecutives to imply that other *waw* consecutives should be taken topically rather than sequentially.[92] Drawing from verse 15 and a few other examples, Irons and Kline conclude, "Thus, temporal recapitulation for the purpose of topical arrangement appears to be a key structural device in Genesis."[93] Though *waw* consecutive may at times reflect temporal recapitulation, their conclusion is overstated and undermines the normal sequential nature of the *waw* consecutive.

Since the context of Genesis 2 clearly indicates that verse 15 resumes the narrative thread of verse 8, both sequential verbs reflect some level of temporal recapitulation. Nevertheless, this recapitulation is restricted by its context. What Irons and Kline do not point out is that both *waw* consecutives are bound to a context that is advanced by a series of 17 *waw* consecutives used sequentially. This is to say, the actual sequential chain to which the two *waw* consecutives in verse 15 belong controls the recapitulation. To review, the narrative line in this pericope begins with the first *waw* consecutive in verse 7 and is advanced by a tight chain of five other *waw* consecutives in verses 7b–9. After the three *waw* consecutives describing the creation of man in verse 7, the next three *waw* consecutives in verses 8–9 picture God's planting a garden in Eden, placing man in the garden, and adorning this garden with various kinds of beautiful trees that had nutritious fruit, as well as including, in the middle of the garden, the tree of life and the tree of knowledge of good and evil. After this brief excursus about the splendor of the Garden of Eden, two *waw* consecutives in verse 15 resume the narrative chain by repeating, as well as expanding on, the *waw* consecutive in verse 8 ("[there he] placed," *wayyāśem*). Consequently, it is preferable to take these two verbs as examples of resumptive repetition.

Genesis 2:15 provides a good context to explain the literary technique of resumptive repetition. In this regard, we should note that both verbs in verse 15 ("took" [*wayyiqqakh*] and "put" [*wayyannikhēhû*]) have some semantic overlap with the second *waw* consecutive in verse 8 ("placed" [*wayyāśem*]).[94] The semantic

91. For example, see U. Cassuto, *A Commentary on the Book of Genesis: Part One — From Adam to Noah,* trans. Israel Abrahams (Jerusalem: Magnes Press, 1961), p. 121; Hamilton, *Genesis: Chapters 1–17,* p. 171; and Wenham, *Genesis 1–15,* p. 67.

92. So Irons and Kline, "Framework View," p. 219–224.

93. Ibid., p. 223.

94. For a discussion of the resumption of the narrative sequence in Gen. 2:15, see Collins, *Genesis 1–4,* p. 133. Niccacci also takes Gen. 2:15 as an example of resumptive

overlap in the vocabulary reflects some form of repetition. Because the two verbs in verse 15 pick up the sequence from verse 8, this is a resumption of the sequential line. By using resumptive repetition, Moses shows how the sequence of verse 15 relates to the overall sequential chain in this account.

Though the description of the *waw* consecutives in verse 15 as examples of resumptive repetition indicates that they do not reflect a strict chronology, this does not mean that chronological constraints have been abandoned by the narrative sequence.[95] Both *waw* consecutives in verse 15 sequentially resume the narrative line. In addition, though the *waw* consecutives in verse 15 are not sequential, the 17 sequential *waw* consecutives in 2:7–25 establish the chronological advancement of this passage. In the final analysis, the two resumptive *waw* consecutives are a non-issue since they practically function like the 17 sequential *waw* consecutives.

Pluperfect Use of *Waw* Consecutive in Genesis 2:19

The third *waw* consecutive used to support a topical interpretation of Genesis 2:4–25 is found in the first part of verse 19 ("[the LORD God] formed," *wayyîtser*). If the narrative line is followed in many English translations, Genesis 2:19a is part of a chronological sequence. The sequential development in verses18–19 is exhibited in the NASB:

> Then the LORD God said [*waw* consecutive], "It is not good for the man to be alone; I will make him a helper suitable for him." [19]And out of the ground the LORD God formed [*waw* consecutive] every beast of the field and every bird of the sky, and brought [*waw* consecutive] *them* to the man to see what he would call them; and whatever the man called a living creature, that was its name.

I have placed in brackets the *waw* consecutive after the appropriate three verbs in verses 18–19. We should observe that the initial *waw* consecutive in verse 19 is translated as a past tense, just like the other two *waw* consecutives in verse 18 and verse 19b. The past tense rendering of *wayyîtser*, "formed," is also followed in the KJV, NKJV, ESV, NRSV, NLT, and NET BIBLE. These translations reflect a narrative sequence in these two verses that looks like this:

1. The LORD God said it is not good for man to be alone.

---

repetition, though he restricts its use to the first sequential verb "took" (*wayyiqqakh*) ("Analysis of Biblical Narrative," p. 187). For a general discussion of resumptive repetition, see Philip A. Quick, "Resumptive Repetition: A Two-Edged Sword," *Journal of Translation and Textlinguistics* 6 (1993): p. 301–304; and Randall Buth, "Methodological Collision Between Source Criticism and Discourse Analysis," in *Biblical Hebrew and Discourse Linguistics,* ed. Robert D. Bergen (Dallas: Summer Institute of Linguistics, 1994), p. 147–148.

95. Young provides a helpful discussion of the chronology of Gen. 2:4–25 as it relates to Gen. 1 (*Studies in Genesis One,* p. 73–76).

2. The LORD God formed every beast of the field and every bird of the sky from the dust of the ground.
3. The LORD God brought every beast of the field and every bird of the sky to man so that man could name them.

Before the sequence in verses 18–19, the narrative chain was initiated by the creation of man, verse 7, then the formation of the Garden of Eden, verses 8–9. Following the sequence in verses 18–19, woman was formed from man, verse 22. According to the apparent sequence in Genesis 2, the beasts and birds were formed after the creation of man in verse 7 but before the formation of woman in verse 22. With this reading, the sequential understanding is in conflict with order in the creation account. On day 5 God created birds (Gen. 1:21–22). On day 6, God initially created wild animals, livestock, and creeping things (v. 24–25), and finally he created man and woman (v. 26–28). If *wayyîtser* is rendered as a past tense, the sequence in Genesis 2:4–25 seemingly contradicts the arrangement in 1:1–2:3. Two solutions to this reputed contradiction will be examined.

One solution that some framework advocates offer is to claim that a topical interpretation of Genesis 2:4–25 resolves this contradiction. This position states that man was created before beasts and birds if *wayyîtser* is used as *waw* consecutives normally function to show chronological sequence.[96] However, since the formation of man before beasts and birds conflicts with a chronological reading of Genesis 1:1–2:3 that has birds and beasts created before man, the past tense translation of *wayyîtser* indicates that the account should be read topically rather than chronologically. According to Kline's framework position, a chronological reading of the sequential verb in 2:19, as well as the two *waw* consecutives in verse 15, is inconsistent with a literal sequence in 1:1–2:3.[97] As such, the account in Genesis 2:4–25 has examples of sequential verbs that indicate a temporal recapitulation, and this indicates, according to Irons and Kline, that the narrative events of Genesis 1:1–2:3 do not correspond to the actual sequence that a literal reading of this text portrays.[98]

A second and preferable solution is to take the first sequential verb in Genesis 2:19a, *wayyîtser,* as a pluperfect, "had formed." With this pluperfect understanding, not only is a sequential, chronological reading of 2:4–25 preserved, but the account also maintains continuity with a literal interpretation of 1:1–2:3.[99] This

---

96. Support for taking *wayyîtser* as a past tense, "formed," has been drawn from S.R. Driver, *A Treatise on the Use of the Tenses in Hebrew* (Oxford: Clarendon, 1892), p. 84–89. Buth has provided further support for this past tense rendering ("Methodological Collision," p. 148–49). For more information about Buth's approach along with a corrective, see C. John Collins, "*Wayyiqtol* as 'Pluperfect': When and Why," *Tyndale Bulletin* 46 (May 1995): p. 128.

97. So Irons and Kline, "Framework Reply," p. 282–283; Ross, "Framework Hypothesis," p. 123–126; and Futato, "Because It Had Rained," p. 10–11.

98. Irons and Kline, "Framework View," p. 222–223.

99. For an alternative that is consistent with a complementary view of Gen. 1:1–2:3 and

view says that *wayyitser,* in the midst of a chain of sequential *waw* consecutives, may be translated as a past perfect, "had formed," reflecting a temporal activity that preceded the mainline sequence in 2:4–25.[100] While the NASB, like many other English versions, translates verse 19a with a past tense: "Out of the ground the LORD God *formed* . . ." (emphasis added), the NIV translates verse 19a with a pluperfect: "Now the LORD God *had formed* out of the ground . . ." (emphasis added). In this context, the NIV best preserves the continuity of 1:1–2:3 and 2:4–25.[101]

Like the two *waw* consecutives in Genesis 2:15, *wayyitser* in verse 19 is an example of temporal recapitulation. But the verses reflect two different types of temporal recapitulation. The sequential verbs in verse 15 are restricted by the immediate narrative sequence in verses 4–25 and are best taken as examples of resumptive repetition. The temporal recapitulation in verse 19 transcends the immediate pericope of 2:4–25 and looks back to the previous pericope in 1:1–2:3. Therefore, it is better to view this as an example of a pluperfect.[102] Various criteria are used to indicate that a *waw* consecutive is used as pluperfect, such as a sequential verb starting a new pericope or paragraph.[103] The context of Genesis 1–2 reflects another criterion for determining if a verb is used as a past perfect. This technique is what Collins calls the "logic of the referent."[104] With this technique, the literary context establishes that the event represented by a *waw* consecutive verb occurred before the situation represented by a prior verb.[105]

From the perspective of some framework supporters, the *waw* consecutive as a pluperfect is not a clear syntactic option in Genesis 2:19. However, what is overlooked by this reasoning is that pluperfect may be used within a sequence of *waw* consecutive verbs to denote an action prior to an immediate narrative sequence. A good example is found in Genesis 12:1. According to the sequential verbs in 11:31, Abram had left Ur of the Chaldeans with his father, Terah, set out for Canaan, and had settled in Haran. However, the *waw* consecutive that initiates 12:1 does not incrementally advance the time-line, but provides a flashback when the Lord had spoken to Abram about initially leaving his father's country in Mesopotamia before moving to Haran (cf., Gen. 15:7 and Acts 7:2). The mainline

---

2:4–25, see Cassuto, *Genesis,* p. 129.

100. Pipa, "Genesis 1:1–2:3," p. 156.

101. It is also possible that the birds and animals mentioned in Gen. 2:19 are a special group of birds and animals that God created after His original creation of birds on day 5 and animals on day 6. This group of animals and birds were the animals that Adam would name and they would have a special role related to the Garden of Eden. With this interpretation there is no conflict with Genesis 1:1–2:3 and *wayyitser* could retain its function as a preterite ("formed," rather than "had formed"). For more support of this view, see Cassuto, *Genesis,* p. 129 and Hamilton, *Genesis: Chapters 1–17,* p. 176.

102. See Collins, *Genesis 1–4,* p. 133–135.

103. Ibid., p. 127–128.

104. Collins, "*Wayyiqtol* as 'Pluperfect,'" p. 128.

105. Ibid., n. 40.

sequence is further interrupted by a series of clauses, verses 1b–3, that contain God's promises to Abram with the narrative sequence being resumed in verse 4. In keeping with this pluperfect use, the NIV translates verse 1a: "The LORD *had said* to Abram . . ." (emphasis added).[106] Although Moses had other syntactic options to convey a pluperfect, his syntactic preference, with this example, was to use a *waw* consecutive for this anterior action.

In closing this discussion of the *waw* consecutives in 2:4–25, the three *waw* consecutives in verses 15 and 19 reflecting temporal recapitulation do not provide a justification for reinterpreting the overall narrative sequence as a dischronologized account. Should these three exceptional uses of *waw* consecutive define the nature of the narrative sequence? Or, should not the 17 normal uses define the mainline narrative? Since the *waw* consecutives in verses 15 and 19 are connected to 17 other *waw* consecutives that demonstrate a normal sequential use of *waw* consecutive, Genesis 2:4–25 should be taken as a sequential, chronological account that has three examples of temporal recapitulation. What defines this pericope is the mainline sequence of 17 sequential *waw* consecutives. In the final analysis, this certainly does not sound like a use of 21 *waw* consecutives that are dischronologized.

To summarize this assessment of the framework's argument that the creation account is controlled by ordinary providence, I have demonstrated that the framework's use of the immediate context of Genesis 2:5 and the surrounding context of 2:4–25 cannot consistently be used to support this argument. To briefly extend my evaluation, there are two other areas of biblical revelation that indicate the tenuous nature of this argument: Genesis 1:1–2:3 and the wider context of Scripture. First, the creation account of Genesis 1:1–2:3 provides no evidence that God worked in this week exclusively through ordinary providence; and, in fact, the specific contextual evidence demonstrates just the opposite: the creation week was dominated by extraordinary providence.[107]

Second, the wider scope of Scripture also opposes this thesis since God has not limited himself in biblical history to work exclusively through ordinary providence. For example, when framework defenders deny a literal interpretation of the creation week by maintaining that Genesis 2:5 denies God had miraculously dried up the ground on day 3,[108] this clearly conflicts with God miraculously drying up the wet ground of the Red Sea when He divided it so that the Israelites, in ordinary providence, could cross it on dry ground

---

106. See Pipa, "Genesis 1:1–2:3," p. 156–157. For more information on the pluperfect use of the *waw* consecutive, see Waltke and O'Connor, *Biblical Hebrew Syntax,* p. 552–553.

107. For example, the Spirit of God, while hovering over the water-covered earth, supernaturally preserved the earth in Gen. 1:2 and God directly intervened to create Adam and Eve in His image in 1:26–28. For additional support of this point, see Pipa, "Genesis 1:1–2:3," p. 164; and Butler, "Question of Genesis 2:5," p. 123.

108. So Kline, "Because It Had Not Rained," p. 152.

(Exod. 14:21–22).[109] Hypothetically speaking, the only way that the creation week could be controlled by ordinary providence is for God to have created everything in a nanosecond.[110] However, the point of the framework position is just the opposite of God creating in a nanosecond. If ordinary providence controlled the creation week, as Kline argues, this strongly implies that the creation "week" involved an extended period of time and not a literal week.[111] A closer reading of the creation account in Genesis 1:1–2:3 reveals that it is more accurate to say that the creation week is governed by extraordinary providence while God is concomitantly establishing the conditions in the created order so that it could begin to operate according to ordinary providence.[112]

In concluding this evaluation of the framework's second thesis, the "unargued presupposition" in Genesis 2:5 that demands the creation week was exclusively controlled by ordinary providence is neither exegetically nor theologically convincing. In contrast to the framework view, Genesis 2:5 explicitly provides the setting for the creation of man on day 6 of the creation week. Therefore, Genesis 2:5 provides no reasonable evidence to abandon the traditional, literal interpretation of Genesis 1:1–2:3.

The Unending Nature of the Seventh Day

The third key premise of the framework position is that the seventh day of the creation week is an unending (or at least long and still continuing) period.[113] Irons states the case like this: "The final exegetical observation that ultimately clinches the case [for the framework interpretation] is the unending nature of the seventh day."[114] Other framework advocates also use this argument.[115] Since 1996, this argument has become a key plank in Kline's more complex two-register cosmology argument.[116] Regardless of whether the extended nature of the

---

109. Pipa, "Genesis 1:1–2:3," p. 163. To use another example, while God used extraordinary providence in the Flood, such as sending rain upon the earth 40 days and nights and breaking open the fountains of the great deep, Noah and his family in ordinary providence built the ark and took care of the animals in the ark for about a year. Again, in the New Testament, Christ performed many miracles, while, in normal providence, he grew up and lived a life of perfect obedience fulfilling the demands of the Law (for a further discussion on this point, see my "Critique of the Framework Interpretation (Part 2)," p. 101–108.

110. See also Michael J. Kruger, "An Understanding of Genesis 2:5," *Creation Ex Nihilo Technical Journal* 11 (1997): p. 109.

111. Kline, "Space and Time," p. 13.

112. So also Pipa, "Genesis 1:1–2:3," p. 163; and Jonathan Sarfati, *Refuting Compromise* (Green Forest, AR: Master Books, 2004), p. 99–100

113. Kline, "Because It Had Not Rained," p. 156; so also Irons, "The Framework Interpretation: An Exegetical Summary, *Ordained Servant* 9 (January 2000): p. 9–10.

114. Irons, "The Framework Interpretation," p. 9.

115. So Blocher, *In the Beginning*, p. 56; Hughes, *Genesis*, p. 26; Ross, "Framework Hypothesis," p. 121–122.

116. Kline, "Space and Time," p. 10–11.

seventh day is treated as a major thesis or as a supporting thesis for Kline's latter argument,[117] this provides significant support for all forms of the framework position.

Explanation

If day 7 is an unending day, it is not a literal, earthly day, but rather a figure that reflects a heavenly time of divine rest. Additionally, if day 7 is a metaphor, then the first six days that are subsidiary to this day are also metaphorical days.[118] The seventh day, according to Kline, "had a temporal beginning but it has no end (note the absence of the concluding evening-morning formula). Yet it is called a 'day,' so advising us that these days of the creation account are meant figuratively."[119] Two observations are said to support the unending nature of day 7. First, while each of the six days of the creation week is concluded by the evening-morning formula, the description of day 7 in Genesis 2:1–3 omits this formula. As Irons states the case, "The seventh day is unique in that it alone lacks the concluding evening-morning formula, suggesting that it is not finite but eternal."[120] According to Blocher, this omission "is deliberate. There can be no doubt about that in a text that has been composed with exact calculation."[121] Second, Hebrews 4 confirms this understanding of day 7 with the motif of an eternal Sabbath rest.[122]

Evaluation

Does the deliberate omission of the evening-morning formula in Genesis 2:1–3 unequivocally indicate that the seventh day of the creation week is an unending heavenly "day"? And, is it biblically legitimate to equate the eternal Sabbath rest of Hebrews 4 with the seventh day of the creation week? Both of these issues must now be addressed.

The Omission of the Evening-Morning Formula on Day 7

Blocher asserts that the open-ended nature of day 7 is the "most simple and natural conclusion" that can be drawn from this deliberate omission.[123] There are six reasons why an open-ended interpretation of day 7 cannot be the "most

---

117. Since Kline's two-register cosmology is not so much an argument supporting the framework view but an explanation that integrates the framework's three major premises with Kline's overall understanding of biblical cosmology as a justification for taking the temporal elements of Genesis 1:1–2:3 as heavenly time, I have not presented this as an argument in this paper. For a discussion of Kline's two register cosmology, see my "Critique of the Framework Interpretation (Part 2)," p. 116–130.

118. Kline, "Space and Time," p. 10; Irons and Kline, "Framework View," p. 245–247.

119. Kline, "Genesis," p. 83.

120. Irons, "Framework Interpretation," p. 9.

121. Blocher, *In the Beginning*, p. 50.

122. Kline, "Space and Time," p. 10.

123. Blocher, *In the Beginning*, p. 56.

simple and natural conclusion."

First, as previously noted, the evening-morning conclusion is one part of a fivefold structure that Moses employed in shaping the literary fabric for each of the days of the creation week. None of the other parts of this fivefold arrangement are mentioned on the seventh day. Moses used this fivefold pattern to represent, in a brief yet accurate manner, God's creation of the heavens, the earth, and all things therein in the space of six, sequentially numbered, literal days. By excluding the fivefold pattern, Moses' theological emphasis was to demonstrate in literary form that day 7 was a day of cessation from divine creative activity,[124] as the two uses of šābat, ("ceased" in NET BIBLE), in Genesis 2:2–3 clearly indicate.[125] This is to say, the omission of the evening-morning conclusion is related to the omission of the other four parts of this fivefold pattern. Since the other four parts are not needed in that God's creative activity is finished, this concluding formula was not needed either. This overall structuring device was not utilized for the apparent reason that God is no longer creating after day 6. But because day 7 is a historic literal day, it is numbered like the previous six days.

Second, the evening and morning conclusion has another rhetorical function that marks a transition from a concluding day to the following day. If the first week was completed, there was no need to use the evening-morning conclusion for transitional purposes. Pipa has precisely summarized this argument: "The phrase 'evening and morning' links the day that is concluding with the next day. For example the morning that marks the end of day one also marks the beginning of day two. Thus, we do not find the formula at the end of the seventh day, since the week of creation is complete."[126] Third, the omission of the evening-morning conclusion as a support for the seventh day being eternal is an argument from silence.[127] Genesis 2:1–3 neither explicitly states nor necessarily implies that day 7 was eternal. God's work of creation is explicitly stated in Genesis 2:2a as being completed "by the seventh day [bayyôm haššᵉbîʿî]."[128] In other words, God's

---

124. Gentry, "Traditional Interpretation of Genesis 1," p. 62.

125. For further discussion, see my "Critique of the Framework Interpretation (Part 2)," p. 112–113.

126. Pipa, "Genesis 1:1–2:3," p. 168.

127. Gentry, "Traditional Interpretation of Genesis 1," p. 62.

128. The prepositional phrase bayyôm haššᵉbîʿî is rendered in some versions as "on the seventh day" (so KJV, NKJV, ESV, NRSV, NLT). Since the semantic range for the preposition bᵉ includes uses such as "in," "at," "within," "on," "by" (HALOT, 1:103–105), this translation has lexical support. However, the translation is not without its difficulties, for it reflects a level of ambiguity in that it implies that God continued His creative work to some point on the seventh day and at that time God finished His creative work. The rendering of the NKJV illustrates this uncertainty: "And on the seventh day God ended His work which He had done." A preferable way to translate this prepositional phrase is "by the seventh day" (so NASB, NIV, TNIV, HCSB, NET BIBLE). What makes this rendering preferable is v. 1: "Thus the heavens and the earth were completed, and all their hosts." In this context, this verse indicates that God's creative work was

creative work is finished before and not on the seventh day.

Fourth, two narrative texts in Exodus dealing with the Sabbath ordinance rule out an open-ended interpretation of day 7. The first text is 20:11: "For in six days the LORD made the heavens and the earth, the sea and all that is in them, and rested on the seventh day; therefore the LORD blessed the Sabbath day and made it holy." The second is 31:17: "For in six days the LORD made heaven and earth, but on the seventh day He ceased *from labor*, and was refreshed." Based upon God's week of creative activity, Israel was commanded, in both passages, to imitate His pattern by working six days and resting on the Sabbath (20:9–10; 31:15–16). Because both passages have been clearly understood as references to man imitating the divine pattern established in the first week of temporal history by working on six consecutive, normal days and resting on a literal seventh day,[129] framework advocates attempt to dodge the force of 20:11 by asserting that even literalists have to take God being "refreshed" in 31:17 as an analogy, rather than a literal statement of God being refreshed.[130] However, God's response of delight, "refreshed," to His cessation from creative activity does not indicate that the days of creation were non-literal. Does something that relates to God's being, which in Exodus 31:17 is certainly analogical since it pictures God as "refreshed," indicate that the creation days were also anthropomorphic? To say that the anthropomorphism of divine refreshment precludes a literal interpretation

---

completed before the seventh day; and v. 2a continues the thought, "*by the seventh day* God completed His work." Translating *bᵉ* with "by" is coordinate with the sense of its governing verb *kalah,* "to finish, complete" (BDB, p. 477–478). However, in the next clause of v. 2, the same prepositional phrase *bayyôm haššᵉbîʿî* is used again and should be preferably translated as "on the seventh day" because its governing verb *shabat,* to "cease" or "rest" (*HALOT,* 2:1407–1409), stresses God's cessation or rest from work during a specific time, the seventh day. NASB appropriately translates this part of v. 2 as "He rested *on the seventh day* from all His work which He had done." For a helpful discussion of this verse, see Mathews, *Genesis 1–11:26,* p. 177.

129. See Hasel, " 'Days' of Creation in Genesis 1," p. 28–30.

130. Irons and Kline, "Framework View," p. 249–250. Irons and Kline's point is that even "literalists" recognize that God's rest cannot be taken literally in Exodus 31:17. Irons and Kline assert that "literalists" (i.e., young-earth creationists) interpret God's "rest" as analogical in Exodus 31:17 and yet still maintain that this non-literal interpretation of God's rest does not eliminate the force of literally keeping the Sabbath. But Irons and Kline contend that their non-literal interpretation of the creation days also does not eliminate the force of the Sabbath command. They further buttress this argument by their appeal to the unending nature of day 7 (Ibid., p. 250). However, this support for their argument is invalid, if day 7 is a literal day, as I have argued above. Furthermore, their previous point is an unacceptable comparison because the use of anthropomorphisms in narrative literature relates to God and not other things, and cannot be used to preclude a literal understanding of a text's basic message. For example, the anthropomorphic descriptions of God looking (Gen. 6:12), remembering (Gen. 8:1) and smelling (Gen. 8:21) do not nullify the literal nature of the description of the events during the year-long, global Flood.

of the days of creation is a comparison of apples and oranges.[131] Since there is no inherent connection between God's nature and the duration of His creative activity, the real issue focuses on whether Scripture affirms that God created on heavenly or earthly time. With a legitimate use of the analogy of Scripture, Exodus 20:11 and 31:17 unequivocally indicate that God did not create on heavenly time, but on earthly time. He created the universe in six, sequentially arranged, normal days. Both passages use an adverbial accusative of time ("in six days"). This grammatical construction indicates the duration of God's creative activity by stating how long it occurred, "*during* six days."[132] This construction, as Benjamin Shaw has correctly noted, "implies both that the days were normal days, and that the days were contiguous. Thus, the 'dayness' of the six days, as well as the seventh, is essential to the meaning of the Sabbath commandment. It is not simply analogy — God rested one period after six periods, so in a similar way we rest one day after six of work. Rather, because God created during the six days and ceased creating on the seventh, we work the six days and rest the seventh."[133] Therefore, the biblical evidence demands that day 7 of the creation week was a literal day.

Fifth, the seventh day must be a literal day because God blessed and sanctified it. If the seventh day is "unending," this means that not only did God bless and sanctify it, but he also, on the same unending day, cursed the earth with the Fall of Genesis 3. From a theological perspective, this is impossible.

Sixth, "all the days that Adam lived were nine hundred and thirty years" (Gen. 5:5) but the first day of his life was before the seventh day. If it was not literal, then just how long did Adam live and how do we make sense of Genesis 5:5? Furthermore, Whitcomb astutely observed, "We must assume that the seventh day was a literal day because Adam and Eve lived through it before God drove them out of the Garden. Surely, he would not have cursed the earth during the seventh day which he blessed and sanctified."[134]

Therefore, the omission of the evening-morning conclusion on day 7 does not imply that this day was unending or longer than a normal day. What Genesis 2:1–3 indicates is that day 7 was substantially different from the preceding six days (characterized by divine creative activity) because "by the seventh day"

---

131. For a refutation against taking the creation days as an analogy, see Hasel, " 'Days' of Creation in Genesis 1," p. 29; and Terence E. Fretheim, "Were the Days of Creation Twenty-Four Hours Long? 'Yes,'" in *The Genesis Debate: Persistent Questions About Creation and the Flood*, ed. Ronald Youngblood (Nashville, TN: Nelson, 1986), p. 20.

132. See Joüon, *Grammar of Biblical Hebrew*, 2:458–459; Waltke and O'Connor, *Biblical Hebrew Syntax*, p. 171; Arnold and Choi, *Biblical Hebrew Syntax*, p. 19.

133. Benjamin Shaw, "The Literal Day Interpretation," in *Did God Create in Six Days?* ed. Joseph A. Pipa Jr., and David W. Hall (Taylors, SC: Southern Presbyterian Press, 1999), p. 217.

134. John C. Whitcomb Jr., "The Science of Historical Geology in the Light of the Biblical Doctrine of a Mature Creation," *Westminster Theological Journal* 36 (Fall 1973): p. 68.

(Gen. 2:2–3) God ceased from this work. Further, since day 7 did not involve a transition to another day of creative activity, there was no need to say "and there was evening and there was morning, the *seventh* day." Day 8 was not a day of divine creation; it could not have been characterized as a day of extraordinary providence. On day 8, the created order was fully functioning according to normal providence and Adam and Eve began their divinely given responsibility of cultivating and maintaining the Garden of Eden. Genesis 2:1–3 has no implication that the seventh day is eternal or thousands or millions of years long. How is this literal interpretation of day 7 to be harmonized with Hebrews 4 where God's eternal Sabbath rest is seemingly equated with Genesis 2:2?

The Motif of God's Rest in Hebrews 4

Some framework proponents equate God's eternal Sabbath rest of Hebrews 4 with the seventh day of the creation week.[135] In contrast to the framework view, the eternal rest in Hebrews 4 cannot be equated with day 7 of the creation week for two reasons.

Initially, this equation of Hebrews 4 with Genesis 2:2 is only legitimate if Genesis 2:1–3 implies that day 7 was unending. Since, as just argued, Genesis 2:1–3 neither explicitly affirms nor necessarily implies that day 7 was an unending day, this interpretation is invalid. Hebrews 4 never states that the seventh day of the creation week is an unending day. In actuality, the use of Hebrews 4 to prove that the seventh day in Genesis 2:1–3 is an ongoing day assumes what needs to be demonstrated. In Hebrews 4:3–11, the author cites Genesis 2:2 and Psalm 95:7–11 as a warning against unbelief. The passage is a call to persevere in the faith. If one does not persevere, he will not enter into God's eternal rest. The eternal rest presented in Hebrews is based on an analogy with God's creative rest in Genesis 2:1–3. The author of Hebrews uses the Mosaic omission of the evening-morning conclusion as a type patterned after God's eternal rest.

Additionally, the actual kind of rest in Genesis 2:2–3 is completely different than the rest in Hebrews 4:3–11. The rest of Genesis 2:2–3 is a cessation from divine creative activity. Only the Creator can cease from that activity. It is absolutely impossible for the creature to experience that cessation. However, the Sabbath-rest of Hebrews 4:3–11 is a rest that the people of God actually experience, and it is spiritual rest. Therefore, the "rest" in both contexts cannot be identical. The framework position assumes that the "rest" of Genesis 2 is identical with Hebrews 4. However, instead of assuming that they are identical, framework advocates need to demonstrate this. Because of the Creator-creation distinction, the only possible relationship between Genesis 2:2–3 and Hebrews 4:3–11 is one of analogy and not identity. Consequently, Hebrews 4:3–11 establishes that God's eternal rest is an analogy drawn from God's rest on the literal seventh day in Genesis 2:1–3. As such, Hebrews 4 does not preclude day 7 of the creation week as a historic literal day.

---

135. Irons and Kline, "Framework View," p. 245.

Neither the omission of the evening-morning conclusion for day 7 nor the use of Genesis 2:2 in Hebrews 4 provide support for the seventh day of the creation week as an unending or otherwise non-literal day. Rather than sustaining the framework's third thesis, the omission of the evening-morning conclusion coupled with explicit references to God's cessation of His work of creation and pronouncement of blessing indicates that the seventh day was a specific, literal day that concluded a week of six, consecutive literal days.

Concluding Remarks

In this essay I have critiqued three major arguments of the framework position. First, the framework position's figurative interpretation that argues for a topical arrangement of the days of the creation week into two triads is incongruous with the exegetical details of Genesis 1:1–2:3 and undermines the literary nature of the creation account as a genuine historical narrative. While Genesis 1:1–2:3 involves a stylized use of Hebrew narrative, the fact that the mainline narrative of this account is predominantly advanced by a sequential narrative verbal form, the *waw* consecutive, unmistakably communicates that it is genuine narrative. When this grammatical feature is coupled with the use of *yôm* (day) modified by sequential numerical adjectives and reference to evening and morning, Moses could not communicate any more clearly that Genesis 1:1–2:3 is the first literal week of literal days in the space and time continuum.

Second, contrary to Kline's "creation-in-process" interpretation of Genesis 1 based on Genesis 2:5 thereby implying that the creation week was controlled by ordinary providence, Genesis 2:5 provides in its grammatical context the setting for the creation of man, by extraordinary providence, on day 6 of the creation week. The evidence from Genesis 1–2 and the overall tenor of Scripture demonstrate that the creation week was characterized by extraordinary providence and that during this week God miraculously established and maintained the conditions for the earth so that, at the end of the six days of divine creative activity, the earth would be able to operate under ordinary providence as a fit habitation for man and all the other living creatures.

Third, the omission of the evening-morning conclusion on day 7, with the explicit reference to God's cessation of His work of creation and God's pronouncement of blessing on day 7, coupled with a legitimate interpretation of Hebrews 4 does not provide adequate evidence to sustain the framework's interpretation of the seventh day is an unending (or still continuing) period. When this evidence is carefully scrutinized in its biblical context, it indicates that day 7 was a specific, literal day that concluded a series of six, consecutive literal days of divine creative activity.

In brief, advocates of the framework position evade the force of the predominant biblical issues associated with Genesis 1–2 by emphasizing a few apparent exegetical and hermeneutical concerns. However, it is not the exegetical data and biblical theology that provide the matrix for their alternative interpretation of the creation account. The real issue is external to Scripture. Until the last two centuries, the witness of orthodox Christianity has almost unanimously supported the literal interpretation of the creation week.[136] What has changed in the last two centuries is that most of the Church has uncritically accepted the scientific establishment's claim about millions of years of "deep time."

Waltke, a framework advocate, reflects a widespread "evangelical" view of modern science:

> The days of creation may also pose difficulties for a strict historical account. Contemporary scientists almost unanimously discount the possibility of creation in one week, and we cannot summarily discount the evidence of the earth sciences. General revelation in creation, as well as the special revelation of Scripture is also the voice of God. We live in a "universe," and all truth speaks with one voice.[137]

But not all truth claims of man are actually true. And young-earth creation scientists do not "summarily discount" the geological evidence; rather they challenge the naturalistic uniformitarian *interpretations* of the evidence. Waltke essentially reduces general revelation to what fallen man says that revelation discloses.[138] This way of thinking doesn't merely equate the "assured results" of scientific opinion with the scriptural revelation from God; it in effect elevates the dominant scientific view to be the hermeneutical authority for understanding Scripture, thereby justifying a figurative reading of the creation account.[139] While Waltke's assessment does not explicitly address the age of the earth, his position supports an old-earth model.

More specifically, Kline has taken the lead in crafting a modern exegetical reinterpretation of the creation account that allows for an old-earth model. Though Irons and Kline claim that those who accept the framework view need not espouse a particular view about the age of the earth,[140] this claim is hollow and misleading. Three items imply that the real "unargued presupposition" of the framework is an old-earth model.

First, if Genesis 2:5 teaches that ordinary providence operated exclusively during the creation period of 1:1–2:3, this suggests that the creation period involved a very extended period of time, as Kline asserts. "Gen. 2:5 reflects

---

136. For a concise historical summary of the interpretation of the creation week, see Duncan and Hall, "24-Hour View," p. 47–52.

137. Waltke, *Genesis,* p. 77.

138. When Waltke states that "contemporary scientists almost unanimously discount the possibility of creation in one week," we should note that this is not a *unanimous* opinion among scientists. See Terry Mortenson, *The Great Turning Point* (Green Forest, AR: Master Books, 2004), p. 236–237.

139. See Andrew S. Kulikovsky, "Scripture and General Revelation," *TJ* 19:2 (2005): p. 27–28; and Noel Weeks, "The Hermeneutical Problem of Genesis 1–11," *Themelios* 4 (1978): p. 13–14.

140. Irons and Kline, "Framework View," p. 217.

an environmental situation that has obviously lasted for a while; it assumes a far more leisurely pace on the part of the Creator, for whom a thousand years are as one day. The tempo of the literalists' reconstructed cosmogony leaves no room for the era-perspective of Gen. 2:5."[141] This certainly intimates an old-earth model.[142]

Furthermore, Kline implies a presumed commitment to modern scientific opinion when he states that traditional interpretations of the creation account are guilty of creating a conflict between the Bible and science.[143] In actuality, a literal interpretation of the creation week is in conflict with naturalistic uniformitarian interpretations of the scientific data and with Kline's interpretation of Genesis 2:5.[144]

Finally, in a context affirming his acceptance of Scripture's authority about Adam's federal headship, Kline states, "In this article, I have advocated an interpretation of biblical cosmogony according to which Scripture is open to the current scientific view of a very old universe and, in that respect, does not discountenance the theory of the evolutionary origin of man."[145] In the final analysis, an old-earth model shaped by our evolutionary age, along with its demand for death and destruction long before the fall of Adam, provides the matrix in which the framework view has been conceived.[146]

If we did not live in this current age, could framework advocates even have dreamed of using "day," "evening," and "morning" figuratively?[147] Because there is no scriptural reason to think that the temporal markers of Genesis 1:1–2:3 should be taken in any way other than a literal use, the complex framework interpretation could not have even been imagined before our modern era. The "deep time" spirit of this age has created a philosophical environment conducive to a reinterpretation of the creation account. The influences that shape such a reinterpretation are clearly external to Scripture because in the overall biblical context, there is no support for the complicated framework view. The only way to conceive of this view is to say that the actual text of Genesis 1:1–2:3 has historically been misinterpreted and a new, enlightened exegetical solution gives the correct interpretation. This type of enlightened exegetical solution is incompatible with "the faith which was once for all handed down to the saints" (Jude 1:3; NAS95). At the end of the day, there is no biblical reason to adopt the framework interpretation.

141. Kline, "Space and Time," p. 13.
142. So also Kenneth L. Gentry Jr., "The Framework Hypothesis Debate," in *Yea, Hath God Said: The Framework Hypothesis/Six-Day Creation Debate,* by Kenneth L. Gentry Jr., and Michael R. Butler (Eugene, OR: Wipf and Stock Publishers, 2002), p. 17.
143. Kline, "Space and Time," p. 14.
144. Walter M. Booth, "Days of Genesis 1: Literal or Non-literal?" *Journal of the Adventist Theological Society* 14 (Spring 2003): p. 116.
145. Kline, "Space and Time," p. 15, n. 47.
146. See Duncan and Hall, "24-Hour Response," p. 258.
147. See Young, *Studies in Genesis One,* p. 100–103.

Therefore, I conclude that the framework view poses more exegetical and theological difficulties than its solves and that the traditional, literal reading provides the most consistent interpretation of the exegetical details associated with the context of the early chapters of Genesis and the overall theological message of Scripture that has a bearing on Genesis 1–2. In refutation of another non-literal interpretation of Genesis 1:1–2:3, a pioneer in the resurgence of young-earth creationism, Dr. John C. Whitcomb Jr., provided a response that is also an appropriate conclusion to this paper: "It is difficult to imagine what more the Scriptures could say to convey the idea that the days of creation were literal days. 'If it were not so, I would have told you.' "[148]

---

148. Whitcomb, "The Science of Historical Geology," p. 68.

Chapter 9

Noah's Flood and Its Geological Implications

William D. Barrick, Th.D.
Professor of OT, The Master's Seminary
Sun Valley, Calif.

In 1965, I first met John Whitcomb during a conference at Beth Eden Baptist Church in Denver, Colorado. At that time I purchased and read The Genesis Flood.[1] *As a recipient of a National Science Foundation grant to pursue wildlife ecology research at Colorado State University's Pingree Park Campus the previous year, I had an intense interest in the created world and its processes. That book captivated my attention and deepened my biblical convictions concerning creation and biblical catastrophism. Little did I know that 11 years later I would be sitting again at his feet in the Doctor of Theology program at Grace Theological Seminary in Winona Lake, Indiana. It is a great privilege to honor my mentor with this essay.*

Genesis specifies the terminus dates for the commencement (Gen. 7:11) and the conclusion (8:14) of the Flood. Therefore, unless one approaches the text with extreme prejudice and modifies it to his or her own liking, the Flood was 371 days in duration. As a global cataclysm, the Flood most likely involved an upheaval of the earth's crust, severe rain, storm surges, gigantic billows of waves, tsunamis, and tectonic denudation. The Flood narrative describes three stages for the event: (1) 150 days of prevailing waters, (2) 165 days of receding waters, and (3) 56 days of drying.

Unless otherwise noted, all Scripture in this chapter is from the NKJV of the Bible.

1. John C. Whitcomb Jr. and Henry M. Morris, *The Genesis Flood: The Biblical Record and Its Scientific Implications* (Philadelphia, PA: Presbyterian and Reformed, 1961, 7th printing 1965).

The Hebrew grammar of Genesis 8:3, I will submit, supports a large-scale, back and forth, circulating motion that could have had profound effects in shaping the new landscape. A detailed examination of the Flood narrative's literary structure and grammar reveals a number of sequential chains of events. Such sequences help to construct a consistent chronology for the Flood. Since geologic processes related to the Noahic Flood have been the subject of considerable debate, such a chronology could be extremely helpful for the placement of stratigraphic Flood boundaries[2] in the earth's rock record.[3]

The *A Priori* Status of the Biblical Record of the Flood

All study of the Flood needs to begin with the biblical record itself. Careful analysis of the record in Genesis 6–8 should be the only basis upon which anyone considers potential geologic implications. However, in spite of the revelatory nature of the biblical record, many evangelical scholars continue to give up valuable ground to secular scientists and liberal biblical critics. Evangelicals too often attempt to baptize secular and humanistic theories in evangelical waters without realizing that those theories and their methodologies have never been converted. While there are valuable kernels of truth buried within contemporary critical and so-called "scientific" studies, evangelicals must take great care to irradiate the material with the Word of God so as not to unknowingly and unintentionally introduce secularized thinking into the Church.

---

2. Obviously, the dates and boundaries of the uniformitarian stratigraphic column with its evolutionary and excessive time scale cannot be accepted as conclusive. Instead, Flood geologists must develop independent stratigraphic columns on the basis of the evidence in the rock record without the taint of uniformitarianism, evolution, and the presumption of an old earth. See, Carl R. Froede Jr., "The Global Stratigraphic Record," in *Creation Ex Nihilo Technical Journal* 11/1 (1997): p. 40-43. That does not rule out the possibility that there might be some degree of overlap between the uniformitarian and biblical stratigraphic columns. For a discussion of potential overlap, see Bernard E. Northrup, "Identifying the Noahic Flood in Historical Geology: Part One," 1:173–179, and "Identifying the Noahic Flood in Historical Geology: Part Two," 1:181–185, in *Proceedings of the Second International Conference on Creationism Held July 30-August 4, 1990*, 2 vols., ed. by Robert E. Walsh (Pittsburgh, PA: Creation Science Fellowship, 1990). Steven A. Austin and Kurt P. Wise, "The Pre-Flood/Flood Boundary: As Defined in Grand Canyon, Arizona and Eastern Mojave Desert, California," in *Proceedings of the Third International Conference on Creationism Held July 18-23, 1994*, ed. by Robert E. Walsh (Pittsburgh, PA: Creation Science Fellowship, 1994), p. 38–39, present five characteristics that should make up the geologic signature of the pre-Flood/Flood boundary.
3. For an earlier publication of some aspects of this study and its geological implications, see William D. Barrick and Roger Sigler, "Hebrew and Geologic Analysis of the Chronology and Parallelism of the Flood: Implications for Interpretation of the Geologic Record," in *Proceedings of the Fifth International Conference on Creationism Held August 4–9, 2003*, ed. by Robert L. Ivey, Jr. (Pittsburgh, PA: Creation Science Fellowship, 2003), p. 397–408.

Far too many evangelicals have allowed the *a priori* nature of the biblical text to slip away by making it subject to external confirmation. In *What Did the Biblical Writers Know and When Did They Know It?* William Dever declares that "one unimpeachable witness in the court of history is sufficient."[4] However, he betrays his prejudice by elevating secular extrabiblical evidence over the evidence of Scripture — he trusts the one and distrusts the other. Robert Dick Wilson, on the other hand, did not see any need for independent confirmation of Scripture from an external historical source. He ably defended the *a priori* nature of biblical evidence in his classical work, *A Scientific Investigation of the Old Testament.*[5] Wilson's view was that the Scripture's testimony is sufficient in and of itself without additional external confirmation. Sadly, Dever's problem is one that he seems to recognize in others, but does not see in himself. Later in the same book he asks, "How is it that the biblical texts are always approached with postmodernism's typical 'hermeneutics of suspicion,' but the nonbiblical texts are taken at face value? It seems to be that the Bible is automatically held guilty unless proven innocent."[6] He almost sounds like Robert Dick Wilson.

Above all else, the evangelical exegete/expositor must accept the OT text as the inerrant and authoritative Word of God. This was one of the principles that John Whitcomb hammered home time and time again in the classroom and in private and public discussion. Adhering consistently to this declaration of faith will require an equal admission of one's own ignorance and of one's inability to resolve every problem. Our ignorance, however, should never become the excuse for compromising the integrity of the OT.

Bernard Northrup, another one of my mentors, warns against building models that lean "too heavily on the authority of historical geology, warping the biblical evidence to fit it."[7] He warns against refusing "to allow the Scriptures to be the final authority in all scientific research."[8]

---

4. William G. Dever, *What Did the Biblical Writers Know and When Did They Know It?: What Archaeology Can Tell Us about the Reality of Ancient Israel* (Grand Rapids, MI: Eerdmans, 2001), p. 118. Dever was commenting specifically about the Merneptah stele (known also as the "Israel Stele" because of its mention of Israel). For a detailed review of this volume, see William D. Barrick, "Review of William G. Dever, *What Did the Biblical Writers Know and When Did They Know It? What Archaeology Can Tell Us about the Reality of Ancient Israel.*" *The Master's Seminary Journal* 13/2 (Fall 2002): p. 275–279.

5. Robert Dick Wilson, *A Scientific Investigation of the Old Testament* (reprint; Chicago, IL: Moody Press, 1959). Unfortunately, Wilson himself did not take an unambiguous stance for a young earth and a universal deluge in Noah's day (ibid., p. 8). He may have been influenced by the so-called scientific evidence of his day that insisted upon the earth being millions of years old. I am not using Wilson for his view on Gen. 1. I am using him for his defense of the *a priori* nature of Scripture.

6. Dever, *What Did the Biblical Writers Know and When Did They Know It,* p. 128.

7. Northrup, "Identifying the Noahic Flood in Historical Geology: Part One," p. 173.

8. Ibid.

An area of substantial abuse by both liberals and evangelicals is the relationship of archaeological evidence to the biblical record concerning the Flood. For some scholars, the various universal Flood accounts are merely the result of "the inclination to offer etiological explanations for mountain lakes and seashell deposits."[9] Brian Schmidt reasons that universal Flood legends are not really a worldwide phenomenon, because of their absence in Egyptian literature.[10] However, as Kenneth Kitchen so aptly observes, the patriarchal tradition was preserved by Israel in Egypt until the Exodus.[11]

The Flood narrative reveals clues about the mechanisms and the timing of geologic processes during the event. The language that permeates this passage clearly indicates that the disruption of the earth's surface was comprehensive and global. Such a description is founded upon semantic clues provided by phraseology, literary devices, and context. Geological implications must be derived from the collective impact of the entire narrative. Apart from the global and catastrophic description inherent in the entire pericope, one element that requires attention is that of chronology. Correlation between the chronology of the Flood and the geologic record must be built upon the bedrock foundation of sound biblical exegesis.

The Biblical Chronology of the Flood Narrative

Although scholars have produced some interesting discussions concerning the Flood's chronology as revealed in the Flood narrative, most of the attention has been given to source criticism.[12] Division of the narrative into two or three hypothetical sources assumes an evolution of the text through a number of redactions before it reached its current canonical form. Such an approach fails to provide an objective exegetical treatment of the text reflecting its inherent unity and integrity. However, even if one were to assume a source-critical approach to the text, the chronological elements cannot be ignored. Barré recognized this fact, declaring:

> Contrary to the opinion [of] some commentators, none of the numbers found in Genesis 7–8 can be regarded as "approximations."

---

9. Brian B. Schmidt, "Flood Narratives of Ancient Western Asia," in *Civilizations of the Ancient Near East*, 4 vols. in 2 vols., ed. by Jack M. Sasson (Peabody, MA: Hendrickson, 1995), 2:2337.

10. Ibid., 2:2338.

11. K.A. Kitchen, *On the Reliability of the Old Testament* (Grand Rapids, MI: Eerdmans, 2003), p. 427.

12. Niels Peter Lemche, "The Chronology in the Story of the Flood," *Journal for the Study of the Old Testament* 18 (Oct 1980): p. 52–62; Frederick H. Cryer, "The Interrelationships of Gen. 5,32; 11,10–11 and the Chronology of the Flood (Gen 6–9)," *Biblica* 66/2 (1985): p. 241–261; Lloyd M. Barré, "The Riddle of the Flood Chronology," *Journal for the Study of the Old Testament* 41 (June 1988): p. 3–20; Schmidt, "Flood Narratives of Ancient Western Asia," p. 2343–2344.

All of the chronological data contained in both J and P cohere only if they are taken literally.[13]

Literary Issues

Moses employed various literary devices in the composition of the biblical account of the Flood. Repetition of words, phrases, and subject matter contribute to the literary structure of the account. For example, Mathews identifies merismus[14] as one of the literary devices that contributes to the global and catastrophic proportions of the Flood: "The immense flood-waters involve the flow of waters from below and from above, a merism indicating the complete transformation of the terrestrial structures."[15]

The text describes the coming catastrophe in a progressively intense series of statements: (1) all flesh will be destroyed (6:7), (2) all flesh and the earth itself are to be destroyed (6:12–13), and (3) everything upon the earth will be destroyed by a great deluge of water (6:17). The description of destruction of life in 7:4 is expanded in the details of 7:10–23. Occasionally there are instances of localized symmetry within the passage. One occurrence is in 7:17–24 where "flood" or "waters" (the equivalent of "flood") occur repeatedly — often followed by "upon the earth."

There are at least three identifiable chiasms[16] within the Flood narrative. They appear to introduce each of the main sections of the Flood narrative proper. In 7:11b the first chiasm is both semantic ("burst open"//"opened" and "all the fountains

---

13. Barré, "The Riddle of the Flood Chronology," p. 16. An endnote indicates that Barré was referring to the view of K. Budde that many of the numbers were approximations (ibid., p. 20).

14. Merismus expresses totality by an abbreviated presentation of extreme pairs like "ladies and gentlemen" (= everyone) or "body and soul" (= the whole person). See Wilfred G.E. Watson, *Classical Hebrew Poetry: A Guide to its Techniques*, Journal for the Study of the Old Testament Supplement Series 26 (Sheffield, England: JSOT Press, 1984), p. 321.

15. Kenneth A. Mathews, *Genesis 1–11:26*, New American Commentary 1A (Nashville, TN: Broadman & Holman, 1996), p. 377–378.

16. By chiasm is meant "a series (a, b, c, …) and its inversion (. . . , c, b, a) taken together as a combined unit. In Hebrew poetry such a unit is generally a parallel couplet, so that the combined (chiastic) unit would be a, b, c // c, b, a. The components of such a series are usually sub-units of the sentence, considered semantically or grammatically. . . . When the components (a, b, c, etc.) are not parts of the sentence but complete lines, then larger chiastic patterns emerge" — Watson, *Classical Hebrew Poetry*, p. 201–202.

The Hebrew structure of 7:11b can be mapped as follows (retaining the English translation in the same order as the wording of the Hebrew):

    A on that day burst open
        B all the fountains of the great deep
        B' and the windows of the sky
    A' were opened.

See U. Cassuto, *A Commentary on the Book of Genesis: Part II — From Noah to Abraham, Genesis V 19–XI 32*, trans. by Israel Abrahams (Jerusalem: Magnes Press, 1992 reprint of 1964 edition), p. 84.

of the great deep"//"the windows of the sky") and grammatical (Niphal perfect verb//Niphal perfect verb and feminine plural subject//feminine plural subject). The structure focuses on the central elements of the chiasm describing the deluge's sources of water. The second chiasm (7:19–20)[17] commences the second major section of the Flood narrative proper. Its focus is on the declaration that all the highest mountains had been covered by the Flood waters. The third chiasm occurs in 8:5.[18] Its focus is on the timing of the Flood, marking the date on which the tops of the mountains reappeared from beneath the waters. Functioning as a pair, the first chiasm marks the commencement of the mechanisms producing the deluge of waters covering the earth while the third marks the uncovering of the earth that resulted from the cessation of those same mechanisms. Thus, these two chiasms balance each other, enhancing the symmetry of the Flood narrative's structure.

Due to apparent parallels throughout the pericope, some commentators identify an extended chiastic (or inverted) parallelism.[19] Gordon Wenham observes

---

17. The structure of 7:19–20 is a 3-part chiasm with each half followed by the same epexegetical *wayyiqtol* verb ("so that . . . covered"; see more discussion in footnote 68, below):

    A The waters
       B prevailed
          C even more over the earth
             D so that all the highest mountains that were under the entire sky were covered.
          C' Fifteen cubits upwards
       B' prevailed
    A' the waters
             D' so that they covered the mountains.

18. The structure of 8:5 is a grammatically matched 3-part chiasm: "waters" as subject // "mountaintops" as subject, "were continually receding" as verb // "appeared" as verb, "until the 10th month" as adverbial modifier // "on the 1st day of the 10th month" as adverbial modifier:

    A The waters
       B were continually decreasing
          C until the 10th month.
          C' On the 1st day of the 10th month
       B' appeared
    A' the mountaintops

19. Gordon J. Wenham, "The Coherence of the Flood Narrative," in *"I Studied Inscriptions from before the Flood": Ancient Near Eastern, Literary, and Linguistic Approaches to Genesis 1–11*, ed. by Richard S. Hess and David Toshio Tsumura (Winona Lake, IN: Eisenbrauns, 1994), p. 437–438; David A. Dorsey, *The Literary Structure of the Old Testament: A Commentary on Genesis-Malachi* (Grand Rapids, MI: Baker, 1999), p. 52. For a critique of Dorsey's chiastic structure, see William D. Barrick, "The Chronology and Mechanisms of the Noahic Flood Based upon an Analysis of the Hebrew Text of Genesis 6–8" (unpublished paper; ETS Far West Region Annual Meeting, April 19, 2002), p. 1–6.

that the periods of time in the Flood narrative "form a symmetrical pattern, 7, 7, 40, 150, 150, 40, 7, 7."[20] He concludes that a "closer examination suggests that some of these time spans are mentioned purely in order to achieve symmetry in the palistrophe."[21] Even without Wenham's larger chiastic arrangement of the full Flood narrative, the three lesser chiasms, the repetitions of terms, and the progressively intense series of statements prove that this passage is a sophisticated and coherent narrative.

Unfortunately, some scholars have attempted to argue for the catastrophic and universal nature of the Flood on the basis of isolated word studies of key terms in the Flood narrative. Responding to the hypothesis that the Hebrew מָחָה (*māḥâ*, "blot out") indicates an obliteration of all evidence of life (including any fossil record),[22] David Fouts and Kurt Wise demonstrate conclusively that such argumentation is invalidated by an adequate analysis of the use of the Hebrew word throughout the Old Testament.[23] In another example, E.A. Speiser declared that the Hebrew גֶּשֶׁם (*gešem*) refers to a "heavy rain" and "signifies abnormal rainfall,"[24] unlike the normal rain usually intended by מָטָר (*māṭār*). However, as Mark Futado (a trained climatologist and Hebraist) points out, "[t]he modern reader can discern no difference between *gešem* and *māṭār*."[25] Due to the significance of rain in the moisture-starved regions of the Ancient Near East (including Canaan), Hebrew possesses a very rich vocabulary that the Old Testament employs for describing such precipitation. Specialized terms for severe rains include זֶרֶם (*zerem*; cf. Isa. 4:6; 25:4 twice; 28:2 twice; 30:30; 32:2; Job 24:8), סַגְרִיר (*sagrîr*; cf. Prov. 27:13), סָפִיחַ (*sāp̄îaḥ*; Job 14:19), and שָׂעִיר (*śā'îr*;[26] cf. Deut. 32:2)[27] — none of which are employed in the Flood narrative.

---

20. Wenham, "The Coherence of the Flood Narrative," p. 437–438.

21. Ibid., p. 439. "Palistrophe" is a synonym for "chiasm."

22. E.g., Steven J. Robinson, "The Flood in Genesis: What Does the Text Tell Geologists?" in *Proceedings of the Fourth International Conference on Creationism Held August 3-8, 1998*, ed. by Robert E. Walsh (Pittsburgh, PA: Creation Science Fellowship, 1998), p. 466.

23. David M. Fouts and Kurt P. Wise, "Blotting Out and Breaking Up: Miscellaneous Hebrew Studies in Geocatastrophism," in *Proceedings of the Fourth International Conference on Creationism Held August 3-8, 1998*, ed. by Robert E. Walsh (Pittsburgh, PA: Creation Science Fellowship, 1998), p. 217–220.

24. E.A. Speiser, *Genesis*, Anchor Bible (Garden City, NY: Doubleday, 1964), p. 53.

25. Mark D. Futado, "גשם," in *New International Dictionary of Old Testament Theology & Exegesis*, [hereafter *NIDOTTE*] 5 vols., ed. by Willem A. VanGemeren (Grand Rapids, MI: Zondervan, 1997), 1:901.

26. For a detailed discussion regarding proposed meanings for this *hapax legomenon*, see Ludwig Koehler and Walter Baumgartner, eds., *The Hebrew and Aramaic Lexicon of the Old Testament* [hereafter *HALOT*], rev. by Walter Baumgartner and Johann Jakob Stamm, trans. and ed. by M.E.J. Richardson (Leiden, The Netherlands: E. J. Brill, 1996), 3:1341–1342.

27. Futado, "גשם," 1:901. In the discussion above I have listed all occurrences of each of the four terms.

Another term subject to much speculation is the word מַבּוּל (*mabbûl*). According to Koehler and Baumgartner's lexicon, מַבּוּל is related to the Akkadian *biblu, bubbulu*, meaning "deluge."[28] The Hebrew word is probably derived from the Hebrew root יבל (*yābal*) meaning "pour rain" or "cloudburst."[29] The Akkadian *biblu* can have the meaning of a "devastating flood."[30] The same meaning has been identified with *bubbulu* (*bibbulu, bumbulu*).[31] It is possible that the word is an example of onomatopoeia, "the imitation of a sound *within the rules of the language* concerned."[32] If it is onomatopoeic,[33] the word might be imitating the gurgling or bubbling sound of falling rain or flowing water.[34] Such a sonic derivation would be similar to that of נֵבֶל (*nēbel*)[35] or בַּקְבֻּק/בַּקְבֻּק (*baqbûq/baqbuq*).[36] Lexicographers recognize both as onomatopoeic.[37] Some earlier experts on semitic languages linked מַבּוּל to the Hebrew root נבל (*nbl*),[38] but such a relationship finds little acceptance today.[39] A problem with the association of מַבּוּל with *biblu* is that these terms are not employed in any of the Akkadian flood stories.[40] The Sumerian flood epic of Atrahasis, for example, utilizes the

---

28. *HALOT*, 2:541.

29. Ibid., 2:383. See, also, Cassuto, *Genesis: Part II*, p. 66–67.

30. Ignace J. Gelb, A. Leo Oppenheim, Erica Reiner et al., eds., *The Assyrian Dictionary of the Oriental Institute of the University of Chicago* [hereafter *CAD*] (Chicago, IL: The Oriental Institute, 1965), 2:221.

31. Ibid., 2:298.

32. Watson, *Classical Hebrew Poetry*, p. 234.

33. A word whose sound is imitative of the sound of the noise or action designated by the word, e.g., gurgle, hiss or meow.

34. נֶשֶׁם might also be onomatopoeic in origin. In Bangladesh (where I served as a missionary for 15 years) the Bengali language contains many words for rain that are related to the respective sounds made by various types of rain. A drizzling rain is *dhop-dhop*, imitating the sound of the drops of water that fall from leaves. A more steady rain may be referred to by *jhim-jhim*, imitating its sound — something that is akin, perhaps to the sound that might be represented by נֶשֶׁם. Association with the English "gush" might not be equivalent since it connotes something that could be far more forceful.

35. *nēbel* I = "jar [for wine or oil]," *nēbel* II = "harp" — I and II represent two different Hebrew root words that are homonyms with two totally different meanings (cp. "through" and "threw" in English).

36. *baqbûq/baqbuq* means "bottle." The word is derived from the sound of an inverted bottle emptying out its liquid contents. In English we often represent such a sound with *glug-glug*.

37. K. Seybold, "נבל," in *Theological Dictionary of the Old Testament* [hereafter *TDOT*], ed. by G. Johannes Botterweck, Helmer Ringgren, and Heinz-Josef Fabry, trans. by David E. Green (Grand Rapids, MI: Eerdmans, 1998), 9:172.

38. Cf. Marcus Jastrow, *A Dictionary of the Targumim, the Talmud Babli and Yerushalmi, and the Midrashic Literature*, 2 vols. (Brooklyn, NY: P. Shalom, 1967), 1:724.

39. P. Stenmans, "מַבּוּל," in *TDOT*, trans. by Douglas W. Stott (Grand Rapids, MI: Eerdmans, 1997), 8:61.

40. Walter C. Kaiser, Jr., "מַבּוּל," in *Theological Wordbook of the Old Testament* [hereafter

word *abûbu*.[41] Occurrences of *abûbu* refer to a devastating cosmic deluge.[42] However, the absence of the phonetic element *l* is problematic for any direct association with מַבּוּל. Therefore, the etymology of מַבּוּל remains uncertain.[43] מַבּוּל could be related to the Akkadian *wabālu* ("wash away [by water]").[44] Other words for "flood" in Akkadian include *butuqtu* ("flood, inundation")[45] and *milu* ("seasonal flooding of the rivers").[46]

In Jewish Aramaic literature, the Hebrew term has been borrowed and utilized unaltered.[47] The most likely reason for the New Testament writers' choice of κατακλυσμός (*kataklusmos*, from whence the English obtains "cataclysm") is that the Septuagint always translated מַבּוּל with κατακλυσμός.[48] However, κατακλυσμός was not reserved just for מַבּוּל. It is also used to translate שֶׁטֶף (*šēṭēp̄*, "flood, torrent, inundation") in Psalm 32:6 (LXX, 31:6) and Daniel 9:26 (Theodotion[49]). By the time of the New Testament, κατακλυσμός had also been used to translate נָהָר (*nāhār*, "river, torrent") in Sirach (Ecclesiasticus) 39:22.[50]

One interpreter concludes that the relationship of the verb גָּבַר (*gābar*, "prevailed"; 7:18, 19, 20, 24) to warfare depicts the Flood waters as being "on the warpath, on a rampage" and "underscores the fearful results of God's judgment."[51] However, in the Qal stem גָּבַר's semantic range includes "be superior," "achieve," and "increase."[52] To impose the connotations of warfare and judgment

TWOT], 2 vols., ed. by R. Laird Harris, Gleason L. Archer, Jr., and Bruce K. Waltke (Chicago, IL: Moody Press, 1980), 1:489.

41. W.G. Lambert and A.R. Millard, *Atra-hasis: The Babylonian Story of the Flood* (London: Oxford University Press, 1969), p. 91 (III.i.37).

42. *CAD* (1964), 1:77.

43. Stenmans, "מַבּוּל," *TDOT*, 8:61. See, also, Michael A. Grisanti, "מַבּוּל," in *NIDOTTE*, 2:835–836. Recent studies in the materials from Ebla have revealed the "bilingual equation A-KUL = *ma-ba-lum*" (Cyrus H. Gordon, "Eblaitica," in *Eblaitica: Essays on the Ebla Archives and Eblaite Language*, ed. by Cyrus H. Gordon, Gary A. Rendsburg, and Nathan H. Winter [Winona Lake, IN: Eisenbrauns, 1987], 1:28; citing *Materiali epigrafici di Ebla*, 272, #640b). This equation "translates Sumerian A 'water' + KUL 'heavy' into Eblaite as *ma-ba-lum*, which calls to mind Hebrew מַבּוּל" (ibid.).

44. H.A. Hoffner, "יבל," in *TDOT*, ed. by G. Johannes Botterweck and Helmer Ringgren, trans. by David E. Green (Grand Rapids, MI: Eerdmans, 1997), 5:364.

45. *CAD* (1965), 2:357.

46. *CAD* (1977), 10:221.

47. Jastrow, *A Dictionary of the Targumim*, 1:725.

48. Cf. Edwin Hatch and Henry A. Redpath, eds., *A Concordance to the Septuagint and the Other Greek Versions of the Old Testament*, 2 vols. (Graz, Austria: Akademische Druck- u. Verlagsanstalt, 1975), 1:734a.

49. Theodotion is the name of one of LXX's daughter translations of the OT into Greek.

50. Ibid., 1:181b.

51. John C. Jeske, "Exegetical Brief: Genesis 7 — The Flood Prevailed," *Wisconsin Lutheran Quarterly* 95/3 (Summer 1998): p. 210–211.

52. *HALOT*, 1:175.

upon its use in the Qal is an unwarranted restriction (or expansion?)[53] of the semantic field of the word.[54]

It is abundantly clear from the language of the Flood narrative that the disruption of the earth's surface was comprehensive and global.[55] Such a description is not dependent upon the imposition of questionable etymological analyses for the individual terms employed in the passage. Individual words in and of themselves make no direct contribution to the task of determining the geologic consequences of Flood mechanisms. Rather, such contributions must be founded upon the sounder semantic clues provided by phraseology, literary devices, and context — the collective impact of the entire narrative.

How long was each mechanism at work on the terrestrial surface and subsurface? Given the specific parameters of their duration, what kind of effect can be expected? Is it possible to identify any correlation between the chronology of the Flood and known geologic stratification? The Flood narrative provides us with the mechanisms and their duration. Such information might be pertinent for constructing a model identifying potential geological results.

Translation with Chronological Notations

The following translation attempts to bring out the sequential nature of the primary layering of *wayyiqtol* verb forms. These verb forms are characteristic of Hebrew narrative and normally indicate a chronological sequence of the actions thus represented.[56]

Introduction to the Flood Narrative Proper (7:6–10)

7:6 Noah was 600 years old when the Flood came — waters *came* upon the earth. **7:7** Thus Noah, his sons, his wife, and his sons' wives went[57] with him into the ark away from the Flood waters. **7:8** The clean beasts and the beasts that were not clean, the flying creatures and all that crept on the ground **7:9** came[58] two

---

53. Some interpreters take the connotation of warfare as being inherent in the Hebrew root word, thus restricting the root to only this type of meaning. However, it is equally possible that the connotation of warfare is an unwarranted expansion of the root, which simply means "prevail" when water is the subject of the verb. Thus, Jeske has abused the root by expanding it to include warfare.

54. For a discussion of such exegetical fallacies with regard to word studies, see D.A. Carson, *Exegetical Fallacies* (Grand Rapids, MI: Baker, 1984), p. 25–66.

55. Henry M. Morris, *The Genesis Record: A Scientific and Devotional Commentary on the Book of Beginnings* (Grand Rapids, MI: Baker, 1976), p. 683–686, lists 100 reasons for understanding the Flood as a truly global catastrophe.

56. "Situations described with *wayyqtl* are mostly temporally or logically succeeding" (Bruce K. Waltke and M. O'Connor, *An Introduction to Biblical Hebrew Syntax* [Winona Lake, IN: Eisenbrauns, 1990], p. 547 [§33.2.1a]). "Most noteworthy in narrative is the way *wayyqtl* traces the thread of discourse" (ibid., p. 549 [§33.2.1c]).

57. This is the first of the *wayyiqtol* verbs that comprise the sequence of events described in the Flood narrative proper following the disjunctive clause of 7:6 that sets the stage.

58. Here the preceding *wayyiqtol* is followed by the same root (בוא, *bô'*) in the suffix

by two to Noah into the ark — male and female just as God had commanded Noah. **7:10** Then **7 days passed** *[600/02/10-600/02/16]*[59] and the Flood waters came upon the earth.[60]

I. First Section of the Flood Narrative (7:11-18)

7:11 In the 600th year of Noah's life, in the 2nd month, on the 17th day of that month[61] *[600/02/17 – day 1]*—on that day the fountains of the great deep burst open and the windows of the sky were opened. [62]

conjugation. This verb is not sequential or consequential to the preceding *wayyiqtol*. It merely represents the action in an unrelated (i.e., grammatically accidental) fashion, viewing it as an independent whole rather than as an action dependent on another action in the immediate context. For a fuller and more detailed discussion, I highly recommend the treatment of Waltke and O'Connor, *An Introduction to Biblical Hebrew Syntax*, p. 455–563 (§§29-33). Their clearest depiction of the distinctive implications of the suffix conjugation (perfect) vs. prefix conjugation (imperfect) is to be found in their discussion of the use of the prefix conjugation in future time (511, §31.6.2a). The same distinctions apply even in narrative past contexts.

59. In the translation, the references to chronological time are in bold font face followed by an italics bracket with the year (based on Noah's age, see v. 6), month, and day. Thus, *600/02/10* = in Noah's 600th year, in the second month, and on the tenth day. This date is not in bold, because it is not identified in this specific fashion in the text — it is deduced from the time reference. In 7:11, however, the text identifies the specific year, month, and day, so those numbers are in bold.

60. An alternative translation would be, "When seven days had passed, the Flood waters came upon the earth." The meaning is not essentially different.

61. This non-*waw* temporal circumstantial clause of 7:11 is paralleled by the same kind of clause in the last verse of this section, 8:14, which constitutes an inclusio marking the structural boundaries of the main Flood narrative. See footnote 63, below.

62. "Great deep": Note the other occurrences of תְּהוֹם רַבָּה (*tᵉhôm rabbâ*) in the OT: Isa. 51:10; Amos 7:4; Pss. 36:7; 78:15. In all of these passages it is clear that the sea is intended. "Great" is not in a qualitative sense, but in a quantitative sense — the concept is that of "a great depth" similar to the concept in the English by "deep sea." Cf. the discussion of this Hebrew phrase in U. Cassuto, *Biblical and Oriental Studies*, 2 vols., trans. by Israel Abrahams (Jerusalem: Magnes Press, 1975), 2:38. Therefore, the "fountains of the great deep" appear at first blush to refer to submarine springs that burst open on the ocean bottom, pouring more water into the ocean basin(s). However, the "great depth" can refer to subterranean as well as submarine sources, as argued by Fouts and Wise, "Blotting Out and Breaking Up: Miscellaneous Hebrew Studies in Geocatastrophism," p. 220–222.

"Burst open": The employment of suffix conjugation verbs (perfects: "burst open" and "were opened") in this verse signal that a new chain of sequential events is being initiated with these verbs as their grammatical head. The verb בָּקַע (*bāqaʿ*) is employed with the same object (מַעְיָן, *maʿᵉyān*) in Ps. 74:15 where it appears to have the sense of emptying out or draining. In Judg. 15:19 [here the verb seems to apply to the rock (not the water) in the hollow place, which was broken open so water could come out]; in Isa. 35:6; 63:12 and Ps. 78:15, the same verb is used to describe the pouring out of

7:12 When[63] the rain came[64] upon the earth **for 40 days and 40 nights** *[600/02/17-600/03/26 – days 1-40]*, **7:13** on that very day Noah, Shem, Ham, and Japheth (Noah's sons), Noah's wife, and his sons' three wives entered the ark with him — **7:14** they and every animal according to its kind, every land animal according to its kind, every crawler creeping on the earth according to its kind, and every flying creature according to its kind (every flying creature of every sort). **7:15** Thus they came to Noah into the ark; two by two out of all flesh in which was the spirit of life. **7:16** The ones coming were male and female out of all flesh. They came just as God had commanded him. So YHWH shut

---

large quantities of water from the earth or from rock. It is obvious, that for the water to come out in such a fashion, the earth or the rock would have to split or divide in some fashion, just like the splitting open of the ground in Num. 16:31 where the same verb is employed. Prov. 3:20 (בְּדַעְתּוֹ תְּהוֹמוֹת נִבְקָעוּ, $b^e\underline{d}a'^e\underline{t}\hat{o}$ $t^eh\hat{o}m\hat{o}\underline{t}$ $ni\underline{b}q\bar{a}'\hat{u}$ — "by His knowledge the deeps burst open") might refer to the creation of dry land in the midst of the waters in Gen. 1:9 or to the passage under discussion (7:11). The Niphal is best translated as an active; cf. Fouts and Wise, "Blotting Out and Breaking Up: Miscellaneous Hebrew Studies in Geocatastrophism," p. 220.

"Windows of the sky were opened": "[T]he expression connotes that during the Flood it did not rain in normal measure, but the windows of heaven were opened wide and the water poured from them in large quantities without any restraint" (Cassuto, *Genesis: Part II*, p. 87). The terminology ("windows of the sky") seems to be a strong indication that the rains were global (Fouts and Wise, "Blotting Out and Breaking Up: Miscellaneous Hebrew Studies in Geocatastrophism," p. 222).

63. The employment of וַיְהִי (*way^ehî*) in 7:12 parallels that of וַיְהִי (*way^ehî*) in the next to last verse of this section, 8:13 — another inclusio confirming the 7:11//8:14 inclusio marking the limits of the Flood narrative (see footnote 61, above).

64. The וַיְהִי (*way^ehî*) construction is followed by the circumstantial clause of v. 13–14 and suffix conjugation (perfect) verb (בָּא, *bā'*). That suffix conjugation verb becomes the lead verb for the series (or, chain) of nine *wayyiqtol* verbs that follow it in v. 15–18. There are nine chronologically sequential actions:

(1) The animals entered the ark (וַיָּבֹאוּ, *wayyā\underline{b}ō'û*) (v. 15a).

(2) Then God shut the door (וַיִּסְגֹּר, *wayyisgōr*) (v. 16b).

(3) Then the deluge came upon the earth for 40 days (וַיְהִי, *way^ehî*) (v. 17a).

(4) Then the waters increased (וַיִּרְבּוּ, *wayyirbû*) (v. 17b) — increase following the 40 days.

(5) Then the ark became sea borne (וַיִּשְׂאוּ, *wayyiś'û*) (v. 17c) — the result of that increase in waters.

(6) Then the ark rose above the land (וַתָּרָם, *wattārām*) (v. 17d) — the result of continuing increase of waters.

(7) Then the waters prevailed (וַיִּגְבְּרוּ, *wayyi\underline{g}b^erû*) (v. 18a) — all landforms finally disappeared beneath the water.

(8) Then the waters increased even more (וַיִּרְבּוּ, *wayyirbû*) (v. 18b) — a clear indication of the mechanisms continuing to produce water.

(9) Then the ark sailed upon the waters (וַתֵּלֶךְ, *wattēlē\underline{k}*) (v. 18c) — the action of the ark until the day it grounded on the mountains of Ararat.

him in. **7:17** Then the flood occurred **for 40 days**[65] upon the earth. The waters continued to increase so that they bore the ark, raising it up off the ground. **7:18** Then the waters prevailed and increased greatly upon the earth so that the ark moved on the surface of the waters.

II. Second Section of the Flood Narrative (7:19–8:4)

7:19 The waters prevailed[66] even more over the earth so that all the highest mountains that were under the entire sky were covered. **7:20** Fifteen cubits upwards the waters prevailed so that they covered the mountains. **7:21** Thus all flesh perished[67] — that which crept upon the earth among flying creatures, beasts, animals, and every swarming thing upon the earth, as well as all mankind. **7:22** Everything possessing the breath of life in its nostrils among everything that was

---

65. "Only one who does not understand the structure of the verse, or its meaning, can regard it as a redundant repetition of what was stated in v. 12" (Cassuto, *Genesis: Part II*, p. 93). This verse refers to the same 40 days as in v. 12, but the focus is on the ark's floating on the waters. The ark was lifted off the surface of the ground on the 40th day, but the mechanisms for submerging the earth continued until the 151st day (8:3). S.E. McEvenue agrees that these 40 days were the period of time required for the ark to become sea borne (*The Narrative Style of the Priestly Writer*, Analecta Biblica 80 [Rome: Biblical Institute Press, 1971], p. 63). According to H. Freedman, Abraham Ibn Ezra (b. 1092) had reached the same conclusion nearly a millennium ago: *"forty days.* This was already stated in verse 12. The repetition teaches that only after forty days of rain was the ark lifted up, but until then it remained stationary" — "The Book of Genesis," in *The Soncino Chumash: The Five Books of Moses with Haphtaroth*, 2nd ed., ed. by A. Cohen (London: Soncino Press, 1983), p. 38–39.

 Jeske writes, "Many Bible readers have the impression that after rising to maximum height during the first forty days, the floodwaters for the next 110 days simply remained sluggishly and sullenly at flood stage" ("Exegetical Brief," p. 210). His description of raging waters upon the earth's surface falls short of the biblical description because he ignores the statement that it was not until the 150th day that the rain and the submarine eruptions of underground water ceased.

66. Verses 7:19–8:4 are a new section. The verb form reverts to a suffix conjugation (perfect) since the chain of *wayyiqtol* verbs have been broken. Just as the verb root נבר (*gbr*, "prevail") had been chosen to express the submersion of all land forms in 7:18a (by implication), so here the same verb root is chosen to express the submersion of all the highest mountains and all terrestrial life forms in v. 19. As a suffix conjugation verb, it views the action as a whole without reference to relationships. The twofold statement (with the *wayyiqtol* וַיְכֻסּוּ [*wayy*ᵉ*kussû*] employed as an epexegetical [cf. Waltke and O'Connor, *An Introduction to Biblical Hebrew Syntax*, §33.2.2) clarifies the preceding reference to prevailing waters and then moves on to the main topic of this section, the submersion of all life forms so that they "expired" (וַיִּגְוַע, *wayyigwa'*). It is also significant that a 3-part chiasm introduces this section break. See footnote 17, above.

67. The difficulty with attempting a chronology regarding the submersion and death of all life forms is that v. 19–22 provide only the submersion of the mountains as the time marker — which could be anywhere between the 40th and the 150th days.

on dry ground — everything — died. **7:23** So He obliterated[68] all living beings from the ground from mankind to beast, to creeping thing, even to flying creature. They were obliterated from the earth. Then[69] only Noah and those with him in the ark were left. **7:24** Thus the waters prevailed[70] upon the earth **for 150 days** *[600/02/17-600/07/16 - days 1-150].*[71] **8:1** Then God remembered Noah and all the animals and beasts that were in the ark with him. God caused a wind to blow over the earth so that the waters began to subside. **8:2** So the fountains of the deep and the windows of the sky were blocked and the rain from the sky was

---

68. Just as the submersion of the mountains involved a double *wayyiqtol* from one root in v. 19–20 (see footnote 62, above), so also the writer employs a double *wayyiqtol* from one root in v. 23 (וַיִּמַח [*wayyimaḥ*] and וַיִּמָּחוּ [*wayyimmāḥû*]) to describe the obliteration of all life forms. Also, just as those previous *wayyiqtols* were epexegetical, so are these.

69. From this point the sequential/consequential *wayyiqtol* chain presents ten sequential actions:

(1) Then only those on the ark remained (וַיִּשָּׁאֶר, *wayiśśā'er*) (7:23b).

(2) Then the waters continued to prevail (וַיִּגְבְּרוּ, *wayyigbᵉrû*) (7:24) to a total of 150 days.

(3) Then God remembered (וַיִּזְכֹּר, *wayyizkōr*) (8:1a) Noah.

(4) Then God caused the wind to blow (וַיַּעֲבֵר, *wayya'ăbēr*) (8:1b).

(5) Then the waters began to subside (וַיָּשֹׁכּוּ, *wayyāśōkû*) (8:1c) — as an immediate result of the wind.

(6) Then the sources for the waters were blocked up (וַיִּסָּכְרוּ, *wayyissākrû*) (8:2a).

(7) Then the rain was withheld (וַיִּכָּלֵא, *wayyikkālē'*) (8:2b).

(8) Then began to recede continually (וַיָּשֻׁבוּ, *wayyāšubû*) (8:3a).

(9) Then they continued to decrease (וַיַּחְסְרוּ, *wayyaḥsᵉrû*) (8:3b).

(10) Then the ark came to rest (וַתָּנַח, *wattānaḥ*) (8:4).

70. N.A. Mundhenk argues that translating 7:24 provides some of the "most serious translation problems" of the Flood narrative ("The Dates of the Flood," *Bible Translator* 45/2 [Apr 1994]: p. 210). He concludes that the translation of the Revised English Bible "is especially unfortunate. It says, 'when the water had increased over the earth for a hundred and fifty days,' which suggests that the waters continued to get deeper for this whole time. For this to be true there would have to be new water coming from somewhere all through this time, even after the rain stopped" (ibid., p. 211). In order to take this position with regard to 7:24, Mundhenk also had to alter 8:2, where it appears that the Flood mechanisms ceased at the end of the 150 days, not at the end of the first 40 days. Regarding 8:2, Mundhenk writes, "Many translations give the impression that the rain and the water from under the earth continued to flow until the time that God made the wind begin to blow. But the time when the source of the Flood stopped is given in 7:17 as 40 days" (ibid.). However, 8:2 is clearly the reversal of 7:11; 8:2 represents the cessation of those mechanisms set in motion in 7:11.

71. These 150 days included the original 40 days. Comparing 7:11 and 8:4 makes this inclusion certain. See, also, Mathews, *Genesis 1:1–11:26*, p. 376; Wenham, *Genesis 1–15*, p. 180. Ibn Ezra was convinced that the text taught that the mechanisms of the Flood continued throughout those 150 days. Freedman's reference drawn from Ibn Ezra states, "Moreover, it continued raining intermittently, whereas during the first forty days it rained incessantly" ("The Book of Genesis," p. 39).

withheld. **8:3** Then the waters were turning back from upon the earth, going and returning *little by little* so that they continued to decrease **at the end of those 150 days**[72] *[600/07/17 – day 151]*. **8:4** Thus, on the **17th day of the 7th month** the ark came to rest in the mountains of Ararat.

III. Third Section of the Flood Narrative (8:5–12)

8:5[73] The waters were continually decreasing until[74] the **10th month. On the 1st day of the 10th month** *[600/10/01 – day 225]* the mountaintops appeared. **8:6** Then **at the end of 40 days**[75] *[600/10/02-600/11/11 – days 226–265]* Noah opened the hatch of the ark that he had made **8:7** and he sent[76] a raven out *[600/11/12 – day 266]*.[77] It went back and forth until the water was dried up from upon the earth.[78] **8:8** Then he sent a dove out from him *[600/11/19 – day 273]* to see if the waters were scant upon the surface of the ground. **8:9** But[79]

---

72. Wenham correctly observes that "the natural way to take the references to the 150 days in 7:24 and 8:3 is that they refer to the same period" ("The Coherence of the Flood Narrative," p. 444).

73. By means of a *waw* + non-verb (disjunctive clause) and a 3-part chiasm (see footnote 18, above), the final major section of the Flood narrative commences.

74. "Until" (עַד, *'ad*) "often indicates not the end of a process but the completion of an important part of it" (Cassuto, *Genesis: Part II*, p. 106). In this particular instance, the significant event is the emergence of the tops of the mountains on day 225.

75. If וַיְהִי (*wayehî*) is taken as macrosyntactical, the following *wayyiqtol* would not be considered sequential and would become the lead verb for the following sequential/consequential *wayyiqtols*. An alternative translation could be: "When 40 days had ended, Noah opened the ark's window that he had made." The meaning is not different, however. If the 40 days began on the same day that the mountaintops emerged, then the dates would be 600/10/01-600/11/10 and would also affect the dates (by one day) for the sending out of the raven and the dove.

76. This *wayyiqtol* verb is the first in a chain laying out three sequential/consequential actions:
     (1) Then Noah sent out (וַיְשַׁלַּח, *wayešallaḥ*) (8:7a) the raven.
     (2) Then the raven flew (וַיֵּצֵא, *wayyēṣē'*) (8:7b) to and fro.
     (3) Then Noah sent out (וַיְשַׁלַּח, *wayešallaḥ*) (8:8) the dove.

77. See 8:10. "[I]t is clear from v. 10 that according to the Biblical narrative seven days passed between the sending forth of the raven and the first time he sent the dove" (Cassuto, *Genesis: Part II*, p. 110; cf., also, Gordon J. Wenham, *Genesis 1–15*, Word Biblical Commentary [Waco, TX: Word, 1987], p. 186).

78. In the case of the raven, it never brought anything back. Every time it was sent out, it returned — until the waters had totally receded. Evidently Noah believed it would be wise to send a second kind of bird since the raven would have been looking for carrion instead of vegetation. It seems from the text that the birds were sent out every seven days and that they probably returned on the same day that they were sent out (cf. 8:11).

79. The negative disjunctive clause interrupts the chain of *wayyiqtol* verbs and brings the first sub-section to a close. The suffix conjugation (perfect) verb (מָצְאָה, *māṣe'â*) becomes the lead verb for the subsequent *wayyiqtol* chain comprising ten sequential/consequential

the dove did not find a resting place for its foot, so it returned to him in the ark because the waters were over the surface of the whole earth. Thus he reached out and retrieved it and brought it into the ark with him. **8:10** When **another 7 days** *[600/11/20-600/11/26 – days 274-280]* had passed, he again sent the dove *[600/11/26 – day 280]* from the ark **8:11** and it returned to him at evening with a freshly picked olive leaf in its mouth![80] Then Noah knew that the waters were scant upon the earth. **8:12** When **yet another 7 days** *[600/11/27-600/12/03 – days 281-287]* had passed, he sent out the dove *[600/12/03 – day 287]* but[81] it did not return to him any more.

Conclusion to the Flood Narrative Proper (8:13–14)

8:13 On the 1st day of the 1st month of the 601st year[82] *[601/01/01 – day 315]*, the waters were drying up[83] from the surface of the ground. So Noah

---

actions:
- (1) Then the dove returned (וַתָּשָׁב, *wattāšāb*) (8:9b) to Noah.
- (2) Then Noah stretched out (וַיִּשְׁלַח, *wayyišᵉlaḥ*) (8:9cα) his hand.
- (3) Then Noah took (וַיִּקָּחֶהָ, *wayyiqqāḥehā*) (8:9cβ) the dove.
- (4) Then Noah brought (וַיָּבֵא, *wayyābē'*) (8:9d) the dove into the ark.
- (5) Then seven more days passed (וַיָּחֶל, *wayyāḥel*) (8:10a).
- (6) Then Noah again sent out (וַיֹּסֶף שַׁלַּח, *wayyōsep šallaḥ*) (8:10b) the dove.
- (7) Then the dove came back (וַתָּבֹא *wattābō'*) (8:11aα) to him.
- (8) Then Noah knew (וַיֵּדַע, *wayyēda'*) (8:11b) the condition of the earth's surface.
- (9) Then seven more days passed (וַיִּיָּחֶל, *wayyiyyāḥel*) (8:12a).
- (10) Then Noah sent out (וַיְשַׁלַּח, *wayᵉšallaḥ*) (8:12bα) the dove for the last time.

80. 8:11aβ is a parenthetical comment introduced by וְהִנֵּה (*wᵉhinnēh*) as a *waw* + non-verb disjunctive clause. As a parenthetical comment providing background information, it does not radically interrupt the *wayyiqtol* chain which picks up after it.

81. Just as in 8:9 (see footnote 73, above), a negative disjunctive clause interrupts the flow of the narrative. This time, however, its suffix conjugation (perfect) verb does not become the lead verb for a subsequent *wayyiqtol* chain. It closes the final sub-section of the narrative (cf. Robert B. Chisholm, Jr., *From Exegesis to Exposition: A Practical Guide to Using Biblical Hebrew* [Grand Rapids, MI: Baker, 1998], p. 127, #7).

82. The וַיְהִי (*wayᵉhî*) is followed by this circumstantial clause of v. 13 and suffix conjugation (perfect) verb (חָרְבוּ, *hārᵉbû*). That suffix conjugation verb becomes the lead verb for the series (or chain) of two *wayyiqtol* verbs that follow it expressing chronologically sequential actions:

(1) Then Noah removed (וַיָּסַר, *wayyāsar*) (8:13bα) the hatch of the ark.

(2) Then Noah observed (וַיַּרְא, *wayyarᵉ'*) (8:13bβ) that the ground was drying up

83. It appears that, on day 315, even though the surface had lost the layer of water over it, it was still too wet below the surface to walk upon it. This is basically the view taken by R.W.L. Moberly, "Why Did Noah Send Out a Raven?" *Vetus Testamentum* 50/3 (2000): p. 351: "The juxtaposition of *ḥrb* in v. 13 with *ybš* in v. 14 clearly indicates a distinction — presumably between a muddy, boggy mess and firm, hard ground — in which *ybš* is the term for the complete disappearance of the flood waters from the earth" on day 371. Both major 11th-century rabbis, Rashi and Ibn Ezra, took the description in v. 13 to refer to the drying of only the top surface of the ground and that

removed the ark's cover. Then he observed that the surface of the ground was drying up.

8:14 On the 27th day of the 2nd month *[601/02/27 – day 371]* the land was dry.[84]

The above translation reveals the sequential nature of the primary layering of *wayyiqtol* verb forms. These verb forms are characteristic of Hebrew narrative and normally indicate a chronological sequence of the actions presented. The temporal circumstantial clause at the beginning of 7:11 is paralleled by the same kind of clause in the last verse, 8:14 — an inclusio marking the structure of the main Flood narrative. The employment of *wayᵉhî* in 7:12 parallels that of *wayᵉhî* in the next to the last verse, 8:13 — another inclusio confirming the 7:11//8:14 inclusio marking the limits of the Flood narrative. Therefore, the introduction to the Flood narrative proper occurs in 7:6–10. The Flood narrative itself is composed of three major sections: (1) 7:11–18; (2) 7:19–8:4; and (3) 8:5–12. The conclusion of the Flood narrative proper occurs in 8:13–14. The difficulty with attempting a chronology regarding the submersion and death of all land-dwelling, air-breathing life forms is that 7:19–22 provides only the submersion of the mountains as the time marker — which occurs sometime between the 40th and the 150th days.

Two-Fold Purpose of the Flood

During the first 150 days, the flood waters destroyed all terrestrial life and obscured the original continent(s). God restrained the heavy rains after the first 150 days (not after 40 days)[85] and He stopped the fountains of the deep and the windows of heaven at that same time. It appears from the text that the significance of the first 40 days of the Flood lies in the floating of the ark on the 40th day.[86] Destruction of all living things outside the ark was the purpose of the first 150 days. The purpose of the next 165 days followed by the 56 days was to make the earth suitable for life — an apparent replication of the original process of creation (1:2–19). The waters returned back to the ocean basins and achieved

---

it left the ground insufficiently firm to walk upon (Freedman, "The Book of Genesis," p. 42). Wenham, *Genesis 1–15*, p. 187. See footnote 78, above.

84. According to Wenham, "Nearly two months elapsed between Noah's looking out of the ark to see the earth is 'drying' חרב till it was 'dried out' יבש. This distinction between the two roots is also attested in Isa. 19:5; Job 14:11; and Jer. 50:38" (*Genesis 1–15*, p. 187). Job 14:11 is a significant pairing of the two roots in that the "verb 'dry up' חרב, speaking of waters (12:15), expresses the result of the action expressed by יבש (Gen. 8:13)" — E. Dhorme, *A Commentary on the Book of Job*, trans. by Harold Knight (Nashville, TN: Thomas Nelson, 1984), p. 200.

85. Contra John Woodmorappe, "Hypercanes as a Cause of the 40-Day Global Flood Rainfall," in *Proceedings of the Fourth International Conference on Creationism Held August 3-8, 1998*, ed. by Robert E. Walsh (Pittsburgh, PA: Creation Science Fellowship, 1998), p. 645–658.

86. Contra Robinson, "The Flood in Genesis: What Does the Text Tell Geologists?" p. 468.

relative stability[87] by day 300.

Overall, the purpose of the Flood is two-fold: (1) The first 150 days are a global cataclysmic judgment; (2) the following 221 days are for cleansing and reconstruction.[88] The statement, "God remembered Noah" (8:1), does not mean that God had forgotten about Noah. It refers to God taking action to make the earth suitable again for the inhabitants of the ark and their descendants.[89] This "remembrance" is first demonstrated by the ark coming to rest on the following day (day 151) during the initial stages of subsidence (8:1–4). At the end of 150 days, the wind and the blocking of the sources caused the waters to subside and continually decline for 221 days. Thus, the purpose of the first 150 days was to obliterate all terrestrial life and the purpose of the next 221 days was to restore the earth to a livable condition.

Prevailing Phase

The destructive phase of prevailing waters during the first 150 days was caused by the eruptions of the fountains of the great deep and torrential rain. The fact that the fountains of the great deep are mentioned before the rains, both here and in 8:1, suggests that the fountains were the primary source of water that flooded the earth.

This Hebrew verb בָּקַע ("burst open") is used in Numbers 16:31 to refer to a small earthquake that took Korah and his family and belongings into the earth. In Judges 15:19 it refers to the breaking of rock to release water, and in Zechariah 14:4 it refers to a major mountain-splitting and valley-forming earthquake. So this word is loaded with geological significance. It indicates that in the prevailing phase of floodwaters there was massive tectonic activity in the crust of the earth. These earthquakes would have caused volcanoes and tsunamis (as earthquakes do today) on a global scale, with incredible destructive power.

The phrase "windows of heaven" (7:11; 8:2) is a Hebrew idiom or metaphor, which apparently means a great pouring out (e.g., 2 Kings 7:19; Isa. 24:18; Mal. 3:10). These processes began on day 1 and ended on day 150. During the first 150 days, rising water is mentioned no less than three times. From day 1, torrential rain and flooding caused the water level to increase and rise. On the 40th day, the water level was sufficient to lift the ark off the ground surface (Gen. 7:17), as previously recognized by Holt.[90] After this, the waters increased greatly so that the ark floated freely on the water surface (7:18). Then the waters continued to rise and all the pre-Flood mountains were covered (7:19–20). After the highest

---

87. "Relative stability" indicates that the environment was stable enough for the dove that Noah sent out from the ark to find a place of rest and security.

88. Bruce K. Waltke, *Genesis: A Commentary* (Grand Rapids, MI: Zondervan, 2001), p. 140.

89. Claus Westermann, *Genesis 1–11: A Commentary*, trans. by J.J. Scullion (Minneapolis, MN: Augsburg Publishing House, 1984), p. 441.

90. Roy D. Holt, "Evidence for a Late Cainozoic Flood/post-Flood Boundary," *Creation Ex Nihilo Technical Journal* 10/1 (April 1996): p. 130.

regions became submerged, all flesh (all land-dwelling, air-breathing creatures) died (7:21). The significance of the first 40 days (7:12, 17) is with raising the ark off the ground surface, not when the rain stopped and not when the land creatures died.

Based on a misunderstanding of 7:4, it is a common misconception that rain (and the whole Flood for that matter) ceased after 40 days. In reality the detailed account of the Flood in 7:11–24 is an expansion of the generalized prophetic announcement of 7:4. It is sequential also: that all life would be destroyed at some point after the 40th day as clearly revealed in 7:11–24. Neither the single verse (7:4) nor the detailed expansion (7:11–24) claim that rain would cease after 40 days. Flood models based upon isolated key word studies are mistaken and so are geologic models based on 7:4 alone.

Subsiding Phase — A Key Interpretative Issue Involving Mechanism

Genesis 8:1 marks the turning point in the Flood. When the mechanisms cease at the end of 150 days, the writer describes a constant back and forth motion of the waters as they return to a relatively stable state over the course of the following 165 days. Studies of the Flood narrative have typically treated 8:3 as though it was nothing but a simple statement of the continuous recession of the waters after the first 150 days. Potentially, this verse has much to contribute to the discussion of Flood hydrodynamics.[91] Best's recent study of the Noahic Flood in the light of the Sumerian epic of Ziusudra focused on 8:3 in one of its appendixes.[92] Although he utilizes the text to support his adherence to a localized riverine flood, he still confirmed that the phrase "going and returning" (translation above for 8:3) is best understood as a reference to "ebbing and flooding."[93] The following three observations lead to the same conclusion.

Observation 1: In the first half of Genesis 8:3 (וַיָּשֻׁבוּ הַמַּיִם מֵעַל הָאָרֶץ הָלוֹךְ וָשׁוֹב, wayyāšubû hammayim mēʿal hāʾāreṣ hālôk wāšôb) the primary verb is וַיָּשֻׁבוּ (wayyāšubû), a verb of motion: "were returning" or "were turning back."[94] An example of such movement is seen in the description of the cycle of winds in Ecclesiastes 1:6 — "The wind blows to the south and goes around to the north; around and around goes the wind, and on its circuits the wind returns (שָׁב, šāb)" (ESV[95]). The same verb root is repeated as the final word (וָשׁוֹב, wāšôb) in this half of the verse, forming a kind of inclusio (or envelope figure) that helps to aug-

---

91. Northrup, "Identifying the Noahic Flood in Historical Geology: Part One," p. 177, notes the significance of the Hebrew text here and discusses one geologic result.

92. Robert M. Best, *Noah's Ark and the Ziusudra Epic: Sumerian Origins of the Flood Myth* (Fort Myers, FL: Enlil Press, 1999).

93. Ibid., p. 281.

94. Waltke and O'Connor, *An Introduction to Biblical Hebrew Syntax*, p. 589 (§35.3.2b-c).

95. *The Holy Bible: English Standard Version* (Wheaton, IL: Crossway, 2001).

ment the focus on this particular motion by delimiting this half-verse.[96] Wenham declares, "Exactly the same description is given of the Red Sea returning to its place in Exodus 14:26, 28, and the Jordan likewise, in Joshua 4:18."[97] However, he must be speaking only of the employment of וַיָּשֻׁבוּ (wayyāšubû), for none of the other passages have the additional double-verb construction (וַיָּשֻׁבוּ ... הָלוֹךְ וָשׁוֹב, wayyāšubû ... hālôk wāšôb).

Observation 2: The combination of two infinitive absolutes in the final phrase (הָלוֹךְ וָשׁוֹב, hālôk wāšôb) is an adverbial hendiadys in which the first verb is the adverbial modifier of the second: "continually returning."[98] The main infinitive (וָשׁוֹב, wāšôb) is functioning as a gerund expressing the circumstance[99] of the primary verb (וַיָּשֻׁבוּ, wayyāšubû): "Then the waters were turning back . . . continually returning." By thus repeating the primary verb with the cognate infinitive absolute, "the writer or speaker wants to indicate that he is especially interested in it or to demand that the reader or hearer give especial attention to it."[100] הָלוֹךְ (hālôk) is an intensifying infinitive absolute (normally paronomastic — playing on the primary verb root or sense).[101] When הָלוֹךְ (hālôk) is employed in this fashion, it normally stresses continuous action.[102] Two different interpretations have arisen from this Hebrew construction. On the one hand, H.C. Leupold claimed that it "amounts to: 'they subsided with a very pronounced fall.'"[103] This appears to be the view upon which Henry Morris depended when he claimed that the Hebrew expression "indicates a quite rapid subsidence."[104] On the other hand, Gordon Wenham explained that it places an emphasis on "the long time in which the waters continued to decline."[105] Such a view was also offered by Umberto Cassuto:

> The process is, of course, protracted: the waters return, *going and*

---

96. Watson, *Classical Hebrew Poetry*, p. 282–285.

97. Wenham, *Genesis 1–15*, p. 184.

98. Frederic Clarke Putnam, *Hebrew Bible Insert* (Quakertown, PA: Stylus Publishing, 1996), §2.3.2.

99. Cf. Gary A. Long, *Grammatical Concepts 101 for Biblical Hebrew: Learning Biblical Hebrew Grammatical Concepts through English Grammar* (Peabody, MA: Hendrickson, 2002), p. 83.

100. T. Muraoka, *Emphatic Words and Structures in Biblical Hebrew* (Jerusalem: Magnes Press, 1985), p. 92.

101. Waltke and O'Connor, *An Introduction to Biblical Hebrew Syntax*, §35.3.2b-c. Cf. E. Kautzsch, ed., *Gesenius' Hebrew Grammar*, 2nd English ed., trans. and ed. by A.E. Cowley (Oxford: Clarendon Press, 1910), §113r-s, u; hereafter referred to as GKC.

102. Ibid. Cf. Putnam, *Hebrew Bible Insert*, §2.3.2; Paul Joüon, *A Grammar of Biblical Hebrew*, trans. and rev. by T. Muraoka, Subsidia Biblica 14/II (Rome: Pontifical Biblical Institute, 1996), §123s.

103. H.C. Leupold, *Exposition of Genesis*, 2 vols. (Grand Rapids, MI: Baker, 1970 reprint of 1942 ed.), 1:310.

104. Morris, *The Genesis Record*, p. 207.

105. Wenham, *Genesis 1–15*, p. 153.

returning — little by little. When the fountains burst forth, the waters gushed out from there with force and speed, and when the windows of the heavens were opened, the water poured down from them fast and furious; but now that these openings, below and above, have been closed, the waters recede slowly, by a gradual and continuous movement, according to the normal way of nature.[106]

In what could be taken as agreement with this second interpretation, some commentators and translators have chosen to bring out the concept of a steady or gradual receding of the waters.[107] Employing Genesis 8:3 as their example, Hans Bauer and Pontus Leander pointed out that the grammar expresses the continual nature of the action of the water as it "subsided more and more" with both a going and a returning motion.[108]

Observation 3: הָלוֹךְ וָשׁוֹב occurs nowhere else in the Hebrew OT. However, there are two similar constructions in the immediate context:

1. verse 5: וְהַמַּיִם הָיוּ הָלוֹךְ וְחָסוֹר (*weḥammāyim hāyû hālôḵ weḥāsôr*):[109] "and the waters were continually decreasing"

2. verse 7: וַיֵּצֵא יָצוֹא וָשׁוֹב (*wayyēṣēʾ yāṣôʾ wāšôḇ*): "[the raven] went back and forth"

The clause in verse 7 is closer in structure and meaning to the clause in verse 3 than verse 5. וַיֵּצֵא יָצוֹא וָשׁוֹב (*wayyēṣēʾ yāṣôʾ wāšôḇ*) is best translated by *flying back and forth*[110] rather than *went out just to come back again (soon)*.[111] In his discussion of verse 7, Moberly concludes that, no matter how one might take the idiom with the infinitive absolutes, "either way the general sense of ceaseless movement is clear."[112] Indeed, this "repeated idiom suggests a possible parallelism between the movement of the receding waters and the flight of the raven."[113] By analogy, therefore, the receding waters are described by the same grammar and phraseology as the raven's flight: as being in continuous

---

106. Cassuto, *Genesis: Part II*, p. 102.

107. Westermann, *Genesis 1–11*, p. 389 ("receded gradually"; cf. NLT and NRSV); Nahum M. Sarna, *Genesis*, JPS Torah Commentary (Philadelphia, PA: Jewish Publication Society, 1989), p. 56 ("receded steadily"; cf. NJPS, NASB, and NIV).

108. ". . . um die Fortdauer der Handlung auszudrücken: . . . 'und sie (kehrten zuruck ein Gehen und ein Zurückkehren, d. h.) verliefen sich immer mehr' " — Hans Bauer and Pontus Leander, *Historische Grammatik der hebräischen Sprache des alten Testamentes* (Halle, Germany: Max Niemeyer, 1922), p. 277 (§36 *e'*).

109. This construction with הָיָה (*hāyâ*) followed by the infinitive absolute הָלוֹךְ (*hālôḵ*), occurs only here in the OT.

110. Waltke and O'Connor, *An Introduction to Biblical Hebrew Syntax*, p. 590 (§35.3.2c).

111. Joüon-Muraoka, *A Grammar of Biblical Hebrew*, §123m.

112. Moberly, "Why Did Noah Send Out a Raven?" p. 350.

113. Ibid., p. 350–351.

motion "*going and returning* — little by little."[114] It is interesting to observe that the same construction in modern Hebrew (*hālôk wāšôb*) refers to a round trip.[115]

The first half of 8:3 speaks of the movement of Flood waters. "Returning" or "receding" describes that motion. Since the first verb (*wayyašubû*) is a *wayyiqtol*, it indicates that this action follows chronologically the cessation of the mechanisms described in 8:2. The description concerns the abating or decreasing of the waters from off the land masses which, at this point, are still submerged. The roots and forms of the last two Hebrew words in 8:3a (*hālôk wāšôb*) present a forceful picture. The two words together focus on the concept of a continual recession of the water. However, it is not a focus on mere recession or abatement. That concept is specified with a related construction and a different second verb in 8:5. That which is involved here is more parallel to what is stated concerning the raven in 8:7 — it was continually going and returning (flying back and forth). Applying this concept to 8:3 reveals that the waters were in a constant back and forth motion.[116]

In conclusion, the apparent intent of the text is to describe the receding waters of the Noahic Flood as being in a constant ebbing and flowing motion. Such movement could be augmented by the absence of extensive land barriers, making for wave motion of grand proportions that could have had a profound effect in the shaping of the earth's surface.[117] Even submerged land masses would feel the scouring and depositional effects of the intermittent surges, retreats, and resurgence of water. Once the water had receded below the highest landforms, massive waves could have been crashing over and against those forms, carving them and forming them into a totally new landscape from that which existed prior to the Flood.

Summary of Chronology

For clarity, the table on the following page presents the chronological summary of the Flood in Genesis 7:11–8:14. For the purpose of this chapter, no detailed defense of the 30-day month will be presented. Support can be found in the sources both in defense of the 30-day month and opposed to it.[118]

---

114. Cassuto, *Genesis: Part II*, p. 102.

115. Best, *Noah's Ark and the Ziusudra Epic*, p. 281.

116. Contra Leupold, *Exposition of Genesis*, 1:310.

117. Whitcomb and Morris, *The Genesis Flood*, p. 100, 269. See, also, Harold W. Clark, *Fossils, Flood, and Fire* (Escondido, CA: Outdoor Pictures, 1968). Unfortunately, this ebbing and flowing movement of the receding waters is totally ignored by Tas Walker, "A Biblical Geologic Model," in *Proceedings of the Third International Conference on Creationism Held July 18-23, 1994*, ed. by Robert E. Walsh (Pittsburgh, PA: Creation Science Fellowship, 1994), p. 584–592.

118. See Jack Finegan, *Handbook of Biblical Chronology: Principles of Time Reckoning in the Ancient World and Problems of Chronology in the Bible* (Princeton, NJ: Princeton University Press, 1964), for arguments supporting the 30-day month in the Israelite

	Passage	Date	Duration	Stage	Flood Days
150	7:11	600/02/17	Rising Waters	Commencement of torrential rain and the bursting open of subterranean water sources (primarily beneath the sea floor)	1st
	7:12, 17	600/03/26	40 days	Rising waters result in floating of the ark	40th
	7:24 (cf. 8:3)	600/07/16	150 days	Continually rising waters due to rain and subterranean sources — all land creatures outside the ark die	150th
165	8:4	600/07/17	Receding Waters	Commencement of subsiding waters after the sources are stopped — ark grounded	151st
	8:5	600/10/01	74 days since ark grounded	Mountaintops appear	225th
	8:6	600/11/11	40 days	Noah opens ark's hatch	265th
	8:7	600/11/12?		Raven released	266th
	8:8	600/11/19?	7 days?	Dove released	273rd
	8:10	600/11/26?	7 days	Dove released and returns with olive leaf	280th
	8:12	600/12/03?	7 days	Dove released and does not return	287th
56	8:13	601/01/01	90 days since mountaintops appeared	Ground surface free of excess water	315th
	8:14	601/02/27	221 days since water sources were stopped	Land dry enough to disembark from the ark	371st

calendar. In addition, Cryer (see footnote 12, above) has adequately covered some of the arguments in support of 30-day months ("Interrelationship," p. 256–257). For a recent critique of a lunar calendar in ancient Israel, see Bruce K. Gardner, *The Genesis Calendar: The Synchronistic Tradition in Genesis 1–11* (Lanham, MD: University Press of America, Inc., 2001). It should be pointed out, however, that even Gardner recognizes that in at least a portion of the Flood narrative, "the use of 30-day numbered months is evident (5 months = 150 days, in Gen. 7:24)" (ibid., p. 183). In actuality, Gardner believes that there are at least two, possibly three, different calendars employed in the Flood narrative (ibid., p. 184, 212–214). This is not a new position, however, a similar observation was made by John Skinner early in the 20th century (*A Critical and Exegetical Commentary on Genesis*, 2nd ed., International Critical Commentary

The verses of Genesis 7:13–16 are not included in the table above because they have no bearing on Flood chronology. "On the very same day" (v. 13) is a reference back to the same day previously noted by year, month, and day in 7:11, the day the Flood mechanisms began. The Hebrew is unambiguous in this emphatic declaration.

The Flood lasted one year and 11 days (or 371 days) based upon a 360-day year (12 months x 30 days/month).[119] It is not known at what hour the Flood began on day 1, nor at what hour Noah left the ark on day 371. But, by definition, a day can mean either a full day or daylight portion thereof (Gen. 1:5). The 7 days prior to the Flood (7:4, 10) do not belong to the Flood chronology per se since they precede the onset of the mechanisms of the Flood. There are two main phases: 150 days of prevailing waters and 221 days of receding waters. The ark was lifted off the earth on the 40th day. After this, the waters kept rising until the antediluvian mountains were submerged. Then all land-dwelling, air-breathing creatures were destroyed. By the end of the 150th day only those in the ark were left (7:23).

The second mention of 150 days in 8:3 is a reference back to the same 150 days in 7:24. The turning point in the Flood is marked in 8:1. The waters began to abate at the end of the 150th day. The waters subsided just enough to allow the ark to land on high ground in the mountains of Ararat. This occurred at some unknown hour during day 151. The tops of the mountains emerged on day 225 (8:5). After this, a more narrow perspective of the earth's condition ensues — the perspective from Noah's viewpoint. Before 8:5 the language of the narrative is global. After the mountains appear, Noah waits 40 days. Then he sends out the birds over the next 4 weeks. The dove returned with the olive leaf on the 280th day, and did not return after it was released on the 287th day. On day 315, Noah observed that the ground surface was drying up. The earth is declared to be dry on day 371.

We may assume that the first vegetation attractive to the dove (the olive tree) had sprouted and had grown sufficiently that the dove could pluck a twig from it 14 days after Noah opened the ark's hatch (54 days after the mountains

[Edinburgh: T. & T. Clark, 1976 reprint of 1930 ed.], p. 167–168). Both Skinner and Gardner were influenced heavily by the documentary hypothesis.

It should be noted that the debate over lunar versus solar calendars in regard to the Flood narrative has been taking place since the very earliest centuries of the Church. In his commentary on Genesis, Ephrem the Syrian (A.D. 308–373) said, "Notice then that even the generation of the house of Noah employed this reckoning of three hundred sixty-five days in a year. Why then should you say that it was the Chaldeans and Egyptians who invented and developed it?" — Genesis 1–11, ed. by Andrew Louth, Ancient Christian Commentary on Scripture: Old Testament 1 (Downers Grove, IL: InterVarsity Press, 2001), p. 143, citing "Commentary on Genesis," 6.11.2–6.12.1, in Fathers of the Church: A New Translation (Washington, DC: Catholic University of America Press, 1994), 91:141–142.

119. See footnote 116, above.

had emerged from the waters and 128 days after the ark had grounded on the mountains of Ararat). Within the next 7 days, the vegetation was strong enough that the dove remained outside the ark because it had a place sufficiently above the fluctuations of the water level to rest itself. Therefore, releasing the raven and the dove involved a period of 21 days.

Noah could see that the surface of the ground was free of water 28 days following the final release of the dove. It was another 56 days before the ground had dried sufficiently that both man and beast could leave the ark and walk safely upon the surface of the earth. Thus, the 371 days of the Flood is more accurately a reference to the period of time that Noah and his family were resident in the ark. In essence, the Flood itself had ended when the surface of the ground was free of water on the 315th day. However, that does not mean that the waters had receded to pre-Flood levels. The water level may have remained significantly elevated for decades or even centuries. Residual effects of the Flood are not touched upon in the Flood narrative and those effects may have had profound results regarding post-Flood topography in many places.

Dissonant Chronologies

The supposed differences between the Masoretic Text, the Septuagint, the Qumran Genesis commentary (4Q252), and the Book of Jubilees are best resolved by understanding that the Hellenistic and Jewish settings produced chronologies that "actually reflect the struggle between the various *milieus* where lunar or solar calendars were in power."[120] It seems fairly universal in the primary sources that the Noahic Flood lasted for approximately one year — whether that is taken as 354, 365, or 371 days.

Geological Inferences

The chronology presented above might present new data to be utilized in resolving some issues regarding geologic mechanisms and the timing of events. The primary geologic mechanisms are the activity of the "fountains of the deep" and the back and forth movements of the receding waters. The torrential rains also would have caused rivers to overflow their banks and produced massive erosion and mud slides even before the ocean waters engulfed the land. The timing of events, which have a bearing on geologic interpretations include (1) the death of terrestrial life, (2) the covering of antediluvian mountains, (3) the emergence of apparent new mountains, (4) the oscillation of receding waters, and (5) the overall sea level.

Global Tectonics

Some Flood geologists identify the fountains of the deep (7:11; 8:2) with both terrestrial and oceanic fountains.[121] To flood all the land-masses of the

---

120. Moshe A. Zippor, "The Flood Chronology: Too Many an Accident," *Dead Sea Discoveries* 4/2 (July 1997): p. 207–210.

121. Fouts and Wise, "Blotting Out and Breaking Up: Miscellaneous Hebrew Studies in

former world with both rain and oceanic waters requires an enormous catastrophic movement of the earth's crust.[122] According to Morris:

> Once the postulated pressure rise caused by the first "fountain" to
> crack open, the pressurized fluid would surge through at this point and
> further weaken nearby boundaries, until soon a worldwide chain reac-
> tion would develop, cleaving open all the fountains of the great deep
> throughout the world.[123]

It is possible that the fountains of the deep that caused the Flood remain
as prominent structures in the crust. Some Flood geologists[124] equate the world
rift system (or spreading centers) with the fountains of the deep. Presently, the
globe-encompassing world rift system does seem to be an obvious choice. Most
of the 70,000-km-long world rift system is below sea level.[125] It is a deep-seated
feature whether it underlies the land (e.g., Dead Sea Rift; East African Rift) or
occurs on the various sea floors (e.g., mid-ocean ridges). Are there any other
features of the crust besides the world rift system, or in conjunction with it,
which could be possibilities? Another question is why and how did the fountains
of the deep get stopped up?

What about orogeny (mountain building processes) during the Flood? As
far as the biblical text is concerned, the mountains of Ararat either were already
formed or were at some stage in the orogenic processes before the end of the first
150 days. Otherwise, how could the ark land there on day 151? Apparently the
mountains of Ararat were forming to some degree during the prevailing phase of
the Flood. Could this mean that some other mountain belts of the world were
also forming during the prevailing phase? Did the mountains of Ararat continue

---

Geocatastrophism," p. 220–222; Whitcomb and Morris, *The Genesis Flood*, p. 242.

122. One theory is a rapid catastrophic subduction of oceanic crust: John R. Baumgardner,
"3-D Finite Element Simulation of the Global Tectonic Changes Accompanying Noah's
Flood," in *Proceedings of the Second International Conference on Creationism Held July
30-August 4, 1990*, 2 vols., ed. by Robert E. Walsh (Pittsburgh, PA: Creation Science
Fellowship, 1990), 2:35–45.

123. Morris, *The Genesis Record*, p. 196.

124. E.g., Steven A. Austin et al., "Catastrophic Plate Tectonics: A Global Flood Model of
Earth History," in *Proceedings of the Third International Conference on Creationism Held
July 18-23, 1994*, ed. by Robert E. Walsh (Pittsburgh, PA: Creation Science Fellow-
ship, 1994), p. 609–621; John R. Baumgardner, "Catastrophic Plate Tectonics: The
Geophysical Context of the Genesis Flood," *Technical Journal* 16/1 (2002): p. 58–63.;
W.T. Brown, *In the Beginning: Compelling Evidence for Creation and the Flood*, 6th
ed. (Phoenix, AZ: Center for Scientific Creation, 1995); Andrew A. Snelling, "Plate
Tectonics: Have the Continents Really Moved Apart?" *Creation Ex Nihilo Technical
Journal* 9/1 (April 1995): p. 18.

125. K.C. Condie, *Plate Tectonics & Crustal Evolution*, 3rd ed. (New York: Pergamon Press,
1989), Plate 1; R.W. and B.B. Decker, *Mountains of Fire* (New York: Cambridge University Press, 1991), p. 21–22.

to grow during the subsiding phase of the Flood and even afterward? On day 225, the tops of other mountains appeared. Did mountain building processes play a role in continental erosion and deposition, and the regressive large-scale back and forth water motion?[126]

Continental Erosion and Deposition

The Flood narrative is very clear that waters rose progressively until all the high hills that were under the whole heavens were covered. Later, the waters receded in a back and forth manner until mountaintops appeared. This means that both subaerial (including fluvial) and submarine erosional and depositional sequences have occurred on the continent(s). But this does not necessarily mean that all the sequences were preserved. Likewise, the great ups and downs, and back and forth nature of waves could have temporarily exposed, then covered and then re-exposed and re-covered land surfaces during both the prevailing phase[127] and the subsiding stage of the Flood.[128]

The prevailing phase of the Flood reformed the earth's surface and killed its terrestrial inhabitants. In the earliest stages of the Flood, it is probable that the pre-Flood world was altered significantly by severe erosion. The torrential rain and subaerial/fluvial geologic processes were probably the most effective during the first 40 days, before oceanic processes prevailed. At the same time, the oceans progressively transgressed the continent(s). Severe erosion was followed by submarine deposition.[129] Do any depositional remnants of the subaerial/fluvial processes (during the Flood's earliest stages) exist? Or were the eroded sediments (carried by fluvial waters) dispersed into oceanic waters when the two met? If so, what are the deposits' characteristics? Perhaps these deposits (if they exist) are buried under transgressive submarine sediments? If they do not exist, were they subducted?[130] From an oceanic perspective, the prevailing phase of the

---

126. Northrup associates crustal movements with the massive oscillation of receding Flood waters ("Identifying the Noahic Flood in Historical Geology: Part One," p. 178).

127. Cf. Berthault's question, "might not these successive tidal waves result from 'the fountains of the deep'?" — Guy Berthault, "Sedimentation Experiments: Is Extrapolation Appropriate? A Reply," *Creation Ex Nihilo Technical Journal* 11/1 (1997): p. 69.

128. E.g., Edmond W. Holroyd III, "Cavitation Processes During Catastrophic Floods," in *Proceedings of the Second International Conference on Creationism Held July 30-August 4, 1990*, 2 vols., ed. by Robert E. Walsh (Pittsburgh, PA: Creation Science Fellowship, 1990), 2:101–113.

129. E.g., Steven A. Austin, ed., *Grand Canyon: Monument to Catastrophe* (Santee, CA: Institute for Creation Research, 1994), p. 69.

130. E.g., Austin et al., "Catastrophic Plate Tectonics: A Global Flood Model of Earth History," p. 609–621; Baumgardner, "Catastrophic Plate Tectonics: The Geophysical Context of the Genesis Flood," p. 58–63. For an empirical study, see Roger Sigler and Van Wingerden, "Submarine Flow and Slide Deposits in the Kingston Peak Formation, Kingston Range, Mojave Desert, California: Evidence for Catastrophic Initiation of Noah's Flood," in *Proceedings of the Fourth International Conference on Creationism Held August 3–8, 1998*, ed. by Robert E. Walsh (Pittsburgh, PA: Creation Science

Flood should be evidenced by an initial transgressive sequence(s) of submarine deposits. This initial sequence should be followed by other sequences of strata that show an earth submerged most of the time. Another issue involves the destruction or alteration of the antediluvian landscape (topographical features and the underlying structures of the crust). When the antediluvian mountains were covered, what was their fate?

As previously discussed, the subsiding phase of the Flood could be referred to (in large part) as the ebb and flow (or ebbing and flooding) stage.[131] Austin reasons from his studies that the receding waters of the Flood "were rushing back and forth with an action resembling tidal movement, as the overall level of water progressively declined."[132] Such movement on a grand (up to continental) scale, augmented by either the absence and/or emergence of land barriers (8:5), would doubtless have a profound effect in the shaping of the earth's surface.[133] This process occurred for at least 165 days.

The back and forth pattern should reveal itself in large-scale regressive and transgressive sedimentary sequences. Overall, the general trend should be primarily regressive. Seventy-five days passed from the time the ark landed until the mountaintops appeared. Apparently, most of the land surface was still submerged most of the time during these 75 days. Why did the waters keep returning? Could increases of submarine sedimentation (on land and in the oceans) with each regression play a role in continued transgressions? If so, could this repetitive process have continued until more volumetric places became available for the waters (e.g., deeper basins: oceanic or continental; land based rifts; caverns and voids within various strata)? After the mountains appeared, the coastlines changed constantly for the remainder of the Flood. Once the water had receded below the highest landforms, waves and currents would naturally rework those forms and rework sediments deposited previously during the Flood. Erosional and depositional sequences moved seaward, left some waters trapped in basins, and eventually gave way to the creation of new river systems.[134] Does an overall regressive sequence exist in the geologic record? Answers to these and other Flood-related questions await further geological studies.

Ultimately, the Flood's forces reshaped the topography of the entire globe. Even Peter recognized this fact when he wrote, "The world that then *existed* perished, being flooded with water" (2 Pet. 3:6; NKJV). Therefore, it is presently impossible to locate antediluvian geographical features such as the garden in Eden or the four rivers of Eden.[135]

Fellowship, 1998), p. 487–501.

131. See also Whitcomb and Morris, *The Genesis Flood*, p. 100.

132. Austin, ed., *Grand Canyon: Monument to Catastrophe*, p. 77.

133. Whitcomb and Morris, *The Genesis Flood*, p. 269.

134. Ibid.

135. Recent research indicates that great river valleys might follow antediluvian rifts in the crust through antediluvian Precambrian basement. But even if this theory accurately identifies the current Tigris-Euphrates river system with the Edenic river system, it might

Paleontological Considerations

Fossilization of land creatures including ichnofossils (i.e., tracks indicating the animal was still alive) may prove to be a key to help determine when certain sedimentary strata were deposited. This study demonstrates that all land-dwelling, air-breathing creatures died by the 150th day of the Flood. Therefore, the types of terrestrial fossils, which are possible during the first 150 days include (1) burial while still alive; (2) burial of dead carcasses; and (3) tracks or footprints. The sorting action of moving water involves dropping out streamlined structures "before rougher textured structures. Bodies with higher specific gravity (heavier for their size) fall before lighter ones. This applies to the sand, silt, etc., as well as to the bodies of dead creatures."[136] In addition, various creatures inhabit different ecologic zones. Robbins describes the resulting order of deposition as follows:

> Creatures living below sea level would naturally be found fossilized in lower layers than those living higher up in altitude. Those living well above sea level would tend to be found in the upper levels of sediments. The mobility of the animals themselves, as well as their method of locomotion, would influence where they most often would be found in the rocks. More mobile, active creatures would tend to escape for a time before being overwhelmed by a flood. Birds, flying insects, etc., having bodies of low specific gravity, would sink more slowly than worms and beetles. Clams, mussels, and the like would be expected to be found in the lowest deposits.[137]

As far as footprints by various land animals are concerned, the following questions must be answered in any interpretation of the earth's strata:

1. Were the tracks definitely made in Flood sediments during the first 150 days of the event?

2. Could the tracks have been made after the Flood (i.e., after the animals left the ark), but **within Flood sediments** while they were still soft (i.e., not lithified)?

3. Were the tracks made during post-Flood catastrophes and within post-Flood deposits?

---

be as much as "200–300 km west" of the antediluvian system and "the topography around the rivers . . . completely changed as a result of the Flood" and the Persian Gulf itself was "smaller in the immediate post-Flood period than it is today." John Woodmorappe, "The Feasible Same-Site Reappearance of the Tigris-Euphrates River System after the Global Flood," *Creation Research Society Quarterly* 39/2 (Sept 2002): p. 109, 114. This theory could also put an end to the dubious claim that the Flood had to be local since the names of two of Eden's rivers were preserved in the post-Flood world.

136. Austin Robbins, "How Were Fossils Formed?" *Bible and Spade* 10/4 (Autumn 1997): p. 74.

137. Ibid.

It is possible that all three scenarios exist in the geologic rock record. Therefore, proper interpretation of the rock record must be based on many criteria.

Sea Level Curve

After the waters rose to their greatest depth, their level began falling at the end of the first 150 days. A sea level was obtained by the Flood's end. Where this sea level was in relation to the modern-day sea level is presently unknown. Could a search for a static shoreline in the upper levels of strata (toward the oceans) in the geologic record be helpful? Would this get us closer to the controversial Flood/post-Flood boundary? What effects might the massive oscillation of receding waters have on the possibility of a non-static shoreline?[138] Though an ice age is not mentioned in Scripture, many creation scientists think that the state of the oceans, land masses, and atmosphere at the end of the Flood would be conducive to producing an ice age that lasted for many centuries. How much would an ice age temporarily lower sea level below what it was at the end of the Flood and its level today? How would an ice age and different sea level aid the dispersion of the animals from the ark? What erosional features and fossilized remains are the result of the advancement and then melting back of glaciers? These post-Flood effects also require further investigations.

Conclusion

The determination of the nature and extent of the geologic consequences of the Noahic Flood are best derived from the primary witness: the scriptural narrative itself. Literary analysis presents a striking picture of a sophisticated, unified, and coherent narrative replete with literary devices designed to provide a structure that is purposefully composed. A formal introduction followed by a double framework of inclusios identifies the limits of the narrative (7:6–8:14). Three chiasms break the narrative into its primary sections:

$$
\begin{aligned}
&\text{7:6–10 – Formal pre-Flood introduction} \\
&\text{7:11–18 – 1st inclusio (7:11a)} \\
&\qquad\quad\ \text{– 1st chiasm (7:11b)} \\
&\qquad\quad\ \text{– 2nd inclusio (7:12)} \\
&\text{7:19–8:4 – 2nd chiasm (7:19–20)} \\
&\text{8:5–12 – 3rd chiasm (8:5)} \\
&\text{8:13–14 – 2nd inclusio (8:13)} \\
&\qquad\quad\ \text{– 1st inclusio (8:14)}
\end{aligned}
$$

Word studies of terms like גֶּשֶׁם (*gešem*) and מַבּוּל (*mabbûl*) provide little upon which to construct a Flood model because terms are more constrained by context and usage within bound phrases than by etymological considerations. Lexical analyses too often pay too little attention to entire phrases and the overall

---

138. See Northrup, "Identifying the Noahic Flood in Historical Geology: Part One," p. 177.

context — both being the better determiners of an individual word's meaning in a particular passage. An objective reading of the Flood narrative in its context impresses the reader with the global and catastrophic nature of the Flood even if the terminology employed within the text is deemed ordinary.

Genesis 8:2 provides one of the principal contributions of the text to the chronology of the Flood. That text describes the reversal of the mechanisms that were first activated in 7:11. If language has any meaning, there can be little doubt that the biblical record presents a full 150 days in which the dual sources (the submarine "fountains" and rain) continued to provide water for the flooding process.

One of the most pertinent and overlooked factors the Flood account relates to the correct translation and understanding of Genesis 8:3. It reveals the ebb and flow of the receding waters. Such hydrologic forces on a global scale over a period of approximately 165 days after the rain and the eruption of submarine waters had ceased has profound significance for constructing a geological model of the Flood. Erosion and sedimentation would have taken place during the first 150 days of the Flood as well as in the last stages of the Flood. This raises a question: Would the ebb and flow of the last 165 days of the Flood and hydrodynamic forces in the post-Flood period produce a more ordered stratification than the original transgression of the waters in the first 150 days?

The Flood narrative's own detailed chronology should inform the placement of stratigraphic Flood boundaries in the earth's rock record. The chronological "dates" and the sequential nature of the *wayyiqtol* verbs employed within the Flood narrative provide a foundation for a linear development of events chronologically. It would be unwise to assume that exact correlations can be made to the various rock system boundaries of the uniformitarian geologic column. Nevertheless, existing Flood models should be revised to reflect the Flood narrative's testimony.

There are some problems that are not resolved by the *wayyiqtol* chains. One such problem involves a time-line for the deaths of the life forms that perished in the Flood waters. In 7:19–24 there are no definite clues to help establish such a time-line. What can be said with confidence is that the death of life-forms in the Flood waters took place before the end of the first 150 days (7:24).

This analysis of the biblical text is but a beginning. Even though there is room for refinement and an expansion of the details involved in the literary and syntactical analysis of the text, there is sufficient material for those with geological expertise to apply the results to the construction of a biblically sound and scientifically viable geologic model.

Chapter 10

Do the Genesis 5 and 11 Genealogies Contain Gaps?

Travis R. Freeman[1]

Since the 19th century, Old Testament scholars have generally expressed the opinion that the genealogies in Genesis 5 and 11 contain generational and chronological gaps. Thus, they cannot be used, as James Ussher did, for chronological purposes. Most of these scholars believe that genealogies experience fluidity over time; that is, names are often added, omitted, or changed in form. Since the earth is older than Ussher thought, they say, names must have been omitted from the Genesis 5 and 11 lists as they were handed down from generation to generation. Thus, in their view, these genealogies do not contradict the generally accepted and quite old dates for the age of the earth and mankind. They certainly cannot be used to help establish the date of creation or the Flood.

Such a view, however, is troubling to some conservative Bible scholars who insist that Genesis 5 and 11 clearly present a continuous and no-gap genealogy and chronology from Adam to Abraham. These texts, they argue, are worded in such a way as to exclude omissions and gaps. To suggest such gaps is, in their view, a violation of a straightforward reading and inerrant view of the passages. Thus, they say, Ussher justifiably used them to help date creation at about 4000 B.C. and modern scholars would do well to follow suit.

Which view is correct? Did fluidity occur during the transmission of the Genesis 5 and 11 genealogies? Were names dropped so that the genealogies now contain generational and chronological gaps?

---

1. This chapter contains substantial portions from my articles "A New Look at the Genesis 5 and 11 Fluidity Problem," *Andrews University Seminary Studies* 42 (2004): p. 259–286; and "The Genesis 5 and 11 Fluidity Question," *TJ* 19(2) [2004]: p. 83–90. They are used with the kind permission of the publishers.

The word "fluidity" as used in this study refers to the practice of omitting names from or adding names to a genealogy, or to the practice of changing the spelling of names. When omissions are made, fluidity results in compression; that is, a shortened list. Sometimes omissions result in symmetry; that is, an equal number of names in each section of a divided genealogy. The terms "chronogenealogy" and "non-chronogenealogy" are used to describe the genre of the various genealogies discussed herein.

The Non-Chronogenealogy View

Historical-Critical Scholars

A number of modern historical-critical scholars think the Genesis 5 genealogy is not an accurate historical record. They see it as the result of an ancient Mesopotamian list of legendary heroes (either a king list, sage list, hero list, or a list of tribal ancestors) that has experienced so much fluidity during the long process of transmission from one generation to the next that most or all of its historical and chronological value, if it ever had any, has been lost. They express similar views concerning the Genesis 11 genealogy. For these scholars, the early Genesis genealogies, if they ever were genealogies, are discontinuous; that is, they contain generational omissions or gaps.

Claus Westermann argues that the ten names listed in Genesis 5 were derived from an ancient tribal oral tradition regarding primeval ancestors.[2] Early in its history this tradition was divided into different segments, and those segments were handed down independently. Westermann locates one segment, or partial segment, in Genesis 4:25–26 (Adam, Seth, Enosh), and another in 4:17–18 (Cain, Enoch, Irad, Mehujael, Methusheal, Lamech) as employed by the Yahwist (J). He thinks these two segments were also used by the priestly author (P) of Genesis 5, and so the names of Genesis 4 and 5 were originally the same. He believes fluidity during transmission of the segments accounts for the differences between Genesis 4 and 5 concerning the spelling of names (Cain/Kenan, Mahujael/Mahalalel, Irad/Jared, Methushael/Methuselah) and the order of names (Cain, Enoch, Irad, Mehujael versus Kenan, Mahalalel, Jared, Enoch). Westermann also argues that P compressed to ten the list of names available to him because this number was "typical and normal for genealogies" in the Ancient Near East.[3]

Jewish theologian Nahum M. Sarna also sees the ten names in Genesis 5 as a result of compression.[4] He points to several other ten-name lists (Berossus's

2. Claus Westermann, *Genesis 1–15: A Commentary*, trans. John J. Scullion (Minneapolis, MN: Augsburg, 1984), p. 348-354. Westermann denies any connection between Mesopotamian king lists and the ancestor names in Genesis 5.

3. Ibid., p. 352. Westermann credits Abraham Malamat, "King Lists of the Old Babylonian Period and Biblical Genealogies," *Journal of the American Oriental Society* 88 (1968): p. 163–173, with demonstrating the common use of a ten-name pattern in ancient genealogies.

4. Nahum M. Sarna, *Genesis*, JPS Torah Commentary (New York: Jewish Publication

list of pre-Flood kings, David's genealogy from Perez in Ruth 4:18-22 and 1 Chron. 2:5, 9–15, and Abraham's genealogy from Seth in Gen. 11:10–26) in ancient records to show that ten-generation genealogies in the biblical world were both artificial and standard. On this basis, he says the "conclusion is unmistakable: we have here [in Genesis 5] a deliberate, symmetrical schematization of history."[5]

Gerhard von Rad says the two genealogies in Genesis 4 and 5 "obviously [came from] one and the same list."[6] The similarity of names provides his evidence. Fluidity accounts for the different order of names and spelling of names. He thinks the list from which the biblical genealogies came probably was a descendant of the Babylonian tradition of ten mythical antediluvian kings, although the Hebrew versions cast the men as patriarchs. Thus, when von Rad calls attention to the "effort of [chapter] 5 to arrange the ages of man and the world,"[7] he does not mean that this text reveals their actual ages. The mythical origin and fluid transmission of the text militate against any such literal interpretation. He simply means the Genesis author provides a fabricated linear view of history in order to challenge the cyclic view of history advocated by many ancient pagan religions.[8]

E.A. Speiser sees similarity between the list of names in Genesis 4 and 5 and surmises these two lists descended from a common Mesopotamian source. He points to the Sumerian tradition of ten antediluvian kings as the probable source, and suggests it was "modified" during transmission to such an extent that the original names were completely replaced by new ones.[9]

John C. Gibson likewise points to ancient tradition as the common source of the Genesis 4 and 5 genealogies. He suggests that the number of names in Genesis 5 probably reflects the number of pre-Flood kings in the Sumerian tradition.[10] Concerning the names in Genesis 4 and 5, Gibson points out that:

> The ancient heroes of Hebrew legend are brought together, presented as related to each other, and little notes are added to identify the fuller stories. The Hebrew lists probably serve as an aid to the memory of Israel's story-tellers or "singers-of-tales." Behind them lies an old Hebrew epic cycle which reflected the views of the early Hebrews on the beginning of the world and rise of civilization.[11]

   Society, 1989), p. 40–41.

5. Ibid., p. 40.

6. Gerhard von Rad, *Genesis: A Commentary*, trans. John H. Marks, Old Testament Library (Philadelphia, PA: Westminster, 1961), p. 69.

7. Ibid., p. 66.

8. Ibid., p. 66–69.

9. E.A. Speiser, *Genesis*, AB (Garden City, NY: Doubleday, 1964), p. 41–42.

10. John C. Gibson, *Genesis*, Daily Study Bible (Philadelphia, PA: Westminster, 1981), 1:155–156.

11. Ibid., p. 156.

In Gibson's view, the men of Genesis 5 probably were not directly related to each other. Their names were simply added to a storyteller's list as the Hebrew epic cycle developed.

Jack Sasson also assumes a common list of names behind the Cainite genealogy of Genesis 4 and the Sethite genealogy of Genesis 5. Sasson further maintains the Hebrews often moved an important figure to the fifth and/or seventh position in a genealogy as a way of emphasizing his importance. He notes, for example, that in the Genesis genealogies Enoch is seventh from Adam, Eber is seventh from Enoch, and Abraham seventh from Eber. For Sasson, examples like this constitute proof of fluidity and, therefore, rule out the possibility of drawing an accurate chronology from Genesis 5 and 11.[12]

Robert Davidson writes that the ten-name list in Genesis 5 is reminiscent of Mesopotamian kings lists, thus implying the dependence of the former on the latter for its names and its ten-member form.[13] He notes further that in Babylonian tradition, Enmeduranna, king of Sippar, was the seventh king, just as Enoch, whose name is similar at its beginning, was seventh from Adam. Seven was considered a sacred number. Shamash had a special fondness for Enmeduranna and blessed him by revealing the secrets of heaven and earth to him, just as the Hebrew deity had a special love for Enoch and blessed him by taking him to heaven. Enoch may have passed from the earth after 365 years, a number which may have been associated with the sun-god.[14] Davidson's points are clear. First, the story of Enoch is dependent on the story of Enmeduranna. Second, the seventh position in ancient genealogies was reserved for outstanding characters which often involved moving a name from its actual position or from a position completely outside the genealogy at hand to the seventh position. Thus, fluidity played a major role in the formation of Genesis 5. Omissions were made to achieve the standard ten-name form, and names were moved for theological purposes.

Evangelical Scholars

Another group of present-day theologians (consisting mostly of evangelicals) argues that the Genesis 5 and 11 genealogies are accurate historical records, but that a certain number of names have been omitted from the lists. Thus, they disagree with the theologians just discussed on the historicity of Genesis 5 and 11, but agree with them concerning the presence of gaps in the genealogies due to fluidity. This group largely echoes the arguments for this viewpoint first set forth by William H. Green late in the 19th century.[15]

---

12. Jack Sasson, "A Genealogical Convention in Biblical Chronography?" *Zeitschrift fur die alttestamentliche Wissenschaft* 90 (1978): p. 171–177.

13. Robert Davidson, *Genesis 1–11*, The Cambridge Bible Commentary (New York: Cambridge University Press, 1973), p. 61.

14. Ibid., p. 61–62.

15. William H. Green, "Primeval Chronology," *Bibliotheca Sacra* 47 (1890): p. 285–303.

Gleason Archer thinks the fact that both Genesis 5 and 11 record exactly ten generations indicates names have been omitted so the list will fit a predetermined symmetrical scheme. He points to Matthew 1 as an example of another genealogy in which names are omitted for the sake of symmetry, probably as a memory aid. While granting the existence of omissions in the Genesis genealogies, Archer insists there must be fewer omissions than names listed. In support of this contention, he notes that other long genealogical lists in the Bible never drop more names than they employ. Matthew, for example, lists at least eight ancestors for Jesus for each one he omits. On this same basis, Archer contends humankind could not have been anywhere near 200,000 years old, as some evangelicals propose, for such an age would mean that an unacceptably large number of Adam's ancestors had been dropped from the Genesis genealogies.[16]

K.A. Kitchen gives three reasons for doubting that Genesis 5 and 11 present continuous lists of descendants.[17] First, archaeological evidence places civilization in Egypt around 3000 B.C. and earlier in Mesopotamia.[18] These dates conflict with a "continuous" reading of Genesis 5 and 11. Second, the word "begat" can refer to a descendant rather than a son. Third, the symmetry of ten names in both lists testifies to schematization.

Gordon Wenham denies the dependence of the Sethite genealogy on either the Cainite genealogy or a Sumerian king list, but embraces the idea of generational and historical gaps in Genesis 5.[19] Although he says emphatically, ". . . the Hebrew gives no hint that there were large gaps between father and son in this genealogy," "archaeological discoveries" and "historical problems" compel him to accept them, thus placing Adam in "very distant times."[20]

Derek Kidner suggests the names in Genesis 5 and 11 are historical persons selected as separate landmarks rather than continuous links. He finds examples of this practice in Matthew 1 and in the genealogical record of modern Arab tribes. The fact that the author of Genesis 5 and 11 does not total his numbers or give the impression that the lives of the patriarchs greatly overlapped each other leads Kidner to doubt that the genealogies could be continuous. Magnifying his doubts are archaeological evidences, which he does not spell out, that "prove" civilization dates to at least 7000 B.C.

John J. Davis thinks the differences between the genealogies of Genesis 4 and 5 far outweigh the similarities, so the names in Genesis 5 are real people,

---

16. Gleason Archer, *A Survey of Old Testament Introduction* (Chicago, IL: Moody, 1994, revised ed.), p. 209–212.

17. K.A. Kitchen, *Ancient Orient and Old Testament* (Chicago, IL: InterVarsity, 1966), p. 35–39.

18. Ibid., p. 37. Kitchen acknowledges that archaeologists depend heavily upon carbon 14 dating methods for these dates. Radiometric dating methods have been strongly challenged in numerous recent scientific works. See the articles listed here: www. answersingenesis.org/home/area/faq/dating.asp.

19. Gordon J. Wenham, *Genesis 1–15*, WBC (Waco, TX: Word, 1987), p. 123–134.

20. Ibid., p. 133–134.

not creations based on the names in Genesis 4.[21] He believes Genesis 5 and 11 mention only key antediluvian figures, not every generation, on several grounds. First, no numerical summation appears at the end of either list. Second, Scripture nowhere totals the years of either list. Third, numbers are included which have little to do with chronology. Fourth, Luke 3:36 lists a man named Cainan as the son of Arphaxad, but Genesis 11 omits him. Fifth, on a literal reading of the text of Genesis 11, Shem outlives Abraham. Sixth, archaeological calculations based on stratigraphy, pottery typology, and carbon 14 readings show that post-Flood human cultures appeared around 12,000 B.C., thus placing the Flood around 18,000 B.C. Seventh, the lists bear the marks of schematic arrangement. Davis thus suspects "considerable" gaps in Genesis 5 and 11, but he suggests that these gaps cannot be nearly large enough to accommodate the "extravagant estimates" of the age of humankind and the earth proposed by evolutionist geologist.[22]

Victor P. Hamilton argues that the names of Cain's descendants vary so much from Seth's in both order and spelling that the former evidently had nothing to do with the construction of the latter; that is, they had separate sources. Neither is the Sethite line connected to any Sumerian list of pre-Flood kings, since the genres differ. Seth's line forms a genealogy, whereas the Sumerian line forms a king list. Hamilton thus sees no reason to doubt that Genesis 5 and 11 recall actual historical men who descended from Seth and later Shem.[23] He doubts, however, that Genesis 5 and 11 record every generation. Expressing the thoughts of many evangelicals, he writes:

> [Recent studies have] shown that these early genealogies in Genesis stem from archetypes among West Semitic tribes from the Old Babylonian period where the ten-generation list is frequent. Applying this observation to Gen. 5 leads us to believe that the names of Gen. 5 need not be understood sequentially. Thus the figures cannot be added to arrive at the age of mankind. Instead what we have here are symmetrical genealogies: ten generations before the flood (Gen. 5) and ten generations after the flood (Gen. 11). So when Gen. 5 says that "X fathered Y" it may mean that "X fathered the line culminating in Y."[24]

Kenneth A. Mathews views the men of Genesis 5 and 11 as historical descendants of Seth and Shem, respectively, but he too thinks fluidity has occurred

21. John J. Davis, *Paradise to Prison: Studies in Genesis* (Grand Rapids, MI: Baker, 1975), p. 102,151.

22. Ibid., p. 28–32, 104, 151. On page 30, Davis acknowledges his dependence on Green.

23. Victor P. Hamilton, *The Book of Genesis, Chapters 1–17,* NICOT (Grand Rapids, MI: Eerdmans, 1990), p. 249–254.

24. Ibid., p. 254. An important study upon which Hamilton draws is Abraham Malamat, "Tribal Societies: Biblical Genealogies and African Lineage Systems,"*Archives europeenes de sociolgie* 14 (1973): p. 126–136.

during transmission, resulting in two compressed and symmetrical genealogies.[25] Mathews notes that traditionally these genealogies have been understood to include every generation from Adam to Abraham, and that "there is nothing explicit in the passage to indicate otherwise."[26] He cannot believe, however, that there are no omissions, because "this would leave us with a very short span of time to accommodate all that we know about human history."[27] Enoch's seventh place position in Genesis 5, which parallels Boaz's position in David's genealogy as presented in Ruth 4, also indicates to Mathews that Genesis 5 and 11 have been schematized, since the number seven symbolizes God's special blessing. Although Mathews fully accepts the idea of gaps in these Genesis genealogies, he insists that the said gaps could not be large enough to accommodate the large ages required by evolutionary paleontology, since such huge gaps would defy the biblical convention of listing more generations than are omitted. Thus, in Mathews's view, humankind is only a few thousand years older than Ussher figured.

Ronald F. Youngblood offers another way in which fluidity might have occurred in Genesis 5. He suggests the names therein might be the names of outstanding pre-Flood dynasties rather than individuals. Presumably, other less important dynasties were omitted. In this interpretation, the numbers have something to do with the lengths of reign of the rulers. Youngblood does not say which set of numbers he is referencing, or what the other sets of numbers might mean. He simply concludes that such an interpretation implies large gaps in the Genesis 5 record.[28]

Non-Chronogenealogy View Summary

In summary, the most often mentioned arguments for gaps due to fluidity in the genealogies of Genesis 5 and 11 are as follows. (1) The genealogies in Genesis 4 and 5 are so alike that they must have evolved from a common source. (2) The symmetrical ten-generation form of the Genesis 5 and 11 genealogies with emphasis on the seventh position indicated schematization in the tradition of ancient Mesopotamian king, sage, and ancestor lists. (3) The lives of the patriarchs overlap too much in a no-gap reading of the text. (4) The oft repeated formula "X fathered Y" should be interpreted to mean that X fathered the line leading to Y. (5) Humankind originated longer ago than a no-gap reading of Genesis 5 and 11 will allow according to extra-biblical evidence.

---

25. Kenneth A. Mathews, *Genesis 1–11:26*, NAC (Nashville, TN: Broadman & Holman, 1996), p. 295–305. On page 302, Mathews acknowledges the classic statement of his view is found in Green, p. 285–303. On page 305, he also notes his dependence on Benjamin B. Warfield, "On the Antiquity and the Unity of the Human Race," *Princeton Theology Review* 9 (1911): p. 1–25.

26. Ibid., p. 302.

27. Ibid.

28. Ronald F. Youngblood, *The Book of Genesis: An Introductory Commentary* (Grand Rapids, MI: Baker, 1991), p. 75.

The Chronogenealogy View

Some modern scholars believe not only that Genesis 5 and 11 contain the names of actual historical figures, but also that those names form a continuous (without generational omissions) linear genealogy from Adam to Abraham. While they readily acknowledge generational gaps due to fluidity as a fairly common occurrence in ancient genealogies, they reason that the occurrence of gaps due to fluidity in some genealogies does not prove gaps due to fluidity in all genealogies. They see the genealogies of Genesis 5 and 11 as two of the many exceptions to the general pattern of generational omissions in ancient genealogies.

The Importance of Genre

In his analysis of early biblical genealogies, the late Samuel Kulling begins by acknowledging that many biblical genealogies, such as those in Ezra 7 and Matthew 1, contain gaps. In his opinion, however, biblical genealogies come in more than one genre. One type of genealogy (for example, Ezra 7) aims mainly at establishing someone's right to a certain office, position, or inheritance, and need not include every generation. Another type includes sufficient details, especially numerical data, to indicate it intends to establish a chronology, although other intentions may be present as well. Kulling finds numerous examples of this genre through 1 and 2 Kings and 1 and 2 Chronicles in those brief passages where a king of Israel or Judah is said to have ruled a certain number of years before being succeeded by his son (or a usurper). When grouped together these passages form a 20-generation chronology for both Israel and Judah, and are often used by theologians for establishing the dates of important events. The passages in Genesis giving the age of Abraham at the birth of Isaac and the age of Isaac at the birth of Jacob provide examples of this genre. These patriarchal passages are also commonly used for chronological purposes.[29]

Kulling then asks to which genre the genealogies of Genesis 5 and 11 belong. He answers that surely the many numerical notations therein, especially the fathers' ages at procreation, place these genealogies in the second category; that is, with the chronological genealogies. Thus, they should be interpreted as possessing no omissions, at least as far as the biblical evidence is concerned.[30]

Brevard S. Childs also sees genre as an important factor in understanding the nature of the Genesis genealogies.[31] He finds two kinds of genealogies in Genesis: vertical (linear) and horizontal (segmented). He analyzes the nature and function of these two types in the context of the 11 *toledoth* (historical records), which he says structure the entire book and unify it as a continuous history (contra

---

29. Samuel R. Kulling, *Are the Genealogies in Genesis 5 and 11 Historical and Complete: That Is, Without Gaps?* (Reihen, Switzerland: Immanuel-Verlag, 1996), p. 30–31. In the case of the kings of Israel, there are actually four or more genealogies, since there were at least four new dynasties. Their chronological value is nevertheless evident.

30. Ibid.

31. Brevard S. Childs, *Introduction to the Old Testament as Scripture* (Philadelphia, PA: Fortress, 1979), p. 145–146.

Westermann). In this history, the function of the horizontal genealogies, such as those dealing with Noah's three sons, Ishmael's offspring, and Esau's descendants (Gen. 10, 25, and 36, respectively), is to show the spread of humanity in general outside the special chosen line. The vertical genealogies (Gen. 5 and 11, mainly), on the other hand, deal with the chosen line of blessing and serve to "trace an unbroken line of descendants from Adam to Jacob, and at the same time to provide a framework in which to incorporate the narrative traditions of the patriarchs."[32] Childs does not say whether he believes the numbers included in these vertical genealogies are accurate and, therefore, suitable for constructing a pre-Abrahamic chronology, but his words as quoted show that he believes the author of Genesis intended to set forth a continuous, no-gap genealogy, and that there is no warrant within the biblical text itself for interpreting it otherwise.

Another scholar who emphasizes the role of genealogical genre identification in the interpretive process is David T. Rosevear.[33] Like Kulling, Rosevear delineates two major types of linear genealogies in the Bible. First, there are incomplete genealogies, which omit generations, and which the ancient writers employed when the inclusion of every generation was not necessary to their task. Conversely, there are complete genealogies, which drop no generations, and which the biblical authors sometimes used to establish a chronological framework for their narratives, among other things. According to Rosevear, the Sethite and Shemite lists bear the marks of the latter type, especially as seen in the consistent record of the number of years between the births of each generation. Again, like Kulling, Rosevear looks to the books which deal with the kings of Israel and Judah for other examples of this genealogical genre.

James Jordan agrees with Kulling, Childs, and Rosevear concerning the importance of genre identification in the process of determining whether gaps due to fluidity have occurred in a genealogy, but he advances their arguments a bit further. He posits that rather than just two types there are actually many different genealogical forms.[34] For example, he identifies continuous and discontinuous genealogies, chronological and non-chronological genealogies, genealogies that omit only a few generations and others that omit almost every generation, genealogies that are no more than a list of names and others that come with historical and biographical notations, 2-generational and 20-generational genealogies, linear and segmented genealogies, and so on. Each has its own functions and characteristics. Jordan reasons that with this vast array of forms available to the author of Genesis, it is unlikely, to say the least, that he would have chosen the form of Genesis 5 and 11 with its careful recitation of the number of years

---

32. Ibid., p. 146.

33. David T. Rosevear, "The Genealogies of Genesis," in *Concepts in Creationism*, ed. E.H. Andrews, Werner Gitt, and W.J. Ouweneel (Welwyn, England: Evangelical Press, 1986), p. 68–77.

34. James B. Jordan, "The Biblical Chronology Question," *Creation Social Science and Humanities Quarterly 2* (1979): p. 1–6.

between each generation unless he believed his list of names was complete and without generational gaps. Jordan further reasons that the mere fact that detailed chronological information is included in Genesis 5 and 11 demonstrates that these texts belong to a genre directly opposed to the idea of generational gaps. In his view, to say there are gaps in these texts is to ignore completely their genre.[35]

Most of the theologians who deny gaps due to fluidity in the genealogies of Genesis 5 and 11 realize their "genre argument," as reasonable as it may sound, will gain credibility only if they can offer reasonable alternative interpretations of the evidence for such gaps. How do they reply to the five main arguments for gaps due to fluidity?

Argument #1: Similarities of the Genesis 4 and 5 Lists

The first argument says the names and order of names in the Genesis 4 and 5 genealogies are so similar that they must have evolved from the same original genealogy, which underwent fluidity during transmission, resulting in two different but similar lists. Theologians opposed to this argument reply that the two lists are really quite different. Furthermore, they say, any similarities probably resulted from the tendency of extended families in the ancient world to use the same or similar names repeatedly.

Wenham points out that, while the Cainite genealogy covers seven generations, only six of the names bear any resemblance to a name in the Sethite list. Of the six, four require the change or addition of at least one consonant to become identical. The only two exact matches, Enoch and Lamech, are distinguished by additional biographical notations. The Lamech of Genesis 4 murders a young man and boasts about it, whereas the Lamech of Genesis 5 acknowledges God in the naming of his son. Little is said concerning the first Enoch, but the second one walked with God for at least three hundred years before being supernaturally taken to heaven by God. Fluidity cannot account for such vast characterization differences. Thus, the two Enochs and the two Lamechs are different men, and there are actually no matches at all. Wenham further points out the differing styles of the two passages. The Cainite passage is a simple genealogy, while the Sethite passage is a chronological genealogy. These differing styles, he posits, suggest two distinct original lists of names.[36]

Mathews agrees with Wenham, but sets forth additional differences which he says cannot be attributed to fluidity.[37] Genesis 4 seems ignorant of the Flood, unlike Genesis 5. Genesis 4 has a segmented genealogy after Lamech, and mentions his daughter, Naamah, unlike Genesis 5. Genesis 5 follows a consistent formula in giving the patriarchs' ages at procreation and death, but the language of Genesis 4 is much less formulaic and the ages are totally missing. Seth's genealogy is closely tied to creation, but Cain's is set in the context of expulsion from

---

35. Ibid., p. 6.
36. Wenham, *Genesis 1–15*, p. 123–124.
37. Mathews, *Genesis 1–11:26*, p. 281–282.

paradise and family.[38] Thus, Mathews concludes that the two chapters reflect different sources; this is, different original lists of names.

Hamilton explains the similarity of names by suggesting that it was not uncommon in ancient times for two people to have the same or similar name at the same time, especially in the same extended family. Parents throughout all ages, including today, have often named their children after uncles, cousins, and so on. Apparently, the Cainites and Sethites did likewise.[39] Hamilton seems to acknowledge the validity of Wilson's theory that form followed function in the use of ancient genealogies; that is, genealogies were often altered to better serve their purpose as social or political tools. Hamilton also agrees with Wilson that Genesis 4 functions to show the spread of sin, whereas Genesis 5 emphasizes the transmission of the divine image. Hamilton complains, however, that Wilson fails to show how changing the number of generations, changing the names, and changing the order of names in either of these genealogies would better serve their functions.[40] Lacking such information, Hamilton sees no reason to posit an original common list of names or fluidity leading to generational gaps.

Among studies which conclude that the Genesis 4 and 5 names descended from different original lists, David T. Bryan's is the most exhaustive.[41] Bryan believes fluidity has occurred in the Genesis genealogies in regard to the spelling of names, but in agreement with the other scholars in this section, he argues strongly and in depth that the similarities of the Genesis 4 and 5 name lists do not necessitate a common original list. Thus, his opinions are included here.

Bryan sees a striking similarity between the names in the two texts as they now stand. He notes most scholars have explained the likeness by positing one original list of names as the basis for both texts. They think, he says, the original may have been the Sumerian King List or a list of important ancestors. On the other hand, he points out that a few scholars have accounted for the likeness in another way. For instance, William H. Green argued in 1895 that the names in these two genealogies probably experienced partial conflation or assimilation at the time they were translated from their original language into Hebrew.[42]

---

38. Mathews does not explain, nor is it clear, why these differences cannot be attributed to fluidity due to function.

39. Hamilton, *The Book of Genesis, Chapters 1–17*, p. 250–251.

40. Ibid., p. 250. Robert R. Wilson's work is addressed more fully later in this study ("The Old Testament Genealogies in Recent Research," *JBL* 94 [1975]: p. 169–189); see also idem for a thorough analysis of the forms and functions of ancient and modern genealogies (*Genealogy and History in the Biblical World* [New Haven, CT: Yale University Press, 1977], p. 11–205).

41. David T. Bryan, "A Reevaluation of Genesis 4 and 5 in Light of Recent Studies in Genealogical Fluidity," *Zeitschrift f die alttestamentliche Wissenschaft* 99 (1987): p. 180–188.

42. William H. Green, *The Unity of the Book of Genesis* (1895), p. 46–47. Apparently, Green did not see name conflation as contrary to the inerrancy of Scripture, since translation from one language to another often involves changes and choices in alphabet and spelling.

Recently, notes Bryan, J.J. Finkelstein[43] and William W. Hallo[44] advanced a similar theory. Pointing to the Sumerian King List and the similar sounding list of pre-Flood sages (*apkallu*) as a case in which two distinct but closely associated lists gradually grew more alike over time, they suggest the same happened to the Cainite and Sethite genealogies.

Bryan believes one thing is obvious. Since the similarity of names between the Cainite and Sethite genealogies is too remarkable to be coincidental, fluidity has occurred. Fluidity either caused one list to develop into two or caused two lists to become more like one. Bryan opts for the latter theory. He notes that in known cases of conflation the two lists are usually still more dissimilar than similar. In cases where one list has evolved into two, the two lists are normally more similar than dissimilar. One might imagine then that one could simply list the similarities and dissimilarities and expect the longer list to indicate the original form. Bryan, however, says this method will not work, because some characteristics of genealogies are more prone to fluidity than others. For example, the spelling of an individual's name is much more likely to change than the biographical comments about the same individual. Thus, some differences, such as name changes, carry less weight in determining the original form than others, such as changes in description. One must consider the weight of each similarity or dissimilarity.[45]

Working on the basis of this principle, Bryan finds two main similarities between the Genesis 4 and 5 texts: some similar names and a similar order of names, both of which are highly prone to fluidity and, therefore, carry diminished weight. He also finds ten dissimilarities. Five of these are prone to change and carry little weight. These five are: (1) the connection to the Flood in Genesis 5 is not found in Genesis 4; (2) Genesis 5 records ten generations, but Genesis 4 only seven, or eight if Adam is included; (3) the segmentation after Lamech in Genesis 4 appears to be part of the rest of the text, but the segmentation after Noah in Genesis 5 appears to be added to the rest of the text; (4) the begetting formulas differ; and (5) the functions differ in that Genesis 4 points to the spread and outcome of sin, whereas Genesis 5 points to the line of the chosen family.

The other five dissimilarities tend to resist fluidity.[46] One is the absence of Noah in Genesis 4. Bryan implies that even a change in function or purpose would not lead to the omission of such an important figure. A second is the inclusion of a segmented generation of three males and a female after Lamech in Genesis 4, which is absent entirely in Genesis 5. A third fluidity-resistant difference is

43. J.J. Finkelstein, "The Antediluvian Kings: A University of California Tablet," *Journal of Cuneiform Studies* 17 (1963): p. 50.

44. William W. Hallo, "Antediluvian Cities," *Journal of Cuneiform Studies* 23 (1970): p. 63–64.

45. Bryan, "A Reevaluation of Genesis 4 and 5 in Light of Recent Studies in Genealogical Fluidity," p. 180–182 .

46. Ibid., p. 183–187.

the stress on the beginnings of certain aspects of culture in Genesis 4, which is totally missing from Genesis 5. A fourth is the numerical data given throughout Genesis 5, but nowhere found in Genesis 4. Bryan comments:

> This is not easily explained by fluidity since even in the [Sumerian King List] the varying traditions of seven to ten kings all have the [numbers] included. The numbers are present even in texts that are fragmented.[47]

The final fluidity-resistant dissimilarity listed by Bryan is the difference in biographical information concerning the two Enochs and the two Lamechs. The Cainite Enoch is associated with the building of a city, but the Sethite Enoch walks with God. The Lamech of Cain's line commits murder and brags about it, but his counterpart fathers righteous Noah and prophesies about it.[48]

Bryan's thesis is that similar features in two name lists point to a common original list, while dissimilar features, especially those that do not lend themselves easily to fluidity, point to separate original lists. In the case of Genesis 4 and 5, Bryan finds only two similar features, but ten dissimilar features, five of which tend to resist fluidity or change over time. Thus, Bryan concludes that the two genealogies did not spring or grow from one original genealogy.

Argument #2: Symmetrical Ten-generaion Form of Genesis 5 and 11

How do theologians who deny fluidity has altered the genealogies of Genesis 5 and 11 answer the second main argument for fluidity? This argument says that the symmetrical ten-generation form of these texts and the prominence of the seventh position in these texts indicate schematization in accord with a standard Ancient Near Eastern pattern. Their replies follow several lines of thought.

Jordan simply states that there is "no reason why Genesis 5 and 11 cannot reflect the actual historical state of affairs; indeed, the inclusion of the father's age at the birth of the son militates against any gaps . . . and thus favors historical accuracy."[49] Jordan does not, however, ignore the ten-generation literary convention of the Ancient Near East. On the basis of P.J. Wiseman's theory that Genesis is structured around and compiled from a number of *toledoth* documents which were recorded near the time of the events and then handed down from generation to generation in ancient times,[50] Jordan suggests that the record preserved

47. Ibid., p. 187.
48. Ibid., p. 187–188.
49. Jordan, "The Biblical Chronology Question," p. 9.
50. P.J. Wiseman, *New Discoveries in Babylonia about Genesis* (London: Marshall, Morgan and Scott, 1958), p. 45–89. See also Duane Garrett, *Rethinking Genesis: The Sources and Authorship of the First Book of the Pentateuch* (Grand Rapids, MI: Baker, 1991), p. 91–125; and R.K. Harrison, *Introduction to the Old Testament* (Grand Rapids, MI: Eerdmans, 1969), p. 63–64, 542–553. On page 552, Harrison asserts, "There can be no real questions as to the immense antiquity of the source material that is to be found in Genesis."

in Genesis 5 pre-dates and may be the source of the convention followed by the other ancient Near Eastern (ANE) lists.[51]

Richard Niessen reasons that just because some ten-generation lists have been schematized does not necessarily mean that all have been. In his view, Genesis 5 and 11 record ten generations each because there actually were ten generations before the Flood and after the Flood to Abraham. He notes that nothing in the texts indicates otherwise, and that the numbers indicate no omissions have been made. Niessen admits that the genealogy in Matthew 1 has been schematized, but since Matthew lists three sets of 14 generations, surely this simply proves that ancient scribes were not locked into a ten-generation form. Niessen also notes that believing Genesis 5 and 11 have been schematized, simply because Matthew 1 has been, ignores the fact that they are different types of genealogies; that is, the Genesis texts have numbers, but Matthew 1 does not. Thus, comparing Genesis 5 and 11 to Matthew 1 is like comparing apples to oranges, and constitutes a basic hermeneutical error.[52]

Kulling highlights an important point that most scholars seem to have overlooked; namely, that the Genesis 5 and 11 genealogies are not really symmetrical. The *toledoth* of Adam contains ten names (Adam to Noah) with the tenth having three sons (Shem, Ham, and Japheth). The *toledoth* of Shem records only nine names (Shem to Terah) with the ninth fathering three sons (Abraham, Nahor, and Haran).

Adam's *toledoth* (Gen. 5:1–32)	Shem's *toledoth* (Gen. 11:10–26)
1. Adam	1. Shem
2. Seth	2. Arphaxad
3. Enosh	3. Salah
4. Kenan	4. Eber
5. Mahalaleel	5. Peleg
6. Jared	6. Reu
7. Enoch	7. Serug
8. Methusalah	8. Nahor
9. Lamech	9. Terah (three sons)
10. Noah (three sons)	

To say that Abraham (Abram) counts as the tenth generation in Genesis 11 is no help to symmetry because consistency would then demand that Shem be counted in Genesis 5 (compare 11:26 with 5:32). The supposed symmetry does not really exist.[53]

---

51. Jordan, "The Biblical Chronology Question," p. 9.

52. Richard Niessen, "A Biblical Approach to Dating the Earth: A Case for the Use of Genesis 5 and 11 as an Exact Chronology," *Creation Research Society Quarterly 19* (June 1982): p. 63.

53. Kulling, *Are the Genealogies in Genesis 5 and 11 Historical and Complete*, p. 33–34.

To these arguments must be added the findings of several well-known and widely respected scholars who do not necessarily support a no-gap view of Genesis 5 and 11, but who nevertheless maintain that these biblical genealogies have no connection to the Sumerian King List, or who conclude that there is in fact no ten-generation pattern among the ancient king, sage, or tribal ancestor lists. A few examples must suffice.

In a carefully reasoned and well-documented article, Gerhard F. Hasel analyzes all the relevant ancient texts and concludes no connection exists, either in fact or in form, between Genesis 5 and the Sumerian King List (SKL).[54] He gives ten reasons.

1. SKL names are distinct from those of Genesis in terms of languages.

2. SKL gives years of reign, not life spans, due to different function.

3. SKL links kings with cities, not fathers with sons.

4. SKL uses much larger numbers

5. SKL argues for the continued political unity of Sumer and Akkad under one king, but Genesis 5 has nothing to do with politics.

6. SKL lists kings, not ancestors.

7. SKL is geographically local in scope, not universal, as Genesis 5.

8. SKL starts with the beginning of kingship, not the first man.

9. SKL ends with a king named Suruppak, not a Flood hero like Noah.

10. SKL does not really exist consistently in a ten-generation form.

In connection with the last reason, Hasel notes that as recently as 1965 a major study concluded that the Hebrew borrowed the ten-generation pattern of Genesis 5 from the SKL.[55] Hasel, however, points out:

> . . . the major rescension of the Sumerian King List (WB 444) contains only eight and not ten kings. One text contains only seven kings (W) and another (UCBC 9-1819) either seven or eight, whereas

---

W.H. Gispen, *Genesis*, vol. 1, Commentaar op het Oude Testament (Kampen, The Netherlands: Kok, 1974), p. 385–386, also acknowledges the lack of symmetry. The Septuagint (LXX) lists an additional patriarch (known as "second Cainan") in Genesis 11, but strong evidence indicates this was a scribal error. This issue is addressed in detail later in this chapter (see the section titled Addendum on Second Cainan).

54. Gerhard F. Hasel, "The Genealogies of Genesis 5 and 11 and Their Alleged Babylonian Background," *Andrews University Seminary Studies* 16 (1978): p. 361–374. See also K. Luke, "The Genealogies in Genesis 5," *Indian Theological Studies* 18 (September 1981): p. 223–244.

55. See W.G. Lambert, "A New Look at the Babylonian Background of Genesis," *Journal of Theological Studies* 16 (1965): p. 287–300, especially 292–293.

a bilingual fragment from Ashurbanipal's library has but nine kings. Berossos and only one ancient tablet (WB 62), i.e., only two texts (of which only one is a cuneiform document), give a total of ten antediluvian kings. On the basis of the cuneiform data it can no longer be suggested that the Sumerian King List originally contained ten antediluvian kings after which the biblical genealogies were patterned.[56]

Hasel makes two additional arresting observations. First, he says, "The supposedly unbroken line of descent in Genesis 5 is in stark contrast to the concurrent or contemporaneous dynasties of the Sumerian King List."[57] Then he reminds his readers that the SKL lists 39 postdiluvians, about four times as many as Genesis 11 lists.[58]

Wenham twice makes references to the different number of pre-Flood kings in the various Mesopotamian versions of the SKL, thus showing his doubt about a ten-generation norm.[59] He does see, especially in T. Jacobsen's reconstructed Sumerian version,[60] a correspondence in the order of events between the Sumerian flood story and Genesis 5–9, 11. To him this demonstrates not dependence of one on the other, but a common early tradition about the beginnings of the world, humankind, civilization, the Flood, and so on. The differences in the genealogical parts of the two versions, he implies, has to do with the purpose for which they were used. A Sumerian story writer may have inverted the names of a number of early kings in a politically motivated effort to justify his city's claim to leadership in Mesopotamia. Other cities may have inserted different names of kings in different numbers to support their claims. The Hebrews meanwhile worked from the same historical framework, but did not insert a king list, since they had no political agenda. Instead, they used the names of their forefathers all the way back to the first man for religious and/or historiographic reasons. The point is that the Hebrew ancestor list of Genesis 5 does not appear dependent on any Sumerian king list for its names or ten-generation form.[61]

Robert R. Wilson argues vigorously that a standard Ancient Near Eastern ten-generation genealogical form simply did not exist, or at least has not yet been demonstrated. Among scholars who think generations have been omitted to make Genesis 5 and 11 fit a standard ten-generation form, the works of

---

56. Hasel, "The Genealogies of Genesis 5 and 11 and Their Alleged Babylonian Background," p. 367.

57. Ibid.

58. Ibid.

59. Wenham, *Genesis 1–15*, p. 124.

60. T. Jacobsen, "The Eridu Genesis," *Journal of Biblical Literature* 100 (1981): p. 513–529.

61. Wenham, *Genesis 1–15*, p. xxxix–xli, p. 123–125. M.B. Rowton, "The Date of the Sumerian King List," *Journal of Near Eastern Studies* 19 (1960): p. 156–162, also suggests a political motive behind the SKL.

Abraham Malamat have been influential.[62] As already mentioned, Westermann credits him with demonstrating the common use of a ten-name pattern in ancient genealogies. Many others also show dependence on Malamat's studies in this regard. In a thorough analysis of Malamat's studies, however, Wilson concludes that while Malamat made some significant contributions to the scholarly analysis of ancient genealogies, his conclusion concerning the ten-generation pattern was extremely unjustified.[63]

Malamat attempted to show similarities between Old Testament genealogical form and Ancient Near Eastern genealogical patterns.[64] He sometimes used studies of modern tribal genealogies to back up his claims of a standard form. An Assyrian king list (AKL) and the Genealogy of the Hammurapi Dynasty (GHD) formed the basis for his comparisons. Malamat said he discovered that these ancient Amorite documents had four divisions, and that these same divisions could also be found in the biblical genealogies as a rule.[65]

The first division, which he labeled "genealogical stock" in the AKL and GHD, contained 12 and 11 names, respectively, after a few adjustments, and consisted of artificial names (sometimes tribal names) arbitrarily linked together. Citing also modern tribal genealogies of 9 to 11 generations, he concluded these were evidence of a standard ten-generation form as found in Genesis, since all of these lists were near ten generations.[66]

The second division, the "determinative line," was used to link the genealogical stock with the rest of the list. Here, the number of names listed amounts to five in the AKL and two in the GHD. In the Bible, it began with Abraham and ended with Judah, only four generations.[67]

The "table of ancestors" formed the third division and was used to link the determinative line to the last division. In the AKL, this division is clearly marked by the superscription, "ten kings who are ancestors," and consists of the genealogy of Samsi-Adad, a well-known king. In the GHD, the division is not clearly marked, but Malamat believed originally it contained ten names, although fluidity had made this unclear. He again cited some modern tribal genealogies near the ten-generation depth. The ten ancestors of David found in Ruth 4 provided a

---

62. Abraham Malamat, "Kings Lists of the Old Babylonian Period and Biblical Genealogies," in *Essays in Memory of E.A. Speiser*, ed. William W. Hallo, American Oriental Series 53 (New Haven, CT: American Oriental Society, 1968), p. 163–173; idem, "Mari and the Bible: Some Patterns of Tribal Organization and Institutions," *JAOS* 82 (1962): p. 143–150; idem, "Tribal Societies," p. 126–136.

63. Robert R. Wilson, "The Old Testament Genealogies in Recent Research," *JBL* 94 (1975): p. 169–189; see also idem for a thorough analysis of the forms and functions of ancient and modern genealogies (*Genealogy and History in the Biblical World* [New Haven, CT: Yale University Press, 1977], p. 11–205).

64. Malamat, "King Lists," p. 163–173.

65. Ibid., p. 164.

66. Ibid., p. 165–168.

67. Ibid., p. 168–169.

biblical example. He also suggested that the Bible meant to preserve ten ancestors of Saul, but he could only find seven.[68]

The final division, the "historical line," consisted of the immediate ancestors of a king or important person who wished to validate his right to a position by linking his line with his predecessors. This division is quite long in the AKL and GHD. He found no example in the Bible, but felt their existence at one time was quite possible.[69]

From this analysis, Malamat concluded that in Amorite culture the ideal form for a table of ancestors was ten generations, just as found in Genesis 5 and 11. A short time later, T.C. Hartman added support to Malamat's conclusion.[70] Hartman argued that Speiser erred in connecting Genesis 5 to the SKL, since there are numerous and basic differences. He also found fault with Speiser for tracing the ten-generation form to the SKL, because most versions of the SKL have fewer than ten names. Based on his consideration of Malamat's work, Hartman concluded that the ten-name form of Genesis 5 probably came from Amorite preference for ten-name genealogies.

Wilson finds major weaknesses in the arguments and conclusions of Malamat and Hartman. First, Wilson points out that the four-division genealogical pattern supposedly found in the AKL and GHD simply does not exist in the Old Testament. For instance, the names of Malamat's second division in the Scripture, Abraham through Judah, never appear together in a linear genealogy in the Old Testament. Furthermore, Malamat himself cannot give an example from the Bible which fits his fourth division.[71]

Second, based on his extensive study of genealogies as used by modern Arab and African tribal societies, Wilson concludes that linear genealogies regularly vary in depth from about 5 to as many as 19 generations. Thus, tribal societies do not favor one particular depth. He implies that Malamat selects only those tribal generations which support his ten-generation theory to use as examples, while ignoring the many genealogies of different depths. Even then the examples vary from 9 to 11 generations and must be adjusted to fit exactly the ten-name form.[72]

Third, Wilson notes that of the eight sections which Malamat says make up the AKL and GHD (four each) only one actually contains 10 names in its present form. The four sections of the AKL contain 12, 5, 10, and 77 names, respectively. The GHD contains 11 names in its first section and two in its second. The third and fourth sections are not clearly marked. Malamat resorts to

---

68. Ibid., p. 169–171.

69. Ibid., p. 164.

70. T.C. Hartman, "Some Thoughts on the Sumerian King List and Genesis 5 and 11B," *Journal of Biblical Literature* 91 (1972): p. 25–32.

71. Wilson, "Old Testament Genealogies," p. 178.

72. Ibid., p. 175–179. For a thorough discussion of modern Arab and African genealogies see Wilson, *Genealogy*, p. 18–55.

arbitrary adjustments and divisions to give the general impression of a standard depth, but none actually exists, whether it is 10 or any other number.[73] In a gross understatement, Wilson concludes, "[Malamat] has not supplied enough evidence to support his claim that those genealogies had a stereotypical ten-generation depth or a four part structure."[74]

Fourth, Wilson points out that the AKL and GHD fall into the king list category. Neither emphasizes kinship relationships, and often names are listed without any genealogical or biographical references. Genesis 5 and 11, on the other hand, show characteristics of a family genealogy. Wilson claims, therefore, that it is methodologically incorrect to compare the AKL and GHD with the Genesis records, since they are different types of literature.[75]

Wilson agrees with Malamat and Hartman concerning the fairly common occurrence of fluidity in ancient and modern genealogies. He cautions, however, that fluidity in some genealogies does not mean fluidity in all genealogies. Each genealogy has a different function and setting, so each must be examined individually. "[N]o generalizations are possible."[76]

Bryan has challenged the idea put forth by Sasson and others that an emphasis on the seventh position in the early Genesis genealogies indicates schematization. Sasson himself acknowledges that absence of such a practice in ancient Mesopotamian genealogies and king lists.[77] He also admits that even the Hebrews failed to use it consistently.[78] Pointing beyond these basic weaknesses in Sasson's theory to a methodological weakness, Bryan writes:

> . . . [Sasson's] methodology is inconsistent. Arguing that Eber is seventh from Enoch, he begins counting with the generations following Enoch. Then when asserting that Abraham is seventh from Eber, he starts counting with Eber. If he were consistent, Abraham would be number six from Eber.[79]

---

73. Wilson, "Old Testament Genealogies," p. 182–88.

74. Ibid., p. 188. Malamat's own tentative language lends support to Wilson's conclusion that Malamat failed to prove his case. For example, in his discussion of the supposed ten-generation form of ancient genealogies, Malamat ("King Lists," p. 165–166) at one point uses eight tentative words or phrases — (1) possible, (2) possibly, (3) may have been, (4) we may also assume, (5) puzzling, (6) we most likely, (7) if we assume, (8) tendency — in the space of just eight sentences. Such language undermines his confident-sounding conclusion that, "The ante and postdiluvian lines [of Adam and Shem, respectively], symmetrically arranged to a ten-generation depth, are undoubtedly the product of intentional harmonization and in imitation of the concrete genealogical model."

75. Wilson, "Old Testament Genealogies," p. 187.

76. Ibid., 189.

77. Sasson, "A Genealogical Convention in Biblical Chronography?" p. 172.

78. Ibid.

79. Bryan, "A Reevaluation of Genesis 4 and 5 in Light of Recent Studies in Genealogical Fluidity," p. 181.

Bryan points out what is, he thinks, another methodological error. Sasson assumes that the Cainite and Sethite genealogies sprang from one original genealogy with Lamech in the seventh position. Once adopted, this assumption leads to the inevitable conclusion that Enoch was inserted into the list. According to Bryan, this kind of reasoning amounts to begging the fluidity question, since the unproved assumption is the main evidence for the conclusion.[80]

Argument #3: Overlapping Lives of the Genesis 5 and 11 Patriarchs

The third main argument for fluidity is that the lives of the Genesis 5 and 11 patriarchs overlap to an unbelievable extent in a no-gap reading of the text. For example, before the Flood, Adam lived until after the birth of Lamech (Noah's father), and all of the patriarchs from Adam to Methusalah for a brief period were contemporaries. After the Flood, Shem almost outlived Abraham, and Eber did outlive Abraham by a few years. How do chronogenealogy advocates explain such an incredible scenario?

Jordan's explanation is typical. He claims there is no objective reason to reject the idea that these patriarchs' lives overlapped to a great extent. Such an idea seems strange to modern scholars, says Jordan, only because they have been conditioned to think that long ages passed between the time of Adam and the time Abraham. Previous generations of scholars saw nothing incredible about overlapping patriarchal life spans at all.[81] For example, Martin Luther wrote:

> But Noah saw his descendants up to the tenth generation. He died when Abraham was about fifty-eight years old. Shem lived with Isaac about 110 years and with Esau and Jacob about fifty years. It must have been a very blessed church that was directed for so long a time by so many pious patriarchs who lived together for so many years.[82]

Jordan acknowledges that Scripture records little about contact between the men of Genesis 5 and 11. He offers two possible explanations for this lack of information. First, such information was unnecessary to the author's purpose. Second, many of the men seem to have migrated to different geographical areas, thus making contact difficult and rare.[83]

According to Jordan, most theologians believe that, because a long period of time (perhaps several millennia) passed between the Flood and the call of Abraham, the knowledge of God was lost, and Abraham was called to restore

---

80. Ibid., p. 182.
81. Jordan, "The Biblical Chronology Question," p. 4.
82. Martin Luther, *Commentary on Genesis*, trans. J. Theodore Mueller (Grand Rapids, MI: Zondervan, 1958), p. 199; quoted in Jordan, "The Biblical Chronology Question," p. 1–2.
83. Jordan, "The Biblical Chronology Question," p. 4. Jordan suggests that the *Gilgamesh Epic* may have a historical basis and may provide an example of one of these rare visits of one patriarch to another. In the epic, Gilgamesh takes a long trip to find the old man who survived the flood, Utnapishtim, who promptly tells him about the flood.

that knowledge. Against this scenario, Jordan notes that Melchizedek and his city seemed to have possessed a full knowledge of God before Abraham, as did Job and his culture, although Job's friends misapplied their knowledge.[84] After Abraham's day, but apparently without contact with Abraham's descendants, Balaam knew about and prophesied in the name of Yahweh. Presumably, other prophets did likewise. For Jordan, such widespread knowledge of God argues against the idea of a long period between the Flood and Abraham, and argues for greatly overlapping patriarchal life spans.[85]

Argument #4: Regularly Repeated Formula in Genesis 5 and 11

The fourth main argument for gaps due to fluidity in the genealogies of Genesis 5 and 11 is that the regularly repeated formula, "When X had lived Y years, he became the father of Z," should be interpreted to mean that X lived Y years and became the father of someone in the list of descent that led to Z. This interpretation leaves room for any number of generations between X and Z. Of all the arguments for gaps due to fluidity, those who deny gaps in Genesis 5 and 11 respond most vociferously to this one. They seem genuinely stunned that an interpretation they consider to be in violation of a basic hermeneutical principle and contrary to the plain words of the text is seriously advocated by so many theologians, including leading conservative evangelicals. Jordan contends knowledgeable theologians would never imagine such an interpretation, let alone advocate it, were it not for their old-earth presuppositions and the resulting pressure to make the text compatible with their old-earth time scale.[86]

According to the reasoning of chronogenealogy advocates, one of the most widely accepted principles of interpretation, especially among those who employ the grammatical-historical method, is that the author's intended meaning is the correct meaning of the text.[87] How does one know the author's intended meaning? His meaning is normally the most obvious sense of his statements, as determined by his target audience and read in context.[88] Throughout Jewish and

---

84. Jordan assumes a date for Job prior to the time of Abraham, at least as far as the heart of Job's story is concerned.

85. Jordan, "The Biblical Chronology Question," p. 4–5. In this view, Joshua's charge that Abraham forefathers worshiped pagan gods (Josh. 24:2) is taken in a general sense, just as charges of idolatry against all Israel by later prophets like Jeremiah and even Jesus are commonly understood to allow for exceptions.

86. Ibid., p. 6.

87. E.D. Hirsch Jr., *Validity in Interpretation* (New Haven, CT: Yale University Press, 1967), p. 1–23, analyzes this principle in depth and concludes that it is undoubtedly correct, since language signs cannot speak their own meaning.

88. Obvious exceptions to this rule can be found in Scripture. For example, Jesus sometimes spoke in veiled language which the unrepentant people of His day misinterpreted. Jesus, however, was by His own admission deliberately avoiding a straightforward presentation of His message. The vast majority of the time, the biblical writers presumably tried to communicate their message as clearly as they could within their space limitations.

church history up until the time of Lyell and Darwin in the 19th century, virtu-ally all believers, the target audience, understood Genesis 5 and 11 as continuous genealogies which recorded a name from every generation between Adam and Abraham and the number of years between those generations.[89] To change the wording of the formula from, "When X had lived Y years, he became the father of Z" to "When X had lived Y years, he begat someone in the line of descent that led to Z," changes the author's intended meaning and constitutes a major violation of a well-established hermeneutical principle.[90]

Did the target audience misunderstand (for thousands of years) the author's intended meaning by overlooking the fact that X fathered Y can mean that X was the ancestor of Y? Surely they did not, say the no-gap advocates, since the ambiguous nature of the word "father" has always been well known. In the case of Genesis 5 and 11, the audience rejected such an interpretation, because the author took great pains to include in his text the number of years between the birth of each man listed and the birth of each man's successor. These numbers are superfluous and entirely without meaning unless the author intended to tie the names together in a continuous sequence of generations.[91]

The correctness of the audience's interpretation is confirmed, according to continuous genealogy advocates, in at least four ways. First, no other reasonable explanation for the presence of the numbers has ever been set forth. Second, ancient literature affords no example in which the formula "X lived Y years and begat Z" can be shown to mean that there were generations between X and Z. Third, the details of the Genesis text itself establish that no generations came between Adam and Seth (5:3), Seth and Enosh (4:26), Lamech and Noah (5:28), Noah and Shem (6:10, 7:13, 8:15, 9:18, 10:1, 11:10), Eber and Peleg (10:25), or Terah and Abraham (11:27–32), thus making generations between the other men unlikely. Fourth, in the New Testament, Jude, apparently an early church leader and half-brother of Jesus, speaks of Enoch as "the seventh from Adam" (Jude 14), thus demonstrating his belief that there were no gaps from Adam to Enoch, and probably indicating the belief that both the genealogy of Adam and the genealogy of Shem are without gaps.[92]

Thus, the rule stands.

89. See Davis A. Young, *The Biblical Flood: A Case Study of the Church's Response to Extra-biblical Evidence* (Grand Rapids, MI: Eerdmans, 1995), p. 1–79. XXX

90. Kulling, *Are the Genealogies in Genesis 5 and 11 Historical and Complete,* p. 25–36; Niessen, "A Biblical Approach to Dating the Earth, p. 61–65; Rosevear, "The Gene-alogies of Genesis," p. 73; Bert Thompson, *Creation Compromises* (Montgomery, AL: Apologetics Press, 1995), p. 175; and Jordan, "The Biblical Chronology Question," p. 5–6.

91. Rosevear, "The Genealogies of Genesis," p. 72–73; Niessen, "A Biblical Approach to Dating the Earth, p. 62-63.

92. Kulling, *Are the Genealogies in Genesis 5 and 11 Historical and Complete,* p. 25–36; Nies-sen, "A Biblical Approach to Dating the Earth, p. 61–65; Rosevear, "The Genealogies of Genesis," p. 73; and Jordan, "The Biblical Chronology Question," p. 5–6.

Argument #5: Extra-biblical Evidence and the Antiquity of Man

The fifth argument for gaps due to fluidity in the genealogies of Genesis 5 and 11 is that, according to extra-biblical evidence (for example, scientific evidence), humankind originated longer ago than a no-gap reading of these two genealogies will allow. The scientific objections against the notion of the evolution of man and against the dating methods that lead the majority of scientist to accept an antiquity for man far beyond the biblical time frame are beyond the scope of this chapter and this book. Interested readers are encouraged to consider the work of Marvin Lubenow, a leading creationist researcher on the issue of human origins.[93] On the unreliability of radiometric dating methods, there is much written for non-specialists (but fully documented for the specialist).[94]

Chronogenealogy View Summary

In summary, those who take the chronogenealogy view insist that the first step in deciding the fluidity question is genre identification. Ancient genealogies came in different forms to serve different functions. Some forms accommodated fluidity, others did not. The inclusion of the age of each patriarch at the birth of his named son marks Genesis 5 and 11 as chronogenealogies, a genre that excludes the type of fluidity that leads to generational gaps.

For chronogenealogy advocates, the second step in deciding the fluidity question consists of exposing weaknesses in the arguments for fluidity. First, they point out that the Cainite and Sethite genealogies have more (and more significant) dissimilarities than similarities, thus indicating that they most probably did not evolve from the same proposed original genealogy. The similarities are best explained by the tendency of extended families to use the same or similar names repeatedly. Second, they maintain that there was no such thing as a standard ten-generation form for ancient genealogies (especially Wilson contra Malamat), nor was emphasis on the seventh position standard. Third, they point out that, while overlapping patriarchal life spans might seem suspect to the modern mind, no one has yet shown why these ancient men could not have been contemporaries, just as earlier theologians thought. Fourth, the chronogenealogy advocates argue that no literary precedent exists for interpreting "X lived Y years and fathered Z" as "X lived Y years and fathered the line leading to Z." They further maintain that this latter interpretation would violate a basic hermeneutical principle and

---

93. See Marvin Lubenow, *Bones of Contention: A Creationist Assessment of Human Fossils* (Grand Rapids, MI: Baker, 2004, 2nd rev. ed.) and his appendix (on dating fossils) from the book's first edition, which is posted at www.answersingenesis.org/docs2006/0816dating-game.asp.

94. See Donald DeYoung, *Thousands, not Billions: Challenging an Icon of Evolution, Questioning the Age of the Earth* (Green Forest, AR: Master Books, 2005), which is a layman's summary of the published results of eight years of research on radiometric dating by an international team of PhD creation scientists. Also consider numerous articles at www.answersingenesis.org/home/area/faq/dating.asp.

render meaningless all of the "Y" numbers given in the formula that is repeated 18 times in Genesis 5 and 11.

Evaluation of the Two Views

Did fluidity leading to generational gaps occur during the transmission of the Genesis 5 and 11 genealogies? Scholarly attempts to answer this question revolve around five issues.

The first issue involves the importance of genre identification in the interpretive process. The foregoing discussion reveals a tendency among gap advocates to see all genealogies as the same genre. Although they often talk of different genealogical forms and functions, in practice they regularly draw conclusions concerning one genealogy by comparing it to a genealogy of a different sort. Their comparison of Matthew 1 (which has no numbers of years mentioned) with Genesis 5 and 11 (which have numbers for each of the 20 generations), along with their subsequent assumption that since Matthew 1 has gaps so Genesis 5 and 11 must also have gaps, provides a prime example of indifference to genre. Such indifference is hermeneutically indefensible. The multitude of genealogical forms extant in the biblical text and ANE world should not only provide scholars clues to different functions, but also to different rules of interpretation. Since no-gap advocates emphasize careful attention and strict conformance to such rules, the high ground on this aspect of the issue goes to them.

Simply calling for genre identification and adherence to appropriate interpretive rules, however, does not insure that one can accurately identify a genre. No-gap advocates identify Genesis 5 and 11 as chronogenealogies primarily because the age at which each patriarch "fathered" the next person on the list is given. Do such procreation ages really mark a genealogy as chronological? No-gap proponents can give only a few examples of genealogical materials which use the age of a father at the birth of a son for chronological purposes. These examples come almost exclusively from the patriarchal accounts in Genesis 12–50. On the other hand, gap proponents can give absolutely no evidence, ancient or modern, biblical or extra-biblical, in which a "father's" age at the birth of a certain son was clearly not meant to convey chronological information. Thus, no precedent exists for understanding the procreation ages in a non-chronological way. On balance then, these ages are best understood as marks of a chronogenealogy.

The second issue scholars debate in an attempt to decide the fluidity question concerns the similarity of the Cainite (Gen. 4) and the Sethite (Gen. 5) genealogies. Did one original list evolve through fluidity into two similar lists? Some scholars believe so, and argue that the similarity of names can only be accounted for in such a way. Other scholars believe not, and argue that the two lists are really quite different, and that any similarities probably resulted from the tendency of extended families to use the same or similar names repeatedly. The fact that there are far more numerous dissimilarities than similarities in the names and in the features that accompany them, some of which are not usually found in two lists that came from the same original, indicates that the Cainite and Sethite genealogies have always been separate and are not the result of one original genealogy that evolved into two.

The third issue of note in the scholarly debate concerning the fluidity question concerns the possible schematization of the Genesis 5 and 11 genealogies to fit a standard ten-generation form with emphasis on the seventh position. Malamat's works on this issue led almost all scholars at one point to believe that such a form was standard in the Ancient Near East, and that the Genesis author dropped names from his genealogical source in order to meet the accepted pattern. Wilson's subsequent work, however, has pointed out significant flaws in Malamat's methods and conclusions, and has shown that both Ancient Near Eastern king lists and modern tribal genealogies vary greatly in the number of generations including the fact that there is no evident preference for any particular length of genealogy. Hasel has shown that the SKL can no longer be used as an example of a standard ten-generation from, since nearly all versions of the SKL are between seven and nine generations. Thus, if a ten-generation pattern ever existed, it has yet to be demonstrated. Scholars no longer have an evidentiary basis for assuming the schematization of Genesis 5 and 11.

The fourth issue debated in relation to the fluidity question pertains to overlapping patriarchal life spans. Gap advocates find the overlaps too large and incredible to be true, while no-gap advocates fail to see any objective reason to doubt them. Since gap advocates give no other reason, their incredulity appears to stem from their commitment to a date for the Flood prior to 3500 B.C. and for the creation of humans prior to 10,000 B.C. Their case then rests not on biblical evidence but on historical and scientific arguments concerning human chronology — arguments that have been strongly challenged in recent years and appear in the eyes of many scholars to be faulty. As far as the biblical literature is concerned, nothing militates against the idea that many of the Genesis 5 and 11 men were contemporaries, just as Luther and other prominent scholars of the past believed.

The fifth issue often discussed in the debate over the fluidity question concerns whether the formula "X fathered Z" should be interpreted to mean that X fathered the line leading to Z. The most telling evidence on this issue is the fact that the latter interpretation was virtually unknown by Jews or Christians prior to A.D. 1800. If the Genesis writer intended for his target audience to understand that there were names omitted from his list, then he failed miserably. There is no doubt that widespread acceptance of Lyellian geology and Darwinian biology in the early and late 19th century, respectively, rather than sound hermeneutical principles, fostered the new interpretation. Green and Warfield, the highly influential sources of the new interpretation, admitted their purpose was to save the credibility of the Old Testament in the face of the supposedly proven scientific evidence for deep time. In attempting to do so, they ignored over two thousand years of interpretive history. Other biblical evidences are telling as well.

The presence of the fathers' ages at the birth of their sons is clearly superfluous, even misleading, if generations are missing between fathers and sons. One strains without success to even imagine why the author of Genesis would include these ages unless he meant to tie the generations together in a continuous sequence. Since no one has yet pointed out another example in all of ancient literature where omissions are known to exist in a genealogy which gives the age of X at the birth of Z, what ground exists for interpreting Genesis 5 and 11 in such a way? To date, no such ground has been offered, let alone established.

Conclusion

The main arguments for gaps due to fluidity in the genealogies of Genesis 5 and 11 suffer from a lack of evidence. While all parties readily acknowledge fluidity in some ancient genealogies, no party has yet presented sound evidence of fluidity in the Sethite and Shemite lists. As far as the biblical evidence is concerned, no omissions or additions have been made to the Genesis 5 and 11 genealogies. There are no gaps there. This conclusion leads to two obvious and important implications for those who trust the Bible. First, the numbers supplied in Genesis 4 and 5 can and should be used for chronological purposes. Second, mankind is only about 6,000 years old. And since Adam and Eve were created on the sixth literal day of creation (as argued elsewhere in this volume), the whole universe is also only about 6,000 years old.

Addendum on Second Cainan

Another issue associated with the fluidity question merits attention as well. Luke 3 mentions two men named Καίναν (hereafter referred to as Cainan), the first as the son of Enos (cf. Gen. 5) and the second as the son of Arphaxad (cf. Gen. 11). Luke's second Cainan does not appear in the Masoretic text of Genesis 11, so Abraham marks the 20th generation from Adam in the Masoretic text of Genesis, but the 21st in Luke. Thus, either the Lukan text lists a man who never existed, or the Masoretic text of Genesis omits a man who did exist. The former option casts doubt on Luke's accuracy, while the latter admits a generational gap in Genesis 5. Did a second Cainan really exist?

The Non-Chronogenealogy View

Non-chronogenealogy advocates find the choice between Luke's accuracy and a Masoretic omission easy to make. John Davis represents most when he writes:

> It should be observed that not all the postdiluvian patriarchs are listed in the present Hebrew text of Genesis 11. In Luke's genealogy of Mary, the name Cainan appears between Sala and Arphaxad (3:36). This one omission makes it impossible to fix the date of the great flood. . . . Genesis 11, then, must have gaps of considerable magnitude, and it is equally probable that the genealogy of Genesis 5 in incomplete.

Therefore, it is impossible to establish a firm date for creation or the flood.[95]

Montague S. Mills notes that the Septuagint includes a second Cainan in Genesis 11, and that many scholars think Luke used the Septuagint rather than a Hebrew text as his genealogical source. The source of Luke's information, however, is of no consequence to Mills, because his presupposition of divine inspiration leads him to believe in the accuracy of Luke's account regardless of the source. From this basis, Mills reasons that Luke confirms the accuracy of the Septuagint and proves the Masoretic text to have omitted the second Cainan.[96]

Many New Testament textual critics have pointed out that a second Cainan appears in several important early uncial manuscripts of Luke such as A, B, L, Δ, Λ, Π, and ‫א‬. These manuscripts date back as far as the fourth century A.D. and constitute strong evidence that Luke included him in his original list. This evidence has caused many evangelical, zealous to protect Luke's integrity, to insist that a second Cainan really existed, and that the Masoretic text omits him.

A Chronogenealogy View[97]

Chronogenealogy proponents obviously reject the option that the Masoretic text omits a name, but that does not mean they believe Luke used a faulty source (the Septuagint) or by mistake listed someone who never existed. They opt for another scenario. They believe that the Masoretic text is correct, a second Cainan never existed, and, contrary to uncial evidence, Luke did not include him in his original text.

Richard Niessen's two main arguments in support of this scenario may be summarized as follows. First, the Septuagint is an inaccurate revision of an earlier Hebrew text.[98] The inaccuracies are especially clear in Genesis 5 and 11. Much more than the adding of one name is involved. Each name in the Septuagint has a completely different set of numbers associated with it, and every single procreation age has been increased by 50 to 150 years. As a result, the Septuagint adds 586 years between creation and the Flood, and another 880 years between the Flood and Abraham. The reason for these inflated numbers is not hard to find. Working under the auspices of Egyptian King Ptolomy Philadelphus II, Manetho published his famous Egyptian king list and chronology shortly before

---

95. John J. Davis, *Paradise to Prison* (Grand Rapids, MI: Baker, 1975), p. 30.

96. Montague S. Mills, "A Comparison of the Genesis and Lukan Genealogies: The Case for Cainan" (Master of Theology Thesis, Dallas Theological Seminary, 1978), p. 9–11.

97. For another case against the existence of a second Cainan, see Jonathan Sarfati, *Refuting Compromise* (Green Forest, AR: Master Books, 2004), p. 295–297.

98. In light of numerous previous studies, this study presupposes the priority and accuracy of the Masoretic text. The Septuagint's numbers in Genesis 5 and 11 are clearly inaccurate. For instance, they make Methusaleh live 17 years beyond the Flood. The discussion given here is not intended to argue that issue, but simply to give the tenor of Niessen's case against a second Cainan.

the Septuagint translation project began in Alexandria. The Septuagint translators were all Jews who lived in the king's palace and were dependent on him for
their daily bread. They undoubtedly felt compelled to make the biblical chronology correspond more closely to Manetho's inflated dates. Evidence suggests the
translators inserted the second Cainan as a "red flag" to indicate that they were
more or less forced to add time to the Hebrew chronology.

> The name "Cainan" in the Hebrew is an extension of the name
> "Cain." "Cain" in Hebrew has the idea of "acquisition" — the LXX
> translators' way of indicating that this particular name, in this particular
> place, was "acquired" or superfluous. There is also a subtle play on words
> in the Greek. The LXX word would be spelled Καίναν, which could be
> a pun on καίνος, which has the idea of "unknown, strange, unheard
> of," or κενος, which means "empty."[99]

In addition, the three numbers assigned to the Septuagint's second Cainan
are exactly the same as those of his son, Salah, which is too much against the odds
to be true, and was probably intended as a sign that he was not real.[100]

Niessen's second main argument is that, while many uncials include a second
Cainan, many do not. For example, Codex Beza, considered one of the five or six
most important witnesses, does not. Likewise, many church fathers omit it from
their commentaries on Luke. Philo, John of Antioch, and Eusebius omit it. Origen
retains it, but marks it in his copy of the Septuagint with an obelisk, which was
his way of labeling an unauthorized reading. One might reasonably conclude,
then, that Luke did not include a second Cainan in his original list.[101]

Niessen offers a suggestion as to how the second Cainan may have gotten
into some early copies of Luke and later became an accepted part of the text.

> The original Gospel of Luke was copied several times, and eventu-
> ally someone noticed that a name seemed to be "missing" from Luke
> 3:36. He consulted the LXX, which was held in high regard by the early
> Christians since they spoke only Greek and no Hebrew, concluded that
> some scribes had accidentally "omitted" the name, and took it upon
> himself to "correct" the text. His manuscript was copied over and over
> and the spurious addition was multiplied.[102]

Samuel Kulling, like Niessen, argues that the second Cainan was a spurious addition to both the Septuagint and the Gospel of Luke. In addition to
Niessen's reasons, Kulling notes that the second Cainan does not appear in any

---

99. Richard Niessen, "A Biblical Approach to Dating the Earth: A Case for the Use of
Genesis 5 and 11 as an Exact Chronology" *Creation Research Society Quarterly* 19 (June
1982), p. 64.

100. Ibid.

101. Ibid.

102. Ibid., p. 64–65.

of the passages in the Masoretic text where the list of Genesis 11 patriarchs is repeated. Neither does he appear in 1 Chronicles 1:18 of the Septuagint nor in some copies of 1 Chronicles 1:24 of the Septuagint, which shows the Septuagint's internal inconsistency. He is also missing from the Targum of Jonathan, the Targum of Onkelos, the old Syrian text, the Latin Vulgate, and all other ancient versions including the Samaritan Pentateuch. One can see, says Kulling, why the Septuagint translators and Lukan copyists might add a name, but one cannot see even a remotely possible reason why the Samaritans and other early writers would omit just one name and leave the rest. Second Cainan, then, must be a spurious addition.[103]

C. Robert Fetter also concludes that Cainan never existed and that Luke did not include him in his original text.[104] After surveying and analyzing all the ancient versions, manuscripts, histories, chronologies, and commentaries which bear on the second Cainan question, and after considering the opinions of many theologians on the question, Fetter summarizes the evidence for the existence of a second Cainan as follows:

1. He is found in most of the best manuscripts of Luke's Gospel.

2. He is found in most of the accounts in the Septuagint.

3. He is included in the *Book of Jubilees.*

4. He may have been included in the chronology of the heathen writer Demetrius.[105]

Fetter summarizes the evidence against second Cainan's existence as follows:

1. Some manuscripts of Luke's Gospel omit the name, including one of the most ancient.

2. The Septuagint is inconsistent within itself in this regard.

3. Neither the character nor the chronology of the *Book of Jubilees* commends its authority on this point.

4. No ancient version except the Septuagint includes the name.

5. With the possible exception of Demetrius, Cainan is recognized by no ancient historian.

---

103. Kulling, *Are the Genealogies in Genesis 5 and 11 Historical and Complete,* p. 33. Kulling rejects the notion that a name was dropped in order to make Genesis 11 symmetrical with Genesis 5 since they are not really symmetrical.

104. C. Robert Fetter, "A Critical Investigation of 'the Second Cainan' in Luke 3:36" (Master of Divinity thesis, Grace Theological Seminary, 1956), p. 1–87. Fetter's extensive study is over 40 years old, but the evidence surrounding the second Cainan question deals with ancient documents primarily, and Fetter has dealt with these in depth. Thus, his research and conclusions still merit consideration.

105. Ibid., 74.

6. He is not mentioned anywhere in the Hebrew Bible.

7. His name is rejected by the early church fathers.

8. There are reasons to believe that the shorter Hebrew chronology is better than that of the Septuagint.

9. His name is omitted from the chronologies of both the Samaritan Pentateuch and Josephus.

10. Two credible motives may be assigned for his inclusion, the Millenary Scheme and the legendary theory, both grounded in historical fact (see next paragraph).

11. Both his name and ages may be based on those of other members of the genealogy and not on fact.[106]

In light of this evidence, Fetter concludes that Cainan almost certainly never existed.

Why was the second Cainan inserted into the text of the Septuagint? Fetter offers two possible explanations. The first explanation is based on the writings of Christian chronologer Theophilus, who was bishop of Antioch A.D. 176–186, and involves a millenary scheme. Many influential theologians at that time, including Theophilus, were chiliasts who believed history was meant to last six thousand years with some great event marking the end of each thousand-year period. Because Peleg's name (Gen. 10:25; 11:18) signifies "division," they surmised history would divide into two equal parts with three thousand years passing before the birth of Peleg's son Reu and an equal period afterward. Unfortunately for their theory, the Septuagint only recorded 2,791 years from the creation of Adam to the birth of Reu. Undaunted, they blamed a copyist's error for the 209-year discrepancy and set out to correct it. They began by adding one hundred years to the age of Adam at the time of Seth's birth, but noticing that Methuselah's procreation age clashed with those of the other pre-Flood patriarchs, they sought to ameliorate this inconsistency by subtracting 20 years. These emendations put 2,871 years between Adam and the birth of Reu. They still needed 129 years to reach the needed three thousand, so they inserted between Arphaxad and Salah the new Cainan, a name they borrowed from a similar position in Genesis 5, and assigned him the age of 130 at the birth of Salah. By assigning the year in which Peleg fathered Reu to the second great epoch of history, they arrived at exactly three thousand years for the first epoch.[107]

Chronologer Martin Anstey reports that some copies of the Septuagint make Methuselah 187 at the birth of Lamech while other copies make him 167. This circumstance tends to confirm, at least in part, Fetter's chiliast explanation.[108]

---

106. Ibid.
107. Ibid., p. 70–72.
108. Martin Anstey, *Chronology of the Old Testament* (Grand Rapids, MI: Kregel, 1973), p. 44.

Fetter states his second possible explanation for the insertion of the second Cainan into the Septuagint as follows:

> . . . as he was included in the *Book of Jubilees* (and no doubt other literature existing at that time) he was thought truly to be the son of Arphaxad and the father of Salah, despite his absence in the Hebrew account, and was therefore to be included in the genealogy wherever possible to do so.[109]

He then adds that "it may have been for both of these reasons, his name first having been inserted to conform with the tradition, and then later his age adjusted to suit the millenary scheme."[110]

Why was the second Cainan inserted into the Book of Luke? Fetter notes that the second Cainan was not in the Septuagint used by many early Christian writers, so he rejects the idea that Luke simply copied indiscriminately from the Greek text of Genesis 11. Fetter thinks, however, that once the second Cainan entered and became an accepted part of the Septuagint, copyists were under pressure to also include him in their copies of the Book of Luke, and at some point they gave in to that pressure.[111]

Evaluation

The majority of important uncial manuscripts include a second Cainan in Luke's genealogy of Christ, but these manuscripts date back to no earlier than the fourth century A.D. Prior to the fourth century, virtually all sources reject him, including Josephus, the secular historians, the early Christian theologians, the ancient versions except the Septuagint, and, quite significantly, the Samaritan Pentateuch. Even some copies of the Septuagint fail to list him in Genesis 11, and all copies of the Septuagint fail to list him consistently in the Old Testament repetitions of the Shemite genealogy. Almost certainly, then, a second Cainan never existed. His name was probably added to Luke's account just prior to the fourth century. The reason for the addition may never be known for sure, but the scenarios offered by Niessen and Fetter seem reasonable. In conclusion, Luke's second Cainan should not be considered reliable evidence of an omission in the Masoretic text of Genesis 11.

109. Fetter, "A Critical Investigation of 'the Second Cainan' in Luke 3:36," p. 73.
110. Ibid.
111. Ibid., p. 83.

Chapter 11

Jesus' View of the Age of the Earth

Terry Mortenson[1]

Introduction

What does Jesus have to say about the age of the earth? That surely should be a question of interest and importance to all Christians and a determining factor in their own belief on the subject.

For Jesus, the Word of God was the bread of life, without which no man could live (Matt. 4:4). He taught that we are like a wise man who built his house on a solid rock, if we hear His words and act upon them (Matt. 7:24–27). As Ravi Zacharias correctly observes in his book refuting atheism, "Jesus claimed to be 'the truth.' Let us test His claims and teachings. If they are true, what He says matters more than anything else in life."[2] The Chicago Statement on Biblical Inerrancy similarly declares about Jesus that, "His words were crucially important; for He was God, He spoke from the Father, and His words will judge all men at the last day." The ICBI scholars added that "the authority of Christ and that of Scripture are one," and that "as He bowed to His Father's instruction given in His Bible (our Old Testament), so He requires His disciples to do."[3]

Unless otherwise noted, all Scripture in this chapter is from the NAS95 version of the Bible.

1. I wish to acknowledge my deep gratitude for the numerous, insightful, and strong criticisms of earlier drafts of this chapter given to me by Dr. Philip Brown, Associate Professor of Bible and Theology at God's Bible School & College in Cincinnati, Ohio. Remaining defects in my argument, of course, are completely my responsibility.

    This chapter was originally published in *The Master's Seminary Journal*, 18:1 (Spring 2007): p. 69–98. It is republished here (with minor changes) by kind permission of the journal.

2. Ravi Zacharias, *Can Man Live Without God?* (Nashville, TN: W Publishing, 1994), p. 131.

3. Norman L. Geisler, ed., *Inerrancy* (Grand Rapids, MI: Zondervan, 1980), p. 499–500. The ICBI statement is reproduced in full in that volume.

Following the teaching and example of the Lord Jesus Christ, every Christian ought to conform his beliefs, teachings, and behavior to the inspired, inerrant, authoritative Word of God.

However, many Christians, even many Christian scholars, seem to be unaware that Jesus said things relevant to the age of the earth. Before considering those statements, it is important to briefly examine what Jesus said about Scripture generally and Genesis 1–11 in particular. This will shed light on how we should interpret the early chapters of the Bible. Then we will examine a number of the writings of young-earth and old-earth scholars to see how they deal with the teachings of Jesus on the subject. It will be argued that Jesus clearly was a young-earth creationist and that if we call Him Lord we should follow Him on this subject (like all others), rather than the contemporary scientific majority or the evangelical theological majority.

Jesus' View of Scripture

In John 10:34–35 Jesus defended His claim to deity by quoting from Psalm 82:6 and then asserting that "Scripture cannot be broken." That is, the Bible is faithful, reliable, and truthful. The Scriptures cannot be contradicted or confounded. In Luke 24:25–27 Jesus rebuked His disciples for not believing all that the prophets have spoken (which He equates with "all the Scriptures"). So, in Jesus' view, all Scripture is trustworthy and should be believed.

Another way that Jesus revealed His complete trust in the Scriptures was by treating as historical fact the accounts in the Old Testament which most contemporary people think are unbelievable mythology. These historical accounts include Adam and Eve as the first married couple (Matt. 19:3–6, Mark 10:3–9), Abel as the first prophet who was martyred (Luke 11:50–51), Noah and the Flood (Matt. 24:38–39), the experiences of Lot and his wife (Luke 17:28–32), the judgment of Sodom and Gomorrah (Matt. 10:15), Moses and the serpent (John 3:14), Moses and the manna (John 6:32–33, 49), the miracles of Elijah (Luke 4:25–27), and Jonah and the big fish (Matt. 12:40–41). As Wenham has compellingly argued,[4] Jesus did not allegorize these accounts but took them as straightforward history, describing events that actually happened just as the Old Testament describes. Jesus used these accounts to teach His disciples that the events of His own death, resurrection, and second coming would likewise certainly happen in time-space reality.

All these above-mentioned statements reflect some aspect of Jesus' attitude toward or belief about the Scriptures. But far more frequently Jesus reveals His conviction about the authority of Scripture. Its authority is shown in the way Jesus used the Old Testament. He constantly quoted it as a basis for His own teaching on such topics as church discipline (Matt. 18:16), marriage (Matt. 19:3–9), God's requirements for eternal life (Matt. 19:16–19), the greatest commandment (Matt. 22:37–39), and the fact that He will cause family divisions (Matt. 10:35–36).

---

4. John Wenham, *Christ and the Bible* (Downers Grove, IL: IVPress, 1973), p. 11–37.

He used the Old Testament as His justification for cleansing the temple (Matt. 21:12–17) and for His disciples picking grain on the Sabbath (Luke 6:3–4). It is the "weapon" He used in His response to the temptations of Satan (Matt. 4:1–10). And in a totally unambiguous manner, He stated that the Old Testament sits in judgment over all the man-made traditions and ideas of public consensus (Matt. 15:1–9). Jesus demonstrated that there is nothing higher than Scripture to which we can appeal as a source of truth and divine standards for what we are to believe and obey (Mark 7:5–13). The thoughts of men are nothing compared to the commandments and testimonies of God. It is a very serious error, according to Jesus, to set them aside in order to submit to some other source of supposed truth, whether human or supernatural.

There is no evidence that Jesus dissected the Old Testament and trusted only the so-called "theological," "moral," or "religious" portions. For Him, all the Scriptures were trustworthy truth, down to the last jot (Matt. 5:18). Nor do we ever find Him appealing to some higher authority to bring out some "hidden meaning" of Scripture. Also, Jesus indicates that the Scriptures are essentially perspicuous: 11 times the gospel writers record Him saying, "Have you not read . . . ?"[5] and 30 times He defended His teaching by saying "It is written."[6] He rebuked His listeners for not understanding and believing what the text plainly says.

Jesus repeatedly and boldly confronted all kinds of wrong thinking and behavior in his listeners' lives, in spite of the threat of persecution for doing so. Even his enemies said, "Teacher, we know that You are truthful, and defer to no one; for You are not partial to any, but teach the way of God in truth" (Mark 12:14). As Wenham cogently argued, Jesus never adapted His teachings to the common, but ignorant and mistaken, beliefs of his audiences.[7] Jesus knew the difference between parables and history, and between the traditions of men and the truth of God's Word (Mark 7:8–13). He spoke in truth (Luke 4:25) because He was and is the truth (John 14:6), and He frequently emphasized this with the introduction, "Truly, truly I say . . ." (e.g., John 3:3). He also explained that believing what He said about earthly, time-space reality was the ground for believing what He said about heavenly realities, such as eternal life, forgiveness of sin and spiritual rebirth (John 3:12). In other words, if we do not believe what He said about things we *can* verify, how can we legitimately believe what He says about the things we *cannot* verify in this life? He also said that believing the writings of Moses was foundational to believing His words (John 5:45–47). Jesus (like

---

5. In these instances Jesus referred to Genesis 1–2, Exodus 3–6, 1 Samuel 21:6, Psalm 8:2, Psalm 118:22, and to unspecified Levitical law — in other words, to passages from the historical narrative, the Law and the poetry of Scripture.

6. Passages He specifically cited were from all five books of the Pentateuch, Psalms, Isaiah, Jeremiah, Zechariah, and Malachi. Interestingly, in the temptation of Jesus, Satan used Scripture literally and, in response, Jesus did not imply that the literal interpretation of Satan was wrong. Rather, He corrected Satan's *misapplication* of the text's literal meaning by quoting another text, which He took literally (cf. Matt. 4:6–7).

7. John Wenham, "Christ's View of Scripture," in Geisler, *Inerrancy*, p. 14–15.

all the apostles and prophets) clearly viewed the Bible's history as foundational to its theology and morality.

Jesus' Teaching on the Age of the Earth

Besides the above-mentioned evidence that Jesus took Genesis 1–11 as straightforward reliable history, the gospel writers record several statements that Jesus made which are relevant to the age of the earth. Those verses, hereafter collectively referred to as the "Jesus AGE verses," show that Jesus was a young-earth creationist (i.e., He believed in a literal 6-day creation a few thousand years ago and the global Flood at the time of Noah). Those verses are:

1. "But from the beginning of creation, God made them male and female" (Mark 10:6).

2. "For those days will be a time of tribulation such as has not occurred since the beginning of the creation which God created, until now, and never will. Unless the Lord had shortened those days, no life would have been saved; but for the sake of the elect, whom He chose, He shortened the days" (Mark 13:19–20).

3. ". . . so that the blood of all the prophets, shed since the foundation of the world, may be charged against this generation, from the blood of Abel to the blood of Zechariah, who was killed between the altar and the house of God; yes, I tell you, it shall be charged against this generation." (Luke 11:50–51)

The key phrases that will attract our attention in these verses are "from (or since) the beginning of creation" and "since the foundation of the world." Old-earth advocates who interact with these verses contend that in them Jesus is not referring to the beginning of the whole creation but only to the beginning of the human race, which they believe was millions of years after the creation of the universe, earth, trilobites, dinosaurs, etc. (a belief that flows from their acceptance of the secular scientists' view of earth and cosmic history). In what follows I will first present my exegetical arguments for concluding that in these verses Jesus is referring to the beginning of the world (the whole creation week). Then later I will come back to these texts as I interact with the writings of the few old-earth proponents who have addressed these verses with respect to the age of the earth.

1. *Mark 10:6* "But from the beginning of creation, God made them male and female."

Commentators agree that in Mark 10:6–8 Jesus is quoting from Genesis 1 & 2. So, the "male and female" he refers to are Adam and Eve. Jesus says they were "from the beginning of creation" (ἀπ ἀρχῆς κτίσεως). To what does that phrase refer — to the beginning of the human race or to the beginning of creation in Genesis 1:1 or something else?

Besides its use in Mark 10:6, "from the beginning of creation" (ἀπ ἀρχῆς κτίσεως) appears in Mark 13:19 and 2 Peter 3:4. In 2 Peter 3:4, Peter is speaking about the past and the future of the whole heavens and earth, not simply of humanity. His reference to the beginning of creation must, therefore, be equally cosmic in extent. In a similar phrase in Revelation 3:14, Jesus says that He is "the beginning (or ruler) of the creation" (ἡ ἀρχὴ τῆς κτίσεως), which certainly applies to all of creation.[8]

The phrase "from the beginning" (ἀπ ἀρχῆς) occurs 20 times in the NT. Of those 20 uses, 5 have the initiation point of the cosmos in view. Never does it clearly refer to the beginning of the human race. It appears three times in 1 John 1:1 and 2:13–14. Comparing the language of these two passages to John 1:1–3 (which uses ἐν ἀρχῇ, "in the beginning") shows that John is referring to the beginning of creation (not merely the beginning of the human race), for he speaks of Christ being in or from the beginning and the Creator of all things.

The phrase ἀπ ἀρχῆς also appears in Matthew 19:4 and 19:8, John 8:44, 2 Thessalonians 2:13, and 1 John 3:8. Matthew 19:4–8 is parallel to the account in Mark 10, so the similar phrases must have the same meaning. John 8:44 and 1 John 3:8 speak about Satan and teach that he has sinned, lied, and murdered from the beginning. This undoubtedly refers to his fall, his deception of Eve, and his behind-the-scenes influence in Cain's killing of Abel. Since we do not know exactly when Satan fell (except that it was before he tempted Eve), these two verses by themselves are too vague to either support or oppose clearly the view that "from the beginning" refers to the beginning of creation. But nothing in the context would restrict the meaning only to the beginning of the human race. Because of Paul's comment on divine election in Ephesians 1:4 (that God chose us "before the foundation of the world"), it seems most reasonable to conclude that in 2 Thessalonians 2:13 he is referring to the same beginning of the whole creation. It seems unlikely that he has merely the beginning of the human race in mind here.

Hebrews 1:10 contains the phrase κατ' ἀρχάς, which is translated as "in the beginning" in the most prominent translations.[9] Since, according to the rest of the verse, this is when the earth was founded or established and the heavens were made, the beginning refers to the events of the whole creation week.

All other uses of "from (or in) the beginning" are irrelevant to the meaning of Mark 10:6, for the context shows that the phrase in these cases refers to either the beginning of the Scriptures (i.e., the time of Moses), or the first hearing of the gospel by some people in the first century, or the beginning of Jesus' earthly

---

8. See David E. Aune, *Word Biblical Commentary, vol. 52: Revelation 1–5* (Dallas: Word, 1997), p. 256, for the different interpretations of ἡ ἀρχὴ here. Either way, the phrase refers to all of creation, which is consistent with the meaning of the other similar phrases.

9. KJV, NKJV, NIV, NAS, ESV, NLT, RSV, and HCSB.

ministry, or the beginning of Paul's life or ministry. Never do these phrases mean the beginning of the human race.[10]

From this discussion, I conclude that when Jesus uses the phrase in Mark 10:6, "from the beginning of creation," He is referring to the beginning of the whole creation, which encompasses the whole creation period described in Genesis 1. Jesus was not merely referring to the creation of the first marriage on day 6.

2. *Mark 13:19* "For those days will be a time of tribulation such as has not occurred since the beginning of the creation which God created until now, and never will. Unless the Lord had shortened those days, no life would have been saved; but for the sake of the elect, whom He chose, He shortened the days."

Like Mark 10:6, this verse uses ἀπ ἀρχῆς κτίσεως. But in 13:19 the phrase is modified by "which God created" (ἣν ἔκτισεν ὁ θεὸς). The relative pronoun (ἣν) is feminine, so the clause modifies either of the feminine nouns, "creation" or "beginning" in the previous phrase. It is doubtful that Jesus is saying that God "created the beginning." Such wording is not used anywhere else in Scripture and it is difficult to see why Jesus would emphasize such a point. Also, the closest antecedent noun of "which" is "creation," linking the two together. Furthermore, Romans 1:18–20 indicates that sinners deny that God is the *Creator*, not that there was a beginning to the physical world. So surely Jesus means the "creation, which God created," with "creation" referring to the whole of creation week during which God created, not just to the events of making Adam and Eve.

Another consideration that supports this conclusion is that in Mark 13:19 Jesus creates a time-line: from the beginning of creation until now and on to the end of this present cosmos (v. 20), when heaven and earth will pass away (v. 31). Mark 13:24–26 and 13:30–32 coupled with Matthew 24:14 and 24:37–39 clearly show that Jesus thinks that the present human experience and the present cosmos will come to an end at essentially the same time (cf. 2 Peter 3). Together, these verses would support the notion that humanity and the rest of creation also began at essentially the same time in the past.

Since the suffering under consideration is human (not animal) suffering, there must have been humans at the beginning of creation in order for Jesus' time-line to make sense. If there were no humans in existence from the begin-

---

10. First John 2:7 is referring either to the beginning of the Scriptures (i.e., the time of Moses) or more likely to the time when John's initial readers first heard the Apostles' preaching or believed the gospel. Likewise, 1 John 2:24, 3:11, and 2 John 5–6 refer to when John's readers became Christians. Luke 1:2 refers to the disciples at the beginning of Jesus' earthly ministry. John 6:64 refers to either the beginning of Jesus' ministry or, less likely, to the beginning of the creation, so the verse is either irrelevant to our discussion or confirms the young-earth view. John 6:25, 15:27, and 16:4 are referring to the beginning of Jesus' ministry. Phil. 4:15 refers to the beginning of Paul's preaching in Philippi. Acts 26:4 refers to the beginning of Paul's life.

ning of creation (supposedly billions of years ago, according to conventional thinking) until the relatively recent past, what would be the point of saying there will be a time of human suffering unsurpassed by any other human suffering since the beginning of the cosmos (when no humans existed, according to old-earthers) until the very end? Jesus could have easily said "since the creation of man until now" or "since Adam," if that is what He meant. His choice of words reflects His belief that man was there at the beginning and human suffering commenced essentially at the beginning of creation, not billions of years after the beginning. His Jewish listeners would have assumed this meaning in Jesus' words, for Josephus's history of the Jewish people indicates that the Jews of the first century believed that both the first day of creation and Adam's creation were about 5,000 years before Christ.[11]

Since Matthew 24:21 is a parallel passage to Mark 13:19, Matthew's wording "since the beginning of the world" (ἀπ' ἀρχῆς κόσμου) must have the same meaning as ἀπ ἀρχῆς κτίσεως, with both accounts accurately reflecting what Jesus meant. While κόσμος (*kosmos*) sometimes refers to this sinful worldly system of man,[12] it often refers to the whole creation,[13] as in Matthew 24:21.

The foregoing evidence demonstrates that Jesus and the NT writers never use the phrase ἀπ' ἀρχῆς to mean "beginning of the human race." Most instances of ἀπ' ἀρχῆς that refer to the ancient past mean the beginning of the whole creation starting in Genesis 1:1, thus supporting the young-earth interpretation of Mark 10:6 and 13:19.

An analysis of the commentary literature on Mark 10:6 and 13:19 yields four views of the phrases relevant to our study. Gundry and Morgan take the phrase in 10:6 to refer to the beginning of the whole creation (not merely the beginning of the human race or the beginning of marriage).[14] Cranfield says the phrase in 10:6 doesn't necessarily mean the beginning of Genesis or the creation narrative, but he gives no justification for his view.[15] McKenna, Evans, and Wessel say the

---

11. See William Whiston, transl., *The Works of Josephus* (Peabody, MA: Hendrickson, 1987), p. 850; and Paul James-Griffiths, "Creation days and Orthodox Jewish Tradition," *Creation* 26:2 (March 2004), p. 53–55, www.answersingenesis.org/creation/v26/i2/tradition.asp.

12. E.g., John 15:18–19, 16:33, 17:6, 17:14, 17:21, and 1 John 2:15–17.

13. E.g., Luke 9:25, John 1:10 (first two uses, cf. 1:3 — Jesus created the world, not the sinful system of man), 13:1 (cf. 6:38, 13:3, and 16:28 — Jesus was not just leaving the sinful world of humanity to be a hermit in the wilderness but leaving the world of time-space physical creation to return to the Father in heaven), John 17:5, 17:24, and Acts 17:24.

14. Robert H. Gundry, *Mark* (Grand Rapids, MI: Eerdmans, 1993); and G. Campbell Morgan, *The Gospel According to Mark* (NY: Fleming Revell, 1927). Neither gives comment on 13:19.

15. C.E.B. Cranfield, *The Gospel According to St Mark: The Cambridge Greek Testament Commentary* (Cambridge: Cambridge Univ. Press, 1959). He makes no comment on 13:19.

phrases refer to the beginning of human history but present no argument for their conclusion.[16] France asserts simply that the phrase in 10:6 refers to "the period before the Fall."[17]

Garland, Lenski, Cole, Gould, Lane, Hare, Edwards, Hendricksen, Brooks, Moule, and Wessel make no comment on these verses, or at least not on the phrases related to the age of the earth, or their comments are too vague to determine what they believed regarding our question.[18]

It is also noteworthy that the most respected Greek lexicon concurs with the young-earth interpretation of Mark 10:6 and 13:19 in its entries for ἀρχή and κτίσις (especially since the compilers are not evangelicals).[19]

3. *Luke 11:50–51* ". . . so that the blood of all the prophets, shed since the foundation of the world, may be charged against this generation, from the blood of Abel to the blood of Zechariah, who was killed between the altar and the house of God; yes, I tell you, it shall be charged against this generation."

---

16. David L. McKenna, *The Communicator's Commentary: Mark* (Waco, TX: Word, 1982); Craig A. Evans, *Word Biblical Commentary: Mark 8:27–16:20* (Nashville, TN: Thomas Nelson, 2001); and Walter W. Wessel, *Mark: The Expositor's Bible Commentary*, Vol. 8 (Grand Rapids, MI: Zondervan, 1984).

17. R.T. France, *The Gospel of Mark* (Grand Rapids, MI: Eerdmans, 2002). He makes no comment on 13:19.

18. David E. Garland, *Mark: The NIV Application Commentary* (Grand Rapids, MI: Zondervan, 1996); R.C.H. Lenski, *The Interpretation of St. Mark's Gospel* (Minneapolis, MN: Augsburg, 1946); R. Alan Cole, *Mark: Tyndale New Testament Commentaries* (Grand Rapids, MI: Eerdmans, 1983);and Ezra P. Gould, *Gospel According to St. Mark: The International Critical Commentary* (Edinburgh: T&T Clark, 1896). On 10:6, Gould only says that "Jesus goes back from the Mosaic Law to the original constitution of things," which would lend support to the YEC view. William L. Lane, *The Gospel of Mark: The New International Commentary on the New Testament* (Grand Rapids, MI: Eerdmans, 1974), does not comment on the phrase in 10:6. On 13:19, he only says that it "is virtually a citation of Dan. 12:1" (p. 471), which is an exaggeration. While the verses are similar, the wording is notably different. Daniel speaks of a time of trouble such as never has been "since there was a nation" whereas Jesus says "since the beginning of creation." See also Douglas R. A. Hare, *Mark* (Louisville, KY: Westminster John Knox Press, 1996); James R. Edwards, *The Gospel according to Mark* (Grand Rapids, MI: Eerdmans, 2002); William Hendriksen, *New Testament Commentary: Exposition of the Gospel According to Mark* (Grand Rapids, MI: Baker, 1975); James A. Brooks, *The New American Commentary: Mark* (Nashville, TN: Broadman Press, 1991); C.F.D. Moule, *The Gospel According to Mark* (Cambridge: CUP, 1965); and Walter W. Wessel, *Mark: The Expositor's Bible Commentary*, Vol. 8 (Grand Rapids, MI: Zondervan, 1984).

19. Walter Bauer, Frederick W. Danker, William F. Arndt, and F. Wilbur Gingrich, *A Greek-English Lexicon of the New Testament* (Chicago, IL: University of Chicago Press, 1979, 2nd ed.), p. 112 and 456, and the 3rd edition (2000), p. 138 and 573.

This statement of Jesus contains the phrase "foundation of the world." The phrase is used ten times in the New Testament: seven times it is preceded by "from" (ἀπὸ) and the other three times by "before" (πρὸ).

In addition to Luke 11:50, the phrase "from the foundation of the world" (ἀπὸ καταβολῆς κόσμου) also appears in Matthew 13:35 and 25:34, Hebrews 4:3 and 9:26, and Revelation 13:8 and 17:8. In Hebrew 4:3, the writer says God's creation "works were finished from the foundation of the world." Verse 4 says that "God rested on the seventh day from His works." The two statements are clearly synonomous: God finished and rested at the same time. This implies that the seventh day (when God finished creating, Gen. 2:1–3) was the end of the foundation period. So, the foundation does not refer simply to the first moment or first day of creation week, but to the whole week.[20] The context, grammar, and lexical evidence in Matthew 13:35 and 25:34, Hebrews 9:26, Revelation 13:8 and 17:8 do not support any alternative sense of the phrase ἀπὸ καταβολῆς κόσμου, particularly the restricted meaning "foundation or beginning of the human race." Since the previous uses of "foundation of the world" include the beginning of creation in Genesis 1:1, we have grounds for concluding that the phrase in these latter verses also refers to the very beginning of creation.

In Luke 11:50–51, "the blood of all the prophets, shed since the foundation of the world" (ἀπὸ καταβολῆς κόσμου) is juxtaposed with the statement "from the blood of Abel" (ἀπὸ αἵματος Ἅβελ). The parallelism in these two verses is clear: "blood" in both verses, the two temporal phrases beginning with ἀπὸ (from or since), and repetition of "charged against this generation." This strongly suggests that Jesus believed that Abel lived very near the foundation of the world.

The phrase, "before the foundation of the world" (πρὸ καταβολῆς κόσμου), appears in John 17:24, Ephesians 1:4, and 1 Peter 1:20. In John 17:24 the sense "before the beginning of all creation" (not merely before the creation of man) best fits the context,[21] for the Father loved the Son eternally before the creation of the heaven and the earth in Genesis 1:1 ("before the world[22] was," John 17:5;

---

20. Heb 1:10 confirms this when it tells us that "in the beginning" God "laid the foundation of the earth" (τὴν γῆν ἐθεμελίωσας literally "founded or established the earth") and "the heavens are the works of His hands," all of which occurred before Adam was made.

21. Those who think this phrase in John 17:5 and 24 refers to the beginning of the whole creation include D.A. Carson, *The Gospel According to John* (Grand Rapids, MI: Eerdmans, 1991); Leon Morris, *The Gospel According to John* (Grand Rapids, MI: Eerdmans, 1971); George R. Beasely-Murray, *John* (Dallas, TX: Word, 1987); R.V.G. Tasker, *John* (Grand Rapids, MI: Eerdmans, 1983); and Roger L. Fredrikson, *John* (Waco, TX: Word, 1985). See also the great 18th century Bible scholar: John Gill, *An Exposition on the New Testament* (London: George Keith, 1774–76).

22. In John 1:9–10, we are told that Jesus came into the world and was in the world that He made. Clearly, in John 1 Jesus is the maker of everything, not simply the human race, and He came into the physical world from His pre-incarnate spiritual life in heaven. In John 11:27, Martha says that she knew Jesus was the Son of God who comes into the world. It is doubtful that she was thinking and meaning anything different than

compare Colossians 1:16–17 for similar teaching). Similarly, given the nature of the foreknowledge of God, we can be certain that in Ephesians 1:4 Paul meant that God chose believers in Christ before anything was created, not just before the first two humans were made.[23] Undoubtedly in 1 Peter 1:20, Peter also meant that Christ was foreknown by the Father before the creation of the earth (and therefore before the creation of anything else, since the earth was created first with the empty heavens). So, in these cases, "foundation of the world" refers to the whole creation week (Gen. 1).

The majority of Lukan commentators do not comment on our phrases under consideration.[24] Marshall's only relevant remark is that ἀπὸ καταβολῆς (from the foundation) is always used in the NT to refer to the beginning of the world.[25] Similarly, Lenski comments that our phrase "implies that God laid that foundation when he called the world into being, and the phrase is used to denote the beginning of time."[26] Both comments support the young-earth interpretation.

Hendriksen says that "the reason why Jesus says 'from Abel to Zechariah' is that according to the arrangement of the books in the Hebrew Bible Genesis (hence 'Abel') comes first; Chronicles (hence 'Zechariah') last."[27] However, the verses are not referring to the books of Scripture, but rather to people.

Jesus did with this language. So "world" (κοσμος) in these verses, as in 17:5, 17:24, and Acts 17:24, is clearly referring to the whole creation, not simply humanity or even the sinful worldly system.

23. See Paul's similar teaching in 2 Timothy 1:9 and Titus 1:2 (NIV and KJV are accurate translations of the time phrase, whereas NAS is not).

24. Alfred Plummer, *Gospel According to S. Luke: The International Critical Commentary* (Edinburgh: T&T Clark, 1901); John Nolland, *Word Biblical Commentary: Luke 9:21–18:34* (Dallas, TX: Word, 1993); Darrell L. Bock, *Luke: The NIV Application Commentary* (Grand Rapids, MI: Zondervan, 1996); Darrell L. Bock, *Luke, Vol 2: 9:51–24:53* (Grand Rapids, MI: Baker, 1996); Walter L. Liefeld, *Luke: The Expositor's Bible Commentary*, Vol. 8 (Grand Rapids, MI: Zondervan, 1984); Leon Morris, *Luke: Tyndale New Testament Commentaries* (Grand Rapids, MI: Eerdmans, 1983); Henry Alford, *The New Testament for English Readers* (Chicago, IL: Moody, ca. 1958); William H. Van Doren, *The Gospel of Luke* (Grand Rapids, MI: Kregel, 1981); Frederic L. Godet, *Commentary on Luke* (Grand Rapids, MI: Kregel, 1981); Norval Geldenhuys, *Commentary on the Gospel of Luke* (Grand Rapids, MI: Eerdmans, 1951); G. Campbell Morgan, *The Gospel According to Luke* (New York: Fleming Revell, 1931); and Joel B. Green, *The Gospel of Luke* (Grand Rapids, MI: Eerdmans, 1997).

25. I. Howard Marshall, *The Gospel of Luke*: NIGTC (Grand Rapids, MI: Eerdmans, 1995), p. 505. He does give one exception to this general statement: Heb. 11:11. But this reference is wrong and probably should read Heb. 11:10.

26. R.C.H. Lenski, *The Interpretation of St. Luke's Gospel* (Minneapolis, MN: Augsburg Publ., 1946).

27. William Hendriksen, *New Testament Commentary: Exposition of the Gospel According to Luke* (Grand Rapids, MI: Baker, 1978).

Furthermore, scholars are not in agreement about which Zechariah this was in history or about when the present order of the OT books became canonical. Furthermore, Jesus does not say "from Abel to Zechariah," but rather "from the blood of Abel to the blood of Zechariah." The emphasis is on the death of the first and last OT prophets.

Most of the commentators on Mark and Luke are silent on our phrases in these verses. Of those who do comment, many support the young-earth interpretation. The others make assertions without offering an argument for their interpretation. Or the argumentation given does not overturn the conclusions of my analysis above.

Preliminary Conclusion about Jesus' View of the Age of the Earth

From the study of these Jesus AGE verses we see that Jesus believed and taught that man has existed essentially as long as the entire cosmos has. Given His evident belief in the literal historical truth of all of Genesis 1–11 and the historical reliability of the rest of the OT (including its chronological information such as contained in the genealogies of Genesis 5 and 11), we have strong grounds to conclude that He believed in a literal six-day creation week which occurred only a few thousand years ago. No other understanding adequately accounts for the Jesus AGE verses and His approach to the historicity of Genesis.

But, as I will seek to demonstrate below, the vast majority of Christian old-earth proponents have not taken into account the Jesus AGE verses. The arguments of the few who have commented on them lack cogency, are inherently self-contradictory, fail to deal with all the evidence, or are inconsistent with the evidence.

Young-earth Creationist References to the Jesus AGE Verses

For decades, young-earth creationist writers have cited these verses in articles and books in defense of the earth being only thousands of years old, emphasizing that the statements of Jesus show that Adam could not have been created billions of years after the beginning, as all old-earth views maintain.[28] Most of these

---

28. Henry Morris, "Christ and the Time of Creation" (*Back to Genesis*, No. 70), *Acts and Facts* (ICR, Oct. 1994), a-b (cites all three Jesus AGE verses); Henry Morris, "The Bible and Jesus Christ" (*Back to Genesis*, No. 125), *Acts and Facts* (ICR, May 1999), c (all three verses); Charles Taylor, "Jesus on Creation," *Creation Ex Nihilo*, 20/2 (March–May 1998), p. 55 (cites Mark 10:6), www.answersingenesis. org/creation/v20/i2/creation.asp; Henry Morris, *Scientific Creationism* (San Diego, CA: Creation-Life Pub., 1974), p. 246 (cites Mark 13:19); Henry Morris, *King of Creation* (San Diego, CA: CLP Publishers, 1980), p. 54 (cites Mark10:6); Henry Morris, *The Biblical Basis of Modern Science* (Grand Rapids, MI: Baker, 1984), p. 113 & 392 (cites Mark 10:6); Henry Morris, *Biblical Creationism* (Grand Rapids, MI: Baker, 1993), p. 148 (cites Mark 10:6, 13:19) and 151 (cites Luke 11:50–51); Henry Morris & John Morris, *The Modern Creation Trilogy* (Green Forest, AR: Master Books, 1996), vol. 1, p. 79–80, 140, 151 & 214 (cites all three verses);

creationist books are still in print.[29] It would appear that either old-earthers are not reading the young-earth literature, as they tell the Church that young-earth creationists are wrong about the age of the earth and about the importance of the subject, or the old-earther proponents are simply overlooking the point being made by young-earthers from the teaching of Jesus on this matter.

Some of the early 19th century defenders of young-earth creationism (called "scriptural geologists") also used these statements of Jesus as they resisted the idea of millions of years that was engulfing geology at that time.[30] In 1834, the Anglican minister Henry Cole argued this way from Mark 13:19:

> Now, is there a geologizing mortal upon Earth who will assert, that the Redeemer is here speaking of "afflictions" experienced by a world of creatures, who lived in a mighty space between "the beginning," and the present race of mankind? Will any geological sceptic, we repeat, dare aver, that our Lord is here referring to a race of beings of whom his disciples had never heard, and whose existence was never known to men or saints, till discovered by wondrous Geologians in the nineteenth

---

John Whitcomb, *The Early Earth* (Grand Rapids, MI: Baker, 1986), p. 36 (cites all three verses); Jobe Martin, *The Evolution of a Creationist* (Rockwall, TX: Biblical Discipleship Publishers, 2002), p. 28–29 (cites Mark 10:6); Douglas Kelly, *Creation and Change* (UK: Mentor, 1999), p. 129–134 (refers to or quotes all the Jesus AGE verses (along with all the other NT verses relevant to the interpretation of Gen. 1-11 and concludes that they indicate nothing "other than the literal, chronological understanding of the six days of creation and the succeeding patriarchal history"); Sid Dyer, "The New Testament Doctrine of Creation," in Joseph Pipa and David Hall, eds., *Did God Create in Six Days?* (Taylors, SC: Southern Presbyterian Press, 1999), p. 222–223 (cites all three verses); Bert Thompson, *Theistic Evolution* (Shreveport, LA: Lambert Book House, 1977), p. 227 (cites Mark 10:6); and Travis Richard Freeman, "The Chronological Value of Genesis 5 and 11 in Light of Recent Biblical Investigation" (PhD thesis, Southwestern Baptist Theological Seminary, 1998), p. 159 and 184 (cites Mark 10:6).

For an Eastern Orthodox perspective, see Fr. Seraphim Rose, *Genesis, Creation and Early Man* (Platina, CA: Saint Herman of Alaska Brotherhood, 2000), p. 150 (cites Mark 10:6) & 228 (cites Luke 11:50–51). In both cases in Rose's work the comments are in the editor's footnotes. This work documents through lengthy quotations that the young-earth view was the unanimous belief of Eastern Orthodox "Church Fathers" until the advent of old-earth evolutionary ideas in the 19th century. See my review of this important book: "Orthodoxy and Genesis: What the fathers *really* taught," *TJ*, Vol. 16/3 (2002) p. 48–53, www.answersingenesis. org/home/area/magazines/tj/docs/v16n3_mortenson.asp.

29. Two of the most prominent young-earth creationists for many years have been Henry Morris and John Whitcomb.

30. See Terry Mortenson, *The Great Turning Point: the Church's Catastrophic Mistake on Geology — Before Darwin* (Green Forest, AR: Master Books, 2004).

century! Must not every scientific, unless he violate every remnant of natural understanding, honesty, and conscience, confess that the Saviour is here speaking to sons of men of the "afflictions" of the same sons of men which have been from the beginning of the Creation of this world? Then, here is the creation of man immediately, manifestly, and undeniably, connected with "the beginning"![31]

But the early 19th century Christian old-earth proponents largely ignored the Genesis text and all of them overlooked the Jesus AGE verses, as they told the church to accept millions of years and to regard the age of the earth as unimportant. As will be seen, old-earth proponents continue to do this.

As part of a thorough survey of evangelical scholarly literature addressing the age of the earth, we consider first commentaries on Genesis, then systematic theology texts, and finally a variety of other scholarly or popular-level books that discuss the issue.

Commentaries on Genesis Regarding the Jesus AGE Verses

1. Young-earth Creationist Commentaries on Genesis

Morris, MacArthur, and Leupold refer to at least one of the Jesus AGE verses to argue for the historicity of Genesis 1–11.[32] This supports their young-earth conclusions about Genesis, although they do not explicitly make the point from these verses about Jesus believing in a young earth. However, Morris's study Bible, *The Defender's Bible* (Grand Rapids, MI: World, 1995) is explicit on this point.[33] Rice says nothing about the Jesus AGE verses.[34]

---

31. Henry Cole, *Popular Geology Subversive of Divine Revelation* (London: J. Hatchard & Son, 1834), p. 46–47. See also George Bugg, *Scriptural Geology* (London: L.B. Seeley & Son, 1826-27), vol 1, p. 108 (uses Mark 10:6). For a summary of Cole's and Bugg's lives and objections to old-earth geology, see my published articles at www.answersingenesis.org/home/area/magazines/tj/docs/tjv13n1_cole.asp and www.answersingenesis.org/home/area/magazines/tj/docs/tjv12n2_george_bugg.asp.

32. Henry Morris, *The Genesis Record* (Grand Rapids, MI: Baker, 1987), p. 103 (Mark 10:6). John MacArthur, *The Battle for the Beginning* (Nashville, TN: Thomas Nelson, 2001), p. 24, references Mark 13:19 in arguing that the New Testament speaks of creation as a past, completed event. H.C. Leupold, *Exposition of Genesis* (Grand Rapids, MI: Baker, 1942, Vol. 1), p. 36, cites Matthew 19:4–6 (parallel of Mark 10:5–9) in arguing that Genesis 1 is "pure history." But he does not discuss the Jesus AGE verses either in Genesis 1 or in his expositions on Genesis 5 and 11.

33. He has notes on Matthew 19:4 (explaining that Jesus took Genesis as literal history), Mark 10:6 (emphasizing that Jesus was a young-earth creationist), Mark 13:19 (mentioning young-earth implications and showing that "beginning of creation" is synonymous with "beginning of the world" in the parallel passage of Matthew 24:21), and Luke 11:50 (pointing out that Abel was at the foundation of the world, not four billion years after the formation of the earth).

34. John R. Rice, *In the Beginning* (Murfreesboro, TN: Sword of the Lord, 1975). The

2. Old-earth Creationist Commentaries on Genesis

Almost all Genesis commentaries by old-earth proponents that I examined apparently overlooked the Jesus AGE verses (most also show little, if any, acquaintance with young-earth literature). These include Kenneth Mathews, John Walton, Bruce Waltke, J. Vernon McGee, Warren Wiersbe, John Sailhamer, Allen Ross, Arthur Pink, Ronald Youngblood, Gordon Wenham, and Griffith Thomas.[35] Space precludes detailed comment on them. However, James Boice's commentary is worthy of brief discussion because (1) he does refer to some of the Jesus AGE verses, and (2) his lack of careful reflection on the issue of the age of the earth is symptomatic of the above commentaries.

In the chapter entitled "Fact or Fiction?" (a question about Genesis which Boice fails to answer clearly), he has a sub-section called "The Teaching of Jesus." Boice there says that, "A special aspect of the attitude of Scripture to Genesis is the teaching of Jesus Christ. This obviously carries special weight. . . . it is surely of interest to those who profess to follow Jesus as their Lord to know what He said. His teaching has special weight if only because we revere the Lord highly."[36] Yes, indeed! How sad then to see that Boice discusses Matthew 19:3–6 but not the parallel passage in Mark 10:2–6, which shows Jesus to be a young-earth creationist. Boice quotes a small part of Mark 13:19 to say that God created. But he does not quote the rest of the verse, which is so relevant to the age of the earth, and he does not comment on Luke 11:50–51. Is this giving special weight to Jesus' teaching on this subject?

Boice rejects theistic evolution, but he also rejects the Flood as the cause of most of the fossil record. He has doubts about the gap theory, and sees problems with the

book claims to give detailed studies on creation vs. evolution, the Flood, etc. It strongly recommends Whitcomb and Morris's *The Genesis Flood*. He argues extensively that the gap and day-age theories are unbiblical and believes that rocks and fossils are the evidence of the Flood, not millions of years. But he does not refer to the apostolic evidence for the historicity of Genesis 1–11 or to the Jesus AGE verses.

35. Kenneth A. Mathews, *Genesis 1–11:26: The New American* Commentary (Broadman and Holman, 1996); John H. Walton, *Genesis: The NIV Application Commentary* (Grand Rapids, MI: Zondervan, 2001); Bruce K Waltke, *Genesis* (Grand Rapids, MI: Zondervan, 2001), p. 31; J. Vernon McGee, *Genesis* (Nashville, TN: Thomas Nelson, 1991), p. 60–61 and 133. Warren W. Wiersbe, *Be Basic: An Old Testament Study* —*Genesis 1–11* (Colorado Springs, CO: Victor, 1998), is uncertain of the age of the creation, but clearly believes it is millions of years. John H. Sailhamer, *Genesis, Expositor's Bible Commentary, vol. 2* (Grand Rapids, MI: Zondervan, 1990); Allen P. Ross, *Creation and Blessing* (Grand Rapids, MI: Baker, 1998); Arthur W. Pink, *Gleanings in Genesis* (Chicago, IL: Moody Press, 1922); Ronald Youngblood, *The Book of Genesis* (Grand Rapids, MI: Baker, 1991, 2nd ed.); Gordon Wenham, *Genesis 1–15* (Milton Keynes, UK: Word, 1991); and W.H. Griffith Thomas (1861–1924, principal of Wycliffe Hall, Oxford), *Genesis 1–25:10* (London: Religious Tract Society, 5th ed., no date).

36. James M. Boice, *Genesis, Volume 1 Genesis 1;1–11:32* (Grand Rapids, MI: Zondervan, 1982), p. 21.

day-age view and framework hypothesis. So he is not sure how to harmonize the Bible with millions of years. In his brief discussion of young-earth creationism's handling of Genesis 1–2, Boice uses quotes from Whitcomb and Morris's *The Genesis Flood* to summarize the view. He then gives several points that should guide one's evaluation of young-earth creationism. He says, "First, there is the concern for biblical teaching. More than this, creationists want to make biblical teaching determinative."[37] Boice is correct, and such a hermeneutic is the necessary corollary of the doctrine of inspiration. Whatever God says should always be determinative for the believer, regardless of the views of other supposed sources of authoritative truth that contradict God's Word. Boice quickly adds that "we have to admit here that the exegetical basis of the creationist is strong."[38] But, as his discussion continues, he reveals that the only reason he rejects the young-earth creationists' sound exegesis is because so-called "science" confidently asserts that the creation is billions of years old.[39] What happened to the authoritative teaching of Jesus, which Boice says is so determinative?

Systematic Theology Texts Regarding the Jesus AGE Verses

1. Young-earth Creationist Systematic Theology Texts

In his discussion on creation, Berkhof argues for literal days and against the gap and day-age views.[40] He does not explicitly state his view on the age of the earth, but uses Exodus 20:11 in defense of his view, rejects theistic evolution, rejects human evolution, and seems to reject old-earth geology.[41] However, he does not refer to the Jesus AGE verses, except to affirm (by reference to Mark 10:6) that the creation had a beginning.[42] Ryrie refers only to Luke 11:51, and then merely in relation to Jesus' view of the extent of the OT canon.[43] Reymond lists many OT and NT references (including Luke 11:51) to support his contention that Genesis 1–11 is reliable history and he refers to Mark 10:6 when he states that "to question the basic historical authenticity and integrity of Genesis 1–11 is to assault the integrity of Christ's own teaching."[44]

2. Old-earth Systematic Theology Texts

For the most part, systematic theology texts written by old-earth proponents also overlook the Jesus AGE verses. If they do refer to the verses, they do

---

37. Ibid., p. 57.
38. Ibid.
39. Ibid., p. 59–60.
40. Louis Berkhof, *Systematic Theology* (Grand Rapids, MI: Eerdmans, 1949, 4th ed.), p. 150–164.
41. Ibid., p. 181–188.
42. Ibid., p. 130.
43. Charles Ryrie, *Basic Theology* (Chicago, IL: Moody, 1986), p. 122.
44. Robert L. Reymond, *A New Systematic Theology of The Christian Faith* (Nashville, TN: Thomas Nelson, 1998), p. 118.

not comment on the implications for the age of the earth. I carefully examined the relevant discussions of Hodge, Feinberg, Thiessen, Erickson, Buswell, and Henry.[45] I will comment on two other texts as representative.

Lewis and Demarest discuss the origin of the world and humanity in their 1996 theology text. In numerous statements, they badly misrepresent the young-earth view,[46] which is not surprising since they do not demonstrate any familiarity with the recent creationist literature (but refer to much recent old-earth literature). It would appear that they did not even read carefully the two older books by Henry Morris (published in 1974 and 1984, respectively), which they cite and both of which refer to the Jesus AGE verses.[47] They argue for the day-age view, concluding that "ultimately, responsible geology must determine the length of the Genesis days."[48] What happened to the principle of Scripture interpreting Scripture? They do refer to Mark 10:6, 13:19 and Luke 11:51, and affirm that "Jesus clearly endorsed the validity of the Old Testament creation

---

45. Charles Hodge, *Systematic Theology* (Grand Rapids, MI: Eerdmans, 1997, reprint of 1871–73 original), Genesis and geology are discussed in vol. 1, p. 570–574 and the antiquity of man in vol. 2, p. 33–39; John S. Feinberg, *No One Like Him* (Wheaton, IL: Crossways Books, 2001), p. 537–624; Henry Thiessen, *Lectures in Systematic Theology* (Grand Rapids, MI: Eerdmans, 1949); Millard Erickson, *Christian Theology* (Grand Rapids, MI: Baker, 1985), p. 367–373; James Oliver Buswell, *A Systematic Theology of the Christian Religion* (Grand Rapids, MI: Zondervan, 1962); Carl F. H. Henry, *God, Revelation and Authority, Vol. VI* (Waco, TX: Word, 1983).

46. Gordon R. Lewis and Bruce A. Demarest, *Integrative Theology* (Grand Rapids, MI: Zondervan, 1996), vol. 2. Under the discussion on the young-earth view, there are several misrepresentations on page 23. They equate "catastrophism" (which is still evolutionary and old-earth) with "flood geology" (which is young-earth in perspective). They falsely accuse young-earthers of believing that "all" the strata, fossils, volcanic activity, and mountain formations were caused by the Flood (informed young-earthers are always careful to say "most"). They say that young-earthers reject "the findings of astronomy and geology," whereas it is the *naturalistic interpretations* of the observational evidence that young-earthers reject. They also say that young-earthers regard "the absence of any developmental mechanisms as essential to theological orthodoxy" and refer the reader to an article by Pattle Pun in the *Evangelical Dictionary of Theology* (p. 390). Pun's article further distorts the young-earth view by saying that young-earthers "ignore the vast amount of data supporting the observable micro-evolutionary processes in nature and the laboratory." In fact, informed young-earth creationists have always believed in "micro-evolutionary" changes due to natural selection and mutations, but they have denied (with supporting arguments) that such changes have any value as evidence in favor of amoeba-to-man "macroevolution." Similarly, Lewis and Demarest assert on page 47 that young-earthers believe that the Flood "accounts for *all* the observable geological evidence by observable evidence from *all* areas *universally*" [emphasis added at the points of misrepresentation].

47. See their footnotes 61 and 67 to chapter 1 of vol. 2 on page 499.

48. Ibid., p. 29.

doctrine"[49] and that "the Lord Jesus Christ and his apostles who wrote the New Testament by the Spirit's inspiration understood the early chapters of Genesis to be informative."[50] However, it is not clear what "endorsed the validity" and "informative" in these statements are meant to convey regarding the truthfulness or proper interpretation of Genesis 1–11. In any case, Lewis and Demarest apparently have failed to grasp the implications of Jesus' words for their view of the age of the earth.

In his *Systematic Theology* Grudem deals with Mark 10:6, but not Mark 13:19 or Luke 11:51. His attempted refutation of the young-earth reasoning from Mark 10:6 is one sentence: "This argument also has some force, but old-Earth advocates may respond that Jesus is just referring to the whole of Genesis 1–2 as the 'beginning of creation,' in contrast to the argument from the laws given by Moses that the Pharisees were depending on (v. 4)."[51] This objection makes little sense; it actually affirms that Adam and Eve were indeed at the beginning of creation, not billions of years after the beginning, just as young-earthers contend. In any case, whatever statements in Deuteronomy 24 the Pharisees were relying on is irrelevant to Jesus' statement and belief about when Adam and Eve were created. Furthermore, Grudem apparently *imagines* how old-earth advocates *might* evade the force of this young-earth argument, but he does not cite and I do not know of any old-earth proponent who has *actually* reasoned the way Grudem suggests. So, the young-earth argument from Mark 10:6 has more than just "some force."

Other Old-earth Writings Regarding the Jesus AGE Verses

The following authors either promote or at least accept belief in millions of years: Snoke, Arnold, Lucas, Forster and Marston, Ramm, Cabal, and Kaiser.[52]

---

49. Ibid., p. 33.
50. Ibid., p. 39.
51. Wayne Grudem, *Systematic Theology* (Grand Rapids, MI: Zondervan, 1994), p. 297.
52. David Snoke, *A Biblical Case for an Old Earth* (Hatfield, PA: Interdisciplinary Biblical Research Institute, 1998). As a day-age proponent, Snoke is an elder in a Presbyterian church and PhD Asst. Prof. of Physics and Astronomy, Univ. of Penn. IBRI is an influential group among evangelical academics and has produced a number of books strongly opposed to the young-earth view. Bill Arnold, *Encountering the Book of Genesis* (Grand Rapids, MI: Baker, 1998) favors either day-age or framework view. Ernest Lucas, *Genesis Today* (London: Scripture Union, 1989), is a professing evangelical and a theistic evolutionist. He has a PhD in chemistry, has been a pastor and is currently vice-principal and tutor in biblical studies at Bristol Baptist College in England. Roger Forster and Paul V. Marston, *Reason and Faith* (Eastbourne, UK: Monarch, 1989), and their revised second edition: *Reason, Science and Faith* (Crowborough, UK: Monarch Books, 1999); Bernard Ramm, *The Christian View of Science and Scripture* (Grand Rapids, MI: Eerdmans, 1955); Ted Cabal, "Evangelicalism and Young-Earth Creationism: Necessary Bedfellows?" a paper given at the annual meeting of ETS in Colorado Springs in 2001 (his paper answers the title question in the negative; Walter C. Kaiser, *Toward an Old Testament Theology* (Grand Rapids, MI: Zondervan, 1978); Walter C. Kaiser,

So do Newman and Eckelmann, E.J. Young, Harris, Mark Ross, Moreland, Scofield, Orr, Hague, Wright, and Mauro, Davis Young, Snow, and Stek.[53] So also do Bradley and Olsen, Blocher, Hugh Ross, Howard Vos, Free, Archer, Sailhamer, Warfield, and Kline.[54] But none of these scholars interact with the

The Old Testament Documents: Are They Reliable and Relevant? (Downers Grove, IL: IVPress, 2001); and Walter C. Kaiser et al, *Hard Sayings of the Bible* (Downers Grove, IL: IVPress, 1996). Kaiser favors the day-age view.

53. Robert C. Newman and Herman J. Eckelmann, *Genesis One and the Origin of the Earth* (Hatfield, PA: IBRI, 1977), advocate the day-gap-day view. E.J. Young, *Studies in Genesis One* (Phillipsburg, NJ: P&R Publ., 1964), wonderfully defends the full historicity of Genesis 1 (and refutes the framework hypothesis) and contends that the days of creation were chronologically sequential (non-overlapping), but he states "The Bible does not state how old the earth is," and "the length of the days is not stated" (p. 102 and 104). R. Laird Harris, "The Length of the Creative Days in Genesis 1," in Pipa and Hall, *Did God Create*, p. 101–111; Mark Ross, "The Framework Hypothesis: An Interpretation of Genesis 1:1–2:3" in Pipa and Hall, *Did God Create*, p. 113–130; J.P. Moreland, *Scaling the Secular City* (Grand Rapids, MI: Baker, 1998). For further critique of Moreland's uncharacteristically superficial comments about the age of the earth, see Ken Ham, Carl Wieland, and Terry Mortenson, "Are (Biblical) Creationists 'Cornered'? — A Response to Dr. J.P. Moreland," *TJ*, 17:3 (2003), p. 43–50, www. answersingenesis.org/docs2003/1001cornered.asp. C.I. Scofield, ed., *The Holy Bible* (Lake Wylie, SC: Christian Heritage Publ., 1994 reprint of 1917 second edition). The writings of Orr, Hague, Wright, and Mauro are in R.A. Torrey, ed., *The Fundamentals* (Grand Rapids, MI: Kregel, 1990). Davis A. Young, *Christianity and the Age of the Earth* (Grand Rapids, MI: Zondervan, 1982). In Howard Van Til et al., eds., *Portraits of Creation* (Grand Rapids, MI: Eerdmans, 1990), Young says nothing about the Jesus AGE verses in his chapter on the perceived tensions between biblical and evolutionary cosmogonies, nor does Robert Snow in his chapter criticizing the creation science movement, nor does John Stek in his chapter on "What Says the Scriptures?"

54. Walter Bradley and Roger Olsen, "The Trustworthiness of Scripture in Areas Relating to Natural Science," in Earl Radmacher and Robert Preus, eds., *Hermeneutics, Inerrancy and the Bible* (Grand Rapids, MI: Zondervan, 1984), p. 285–317. Henri Blocher, *In the Beginning* (Downers Grove, IL: IVPress, 1984), advocates the framework hypothesis. Hugh Ross, *The Genesis Question* (Colorado Springs, CO: NavPress, 1998) and *Creation and Time* (Colorado Springs, CO: NavPress, 1994). For a thorough critique of Ross' teachings on creation and the age of the earth see Jonathan Sarfati's *Refuting Compromise* (Green Forest, AR: Master Books, 2004). Howard Vos, *Genesis* (Chicago, IL: Moody Press, 1982); Joseph P. Free and Howard F. Vos, *Archeology and The Bible* (Grand Rapids, MI: Zondervan, 1992); Gleason Archer, *Encyclopedia of Bible Difficulties* (Grand Rapids, MI: Zondervan, 1982); Gleason Archer, "A Response to The Trustworthiness of Scripture in Areas Relating to Natural Science," in Earl Radmacher and Robert Preus, eds., *Hermeneutics, Inerrancy and the Bible* (Grand Rapids, MI: Zondervan, 1984), p. 321–334; and Gleason Archer, *A Survey of Old Testament Introduction* (Chicago, IL: Moody, 1994, see also all his earlier editions back to the 1964 original); John H. Sailhamer, *Genesis Unbound* (Sisters, OR: Multnomah, 1996). On Warfield, see Mark Noll & David N. Livingstone, eds., *Evolution, Science, and Scripture: B.B. Warfield,*

Jesus AGE verses and most of them do not consider at all the New Testament teaching relevant to the correct interpretation of Genesis 1–11. Other authors who do the same deserve some comment. Their handling of Scripture on this subject is illustrative of the works above.

In *Evolution and the Authority of the Bible*, Nigel Cameron presents some strong arguments in favor of the young-earth view, although he does not explicitly endorse it. He considers Matthew 19:4 to be a "strong testimony to an historical reading of Genesis by Jesus himself."[55] After discussing other relevant NT verses he concludes:

> The New Testament view of the early chapters of Genesis, both as to the essentials (that Adam was a real man and that he really fell) and also as to certain details (such as the order of creation and Fall — Adam created first, Eve first to fall), is that an historical reading of the narrative is the appropriate one. . . . Evangelical Christians who desire to interpret Scripture faithfully will follow the New Testament writers in treating Genesis 2 and 3 as history. If they reject this reading, they do so at their peril.[56]

Cameron gives no reason for limiting his conclusion about historicity to Genesis 2–3, instead of applying it to all of Genesis 1–11. He seems to imply that the historicity and fall of Adam are the only essentials taught in the early chapters of Genesis and that only "certain details" (of the order of creation and fall of Adam and Eve) are important, straightforwardly clear and trustworthy, but that the details about creation in six days, the global Flood, and the genealogies of Genesis 5 and 11 are not. He fails to provide any rationale for such a selective reading of the details of the text. The New Testament writers clearly indicate that they treated all those chapters (and their details) as literal history. Is it not also to our peril, if we reject or ignore the *details* of the creation narrative or the Flood account? And should we not consider Jesus' view on these matters, as well as the views of the NT writers? Cameron has not heeded his own very appropriate warning.

Given Cameron's affirmation of the authority of Scripture, I wanted to find out more about his views after reading his 2001 email to a colleague of mine, in which Cameron said this about his above-mentioned book: "I have long taken the view that it is open to us to be agnostic on the 'alternative' we put in place

---

Selected Writings (Grand Rapids, MI: Baker, 2000), which contains all of Warfield's writings on the subject. Warfield's writings that deal directly with the age of man and the earth can be found on pages 211–229 and 269-287. Meredith G. Kline, "Space and Time in the Genesis Cosmogony," *Perspectives on Science and Christian Faith*, 48/1 (March 1996): p. 2–15.

55. Nigel M. de S. Cameron, *Evolution and the Authority of Scripture* (Exeter, UK: Paternoster Press, 1983), p. 85.

56. Ibid., p. 90–91.

of the standard evolution position. It's fair to say that when I wrote that book I was more sympathetic to the young-earth view than I am now, but I was not committed to it even then."[57] So in January 2004, I wrote Dr. Cameron to clarify his position on the age of the earth and whether he still held to the arguments presented in his book. He replied, "My position has all along been somewhat agnostic, and indeed I do not think we are obliged to come up with alternative scenarios. So I don't think my position has changed!"[58]

This is doubly perplexing when we note two more things. First, Cameron explains that the rapid, 19th-century compromise of the Church with millions of years was because "first in geology and then in biology . . . nincteenth century, biblical commentators hastened to accommodate their interpretation of Scripture to the latest orthodoxy in science."[59] Secondly, he gave a glowing endorsement (on the back cover) of Douglas Kelly's defense of young-earth creationism (which includes reference to the Jesus AGE verses and other NT references to Gen. 1–11), *Creation and Change* (1997), saying "A highly intelligent engagement with these crucial verses with which God declares himself to be a speaking God who is our maker. The discussion is scholarly but accessible, a model of the kind of exegetical theology which the church of our day needs." Surely, Cameron's inconsistent reasoning (revealed in his book, emails, and endorsement of Kelly's book) creates problems for our commitment to the authority of the Bible and of Jesus, our Lord, not to mention for our ability to articulate the gospel in an intellectually rigorous and coherent way to a skeptical world.

In *Genesis in Space and Time*, Francis Schaeffer says that the Bible "*is* a scientific textbook in the sense that where it touches the cosmos it is true, propositionally true" and "wherever it touches upon anything, it does so with true truth, but not with exhaustive truth. That is, where it speaks of the cosmos, science, what it says is true. Likewise, where it touches history, it speaks with that [sic] I call true truth, that is, propositional, objective truth."[60]

He argues that Genesis 1 and 2 are united descriptions of one creation account and he refers to Mark 10:6–8 to support that view.[61] He argues for the historicity (even the "historicity of the details") of the account of Adam and Eve[62] and the historicity of the Flood and even (rather weakly) defends it as being global.[63] However, he devotes merely one paragraph to the question of the

---

57. Cameron's email to my friend, dated Sept. 4, 2001, copy on file.
58. Cameron's email to me, dated Jan. 7, 2004, on file.
59. Cameron, *Evolution and Authority*, p. 72.
60. Francis Schaeffer, *Genesis in Space and Time* (Downers Grove, IL: IVPress, 1972), p. 35 (his emphasis) and 76.
61. Ibid., p. 39–40.
62. Ibid., p. 41–43.
63. Ibid., p. 33–34. He shows no evidence of having read Whitcomb and Morris's *The Genesis Flood*, even though it was a landmark book that spawned the modern creationist movement and was published ten years earlier by Schaeffer's fellow Calvinists at Presbyterian and Reformed Press. *The Genesis Flood* deals not only with the extent of

length of days in Genesis 1, and only asserts that "day" (*yôm*) can mean a long period as well as a normal day and so "we must leave open the exact length of the time indicated by *day* in Genesis."[64] He gives absolutely no exegesis to defend this view. Following the views of William Henry Green and B.B. Warfield, he briefly argues that the genealogies of Genesis 5 and 11 have gaps.[65] But nowhere does he discuss the verses showing Jesus to be a young-earth creationist.

In his *No Final Conflict* (1975) Schaeffer said this book should be studied with the above book as a unity.[66] But he says this book:

> . . . deals with the *possibilities* open to us where the Bible touches science in the first chapters of Genesis — that is, the possibilities that exist if we hold to the historic Christian view that both the Old and New Testaments in their entirety are the written Word of God without error in all that they affirm about history and science as well as about religious matters.[67]

Schaeffer affirms the "space-time" historicity of Genesis 1–11 and unity of the whole book. In defending this he cites the *toledoths* in Genesis[68] and 14 New Testament verses. He says that "absolutely every place where the New Testament refers to the first half of Genesis, the New Testament assumes (and many times affirms) that Genesis is history and that it is to be read in normal fashion, with the common use of words and syntax."[69] Nevertheless, although he rejects the gap theory, he does still allow it as a "theoretical possibility."[70] He accepts the day-age view as possible, as well as the literal-day view, and says that he is not sure about the matter. He appears to lean toward a global Flood, but is hesitant about how to relate it to geological ages. And he accepts that animals could have died peacefully before the Fall, but that there would not have been violence and agonizing, cruel death (as in one animal chasing down another) before Adam's sin. But he fails to mention and take account of the Jesus AGE verses. Failing to take account of them certainly makes it easier to accept Schaeffer's *possibilities* for harmonizing the Bible and millions of years. But that is a serious oversight.

Geisler's helpful encyclopedia of apologetics has three articles relevant to our discussion. In "Genesis, days of" (where he argues against young-earth

---

the Flood, but also the date of the Flood (based on population growth rates, by which Schaeffer also reasons, although he does not do the math and so only limits the date of the Flood to less than 20,000 years ago).

64. Ibid., p. 57.
65. Ibid., p. 122–124.
66. Francis Schaeffer, *No Final Conflict* (1975), reprinted in volume 2 of *The Complete Works of Francis A. Schaeffer* (Westchester, IL: Crossways, 1982), p. 120.
67. Ibid., emphasis in the original.
68. The Hebrew word behind the phrase "these are the generations" (or "this is the account") in Genesis 2:4, 5:1, 6:9, 10:1, etc.
69. Ibid., p. 126.
70. Ibid., p. 132.

creationism) and "Genealogies, Open or Closed" (where he argues for gaps in the Genesis genealogies) he does not deal with the Jesus AGE verses.[71] In the article "Creation and Origins," he does refer to and even quote Mark 10:6 and 13:19, but he uses them to state only that creation was a past singular event, rather than a continuing process.[72] However, this contradicts Geisler's endorsement of Hugh Ross and the idea of millions of years, because the evolutionary astronomers and geologists (whom Ross relies on) argue for millions of years on the basis of *presently* observed physical and chemical processes going back in an unbroken sequence to the beginning of time. In other words, the evolutionists deny that the creation activities are different from present-day processes, in contrast to what Geisler (rightly) believes.

In a basic apologetics book, Geisler and Bocchino say that the order of creation in Genesis "does offer an extremely accurate account of the order of creation as compared to the discoveries of modern science" (i.e., of *evolutionary* cosmology and geology).[73] However, their supposedly wonderful harmonization fails to mention the creation of the birds, sun, moon, or stars![74] So, once again we see a lack of careful attention to the biblical text. They tell their readers that they will not deal with the technical Hebrew details to defend their old-earth view. But they do not say where such details are discussed and unfortunately they fail to reckon with the Jesus AGE verses and the other NT teaching germane to the age of the creation. Nevertheless, they do urge their young-earth readers to "stop the infighting over the question of age" because "many sincerely honest and intellectually gifted scholars" argue for an old earth.[75] Unfortunately, neither sincerity, nor honesty, nor intellectual giftedness, separately or combined, ensures correct (biblical) thinking, and history affords many examples of times when many, or even the majority of, scholars were wrong.[76]

---

71. Norman L. Geisler, *Baker Encyclopedia of Christian Apologetics* (Grand Rapids, MI: Baker, 1999). Geisler does not indicate which old-earth interpretation of Genesis he favors.

72. Ibid., p. 165–166.

73. Norman Geisler and Peter Bocchino, *Unshakeable Foundations* (Minneapolis, MN: Bethany House, 2001), p. 174–175.

74. They continue to ignore the birds, sun, moon, and stars in their chart of progressive creationism on page 178.

75. Ibid., p. 175, fn. 6.

76. For example, Athanasius was exiled five times before he almost single-handedly convinced the majority that Arius' view of the nature of Christ was wrong. Most of the visible Church was wrong about the doctrines of salvation and indulgences at the time of Martin Luther's conversion. Most scholars in the world presently accept Darwinian evolution (though most OEC Christians do not). In the 18th century, most physicians believed that bleeding was an almost universal cure for sickness. Also in the late 18th century, most chemists believed that when a material was burned it released a substance called phlogistron. Joseph Priestley's discovery of oxygen proved them wrong.

In his recent book on science and faith, Collins does address some of the Jesus AGE verses, saying that "if this [young-earth] argument is sound, I'm in trouble."[77] This is because he rejects the literal, six-day creation view. After summarizing accurately the young-earth argument from the Jesus AGE verses, he says that it "finds its credibility from the way the English 'from *the* beginning' seems so definite; but the Greek is not so fixed."[78] He then discusses several verses to argue that "from the beginning" in Matthew 19:4 and 8 is referring to the beginning of the human race. He says that the phrase found in 1 John 1:1, and 2:13–14 relates to Christ and refers "to a 'time' before the world began." The same phrase used in 1 John 3:8 and John 8:44 in relation to Satan refers, he contends, "to the beginning of the world or perhaps to the beginning of his own rebellion."[79] On the other hand, he observes that 1 John 2:7, 24, and 3:11 refer to the time when John's readers became Christians or to the beginning of the Apostles' ministry. Without further comment Collins then concludes, "If we apply this insight to the verses in Matthew 19, we find that they most naturally refer to 'the beginning' of the human race."[80]

Attempting to neutralize the young-earth argument from Mark 10:6, he refers to Matthew 24:21 ("from the beginning of the world") and its parallel passage in Mark 13:19 ("from the beginning of the creation"). He says that these phrases here cover all of time or at least all of the time that humans have existed to experience tribulation. But he contends that the total time since the absolute beginning is irrelevant to Jesus' point in Mark 10:6. So he concludes that these discussed verses "have no bearing on the age of the earth."[81]

Several things can be said in response. First, we might ask how Collins knows that young-earthers only build their argument from the italicized word ("the") in the English phrase "from *the* beginning." None of the young-earthers cited in this essay argue that way. But in any case, the English phrase is no more definite than the Greek phrase. Second, in 1 John 1:1 and 2:13–14, John easily could have said "He who was *before* the beginning" (cf. John 17:24 and 1 Peter 1:20). But he rather says "He who was *from* the beginning." Given the opening of John's gospel, which refers to the creation of *all* things in the beginning, there is no reason whatsoever to see these verses as lending support to the restricted meaning of "the beginning of the human race." Third, none of Collins' suggested meanings of the verses about Satan (1 John 3:8 and John 8:44) and the verses about Christians (1 John 2:7, 2:24, and 3:11) supports his restricted interpretation. Since we don't know precisely what "from the beginning" refers to with respect to Satan, those verses cannot be used to support Collins' particular interpretation of "from the

---

77. C. John Collins, *Science and Faith: Friends or Foes?* (Wheaton, IL: Crossways, 2003), p. 106.
78. Ibid., p. 106.
79. Ibid.
80. Ibid., p. 107.
81. Ibid.

beginning of the human race." But also, while that verse and the ones related to Christians in 1 John may be construed to give "insight" to Collins' interpretation of Matthew 19:4, they do so only because he has ignored the additional words "of creation" in the parallel passage of Mark 10:6.

Lastly, Collins overlooks Luke 11:50–51, which is relevant to his argument about Mark 10:6. It should be noted that neither I nor any other young-earther has argued that the age of the earth is "the point" of any of these Jesus AGE verses. Although the particular phrases we are studying are incidental to the main thrust of Jesus' statements, they nevertheless do reveal something of Jesus' worldview (i.e., that He was [and still is] a young-earth creationist). In Luke 11, Jesus could have said merely that "the blood of all the prophets will be charged against this generation, from the blood of Abel . . ." and left out the words "shed from the foundation of the world." This latter phrase is unnecessary to warn people of judgment, but its presence reveals an aspect of Jesus' worldview. The same applies to the additional but unnecessary (if Jesus is only referring to the beginning of the human race) words "of creation" in Mark 10:6 and 13:19. Furthermore, it is very doubtful that any Pharisees and any Christian readers of the Gospels prior to the 19th century would have thought that Jesus was referring to only the creation of man or the beginning of the human race, for there is no biblical evidence that long ages of time elapsed between the absolute beginning in Genesis 1:1 and the creation of man in Genesis 1:26 and, as we noted earlier, Jesus always treated the OT narratives as straightforward history.

We therefore have good reasons to reject Collins' attempts to avoid the clear implications of the Jesus AGE verses for our understanding of the age of the earth. Also, it is clear from his book that the driving force behind Collins' old-earth interpretations of Scripture is his unquestioning trust in the claims of the evolutionary geologists about the age of the rocks. At the end of his four-page discussion of geology he states, "I conclude, then that I have no reason to disbelieve the standard theories of the geologists, including their estimate for the age of the earth. They may be wrong, for all I know; but if they are wrong, it's not because they have improperly smuggled philosophical assumptions into their work."[82] But, as I argue elsewhere,[83] smuggling philosophical assumptions into their work is precisely what geologists have done (usually unknowingly because of the educational brainwashing they received). Without the uniformitarian assumptions of philosophical naturalism, which have controlled geology (and astronomy) for the past two centuries, there would be no "evidence" for millions of years.

---

82. Ibid., p. 250.

83. See my earlier chapter in this book and also Terry Mortenson, "Philosophical Naturalism and the Age of the Earth: Are they related?" *The Master's Seminary Journal*, 15:1 (Spring 2004), p. 72–91, www.answersingenesis.org/docs2004/naturalismChurch.asp.

Endorsed by Hugh Ross, Don Stoner promotes the day-age theory and attempts to refute the young-earth arguments from the Jesus AGE verses.[84] First of all, he says that "Adam was created on the sixth day of creation, not the first. This was not the beginning of creation no matter how long or short the creation days were." But, as noted before, "the beginning of creation" refers to the whole first week and when Jesus said these words 4,000 years after the beginning, the sixth day was truly at the beginning of creation, on the level of precision that He was speaking (everyday language to a non-scientific audience).

Secondly, Stoner argues that κτίσις ("creation") in Mark 10:6 should be translated as "institution" so that Jesus should be understood to be talking about the beginning of the institution of marriage, not the beginning of creation. He bases this interpretation on the fact that in 1 Peter 2:13 κτίσις is translated in the NIV as "authority instituted." But Stoner is mistaken because he did not pay careful attention to his own English quote of Peter, where it says "to every authority instituted *among men*," i.e., to every human authority or "to every human institution" (as in NASB). The Greek text is clear: in πάσῃ ἀνθρωπίνῃ κτίσει the adjective ἀνθρωπίνῃ (human) modifies κτίσει (creation). An institutional authority (such as kings, governors, and slave masters, which Peter discusses in the context) is indeed a "human creation" (the literal translation of Peter's Greek words). But this is a very different contextual use of κτίσις than we find in Mark 10:6. Furthermore, Jesus could have easily said "from the first marriage" or "from the beginning of marriage" or "since God created man," if that is what He meant. Also, if we give κτίσις in Mark 10:6 the meaning "authority" or "institution," it makes no sense. What would "from the beginning of authority" or "beginning of institution" mean? To make it meaningful, Stoner would have to add a word to the text, which has no clear contextual justification.

Finally, Stoner ignores Mark 13:19 and Luke 11:50–51, which were discussed in two of Henry Morris' books cited by Stoner and which also expose the error of his interpretation of Mark 10:6. It is also noteworthy that neither the NASB nor the NIV (nor any other English translation I consulted) uses "authority" or "institution" as a translation for κτίσις in Mark 10:6. All of the above applies equally to the reasoning of Geisler and Ankerberg,[85] who in their opposition to the young-earth view, reason essentially the same as Stoner and Ross do on Mark 10:6.[86]

In their little 1991 booklet on evolution, Ankerberg and Weldon mention

---

84. Don Stoner, *A New Look at an Old Earth* (Eugene, OR: Harvest House, 1997), p. 53–54.

85. John Ankerberg and Norman Geisler, "Differing Views on the 'Days' of Genesis," www.johnankerberg.com/Articles/science/SC0704W1.htm. Also, see question 28 at www.johnankerberg.org/Articles/science/creation-questions/SC-creation-questions. htm. Geisler and Ankerberg also do not refer to Luke 11:50–51 and Mark 13:19.

86. See my response to the Geisler/Ankerberg article at www.answersingenesis.org/docs2004/1101ankerberg_response.asp.

Matthew 19:4–5 (parallel to Mark 10:6) as part of their defense of the young-earth view. They even state that they have studied the various old-earth reinterpretations of Genesis "in detail and believe they all have fatal biblical flaws."[87] Unfortunately, Ankerberg has since ignored Jesus' teaching, and his own reasoning based on it, and has abandoned the young-earth view by sympathizing with Hugh Ross's old-earth views in an October 2000 TV debate between Ross and Kent Hovind.[88] He has continued to promote Ross's teaching in a 2004 TV series and in another series with Kaiser and Ross in 2005[89] and by moderating (but not impartially) the 8-part TV series "The Great Debate" between Ken Ham and Dr. Jason Lisle from Answers in Genesis and Drs. Kaiser and Ross, which was televised starting in January 2006.[90]

Wenham contends correctly that Jesus "consistently treats the historical narratives as straightforward records of fact."[91] In his discussion that follows this statement he cites more than 50 passages from the gospels and refers once to Mark 10:6 and three times to Luke 11:50–51. After one mention of the latter passage Wenham states, "This last passage brings out his [Jesus'] sense of the unity of history and his grasp of its wide sweep. His eye surveys the whole course of history from 'the foundation of the world' to 'this generation.' "[92] Wenham notes that "Curiously enough, the narratives that are least acceptable to the so-called 'modern mind' are the very ones that he seemed most fond of choosing for his illustrations."[93] But then he strangely reasons later, on the same page in reference to Mark 10:2, that "the references to the ordinance of monogamy 'from the beginning of creation,' for instance, do not seem to necessitate a literal interpretation of chapters 1 and 2 of Genesis for their validity." However, in the process of justifying this view he overlooks Mark 10:6 and instead focuses on the laws of Moses referred in Mark 10:3–4 (cf. Deut. 24:1, 3). He seems not to have applied his own true statement to his thinking on origins: "Thus to our Lord the Old Testament is true as to its history, it is of divine authority, and its

---

87. John Ankerberg and John Weldon, *The Facts on Creation vs. Evolution* (Eugene, OR: Harvest House, 1991), p. 43.

88. See an analysis of this Ross-Hovind debate by Jonathan Sarfati at www.answersingenesis. org/news/ross_hovind_analysis.asp.

89. His two TV series on science and the Bible ("Why is the Big Bang Evidence that God Created the Universe?" [five programs in 2004] and "Can the Biblical Account of Creation be Reconciled with Scientific Evidence Today?" [four programs in 2004]) promoted the old-earth, day-age teachings of Hugh Ross. The 2005 series of five programs with Kaiser and Ross was "Are the Genesis Creation Days 24 Hours or Long Periods of Time?"

90. See www.ankerberg.com. The unedited debate is on DVD with my audio critical commentary (exposing many errors of fact and logic in the comments of Drs. Ross and Kaiser) and is available at www.answersingenesis.org/p/90-7-300.

91. John Wenham, *Christ and the Bible* (Downers Grove, IL: IVPress, 1973), p. 12.

92. Ibid., p. 12–13.

93. Ibid., p. 13.

:itings are inspired by God himself."[94]

:nham presents the same arguments in summary form in his contribution
lefense of inerrancy.[95] He gives good reasons for rejecting the notion that
:commodated His teachings to the (supposed) erroneous beliefs of His
poraries. He cites Luke 11:50–51 three times (quoting it in full once)
n that "Jesus consistently treats Old Testament historical narratives as
forward records of fact."[96] But in his listing of 27 gospel passages, he
:th Abel (instead of Adam) and again overlooks Mark 10:6 and 13:19.
e later does refer to Mark 10:2ff, he states:

> The teaching of monogamy as being God's plan from "the beginning
> eation" perhaps does not necessitate a literal interpretation of chapters
> 1 2 of Genesis for its validity; but subsequent reference to the changed
> situation under Moses seems to require it. Seldom can a non-literal mean-
> ing be applied without some loss of vividness and effectiveness.[97]

Sadly, Wenham's scholarly understatement weakens the authority of our
Lord's straightforward records of fact. And nowhere in his discussion does
Wenham explain on what grounds he does not accept the literal interpretation
of Genesis 1 and 2.

In a 1989 article on the history and future of evangelicalism, Wenham begins
with these words: "Many devout and thoughtful people are deeply worried as to
where evangelicalism is going."[98] He recounts with sadness the fact that many
evangelicals have slid into liberalism or at least a denial of inerrancy. He decries
the fact that the Christian faith and morals have lost much ground in the 20th
century. He admits that "Darwin raised problems for biblical Christianity which
neither the Victorians nor ourselves have ever wholly solved," but he strongly
rejects young-earth creationism. He considers it to be "far saner and healthier"
to reject Darwinism while still accepting the millions of years demanded by
evolutionary geologists and cosmologists, though he does not endorse any particular old-earth reinterpretation of Genesis.[99] In his proposed plan of action to
revive evangelicalism, he says that "we shall probably have to work again and
again at Genesis 1–11," but apparently that means coming up with new alternative old-earth reinterpretations, rather than accepting the straightforward literal
interpretation which Jesus and the apostles affirmed.[100] He concludes by saying,
"We want the Church united in utter loyalty to Christ and his revelation . . .

94. Ibid., p. 28.
95. John Wenham, "Christ's View of Scripture," in Geisler, *Inerrancy*, p. 3–38.
96. Ibid., p. 6.
97. Ibid., p. 7–8.
98. John Wenham, "Fifty Years of Evangelical Biblical Research: Retrospect and Prospect,"
    The Churchman, Vol. 103/3 (1989): p. 209. This influential paper was read at the
    prestigious Tyndale House Open Day at Cambridge University, May 14, 1988.
99. Ibid., p. 212.
100. Ibid., p. 217.

without compromising biblical principles."[101] But is it loyalty to Christ for us to ignore or reject our Lord's teaching regarding the literal truth of Genesis and the age of the earth?

Conclusion

The sayings of Jesus recorded in the gospels demonstrate that Jesus was clearly a young-earth creationist. Further evidence of Jesus' young-earth view can be seen in the NT writings of His faithful disciples, as will be seen in the next chapter. There is nothing in His teachings that would support an old-earth view (that Adam was created long ages after the beginning of creation).

These two figures illustrate the importance of Jesus's statements on this subject.

Figure 1

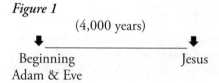

(4,000 years)

Beginning   Jesus
Adam & Eve

Figure 2

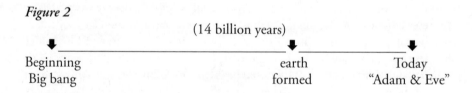

(14 billion years)

Beginning   earth   Today
Big bang   formed   "Adam & Eve"

As figure 1 illustrates, the time from when Jesus spoke these words as recorded by Mark and Luke back to the first day of creation would be about 4,000 years, assuming that there are no gaps in the Genesis genealogies. Jesus taught that Adam was at the beginning of creation (the 6th day on a 4,000-year time scale would be the "beginning of creation" in the non-technical everyday language that Jesus was using).

Contrast this to the evolutionary view, illustrated in figure 2, that all old-earth proponents embrace, namely that the big bang happened about 14 billion years ago, earth came into existence about 4.5 billion years ago and true *Homo sapiens* came into existence only a few hundred thousand years ago (or less). On a 14-billion-year time scale, this would mean that man came into existence at the *very tail end* of creation to-date.

So we cannot believe Jesus' view and the evolutionary view on the age of the earth at the same time. They are diametrically opposed to each other.

As noted before, early 19th century young-earth creationists (the scriptural

---

101. Ibid., p. 218.

geologists) pointed this out when the Church was quickly compromising with the new geological theory of millions of years.[102] Twentieth-century young-earth creationists have been using the Jesus AGE verses in support of this view for decades.

On the other hand, of the 61 old-earth proponents examined (many of them among the top scholars in evangelicalism) only three (Grudem, Collins, and Stoner) dealt with the Jesus AGE verses and attempted to rebut the young-earth creationist interpretation of them. But their old-earth arguments were found wanting. Sadly, many of these old-earth proponents refer to each others' writings (therefore circulating their misguided arguments). The vast majority of them do not attempt to refute the best young-earth arguments and in fact give little or no evidence of having even read the most current, leading young-earth writings.

There is only one reason that the above 61 old-earth authors hold on to the idea of millions of years. It is not because the idea of millions of years is taught in the Bible, for it is not. It is, as many of these men plainly indicate, because they are operating with the assumption that the evolutionary geologists and astronomers have proven scientifically that the creation is billions of years old. In addition to the statement by C. John Collins earlier in this essay, many other examples could be cited. Meredith Kline stated, "In this article I have advocated an interpretation of biblical cosmogony according to which Scripture is open to the current scientific view of a very old universe and, in that respect, does not discountenance the theory of the evolutionary origin of man."[103] But this assumption that the scientists have proven millions of years is simply false, as many of the resources cited in an appendix to this work demonstrate. I plead with my old-earth Christian readers to become acquainted with these scientific arguments for a young earth.

In light of this study, Mark Noll's scathing criticism of young-earth creationism is shown to be grossly in error. In his widely acclaimed book denouncing young-earthers for the alleged scandalous misuse of their minds, he states that they use

> . . . a fatally flawed interpretive scheme of the sort that no responsible

---

102. See footnote 30.

103. Kline, "Space and Time in the Genesis Cosmogony," p. 15, fn. 47. Likewise, James M. Boice said, "We have to admit here that the exegetical basis of the creationists is strong. . . . In spite of the careful biblical and scientific research that has accumulated in support of the creationists' view, there are problems that make the theory wrong to most (including many evangelical) scientists. . . . Data from various disciplines point to a very old earth and an even older universe." See Boice, *Genesis*, 1:57–62. Similar statements are Gleason Archer, *A Survey of Old Testament Introduction* (Chicago, IL: Moody, 1985), p. 187; J.P. Moreland, *Scaling the Secular City*, p. 219–220; Geisler, *Encyclopedia of Apologetics*, p. 270–272; Sailhamer, *Genesis Unbound*, p. 15; and Pattle P.T. Pun, "A Theory of Progressive Creationism," *Journal of the American Scientific Affiliation*, Vol. 39 (March 1987): p. 14. Many others could be cited.

Christian teacher in the history of the church ever endorsed before this century came to dominate the minds of American evangelicals on scientific questions . . . [These young-earthers are] almost completely adrift in using the mind for careful thought about the world. . . . thinking they are honoring the Scriptures, yet who interpret the Scriptures on questions of science and world affairs in ways that fundamentally contradict the deeper, broader, and historically well-established meanings of the Bible itself.[104]

Sadly, Noll largely bases his indictment of young-earth creationists on the historical interpretations of a secular historian of science, Ronald Numbers,[105] whom (amazingly) Noll describes as a "truly professional" historian who has "few bones to pick with basic Christian teachings."[106] Numbers is certainly a justifiably respected historian of science. But as a self-proclaimed agnostic (and former Seventh Day Adventist who was taught young-earth creationism), Numbers is far from being unbiased or neutral on basic Christian doctrines — he rejects most, if not all, of them! Furthermore, Noll also accepts the condescending evaluation of young-earthers by James Moore (a former evangelical, turned skeptic), and many other non-Christian historians. He offers no substantive exegesis of Scripture to defend his old-earth views and completely overlooks the Jesus AGE verses as he harangues young-earthers for shallow thinking and lack of scholarship. Judging from his text and footnotes, we might justifiably conclude that the only young-earth literature he has read is the introduction to Whitcomb and Morris's *The Genesis Flood* (published 33 years before Noll's book!), although he seems to have read a considerable amount of literature from theistic evolutionists and progressive creationists. So where does the scandalous use of the evangelical mind really lie? And just who is using a fatally flawed hermeneutic to interpret Genesis? It is truly sad to see such a justly respected Christian historian ignore the overwhelming witness to young-earth creationism in the first 18 centuries of Church history.

We need to heed the words spoken by God to Peter, James, and John on the Mount of Transfiguration. While the gospel writers record different aspects of God's declaration about the nature of Jesus' Sonship (Luke 9:35, Mark 9:7,

---

104. Mark A. Noll, *The Scandal of the Evangelical Mind* (Grand Rapids, MI: Eerdmans, 1994), p. 13–14. He said essentially the same thing in his widely read article: Mark A. Noll, "The Scandal of the Evangelical Mind," *Christianity Today* (Oct. 25, 1994): p. 29–32.

105. Numbers does not discuss history before the 1850s. He therefore draws the erroneous conclusion that the young-earth view is a modern invention. Perhaps at the time he wrote this book he knew nothing about the young-earth "scriptural geologists" of the early 19th century. As my book *The Great Turning Point* (Green Forest, AR: Master Books, 2004) shows, it is the old-earth view that is novel in the Church. Shortly after publication, I sent Numbers a copy, so he knows now.

106. Noll, *Scandal*, p. 14.

Matt. 17:5), they precisely agree in their quotation of God's command: "Listen to Him!" Evangelicals, and especially evangelical scholars, need to listen to what Jesus says about Genesis 1–11 and the age of the earth.

I return to a quote, which I used at the beginning of this essay, but which is worth repeating. Ravi Zacharias is correct to say that, "Jesus claimed to be 'the truth.' Let us test his claims and teachings. If they are true, what He says matters more than anything else in life."[107] Jesus made some sobering statements about the importance of believing His words. In John 8:31–32 we read, "So Jesus was saying to those Jews who had believed Him, 'If you continue in My word, then you are truly My disciples; and you will know the truth, and the truth will make you free.'" And in John 12:47–50 He warns:

> If anyone hears My sayings and does not keep them, I do not judge him; for I did not come to judge the world, but to save the world. He who rejects Me and does not receive My sayings, has one who judges him; the word I spoke is what will judge him at the last day. For I did not speak on My own initiative, but the Father Himself who sent Me has given Me a commandment as to what to say and what to speak. I know that His commandment is eternal life; therefore the things I speak, I speak just as the Father has told Me.

Among the words which the Father commanded Jesus to say were those in Mark 10:6, 13:19, and Luke 11:50–51. Those verses are also relevant to Paul's warning about how we respond to the teaching of Jesus: "If anyone advocates a different doctrine and does not agree with sound words, those of our Lord Jesus Christ, and with the doctrine conforming to godliness, he is conceited and understands nothing" (1 Tim. 6:3–4). And in John 5:45–47, Jesus says, "Do not think that I will accuse you before the Father; the one who accuses you is Moses, in whom you have set your hope. For if you believed Moses, you would believe Me, for he wrote about Me. But if you do not believe his writings, how will you believe My words?"

Given this study, it seems legitimate to conclude that if we do not know and believe Christ's words about the age of the earth, then we may not believe Moses' words either. But if we do believe and submit to the authority of Jesus' clear and straightforward words concerning the age of the earth, then we must believe Moses' clear and straightforward words about the details of creation week, the Fall, the Flood, the Tower of Babel, and the other historical facts in Genesis 1–11.

We cannot with consistency follow the teachings of our Lord Jesus Christ and at the same time follow the teachings of the evolutionary geologists and astrophysicists (and the Christian geologists and astrophysicists who promote their old-earth teachings in the Church). As the old-earth proponent C. John Collins rightly reasons, if millions of years indeed transpired before Adam was

---

107. Zacharias, *Can Man Live*, p. 131.

created and Jesus believed Adam was at the beginning of creation, "then we must conclude that Jesus was mistaken (or worse, misleading), and therefore he can't be God."[108]

Let us no longer ignore our Lord's teaching. If we call Him Lord, can we have a different view of Genesis and the age of the earth than He had and in addition say that the age of the earth does not matter?

---

108. Collins, *Science and Faith*, p. 106.

Chapter 12

Apostolic Witness to Genesis Creation and the Flood

Ron Minton

Introduction

My outlook on creation studies was influenced when, in 1970, I read *The Genesis Flood* by Drs. John C. Whitcomb and Henry Morris. I was a young sailor, and eager to learn the Word of God. One of my teachers at a Christian Servicemen's Center in New London, Connecticut, taught a series of lessons using that book. When I got out of the navy, I wanted a degree in Greek so I went to Grace College in Winona Lake, Indiana. Before classes started, my wife and I attended some sessions at the old Winona Lake Bible Conference. There, on several occasions, we heard John Whitcomb speaking in an outdoor amphitheater and were amazed at his teaching ability and his commitment to the truth of the Word of God. As it turned out, Dr. Whitcomb and Norma were our neighbors, living just a few blocks down the road for the eight years I was at Grace College and Grace Theological Seminary. After I finished college, I completed the M.Div and ThM from Grace, taking several classes from Dr. Whitcomb. No one has enabled me to appreciate the truth about God's creation more than Dr. John C. Whitcomb. I hope that my small contribution to this book will help others also.

What did the Apostles think about creation week, Noah's Flood and the age of the earth? Every Christian should examine the apostolic teachings found in Acts, the New Testament epistles, and the Book of Revelation, and note what they said about these subjects. Old-earth creationists (OEC), whether they are theologians, Genesis commentators, or scientists, have generally neglected the witness of the Apostles. James Buswell's theology text has no discussion of the

Apostles' views on the historicity of Genesis or age of the earth.[1] Wayne Grudem has a more thorough discussion about creation and the age of the earth, but also does not consider the apostolic teaching on this point.[2] The same is true of Lewis and Demarest.[3] In his popular commentaries, J. Vernon McGee rejects biological evolution and believes Noah's Flood was global but accepts the billions of years for the age of the earth.[4] However, he does not discuss the chronological implications of the Genesis 5 and 11 genealogies, Exodus 20:11, or the Apostles' teaching related to the literal historicity of Genesis. Kenneth Mathews[5] and John Skinner[6] prefer the day-age view and place geology over Scripture when it comes to the age of the earth, but they ignore the words of the Apostles in this area. Creationists who espouse the Intelligent Design (ID) movement have also not dealt with the apostolic teaching.[7]

One can only wonder why OEC overlook the Apostles' teaching on this subject. As will be seen in this study, there is not a single statement in the apostolic writings that would incline one toward believing the earth is millions of years old or that the Flood of Noah was anything less than global in extent. On the contrary, the NT writers teach both recent creation and a worldwide Flood, just as Jesus and the OT writers did. Even though other portions of Scripture speak of the creation and the Flood in more detail, the voice of the Apostles is important and should be heeded. Most NT books refer to, quote, or allude to the creation account in Genesis 1–2. Of the NT epistles, Romans

---

Unless otherwise noted, all Scripture in this chapter is from the NKJV of the Bible.

1. James Oliver Buswell, *A Systematic Theology of the Christian Religion* (Grand Rapids, MI: Zondervan, 1962).

2. Wayne Grudem, *Systematic Theology* (Grand Rapids, MI: Zondervan, 1994), p. 275–306. Grudem seems to lean toward the day-age view.

3. Gordon R. Lewis and Bruce A. Demarest, *Integrative Theology* (Grand Rapids, MI: Zondervan, 1996), Vol. 2:29, 39ff. They prefer the day-age view and also depend on geologists for their views on the earth's age: "Geology must determine the length of days in Genesis" (p. 29).

4. J. Vernon McGee, *Genesis* (Nashville, TN: Thomas Nelson, 1991), p. 60–61, 133.

5. See the long introduction to Kenneth A. Mathews, *Genesis 1–11:26: The New American Commentary* (Nashville, TN: Broadman and Holman, 1996). Under the question of whether Genesis 1 is history or story, he favors the framework hypothesis, but also concludes "that the creation narrative claims historicity" (p. 111). He discusses the nature of Genesis in light of critical scholarship and Ancient Near Eastern literature. He also mentions the modern creation-evolution debate, but he says nothing about the Apostles' views on Genesis.

6. John Skinner, *Genesis: The International Critical Commentary* (Edinburgh: T&T Clark, 1930, 2nd ed.) takes a view that Genesis is a mixture of history, legend, and myth. But he considers no evidence from the Apostles on the matter.

7. In William A. Dembski, *Intelligent Design* (Downers Grove, IL: Inter Varsity, 1999), p. 187–236 (chapters 7 and 8, the last two in the book), is found a discussion about science and religion, but no analysis of the apostolic teaching on creation, the Flood, and the age of the earth.

and Hebrews speak the most about creation, while the shorter books generally refer to creation less.[8]

The NT writers held that a personal God directly created the world — a view that was not held by philosophers and/or unbelievers in the first centuries B.C. and A.D.[9] While most comments made in the epistles about creation say nothing with regard to the age of the creation, a few passages do show that NT writers indeed held to a recent creation. Only by resorting to eisegesis and by ignoring contexts do old-earth proponents "find" evidence for their views in Acts and the NT epistles.

NT Passages

The NT passages which make comments that help us in formulating a doctrine of creation, the Flood, and the age of the earth are quoted and discussed below in the order in which they appear in the NT. In many cases it will be sufficient to make only a few comments since the teaching of the passages is quite obvious, but key passages will require careful but limited examination.

Acts 3:21: . . . whom heaven must receive until the times of restoration of all things, which God has spoken by the mouth of all His holy prophets since the world began.

Peter speaks of the "restoration of all things" (ἀποκαταστάσεως πάντων, *apokatastaseos panton*). The genitive neuter construction πάντων ("of all things") indicates that Peter is referring to all of creation, not just people. And, as he says, the OT prophets did speak about this restoration of all things. Several passages (Isa. 11:6–10; 35:1–10; 65:24–25; Ezek. 34:23–31) indicate that this restoration will affect the animals, making them no longer carnivorous or dangerous to man. Peter makes this statement in the midst of his proclamation of the redemptive work of Christ. He thereby indicates that the Fall had an adverse affect on all of creation (including man and animals) so that it is now waiting to be restored when Jesus Christ returns. Paul and John teach the same in Colossians 1, Romans 8, and Revelation 21 and 22 (to be discussed later). Peter's reference to "restoration" strongly implies that in the future the creation will be very similar to the pre-Fall world,

---

8. See also Ekkehardt Mueller, "Creation in the NT," *Journal of the Adventist Theological Society* 15:1 (Spring 2004): p. 47. He agrees that Galatians, Philippians, 1 and 2 Thessalonians, 2 Timothy, Titus, Philemon, and 1, 2, 3 John do not directly refer to creation.

9. Around A.D. 180, the apologist Theophilus of Antioch said, "On the fourth day, the luminaries were made. This was because God, who possesses foreknowledge, knew the follies of the vain philosophers. He knew that they were going to say that things that grow on the earth are produced from the heavenly bodies. For in this way, the philosophers exclude God." *See Theophilus*, 2:90, in David W. Bercot, ed., *A Dictionary of Early Christian Beliefs* (Peabody, MA: Hendrickson, 1998), p. 179. See also Ernest L. Abel, *Ancient Views of the Origins of Life* (Cranbury, NJ: Associated University Presses, 1973), p. 66–76.

when, as Genesis 1:29–30 teaches, animals were herbivores. The entire earth, even the universe was affected by the Fall and so the restoration will affect the same.

> **Acts 14:15–17:** (15) and saying, "Men, why are you doing these things? We also are men with the same nature as you, and preach to you that you should turn from these useless things to the living God, who made the heaven, the earth, the sea, and all things that are in them, (16) who in bygone generations allowed all nations to walk in their own ways. (17) Nevertheless He did not leave Himself without witness, in that He did good, gave us rain from heaven and fruitful seasons, filling our hearts with food and gladness."

Paul boldly declares to these polytheists that God made the heavens, earth, the oceans, and everything in them. The Greek language translated at the end of verse 15 as "made the heaven, the earth, the sea, and all things that are in them" is identical to the wording of the Greek translation of Exodus 20:11 found in the Septuagint, the version used by Jesus and the Apostles. That exact wording is used nowhere else in the OT. So Paul was clearly quoting from that verse, which says that God created in six days.[10] Paul's statement about God's creative acts is the basis of his teaching about the gospel. God has borne witness to himself in the creation, especially in graciously giving people rain, food, and joy.

> **Acts 17:24–31:** (24) "God, who made the world and everything in it, since He is Lord of heaven and earth, does not dwell in temples made with hands. (25) Nor is He worshiped with men's hands, as though He needed anything, since He gives to all life, breath, and all things. (26) And He has made from one blood every nation of men to dwell on all the face of the earth, and has determined their preappointed times and the boundaries of their dwellings, (27) so that they should seek the Lord, in the hope that they might grope for Him and find Him, though He is not far from each one of us; (28) for in Him we live and move and have our being, as also some of your own poets have said, 'For we are also His offspring.' (29) Therefore, since we are the offspring of God, we ought not to think that the Divine Nature is like gold or silver or stone, something shaped by art and man's devising. (30) Truly, these times of ignorance God overlooked, but now commands all men everywhere to repent, (31) because He has appointed a day on which He will judge the world in righteousness by the Man whom He has ordained. He has given assurance of this to all by raising Him from the dead."

---

10. Those were literal days, as Trevor Craigen has argued in this volume regarding Exodus 20:11. There is no evidence in all of Paul's references to creation that he would have taken Exodus 20:11 to mean anything other than literal days, just as the Jews in his day did (as Josephus indicates in his *The Antiquities of the Jews*, Book 1, Chapters 1–3).

Here, Paul teaches the Athenian philosophers that God made not only the world, but also everything in it (v. 24). "World" here in Greek is κόσμος (*kosmos*), and in the context is synonymous with "heaven and earth." In verse 26 Paul says all people came from one man, Adam,[11] which again indicates that Paul accepted the Genesis creation account as factual. He also says Jesus will judge the world (31) in righteousness, indicating that he held to a literal future judgment.

> **Romans 1:18–25:** (18) For the wrath of God is revealed from heaven against all ungodliness and unrighteousness of men, who suppress the truth in unrighteousness, (19) because what may be known of God is manifest in them, for God has shown *it* to them. (20) For since the creation of the world His invisible *attributes* are clearly seen, being understood by the things that are made, *even* His eternal power and Godhead, so that they are without excuse, (21) because, although they knew God, they did not glorify *Him* as God, nor were thankful, but became futile in their thoughts, and their foolish hearts were darkened. (22) Professing to be wise, they became fools, (23) and changed the glory of the incorruptible God into an image made like corruptible man — and birds and four-footed animals and creeping things. (24) Therefore God also gave them up to uncleanness, in the lusts of their hearts, to dishonor their bodies among themselves, (25) who exchanged the truth of God for the lie, and worshiped and served the creature rather than the Creator, who is blessed forever. Amen.

Paul boldly declares that the world was created by God and that everyone knows it,[12] but he says much more. Many commentaries on this passage describe how all people are responsible for their unbelief because the fingerprints of God are found everywhere in His creation. Most, however, say little or nothing about the time aspect in the words "since the creation of the world" (ἀπὸ κτίσεως κόσμου *apo ktiseos kosmou*).[13] Old-earth advocates generally believe the earth

---

11. First Corinthians 15:45 makes this very clear.

12. In Rom. 1:25, God is called the Creator by using the participle form of the verb κτίζω (*ktizo*, "to create"). However, 1 Pet. 4:19 has the only NT use of κτίστης (*ktistes*, a masculine noun) meaning "creator." The verb κτίζω is used 13 times in the NT (10 by Paul), and in all 13 references God the Father or God the Son is the Creator (Mark 13:19; Rom. 1:25; 1 Cor. 11:9; Eph. 2:10, 15, 3:9, 4:24; Col. 1:16, 3:10; 1 Tim. 4:3; Rev. 4:11, 10:6).

13. For example, see John Brown, *Romans* (Minneapolis, MN: James Family Christian Publishers, 1883, reprint 1979), p. 13ff; Charles Hodge, *Commentary on the Epistle to the Romans* (Grand Rapids, MI: Eerdmans, 1886, reprint 1950), p. 37; John Murray, *The Epistle to the Romans* in *NICNT* (Grand Rapids, MI: Eerdmans, 1959), p. 38–40; Manford G. Gutzke, *Plain Talk on Romans* (Grand Rapids, MI: Zondervan, 1976), p. 16–17; William Hendriksen, *Exposition of Paul's Epistle to the Romans* (Grand Rapids, MI: Baker, 1980), p. 69–71; Ernst Kasemann, *Commentary on Romans*, trans. and ed.

was in existence millions of years before man. However, Paul's wording indicates that man is as old as the creation itself, and that people have been able to observe God's witness to himself in creation right from the very beginning of creation.

The phrase ἀπὸ κτίσεως κόσμου in verse 20 is translated as a temporal genitive ("since the creation of the world") in many translations.[14] Some translations render it as "from the creation of the world,"[15] which when combined with the present participle νοούμενα (*noomena*, "are understood") and the present indicative verb καθορᾶται, *kathoratai*, "are clearly seen") might lead one to interpret it as a genitive of means "from (or, by) looking at the present created world." But several considerations favor the temporal sense, which would mean "ever since the time when the world was created at the beginning."[16]

by Geofrey W. Bromiley (Grand Rapids, MI: Eerdmans, 1980), p. 37ff; F.F. Bruce, *Romans* (Grand Rapids, MI: Eerdmans, 1985, revised ed.), p. 79–80; James D.G. Dunn, *Romans 1–8* in *Word Biblical Commentary* (Dallas, TX: Word, 1988), p. 57–59; John MacArthur, *Romans 1–8* (Chicago, IL: Moody, 1991), p. 78–82. MacArthur gives three pages of evidence for God's creation, but does not mention that men saw the evidence soon after the creation. See also James R. Edwards, *Romans* in *NIBC* (Peabody, MA: Hendrickson, 1992), p. 50–52, and Joseph A. Fitzmyer, *Romans* in *The Anchor Bible* (New York: Doubleday, 1993), p. 280. But Fitzmyer does say "*apo* . . . is preferably taken in a temporal sense." Others favoring the temporal interpretation include William S. Plummer, *Commentary on Romans* (Grand Rapids, MI: Kregel, n.d., reprint 1993), p. 64–65; Douglas Moo, in *The Epistle to the Romans*, in *NICNT* (Grand Rapids, MI: Eerdmans, 1996), p. 104–106.

14. ESV, NKJV, NAS, NIV, NLT, and NRSV. See also James H. Moulton, *A Grammar of New Testament Greek*, Vol. 3 (Edinburgh: T&T Clark, 1963), p. 259, where Moulton lists a number of examples of the temporal sense of ἀπὸ including Rom. 1:20, and Frederick William Danker, *A Greek-English Lexicon of the New Testament and other Early Christian Literature* (Chicago, IL: Univ. of Chicago Press, 2000, 3rd ed. *BDAG*), p. 105, where Romans 1:20 is listed under ἀπὸ, "of time *from* . . . *(on), since.*" Dan Wallace concurs in his *Greek Grammar Beyond the Basics* (Grand Rapids, MI: Zondervan, 1996), p. 123, noting that emphasis "is placed on the beginning."

15. KJV, KJ21, HCSB.

16. Others agree that the temporal phrase is in view and is important. See C.E.B. Cranfield, *Commentary on Romans*, in *ICC* (Edinburgh: T&T Clark, 1975), p. 114–115. F. Godet, *Commentary on St. Paul's Epistles to the Romans* (New York: Funk and Wagnells, 1883), p. 103, says ἀπὸ "indicates that the time of creation was the point of departure for this revelation which still lasts." Similar explanations are found in Robert Haldane, *Exposition of the Epistle to the Romans* (London: Banners of Truth Trust, 1835, reprinted 1958), p. 58; John Gill, *An Exposition of the Epistle of Paul to the Romans* (Springfield, MO: Particular Baptist Press, 2002 reprint of 1746 edition), p. 28, notes," this is no new discovery, but what men have had . . . ever since the world was created." In *Romans*, p. 105, Moo does not say whether he thinks the creation was thousands or billions of years ago, but, following Fitzmyer, Moo does explain that we have known God *since* the creation event. The creation event marks the time when the information began to be known by men.

First, Paul surely would have had in mind such passages as Job 12:7–10, Psalm 19:1, and Psalm 97:6. Writing about a thousand years before Paul, the Psalmist declares that the heavens show forth God's glory and righteousness. A thousand years before that, Job said that the beast, birds, fish, and earth itself tell us of the Creator and His life-giving power. So this witness of creation was seen by men long before Paul. Secondly, if Paul was only referring to the present witness of creation in his day, then most of mankind in history would be exempt from his condemnation here. But that would be inconsistent with the whole tenor of his argument through the first five chapters of Romans. Paul is speaking about the whole human race throughout history. Furthermore, Paul says here that since that time, God's invisible attributes have always been clearly seen and they are understood continuously (present tense).[17] As Moo points out, "Those who perceive the attributes of God in creation must be the same as those who suppress the truth in unrighteousness and are therefore liable to the wrath of God."[18] Murray concurs, saying that this witness of creation is made "to all men, at all times . . . without any limitation of time or persons."[19] Furthermore, Paul indicates in his statements in Lystra (Acts 14:15–17) and Athens (Acts 17:18–31) that God has throughout history revealed His existence and goodness by sending rain and giving food to people and establishing the boundaries of their habitation.

It is unlikely that Paul's words ἀπὸ κτίσεως κόσμου mean merely "from the present creation" or "by looking at the present creation," as seen in Paul's day, for in this case most people who have ever lived would not be held accountable to God for suppressing the truth of the creation's witness to Him. Also, if Paul is only speaking of the creation visible in his day, he could have said ἀπὸ νῦν κόσμου ("from the present world") or ἀπὸ νῦν κτίσεως ("from the present creation").[20] The aorist verbs in this section (verses 18–32), which in English translations are translated as past tense, further support the conclusion that ἀπὸ κτίσεως κόσμου is a temporal phrase. Most commentaries agree on the temporal aspect.[21] Therefore, Paul is referring to unrighteous people throughout history who have

---

17. The Greek word νοούμενα ("being understood") is a gnomic present participle and the emphasis is on the continual availability of the information about God. It is true all the time. See Wallace, *Greek Grammar*, p. 523, for more information on this kind of construction.

18. Moo, *Romans*, p. 105.

19. Murray, *Romans*, p. 38. Schreiner also agrees that Paul is looking back through time to creation week. See Thomas Schreiner, *Romans* (Grand Rapids, MI: Baker, 1998), p. 84–85. In the 2008 edition of his notes, Constable said that the message "has gone out since the creation of the world in every generation," www.soniclight.com/constable/notes/pdf/romans.pdf.

20. Paul and Peter both use this kind of language to refer to their contemporary world: 1 Tim. 6:17, 2 Tim. 4:10, Tit. 2:12, and 2 Pet. 3:7.

21. This is noted in R.C. Sproul, John Gerstner, and Arthur Lindsley, *Classical Apologetics* (Grand Rapids, MI: Zondervan, 1984), p. 44–45.

seen this witness of creation to God and have rejected it. Thus, the NAS and NIV translations of "having been clearly seen being understood through what has been made," accurately convey the sense of Paul's words.

Finally, verses 23 and 25 indicate that the eternal God is the Creator — there is a contrast between created beings and the Creator. Satan first exchanged God's truth for a lie (Gen. 3:1–4), and this form of idolatry (making God what one wants Him to be) has been practiced by every generation since. Indeed, Paul's reference to the conscience in Romans 2:14 and his indictment of all Jews and Gentiles in chapter 3 shows that this unrighteous suppression of truth applies to all the descendants of Adam.

So Paul is speaking of the witness of creation from his day all the way back to creation week in Genesis 1, which implies that mankind is as old as the rest of creation. This is incompatible with the evolutionary view that most of the creation existed for millions of years before man came into existence. Man was not created 10 billion years after the first stars were born and 4.5 billion years after the earth formed and millions of years after the dinosaurs, as evolutionary time scales indicate. Romans 1 is simply incompatible with any attempt to insert millions of years into Genesis. It shows that man was there at the beginning of creation (on the sixth literal day of history) to observe the handiwork of God's eternal power and wisdom.

> **Romans 5:12–14, 19:** (12) Therefore, just as through one man sin entered the world, and death through sin, and thus death spread to all men, because all sinned— (13) For until the law sin was in the world, but sin is not imputed when there is no law. (14) Nevertheless death reigned from Adam to Moses, even over those who had not sinned according to the likeness of the transgression of Adam, who is a type of Him who was to come. . . . (19) For as by one man's disobedience many were made sinners, so also by one Man's obedience many will be made righteous.

Paul says that sin, and then death, came into the human race as a result of Adam's disobedience, and there was nothing other than man's sin that caused death to originate.[22] It is clear that Paul accepted the Genesis account of sin and the Curse as literal history, and there is no reason to suppose he would not have accepted all of the Genesis record as accurate. Romans 5 speaks of human death, but in chapter 8 Paul explains further that it was more than humans that were affected by Adam's sin. There was no death in the world, until Adam sinned.[23]

---

22. John C. Whitcomb, *The Early Earth* (Grand Rapids, MI: Baker, 1986, rev. ed.), p. 32, summarizes what many have said, "Every effort to accommodate the long ages of evolutionary geology, whether before, during, or between the days of creation, hopelessly compromises the biblical concept of the curse and death coming into the world only after man's rebellion (cf. Rom. 5:12; 8:18–23)." Romans 5:12 leaves no doubt about the relationship of sin and human death.

23. The NT word κόσμος ("world") refers primarily to people, as in John 3:16, but the

"Until the law" (5:13) means from Adam to Moses. Therefore, sin was from Adam, and no person has avoided the effects of sin.[24]

Stambaugh discusses the relationship between sin and death in the next chapter of this book.[25] Similar concepts concerning Adam and Eve, sin, the Fall, and death can be found in other passages later in the chapter.[26] In summary, Paul accepted the Genesis account of man's sin as factual. Adam sinned and that brought both spiritual and physical death into the human race.

> **Romans 8:19–23:** (19) For the earnest expectation of the creation eagerly waits for the revealing of the sons of God. (20) For the creation was subjected to futility, not willingly, but because of Him who subjected *it* in hope; (21) because the creation itself also will be delivered from the bondage of corruption into the glorious liberty of the children of God. (22) For we know that the whole creation groans and labors with birth pangs together until now. (23) Not only *that*, but we also who have the first-fruits of the Spirit, even we ourselves groan within ourselves, eagerly waiting for the adoption, the redemption of our body.

Here Paul speaks about three aspects of the creation: its past curse, present suffering, and future restoration. Groaning is prominent here. Groaning is a very deep inward and personal response to pain, frustration, or agony.[27] It is a universal language — even God's Spirit groans (Rom. 8:26). For all of creation, groaning cannot be avoided because it is part of God's bigger plan. Paul says that the creation is groaning in bondage to corruption. What does he mean by the word κτίσις (*ktisis*, "creation")?

The context of κτίσις is always important in determining who or what it refers to. The word has several meanings in the NT:[28] (1) everything that has

---

physical universe was affected by sin as well. See the discussions below.

24. Numerous interpreters have given up the authority of Scripture (Rom. 5:12) because modern science seems to contradict the Bible in this area. This has been observed by many. See Whitcomb, *The Early Earth*, p. 77, 79, 119, and 142.

25. For another helpful discussion of the sin and death issue, see Fred VanDyke, "Theological Problems of Theistic Evolution," *Journal of the American Scientific Affiliation*. 38:1 (March 1986): p. 11–18 (http://www.asa3.org/ASA/PSCF/1986/JASA3-86VanDyke.html). He shows that "In the biblical view, 'death' (both physical and spiritual) and sin are inseparably linked, with the former, being the explicit, ultimate manifestation of the latter" (cf. Rom. 6:23). Although he does not mention the day-age theory, on page 16 he does correctly say, "Objections raised so far apply not only to theistic evolution, but to the gap theory and progressive evolution as well."

26. See Rom. 8:1–22; 1 Cor. 11:3–12; 1 Tim. 2:11–14; 1 Pet.3:18–20; 2 Pet. 2:4–9, 3:3–7; Jude 14.

27. For a good discussion, see Bob Deffinbaugh, "From Groaning to Glory" at www.bible.org/page.php?page_id=2306, accessed April 3, 2008.

28. The word κτίσις is found 18 times in the NT, 10 of which refer to the whole of creation. In our passage, verses 19, 20, and 21 all have this first meaning — "the whole

been created, (2) an individual living or non-living creature, (3) all humans collectively (may be figurative for a group), (4) born-again people (Christians), or (5) a government institution.[29] Some identify the groaning with the subhuman creation or "nature." Moo notes that the reason creation is eagerly anticipating is that "the subhuman creation itself is not what it should be, or what God intended it to be. It has been subjected to frustration. In light of Paul's obvious reference to the Genesis 3 narrative — Murray labels these verses 'Paul's Commentary on Genesis 3:17–18' . . . Humanity's fall into sin marred the 'goodness' of God's creation, and creation has ever since been in a state of 'frustration.' "[30] Morris comes to the same basic conclusion.[31] Nelson says, "Paul's reference in Romans 8:19 is probably the widest possible, without intention to exclude any category."[32] This fits Paul's language of "the whole creation" in verse 22.

However, not everything God created was "subjected to frustration" because of Adam's sin. Satan and demons are creatures, but they fell when they sinned of their own will, which must have happened before Adam sinned. Neither they nor the angels will be part of the redemption that is spoken of here.[33] The unsaved will not be "delivered from bondage" (v. 21), neither do they eagerly await Jesus' return. Therefore, they are not in Paul's focus here. Neither are the saved, for in this passage Paul is comparing and contrasting "the creation" with believers. We conclude then that Paul is referring to the whole subhuman creation.[34]

---

of creation." Yet even here, as will be seen, there may be more precision in what we mean by "all creation."

29. These are my categories, but other lists are similar. See BDAG, p. 456; Harry A. Hahne, *The Birth Pangs of Creation: The Eschatological Transformation of the Natural World in Romans 8:19–22* (Toronto: Tyndale Seminary, 1999). For full details, see Harry Alan Hahne, *The Corruption and Redemption of Creation. Nature in Romans 8:19–22 and Jewish Apocalyptic Literature* (Edinburgh: T&T Clark, Library of NT Studies 336 — also his ThD. Dissertation, University of Toronto, 1997), p. 353–361. The NT usage is this: (1) everything that has been created (Mark 10:6, 13:19; Rom. 1:20, 8:19–21; Col. 1:15; Heb. 9:11; 2 Pet. 3:4; Rev. 3:14) , (2) an individual created thing (living or non living) (Rom. 1:25, 8:39; Heb. 4:13), (3) all humans collectively (may be figurative for a group, Mark 16:15; Col. 1:23), (4) newborn people (Christians) (2 Cor. 5:17; Gal. 6:15), (5) government institution (1 Pet. 2:13).

30. Moo, *Romans*, p. 515–516.

31. Leon Morris, *The Epistle to the Romans* (Grand Rapids, MI: Eerdmans, 1988), p. 320–322, argues that all of the non-human creation was cursed, not just humans.

32. Joseph Lee Nelson Jr., "The Groaning of Creation: an Exegetical Study of Romans 8:18–27" (Th.D. Dissertation, Union Theological Seminary of Virginia, 1969), p. 192 and 253. However, he also says that because of the words οὐχ ἑκοῦσα (*ouch hekousa*, "not willingly"), the creation in this reference should probably be limited to the non-human order (p. 195).

33. Demons do not eagerly await the coming of Jesus (v. 19). Also, unfallen angels have not been affected and subjected to the corruption that Paul mentions (v. 20–21).

34. The KJV translation of κτίσις as "creature" in verses 19, 20, and 21 (but as "creation" in v. 22) is therefore not as clear as those translations which render this word as "creation"

When did the creation come into this bondage? Paul indicates that this bondage commenced when God cursed the creation at the Fall.[35] Several considerations point to this conclusion. First, the description of the present creation in Romans 8 certainly does not fit the description at the end of Genesis 1, namely, that the whole creation was "very good." Second, Paul's language of "groans and labors with birth pangs" is reminiscent of the judgment made against Eve in Genesis 3:16. Third, since the liberation of the creation (and its eager expectation of that freedom from decay) is connected to the final redemption of believers' bodies (and their eager expectation of that freedom from death), it seems clear that the curse on nature (bondage to corruption) began with the fall (bondage to sin) of man. The phrase "the creation was subjected to futility" is a divine aorist passive: God is the one who subjected the creation to the curse.[36] Contrary to what some OEC say,[37] man's sin ruined God's magnificent creation. If the world existed for millions of years with animal death and extinction and other natural evils, then God's curse on creation did nothing.

The groaning of creation is man's fault because it came about only when man sinned. It is an irreversible process of decay and corruption — all of creation is aging and dying.[38] This leads to futility and nothing we can do can change this. Yet it was God who subjected creation to futility (Rom. 8:20), and Paul says it was "in hope." This seems impossible because futility is the opposite of hope. The reason God did this was because of love — He created all things for full potential and fellowship. The only means of restoring creation to God's original plan was to have Christ redeem it. This is real hope, and Paul uses the word hope not only here in verse 20, but five more times in this context (verses 24–25).

---

throughout this passage.

35. As we will see, this happened when Adam sinned. Edwards, *Romans*, p. 213, says it "probably refers to curse of creation in Genesis." Godet, *Romans*, p. 314–317 (and numerous other writers) concur.

36. On the divine passive, also called theological passive, see Wallace, *Greek Grammar*, p. 437–438. See Moo, *Romans*, p. 516, "Paul must be referring to God, who alone had the right and the power to condemn all of creation."

37. Hugh Ross, *Creation and Time: A Biblical and Scientific Perspective on the Creation-Date Controversy* (Colorado Springs, CO: NavPress), p. 55 and 65, believes that sin had little affect on the physical world.

38. Some have hinted that man's pollution and abuse of the planet are the cause of the "futility" Paul speaks of. However, in "Theological Problems of Theistic Evolution," VanDyke observes, "Likewise, the 'futility' to which creation is subjected (Rom. 8:19ff) cannot be referring only to human exploitation and pollution of creation. The society of that writer's day was no match for its modern counterpart in these activities. At that time major portions of the planet were still largely unaffected by any significant human exploitation. Yet the 'whole creation' groans in its longing for redemption. The futility and corruption, to which creation is now enslaved, is something which, though originating in man, now exists independent of human activities" (p. 16).

Paul leaves no doubt that the deliverance from the condemnation is in the future. He uses the phrases "eagerly awaits" (v. 19), "will be delivered" (v. 21), "until now" (v. 22), and "eagerly awaiting" (v. 23). This deliverance of the creation will happen when believers receive their immortal glorified bodies.[39] In reference to the believer's future bodies and Romans 8:19–23, Grudem correctly reasons, "There will be no more thorns or thistles, no more floods or droughts, no more deserts or uninhabitable jungles, no more earthquakes or tornadoes, no more poisonous snakes or bees that sting or mushrooms that kill."[40] He acknowledges that the corruption of nature came because of Adam's sin.[41] But his thinking is inconsistent because he leans toward one of the old-earth views, thereby accepting that this death and corruption have gone on for millions of years. Such a view cannot be harmonized with the "very good" pronouncement of Genesis 1:31.

Colossians 1:15–20: (15) He is the image of the invisible God, the firstborn over all creation. (16) For by Him all things were created that are in heaven and that are on earth, visible and invisible, whether thrones or dominions or principalities or powers. All things were created through Him and for Him. (17) And He is before all things, and in Him all things consist. (18) And He is the head of the body, the church, who is the beginning, the firstborn from the dead, that in all things He may have the preeminence. (19) For it pleased *the Father that* in Him all the fullness should dwell, (20) and by Him to reconcile all things to Himself, by Him, whether things on earth or things in heaven, having made peace through the blood of His cross.

Referring to Christ, Paul says that the entire universe came into existence by His creative power. Christ created all things. It is also important to note the repetition of τὰ πάντα (*ta panta*, "all things") in verse 16 (twice), 17, and 20. In verse 18, "in all things" (literally "in everything") is also found. Paul is clearly certain that as Jesus both created and sustains everything, so He will also redeem all things by the blood of His cross. As in Romans 8, Paul indicates that the consequences of the Fall will be removed when Christ finishes His redemptive work.

Hebrews 4:1–10: (1) Therefore, a promise being left to enter into His rest, let us fear lest any of you should seem to come short of it. (2) For also we have had the gospel preached, as well as them. But the Word *preached* did not profit them, not being mixed with faith in those who heard *it*. (3) For we who have believed do enter into the rest, as He said,

---

39. This understanding of Romans 8:19–23 has been commonly held throughout the Christian era, and is obviously the correct meaning. See Murray, *Romans*, p. 301–302; Moo, *Romans*, p. 513–516; Thomas Schreiner, *Romans*, p. 434–435.
40. Grudem, *Systematic Theology*, p. 836.
41. Ibid., p. 835.

"I have sworn in My wrath that they should not enter into My rest;" although the works were finished from the foundation of the world. (4) For He has spoken in a certain place of the seventh *day* in this way: "And God rested on the seventh day from all His works" (5) and again in this place: "They shall not enter My rest." (6) Since therefore it remains that some *must* enter it, and those to whom it was first preached did not enter because of disobedience, (7) again He designates a certain day, saying in David, *"Today,"* after such a long time, as it has been said: "Today, if you will hear His voice, Do not harden your hearts." (8) For if Joshua had given them rest, then He would not afterward have spoken of another day. (9) There remains therefore a rest for the people of God. (10) For he who has entered His rest has himself also ceased from his works as God *did* from His.

Many OEC proponents try to use this passage to say that since God is still resting, the seventh day is still continuing and therefore the days of creation in Genesis 1 are not literal 24-hour days. Only by taking verse four out of context can someone find support for an old-earth view in this passage. Psalm 95, likely written by David, refers to the wilderness wanderings of Israel in the time of Moses. The unbelieving wandered for 40 years (95:10), but were not allowed into God's "rest" (95:11). Clearly, the rest Moses spoke of referred to entering the Promised Land. Using Psalm 95:11 (also cited in Heb. 3:11), the writer of Hebrews declares that those to whom the promise of rest was made will not have God's rest (salvation) because of unbelief. Rather, those who believe the gospel will enter into that rest. Morris notes that, "God's rest was available from the time Creation was completed."[42]

Exodus 20:8–11 says God created the world in six days and rested on the seventh day. This is therefore a pattern for man: work six days and rest the seventh day. The author of Hebrews is showing that there is a spiritual rest for God's people, and he refers to Genesis 2:2 where God rested. Obviously, God's rest indicated satisfaction, not weariness. But it is important to note that God "rested" (the Greek is aorist tense in v. 4, consistent with the past tense rendering of the Hebrew in Gen. 2:2). His acts of creating for six days and resting one are not ongoing; the seventh day "rest" was an historical event that lasted one 24-hour day like the other six.[43] Hebrews 4:10 says this also. God's rest, which occurred on the seventh day, and our rest, which occurs at salvation, are statements of

---

42. Morris, *Hebrews* in *Expositor's Bible Commentary*, ed. by Frank E. Gaebelein (Grand Rapids, MI: Zondervan, 1981), p. 41.

43. In Genesis 2:2 and 2:3, the phrase "the seventh day" is spoken of in the same way as "the first day," etc. in Genesis 1. Genesis 2:3 says God blessed the seventh day because he finished his creative work. This creative work did not take ages, but literal days. In Mark 2:2, Jesus says the seventh day was made for man — obviously a 24-hour day. When Moses wrote the seventh day regulations, every Jew knew he spoke of only a 24-hour day.

past accomplishment and finality. It is true that when verse 10 says the believer has "ceased from his works as God *did* from His," the word "*did*" is in italics because it is not in the Greek text. However, the context and the aorist tense of the leading verb κατέπαυσεν (*katepausen*, "ceased") show that the supplied past tense verb in "God *did*" is an accurate translation.

MacArthur notes "God's own rest from His work of creation, and the rest He gives us in Christ, are not the rest brought on by weariness or the rest of inactivity, but the rest of finished work."[44] Bruce says: When we read that God "rested on the seventh day from all his work which he had made" (Gen. 2:2), we are to understand that He *began* to rest then; the fact that He is never said to have completed His rest and resumed His work of creation implies that His rest continues still, and may be shared by those who respond to His overtures with faith and obedience. This interpretation . . . views the divine Sabbath as beginning from the moment when creation's work came to an end and going on to the present time.[45]

Bruce implies that God's continuing "divine Sabbath" is the same thing as His rest from His creative work on the seventh day. But the text does not say that the seventh day of creation week is still continuing. Rather, it says that God's rest (or cessation) from His creation work is what continues to the present. Yet others have picked up on this and similar comments and used it to defend their old-earth views. For example, Davis A. Young quotes part of Bruce's statement and then says in his own defense of the day-age view, "Hebrews 4 thus tells us that the seventh day is still in progress and therefore cannot have lasted 24 hours."[46] Yet, it does not appear that Bruce is using this passage as an apologetic to defend the day-age theory, but is saying that the "rest" of God (i.e., salvation or eternal life) is available to all people of all ages, if they believe. In fact, Bruce had already said, "The promise of entering the 'rest' of God remains open. The practical implication is clear: it is not the hearing of the gospel by itself that brings final salvation, but its appropriation by faith. . . . It is for those who have accepted the saving message by faith, then, that entry into the 'rest' of God is intended."[47] Bruce is here less ambiguous and accurately interprets the text to say that the rest is a spiritual blessing for the believer. It is not an extended measure of time. Indeed, the unsaved do not experience the rest at all even though they live through time, just as believers do.

44. John F. MacArthur, *Hebrews* (Chicago, IL: Moody, 1983), p. 101.

45. F.F. Bruce, *The Epistle to the Hebrews* (Grand Rapids, MI: Eerdmans, 1984), p. 74.

46. Davis A. Young, *Creation and the Flood* (Grand Rapids, MI: Baker, 1977), p. 86. Other old-earth proponents also use this passage to say that the first Sabbath was not 24 hours and so the other six days were also not 24 hours long either. Therefore, the days in Genesis were ages. For example: Robert C. Newman and Herman J. Eckelmann Jr., *Genesis One and the Origin of the Earth* (Hatfield, PA: IBRI, 1977), p. 65; and C. John Collins, *Science and Faith: Friends or Foes?* (Wheaton, IL: Crossway Books, 2003), p. 85.

47. Bruce, *Hebrews*, p. 72–73.

Joshua's rest was not a chronological continuation of the Sabbath day. There is no hint of this in the Hebrews text. Even after being in the Promised Land for hundreds of years, God was still promising His rest (Ps. 95). This shows that Joshua's rest was not God's final spiritual rest. Kent explains that the author's contention is that Joshua did not provide Israel with rest in the fullest (spiritual) sense of Psalm 95:11, even though he did lead the people into the Promised Land. In fact, the Old Testament asserts that he led them into rest of a limited sort — rest from fighting their enemies (Josh. 21:44, 22:4, 23:1). However, God had planned for His people to experience a much greater rest — a spiritual rest in eternal salvation, which is the possession as well as the prospect of all true believers. This was beyond Joshua's capability to bestow.[48]

It is clear that Hebrews 4:1–10 speaks of God's rest as a blessing for those who have faith in Jesus. Bruce explains that it is not just something God bestows on believers; it is something God himself enjoys.[49] Thus the rest is a qualitative gift from God, not the quantity[50] of time (i.e., an unending day). God, being eternal, has always possessed this quality. The whole concept of a Sabbath day was to celebrate God's final day of creation week. But the Sabbath day system was intended to be short-lived. MacArthur explains, "Sabbath rest was instituted as a symbol of the true rest to come in Christ. That is why the Sabbath could be violated by Jesus, and completely set aside in the New Testament."[51] There is no literal or spiritual Sabbath *day* that has continued since creation week. There is, however, a spiritual rest available now by faith in Christ alone.

Moffatt says that all references to God's rest in Hebrews (3:11–4:11) refer to "the blissful existence of God's faithful in the next world."[52] Guthrie comments on this passage that "rest is a quality which has eluded man's quest, and in fact cannot be attained except through Christ. Jesus himself invited men to come to Him to find rest (Matt. 11:28–30)."[53] This is nothing other than salvation in Christ, which unbelievers never enter or experience. Yet Young strangely says "the seventh and concluding day of the week has not yet ended, and, in fact, will continue into the eternal state."[54] He then makes his analogy in favor of the day-age theory, perhaps realizing that "eternal" is out of place here.

48. Homer A. Kent, *Epistle to the Hebrews* (Winona Lake, IN: BMH Books, 1972), p. 84.
49. Bruce, *Hebrews*, p. 73. Bruce also explains that the "rest" of God is the same rest as our eternal salvation. It goes on forever. Therefore, Bruce cannot be saying this is only a long rest (millions of years) as the OEC do. The seventh day cannot last eternally.
50. It is true that time can be involved in a limited way. The Sabbath day in Genesis was 24 hours, and the millennium can be thought of in a certain sense as a rest (from evil) of 1,000 years. However, these facts do not in any way help the OEC views.
51. MacArthur, *Hebrews*, p. 101.
52. James Moffatt, *Epistle to the Hebrews* (Edinburgh: T&T Clark, 1924), p. 53.
53. Donald Guthrie, *The Letter to the Hebrews* (Grand Rapids, MI: Eerdmans, 1983), p. 113.
54. Young, *Creation and the Flood*, p. 86.

Inasmuch as the seventh day is seen as a long, indeterminate period (it is really a figurative day), there is no pressing reason to conclude that the six creative days were other than long, indeterminate periods of time. The seventh day is therefore the key to understanding the creation week. The creation week is best seen as a figurative work, a figurative divine week which serves as the pattern for man's ordinary, repetitive, 168-hour weeks.[55]

One problem this interpretation immediately presents is that the other six days are not eternal. Young had just said the seventh day is "the key to understanding the creation week." He then tries to support the day-age idea, reasoning that the Sabbath is God's rest day, so it is eternal or at least an extended time not yet finished. Then he makes the application to each of the other six days as well. But this is inconsistent, for it would imply that the six days of creation are eternal or unending also. This simply does not follow logically, since they are not included as God's rest days. Young uses his extensive Sabbath day to transform the other six days into long ages simply because he sees no reason not to do so and it fits his old-earth view. However, Kent correctly says, "each of the six days of creation had its beginning and ending marked by the words 'the evening and the morning,' but the seventh day had no mention made of its terminus. . . . this does not imply that the seventh day was not a literal day with an evening and a morning, just as the previous six days of creation."[56] Indeed, Genesis 2:1–3 is emphatic (by the use of repetition) that God ceased His creative work. There is no evidence in Genesis or elsewhere that God resumed creative work on day eight and then rested on the next seventh day and so on. The absence of the words "there was evening and there was morning, the seventh day" actually reinforces the emphatic statements about God ceasing His creative work. If the refrain were there, it might lead readers to suspect that God resumed creating on day eight.

As was noted, one obvious difficulty with Young's view is that he wants the Sabbath day to be both eternal and not eternal. Old-earth creationist Hugh Ross reasons in similar ways in defense of the day-age view, but apparently seeing the pitfall of the "eternal state" he says the Sabbath is "open ended but finite."[57] But as other chapters in this book have argued, the seventh day was no longer than any of the other six, and there is nothing to indicate they were extended in time. Responding to Ross, Kelly says:

> . . . to say the least, this places a great deal of theological weight on
> a very narrow and thin exegetical bridge! Is it not more concordant with
> the patent sense of the context of Genesis 2 (and Exodus 20) to infer that

---

55. Ibid.

56. Kent, *Hebrews*, p. 82. He goes on to say that "God's Sabbath rest has never ended." The seventh day ended, but God's rest (salvation) never ends.

57. Ross, *Creation and Time*, p. 49; Ross, *The Fingerprint of God* (Orange, CA: Promise, 1991, 2nd ed.), p. 149.

because the Sabbath differed in quality (though not — from anything we can learn out of the text itself — in quantity), a slightly different concluding formula was appended to indicate a qualitative difference (six days involved work; one day involved rest)? The formula employed to show the termination of that first Sabbath: "And on the seventh day God ended His work which He had made; and He rested on the Sabbath day from all His work which He had made" (Gen. 2:2) seems by the normal rules of biblical interpretation to intend an end just as definite as that of "and the evening and the morning were the first day."[58]

There is another problem with interpreting the seventh day as still continuing. If that is so, then God is still in a state of resting. Therefore, the current processes that scientists study in the world are not the processes/methods by which God actively created during the first six days. So, to extrapolate evolutionary interpretations[59] of the present behavior of creation into the past cannot be accepted as the way God brought the universe and living creatures into existence in the beginning.

In summary, the "rest of God" is not a chronology statement about creation week; it is an offer of God to share eternal life with all who believe. Kent asks, "What is this rest of God?" After a brief discussion he says "at the conclusion of creation, God 'rested' from His project because it was accomplished; and because His work was good, His rest was also one of satisfaction and enjoyment. This rest of eternal blessedness and fulfillment is what God wants to share with His children."[60] There is no hint of a day-age concept in this passage. It never entered the mind of the biblical writer. God instituted His salvation rest on the first literal Sabbath day. That rest is eternal life and can continue to be offered and experienced even though the seventh day of creation ended after 24 hours.

Hebrews 9:25-26: (25) not that He should offer Himself often, as the high priest enters the Most Holy Place every year with blood of another— (26) He then would have had to suffer often since the

---

58. Douglas F. Kelly, *Creation and Change* (Ross-shire, Scotland, UK: Mentor, 1997), p. 111.

59. Those who hold to the day-age theory generally accept these evolutionary interpretations, at least with respect to the formation of the heavenly bodies and the rock layers of the earth, if not also with regard to the origin of living creatures. However, present observable processes are not how God created. God created supernaturally in the beginning and He established "natural" providential processes that now hold the universe together. This is clear in Genesis 1. He brought the first plants into existence supernaturally by His Word, but later plants came from the seeds in the fruit of those plants. He similarly supernaturally created the first creatures in the sea, air, and land and the first humans, but then ordered them to sexually reproduce to produce more creatures "after their kind."

60. Kent, *Hebrews*, p. 82.

foundation of the world; but now, once at the end of the ages, He has appeared to put away sin by the sacrifice of Himself.

The world had a beginning or a time of foundation. But the writer indicates here that the foundation must have been very close in time to the creation of Adam and Eve. He says that if Jesus' sacrifice had not been of infinite value, and therefore different from the sacrifices that the Jewish high priest continually offered, then Jesus would have had to suffer often "since the foundation of the world." Here "world" κόσμου must be referring to the physical creation, not just mankind. Hebrews 4:3–4 has already used the same phrase ἀπὸ καταβολῆς κόσμου "since the foundation of the world" to refer to the whole creation week of Genesis 1. So without clear indication to the reader of a different meaning in 9:26, the reader ought to expect a similar meaning as when the phrase appeared in 4:3. Man has needed a savior ever since Adam sinned, which is here implied to have been at the foundation of the world. So man must have been created very soon after the rest of creation.[61] And sin must have happened very soon after man was created. This is another indication of the problem of placing the creation, death, and decay millions of years before man and sin existed, as all old-earth creationist views do.

> **2 Peter 3:3-8:** (3) knowing this first: that scoffers will come in the last days, walking according to their own lusts, (4) and saying, "Where is the promise of His coming? For since the fathers fell asleep, all things continue as *they were* from the beginning of creation." (5) For this they willfully forget: that by the word of God the heavens were of old, and the earth standing out of water and in the water, (6) by which the world *that* then existed perished, being flooded with water. (7) But the heavens and the earth *which* are now preserved by the same word, are reserved for fire until the day of judgment and perdition of ungodly men. (8) But, beloved, do not forget this one thing, that with the Lord one day *is* as a thousand years, and a thousand years as one day.

Peter affirms in 1 Peter 3:18–20 that only eight people survived the Flood. In his second epistle (2:4–9), he reiterates this fact and indicates that the account of the Flood was just as historical as the judgment on Sodom and Gomorrah and Lot's escape from it.[62] Here in chapter 3 we first note that Peter says that scoffers

---

61. See Whitcomb, *The Early Earth*, p. 36 for similar views on this passage. Morris, *Hebrews*, p. 92, says, "The reference to 'creation' carries the idea right back to the beginning."

62. The "ancient world" (ἀρχαίου κόσμου) and "world of the ungodly" (κόσμῳ ἀσεβῶν) in 2:5 refers to the people living in Noah's time. See Edwin A. Blum, "2 Peter" in *The Expositor's Bible Commentary*, ed. by Frank E. Gaebelein (Grand Rapids, MI: Zondervan, 1981), p. 278. The language in this verse, by itself, is too ambiguous to determine if the Flood was local or global. It neither confirms nor rules out either view. Only by comparing all the scriptural teaching on the Flood can we answer that question.

will come, denying the second coming of Christ. Peter affirms that God created by His spoken Word, not by the natural processes that the scoffers say have continued since the beginning of creation. They reject the supernatural second coming of Christ and ending of the world because they reject the supernatural beginning of the creation and the worldwide judgment at the time of Noah, which Jesus believed and taught was a sure sign of His second coming (Matt. 24:35–37). Peter indicates that the Flood was global in scope by the fact that he links the Flood to the coming judgment, which will be global. Conversely, there is nothing in Peter's three passages on the Flood that give any indication that it was restricted to a relatively small geographical area on the earth. Everything he says indicates that he took the Flood account in Genesis as it naturally reads — a global catastrophe. Furthermore, Peter's use of the verb κατακλυσθείς (*kataklustheis*, 3:6) and the noun κατακλυσμὸν (*kataklusmon,* 2:5) for deluge or flood is significant. This same word (from which we get "cataclysm") is used 12 times by the LXX for the Hebrew (מַבּוּל, *mabbul*) in Genesis 6–11, and it is the only word used in the OT to refer to Noah's Flood.[63]

But Peter says these scoffing people willingly forget the fact of creation and the Flood. The scoffers were advocating a way of looking at history which is very prevalent today; it is called "uniformitarianism." They think that all present physical processes have always continued in the past without interruption or change. Peter says they forget that God intervenes in history to accomplish His will. That same kind of thinking has dominated science for the last 200 years and as an uneducated fisherman without a single class in geology, Peter has described in laymen's terms the way evolutionary scientists now think about the history of the earth. When Peter wrote, it had been approximately 40 years since Jesus had died, and many Christians had died as well. This gave some strength to the scoffers' claim that Jesus was not coming again. Peter assures his readers this is not the case and that the scoffers are willingly ignorant because they rejected the Word of God.

Peter's statements indicate that the people living in Noah's time were wicked sinners. A local Flood would be meaningless if we assume people were living outside the flood plain. Just as the population of earth will one day be purged, so the entire pre-Flood population (except eight people) perished. Peter is making a connection between creation of the whole earth (and the heavens) and the global extent of the Flood, on the one hand, and the global (and heavenly) extent of the consequences of the second coming of the Lord, on the other. Creation week was not restricted to a limited geographical part of the earth, and the second coming of Christ will not affect a geographically limited part of the earth. The creation week did, and the Second Coming will, involve the whole universe. So in this context there is strong reason to conclude that Peter believed in a global Flood.

---

63. The word is also used for Noah's Flood in Psalm 29:10. Other Hebrew words are used in the OT to refer to local floods.

Hugh Ross defends his old-earth view by citing 2 Peter 3:5 and Habakkuk 3:6 as "explicit statements of earth's antiquity."[64] Ross makes this remark as the last of his nine points in chapter five, the "Biblical Basis for Long Creation Days." Amazingly, 2 Peter 3:5 and Hebrews 4 (see above) are the only passages from the NT epistles that Ross uses in his "biblical basis" arguments. But careful attention to Peter's words here will not support any old-earth view. Contrary to what Ross wants, the words "were of old" in verse 5 contain nothing that suggests the world is millions of years old. The words "were of old" (KJV) or "existed long ago" (NASB and NIV) are a translation of the Greek verb ἦσαν (esan, which means "were" or "existed") and the Greek adverb ἔκπαλαι (ekpalai which means "for a long time" or just "a long time"[65]). The only other NT use of this adverb is found in 2 Peter 2:3, where Peter says that the judgment coming to these false teachers has been waiting for them "for a long time." But this reference to time surely must be within human history, evidenced by the examples Peter gives in the following verses about the Flood and the destruction of Sodom and Gomorrah — only a few thousand years before Peter's time. So, there is no biblical support for interpreting ἔκπαλαι to mean millions of years, as Ross believes.

Peter also implies, with the phrases "long ago" in 3:5 and "at that time" in verse 6, that relatively speaking, in Peter's day, the creation and the Flood were closer together than Peter was to those events. The language does not fit with the idea that creation week was millions of years before the Flood, as old-earth proponents believe.

Many Bible teachers and other Christian leaders have used 2 Peter 3:8 to support their old-earth views, especially the day-age theory. But this is as unjustified as saying that because of this verse we must conclude that Jonah was in the fish 3,000 years or Joshua walked around Jericho for 7,000 years. Close attention to Peter's text leads us to reject this old-earth interpretation of his words. Peter is not defining the length of the creation days in Genesis 1 (nor is Moses in Psalm 90:4, to which Peter possibly alludes). Peter says a day is as (like) a thousand years and then reverses it to say that a thousand years is as (like) a day. So Peter (like Moses in Psalm 90) is saying something about the timeless nature of God and that He does not work in the world according to our timetable of when events should occur. The second coming of Christ seems like a distant future event to believers, but to God it is a short time away.[66] He is waiting for the church to accomplish her task of taking the gospel to the whole world and for people to

---

64. Ross, *Creation and Time*, p. 52, is clearly wrong here. See Jonathan Sarfati, *Refuting Compromise: A Biblical and Scientific Refutation of "Progressive Creationism" (Billions of Years) As Popularized by Astronomer Hugh Ross* (Green Forest, AR: Master Books, 2004), p. 323–325.

65. *BDAG*, p. 307. It simply refers to a time prior to the current moment.

66. Douglas Moo, *2 Peter and Jude* (Grand Rapids, MI: Zondervan, 1996), p. 186, says, "What seems like long ages to us is a mere blip in time to him."

be saved out of every tribe, tongue, people, and nation. Furthermore, even if this verse were speaking about the length of the days of creation, it could only say that each day was about 1,000 years long. But that does not harmonize the Bible with the evolutionist time scale and it also creates other difficulties. For example, how could plants survive for 500 years of darkness, if the third day was 1,000 years long?

> **Rev. 14:6–7:** (6) And I saw another angel flying in the midst of heaven, having the everlasting gospel to preach to those who dwell on the earth — to every nation, tribe, and people — (7) saying with a loud voice, Fear God and give glory to Him, For the hour of His judgment has come; and worship Him who made heaven and earth, the sea and the springs of water.

In this last reference to the gospel in the NT, John reports that the angel said three things: fear God (believe who He is), glorify God (obey and honor Him), and worship God, who is the Creator. It is noteworthy that John again brings in the Genesis account of creation as a vital element in the gospel and the work of God. His reference to "made heaven and earth, the sea and the springs of water" seems to be an allusion to the fourth commandment in Exodus 20:11. The God of the Bible is not just a personal God; He is the personal Creator God.

> **Rev. 21:1-5:** (1) Now I saw a new heaven and a new earth, for the first heaven and the first earth had passed away. Also there was no more sea. (2) Then I, John, saw the holy city, New Jerusalem, coming down out of heaven from God, prepared as a bride adorned for her husband. (3) And I heard a loud voice from heaven saying, "Behold, the tabernacle of God *is* with men, and He will dwell with them, and they shall be His people. God Himself will be with them *and be* their God. (4) And God will wipe away every tear from their eyes; and there shall be no more death, nor sorrow, nor crying. There shall be no more pain, for the former things have passed away." (5) Then He who sits on the throne said, "Behold, I make all things new." And He said to me, "Write, for these words are true and faithful."

Certainly, John must consider that he is part of the first heaven and first earth where he has witnessed many tears, mourning, pain, and death. Since these things came into the creation at the Fall, John's statement implies that the time before the Fall was so short (only a few days) as to be inconsequential in describing the creation in this context. So, John indicates that "the first heaven and the first earth" includes everything from the initial creation to a point after the millennium. In the future, John says, there will be no more death, sorrow, etc., indicating that the curse in Genesis 3 will be finally removed (Rev. 22:3).

This ties in well with Acts 3:21 and Colossians 1:20 and reminds us of the allusions to the restored state of affairs in Isaiah 11:9 and 65:25. There will be no darkness (Rev. 21:23, 22:5) because one source (the Son of God) provides the light. Just as was the case during the first three days of Genesis 1, so in the future there will be light without the sun.

> **Rev 22:2–3:** (2) In the midst of its street, and of the river, from here and from there, *was* the Tree of Life, which bore twelve fruits, each yielding its fruit according to one month. And the leaves of the tree were for the healing of the nations. (3) And there shall be no more curse, but the throne of God and of the Lamb shall be in it, and His servants shall serve Him.

Here John mentions the "tree of life." The reference to the "tree of life" in Genesis and here ties the Bible together and shows that in a real sense paradise lost will be paradise restored. The new world, after the completion of all Christ's redemptive work, will be similar to the original creation, but better than the original in that there will not be even the possibility of sin and death in the future. He says that the Curse is finally lifted. It is noteworthy that the restoration had never happened from the early days of creation to the time John speaks about in his book. Sin, which had troubled man since the Fall in the garden, will be gone forever. John surely recognized the Genesis account as factual and he never hesitated to speak about it.

Other Apostolic Teaching on Creation

The Apostles' writings we have considered so far show that they accepted the early chapters of Genesis as literally true and authoritative history. Other comments scattered in their writings confirm this. It was upon the foundation of these Genesis texts that they built much of their teachings. Paul condemns immorality in 1 Corinthians 6:16 because Genesis says a married couple is one flesh, as Genesis 2:24 teaches. In 1 Corinthians 11:3–12 and Ephesians 5:31, he bases his teaching about roles in marriage on the Genesis facts that Eve was made after Adam, for Adam, and from Adam.

In 1 Corinthians 15:21–22 and 15:45, Paul affirms what he teaches in Romans 5:12, namely, that death came through Adam. Adam was just as historical as Jesus, and the historicity of Adam and his rebellion is foundational to the work of Christ, the Last Adam, who by His death and resurrection solved the problem started by the first Adam.

Knowing that Satan has never changed his tactics that he used on Eve, Paul warns in 2 Corinthians 11:3 that Christians should not be led astray from the simplicity of trusting and obeying Christ and His Word. The reality of the deception of Eve is also the basis of Paul's teaching on church leadership in 1 Timothy 2:12–15. Paul clearly believed that the Fall recorded in Genesis 3 was literal history.

In agreement with John 1 and Colossians 1, Hebrews 1:2 and 10 teach that Jesus Christ was involved in creation in the beginning.[67] In Hebrews 11:3–4 the writer affirms that God created *ex nihilo* (out of nothing) by His Word, as Genesis 1 teaches. Also, the Genesis account of Abel and his experience with Cain is considered just as historical as the life experiences of Enoch, Noah, Abraham, Sarah, Isaac, Jacob, Joseph, Moses, David, and the other godly men and women mentioned in this "Hall of Faith" chapter.

James 3:9 affirms that man was created in the image of God and even in our sinful state that should affect how we use our tongue in speaking about and to other people. Jude 14 says that Enoch was the seventh from Adam. While that does not prove that the Genesis 5 genealogy has no gaps, this certainly is the most natural reading of Jude's statement.

Revelation 4:11 says that God is worthy of worship because He created and sustains all things. In Revelation 12:9 and 20:2, John identifies Satan with the serpent of old, clearly the one who deceived Eve, as he has the rest of the world ever since.[68]

These NT teachings are stripped of their authority and the reliability of the NT writers is undermined, if Genesis 1–11 is not true history. Some might object that the Apostles, as children of their pre-scientific times, could not distinguish between myth and history. But 1 Timothy 1:4, 4:7, 2 Timothy 4:4, Titus 1:14, and 2 Peter 1:16, all of which use μῦθος (*mythos*, from which we get "myth"), show that the Apostles clearly understood the difference between history and myth and between truth and error.

Conclusion

The Apostles and other writers of the NT do not teach an old-earth view of creation. Admittedly, they do not give as much information about the time of creation as other sections of the Bible. But when they do speak, their voice

---

67. The Greek phrase in Hebrews 1:2 is τοὺς αἰῶνας (*tous aionas*). The word αἰών means age, world, or eternity. See *BDAG*, p. 32–33. It is found about 40 times in the NT and in most of the occurrences it means, directly or figuratively, the physical world or universe. The NIV and the HCSB translate this as "the universe." The KJV and NKJV rendering "worlds" means the same thing in this context. Morris, *Hebrews*, p. 13, adds "While the universe may well be in mind, (it is the natural object of the verb 'made'), it will be the universe as 'the sum of the periods of time, including all that is manifest in them.'" The word αἰών does mean ages or past generations in some contexts. See Eph. 2:7 "in the ages to come," Eph. 3:5 "in other ages was not made known," Eph. 3:21 "to all generations," Col. 1:26 "has been hidden from ages." Jesus did, in fact, create time, but the context and word usage favor the universe here.

68. The Greek ὁ ὄφις ὁ ἀρχαῖος (*ho ophis ho archaios*) simply means "serpent of old" or "ancient serpent." The NT use of the adjective ἀρχαῖος does not support an interpretation of millions of years. It means "old" or "ancient" in a relative sense and is used in reference to the people at the time of Moses (Matt. 5:21), a mature believer (Acts 21:16), and the time of the OT prophets after Elijah (Luke 9:8, 19).

strongly supports, and in no way contradicts, the young-earth view. An analysis of all the relevant passages in Acts through Revelation gives no support whatsoever for the acceptance of millions of years, in any old-earth creationist or theistic evolutionist scheme. In fact, the Apostles use Genesis 1–11 as the foundation of some of their most important teachings: creation, death, redemption, male headship in the home and church, marriage, the second coming of Christ, and the judgment to come. To accept millions of years we must reject the teaching of the Apostles on this subject, which seriously undermines their trustworthiness and authority on any other subject.

From Acts to Revelation, the Apostles continually declare that the creation is of God, and that the early chapters of Genesis are straightforward history. They never hint that the creation is much older than mankind. Modern scholars lack their insight. Philip Johnson says, "John 1 and Romans 1 provide the metaphysical basis for a Christian understanding of both science and pseudoscience."[69] He shows that Darwinian evolution is as much a religion as any organized religion, but Johnson's assertion that we should start with John 1 and Romans 1 instead of Genesis 1 leaves John, Paul, and the other Apostles shorthanded. Johnson does not consider all that the Apostles bring to the table. Johnson makes impressive arguments against important aspects of Darwinian evolution. However, there is no biblical justification for Johnson's assertion that John 1 and Romans 1 have preeminence over Genesis 1.

It is true that Romans 1 does declare God to be an intelligent designer. However, creation also shows God to be divine and eternally powerful, and Job 12:7–10, Psalm 19:1–2, and Psalm 97:6 show that creation reveals other attributes of the God of the Bible, not just some vaguely defined "intelligent Designer."

Romans 1:18–20 indicates mankind is essentially as old as the creation. Man has been able to see the witness of the creation to its Creator from the beginning of creation and time.

Romans 5 and 1 Corinthians 15 declare that human death came into the world because of Adam's sin. But Romans 8, Acts 3:21, and Revelation 21 and 22 indicate that the Fall had a cosmic impact on the whole creation, so that it is now cursed and in bondage to corruption, waiting to be redeemed and set free at the second coming of Jesus Christ. This clearly implies what Genesis 1:29–30, 3:14, and other OT passages indicate, namely that there was no animal death before the Fall either. As will be discussed further in the next chapter of this book, this is a major problem for all old-earth views because they all accept the claim of the scientific establishment today that the earth existed millions of years before Adam and that in those millions of years billions of animals died in natural disasters, disease, and carnivorous behavior. But such a view is not consistent with the NT testimony about the Fall and about the future cosmic effects of the full redemptive work of Christ.

---

69. Phillip E. Johnson, *The Wedge of Truth* (Downers Grove, IL: Inter-Varsity Press, 2000), p. 154.

We have seen that Hebrews 4, a passage used by some old-earth proponents, does not support that view. God's rest, eternal salvation, is still available to the believer, but the seventh day of creation (the first Sabbath day) was a normal 24-hour period, ending before the eighth day of history.

The Apostles freely used Genesis 1–11 as a foundational base for their own doctrine, and they taught that mankind was essentially as old as the whole universe which, as Genesis teaches, is only a few thousand years, and that Noah's Flood was a global catastrophe which destroyed the surface of the earth and all land animals, birds, and humans not in the ark. Today's Christians should believe, teach, and defend the same truths.

Chapter 13

Whence Cometh Death?
A Biblical Theology of Physical
Death and Natural Evil

James Stambaugh

Physical death is a sad reality in our world today. All one needs to do is to watch the news on a daily basis. We hear of people who die of disease, storms, volcanoes, earthquakes, car accidents, crime, and war. Physical death occurs to humans independent of their age, nationality, wealth, or religion. Those who survive suffer from grief and it may be intense.

However, humans are not the only victims of physical death. Animals succumb to physical death, and many times it is our beloved pets that have to be put to sleep to ease suffering. Animals die along our roadways and kill other animals for food. We see even more death in the rocks of the earth. Billions of fossils in sedimentary strata bear a sobering testimony to disease, death, and extinction of animals in the earth's history.

Often people ask, "Why is there all this death?" The general assumption is that physical death is simply built into the fabric of our existence, and if God truly cared about His creatures, He would do something about it. But alas, the heavens are apparently silent when we ask why there is death. All of creation, as our experience testifies, suffers under the burden of physical death and the physical and emotional pain which results from physical death.

All too often we do not think theologically about life and death on earth. We tend to forget (or worse, reject) some of the watershed events that the Bible says have shaped the earth and significantly affected the plants, animals, and humans. Have you ever seen a *National Geographic* special that featured a lioness chasing a gazelle and eventually eating it? The gazelle is fleeing for its life with terror in its eyes. We react negatively to news of a natural disaster in which many are killed and suffer, both physically and emotionally. There seems to be an unspoken assumption that creation has always been the way we currently see it. This assumption has caused many to question the reality of God's existence. The question may be stated this way: "If God exists, why is there so much suffering and death? Why did He make a world like this? He must not be powerful enough to deal with this problem or He does not care enough to solve it." This is called "the problem of evil" and the response is called a "theodicy."[1] The issue casts doubt on the character and ability of God; it lays the blame for the condition of the creation at His feet.

Today, a growing number of Christians seem to suggest that God, not man, is to blame for the condition of the world. Ross puts it this way:

> While the sin we human beings commit causes us all naturally to react negatively to decay, work, physical death, pain, and suffering, and while ultimately all this is somehow tied to God's plan to conquer sin permanently, there is nothing in Scripture that compels us to conclude that none of these entities existed before Adam's first act of rebellion against God. On the other hand, God's revelation through nature provides overwhelming evidence that all these aspects did indeed exist for a long time period previous to God's creating Adam.[2]

His statement reveals the belief that the operating system of the world, as we currently observe it, was created by God and was this way before man sinned. But is that way of thinking correct? Is that consistent with the Bible's teaching? And if we, as Christians, believe that God originated death, pain, and suffering, can we have anything to say to the skeptic who raises the problem of evil? To answer these questions, we need to understand the origin and nature of physical suffering and death, according to the Scriptures. Only then will we have a consistent theodicy and theology and an effective witness.

1. What is Physical Death?

We first need to examine the biblical vocabulary for "death." A consideration of the English words leads to different conclusions than those reached by examining the Greek and Hebrew words for death in the Bible.

Unless otherwise noted, all Scripture in this chapter is from the NIV of the Bible.

1. Theodicy seeks to explain the ways of God to man expressly concerning the origin of evil. Evil may be subdivided into "moral" evil and "natural" evil. "While the two are distinct, they are not separate as natural evil is a consequence of moral evil." s.v. ,Theodicy", by John S. Feinberg, *Evangelical Dictionary of Theology* (Grand Rapids, MI: Baker Academic, 2001, 2nd ed.).

2. Hugh Ross, *Creation and Time* (Colorado Springs, CO: NavPress, 1994), p. 69. See a similar statement in John C. Munday, "Creature Mortality: From Creation or the Fall" *JETS* 35 (March 1992): p. 51–68.

Webster's Dictionary gives the English word "death" a range of nine various shades of meaning.[3] The first definition is most relevant for our study: "the act or fact of dying; permanent cessation of life in a person, animal, or plant in which all vital functions cease permanently." It is clear that the English language communicates that plants have the ability to die, as do animals and humans.

But when we look at the biblical definition of what is "living" and what "dies," we get a different picture, and that picture is confirmed when one examines the world God created. We can see that when the Bible describes something as living, it must have three characteristics. First, there must be consciousness. The Hebrew word reflecting this is נֶפֶשׁ *(nephesh)* and the Greek word is ψυχή *(psuche),* both of which are frequently translated "soul." So a living thing must be conscious of itself and its environment. The second component necessary for something to be considered "living," according to the Bible, is respiration. This simply is the use of some apparatus for gas exchange. This is described in the Bible using the phrase "breath of life." It is used to describe humans and animals, but not plants.[4] The last item that must exist in "living" things is blood. Leviticus 17:11 says that "the life of the flesh is in the blood." People and animals have these three qualities. But plants lack two of the three components. The only component that some plants have is blood. There are certain bean families that use hemoglobin to fix nitrogen in the roots of beans; the blood is not throughout the entire plant, however, as it is in animals and people. So whereas in English usage "living" is broad and includes humans, animals, and plants, in Scripture, plants are not afforded the status of "living creatures," as humans and animals are.[5] However, some Christians have raised the issue that plants are said to "die" and this is the next issue at hand.

The main Hebrew word for death in the Old Testament is מוּת *(mût).*[6] It is used both as a noun (161 times) and verb (630 times in Qal form). *HALOT*[7]

---

3. s.v. "Death," *Webster's New Twentieth Century Dictionary of the English Language* (New York: Collins Word, 1976, 2nd unabridged edition), edited by Jean L. McKechnie.

4. One can see, for example,: Gen. 2:7, 6:15, 7:15. The same holds true if one looks at the word "breath" alone. See 1 Kings 17:17, Eccles. 3:19, 3:21, etc.

5. For a fuller treatment, see Jim Stambaugh, "'Life' According to the Bible and the Scientific Evidence," *Creation Ex Nihilio Technical Journal* 6 (1992): p. 98–121, available at www.answersingenesis.org/tj/v6/i2/life.asp. It would appear that the origin of the classification of plants as "living" things goes back to Aristotle. Aristotle seeks the lowest common denominator for his definition of something that has "soul" or life. He observes: "Consequently all plants are considered to live, for they evidently have in themselves a capacity and first principle by means of which they exhibit both growth and decay in opposite directions; for they do not grow up and not down, but equally in both directions, and in every direction, and they are nourished and continue to live as long as they are able to absorb food." Aristotle, *On The Soul,* translated by W.S. Hett, Loeb Classical Library, (Cambridge: Harvard University Press, 1964), p. 75.

6. The synonyms are more picturesque in their description of human death. Often the words focus on a physical ruin, to the euphemism of "sleep."

7. Ludwig Kohler and Walter Baumgartner, *The Hebrew and Aramaic Lexicon of the Old Testament* (Leiden: E. J. Brill, 2001), p. 562. Hereafter referred to as *HALOT.*

gives four definitions for the verb in the Qal stem[8] and six definitions for the noun[9]. Smick notes that

> *mût* may refer to death by natural causes or to violent death. The latter may be as a penalty or otherwise. The root is not limited to the death of humans although it is used predominantly that way. This is a universally used Semitic root for dying and death.[10]

The common significance of the Old Testament uses of מוּת or its synonyms is to suggest simply the departure of life.[11] It is used primarily with reference to humans, although animals are also said to die. The only OT passage which uses מוּת to describe plant death is Job 14:8, which we will consider shortly.

The New Testament uses primarily two different Greek words to signify "death." They are the nouns θάνατος (*thanatos*) and νεκρός (*nekros*) plus the verbal forms of these words. The primary distinction between these words is that θάνατος is a more generic word that is used to convey physical death and spiritual or eternal death.[12] There is one place where animals are said to have died (Rev. 8:9) and the word used a verbal form of θάνατος (ἀποθνῄσκω, *apothnēskō*). The word νεκρός, on the other hand, is used to convey the idea of physical death or used metaphorically of something that becomes useless.[13] Davids notes two ways this word, νεκρός, is used theologically. He states: "either in its physical aspects as the cessation of bodily life or in its spiritual aspects as separation from God."[14] In keeping with the OT, these Greek words are used of humans.

The reader might be thinking that some passages in his English OT and NT use "death" in reference to plants. This is true, but the question that must

---

8. (1) natural death of animals or plants; (2) violent death, death penalty; become mortal (of gods); (3) in phrases impatient to die, mortally ill; (4) participles: dying, dead; a dead man, one who is going to die, (anyone) subject to death, stillborn; sacrifices offered to the dead. The only OT reference to plant death given is Job 14:8.

9. (1) singular: death, dying; (2) plural intensive: death; (3) a superlative: to the utmost:; (4) mortal illness, epidemic, pestilence; (5) personified, Death; (6) realm of the dead.

10. *Theological Wordbook of the Old Testament*, edited by R. Laird Harris (Chicago, IL: Moody Press, 1980) s.v. "מוּת" by Elmer B. Smick. Hereafter referred to as *TWOT*.

11. *Theological Dictionary of the Old Testament*, edited by G. Johannes Botterweck (Grand Rapids, MI: Eerdmans Publishing Company, 1997) s.v. "מוּת" by H. Ringgren. Hereafter referred to as *TDOT*.

12. Frederick W. Danker, *A Greek-English of the New Testament and other Early Christian Literature*, 3rd edition (Chicago, IL: University of Chicago Press, 2000), s.v. "θάνατος" This word appears about 120 times in the NT. Hereafter referred to as *BDAG*.

13. *BDAG*, s.v. "νεκρός." With respect to the metaphorical meaning, James uses this word to suggest that faith is useless if it is not accompanied by works. This word appears about 130 times in the NT.

14. Walter Elwell, ed., *Evangelical Dictionary of Theology* (Grand Rapids, MI: Baker Academic, 2001, 2nd ed.), s.v. "Death," by P.H. Davids.

be answered is, what are the Hebrew and Greek words translated as "death" in these cases and how are these terms used? The OT uses the word מוּת once in reference to plants dying. The NT word used to describe plants as dying is ἀποθνήσκω (*apothnēskō*), which occurs in two verses. No form of νεκρός is used in reference to plants, and only the above variation of θάνατος (*thanatos*) is used for plants. Let's consider these few texts carefully.

The only OT passage that uses "death" (מוּת) to refer to plants is Job 14:8. As we examine this passage we need to look at verses 7–12 to provide the context for the verse. The text:

> [7]At least there is hope for a tree: If it is cut down, it will sprout again, and its new shoots will not fail. [8]Its roots may grow old in the ground and its stump die in the soil, [9]yet at the scent of water it will bud and put forth shoots like a plant. [10]But man dies and is laid low; he breathes his last and is no more. [11]As water disappears from the sea or a riverbed becomes parched and dry, [12]so man lies down and does not rise; till the heavens are no more, men will not awake or be roused from their sleep.

Here Job wishes that man was like a tree — it might look as if it is dead but it can be revived when water is added. However, when a man dies there is no hope of being revived.[15] The point Job makes is that the tree, while it gives the appearance of being dead, is not. Cline says it well: "Human loss of power after death is contrasted with a tree's continuing vitality after it is cut down."[16] So while מוּת is used to describe the plant dying, this passage recognizes a vital difference between plant death and human death (and, we could add, animal death). Plants do not die in the same sense as humans and animals do, because plants are not living in the same sense as humans and animals either.

There are two NT passages where the authors use "death" in reference to plants. The first one is John 12:24, in the context of verses 20–33. This text reads:

> [20]Now there were some Greeks among those who went up to worship at the Feast. [21]They came to Philip, who was from Bethsaida in Galilee, with a request. "Sir," they said, "we would like to see Jesus." [22]Philip went to tell Andrew; Andrew and Philip in turn told Jesus. [23]Jesus replied, "The hour has come for the Son of Man to be glorified. [24]I tell you the truth, unless a grain of wheat falls to the ground and dies, it remains

---

15. See John E. Hartley, *The Book of Job*, NICOT (Grand Rapids, MI: Eerdmans, 1988), p. 233–235; Samuel R. Driver, *A Critical and Exegetical Commentary on the Book of Job Together With a New Translation*, ICC (Edinburgh: T & T Clark, 1964), p. 127–128; and Robert L. Alden, *Job*, The New American Commentary (Nashville, TN: Broadman & Holman, 1993), p. 166–169.

16. David J.A. Clines, *Job 1–20*, Word Biblical Commentary (Dallas, TX: Word Books, 1989), p. 329.

only a single seed. But if it dies, it produces many seeds. [25]The man who loves his life will lose it, while the man who hates his life in this world will keep it for eternal life. [26]Whoever serves me must follow me; and where I am, my servant also will be. My Father will honor the one who serves me. [27]Now my heart is troubled, and what shall I say? 'Father, save me from this hour?' No, it was for this very reason I came to this hour. [28]Father, glorify your name!" Then a voice came from heaven, "I have glorified it, and will glorify it again." [29]The crowd that was there and heard it said it had thundered; others said an angel had spoken to him. [30]Jesus said, "This voice was for your benefit, not mine. [31]Now is the time for judgment on this world; now the prince of this world will be driven out. [32]But I, when I am lifted up from the earth, will draw all men to myself." [33]He said this to show the kind of death he was going to die.

Some would argue that Jesus makes it very clear that a seed "dies" and therefore plants as a whole can die. On the surface this appears to be persuasive. Yet as one examines the passage more closely it is apparent that Jesus was using the language of appearance.

The point that Jesus is making, using the language of appearance, can be demonstrated in three ways. First, the context of His comment about grain death is the "glorification" of Jesus through His death. Verse 24 is therefore thought to be a parable or a symbol of the future resurrection.[17] Second, the phrase "truly, truly" occurs 25 times in the Gospel of John and when Jesus uses it He gives a statement regarding the kingdom or Himself as the king (i.e., Messiah). So Jesus is the focus of the passage, not plants. Third, the point is not that the seed "dies" (as a man would), as no one would consider a seed to be living in itself. It only has the potential of "life" in it: it must germinate in order to have "life." Jesus uses the illustration to say that as the seed must be buried to bring forth fruit, so in an analogous way, the Son of Man must be buried and then He will bear fruit as many will believe on Him and receive His resurrection life.[18] So Jesus uses the illustration of burying a seed as a picture of His death and Resurrection

---

17. George R. Beasley-Murray, *John*, Word Biblical Commentary (Waco, TX : Word Books, 1987), p. 210; Raymond E. Brown, *The Gospel According to John 1–12*, Anchor Bible (New York: Doubleday, 1966), p. 472; Gerald L. Brochert, *John 12–21*, New American Commentary (Nashville, TN: Broadman Publishing, 2002), p. 50; and Andreas J. Kostenberger, *John*, Baker Exegetical Commentary on the New Testament (Grand Rapids, MI: Baker Book House, 2004), p. 378.

18. Kostenberger, Brochert, Brown, and Beasley-Murray make this observation. See also, D.A. Carson, *The Gospel According to John*, Pillar New Testament Commentary (Grand Rapids, MI: Eerdmans, 1991), p. 438; Leon Morris, *The Gospel According to John*, NICNT, rev. ed. (Grand Rapids, MI: Eerdmans, 1995), p. 527; and William Hendriksen, *The Gospel of John*, New Testament Commentary (Grand Rapids, MI: Baker Books, 1953), p. 196.

which results in the flowering of the Church. He is not stating that plants or their parts die in the same sense as people (or animals) do.

The next passage is Jude 12, where Jude seems to suggest that a tree could be "twice dead." In context it reads:

> [11]Woe to them! They have taken the way of Cain; they have rushed for profit into Balaam's error; they have been destroyed in Korah's rebellion. [12]These men are blemishes at your love feasts, eating with you without the slightest qualm — shepherds who feed only themselves. They are clouds without rain, blown along by the wind; autumn trees, without fruit and uprooted — twice dead. [13]They are wild waves of the sea, foaming up their shame; wandering stars, for whom blackest darkness has been reserved forever.

Jude begins by pronouncing a curse on the false teachers (apostates) who are plaguing his Christian readers. He gives two OT examples and four natural examples of their character. With each of the examples, Jude identifies the things and tells how the apostates are like them. The clouds suggest that these people are unstable in that they are blown around. The waves that produce foam are a picture of the way they produce shame. They are like wandering stars and are destined for eternity without God.

Of interest to us is Jude's analogy about trees, in which he places the phrase "twice dead" (ἀποθανόντα ἐκριζωθέντα) in an emphatic position.[19] Jude describes these false teachers as trees that are in a state of deadness (spiritually) and they will die in the second death. Mayor seems to be the only commentator who takes the reference of "twice dead" to refer to both trees and the apostates.[20] The other commentaries surveyed follow the sentiment of Bauckham when he says, "It is hard to give 'twice dead' a botanical meaning."[21] It would appear that Jude,

---

19. The fact that Jude places these words at the very end of this verse suggests that he wants the reader to pay very close attention to the ultimate condemnation upon these false teachers.

20. Joseph B. Mayor, *The Epistle of St. Jude and the Second Epistle of St. Peter* (Grand Rapids, MI: Baker, 1965), p. 43. He is less than convincing when he says, "This does not however explain the words in their first application to the trees. These may be called doubly dead, when they are not only saples [saplings], but are torn up by the root, which would have caused the death of even a living tree. The figure of a tree is often used to illustrate the consequences of a good or evil life." So Mayor sees the use of "twice dead" referring both to trees and humans. However, it would make better sense to see "twice dead" referring to humans both in this life and in the life to come and the function of trees in this passage is a picture of that (pulled up and thrown into the fire), not a propositional statement regarding the life and death of trees.

21. Richard J. Bauckham, *Jude and 2 Peter*, WBC (Waco, TX: Word Books, 1984), p. 88. See also Thomas R. Schreiner, *1,2 Peter, Jude*, New American Commentary (Nashville, TN: Broadman & Holman, 2003), p. 466; Douglas J. Moo, *2 Peter and Jude*, NIV Application Commentary (Grand Rapids, MI: Zondervan, 1996), p. 260; E.M. Sidebottom,

like Job, uses trees as an analogy to humans who die. The point Jude makes is that trees can have two actions applied to cause a physical ruin, but the false teachers are already judged. It would seem that the reference to "twice dead" might be a means of communicating "second death." Because these false teachers incur both present and future judgment, Jude speaks out so strongly against them. Trees cannot be said to die twice as only humans are capable of this kind of death. When the NT passages speak of plant "death," the point is a word picture, not a propositional statement regarding plant death. Neither passage can be used to demonstrate that plants "die" in the same sense that animals and people do (both of which, unlike plants, are living creatures [נֶפֶשׁ חַיָּה, *nephesh chayyah* in Genesis 1:20–21, 1:30, 2:7]).

So, the biblical language related to death suggests a wide range of meanings. As we have seen, the OT uses one word predominantly, but others too, with respect to human and animal death. The words frequently used to describe the demise of plants are more descriptive such as "wither" or "fade." Biblically speaking, there is a sharp and significant difference between, on the one hand, humans and animals (which live and die in the same physical sense), and on the other hand, plants (which do not live and die in that same sense). The NT words for death reflect the OT usage in that the words describing death are used of humans and animals. It is noteworthy that there are a total of three passages in the OT and NT which superficially suggest that plants are capable of death. But it was discovered upon closer examination that what the biblical authors meant to communicate was a very rudimentary and contrasting analogy between man and plants, not to state a fact that plants die in the same sense as man. How all this relates to the age of the earth will be discussed below.

2. Was the Original Creation Subject to Physical Death?

Two related questions need to be examined here. Was the original creation subject to death? That is, did animals die before Adam and Eve sinned? And did Adam and Eve need to eat from the Tree of Life in order to avoid death? One will observe a variety of scholarly opinions on these points. However, what one believes does have a significant impact upon the consistency of one's overall theology and how it squares with the biblical text.

Some hold the view that Adam was created mortal and that he needed to eat from the Tree of Life to keep him alive.[22] Most theologians state that Adam was created in such a manner that he would not physically die.[23] However, there

James Jude, 2 Peter, The New Century Bible Commentary (Grand Rapids, MI: Eerdmans, 1982), p. 89–90; Charles Bigg, *A Critical and Exegetical Commentary on the Epistles of St. Peter and Jude*, ICC (Edinburgh: T & T Clark, 1978), p. 335.

22. See Henri Blocher, *In The Beginning: The Opening Chapters of Genesis* (Downers Grove, IL: IVP, 1984), pP. 124, and John C. Munday, "Creature Mortality: From Creation or the Fall" *JETS* 35 (March 1992): pP. 51–68.

23. See Norman Geisler, *Systematic Theology: Sin-Salvation* (Minneapolis, MN: Bethany House, 2004), p. P. 123; Wayne Grudem, *Systematic Theology* (Grand Rapids, MI:

is one notable exception. Strong expressly states that Adam was condemned to die as a result of his creation by God.[24] But it is hard to see how this could be true of God's "very good" creation of Adam. Furthermore, Strong's conclusion did not come from careful exegesis of the biblical text but from allowing his belief in evolution to control his interpretation of Scripture.[25] Those who believe that man was created mortal suggest that Adam and Eve would need to eat on a regular basis from the Tree of Life so they would not die. The implication is that there was something in the nature of the fruit itself that would provide this aid. The corollary to this is that there was something within the nature of the fruit from the Tree of the Knowledge of Good and Evil that would provide the knowledge of evil. However, this approach raises a significant problem as it relates to the character of God. The issue begins with hermeneutics. Both trees need to be treated in the same manner, as we have no textual warrant to think of one as physical and the other as figurative. If both trees are actual trees, and the fruit from those trees have within them, or ontologically, a life-giving power or knowledge-giving power, the trees and fruit were given these characteristics by the hand of God. If it was not the act of disobedience by Adam and Eve, but simply the ingestion of the fruit that brought about the knowledge of evil, then God must have created evil! If there was something present in the fruit that brought the knowledge of moral evil when eaten, then God created the moral evil within that fruit. This is contrary to the character of God, and some use this point to suggest that God is capable of moral evil. There is no way around this problem. The problem is solved if one accepts the idea that it was the act of eating the fruit that brought the knowledge of moral evil. This would also apply to the Tree of Life, as it would have given eternal life to the eater because of the promise of God.

Some of those mentioned above would accept the approach that suggests that animals and humans certainly died before the Fall because the nature of creation stresses the deterioration we observe in nature.[26] There is a decay principle in operation, known as the second law of thermodynamics, or the law of entropy. Put simply, there is a net loss of available energy in systems to accomplish work. The argument suggests that of physical necessity this process of decay was present from the very beginning. Thus, advocates of this view contend that

Zondervan, 1994), p. 516; J. Rodman Williams, *Renewal Theology* (Grand Rapids, MI: Zondervan, 1996), 1:216; Millard J. Erickson, *Christian Theology* (Grand Rapids, MI: Baker, 1985), p. 613; and Gordon Lewis and Bruce Demarest *Integrative Theology* (Grand Rapids, MI: Zondervan, 1996), 2:195.

24. Augustus Hopkins Strong, *Systematic Theology* (Philadelphia, PA: Judson Press, 1907), p. 527.

25. Ibid., p. 527. His reason is that "science shows that physical life involves decay and loss." He also accepted the idea of human evolution, since this too was something that science has supposedly proven.

26. See Ross, *Creation and Time*, p. 69; Munday, "Creature Mortality," p. 57; or Strong, *Systematic Theology*, p. 527.

it is certain that animals and even Adam and Eve must have started dying the moment after they were created since this is consistent with the current laws of physics. For example, Munday reasons, "Decay processes of a general sort can also be inferred from earlier in the creation week. When the land was divided from the water at the creation of the continents and seas, heat exchanges must have been operative."[27] Another good example of this process of entropy would be the heating of the oceans during the day, and cooling at night. Virtually all informed young-earth creationists today are in agreement with this perspective in some senses. Entropy would have occurred when humans or animals ate and digested plant food or when Adam worked in the garden before the Fall. Henry Morris also acknowledges this: "In the primeval creation, however, even though what we might call 'decay' processes certainly existed (e.g., digestion, friction, water erosion, wave attenuation, etc.), they must all have balanced precisely with 'growth' processes elsewhere either within the individual system, so that the entropy of the world as a whole would stay constant."[28] So, there would be entropy in the physical universe during creation week. But whether human and animal death and disease were part of this entropy before the Fall, that is, in God's "very good" creation, is another question. It should be noted that the causes of aging are not well understood.[29] There is neither scientific warrant nor biblical warrant to think that aging, as a decay process, was part of the original creation. So, the second law was certainly functioning before the Fall. But that does not mean there was decay and physical death among the living creatures (man or sea and land animals, and birds — the *nephesh chayyah*) before the Fall.

3. When Did Physical Death Begin?

It is now time to explore what the Scriptures teach about the origin of physical death and natural evil and attempt to offer a consistent theodicy that explains it. Paul states, in Romans 8:19–21, that the creation was placed under a harsh task master called ματαιότης (*matiaotes*), which is translated variously as "frustration" (NIV) or "corruption" (NAS) or "vanity" (KJV). As we examine the world, it is in many ways not a good place to call home. We see such things as disease carried by mosquitoes, HIV virus, earthquakes, tsunamis, and hurricanes. Many have

---

27. Munday, "Creature Mortality," p. 57.
28. Henry M. Morris, *The Biblical Basis for Modern Science* (Grand Rapids, MI: Baker, 1986), p. 195.
29. Consider the opening paragraph of Caleb E. Finch, *Longevity, Senescence, and the Genome* (Chicago, IL: University of Chicago Press, 1990), p. x. "This project really originated in a literature review for my Ph.D. dissertation, in which I considered the then heretical positions that senescence might not be pervasive in cells throughout the body; that many cellular changes during senescence in mammals were driven by changes in hormones or other regulatory factors, rather than by random degeneration of the genome in somatic cells or random disturbances of macromolecular biosynthesis, and that there might be fundamental differences between species in the mechanisms of senescence."

asked down through time, "Is God to blame for this condition?" According to the Bible, in Genesis 1:31, God said that everything that He created was "very good" thereby placing upon it His stamp of approval.[30] Yet, as observers, we see a vast amount of evidence which would suggest that there truly is an "evil" that exists in the natural world.

The theodicy that is consistent with both the biblical text and Christian theology is the belief that physical death and natural evil came into existence *only* after the Fall of Adam. The issue of the origin of physical death and natural evil will impact both the character of God and the plan of God.

First, is the issue of the character of God. If there was suffering built into the creation, it would seem that God enjoys seeing animals and humans suffer by calling it very good. In this case, God could be thought of as the original Marquis De Sade,[31] which fits exactly with the character of the pagan gods. Yet the biblical portrait of God is that He is gracious, loving, and compassionate, even to animals. We observe the concept of God's care for creation beginning with the dominion mandate as man is to be a caretaker for the earth (Gen. 1:26). God commands a Sabbath rest be given to a man's animals (Exod. 23:12). He condemns men who are cruel to their animals (Prov. 12:10), and He cares for creatures in this fallen world (Ps. 104:14–16 and 27–28). Christ also speaks of God's care for the "lilies of the field" and "birds of the air" in Matthew 6:26–28.

In this consistent biblical view, when God said "very good" in Genesis 1:31, He meant to convey that creation was in an idyllic condition. Genesis 1:29–30 tells us that both man and the animals and birds were vegetarian. The text clearly distinguishes those creatures which have life (*nephesh chayyah* is used here in v. 30) from the plants they were given to eat. Man did not eat animals and animals did not eat each other. In fact, the permission for man to eat animals was not given until after the Flood (Gen. 9:3). So when Adam fell, creation underwent a significant change for the worse. The suffering that exists today originated from man's rebellion and God's judgment, not from God's creative goodness. Since the moment that sin stained His creation, God has been seeking a people who will be His through faith. This observation will allow the apologist to present the good news of Christ to the inquiring skeptic.

The second is the issue of the plan of God. Scripture speaks of the renewal of the creation at some point in the future. There are many passages which make this point. Paul speaks of the future renewal of creation in Romans 8:19–25. As the majority of commentators on Romans have concurred, Paul is referring

---

30. See Jim Stambaugh, "Creation and the Problem of Evil" (a paper presented at the national meeting of the Evangelical Theological Society, Philadelphia, PA., November 1995). The majority of the paper is available online at www.answersingenesis.org/tj/v10/i3/suffering.asp. The on-line version of the paper omits the section showing the connection of the biblical model with the scientific model.

31. De Sade is well known for his enjoyment of the abuse of women for his pleasure. It is from his name that the word "sadism" derives.

to Genesis 3;[32] Adam's act of rebellion brought a curse upon nature so that its "potentialities are cribbed, cabined, and confined."[33] But Paul says that when Christ completes His work of redemption and gives believers their resurrection bodies, the whole creation will be changed and renewed.[34] Acts 3:21 and Colossians 1:15–20 further illustrate the future of creation because of the work of Christ. Both passages state that there will be a "restoration" and "reconciliation" of all things because of Christ's work on the Cross. This restoration will happen when the Messiah is fully present and reigning in His Kingdom. The very word "renewal" suggests that the creation is going back to a state of existence that is very similar to what it enjoyed previously.

Another passage about this future renewal of creation is Isaiah 11:6–8. Here we observe various changes in nature: 1) presently carnivorous animals will be changed into herbivores and live in peace with animals that are now their prey[35] and 2) animals now dangerous to man will live in harmony with people. The change will be a literal restoration of the animal kingdom as it was before the Fall of man into sin.[36]

Finally, Revelation 21–22 discusses the changes in the new heavens and new earth. In chapter 20, God judges all non-believers, so sin is vanquished from this new creation. In 21:4 we are told that there will be "no more . . . mourning or crying or pain, for the old order of things has passed away." Much of the crying and pain in today's world is due to natural evils, such as tornados, hurricanes, tsunamis, insect-carried diseases, etc. This will all be gone and Revelation 22:3 says why: the Curse will be done away. The point seems clear — with sin and

---

32. Douglas Moo, *The Epistle to the Romans* (Grand Rapids, MI: Eerdmans, 1996), p. 513–514; John Murray, *The Epistle to the Romans* (Grand Rapids, MI: Eerdmans, 1968), p. 301–302; Thomas Schreiner, *Romans* (Grand Rapids, MI: Baker, 1998), p. 435–438.

33. William Hendriksen, *An Exposition of Paul's Epistle to the Romans* (Grand Rapids, MI: Baker, 1981), p. 268.

34. John G. Gibbs, *Creation & Redemption: A Study in Pauline Theology*, (Supplements to *Novum Testamentum* v.26, (Leiden: E. J. Brill, 1971), p. 41. See also Harry Alan Hahne, *The Corruption and Redemption of Creation: Nature in Romans 8:19–22 and Jewish Apocalyptic Literature*, Library of New Testament Studies, v. 336 (London : T & T Clark, 2006), p. 196. Hahne says, "Since death is an inescapable part of the cycle of nature since the fall, futility is a pattern of life in this age. This present enslavement of creation to corruptibility is contrasted to the future freedom that creation will share with glorified believers."

35. Many ancient stories speak of carnivorous animals in a future vegetarian state. See Claus Westermann, *Genesis 1–11* (Minneapolis, MN: Augsburg Publishing, 1987), p. 163.

36. E.J. Young, *The Book of Isaiah* (Grand Rapids, MI: Eerdmans, 1981), 1:390. See also Alec Motyer, *The Prophecy of Isaiah* (Leicester, UK: IVPress, 1993), p. 124–125; Otto Kaiser, *Isaiah 1–12, Old Testament Library* (Philadelphia, PA: Westminster Press, 1972), p. 160–162; John N. Oswalt, *The Book of Isaiah Chapters 1–39, NICOT* (Grand Rapids, MI: Eerdmans, 1986), p. 283. This point holds true no matter what millennial position one takes. If it is not literal, it is difficult to comprehend what the prophecy might mean.

God's Curse these negative things came into being, and in the absence of sin and the Curse an idyllic creation is restored.

Those who reject this understanding of the Fall and its impact on all of creation and who accept the "scientific" idea that millions of years have occurred since the creation of animals have only one other option. They must somehow assign natural evil, including the death, pain, and suffering to Genesis 1 when God spoke the universe into existence.

But there are serious problems with the various versions of this alternative. Those who would place the origin of death, pain, and suffering in Genesis 1 cannot adequately harmonize natural evil and Christian theology.[37] They try to hold to some of the orthodox moorings of Christian theology, yet they include many doctrines that contradict what they say they believe.

One recent attempt at such a harmony uses evolution and Eastern mysticism as building blocks. Betty states that the purpose of God in creation was to "create others sufficiently distinct from Himself to experience the divine life as uniquely their own."[38] Betty describes this process of creating others:

> In like manner a soul is being cultivated by its contact with a body — the body of a protozoan, for example. When the "particle" or "wave" of Spirit that is in contact with the protozoan body departs the body at death, it returns to undifferentiated Spirit. But the particle is not the same as before. It is true that it loses its intactness as a distinct unit, which at this early stage is dependent on its being united with a specific material body; but it is closer to individuation, than before.[39]

This kind of theodicy actually creates more problems for Christian theology than it solves. Although it does appear to be internally consistent, it seems to be based more on a concept of spiritual reincarnation than on the teaching of the Scriptures. Betty attempts to offer a "best way" to the "greatest good," yet there does not seem to be any fundamental difference between her view and that of a Hindu or Buddhist.[40]

---

37. The concept of "moral evil" (evil as a result of human choices, such as murder, rape, abortion, robbery) is easily accounted for by the Fall of man. Yet many who attempt to harmonize the problem of "natural evil" seem to resort to special pleading, and many of these attempts run contrary to what we know of nature. One can see this approach in the writing of John Hick, *Evil and the God of Love*, rev. ed. (New York : Harper & Row, 1978). He argues that through our experience of evil, both moral and natural, we have our souls built so that we are more conforming to what God wants for His creatures. He assumes that natural and moral evil are a necessary part of this world and part of God's plan for us to grow.

38. L. Stafford Betty, "Making Sense of Animal Pain: An Environmental Theodicy" *Faith & Philosophy* 9 (1992): p. 71.

39. Ibid., p. 73.

40. Yew-Kwang Ng, "Towards Welfare Biology," *Biology and Philosophy* 10 (1995): p. 280–282.

Some of the old-earth theodicies try to explain the presence of death, pain, and suffering as actually beneficial or benign in its effects. So, these were part of God's creation but may not have affected man.[41] This seems to be a popular approach in harmonizing theology and science among believers, so several variations of this approach will be analyzed.

Bernard Ramm was one of the pioneers promoting this idea. He states:

> God did not say that creation was perfect, but that it was good. In Scripture it is heaven which stands for perfection. The earth is the scene of man's probationary existence, and it is good but not heavenly perfect. Creation is a system which involves certain features, and necessarily so, which appear to us as dysteleological[42] (diseases, storms, tornadoes, etc.). . . . The universe must contain all possible ranges of goodness. One of these grades of goodness is that it can fail in goodness. . . . The system of creation or the perfection of the universe requires that which is corruptible and that which can fail in goodness. Creation is not the best in every single part for, as indicated, animals are not immortal. But this is the best creation when seen as a whole, an entirety. If there were nothing corruptible or if there were no evil men, many good things would be missing in the universe. The lion lives because he can kill the ass and eat it. Avenging justice could only be praised if there were injustice; and patient suffering could be a virtue only in the presence of injustice.[43]

So, according to Ramm, a good creation cannot exist without animal death, and humans can only see and appreciate God's goodness and love when they are confronted by the wrath and hatred of man. As such, death, pain, and suffering were part of God's natural order and necessary so that man may see the provision of God in contrast to way of nature. This is a good example of assuming his conclusion is correct before he makes his argument. So when one encounters those who are terminally ill, one should simply tell them to buck up, as this is the world God made and who are we to question Him?

John Wenham expresses a similar view when he writes concerning emotional suffering of animals and man:

---

41. One of the ideas that would support this is that the Garden of Eden was only a localized paradise, and that the world outside it was similar to our world today with death, pain, and suffering. For a presentation of this view, see Arthur H. Lewis, "The Localization of the Garden of Eden" *BETS* 11 (1968): p. 169–175.

42. Dysteleology is the philosophical view that existence has no *telos* or final (ultimate) cause.

43. Bernard Ramm, *The Christian View of Science and Scripture* (Grand Rapids, MI: Eerdmans, 1954), p. 93–94. This view is similar to the "soul making" approach of John Hick. It also begs the question about the original diet of animals. For more on this see Jim Stambaugh, "Creation's Original Diet and the Changes at the Fall," *Creation Ex Nihilo Technical Journal* 5 (1991): p. 130–138, www.answersingenesis.org/tj/v5/i2/diet.asp.

Demonstrable suffering is at its worst when animals are in closest touch with man. The anxieties felt by captive animals when approached by a cruel master are simply not paralleled in nature, nor are the worst features of factory farming or vivisection. Animals in their natural habitat experience fear, but it is a wholesome fear. Among ourselves there is a fine dividing line between fear which gives a great thrill and the fear which is too much and leaves mental wounds. A healthy animal's escape when hunted may well produce an exhilaration akin to that experienced by a daring young man who brings off a dangerous escapade.[44]

Wenham is correct in that not all fear, or emotional experiences, may be classified as "bad." However, we know from recent observation and experimentation that animals, even in a natural habitat, do experience great emotional suffering.[45]

There have been other attempts to harmonize suffering with Christian theology. These seem to suggest that the suffering present in nature is a metaphor in God's overall program. This view, by implication, would caution the scientist or theologian, not to take what they observe in nature as a literal reflection of God's character.[46] Rice elaborates on the application of this metaphorical approach to nature:

We can obtain factual information about nature through the scientific method. But human observers feel irresistibly drawn to impose metaphorical interpretations on nature. . . . This procedure is metaphorical because it causes us to seek illustration of Christian themes which

---

44. John W. Wenham, *The Goodness of God* (Downers Grove, IL: IV Press, 1974), p. 205. Wenhem makes it clear that the world outside of Eden is the same world we see today. Note as he says on page 196–197: "Harm comes when man, out of touch with his Maker, is in the wrong place at the wrong time. Man in touch with his Maker, is in the right place at the right time, enjoys divine protection, so that Jesus could safely sleep in the storm. The earth is an awesome and magnificent home for man, but it is far too dangerous for him to venture out of Eden on his own." Consider also Theodore Wood's account of the "apparent" cruelty in nature. "As far as the animals are concerned, (the world) is one huge, perpetual, battle-field; one wide, vast, endless, scene of almost universal carnage and blood. Thousands are dying that one may live, and the battle is always to the strong. And certainly death, in many forms which it is inflicted, seems terrible and painful enough to substantiate the charge of cruelty against Nature." Theodore Wood, "The Apparent Cruelty of Nature," *Journal of the Transactions of the Victoria Institute* 25 (1891–92): p. 254.

45. See Stambaugh, "Creation and the Problem of Evil," p. 17–36.

46. Stanley Rice, "On the Problem of Apparent Evil in the Natural World" *Perspectives on Science and Christian Faith* 39 (1987): p. 156. This kind of suggestion causes more problems as the biblical text says the nature is a picture of God's glory, thereby a reflection of His character.

are not literally connected with either the origin or operation of the natural systems so studied. If we employ this procedure, it does not matter whether we can demonstrate that nature has a Designer or whether evolutionary theory is correct or not. . . . The apparent contradiction between a good God and "evil" in the natural world also vanishes. For nature is His great work of fiction, He need not approve of all the activities of the participants in the story any more than a novelist need approve of all the actions of his characters.[47]

This approach seems to deny the explicit teachings of Scripture that nature does reflect God's glory and character. If we follow this apologetic, we would be forced to maintain that Christianity is just like any other Eastern religion, because one must deny any connection between objective physical reality (as presented through nature) and truth.

Rice offers yet another option, in which one may examine the harsh reality of creation as adversity and yet even within adversity God's hand of blessing is present. He says:

However, the main purpose of this article is to demonstrate that God's creative mechanism in the natural world has been the same as His creative mechanism in human experience: to bring blessing out of adversity. Adversity in the natural world, such as privation, disease, injury, results when God operates through the laws of nature. As a general rule, individual organisms and whole species respond creatively to and triumph over their circumstances.[48]

While it is true that God does use adversity in the post-Fall world to illustrate His purposes, this begs the question as to the origin of these adverse conditions. Rice, and those who accept this viewpoint, must view them as part of God's "very good" original creation, which is theologically problematic.

A novel approach to theodicy views the fall of angels as the cause for natural evil. Gary Emberger articulates:

The angelic fall introduced extensive changes. Parasites, pathogens, predators, and death became perversions (perhaps through a satanically guided evolutionary process) of God's plan. Angelically caused imbalances led to the extinction, as evidenced by fossils, of various species over time — perhaps even dinosaurs! For reasons discussed, God permitted these disruptions and has worked to bring good out of these evils. . . . Death became seen as an evil only after man's fall. At that point, because of man's broken relationship with God, death was viewed as an enemy,

47. Rice, "Apparent Evil," p. 156–157.
48. Stanley Rice, "Bringing Blessings Out of Adversity: God's Activity in the World of Nature" *Perspectives on Science and Christian Faith* 41 (1989): p. 3. Rice says on p. 6 that this model works for all systems except young-earth creationism.

as a rejected good. As a result, all death — past (fossils), present, and future — is interpreted as evil.[49]

This option has certain observations to commend it for our consideration. First, it does offer an internally consistent theodicy, as it insists that angels, not God, are the moral cause of natural evil. Second, it is able to offer us a corresponding explanation for the data of the natural world (e.g., the fossil record). The major obstacle is that this theodicy goes far beyond what is stated in the biblical text. Scripture places man as God's vice-regent over the creation and teaches that it was Adam's sin that resulted in natural evil. Nothing in Scripture suggests that the fall of angels resulted in divine actions against the earth and the rest of creation. This view also breaks the tight biblical connection between the sin of the first Adam and the full redemptive work of the Last Adam, Jesus Christ. So, while it might look appealing to view the fall of angels as the cause of natural evil, biblically speaking, it is man's responsibility.

A more recent and novel approach is presented by William Dembski in his recent web article.[50] He accepts as fact that the earth is old and that natural evil occurred before the Fall of man. This way of looking at the world is what he calls "our noetic environment."[51] By this he means that science has proven, beyond any reasonable doubt, that the earth and universe are billions of years old. But he also accepts the Bible's teaching that the Fall resulted in the divine curse on the whole creation. After nicely demolishing other old-earth theodicies, he proposes that because of God's foreknowledge of Adam's sin, He cursed the non-human creation in anticipation of Adam's sin. He observes:

> But this requires that God act preemptively to anticipate the novel events induced by God's prior actions (priority here being conceived not temporally or causally [*chronos*] but in terms of the teleological-semantic logic [*kairos*] by which God orders the creation.[52]

So, Dembski argues that there are two kinds of "time" (based on two New Testament Greek words, *chronos* and *kairos*): 1) a sequential or chronological time which we experience, and 2) the "time" which is a-temporal and is linked to God's plans. Dembski states very plainly that the "days" of Genesis 1 are to be seen as non-chronological. "Genesis 1 is therefore not to be interpreted as ordinary chronological time (*chronos*) but rather as time from the vantage of God's purposes (*kairos*).[53] He likens this view of time to Christ being "slain

---

49. Gary Emberger, "Theological and Scientific Explanations for the Origin and Purpose of Evil" *Perspectives on Science and Christian Faith* 46 (September 1994): p. 157.

50. William A. Dembski, "Christian Theodicy in Light of Genesis and Modern Science" Version 2.3 March 17, 2007, 38. www.designinference.com/documents/2006.05. christian_theodicy.pdf, accessed July 29, 2008.

51. Dembski, "Christian Theodicy," p. 1–2.

52. Ibid., p. 37.

53. Ibid., p. 39.

before the foundation of the world" (Rev. 13:8).[54] The theodicy Dembski has suggested is an improvement over many theodicies, and it does seem to answer many of the problems.

However, there are three problems that make this suggestion unworkable as a consistent Christian theodicy. First is his illustration of the analogy found in the phrase "before the foundation of the world." If this phrase indeed modifies "slain" (rather than "written," as the NAS, HCSB, and ESV translate the Greek syntax in this verse), Christ was only slain before the foundation of the world in the *mind and purposes* of God, not in actual time-space history. Christ actually died long *after* Adam sinned, and the benefits of His death were not initiated until *after* Christ's crucifixion and resurrection.[55] If the analogy Dembski suggests were followed, the benefits of Christ's death would have been initiated from the time of Adam and Eve. More importantly, there is no example in Scripture where God judged a person or group of people for a sin *before* they actually committed that sin. To do so would have contradicted the laws of justice that He gave to Israel, and to think that God would do this would bring a revolt in most people's mind as being most unjust and contrary to the nature of God revealed in Scripture.

The second problem can be found in the Hebrew narrative of Genesis 1. The style of writing is historic narrative in that there is no substantive change in style from Genesis 1 through to 2 Chronicles.[56] We should expect that if there were a difference between the chronological view and the kairological view of Genesis 1 it should be observed in the text. This is the case in a change from narrative to poetic style, for example. Deuteronomy 32 is poetic, but this change is clear in the text. If Dembski's point were accepted, it would imply that God is being somewhat deceptive as He gives us the biblical text. This view is amazingly very similar to the "literary-framework hypothesis," although Dembski tries to distance his view from it.[57]

The last problem is a consistent understanding of the noetic environment and the kairological understanding of Scripture. Our current noetic environment insists that it is foolish to believe that dead men come back to life. That they do not do so has been demonstrated over and over again in our human experience. So the fact that the biblical authors all testify to a physical Resurrection of Jesus must be understood in a kairological manner (i.e., not as a space-time event in chronological time). This way of looking at the Resurrection would be contrary

---

54. Ibid., p. 46.
55. This is not to suggest that OT believers could not be saved. They were saved, just as we are, by believing the promises of God.
56. There are portions of books that will shift into a poetic style (an example is Deut. 32), but on the whole, the historical books are written as Hebrew historical narrative.
57. Meredith Kline in several of his writings suggests that the advantage of the "framework" view is that it emphasizes theological concern over historical concern. This is exactly the point Dembski suggests.

to Dembski's own apparent faith in the actual bodily Resurrection of Jesus and would be very consistent with Dembski's approach to the theodicy problem, but it also destroys biblical Christianity. If we do not have a literal physical Resurrection of Christ, then we do not have biblical Christianity. It seems that Dembski desires to mesh his thinking about Scripture with the contemporary noetic environment in some areas of theology, but not in others. The issue is that he cannot be consistent with his system without some special pleading in other areas.

The last approach to theodicy would suggest that we, as interpreters of God's Word or God's world, ought not to get caught up in the details of its operation, but simply concentrate on God's love. Karl Krienke puts it this way:

> Why does God allow such an idea as evolution? God allows sin and suffering, within the purpose of his creation, in order to make possible true love. As a result of this choice, God bore the suffering of all mankind! Similarly, to allow true freedom and true love, God also allows a system such as evolution to exist, free of the requirement of God's existence, as necessary in order to preserve that same purpose of creation, free choice, true love. Then let us concentrate on God's great love, on God's great love as demonstrated in his suffering for us. And let us concentrate on appreciating the greatness of God as revealed by science, by revelation, and by our personal reconciliation to fellowship with him.[58]

The suggestion that Krienke seems to be making is that we ignore the harsh reality around us and focus on the "warm fuzzies" of God's love for us. While the contemplation of the love of God is an excellent task for the believer, it is entirely another thing to belittle the data of the real world in order keep a theological system. This is the cry of the New Age movement that we all should "create our own reality." The command of Paul stands in contrast to this: "Test everything. Hold on to the good" (1 Thess. 5:21).

Those who hold to any of the above theodicies would look at death and natural selection as being a vital part of God's original creation Some suggest that natural selection (which may be thought of as the elimination of the weak and sickly, while preserving the strong) was a functioning part of the creation from the very beginning. However, natural selection contains certain "evil" underpinnings as Pattle Pun points out:

> The fact that animals and man had to eat, as recorded in the creation account, suggests a kind of death for that which had been eaten. Although carnivorousness was not mentioned before the Fall, this does not eliminate the possibility of animal death. The fossil record is

---

58. Karl Krienke, "Theodicy and Evolution" *Perspectives on Science and Christian Faith* 44 (December 1992): p. 257.

replete with carnivores who existed long before the appearance of man. God used natural selection to propagate those species most adapted to survive, thereby ensuring that the resources of His creation not suffer from depletion and that the population of the creatures remains under control. He has allowed natural selection to maintain a finely tuned ecological balance.[59]

Pun points out that natural selection involves death, pain, and bloodshed. Also, there is a competition for what may be scarce resources within the ecosystem. These things might abhor us but they do seem to be consistent, in Pun's mind, with God's "very good" original, pre-Fall creation. Pun must assume two things in order to draw this conclusion. First, he must believe that plants "die" in the same sense that humans die. This has been shown to be a false assumption. Second, as he suggests, animals must have eaten each other. However, Pun has no explicit scriptural support for this belief and this is contrary to the clear implications of the language God used for man and animals concerning their diet in Genesis 1:29–30.

One might suppose that the secular community would applaud the integration of natural evil and/or natural selection with Christian theology. Yet the reaction of the secularists has been one of hostility. There is a growing plea within the Christian community to concede the "age issue," thereby giving the scientific apologist a better foothold with the secular community for an apologetic message. The secular community is very much aware of these integration attempts and it would seem that they want nothing (and will accept nothing) but a total annihilation of any Christian apologetic.[60] For example, note the sentiment of Lynn Margulis as she writes in Bennett's article:

> The result is treacherous. Authentic scientific and didactic principles have been put to nefarious use, for the writers' ultimate purpose is to coax us to believe in the ASA's particular creation myth.[61]

While the ASA text is advocating a form of theistic evolution, it is clear that

---

59. Pun, "Progressive Creationism," p. 17. Pun seems to allow a biological definition of life to be prescriptive, however the biblical definition would exclude plants and single-celled animals. See Jim Stambaugh, " 'Life' According to the Bible and the Scientific Evidence" *Creation Ex Nihlio Technical Journal* 6 (1992): p. 98–121, www. answersingenesis.org/tj/v6/i2/life.asp. Furthermore, it would seem that some animals which appear to be carnivorous may not necessarily be so. See Stambaugh, "Creation's Original Diet," p. 133–136, and David Catchpoole, "Skeptics Challenge: A 'God of Love' Created a Killer Jellyfish?" *Creation* 25:4 (Sept. 2003), p. 34–35, www.answersingenesis.org/creation/v25/i4/killer.asp.

60. An example of this is the reception of the ASA's publication *Teaching Science in a Climate of Controversy* . See William Bennett, ed., "Scientists Decry a Slick New Packaging of Creationism," *Science Teacher* 54 (May 1987): p. 36–43.

61. Bennett, "Scientists Decry," p. 40.

Margulis and the others writing in this article want no hint of any form of theism to be present when considering the topic of origins.

The reason for the hostility, apparently, is that the secularist observes an inconsistency relating to the character of God, when one tries to integrate natural evil and/or natural selection and Christian theology. While the old-earth view distances itself from evolution, it accepts as standard operating procedure mutation and natural selection. But these two things are a major source of suffering. The Nobel laureate and French biologist Jacques Monod brings out this very point:

> [Natural] selection is the blindest and most cruel way of evolving new species, and more and more complex and refined organisms. . . . The struggle for life and elimination of the weakest is a horrible process, against which our whole modern ethics revolts. An ideal society is a non-selective society, one where the weak is protected; which is exactly the reverse of the so-called natural law. I am surprised that a Christian would defend the idea that this is the process which God, more or less, set up in order to have evolution.[62]

Monod observes that biblical Christianity cannot be integrated with natural selection and still have a good and loving God. Although Monod specifically states "evolution," the same conclusion can be applied to any old-earth model, because such models accept the evolutionary history of death, disease, and extinction of billions of animals over millions of years. Monod notes that if God used this method to create, then modern society is more ethical than God. The late geologist at Harvard, Stephen Jay Gould, echoes this sentiment when he writes:

> Moreover, natural selection, expressed in inappropriate human terms, is a remarkably inefficient, even cruel process. Selection carves [sic] adaptation by eliminating masses of the less fit — imposing hecatombs of death as preconditions for limited increments of change. Natural selection is the theory of "trial and error" externalism — organisms propose via their storehouse of variation, and environments dispose of nearly all — not an efficient and human "goal-directed internalism" (which would be fast and lovely, but nature does not know the way).[63]

Arthur Falk, a secular humanist, reasons similarly when he says, "So natural selection seems smart to those who see only the surviving products, but as a design

---

62. Jacques Monod, "The Secret of Life," an interview with Laurie John, Australian Broadcasting Commission, June 10, 1976, quoted in Henry Morris, *That Their Words May Be Used Against Them* (San Diego, CA : Institute for Creation Research, 1997), p. 417.

63. Stephen Jay Gould, "The Power of This View of Life," *Natural History* 103 (June 1994): p. 6.

process it is idiotic. And the raw brutality of the process is offensive."[64] Richard Dawkins frequently uses the "truth" of scientific data to take verbal swipes at theism. Consider his thinking:

> The total amount of suffering per year in the natural world is beyond all decent contemplation. During the minute that it takes me to compose this sentence, thousands of animals are being eaten alive, many others are running for their lives whimpering with fear, others are slowly devoured from within by rasping parasites, thousands of all kinds are dying of starvation, thirst, and disease. It must be so. If there is ever a time of plenty, this very fact will automatically lead to an increase in population until the natural state of starvation and misery is restored.[65]

Dawkins points out, and rightly so, that natural selection or natural evil, which in the old-earth models is believed to have existed from the beginning in Genesis 1, is the natural state of creation. This concept has dreadful ethical consequences, if it is followed consistently. One may consider the idea of "might makes right" or "only the strong survive" as being the motto of an ethical system built from the concept of natural selection. If we place natural selection and/or natural evil within Genesis 1, it affects our ethical system and our view of God's character. So when the apologist accepts the notion that God created death and natural selection and then mixes that idea with Christian theology, he can give no consistent answer to the unbeliever who sees natural evil as incompatible with the God of Christianity.

The implications of God creating death and natural selection for ethics is bad; yet even worse is the impact on personal piety. The kind of god that would have created the world with natural selection as part of the operating system could hardly garner support from the faithful, as the philosopher David Hull observes:

> Whatever the God implied by evolutionary theory and the data of natural history may be like, He is not the Protestant God of waste not, want not. He is also not a loving God who cares about His productions. He is not even the awful God portrayed in the book of Job. The God of the Galapagos is careless, wasteful, indifferent, and almost diabolical. *He is certainly not the sort of God to whom anyone would be inclined to pray.*[66]

Even the thought of the Fall and Curse may be examined skeptically, if natural evil is part of the created order. Holmes Rolston observes:

---

64. Arthur Falk, "Reflections on Huxley's Evolution and Ethics," *Humanist* 55 (Nov/Dec 1995): p. 24.

65. Richard Dawkins, "God's Utility Function," *Scientific American* 273 (November 1995): p. 85.

66. David L. Hull, "The God of the Galapagos" *Nature* 352 (August 8, 1991): p. 486, emphasis added.

Biologists believe in genesis, but if a biologist begins reading Genesis, the opening story seems incredible. The trouble is not so much the six days of creation in chapters one and two, though most of the controversy is usually thought to lie there, as in chapter three, where, spoiling the Garden Earth, the first couple fall and Earth becomes cursed. A biologist realizes that pre-scientific peoples expressed themselves in parables and stories. The Earth arising from a formless void, inspired by a command to bring forth swarms of creatures, generated in the seas, filling the land, multiplying and filling the Earth, eventuating in the appearance of humans, made of dust and yet remarkably special — all of this is rather congenial with the evolutionary genesis. The real problem is with the Fall when a once-paradisical nature becomes recalcitrant as a punishment for human sin. That does not fit into the biological paradigm at all. Suffering in a harsh world did not enter chronologically after sin and on account of it. There was struggle for long epochs before the human arrival, however problematic the arrival of sinful humans may also be.[67]

It would appear that the old-earth view of creation gives away the very heart of the Christian apologists' message — Christ came to redeem fallen humanity and the fallen creation.

As certain members of the Christian community examine the prospect of natural evil or how benign natural selection may be, there is a marked shift. In a book dedicated to examining the problem of evil, John Feinberg states:

> What is the point of appealing to the race's fall into sin? The point is that we live in a fallen world. In a fallen world, people die as God said they would. But if people are going to die, they must die of something. One of the causes of death is disease. Some of those diseases may be contracted early in life and others may arise only later. Some diseases may kill slowly, whereas others kill quickly. Some diseases are genetically based, while others result from germs in our world. People may also die in fires, floods, earthquakes, or famines. Had sin not entered the world, I take it that the biblical teaching implies that natural processes would not function in ways to contribute to or cause death. *What this means is that the ultimate reason for these unattached natural evils is that we live in a fallen world.*[68]

While Feinberg examines the concept of natural evil as a whole, Richard Young examines the food chain and, by implication, the concept of natural selection. Young observes:

---

67. Holmes Rolston, "Does Nature Need to be Redeemed?" *Zygon* 29 (June 1994): p. 205.

68. John S. Feinberg, *The Many Faces of Evil: Theological Systems and the Problem of Evil* (Grand Rapids, MI: Zondervan , 1994), p. 147–148, emphasis added. The same sentiment is expressed by D.A. Carson, *How Long, O Lord?: Reflections on Suffering and Evil* (Grand Rapids, MI: Baker, 1990), p. 51–68.

Most ecologists would contend that the absence of death is impossible because all life forms we know depend on the death of other life forms. Most notable are the complex food chains for both plants and animals, chains which are maintained by death and decay. This law, however, does not need to be absolute in a theistic universe. Scriptures teach that all life ultimately comes from and is sustained by the God of life. Death is the enemy of life, not its friend. It is true that life, as we know it, is partially sustained by the death of something else, but this certainly does not represent the ideal state. Just because the prelapsarian ecological harmony spoken of in Genesis is unknown in a postlapsarian world[69], and thus unknown to science, does not preclude the possibility of its being true.[70]

Nigel Cameron illustrates how harmonistic theodicies undermine consistent Christian theology:

For the problems to be solved, its terms [specifically, how evolution can be accommodated into theology] must be changed. On the one hand, it is possible to admit that Adam was under the effects of what Scripture terms the curse right from the start, before as well as after his decision; but this overthrows the sin-death causality, and in so doing pulls the rug from under the atonement. . . . However . . . the world which God made for man to inhabit was "very good." It had been prepared to receive him as its crown, and the setting was constructed so as to be ideal for probation to which Adam and Eve were called. The world was not created with the Fall in prospect, still less with the curse already let loose.[71]

The idea of a "perfect" creation seems to be fundamental for a consistent Christian theology or theodicy.[72] These three quotes illustrate the views of many

---

69. Prelapsarian means "before sin entered the world.'" Postlapsarian means "after sin entered the world.'"

70. Richard A Young, *Healing the Earth: A Theocentric Perspective on Environmental Problems and Their Solutions* (Nashville, TN: Broadman & Holman, 1994), p. 144–145.

71. Nigel M. de S. Cameron, *Evolution and the Authority of the Bible* (Exeter: Paternoster Press, 1983), p. 66, bracketed phrase added. While Cameron's main topic is evolution, the same argument applies to any old-earth model.

72. For those who suggest the idea that creation was "perfect" see Norman L. Geisler and Ronald M. Brooks, *When Skeptics Ask* (Grand Rapids, MI: Baker, 1990), p. 61–62. Norman L. Geisler, *Systematic Theology: Sin Salvation* (Minneapolis, MN: Bethany House, 2004), p. 17–26. Ironically, Geisler is inclined to accept the geological time scale of great antiquity for the earth. He apparently doesn't see the inconsistency of millions of years of death, as evidenced by the fossil record, with his belief in a pre-Fall perfect creation.

who point out that any natural evil, and specifically natural selection, is not consistent with the notion of the original "very good" creation before the Fall.

The only consistent option for the careful Bible student is to place the origin of natural evil and natural selection at the Fall and the resulting Curse. Those who would place the origin of suffering in Genesis 3:17–19 (as do Feinberg, Young, and Cameron) do not have the difficulties expressed above and are able to harmonize this concept with the total teaching of Scripture.

Conclusion

In the course of this essay we have examined the issue of death biblically and theologically. We have examined the question of what death is, and have seen that it is a separation of body and soul. Three biblical passages appear to suggest that plants live and die, just like animals and people do. But on closer examination we found that they do not teach this. Biblically speaking, plants are categorically different from animals and people. So while plants were capable of "withering" and "fading," plants are not capable of dying in the biblical sense. The Bible makes it clear that animals and people did not die as part of God's "very good" creation.

We also noted that Adam was created immortal and that the law of entropy was in operation during creation week. So, for example, entropy occurred during the process of digesting plant food or breathing air, but the deleterious effects of entropy were not in existence in Genesis 1.

Finally, we examined the question of when did animal and human death and natural evil begin. The unified voice of Scripture is that the "subjection to futility" spoken of in Romans 8:19–21 began in Genesis 3, not in Genesis 1. The many old-earth theodicies designed to fit the millions of years into the Bible simply are not consistent with what we observe in the biblical text. Only if we believe that God created the world without the presence of death, pain, and suffering can we construct a consistent theodicy and have a biblically faithful message to the world.

We began this essay with a question about the past: Whence cometh death? Yet, the question also relates to the future: the hope that we have in Jesus Christ. This is truly the hope that Peter spoke of in 1 Peter 3:15, and for which the Christian apologist can give an adequate answer, if he embraces the biblical teaching about sin, death, the Curse and redemption. But we cannot give an adequate, coherent answer or be faithful to the biblical teaching if we accept as a "scientific" fact that millions of years of disease, violence, death, and extinction occurred in the animal world before Adam was created. A theodicy that is truly biblical and internally consistent requires us to reject the widely accepted idea of millions of years and its resulting death, pain, and suffering of animals and humans.

Chapter 14

Luther, Calvin, and Wesley on the Genesis of Natural Evil: Recovering Lost Rubrics for Defending a *Very Good* Creation

Thane Hutcherson Ury

Traveling in Sichuan, China, in the summer of 2008, I was deeply unnerved to feel generous aftershocks from the decimating earthquake that had recently rocked the province. My edginess was of course nothing compared to the full brunt of panic that China experienced in the wake of the quake itself, which claimed more than 80,000 citizens on "5/12." Death is tragic; mass fatalities all the more so. My numbed host had lost count as to how many friends he had lost. Two medical doctors told me of scenes too hideous to repeat, and of the debilitating effect that the stench of death later had on rescue workers. Stupefaction, hot tears, and fist-shaking at heaven are sometimes the only responses our traumatized souls can muster in the wake of such calamities; words are often rendered powerless to the task. Such could be seen after China had a chance to process its grief. Exactly one week after the quake, we watched TV as cameras panned across seas of bowed heads across the nation. The country stood frozen for three minutes in a symbolic, if not eerie, gesture of grief and solidarity over the huge death toll.

Such losses are not new to Asia. In Shaanxi Province, a quake in 1556 took 830,000 lives,[1] while more recently in nearby Myanmar, 130,000 perished in

---

1. This is the deadliest quake in recorded history. Sites of other notable Chinese quakes include Chihli, Sept. 1290 (100,000 killed); Gansu province, Dec. 16, 1920 (200,000 killed) and Dec. 25, 1932 (70,000 killed); Xining, May 22, 1927 (200,000 killed); Yunnan Province, Jan. 5, 1970 (10,000 killed); and Tangshan, July 28, 1976 (unofficial estimate, 655,000 killed).

Cyclone Nargis. And who can forget the 230,000 victims from the 2004 tsunami? Such calamities are compounded all the more by survivors crippled for life, post-traumatic stress disorders, resulting diseases, animal deaths, mass structural damage, and economic upheaval. What can be said of an earth history constantly perforated with similar catastrophes? More pointedly, in light of such carnage, how can we claim that God really exists, much less that He is good and loving?

Whether it is a brain tumor of an Iraqi infant, an AIDS-ravaged village in Nigeria, or a Thai tsunami, nothing kindles angst, or cuts as thoroughly across culture, time, and creed, like the problem of evil. Layman and scholar, believer and cynic, ask: "If God exists, why so much evil?" Answers to this foreboding question have toggled between extremes. Some atheists use such evils as "exhibit A" in their polemic against theism. Even some theists have plotted out trajectories very different from the Church fathers and reformers; proposing daring reinterpretations of evil, God's goodness, and the meaning of *very good*.

An attempt to answer the problem of evil is called a *theodicy*.[2] Christian theodicies focus on reconciling this dilemma: how can a good, all-powerful God co-exist with, allow, or even initiate various forms of evil, suffering, and death? Whether caused by moral or natural agency, thinking people want answers. Stephen Davis sees little doubt that this problem "is *the* most serious intellectual difficulty for theism."[3] If he is correct, then sober reflection on the matter is obligatory for evangelicals. But surprisingly, few wrestle with the issue to the point where they personally grasp the stakes, much less respond satisfactorily. Such reticence may stem from either failing to see it as a problem, intellectual laziness, or a subconscious hunch that a theodicy is "the most ambitious of all human intellectual enterprises and the one that seems most destined to failure."[4] Capon aptly warns it is reserved "for people with very strong stomachs,"[5] whereas Brunner sees an implied arrogance in a creaturely defense of the Creator to other creatures.[6] Be that as it may, 1 Peter 3:15 allows no escape hatch: Christians must give a defense.

Central Issues in Christian Theodicy

While answers differ radically, all religions propose some theodicy. Hindus merely defer to bad *karma* to explain evil; pantheists chalk it up to illusion; Buddhists see evil as an inescapable by-product of being. In the West, finite-theists attempt

---

2. In a 1697 letter, Gottfried Leibniz first joined the Greek words for *God* and *just* to form *théodicée*. The idea being, in light of all manner of evils, how do we "justify God," while keeping His attributes of omnipotence and omnibenevolence intact?

3. Stephen T. Davis, ed., *Encountering Evil: Live Options in Theodicy* (Atlanta, GA: J. Knox Press, 1981), p. 5.

4. Donald Bloesch, *God the Almighty* (Downers Grove, IL: InterVarsity Press, 1995), p. 128.

5. Robert Farrar Capon, *The Third Peacock* (Garden City, NY: Image Book, 1972), p. 18.

6. Emil Brunner, *The Christian Doctrine of Creation and Redemption* (Philadelphia, PA: Westminster, 1952), p. 176f.

to expiate God by limiting His power, as open-theism curbs His foreknowledge. While these tacks may be system-coherent, they are pretty thin soup when it comes to providing comfort for the human condition at ground zero or in the aftermath of the Sichaun quake. Historic Christianity, however, offers a riskier theodicy, as we shall see, and has thus been much more scrutinized.

Before going on, we need to lay out three key theodical axioms: (1) The three-personed God of Christianity is infallibly benevolent,[7] (2) He is not limited in power, and (3) evil exists. To affirm any one or two of these propositions creates no problem. Yet Christianity has been obliged to affirm them all, thus requiring a nuanced theodicy. In other words, it is precisely *because* the Christian God is allegedly personal, all-powerful, *and* all-loving[8] that a problem arises in the first place.

It is also important to distinguish moral evil from natural evil. *Moral evil*, on a Christian view, means those volitional, wrongful acts that are directly attributable to rational free agency, such as lying, stealing, murder, torture, rape, etc. On this count, any evil presupposes an absolute meta-ethical standard by which alleged evils can be judged. But *natural evils* are linked to impersonal causes, and may be called amoral. Included here are meteorological disasters, most physical ailments, or animal attacks, resulting in the suffering, detriment, or death of sentient beings. The consensus used to be that both moral and natural evils were intrusions into God's perfect creation. But in strong dissent, modern geological theory posits all manner of deep-time, pre-human pain, death, and extinctions. If true, how are we to defend the very goodness of God and His creation?

In the previous chapter, James Stambaugh provided an overview to theodicy. Here we turn to the viewpoints of Luther, Calvin, and Wesley, and how they informed the early 19th century controversy about the age of the creation. Hall showed in his chapter that from the Reformation to Lyell, the Church basically saw Genesis 1–11 as real history, seeing the creation week as recent and composed of six normal days, and the Flood as global and catastrophic. Luther, Calvin, and Wesley strongly concur, convinced that Genesis 1:31 did not allow for prelapsarian[9] natural evil. The late E.L. Mascall affirmed that until recently, it was

> *almost universally held that all the evils, both moral and physical . . .* are in some way or another derived from the first act by which a bodily creature endowed with reason deliberately set itself against what it knew to be the will of God.[10]

---

7. "Infallibly benevolent" means perfectly benevolent or moral, wholly good, limitlessly good, etc. The attribute *omnibenevolence* refers to God's unlimited love, with the idea that His intrinsic nature puts Him beyond moral culpability.

8. I.e., a God who portrays Himself as a caring Creator and loving Father, whose concern extends to sparrows and the lilies of the field (Matt. 6:26–30, 10:29–31).

9. Prelapsarian means before the sin of Adam and Eve, whereas postlapsarian means after the Fall.

10. E.L. Mascall, *Christian Theology and Natural Science* (New York: Ronald Press Co, 1956), p. 32.

In other words, prior to the development of modern geology and the advent of higher criticism in biblical studies, the majority view was that natural evil is due to sin. This consensus natural reading of Genesis is described by Pattle Pun as "the most straightforward understanding of the Genesis record, without regard to all of the hermeneutical considerations suggested by science [i.e., geology and astronomy]." Pun adds that this view was that "God created heaven and earth in six solar days . . . that death and chaos entered the world after the Fall of Adam and Eve, [and] that all of the fossils were the result of the catastrophic universal deluge."[11]

But uniformitarianism touted a deeply crimson reading of the fossil-bearing layers of the geologic record;[12] the rocks crying out of a natural history that did not seem *very good*. This emerging paradigm indicated a harsh reality of deep-time prelapsarian pain, struggle, predation, disease, death, and catastrophic mass-extinctions in the non-human realm. And being posited as an empirically backed portrait of history, new theodical pressure was applied to a Church which had never before been confronted with the idea of paleonatural evil.[13] If natural evils preceded Adam (erasing a penal link to original sin), then believers needed to justify why God and His creation are still good. Would geology initiate a great turning point in the Church's understanding of God's goodness?

Two early 19th-century British groups saw the problem. The *traditionalists* held the time-honored view that the Fall impacted the whole creation; viewing natural evil as intrusive to the original creation. In the other corner were the *accommodationists*, who in their attempt to fit deep time into Genesis, had to see natural evil as non-intrusive. These contrasting perspectives on what Genesis and geology say about divine creative activity, demonstrates a strong shift in perspective from the Reformation era.

Early Protestant Perspectives on the Original Created Order and the Effects of the Edenic Curse

To establish a backdrop for comparing these opposing views which began jousting in the early 19th century, it is necessary to review how three key

---

11. Pattle Pun, "A Theology of Progressive Creationism," *Perspective on Science & Christian Faith* 39 (Mar. 1987), p. 14.

12. Secular consensus puts the earth at about 4.5 billion years old, and that natural history is largely characterized by uniformitarian processes. Conventional paleobiology and geology claim that there have been five massive extinctions in the past, each resulting in tremendous loss of life and species extinction. They are, according to accepted evolutionary dating, the Late Ordovician (440 million years ago), Late Devonian (365 mya), Permian-Triassic (245 mya), Late Triassic (210 mya), and Cretaceous-Tertiary (65 mya). Evolutionists claim each extinction "event" killed 60–90 percent of the creatures living at the time.

13. I coined the term "paleonatural evil" in 2001 to mean ancient natural evils reflected in the geologic column, such as mass extinctions, evolutionary cul-de-sacs, and alleged pre-Adamic predation and death. Paleonatural evil includes any deep-time physical event, entity, or state of affairs believed to have occurred before the creation of Adam, which caused the suffering, death, or significant detriment of sentient beings.

Protestant theologians, Luther, Calvin, and Wesley, understood the origin of natural evil. Their thoughts will provide a historic vantage point against which later theodicies can be compared.

Martin Luther (1483–1546)

The fact that Luther invested a decade on his Genesis commentary hints at how pivotal he saw this book as preparatory for the understanding of the rest of Scripture. He was committed to the *sensus literalis* of Genesis, and expressed concern over the likes of Origen, Jerome, and Augustine, who had a propensity to allegorize. In spending "too much time on allegories," Luther believed these writers tempt some away

> and make them flee from the historical account and from faith, whereas allegories should be so treated and designed that faith, to which the historical accounts point in every instance, may be aroused, increased, enlightened, and strengthened. As for those who do not pay attention to the historical accounts, it is no wonder that they look for the shade of allegories as pleasant bypaths on which to ramble.[14]

On the creation days, Luther thought it obvious that Moses used *day* and *evening* without

> allegory, just as we customarily do. . . . We assert that Moses spoke in the literal sense, not allegorically or figuratively, i.e., that the world, with all its creatures, was created within six days, as the words read. If we do not comprehend the reason for this, let us remain pupils and leave the job of teacher to the Holy Spirit.[15]

But what of Luther's view of sin's impact on nature? He warns us of the conjecture of many objections, since Genesis records the "history of the time *before* sin and the Deluge," while "we are compelled to speak of conditions as they are *after* sin and *after* the Deluge."[16] Thorns and thistles were not part of the "uncorrupted creation,"[17] therefore, but came in by sin.[18] For Luther, if it were not for the Fall, "the earth would have produced all things, unsown and uncultivated;" the earth "would gladly produce the best products, but is prevented by the curse;" no part of the earth would be barren, but all of it would have remained "amazingly fertile and productive." But, as it is, husbandry is plagued by weeds, not to mention "the almost endless troubles from the sky, the harmful animals, and similar things, all of which increase . . . sorrow and hardship."[19]

---

14. J. Pelikan, ed., *Luther's Works*, (St. Louis, MO: Concordia, 1960), 2: p.164.
15. Pelikan, *Luther's Works*, 1: p. 3, 6.
16. Ibid., p. 88; italics added.
17. Ibid., p. 77, 206.
18. Ibid., p. 76.
19. Ibid., p. 205–206.

Even pernicious insects, said Luther, are due to sin.[20] On queries about "harmful worms and vermin," he replied that such did not exist prior to the Fall, "but were brought into being . . . as a punishment for sin."[21] Note the following important affirmation:

> Wolves, lions, and bears would not have acquired their well-known savage disposition. Absolutely nothing in the entire creation would have been either troublesome or harmful for man. For the text states plainly: "Everything that was created by God was good." And yet how troublesome they are! How many great afflictions of disease affect our body! . . . And how great the dangers are from the other fierce and poisonous animals![22]

Luther felt that in man's innocent state, creation coexisted in perfect peace, and had he stayed obedient, "there would have been no fear of the flood."[23] How abominable, he thought, to suggest that Adam might "kill a little bird for food."[24] Before "that wretched depravity which came in through sin," creation was "far different," in an "unimpaired"[25] state of innocence and perfection; a golden age having "neither thorns of thistles, neither serpents nor toads; and if there were any, they were neither venomous nor vicious."[26] Likewise, things like "water, fire, caterpillars, flies, fleas, and bedbugs" are heralds that "preach to us concerning sin and God's wrath, since they did not exist before sin, or at least were not harmful or troublesome."[27] Creation's purity and innocence hinged, therefore, on Adam and Eve's continued purity and innocence.

> If Adam had not eaten of the forbidden tree, he would have remained immortal. But because he sinned through disobedience, he succumbs to death like the animals which are subject to him.[28] Originally death was not part of his nature. He dies because he provoked God's wrath. Death is, in his case, the inevitable and deserved consequence of his sin and disobedience.[29]

20. Ibid., p. 72.
21. Ibid., p. 54.
22. Ibid., p. 77.
23. Ibid.
24. Ibid., 2: p. 134.
25. Ibid., 1:78.
26. Ibid., p. 77.
27. Ibid., p. 208. By water here, Luther certainly means the harmful variety (i.e., floods, drowning, and storms).
28. We must note that Luther did in fact allow for animal death before the Fall, "not because God is angry at them. On the contrary, for them death is . . . a sort of temporal casualty, ordained indeed by God but not . . . as punishment. Animals die because for some other reason it seemed good to God that they should die" (ibid., 13: p. 94).
29. Pelikan, *Luther's Works*, 13: p. 94.

In his idyllic state, Luther continues, Adam "was free from sin, death,[30] and every curse."[31] And just as he was affected "on account of sin, the world, too, has begun to be different; that is, the fall of man was followed by the depravation and the curse of the creation."[32] The entrance of "endless evils" all point to "the enormity of original sin."[33] All "harmful plants . . . such as darnel, wild oats, weeds, nettles, thorns, thistles," as well as poisons, the injurious vermin, and whatever else there is of this kind . . . were brought in though sin."[34]

Commenting on sermons on sin, Luther felt "almost the entire creation was full of such sermons,"[35] and to the degree that the Flood impacted orogeny, then mountains too are reminders of God's wrath. It alarmed him that despite this wrath being evident in the earth and every creature, that we have such a "smug and unconcerned attitude."[36] Interestingly, for Luther, the Flood was the even "greater curse," utterly ruining "Paradise and the entire human race."[37] This cataclysm left no vestige of the world's former state,[38] leading him to rhetorically ask: "If today rivers overflow with such great damage to men, cattle and fields, what would be the result of a worldwide flood?"[39]

John Calvin (1509–1564)

Calvin also believed that Genesis taught a recent, literal six-day creation and global Flood. Addressing the error that the world was made in a moment,[40] Calvin wrote:

> For it is too violent a cavil to contend that Moses distributes the work which God perfected at once into six days, for the mere purpose of conveying instruction. Let us rather conclude that God himself took

---

30. According to Luther, while man was free from disease and death (even with no wrinkles on his head) he would eventually be "translated from the physical life to the spiritual" (Pelikan, *Luther's Works*, 1: p. 92).

31. Pelikan, *Luther's Works*, 1: p. 89. Luther believed there was no apoplexy, leprosy, epilepsy, and other pernicious evils like "snakes in the belly" or "worms in the brain" in the first world (ibid., 1: p. 207).

32. Ibid., 1: p. 77–78.

33. Ibid., 1: p. 71.

34. Ibid., 1: p. 204.

35. Ibid., 1: p. 209.

36. Ibid., 1: p. 208. All creation is a collective indictment on original sin; yet some interpreters are still able to maintain an "amazing insensibility" to this fact (ibid., p. 209).

37. Ibid., 1: p. 90.

38. John Nicholas Lenker, ed., *Luther on the Creation* (Minneapolis, MN: Lutherans in All Lands, 1904), 1: p. 164.

39. Pelikan, *Luther's Works*, 1: p. 90.

40. Given his allusions to Augustine in his *Institutes*, Calvin likely has him primarily in mind. See Valentine Hepp, *Calvinism and the Philosophy of Nature* (Grand Rapids, MI: Eerdmans, 1930), p. 203–204.

the space of six days, for the purpose of accommodating his works to the capacity of men.[41]

Regarding the earth's age, Calvin clearly believed in a span of not quite 6,000 years. In fact, he sounds very much like he is laying the foundation for Ussher when he writes that "time was first marked so that by a continuing succession of years believers might arrive at the primal source of the human race and all things."[42] He sees this knowledge as

> especially useful not only to resist the monstrous fables that formerly were in vogue in Egypt and in other regions of the earth, but also that, once the beginning of the universe is known, God's eternity may shine forth more clearly, and we may be more rapt in wonder at it. And indeed, that impious scoff ought not to move us: that it is a wonder how it did not enter God's mind sooner to found heaven and earth, but that he idly permitted an immeasurable time to pass away, since he could have made it very many millenniums earlier, albeit the duration of the world, now declining to its ultimate end, has not yet attained six thousand years.[43]

He warns that these same "impious scoffers" make a mad leap when they

> carp at God's idleness because he did not in accord with their judgment establish the universe innumerable ages before. . . . As if within six thousand years God has not shown evidences enough on which to exercise our minds in earnest meditation. . . . For by this circumstance [six-day creation] we are drawn away from all fictions to the one God who distributed his work into six days that we might not find it irksome to occupy our whole life in contemplating it.[44]

Calvin held that light preceded the sun, Adam was made from dust and Eve from his rib,[45] the Fall cursed all creation, and all land-dwelling, air-breathing animals not on the ark died.[46] So complete was the "confusion and disorder which had overspread the earth," that he felt "that there was the necessity of some renovation" on God's part.[47]

---

41. John Calvin, *Genesis* [1554], trans. and ed. John King (Edinburgh: Banner of Truth Trust, 1984), p. 78.

42. John Calvin, *Institutes of the Christian Religion*, J.T. McNeil, ed. (Philadelphia, PA: Westminster, 1960), 1: p. 160.

43. Ibid.

44. Ibid., 1: p. 161.

45. Despite the fact that this method of forming a woman seems "a great absurdity" to "profane persons," nonetheless Adam "lost . . . one of his ribs" (Calvin, *Genesis*, p. 132–133).

46. "God certainly determined that he would never more destroy the world by a deluge" (ibid., p. 283).

47. Ibid., p. 286.

On natural evils, Calvin saw "inclemency of the air, frost, thunders, unseasonable rains, drought, hail, and whatever is disorderly,"[48] as due to human sin. In short, there is

> nothing certain, but all things are in a state of disorder. We throw heaven and earth into disorder by our sins. For if we were in right order as to our obedience to God, doubtless all the elements would be conformable to us and we should thus observe . . . an angelic harmony.[49]

As to predation, Calvin asked: "Whence comes the cruelty of brutes, which prompts the stronger to seize and rend and devour with dreadful violence the weaker animals?"[50] He held that if "the stain of sin had not polluted the world, no animal would have been addicted to prey on blood, but the fruits of the earth would have sufficed for all, according to the method which God had appointed."[51]

For Calvin, the Fall perverted "all regions of the world," carrying "the most filthy plagues, blindness, impotence, impurity, vanity and injustice."[52] Adam "consigned his race to ruin by his rebellion when he perverted the whole order of nature in heaven and on earth. . . . There is no doubt that . . . [the creatures] are bearing part of the punishment deserved by man, for whose use they were created."[53] By sin "the earth's fertility was diminished and such things as briers, thorns and bugs came into being,"[54] and originally docile animals became savage, threatening, and "liable to vanity, not willingly, but through our fault."[55] Thus, Calvin asserted that the natural evils presently observed are distortions, and not part of its original "furniture." In Adam's fall from his original state

> it became necessary that the world should gradually degenerate from its nature. We must come to this conclusion respecting the existence of fleas, caterpillars, and other noxious insects . . . [which proceed] from the sin of man than from the hand of God. Truly these things were created by God, but by God as an avenger.[56]

---

48. Ibid., p. 177. Inclemency of air refers to scorching heat. See also *Institutes* 1: p. 604.

49. John Calvin, *Commentary on Jeremiah* (Grand Rapids, MI: Eerdmans, 1950), 5: p. 25.

50. John Calvin, *Commentary on Isaiah*, trans. William Pringle (Grand Rapids, MI: Eerdmans, 1948), 1: p. 383.

51. Ibid., p. 216. Marcos Terreros asserts that for Calvin, Isaiah's eschatological peace between men and beasts is a mere return to prelapsarian conditions. "Death Before the Sin of Adam: A Fundamental Concept in Theistic Evolution and Its Implications for Evangelical Theology" (Ph.D. dissertation, Andrews University, 1994), p. 71.

52. Calvin, *Institutes of the Christian Religion*, 1: p. 246.

53. Ibid.

54. Calvin, *Genesis*, p. 104.

55. Ibid., p. 105.

56. Ibid., p. 104.

Calvin affirmed further

> that if the earth had not been cursed on account of the sin of man, the whole — as it had been blessed from the beginning — would have remained the fairest scene both of fruitfulness and of delight; that it would have been, in short, not dissimilar to Paradise, when compared with that scene of deformity which we now behold.[57]

In relation to the origin of thorns and thistles, he wrote that the world will

> not be the same as it was before, producing perfect fruits; for he declares that the earth would degenerate from its fertility, and bring forth briars and noxious plants. Therefore, we may know that whatsoever unwholesome things may be produced, are not natural fruits of the earth, but are corruptions which originate from sin.[58]

Thus, as with Luther, the key to Calvin's theodicy is the idea that *all* natural evils are all the result of sin.

John Wesley (1703–1791)

Wesley did not belabor the length of the creation days, likely seeing the matter as too obvious to need defending. But there is no doubt what he believed when contending

> that in six days God made the world. We are not to think but that God could have made the world in an instant: but he did it in six days, that he might shew himself a free agent, doing his own work, both in his own way, and in his own time; that his wisdom, power and goodness, might appear to us, and be meditated upon by us, the more distinctly; and that he might set us an example of working six days, and resting the seventh.[59]

Wesley affirmed that the Flood came in "the six hundredth year of Noah's life" and was "1,656 years from the creation,"[60] and a quick perusal of his notes on Genesis 7–9 clearly indicates, as with Luther and Calvin, that he took the Flood details as literal history.

Wesley saw sin corrupting all creation, writing that by God's "own declaration it is infallibly certain, there was no natural evil in the world, till it entered as the punishment of sin."[61] Taking God's approbation[62] of His finished creation

---

57. Ibid., p. 120.

58. Ibid,, p. 174.

59. www.ccel.org/ccel/wesley/notes.ii.ii.ii.ii.html

60. www.ccel.org/ccel/wesley/notes.ii.ii.viii.ii.html.

61. *The Works of the Rev. John Wesley* (London: Thomas Cordeux, 1812), 15:149. Hereafter, *WJW.* See also Wesley's treatise, The *Doctrine of Original Sin*, written soon after the Lisbon quake, ibid., 5: p. 315.

62. Approbation refers to the action of approving a thing as good or true.

as *very good*, Wesley noted the present state of things: "In what condition is the whole lower world! To [sic] say nothing of inanimate nature, wherein all the elements seem to be out of course, and by turns to fight against man. Since man rebelled against his Maker; in what a state is all animated nature?"[63] Wesley held that before sin there was no natural evil;[64] the Fall subjected all creatures "to vanity, to sorrow, to pain of every kind, to all manner of evils."[65] On "the present state of things,"[66] and the premise that God is merciful toward all living things, Wesley asked:

> How comes it to pass, that such a complication of evils oppresses, yea, overwhelms them? How is it, that misery of all kinds overspreads the face of the earth? This is a question which has puzzled the wisest philosophers in all ages. And it cannot be answered without having recourse to the Oracles of God.[67]

Answering his own query about why there is pain in the world, Wesley answered: "Because there is *sin*: had there been no sin, there would have been no pain."[68] Before the Fall, Adam was immune from pain, death,[69] weariness,[70] and wrinkles.[71] Also, there were "no impetuous currents of air, no tempestuous winds; no furious hail, no torrents of rain, no rolling thunders or forky lightnings."[72] In the plant realm, "there were no weeds, no useless plants, none that encumbered the ground; much less were there any poisonous ones, tending to hurt any one creature: but every thing was salutary."[73] Lunar tides, Wesley thought, "had no hurtful, no unwholesome influence on any living creature."[74] While some "ingenious men have imagined" that stars are "ruined worlds," Wesley countered that "they did not either produce or portend any evil."[75] Wesley plainly saw our present natural order as cursed, and horribly different from its once perfect state.[76]

---

63. *WJW* (1811), IX: p. 194.
64. John Wesley, *The Arminian Magazine*, vol. V (London: J. Paramore, 1782), p. 11.
65. *WJW*, IX: p. 194.
66. Ibid., p. 190f.
67. Ibid., p. 190.
68. Ibid., p. 143. Since birth pangs greatly increased at the Fall, some say this proves prelapsarian pain. Whether this was more or less mere discomfort is anyone's guess, but it seems rash to use this to rubberstamp all manner of prelapsarian pain.
69. Ibid., p. 136.
70. Ibid.
71. Ibid., p. 150.
72. Ibid., p. 137.
73. Ibid.
74. Ibid., p. 138.
75. Ibid.
76. Wesley averred that before the Flood the earth "retained much of its primeval beauty and original fruitfulness," and that "the globe was not rent and torn, as it is now" (*WJW* [1811], VII: p. 281).

Wesley thought it "an evident truth, that the whole animate creation is *punished* for Adam's sin,"[77] the "very foundations" of animal nature now "out of course, are turned upside down."[78] Little remains of the primal goodness "in any part of the brute creation," since sin brought in "savage fierceness" and "unrelenting cruelty . . . invariably observed in thousands of creatures,"[79] that now rip flesh, suck blood, and crush bones.[80] The present bent of the "immense majority of creatures, perhaps a million to one"[81] is to

> devour one another, and every other creature which they can conquer. Indeed, such is the miserably disordered state of the world at present, that innumerable creatures can no [*sic*] otherwise preserve their own lives than by destroying others. But in the beginning it was not so. The paradisiacal earth afforded a sufficiency of food for all its inhabitants: so that none of them had any need or temptation to prey upon the other. The spider was then as harmless as the fly, and did not lie in wait for blood. The weakest of them crept securely . . . [without anything] to make them afraid. Mean time, the reptiles of every kind were equally harmless. . . . There were no birds or beasts of prey: none that destroyed or molested another: but all the creatures breathed . . . the benevolence of their great Creator.[82]

For Wesley, the *very good* creation was free of predation, creaturely fear, and any of the beastly "red in tooth and claw" proclivities now observed.

Human sin brought not only death into the sub-human realm, said Wesley, "but all its train of preparatory evils: pain, and ten thousand sufferings."[83] Anticipating the objections of some who might use natural evil against God's goodness, he held that the "cavils of minute Philosophers" and *"vain men"*[84] hinge upon this one huge mistake

> that the world is now in the same state it was at the beginning. And upon this supposition they plausibly build abundance of objections. But all these objections fall to the ground, when we observe this supposition cannot be admitted. The world at the beginning was in a totally different state, from that wherein we find it now. Object, therefore, whatever you please to the present state, either of the animate or inanimate creation, whether in general, or with regard to any particular instances; and the answer is ready, These [*sic*] are not now as they were in the beginning.[85]

---

77. *WJW* (1812), XIV: p. 147.
78. *WJW*, IX: p. 195.
79. Ibid.
80. Ibid.
81. Ibid., p. 196.
82. Ibid., p. 139–140.
83. Ibid., p. 196.
84. Ibid., p. 140.
85. Ibid.

In Wesley's view, God made things "unspeakably better than it is at present. . . . without blemish . . . [or] defect. He made no corruption, no destruction in the inanimate creation. He made no death in the animal creation, neither its harbingers, sin and pain."[86] Responding to Soame Jenyns' view that natural evils "must exist in the very nature of things," Wesley thought it shameful to make miserable excuses for the Creator who "needs none of us to make apologies, either for him, or for his creation."[87] Wesley's is a *lapsarian theodicy*, tracing all natural evil back to a cosmic Fall. As to other questions, like "How can the invisible things of God be clearly seen from such a ruined creation?" Wesley asserted that "the scriptural account of *natural*, flowing from *moral* evil, will easily and perfectly solve them."[88]

In sum, a trajectory of three key Protestant thinkers has been plotted, focusing primarily on their theodicy for natural evil. With this historical backdrop established, we are positioned to consider later opinions on the origin of natural evil.[89]

A Brief Introduction to Two Contrasting Early 19th-Century Schools of Thought

Adding deep time to the early 19th-century dialogue on earth history meant theodicies for natural evil then had to address paleonatural evil, and two British groups spoke to the issue. Despite some unity, wide disagreement surfaced in three areas. First, are science and nature equal authorities with Scripture? In other words, where conflict arises, does special revelation or natural revelation have final veto power? If they are not coequal or symbiotic, are they subservient to a third standard, such as tradition? Second, what should be our hermeneutical method in the creation and Flood accounts? And, third, what was the genesis of natural evil? Listening for their answers to such questions will delineate the general contours of each group's theodicy. If these theodicies differ significantly, evangelicals will want to know which is most faithful to Scripture and consistent with the historic teaching of the Church.

---

86. Ibid., p. 140–141. Wesley here urges the reader to consult Horace's first poem to Virgil.

87. Ibid., p. 141. Jenyns, a Member of Parliament, poet, and essayist, flaunted his skepticism on infallibility, etc. Wesley targeted him in the famous quote: "If there be any mistakes in the Bible, there may as well be a thousand" (journal entry, Aug. 24, 1776). Given Jenyns' criticisms, Wesley thought it unclear whether he was Christian, deist, or atheist. If he was a Christian, then Wesley felt "he betrays his own cause." See Soame Jenyns, *A Free Inquiry into the Nature and Origin of Evil* (London: R. and J. Dodsley, 1757), p. 15–17, 108–109; and *A View of the Internal Evidence of the Christian Religion* (London : J. Dodsley, 1776, 2nd ed.).

88. *WJW*, XIV p. 150. Wesley's italics.

89. Some may propose that these men would have been less dogmatic if they saw the modern evidence. But this begs the question, assumes paleo-exegesis is trumped by newer (and nature), and infers that these figures could not have integrated the data into their frameworks. Further, there is no hint from their pens that they gave reason, tradition, or experience near the same authority as special revelation.

Few in the early 1800s deserve the label "traditionalist" more than the "scriptural geologists."[90] In fact, most of the debate within the Church over the last two centuries regarding the compatibility between science and theology may stem from the adjectival half of this idiom. They were called scriptural geologists for many reasons, but mostly due to an intransigence in taking a natural reading of Genesis. As an accommodationistic spirit had been brewing already for more than half a century, they believed that the hard-fought gains of the Reformation would be nullified by subordinating Genesis to geological speculation. But the accommodationists, armed with the "assured results of geological science" — and flying the banner "have we learned nothing from the Galileo affair?" — did not accord Genesis 1–11 the same level of historicity as the reformers had.

Key British scriptural geologists include George Bugg, William Cockburn, Henry Cole, George Fairholme, Thomas Gisborne, John Murray, Granville Penn, William Rhind, Joseph Sutcliffe, Sharon Turner, Andrew Ure, and George Young.[91] They all held to 24-hour creation days and a global Flood; they wrote substantial, widely read books; and they did not think natural evils were part of God's *very good* creation, but were instead intrusions into a perfect creation. We will take Bugg, Ure, and Young's views on paleonatural evil as representative of the others.

Similarly, we will take William Buckland, John Pye Smith, and Hugh Miller as major Christian accommodationists, since they deftly addressed natural evils and had a wide readership. They did not take the Genesis days literally, nor the Flood as global or geologically significant, and saw natural evil as something divinely intended.

Our primary foci will be on each group's view of the finished creation's goodness, the genesis of natural evil, and the scope of both the Fall and Flood.[92] To

---

90. For an in-depth and sympathetic treatment of the scriptural geologists, see Terry Mortenson, *The Great Turning Point* (Green Forest, AR: Master Books, 2004). For shorter and secular analyses, see Richard Millhauser, "The Scriptural Geologists: An Episode in the History of Opinion," *Osiris* 11 (1954): p. 65–86. Other works that comment on the scriptural geologists are Jan Marten Ivo Klaver, *Geology and Religious Sentiment: The Effect of Geological Discoveries on English Society and Literature between 1829 and 1859* (Leiden, Netherlands: Brill, 1997); James Moore, "Geologists and Interpreters of Genesis in the Nineteenth Century," in *God & Nature*, David C. Lindberg and Ronald L. Numbers, eds. (Berkeley, CA: University of California Press, 1986), p. 322–350; Nicholaas Rupke, *The Great Chain of History* (Oxford: Oxford University Press, 1983), p. 42–50; and Davis A. Young, *The Biblical Flood: A Case Study of the Church's Response to Extrabiblical Evidence* (Grand Rapids, MI: Eerdmans, 1995), p. 124–136.

91. These are some of the 30 such authors that Mortenson discusses. Although there were a few American scriptural geologists (e.g., David Lord and Eleazar Lord), Britain was the center of the Genesis-geology controversy.

92. Space precludes a fuller treatment, which will be found in my forthcoming book, *The Evolving Face of God: Early Nineteenth-Century Traditionalist and Accommodationist Theodical Responses in British Religious Thought to Paleonatural Evil in the Fossil Record.* Cf. Mortenson's *The Great Turning Point*.

what degree did geology and exegesis impact their view of God's character? In analyzing these responses to paleonatural evil we hope to trace a subtle evolution of the Church's understanding of divine goodness. While accommodationists and traditionalists did share some common ground, stark differences persisted. In his earlier chapter, Mortenson has already pointed out their differences regarding the length and recency of the creation days and the extent and violence of the Flood. Here our accent is on seven theodicy-related contrasts.

Contrast One: In What Manner was the Finished Creation *Very Good*?

One area of discord related to nature's pre-Fall economy and the Creator's approbation, "*very good*." Traditionalists held that before sin everything was absolutely perfect, needing no improvement, and there would "have been no prior revolutions and destructions" of God's works.[93] Accommodationists, on the other hand, held the inverted thesis that before the Fall, creation's perfection and goodness were relative. This meant that natural evils were created things which perfectly fulfill their *intended purpose*, serving as evidence not only for mere design, but even benevolent design.

Our three theologians, while poles apart soteriologically, were in lockstep regarding God's approbation. Luther believed God gave man an abode where nothing was "lacking for leading his life in the easiest possible manner," but sadly, "all these good things have, for the most part, been lost through sin."[94] Calvin saw a "very good" golden age that would continue, had it not been for sin's corruption.[95] Wesley held it as "unspeakably better than it is at present,"[96] believing that no prelapsarian blemish, destruction, or natural evil existed.

Perusal of these early 19th century views has of necessity been truncated. Our thrust is only to sketch the broad strokes for discerning which group more closely aligned with the reformers on Genesis 1:31.[97]

Contrast Two: Does the Postlapsarian World Bear Penal Scars?

Given the varying views on the meaning of creation's original goodness mentioned above, a second difference is further implied: namely, does the natural order bear penal scars. For traditionalists, sin brought in everything from thorns to volcanoes; from vermin to predation; from disease to death. Nothing existed prior to the Fall that could be construed as tumultuous in the realms of meteorology, geology, or biology. Thus, prior to sin, neither geophysical catastrophism, nor pain and death in the animal realm existed.

---

93. George Bugg, *Scriptural Geology* (London: Hatchard & Son, 1826–1827, 2 vol.), 1: p. 143.
94. Pelikan, *Luther's Works*, 1: p. 73.
95. Calvin, *Jeremiah*, 5: p. 25.
96. *WJW*, IX: p. 140.
97. I do not want to play loose with accepted nomenclature, but have occasionally placed Wesley under the label "Reformer." This is solely for brevity, and here I mean nothing more than *early evangelical trailblazer.*

Accommodationists held that sin had little role, if any, in corrupting nature. Things like fire, hail, and snow are attributable to "the will of the same Creator" who made the world.[98] Further, serial catastrophism with its attendant suffering, death, and extinction was intended, necessary, and preparatory; providentially woven into creation's original tapestry. Collateral losses along the way were the unavoidable cost of securing a greater good. Any idea of a golden age is sheer sentimentalism wrapped in naïve literalism.

But for Wesley, creation was originally "in a totally different state from that wherein we find it now."[99] Calvin also saw natural evil as representing a corruption and degeneration from the original creation, and that "many things which are now seen in the world are rather corruptions of it than any part of its proper furniture."[100] Such theodical convictions were not shared by the later accommodationists.

Contrast Three: The Cause of Deep-Time Serial Catastrophism

The origin of geophysical revolutions is another telling contrast. The traditionalist model admits of no catastrophic upheavals among the secondary strata.[101] Instead, one catastrophic Flood formed most of the geologic column and its fossil-bearing strata.

But the accommodationists tacked the Flood on as merely the last of many catastrophes, each of which could cause mass extinctions, but none of which were global. *Collectively* those pre-Adamic catastrophes formed the geologic column and its fossiliferous rock layers. These men also saw no substantial geophysical change to nature's economy after sin. All things continue as they were from the beginning.

But for Luther, before sin there was no "settling of the ground" or "earthquakes."[102] Wesley posited a future restoration to pre-Fall conditions, where *once again* there would be no "jarring or destructive principles like earthquakes, horrid rocks, [or] frightful precipices."[103] By comparison, then, the traditionalists' position dovetails with the reformers. But in advocating as many as 50

---

98. William Buckland, *An Inquiry Whether the Sentence of Death Pronounced at the Fall of Man Included the Whole Animal Creation, or Was Restricted to the Human Race*, (London, John Murray, 1839), p. 9. Cf. *Luther's Works*, 1: p. 208; Calvin, *Genesis*, p. 177; and *WJW*, IX: p. 137.

99. *Wesley's Works*, 6: p. 210.

100. Calvin, *Institutes*, 1: p. 104, 246

101. Bugg, *Scriptural Geology*, 1: p. 55. The deeply situated Primary strata were devoid of fossils and deemed creation rocks; whereas many or most of the Tertiary deposits were thought to be possibly post-Flood. These formations roughly correspond to today's respective classifications, Pre-Cambrian and Cenozoic. The Secondary strata roughly refers to the modern designations of the Paleozoic and Mesozoic periods.

102. Pelikan, *Luther's Works*, 1: p. 206.

103. *WJW*, IX: p. 253. Cf. Charles Wesley, *The Cause and Cure of Earthquakes*, (London: Strahan, 1750). Often mistakenly attributed to John, this sermon represents the Wesleys' shared convictions. Quakes were often penal, thought Charles, and repentance is the "cure."

prelapsarian geophysical revolutions, the accommodationists contravene the views of the reformers on the tranquility of the original creation order, and the corruption of this peaceable kingdom by sin.

Contrast Four: The Cause of Physical Maladies and Diseases

The root of all maladies and diseases is a fourth contrast. Were these the fruit of sin, or in the Architect's blueprint from day one? Young embodied the traditionalists' view that Scripture teaches that sin "brought death into the world, with *all our woes*."[104] He took Genesis to teach that "the misery and destruction of the creatures are represented as the bitter fruits of man's transgression,"[105] and would have labeled as unscriptural any idea that such "woes" preceded sin or were in operation through deep time.

Accommodationists, like Buckland, saw nature as "crowded with evidences of death" and extinction,[106] which were "in no way connected" to human misconduct.[107] He held that the penalties of the Curse were "strictly and exclusively" limited to man,[108] which logically makes God the author and intender of all maladies, suffering, and death in the non-human realm.

Wesley was convinced that creatures were "subjected to vanity, to sorrow, to pain of every kind, to all manner of evils," due to sin,[109] prior to which no "evil of any kind" existed.[110] Luther made frequent allusion to the fact that diseases have their primordial cause in original sin. Calvin also saw the "primary cause of diseases" to be sin.[111] The Edenic Fall perverted every quarter of creation, freighting in "the most filthy plagues, blindness, impotence, impurity, vanity and injustice . . . miseries"[112] on her train. The reader must decide whether the traditionalists or accommodationists paralleled Reformationist precedent on this theodical facet. But it seems the accommodationists clearly plotted out theologically risky territory quite different from that of Luther, Calvin, and Wesley.

Contrast Five: The Origin of Predation

Another contrast relates to predation. Traditionalists thought Eden was predation-free, and that all animals were herbivores.[113] Bugg held that God had

---

104. George Young, *Scriptural Geology* (London: Simpkin, Marshall and Co, 1838), p. 41–42, my emphasis.

105. George Young and John Bird, *A Geological Survey of the Yorkshire Coast* (Whitby: R. Kirby, 1828), p. 342.

106. Buckland, *An Inquiry*, p. 11.

107. Ibid.

108. Ibid., p. 15.

109. *WJW*, IX: p. 194.

110. Ibid., p. 190f.

111. Calvin, *Genesis*, p. 177.

112. Calvin, *Institutes*, 1:246.

113. Andrew Ure, *A New System of Geology* (London: Longman, Rees, Orme, Brown & Green, 1829), p. 500.

originally "granted to *all the animals, only vegetable food*,"[114] but degenerated into a state of carnivory, and it is "the grossest insult to the wisdom and goodness of God, to suggest otherwise."[115] This fits with the view of Luther, et al, that carnivory resulted directly from the Fall.[116]

Accommodationists erased any link of carnivory to the Fall; predation long pre-dating man, on their view. Buckland saw carnivory as effecting "the destruction of life;"[117] a "law of universal mortality [as] being the established condition, on which it has pleased the Creator to give . . . to every creature on earth."[118] Miller felt that predatory apparatuses which cut, pierce, torture, and kill had always existed and functioned for those purposes from the beginning.[119] And Smith found incredulous the idea that there was no carnivory before Adam, claiming that, "in a thousand instances, [it was] the immediate cause of inestimable benefits to man."[120] Thus, once again the traditionalists are in harmony with their forefathers on the cause of predation, while the accommodationists, compelled more by geological philosophy than exegesis, adopted a much different perspective.

Contrast Six: The Cause of Human and Animal Death

Close to the previous category, a sixth contrast concerns whether human death and animal death are intended or intrusive. The traditionalists' canon saw death as having a penal cause. Bugg saw all death as part of a fuller degeneration from an original perfection: "*Man* has degenerated and all nature with him, from their original *perfection*; and the tendency of his *nature* is to grow worse and worse."[121]

Yet the accommodationists saw death as "a way of life," believing that the "rocks cry out" no other reasonable inference. Death was built in at the beginning in all levels of creation. On the origin of human death, accommodationists hint that had man never sinned, humanity would not have tasted physical death. But they are not nearly as explicit as the traditionalists, and do not rule out that *all* things were designed to die.

Wesley, Calvin, and Luther agreed on the genesis of carnivory. Referring to sin's "horrible curse," Calvin said "All the harmless creatures from earth to heaven

---

114. Bugg, *Scriptural Geology*, 1: p. 146.
115. Ibid., 1: p. 147.
116. Cf. Pelikan, *Luther's Works*, 1: p. 78, 210; Calvin, *Genesis*, p. 104; and WJW, IX: p. 189–203. Luther varies a little from Calvin and Wesley here, but all agree that post-lapsarian beasts differ radically from their pre-Fall disposition.
117. Buckland, *Geology and Mineralogy Considered with Reference to Natural Theology* (London: William Pickering, 1836), 1: p. 130.
118. Ibid.
119. Hugh Miller, *The Testimony of the Rocks; or Geology in Its Bearings on the Two Theologies, Natural and Revealed* (Edinburgh: Thomas Constable & Co., 1857), p. 66, 69–70.
120. John Pye Smith, *The Relation Between the Holy Scriptures and Some Parts of Geological Science* (Philadelphia, PA: Robert E. Peterson Press, 1850), p. 67.
121. Bugg, *Scriptural Geology*, 1: p. 152.

have suffered punishment for our sins."[122] Wesley went so far as to say that there would be no pre-Fall death (at least not from predation) even at the insect level! In the Edenic realm there was

> a sufficiency of food for all its inhabitants: so that none of them had any need or temptation to prey upon the other. The spider was then as harmless as the fly, and did not lie in wait for blood. The weakest of them crept securely . . . [without anything] to make them afraid. Mean time, the reptiles of every kind were equally harmless. . . . There were no birds or beasts of prey: none that destroyed or molested another: but all the creatures breathed . . . the benevolence of their Creator.[123]

The traditionalists, accommodationists, and reformers had some unity on the origin of human death, but differed strongly on paleonatural evil and violent animal death. Traditionalists felt such elements contradict Genesis, but accommodationists allowed for a pre-Fall order "red in tooth and claw,"[124] even having no problem with the idea that mankind was also designed to die.

Contrast Seven: The Bearing of Paleonatural Evil on God's Character

All the above contrasts set the stage for this one: the bearing of paleonatural evil on what we will call "the face of God." Most Christians join Stanley Rice in presuming that "the Creator wanted to express His personality in the creation in part so that we . . . could learn about Him."[125] All six of our 19th-century figures concur in this: the finished creation displayed God's power, wisdom, and benevolence. But to say that creation is now in a fallen state due to sin (traditionalist view), as opposed to saying the present creation is exactly the way an all-loving, all-powerful God intended it from the beginning (accommodationist view), is to paint two conflicting portraits of a good God.

For Bugg, Young, and Ure, it was not theodically credible to interpret the travail of *nature red in tooth and claw* as being the best of all possible designs that one would expect from the God reflected in a careful reading of Scripture. This was certainly not the God embraced by Luther, Calvin, and Wesley. How could an omnibenevolent and omnipotent being, with the best of all possible creative options at His disposal, design as His preferred method, deep-time, serial catastrophe, pain, disease, and death in such an apparently profligate, if not pernicious, manner to bring about and maintain the economy of sentient creation? What can be said of a Designer with a serrated hand?

---

122. John Calvin, *Commentary on Romans* (Edinburgh: Calvin Translation Society, 1844), p. 218.

123. *WJW*, IX: p. 139–140.

124. The oft-quoted phrase is from stanza 56 of Alfred Tennyson's 1850 poetic masterpiece, *In Memoriam*, perhaps the most popular English theodicy of the mid-19th century.

125. Stanley Rice, "On the Problem of Apparent Evil in the Natural World," *Perspectives on Science & Christian Faith* 39 (September 1987): p. 150.

Modern skeptics voice surprise at any accommodationist-like theodicy that suggests such an uncaring Creator. Regarding theists who embraced a God of natural selection, famed 20th century atheist Bertrand Russell ponders:

> Religion . . . has accommodated itself to the doctrine of evolution. . . . We are told that . . . evolution is the unfolding of an idea which has been in the mind of God throughout. It appears that during those ages . . . when animals were torturing each other with ferocious horns and agonizing stings, Omnipotence was quietly waiting. . . . Why the Creator should have preferred to reach His goal by a process, instead of going straight to it, these modern theologians do not tell us.[126]

Philosopher David Hull is equally non-plussed, in noting that the process of natural selection "is rife with happen-stance, contingency, incredible waste, death, pain and horror. . . . The God implied by . . . the data of natural history . . . is not a loving God. . . . He is . . . careless, indifferent, almost diabolical."[127]

Jacques Monod, the Nobel-prize winning atheist biologist, sees natural selection as "a horrible process," expressing surprise "that a Christian would defend the idea that this is the process which God more or less set up."[128] Renowned biologist Theodosius Dobzhansky, self-avowed creationist and evolutionist, also stated:

> The universe could have been created in the state of perfection. Why [then] so many false starts, extinctions, disasters, misery, anguish, and finally the greatest of evils — death? The God of love and mercy could not have planned all this. Any doctrine which regards evolution as predetermined or guided collides head-on with the ineluctable fact of the existence of evil.[129]

He added later, "What a senseless operation it would have been, on God's part, to fabricate a multitude of species *ex nihilo* and then let most of them die out! . . . Was the Creator in a jocular mood . . . ?"[130] Such an operation, we agree, does not lend itself to a perspective that is consistent with the loving Creator's self-revelation in Scripture.

Bearing in mind the implications behind the assertions of Russell, Hull, Monod, and Dobzhansky, the reader will perhaps agree with the following notion:

---

126. Bertrand Russell, *Religion and Science* (New York: Oxford University Press, 1961), p. 73.

127. David Hull, "The God of the Galápagos," *Nature* 352 (August 8, 1992): p. 486.

128. Jacques Monod, interviewed by Laurie John, Australian Broadcasting Commission, June 10, 1976, quoted in Ted Peters, "Evolutionary Evil," *Dialogue* 35 (Fall 1996): p. 243.

129. Theodosius Dobzhansky, *The Biology of Ultimate Concern* (New York: New American Library, 1967), p. 120.

130. Theodosius Dobzhansky, "Nothing in Biology Makes Sense Except in the Light Evolution," *The American Biology Teacher* 35:3 (1973): p. 126–127.

the traditionalists' defense of a six-day creation, literal Fall, and a global Flood, may have sprung primarily from a need to defend God's character, instead of from any pre-scientific, puppet-like adherence to a crass literalism, as is often inferred. This is certainly the case with the scriptural geologists. Bugg understood this well:

> Hence then, we have arrived at the wanton and wicked notion of the Hindoos, viz., that God has *"created and destroyed worlds as if in sport, again and again"*!! But will any Christian Divine who regards his Bible, or will any Philosopher who believes that the Almighty works no "superfluous miracles," and does nothing in vain, advocate the absurdity that a wise, just, and benevolent Deity has, "numerous" times, wrought miracles, and gone out of his usual way for the sole purpose of destroying whole generations of animals, that he might *create others* very like them, but yet differing a little from their predecessors!![131]

The depth of Granville Penn on this flank cannot be overstated, and you will be rewarded by deeply reflecting on the following emphases:

> To assume arbitrarily, *a priori*, that God created the matter of this globe *in the most imperfect state to which the gross imagination of man can contrive to reduce it*, which it effectually does, by reducing the creative *Fiat* to the mere production of an *amorphous elementary mass*; and then to pretend, that His intelligence and wisdom are to be collected from certain hypothetical occult laws, by which *that mass worked itself into perfection of figure and arrangement after innumerable ages*; would tend to lessen our sense either of the divine *wisdom* or *power*, did not the supposition recoil with tremendous reaction upon the *supposers*, and convict them of the clumsiest irrationality. The supposition is totally *arbitrary*; and not only arbitrary, *viciously* arbitrary; because, it is totally *unnecessary*, and therefore betrays a *vice of choice*. For, the laws of matter could not have *worked perfection* in the mass which the Creator is thus supposed to have formed *imperfect*, unless by a power imparted by *Himself* who established the laws. And, if He could thus produce perfection *mediately*, through their operation, He could produce it *immediately*, without their operation. Why, then, wantonly and viciously, without a pretence of authority, *choose* the supposition of their mediation? It is entirely a decision of *choice and preference*, that is, of *the will*; for, *the reason* is no party in it, neither urging, suggesting, encouraging, or in any way aiding or abetting the decision, but, on the contrary, positively denying and condemning it. The *vast length of time*, which this sinistrous [sic] *choice* is necessarily obliged to call in for its own defense, could only be requisite to the Creator *for overcoming difficulties obstructing the perfecting process*; it *therefore chooses to suppose*, that He *created obstructions* in matter, to

---

131. Bugg, *Scriptural Geology*, 1: p. 318–319.

resist and retard the perfecting of the work which He designed; whilst at the same time he [sic] might have perfected it without any resistance at all, by *His own Creative Act*. . . . To suppose then, *a priori*, and without the slightest motive prompted by *reason*, that His wisdom willed, at the same time, both the *formation* of a perfect work, and a series of resistances to *obstruct* and *delay* that perfect work, argues a gross defect of intelligence *somewhere*; either in the *Creator* or in the *supposer*; and I leave it to this science, to determine the *alternative*.[132]

While accommodationists tried to exonerate God from the unsavory nuances implied by paleonatural evil, they appeared undeterred by the sheer amount of paleonatural death, seemingly open to including *any* level of non-human suffering, death, and mass extinction in the Creator's approbation, "very good." Such believers look prepared to give God a free pass "even if he multiplied the world's pain a billionfold."[133] And thus we cannot help but ask if the skeptic will be impressed by a panglossian theodicy in which *any* level of natural evil can be made to fit Genesis 1:31.[134]

Seven Findings from Our Study

1. Paleonatural Evil Was a Problem Recognized in the Early 19th Century

As deep-time geological interpretations gained a toe hold, a theodicy for paleonatural evil was needed: would the Christian God have intentionally devised a process so rife with "happen-stance, contingency, incredible waste, death, pain, and horror"?

2. The Responses to Paleonatural Evil Come under Two Basic Groupings

The early 19th century theodicies fall under two major headings: traditionalists and accommodationists. Each proposed starkly contrasting theodicies which essentially mirror the present-day debate: fiat creationists (young-earth advocates) versus progressive creationists and theistic evolutionists (deep-time proponents).

3. Some Saw Paleonatural Evil as Clashing with a Plain Reading of Genesis

The traditionalists thought paleonatural evil exacted too high a price on the face of God, and urged the Church to take Scripture at face value. Every

---

132. Granville Penn, *A Comparative Estimate of the Mineral and Mosaical Geologies* (London: J. Duncan, 1825), I: p. 124–127.

133. Winslow Shea, "God, Evil and Professor Schlesinger," *Journal of Value Inquiry* 4 (1970): p. 228.

134. In Voltaire's satirical *Candide*, Dr. Pangloss rationalizes away all bad things, insisting that they serve some good purpose in our best of all possible worlds. The term *panglossian* refers to any bent for labeling evils as *very good*. Evangelical old-earthers are panglossian in that their philosophical starting point logically obliges them to accept all manner of paleonatural evil as divinely approved.

discernable impulse of this group was to embrace what Scripture's original recipients would have most likely taken as historical fact. When alleged conflicts arose between Scripture and geology, traditionalists suggested plausible interpretations of the geological evidence which would not sacrifice a natural reading of the creation, Fall, and Flood accounts. Tethering Genesis to the ever-evolving theories of a young scientific discipline was simply an unacceptable hermeneutic for the traditionalists.

4. Some Saw Paleonatural Evil as Consistent with Genesis

Accommodationists instead took more hermeneutical license to wed old-earth theories with the Bible. They not only saw paleonatural evil as an issue worth appraising, but did not see it as detrimental to the Creator's goodness. In forging theodical, theological, and hermeneutical constructs amenable to paleonatural evil, their theodicy took on a strong panglossian tinge.

5. The Traditionalists' Theodicy Dovetailed with Earlier Protestant Theodicies

The early 19th-century traditionalist theodicy was congruent with the earlier classic understandings of God's beneficence as revealed through His creative method. Like Luther, Calvin, and Wesley, the scriptural geologists also saw intense pain, death, or natural evils as having no place in a *very good* creation, but were post-Fall intrusions. There can be no reasonable doubt that the reformers and traditionalists embraced the same general theodical rubrics.

6. Accommodationists Had Little Continuity with Earlier Protestant Theodicies

Accommodationists saw natural evils as intended, non-intrusive agents in the *very good* creation. With the sin-death nexus now severed, they had to adopt a panglossian theodicy quite divergent from those of the reformers.

7. These Dueling Theodicies Paint Very Different Portraits of God's Face

Lastly, these contrasting philosophies of divine creative method provide conceptual and historical perspectives by which to trace *the evolving face of God*; i.e., to detect a shift in how His beneficence was understood from the Reformation era to the early 19th century.[135] This chapter has shown that the traditionalists recognized severe theodical difficulties with paleonatural evil. Though our nine key thinkers all in some way held that God's goodness could be derived from the study of nature, they were at odds over how this goodness was to be framed. The metaphor of "God's face" differentiates the God of the traditionalists from that of the accommodationists. Traditionalists picture a God whose "face" is inviting, and which reflects tender compassion and protective grace. However, while the visage of deep time's God can be given a panglossian face lift, another

---

135. It would require another essay to document that old-earth thinking of the early 19th century was also a shift away from pre-Reformation thinking in the Church about the nature of the beneficence of the Creator. But Mook's earlier chapter on that period steers future researchers in a very healthy direction.

whole range of expressions naturally arise which do not illicit a sense of paternal comfort, wisdom, and moral uprightness.

In the wake of the new geology, the accommodationists appear overly optimistic in their "handling of the difficult problem of pain, disease, disaster, and death in creation. Generally, they either ignored the problem or dealt with it superficially, attributing the evil in a mysterious way to divine beneficence."[136] They were left to see paleonatural evil as the blessed condition of divine creative method, not the result of sin, and as such followed a more eisogetical path to fit deep-time serial catastrophism, suffering, death, and extinction with the Mosaic record.

Conversely, Luther, Calvin, Wesley, and the traditionalists defended a caring Creator who set up a creation reflecting His own very good, loving nature; and thus of necessity free of disease, death, and natural evils. The traditionalists mirrored the theodicy which the reformers used for defending a *very good* creation. Though privy to the same hard data as the accommodationists, the traditionalists felt comfortable exegeting the rocks differently. They objected that the paleonatural evil implied by uniformitarianism conflicted with the perspicuity of Genesis. And such a twisted view of the genesis of natural evil could lure believers to accept completely unbiblical ideas about earth history and God's nature.

Conclusion

In sum, our assessment and brief historical analysis above supports this conclusion: the early 19th-century interpretation of the fossiliferous geologic strata initiated a re-evaluation of the origin of evil. Recalibrations may have been ever so slight at first, but a perilous precedent was set, because by the mid-1800s, only a fraction of the world's bone yards had been quarried. Yet with the unearthing of highly concentrated bone beds yet to come (e.g., South Africa's Karoo formation[137]), the incompatibility between natural evil and God's character showed promise of becoming all the more acute.

This chapter has highlighted several areas of contrast between two groups of Christians and their responses to this problem: if nature has been *red in tooth and claw* for deep time, why then would God call it *very good*? If paleonatural evil was deemed "very good," then the new geology could be credited with generating a new face for God, by which is meant a significant shift away from traditional understandings of God's omnibenevolence and the goodness of the original creation. The Creator revered by Luther, Calvin, Wesley, and the 19th-century traditionalists differs significantly from the accommodationists' God who created

---

136. Mortenson, *Great Turning Point*, p. 39.

137. One evolutionist estimated that 800 million vertebrates (ranging in size from small lizards to cow-sized creatures) are buried in this jumbled grave. Although this figure is likely exaggerated (and actually unverifiable), the Karoo formation is nevertheless a massive fossil graveyard that is explained well by Noah's Flood but is very difficult to explain within any evolutionary framework. See John Woodmorrappe, *Studies in Flood Geology* (El Cajon, CA: Institute for Creation Research, 1999, 2nd ed), p. 18.

whole species whose main purpose seems to have been to serve as nothing more than roadkill on the evolutionary highway.[138]

Considering the staggering levels of natural evil unearthed by geology since Lyell's day, it must be asked how much more ground accommodationists will cede in their theodicy. In forfeiting the time-honored natural reading of Genesis to comport with the alleged scientific fact of deep time, we must ask this: have well-meaning evangelicals set a precedent for further accommodations to all subsequent edicts of scientific consensus? What will these believers do when science says they cannot believe that an axe head floated, or the Red Sea parted, or the sun stood still, or that Jesus actually walked on water? When we stroll along with any scientific discipline as more authoritative than Scripture, then what consistent rationale can be given for not going a second mile as well? To the extent that modern accommodationists remain ambiguous here, it seems just a matter of time before the "face of God" evolves once again.

Please recall the suggestion above that God wants us to detect something of His personality in creation,[139] and couple this with the accommodationist contention that God designed serial catastrophism, natural evils, and death; going further by labeling His finished work *very good*. How would such a divine *face* reassure history's millions of victims of congenital deformities, or the sentient creation ravaged by cancer for many trillions of collective hours, or the most recently traumatized survivors of the Sichuan quake?

Naturally, in the wake of life's tragedies we should not just trot out proof texts, or quote some lofty figure on Genesis 1:31. Agonizing persons deserve better. Ministerial tact should always be Spirit led, multifaceted, context-sensitive, and never perfunctory. Still, when bad things happen to good people, Evangelicals would do well to recover and imbibe the theodical underpinnings taken as scripturally self-evident by the early church and the reformers — that all natural evils are the result of the sin with no place in the finished creation. Pastorally, more needs to be shared, of course, but it carries much therapeutic weight to affirm that such thorns in the flesh were not originally intended by the Creator. Yet, the bedside manner of modern accommodationists, whereby death and its ilk are somehow *very good* (being designed and called such by the heavenly Physician), can hardly be expected to infuse hope into the aching heart. When encountering natural evils of every stripe, would it not be healthier theologically and pastorally to affirm with Wesley that "in the beginning it was not so"?

138. This graphic metaphor comes from Del Ratzsch, *The Battle of Beginnings: Why Neither Side Is Winning the Creation-Evolution Debate* (Downers Grove, IL: InterVarsity Press, 1996), p. 189.

139. Stanley Rice, "On the Problem of Apparent Evil in the Natural World," p. 150.

Epilogue

Since the Enlightenment, reason and science have progressively usurped theology and revelation as the arbiters of truth and knowledge. Through the powerful cultural influence of science, the whole world has been taught that evolution and millions of years are demonstrable, unquestionable scientific fact. The pressure to comply is great, and those who do not are ridiculed as ignorant, flat-earth fundamentalists. Darwinism and deep time have influenced almost all major academic disciplines, and have thus slowly shaped every tier of society.

Most Christians do not accept the Darwinian view that all plants and animals are descended from common ancestors, first because it so clearly contradicts Genesis, but also presumably because the scientific evidence has been weighed and found wanting. However, it appears that a majority of those in Christian academia, along with many pastors and laypeople, have embraced the idea of millions of years. A major reason is their confidence (very often publicly stated) that all the relevant evidence indisputably points toward an ancient earth and even older universe. They are equally persuaded that there is no contradiction between deep time and Scripture. But no matter how sincerely these views are held, they open the door for students of these professors to accept evolution. The consequences have been socially and spiritually significant.

Dangerous ideas have always had negative consequences, as is tragically seen in the 20th century, which reaped so much bitter fruit in the wake of philosophies which implemented Darwin's ideas. Few more chilling examples of the fallout of Darwinism can be found than Nazism and communism, which consciously applied Darwinian principles, and radically affected millions of lives. Our Western world, once so firmly grounded on Judeo-Christian principles, is now deeply into its post-Christian phase illustrated by partial-birth abortions, marriage radically redefined, euthanasia, etc. This decline shows no sign of abating.

In his highly influential 1985 scientific critique of evolution, non-Christian microbiologist, Michael Denton said, "Today it is perhaps the Darwinian view of nature more than any other that is responsible for the agnostic and skeptical outlook of the twentieth century."[1] That is an astute insight for one who at

---

1. Michael Denton, *Evolution: A Theory in Crisis* (London: Burnett Books, 1985), p. 358. Denton is a medical doctor and PhD molecular biologist from New Zealand.

the time was himself an agnostic. But skepticism and the resulting widespread rejection of the gospel and Christian morality did not start with Darwin: it was "already in the air."[2]

The late Harvard biologist Ernst Mayr, a renowned atheist evolutionist, made the connection that Christians often miss: "The [Darwinian] revolution began when it became obvious that the earth was very ancient rather than having been created only 6,000 years ago. This finding was the snowball that started the whole avalanche."[3] While the idea of millions of years was not a "finding" of science, but an invention rooted in anti-biblical assumptions about the past, we agree that the rejection of the biblical chronology set a whole chain of events in motion.

There is a strong irony in the above statement, in that it was made by a Harvard scholar; a school with the early motto *"Veritas pro Christo et Ecclesia" (Truth for Christ and His Church)*. Harvard was America's first university, chartered in 1636, where every applicant was required to know Latin and Greek *before* coming, so that they could better study the Bible. During its first century, more than half of its graduates became pastors. One of the saddest and most well-attested facts in the West is that formerly Christ-centered institutions, like Harvard, slowly absorbed the zeitgeist of modernity — an anti-supernatural, deep-time, evolutionary dogma — which infected their curriculum and eventually killed their view of Scripture and their statements of faith. A brief perusal of the founding canons of our nation's oldest, most prestigious academic institutions demonstrates their one-time adamant Christian character. All except two of America's first 108 universities were strongly Christian, often sharing the common objective of training students competently in God's Word for the expressed purpose of winning the world for Christ. Today, they are bastions of anti-Christian unbelief which their founders would scarcely recognize.[4]

Considering this long and winding trail of compromise, we leave it to our readers' judgment to ponder this: what are the risks that schools take today when they hire professors who are sympathetic to evolutionary and deep-time thinking, and sow such philosophical seeds throughout their curriculum? How many institutions do you know that have ever drifted to the right? And as the academy goes, so go the denominations eventually. Today's liberal Protestant denominations were once orthodox, believing in the inspiration and inerrancy of Scripture, the miracles in the Bible, Jesus atoning death, and His bodily resurrection. But history shows that the slippery slide started with the absorption of anti-biblical

---

2. Cf. Milton Millhauser, *Just Before Darwin* (Middletown, CT: Wesleyan University Press, 1959), chapter 3.

3. Ernst Mayr, "The Nature of the Darwinian Revolution," *Science*, vol. 176 (2 June 1972): p. 988.

4. For a thorough survey of the de-Christianization of the American universities, see Jon H. Roberts and James Turner, *The Sacred and the Secular University* (Princeton, NJ: Princeton University Press, 2000).

naturalistic (deistic and atheistic) philosophical assumptions through the one-two punch of higher criticism and old-earth geology.

The authors of this book are convinced that no properly interpreted scientific facts will ultimately contradict a straightforward reading of Genesis. We have shown that the Bible, God's "special revelation," teaches that creation reveals to us the existence of God and at least some of the His attributes. This "general revelation" is about God. Not everything that scientists "discover" about God's creation is general revelation. Nor does everything the majority of scientists believe to be true fall under that label. Scripture does not teach that by a study of general revelation alone, without any reference to special revelation, we can hammer out the time frame of the creation or the manner in which God brought it into being. *Sola Scriptura* provides the protective parameters for interpreting our observations of creation, not the other way around.

We strongly affirm J.I. Packer's insistence, that inerrantists must have "an advance commitment to receive as truth from God all that Scripture is found on inspection actually to teach."[5] We must compare Scripture with Scripture, exegete it carefully and in context, seek for authorial intent, and have a prior commitment to submit to its teachings. Provided the texts are interpreted correctly, the results should serve as a lens to judge everything else, including our own personal theological provincialisms. If not, how could we affirm that *any* miracle took place in space and time? By way of exact parallel, Genesis, properly interpreted, is a pair of glasses to correctly observe, filter, and interpret God's creation.

Any reconstruction of the history of our universe that contradicts the truths of Scripture must be judged as erroneous. But when we study the created world of living things, rocks, and stars within this biblical framework, it makes sense of what we see. We can readily observe in biology that God indeed created plants and animals to reproduce after their distinct kinds, not to change into different kinds. Our minds recognize that the scientific evidence is consistent with a global catastrophic Flood. Using biblically derived assumptions, we also detect the earmarks of design, and that physical evidence points to a recent creation. And in holding consistent scriptural presuppositions, God's Curse is evident throughout creation, joining the refrain of the reformers that these things were not always so.

We have shown that young-earth creationism is the historic, orthodox teaching of the Church. For 1,800 years, the almost universal belief of Christians was that God created in six literal days about 6,000 years ago, and that He destroyed the world with a global Flood at the time of Noah. But in the early 19th century, deistic and atheistic geologists and astronomers, armed with anti-biblical assumptions, began to advance their old-earth and old-universe theories. There were dissenting voices, of course, but when this Pandora's box was opened in the Church, believers began to embrace gap, day-age, local Flood, and framework theories, and other tenets not immediately apparent from a natural reading of Genesis 1–11. Who can calculate the damage this has done to Christendom?

---

5. J.I. Packer, "Hermeneutics and Biblical Authority," *Themelios*, 1 (1975): p. 11.

The price tag of inserting millions of years into the Bible has been quite costly. First, we are asked to ignore many details of the biblical text in Genesis and elsewhere in Scripture, as discussed in this volume. Second, we must also reject, ignore, or otherwise suppress the plain teaching of Jesus and the Apostles. Third, by incorporating "deep time" into our thinking, we undermine the Bible's teaching on the origin of death. Fourth, we sully the character of God by adopting a view that has no other recourse but than to affirm that the natural evil we presently observe was designed and called *very good* by the Creator. Fifth, we are left with many other thorny conundrums, not the least of which is this: if our omnipotent Creator's finished work was not death-free (death even seen as "good"), then what assurance do we have that the new heavens and new earth will be death-free? Why trust Scripture on the eschaton, but not the beginning? No matter how sincere one's motives are, or how unintentional the fallout, tethering deep time to Scripture ultimately undermines the gospel of Jesus Christ, which is rooted in the literal history of Genesis, and the hope of the gospel in the eternal state, where there will be no more natural or moral evil.

We believe the arguments presented here provide compelling biblical reasons to believe that the Church was correct during its first 18 centuries. The resources in the appendix provide some of the scientific evidence for believing this also. We urge our readers to become familiar with that material.

In 1990, in a Wheaton College symposium on Christianity and science, Davis Young made a stunning admission. As a former day-age proponent (but still an old-earther) he lamented that "there were some textual obstacles the day-agers developed an amazing agility in surmounting." He frankly confessed that he "repented of that textual mutilation a few years ago," and decided to move on "without further embarrassing [him]self." He colorfully depicted those who force harmony between Scripture and old-earth evolutionism, as engaging in "the usual subterfuge," and "exegetical gymnastic maneuvers" which have caused "damage to the theological musculature." He said he did not particularly like to admit it, but these "concordistic harmonizations have generally failed," and as "genius as all these schemes may be, one is struck by the forced nature of them all." With all this confession of mishandling the Word of God, one might think Young is now a young-earth creationist. But sadly he has moved even further from Scripture. His conclusion in that Wheaton lecture (and evidently still today) is that Genesis 1–11 "may be expressing history in nonfactual terms."[6]

---

6. The context of the quoted phrases is here. "The Day-Age hypothesis insisted with at least a semblance of textual plausibility that the days of creation were long periods of indeterminate length, although the immediate context implies that the term, *yôm*, for 'day' really means 'day.' . . . There were some textual obstacles the Day-Agers developed an amazing agility in surmounting. . . ." After discussing some examples of contradiction in order of events between Genesis 1 and evolution history, he continued, "This obvious point of conflict, however, failed to dissuade well-intentioned Christians, my earlier self included, from nudging the text to mean something different from what it says. In my case, I suggested that the events of the days overlapped. Having publicly

Such a logically challenged idea as "non-factual history" is the fruit of Young's acceptance of geological "facts" that are actually *interpretations* based on anti-biblical, naturalistic, uniformitarian, philosophical assumptions, which he absorbed during his academic training (or "brainwashing," as Derek Ager put it[7]) under secular evolutionary geologists. Unfortunately for the Church, many Bible scholars have trusted Young's writings because of his geological credentials and probably also due to the fact that his father was the respected Old Testament scholar, E.J. Young. As a result, those theologians have not believed God's Word about the age of the earth. We can only hope that these scholars would consider carefully the young-earth view of the equally qualified PhD geologists, whose books and DVDs are listed in the appendix.

In more recent years, the Intelligent Design movement (IDM) has become popular in the Church. Most of the books generated by leaders in this movement have been published by evangelical publishers and have been widely read in the Church. We greatly value the IDM arguments which expose the flaws of Darwinian evolution, and the sophisticated analysis which enables us to recognize design in nature (in contrast to what time, chance, and the laws of nature produce). These arguments have greatly supplemented the design arguments that young-earth creationists have used for decades both before and after the IDM arose.

We also appreciate the attention that the IDM has drawn to the influence of naturalism in Darwinian science. Ben Stein's provocative 2008 movie *Expelled* is a timely exposé, demonstrating that the "evolution versus creation/design" debate is actually a worldview conflict, not a "science versus religion" debate. We believe that *Expelled* is extremely helpful and will open many people's minds to the nature of the battle. So we will continue to warmly appreciate and use much of what the IDM has produced and encourage them to press on in the battle.

Having said this, we must also highlight briefly our concerns about the impact that the IDM is having on the Church. First, from our reading and experience

---

repented of that textual mutilation a few years ago, I will move on without further embarrassing myself." Following an examination of other unsuccessful techniques for harmonizing Genesis with old-earth geology, Young confessed "Genius as all these schemes may be, one is struck by the forced nature of them all. While the exegetical gymnastic maneuvers have displayed remarkable flexibility, I suspect that they have resulted in temporary damage to the theological musculature. Interpretation of Genesis 1 through 11 as factual history does not mesh with the emerging picture of the early history of the universe and of humanity that has been deciphered by scientific investigation. Dickering with the biblical text doesn't seem to make it fit the scientific data. . . . The Bible may be expressing history in nonfactual terms." See Davis Young, "The Harmonization of Scripture and Science," quoted at length in Marvin Lubenow, *Bones of Contention* (Grand Rapids, MI: Baker, 1992), p. 232–234. Terry Mortenson has the complete lecture on audio CD.

7. See the end of Mortenson's chapter on the historical developments, earlier in this volume.

we believe it influences Christians to downplay the Word of God on this issue of the age of the earth, leading them to think it is somehow less clear in its teachings than science is. Books by IDM scholars might make some general reference to the Bible, but this often looks like an afterthought, or proof-texting, instead of seriously engaging the best exegesis related to the age of the earth, especially on Genesis. Also, many IDM leaders lecture in Christian contexts (churches, Christian universities, seminaries, Christian radio and TV, etc.). In those settings they either generally ignore Genesis (or at least one read naturally) as they promote old-earth views. This is not surprising since many in the movement are not evangelicals or necessarily even Christians. Leaders at the IDM's primary think tank, *The Discovery Institute*, are very frank about the fact that the movement has no religious boundaries.[8] This ignoring of the biblical text would not be a problem if Scripture said nothing related to geology, cosmology, and the age of the creation. But it does. And no serious follower of Christ can justifiably ignore His Word or superficially examine the relevant Scriptures on this subject.

Second, while the IDM leaders are good at highlighting the heavy influence of philosophical naturalism in biology, they ignore its equal domination of geology and astronomy, which is why most IDM proponents have accepted the millions of years as proven scientific fact. But, as we've shown, naturalism took control of geology and astronomy over 50 years before it took control of biology through Darwinism. In fact, the former laid the foundation for the latter, which then has been the basis for evolutionizing every other field of study in the academy. So the age and history of the creation strikes at the very heart of the stranglehold of science by philosophical naturalism. Evolution is like a rope made of three inseparable cords: biological evolution (origin and historical development of life), geological evolution (origin and historical development of planet Earth), and astronomical evolution (origin and historical development of the cosmos and heavenly bodies). Christians are not really dealing adequately with evolution or philosophical naturalism if they do not realize this and deal with the biblical teaching on the age of the creation.

Third, because IDM arguments only focus on design, they do not seem to fully appreciate the theological importance of the origin of the natural evil we see in the world or, if they grasp the problem, they do not offer an adequate answer that is consistent with scriptural teaching about the Fall. Evolutionists have long pointed to disease, mutations, and natural disasters, concluding that if this is the work of an intelligent designer, he is sadistic. These sentiments go back as far as Darwin, who in an 1856 letter to Joseph Hooker, wrote, "What a book a Devil's Chaplain might write on the clumsy, wasteful, blunderingly low and horridly cruel works of nature."[9] Unless we believe what Genesis says about the initially perfect creation where there was no animal or human death and

---

8. See the movie *Expelled* for many statements that reflect this fact.

9. Frederick Burkhardt and Sydney Smith, eds., *The Correspondence of Charles Darwin*, vol. 6, 1856–1857, (Cambridge: Cambridge University Press, 1990), p. 178.

what it says about the cosmic impact of the Fall of Adam in sin, then we are not offering a fully biblical theodicy to the most common objection to the Christian faith (i.e., how can there be a loving God with all the death and suffering and natural evil [e.g., hurricanes, earthquakes, tsunamis] in the world?)

Fourth, the IDM arguments do not constitute a real alternative to old-earth evolutionism because the IDM arguments do not have a history attached to them. Inevitably, questions arise. *When* did the "intelligent designer" do the creative work? Was everything created in one act? If so, how long ago? If not, what order were things created and how much time was between each creative act? Did "he" create only simple living cells and all plants and animals evolved from there with (or without) "his" providential control or intervention? Or did "he" make separate kinds of plants and animals in adult form? Without some tangible narrative, the IDM arguments are no match for the evolutionist theory to explain all of reality. We submit that only a fully biblical view of origins and history is an adequate alternative to deep-time evolutionism.

Fifth, while creation certainly does point to a designer, it does more than that, according to Scripture. It points to the God of the Bible (Rom. 1:18–20). But IDM leaders either downplay this fact or in effect deny it, which is why evolutionists (who are not spiritually discerning) continually charge that the IDM is a covert form of young-earth creationism. In reality, most IDM leaders are quite strongly opposed to the young-earth view.

Finally, and fleshing out the previous point, the IDM arguments can only lead a person to belief in some vaguely defined "intelligent designer." According to Michael Behe, a leader in the IDM, the design arguments alone do not preclude the conclusion that the designer was a group of alien beings in outer space.[10] Scripture, on the other hand, says that the creation bears clear witness to the true and living God, Creator of heaven and earth.[11] The IDM, therefore, is overlooking much of the evidence (which points to God's holiness, justice, and wrath, as well as his love and intelligence and power). As a result, there are strange bedfellows in the IDM: deists, pantheists, and various kinds of theists.

This approach of just looking for design and using it in defense of the existence of God (however vaguely He may be defined) was tried in the early

---

10. Michael Behe, "The Evolution of a Skeptic," www.origins.org/mc/resources/ri9602/behe.html, updated February 6, 1999, accessed August 18, 2008. He said this in response to the penultimate question in the interview: "If Francis Crick claimed intelligent aliens not only seeded life but actually designed life that is on the earth, I could not point at a biochemical system and argue against him. I might think it was a little far-fetched, but I would have to go to philosophical or theological or historical arguments to rebut that."

Most of the key players in the IDM personally believe the designer is the God in the Bible, but we are just emphasizing that this is not a necessary conclusion from ID premises, but rather a subjective religious view flowing from factors beyond anything inherent to mere intelligent design.

11. E.g., Ps. 19:1-6, Rom. 1:18–21 and Acts 17:22–31.

1800s in England, primarily by Christians and Deists who accepted the idea of an earth much older than the Bible teaches. These intelligent design arguments failed miserably to convert infidels or to stop the cultural slide away from biblical Christianity toward atheism. We think it failed precisely because the theology was fuzzy and there was a shallow and divorced-from-Scripture analysis of the philosophical assumptions of old-earth geological and old-universe astronomical theories.

So the IDM arguments do not necessarily lead people to Christ. If they do open a person to the idea that God exists, culminating later in conversion to Christ, such a person may have a struggle in believing Genesis because he has likely only had an accommodationist hermeneutic modeled for him. If his main mentors have shied away from "divisive readings of Genesis," where will a proper hermeneutical approach to Scripture be acquired? It is likely that he will have a lingering emotional attachment to IDM authors and their books which have helped him to believe in a Designer. In contrast, many people (and not a few scientists) are being won to Christ, and Christians are being won back to full confidence in Genesis by young-earth creationist presentations which employ both scientific and biblical arguments.[12]

We understand the IDM strategy is to engage the materialists on the scientific level only, because (it is assumed) the materialists will not accept arguments based on scriptural authority. But young-earth creationists know how to discuss only the scientific evidence in a secular public setting, such as a lecture or debate at a university or in a public school. Many young-earth creationists have been doing this for years, long before the IDM movement was born. But even in these secular contexts, young-earth creationists have found that many unbelievers are open to and interested in knowing what the Bible says on the subject, even if they do not yet believe it is the inspired Word of God. While we do not require the non-Christian to accept biblical authority without any apologetic arguments, neither do we hide or apologize for our biblical starting points. Rather we show that the scientific evidence powerfully confirms the Bible's teaching, just as we would expect, since God inspired Scripture and perfectly knows the history of the creation. However, when speaking to Christians (e.g., in books, churches, seminaries, or Bible colleges), as some IDM leaders do, we must help believers to consider first and foremost what the Word of God says about this whole subject of origins.

IDM leaders have a vision, represented by what Johnson calls the "wedge" strategy.[13] The reasoning seems to be that if we start by dismantling the evolutionary paradigm in biology and getting biologists to embrace the intelligent designer concept, then later on we can work on the questions of the Creator's identity and the age of the creation. If we get the wedge into the log of the evolution

12. E.g., "A Testimony: 'Joel Galvin' — Faith Shipwrecked by Compromising 'Christian' Colleges; Restored by Answers in Genesis," www.answersingenesis.org/home/area/feedback/joel_galvin_testimony.asp.

13. Phillip E. Johnson, *The Wedge of Truth* (Downers Grove, IL: InterVarsity Press, 2000).

paradigm and open that crack big enough, then the log will split, it is hoped. But, we contend, this is a mistaken vision, because the Bible says that people who are not in right relationship with God are suppressing the truth in unrighteousness (Rom. 1:18–20). The majority of biologists will never be won over to the intelligent design position, because ultimately this is a spiritual, worldview conflict, not a scientific debate. Furthermore, in this long and fruitless effort to get most biologists to embrace intelligent design, how many Christians will loose their confidence in the Word of God and assimilate naturalistic presuppositions into their thinking as a result of accepting the deep-time theories of geology and cosmology? And how many non-Christians will never believe the Bible (and the gospel) and will die in their sins (lost for eternity) because they think geology and cosmology have proven that the early chapters of Genesis are myth?

Atheistic science may be replaced by pantheistic science or deistic science (though we doubt it will). But the biblical worldview and the creation model of origins will never be accepted by the majority. No matter how strong our logic and scientific evidences are, most people will not be persuaded by them, not for intellectual reasons but for moral and spiritual reasons. This is a spiritual battle, first and foremost. That must be our conclusion, if we take the Bible's teaching seriously about God and the nature of man and the world system.

Stephen J. Gould, late professor of geology and paleontology at Harvard University and a strong anti-creationist, summarized the early developments in geology and its impact on biblical interpretation this way:

> Traditionally, non-biblical sources, whether natural or historical, had received their true meaning by being fitted into the unitary narrative of the Bible. This relationship now began to be reversed: the biblical narrative, it was now claimed, received its true meaning by being fitted, on the authority of self-styled experts, into a framework of non-biblical knowledge. In this way the cognitive plausibility and religious meaning of the biblical narrative could only be maintained in a form that was constrained increasingly by non-biblical considerations. . . . At least in Europe, if not in America, those geologists who regarded themselves as Christians generally accepted the new biblical criticism and therefore felt the age of the earth to be irrelevant to their religious beliefs.[14]

Ultimately, what is at stake in this controversy about the age of the earth is the perspicuity and authority of Scripture. It simply does not teach deep time or gradual creation or a local Flood. It clearly teaches six literal days of supernatural creation only a few thousand years ago, and a global catastrophic Flood that radically altered the surface of the earth, destroying billions of plants,

---

14. Cited in Martin, J.S. Rudwick, "The Shape and Meaning of Earth History," in David C. Lindberg and Ronald L. Numbers, eds., *God & Nature* (Berkley, CA: University of California Press, 1986), p. 306 and 311.

animals, and people in the process. Genesis 1–3, Romans 8:19–23, and other related passages just as clearly teach that His finished creation was *very good* and free of human and animal death. Furthermore, Scripture's testimony about the goodness, wisdom, power, justice, faithfulness, and grace of God makes it very difficult to comprehend how He could have created and destroyed countless species over the course of millions of years before creating man, who was commanded to rule over the creatures, most of whom (on this view) lived and died before Adam came on the scene. There is no scriptural warrant for this idea. To advocate it is to put an incompetent, wicked, or even sadistic face on God.

So, do we interpret Scripture by Scripture or do we use the outside higher authority of "science" to interpret Scripture? Will we believe the Word of God, who was there at the creation and the Flood, who knows everything, who never makes mistakes, who always tells the truth, and who inspired men to write the Scriptures without error so that Old Testament Jews, the Church fathers, the Reformers, and today's Christian would know the truth about how the creation came into existence and why it is the way it is today? Or will we place more confidence in the words of scientists, who weren't there during the early history of the earth, who don't know everything, who repeatedly make mistakes (which is why they must continually revise their textbooks), and most of whom are in rebellion against their Creator, trying to explain the world without God so they do not have to feel morally accountable to Him?

A few years ago, one of the editors of this book had a private meeting with a well-known, godly leader of a large evangelical ministry. This leader wanted to hear why the editor believed the age of the earth was vitally important. Some of the points in this book were raised in their conversation. At the end of the discussion, this leader said, "I believe God could do anything. I believe He could create in six seconds, six days, or six million years." On first glance that appears to be a statement of great faith. But in reality it is not, in spite of the godly sincerity of this Christian statesman, because the issue is not what we believe God *could* do or *could have* done. The issue is what God *said* that He *did do*. And so the question is this — will we believe what He said? If scientific theories convince us to adopt interpretations of Genesis which the original Hebrew readers would never have considered, then what's next? If we reinterpret the Scriptures on the creation days, Fall, and Flood, where will the process stop? Why stop with Genesis? What about the virgin birth or Resurrection of Jesus Christ? Perhaps we will remain faithful on these latter points, but will our children and students and schools and churches do so after we are gone?

Martin Luther is reported to have once expressed the following:

> If I profess, with the loudest voice and clearest exposition, every portion of the truth of God except precisely that little point which the world and the devil are at the moment attacking, I am not confessing Christ, however boldly I may be professing Christianity. Where the

battle rages the loyalty of the soldier is proved; and to be steady on all the battle-field besides is mere flight and disgrace to him if he flinches at that one point.[15]

Will we contend for the truth of God at that point that is one of the greatest points of attack today across the globe — the attack on the divine supernatural creation of the original world, the biblical chronology, and the Flood? Will we believe and contend for the truth of the Word of God, from the very first verse? God says through the prophet Isaiah"

> Thus says the LORD, "Heaven is My throne, and the earth is My footstool. Where then is a house you could build for Me? And where is a place that I may rest? For My hand made all these things, thus all these things came into being," declares the LORD. "But to this one I will look, to him who is humble and contrite of spirit, and who trembles at My word" (Isa. 66:1–2; NASB).

In the last 200 years, many in the Church have trembled at the words of the apologists for deep time. But historically, those who have worshiped the God of Abraham, Jacob, and Isaac, the God and Father of our Lord Jesus Christ, have demonstrated their loyalty by trembling at *His* Word. Would this be a time of soul-searching, humility, and contrition for you? The time is once again at hand for us to take the Creator at His Word. Evangelicals believe Scripture is the active voice of the only wise and living God. We thus agree that He has spoken in Genesis — that much is certain. But will we humble ourselves and reject whatever is preventing us from trembling at and believing His inerrant Word in Genesis 1–11, regardless of what the world and other believers think? That is the vital question we each must answer.

— The editors

---

15. This famous statement is quite often quoted, but hardly ever with proper documentation. It can be found in secondary sources like Elizabeth Rundle Charles, *Chronicles of The Schönberg-Cotta Family* (London: T. Nelson and Sons, 1864), p. 276. Many writers mistakenly attribute the quote to *D. Martin Luthers Werke: Kritische Gesamtausgabe*, ed. J.K.F. Knaake, et al. (Weimar: H. Böhlau, 1883), *Briefwechsel*, vol. 3, p. 81f., which expresses only similar sentiments. Cf. Luther's 1523 comment, in the original German, in *Briefe, Sendschreiben und Bedenken* (Berlin: G. Reimer, 1826), p. 345.

A Biographical Tribute to Dr. John C. Whitcomb Jr.

Paul J. Scharf

The life story of Dr. John C. Whitcomb Jr. is filled with paradoxes. Whitcomb is a gentle man with intense convictions. He is a famous scholar and author and a humble professor; a man who has traveled the world and yet spent more than 40 years at one seminary; a peaceful man who has never run from righteous conflict; a light-hearted man who has endured tumultuous crises. The son and grandson of army officers, he served in the infantry and then trained for a career as a diplomat. But he found fulfillment as an ambassador of a higher kingdom. Taught from childhood to be an evolutionist, he devoted his life to studying and teaching creationism.

When Whitcomb was born on June 22, 1924, at Walter Reed Army Medical Center in Washington, DC,[1] no one would have been surprised at the thought that his life would become a success — that was simply assumed. The manner in which Whitcomb ultimately achieved notoriety, however, could not have been foreseen by anyone during the early years of his life.

"Great things were expected of me," Whitcomb said of the circumstances into which he was born.[2] His father, John Clement Whitcomb Sr., was a graduate of the United States Military Academy at West Point, where he also taught Spanish in the early 1920s. He served in both World Wars and attained the rank of full colonel of infantry in Gen. George Patton's Third Army in Europe.[3]

---

1. Unless otherwise noted, the information included in this writing is taken from interviews conducted by the author with Dr. Whitcomb on the subject of his biography since May 30, 2003. A condensed version of Dr. Whitcomb's biography, entitled "Dr. John C. Whitcomb: Hero of the Faith," has been published in the Fall Quarter 2005 issue of the *Gospel Herald and the Sunday School Times* magazine (Cleveland, OH: Union Gospel Press), p. 12–13.
2. Quotation taken from Whitcomb's sermon "God's Truth Circles" (Part 1), given at First Baptist Church of Kingsbury, IN, on June 12, 2004.
3. The Whitcomb family actually lived next door to Gen. George Patton from 1939 to 1941 in Ft. Benning, GA.

Whitcomb's grandfather, Clement Colfax Whitcomb, was a graduate of Bowdoin College and an Army surgeon,[4] and was placed in charge of all medical supplies in Europe during World War I. His military service took him to the Philippines (where he served during the Spanish-American War) and Cuba (where John C. Whitcomb Sr. was raised from 1906 to 1909 and where he learned to speak Spanish fluently) — forging connections that would impact the younger Whitcomb's life and ministry many years later.

Whitcomb himself was raised in China from 1927 to 1930, where his father served in a United States Army regiment, protecting American citizens from warlords.[5] While there, the younger Whitcomb became fluent in Mandarin Chinese. (This, too, would serve as a catalyst for some of Whitcomb's later ministry activities.) Other stops during his childhood included Governor's Island, New York; Ft. Benning, Georgia; Ft. Leavenworth, Kansas; and Seattle, Washington. "I hit the ground running when I was born," he said, thinking of his youth. "You look back at your father and your grandfather, and see how God arranged your own background — providentially — to be able to do things He wanted you to do later that you can't explain in terms of your own life."

His parents' desire to see greatness in their only child caused them to send Whitcomb to McCallie School — a Christian preparatory school in Chattanooga, Tennessee, where he would hear the gospel for the first time in the chapel services.[6] They had hoped that their son would attend West Point like his father, but poor eyesight made that impossible. The next best alternative, in their opinion, was Princeton University, where Whitcomb was to study at the John Foster Dulles School of Public and International Affairs, hopefully preparing for a career as a diplomat for the United States government.

He entered the prestigious school in June of 1942 to begin an accelerated program.[7] "Little did I realize," Whitcomb stated, "that in the mystery of God's providence, before the end of my first year at the university I would become an ambassador for Christ through salvation."[8]

During that first year at Princeton, Whitcomb was fascinated by his science courses, particularly those dealing with evolutionary geology. The training he received there impacted him deeply, engraining him with a passion for exacting historical study. To this day, he shares many stories and illustrations from his

---

4. Whitcomb's great-grandfather also served in the Army, having lost a leg in the Civil War.
5. Whitcomb Sr. also served as the United States military ambassador to Peru from 1948 to 1951.
6. The principal of the school was Dr. J.P. McCallie, a committed Christian. Whitcomb's parents were members of an Episcopal church, which they rarely attended.
7. By the time of his graduation, Whitcomb's major had changed to ancient and European history.
8. Quotation taken from Whitcomb's sermon, "God's Truth Circles" (Part 1), given at First Baptist Church of Kingsbury, IN, on June 12, 2004.

time at Princeton, where he moved among some of the world's foremost thinkers and scholars.[9]

Of all the people who impacted Whitcomb at Princeton, however, the man who made the greatest mark was a most unlikely candidate. Dr. Donald B. Fullerton was a 1913 graduate of Princeton University and a Plymouth Brethren missionary to India and Afghanistan. In 1931, he returned to the United States due to health concerns, and established the Princeton Evangelical Fellowship. Amazingly, he would go on to hold Sunday afternoon Bible classes on the university campus for the next 50 years — until 1981 — leading hundreds of students to the Lord.

It was during Whitcomb's freshman year at Princeton that a former classmate from McCallie School, then a sophomore at Princeton, invited him to attend one of Fullerton's Bible classes in the student center at Murray-Dodge Hall. "That was the transformation of my life forever," Whitcomb said in retrospect. After several weeks of attending the meetings, and especially a private session with Dr. Fullerton in his dormitory room at Pyne Hall, Whitcomb placed his trust in Jesus Christ, and passed from spiritual death unto life, in February of 1943.[10]

"I was just overwhelmed by what I heard from that man of God," Whitcomb said. "God had prepared me for this. When he [Dr. Fullerton] opened the Bible and told me who the Lord Jesus Christ was, and what He had done for me on the Cross, I could not resist the work of the Holy Spirit in my life — and accepted Jesus as my Savior. The next morning I was overwhelmed by the magnificence of the universe around me," he recalled. "The sun, the clouds, the sky, the trees, flowers, squirrels, people, everything — and now I realized that God had made them."

From the moment Whitcomb trusted Christ, Fullerton had a dramatic impact on his thinking that has lasted until the present hour.[11] It was under Fullerton that Whitcomb had his first experiences with witnessing and apologetics, and it was Fullerton who initially pointed Whitcomb in the direction of dispensational theology.

One area that still remained unclear to him, however, was the real meaning of the early chapters of Genesis. "When Donald Fullerton came to tell me about the Lord," he said, "the obvious conflict between evolutionary theory and the Book of Genesis sort of shocked me." That conflict would boil within

---

9. Among them was Albert Einstein, to whom Whitcomb gave a piece of Christian literature at a meeting of the Princeton Evangelical Fellowship in 1947 where the Moody Institute of Science film, "The God of Creation," was shown.

10. For a complete firsthand account of Whitcomb's conversion experience, see John C. Whitcomb, *The Conversion of an Evolutionist*, Whitcomb Ministries, Inc., n.d., videocassette.

11. To this day, a treasured photograph of Fullerton standing with Whitcomb hangs in his study.

Whitcomb's heart for ten years before he would be able to pour his energy into studying it to his satisfaction.

Whitcomb noted that he had a desire to serve the Lord from very early in his Christian experience. "I wanted to get training to be a Bible teacher," he said. "If God's Word could do that to me, what could it do for others?"[12]

Those dreams would be interrupted, however, as Whitcomb, like so many of his generation, was called into military service during his sophomore year at Princeton. In April of 1943 he was drafted into basic training at Fort Bragg, North Carolina. He was sent off for additional training in army engineering at Virginia Polytechnic Institute, and then to basic infantry training in Louisiana before being shipped to Europe in October of 1944.

Whitcomb has incredible stories to tell about his experiences during those days. His service in the war, like that of so many thousands of his comrades, was profoundly life-transforming. Since he had studied German at Princeton, he was made a German interpreter, and was able to share the gospel as he dealt with German prisoners-of-war as a member of the Red-Ball Express — a supply line unit that delivered food and ammunition off of ships all the way to the front lines — in the fall of 1944. "That was my introduction to be a missionary in Europe," he said.

Whitcomb's most dangerous activities during the war involved his service in a field artillery fire-direction center in Belgium. During the German counter-attack in the Battle of the Bulge in December of 1944, he worked there with forward observers and artillery men. One moment that he will never forget occurred during that battle. An artillery shell exploded near the place where he had previously been on guard — only seconds after he had gone down into a basement to the fire-direction center. He realized immediately that God had protected him. "You owe your life to Me," was the message that he was sure that God communicated to him through that incident.

"God spared my life and gave me a hunger and thirst for missions in Europe through that war," Whitcomb said, looking back across the decades. He left Europe in January of 1946,[13] and returned to Princeton that summer. Amazingly, he left with a zeal for the evangelization of the German people that would stay with him for the rest of his days.

Whitcomb now counts his tie to the German people as one of several strong "connections" that God gave him to foreign lands that have led to significant ministry opportunities. "I just say, 'Thank You Lord. In Your providence, You had led me to spend one year studying German at Princeton University,'" he

---

12. For an account of Whitcomb's early attempts at witnessing (and how they later impacted his view of apologetics) see John C. Whitcomb Jr., "Contemporary Apologetics and the Christian Faith — Part I: Human Limitations in Apologetics," *Bibliotheca Sacra*. vol. 134, no. 534 (April 1977): p. 99–103.

13. Whitcomb attained the rank of technical sergeant during his service in the army. He left with no desire for a military career.

said. "Through this means, God gave me a further incentive and motivation to become involved with Germany."

In 1948, Whitcomb graduated with honors from Princeton, two years later than originally planned, but already with a virtual lifetime of experience. He had a desire to continue his studies at a seminary, and was considering Fuller Theological Seminary in Pasadena, California, which was ready to begin its second year of classes. Fullerton, however, pointed Whitcomb toward Grace Theological Seminary in Winona Lake, Indiana, which was just beginning to gain a high reputation within the evangelical world. "Dr. Fullerton urged me to consider Grace Seminary as the finest school in America for learning the whole Bible," stated Whitcomb. "He had heard wonderful reports of (founder and president) Alva J. McClain, Herman A. Hoyt, and Homer Kent Sr."

"God shapes every life uniquely," Whitcomb has remarked. When he went to Grace Seminary in the fall of 1948, he had no reason to think that God was shaping him to remain at that school as a student and professor for the next 42 years. He actually wanted to return to China as a missionary (before the Communist government expelled all foreign missionaries in 1950). His "Chinese connection" extends back to the three years that he spent there early in his life. "I had a fascination with the Chinese people, that they need the Lord," he stated. Though that door was closed, Whitcomb's interest in the souls of Chinese people would endure.

Still single, and without any particular plans for the future, Whitcomb was asked to meet with two of his most respected professors — Drs. McClain and Hoyt — on the morning following his seminary graduation in May of 1951. Dr. Robert Culver, Whitcomb's Old Testament professor, had resigned the night before, and his two mentors asked Whitcomb to stay at the school and teach the Old Testament and Hebrew. He agreed, and also continued his own studies at Grace, receiving the master of theology degree in 1953[14] and the doctor of theology degree in 1957.

"I love teaching the Old Testament," Whitcomb said, thinking back to those times. The excellence in teaching and skill in communicating for which he has come to be known were forged in those difficult days in which he combined the task of teaching students nearly his age with his own academic pursuits.

One area of Whitcomb's teaching, in fact, was the object of particular scrutiny among his own students. Since his conversion, Whitcomb had struggled to harmonize the creation account of Genesis with the teachings of evolution that he had been assured of all his life. He taught the famous gap theory of Genesis 1:1–2 to his students for two years, but was challenged on occasion as to how that view fit within the whole context of Scripture. Whitcomb would soon use

---

14. Whitcomb's Th.M. thesis was on the subject of the Jerusalem Temple. In 1951, he had written his bachelor of divinity thesis on the identity of Darius the Mede in the Book of Daniel. That work was published by Eerdmans in 1959 (see bibliography), and remains a definitive study of the topic.

the opportunity to write a doctoral dissertation to settle his questions related to the early chapters of Genesis and origins.

Meanwhile, Whitcomb's life was taking shape in other areas as well. In 1953, he married Edisene Hanson, whom he called a "wonderful Christian lady." Their first son, David, was born in 1955, followed by Donald in 1957, Constance in 1958, and Robert in 1960.

Those were busy times for Whitcomb as he balanced family responsibilities with his teaching career and the continuation of his own doctoral studies. The road that he would take in preparing his doctoral thesis, however, was greatly impacted by a man who came to speak at the Grace Seminary campus in September of 1953.

That visitor was a young engineering professor named Dr. Henry Morris. Whitcomb was acquainted with Morris' first book, entitled *That You Might Believe*,[15] and anticipated the opportunity to meet him.[16] While at Grace, Morris lectured on Flood geology, a topic that few had broached prior to that time.[17] McClain and Hoyt were receptive to Morris's ideas. Morris pointed out the scientific inadequacies within Whitcomb's writing, and thus the two began to work together. What followed were nearly 200 letters and two more personal meetings between Whitcomb and Morris, all of which culminated in the publication of *The Genesis Flood* in 1961.

"My evolution background at home and at Princeton was God's means to fascinate me with the origins issue, which I have never ceased to study and lecture on and write on to this day," Whitcomb said. *The Genesis Flood* was rejected by two evangelical publishers before being accepted by Presbyterian & Reformed Publishing Company. It would be difficult to overstate the impact that the book has since had on the development of the biblical and scientific creation movements

---

15. Henry M. Morris, *That You Might Believe* (Westchester, IL: Good News Publishers, 1978), 188 pages. The book was first published by Good Books, Inc., a division of Good News, in 1946. The background to its writing, and to its impact upon Whitcomb, is described in Henry M. Morris, *History of Modern Creationism* (San Diego, CA: Master Book Publishers, 1984), p. 93–99. (Morris also discussed his ongoing relationship with Whitcomb at length throughout that book.) Whitcomb gives the background to his historic encounter with Morris in John Whitcomb, *The Importance of Genesis — ICR's 25th Anniversary*, cassette, Institute for Creation Research, Nov. 10, 1995.

16. For a complete firsthand account of the history behind the partnership of Whitcomb and Morris, see John Whitcomb and Henry Morris, *ICR presents Fireside Chats*, Institute for Creation Research, n.d., DVD, 2003.

17. One work that had impacted that field of study prior to that time was Alfred M. Rehwinkel, *The Flood* (St. Louis, MO: Concordia Publishing House, 1951; rev. ed. 1957), 374 pages. Rehwinkel was a Missouri-Synod Lutheran scholar and professor of theology at Concordia Seminary in St. Louis. Whitcomb still points to Rehwinkel as being an early authority on the universality and significance of the Noachian Flood.

— to say nothing of the impact it had on the personal circumstances of Whitcomb and Morris.[18] "That changed our lives forever," Whitcomb summarized.

Whitcomb taught thousands of students during his years in Winona Lake, even earning the honorary title "Mr. Grace Seminary."[19] His reputation for teaching the Old Testament and theology drew many students to the school, and had a great impact on many lives. There are hundreds of pastors and missionaries still out in God's harvest fields that sat under his teaching — absorbing his theology and philosophy, and adopting his views in areas such as young-earth creationism, presuppositional apologetics, traditional dispensationalism, premillennial eschatology, and Old Testament theology.

During those years, Whitcomb held numerous positions at Grace, including professor of Old Testament and theology, chairman of the department of theology, director of doctoral studies, managing editor of the *Grace Journal* (from 1960 to 1973) and editor of the *Grace Theological Journal* (from 1980 to 1989). Some of his most treasured experiences related to his interaction with doctoral students. "I felt profoundly grateful to God that I was privileged to teach the Old Testament," Whitcomb said. "To study and teach the Old Testament on a seminary level for nearly 40 years is an extremely rare event in the evangelical world."

Whitcomb's years of teaching at Grace, however, were not without their share of trials. His greatest time of difficulty came as a result of the illness of his wife Edisene. She contracted a rare liver disease which was treated superficially as jaundice for ten years before an exploratory surgery was performed in the fall of 1968. Doctors determined as a result of that surgery that it was too late for treatment, and Edisene died in June of 1970.

During that time, however, God marvelously provided, not only for the future of the Whitcomb family, but also for another family that experienced a severe trial as well. One of Whitcomb's doctoral students, Robert Pritchett, died of an apparent heart attack while jogging late one evening in April of 1969. Pritchett and his wife Norma had been missionaries in the Philippines for 11 years, first serving as church planters south of Manila for 5 years, and then teaching for 6 years at the Far Eastern Bible Institute and Seminary.[20]

The couple and their two sons, Daniel and Timothy, moved to Winona Lake in the fall of 1968 for Robert to undertake a doctor of theology program, which would benefit his work at F.E.B.I.A.S. Whitcomb, as a representative

---

18. In 2006, *Christianity Today* named the book number 22 among "The Top 50 Books That Have Shaped Evangelicals" in "the last 50 years." The story may be found at www.christianitytoday.com/ct/2006/october/23.51.html.

19. Robert Delnay, *What Happened at Grace Seminary* ("Contemporary Christianity," Course Notes, p. 2), Faith Baptist Theological Seminary, Ankeny, IA, April 1995.

20. Norma Whitcomb came from a Christian and Missionary Alliance church background, and graduated from Houghton College in Houghton, NY (where she met her first husband), in 1949. They went to the Philippines in 1956 under China Inland Mission, which is now known as Overseas Missionary Fellowship. China Inland Mission had put them on loan to Send, International, which oversaw the work of F.E.B.I.A.S.

of the seminary, was called by the local authorities to identify Robert and to notify Norma and her sons of his death. "She was magnificent in that crisis," Whitcomb said of Norma. "She didn't fall apart. She knew that somehow God had a plan."

The two families had known each other before Robert died, and Edisene Whitcomb, as she was dying, informed her husband that it would please her if he would marry Norma after her passing. The couple wed in 1971, and formed a family that included children ages 10, 12, 13, 14, 15, and 16 at the time.[21] "Thank You, Lord," said Whitcomb, looking back on his family life after several decades had passed since he and Norma were first married. They can now take great delight in their 6 children, 17 grandchildren and 2 great-grandchildren.

Whitcomb was never one to do merely what was necessary to get by as a seminary professor. In addition to his teaching responsibilities, he continued to travel and speak, gaining notoriety particularly for his lectures on creationism, but also being asked to speak regularly on the subjects of Bible prophecy and apologetics.

Throughout his ministry, Whitcomb has focused much time and effort on world missions. The Whitcombs returned to the Philippines for mission trips on four occasions: 1982, 1983, 1987, and 1993. He served as president of the board of the Spanish World Gospel Mission from 1959 to 1990,[22] and was also president of the board and board member of the Foreign Missionary Society of the Fellowship of Grace Brethren Churches[23] from 1967 to 1987. He has lectured in Argentina, Australia, Brazil, the Central African Republic, Ecuador, England, France, Guatemala, Germany, Hong Kong, Italy, Japan, Korea, Luxembourg, Malaysia, Mexico, Peru, the Philippines, Puerto Rico, Singapore, Scotland, Spain, Taiwan, and Wales, and continues to receive words of testimony from people that he ministered to in those lands.

Whitcomb also continued to write, and wrote several books for major evangelical publishers. Foremost among these were *The Early Earth* and *The World That Perished* (Baker Book House) and commentaries on Esther and Daniel (Moody Press). His background in history carried over directly to his study of Scripture, and his interest in Bible chronology led him to produce his well-known Bible charts, more than a million copies of which have been printed in various forms. Whitcomb also contributed numerous articles to the *Grace Theological Journal* and *Bibliotheca Sacra* during the 1970s and 1980s.

In his final years at Grace, however, Whitcomb began to have concerns about the school he loved. The professors under whom he had studied, and with whom he had ministered, were passing off the scene. Dr. McClain had been dead for

---

21. For Norma's perspective on the merging of the two families, check her CD, *Brushstrokes of the Master Artist* (Whitcomb Ministries, Inc.).

22. This group is now known as Spanish World Ministries, Inc. Until 1973, it was known as Spanish World Gospel Broadcasting, Inc.

23. This group is now known as Grace Brethren International Missions.

about two decades,[24] and Drs. Hoyt and James L. Boyer had reached retirement age. By the middle of the 1980s, Whitcomb had become a senior member of the faculty, and believed that some of the core teachings that the seminary had historically stood for were no longer held unconditionally by all faculty members. He found himself in conflict with the positions of the school's administration. Finally, after 38 full years of teaching at Grace Theological Seminary — and after being coaxed out of resignation the summer before — Whitcomb's career at the seminary came to a most unexpected end in February of 1990.

That school year began on an ominous note, with Whitcomb suffering from blood clots in his right leg in France in August of 1989. He had been there to teach in Grace Seminary's European extension school for the fourth time,[25] but nearly died from this experience.

After 17 days in a French hospital, Whitcomb returned home to teach for another year, but during that time his disagreements with the administration came to a breaking point. He was asked to decide whether or not he would agree to continue at the school under the administration's constraints, which he could not do.

After more than 38 and one-half years on the faculty, the man who had become almost synonymous with Grace Theological Seminary was terminated in his final semester, just before retirement. The immediate cause for his removal was that he attended a meeting of conservative Grace Brethren pastors who shared some of his concerns over the direction of the seminary and the Fellowship of Grace Brethren Churches.[26] "It's unpleasant to be dismissed from a school where you've spent much of your life," Whitcomb stated, "but looking back I can say, 'That was one of the most blessed events in my whole life.'"

Whitcomb can now clearly see that much good came out of those unpleasant circumstances — including the fact that they gave him a special motivation to do the work in which he is now fully engaged. "At the time it was a tragedy," Whitcomb said. "Now I look back and say, 'Lord, if I hadn't left that place — totally, completely — I would never have been pressured into doing all these other things that now obviously were Your plan for the remainder of my life.' If I had just normally retired, I wouldn't have sensed the urgency that I have sensed to put all of my lectures on videotape."

The Whitcombs soon began Whitcomb Ministries, Inc. Whitcomb continued to research and write, while still also traveling to teach and preach in churches and schools in many parts of the world.[27] In fact, Whitcomb's opportunities

---

24. Dr. Alva J. McClain died in 1969. A biography of his life entitled *A Saint in Glory Stands* was written by Norman B. Rohrer (Winona Lake, IN: BMH Books, 1986).

25. The previous trips were in 1985, 1986, and 1987.

26. For a news article related to these events, see, "Grace Seminary Cuts Program," *Christianity Today* (January 11, 1993): p. 46.

27. Dr. and Mrs. Whitcomb traveled abroad for the final time in the spring of 1999 when they went to London.

were to become even greater than he ever anticipated. In the early 1990s, several Grace Brethren pastors and former students at Grace Seminary encouraged him to give serious thought to putting the courses that he had taught throughout his career onto videotape so that they could be preserved for future use. Soon that idea became a project, and the project was given a name — Christian Workman Schools of Theology.

"Pastors came to me and said, 'Dr. Whitcomb, we need to preserve traditional Christian theology and exegesis and hermeneutics from the days of McClain and Hoyt and the other founding fathers of Grace Seminary,'" Whitcomb stated. "The Grace Brethren had achieved international respect for their solid theological position at Grace Seminary through all those years, and that desperately needed to be preserved, and perpetuated, and protected from complete neglect."

At present, Whitcomb has recorded almost every class that he has ever taught, along with some new courses as well. He and Pastor Jeffrey Brown of Middl-ebranch, Ohio, have also recruited other highly qualified professors to record their lectures, and a complete seminary-level curriculum is being assembled for use in a variety of settings. The materials, in fact, are being used by a number of seminaries, overseas missionaries, and home-schoolers, as well as local churches. "That, in retrospect, showed God's hand in my departure from Grace Seminary," Whitcomb stated.

In addition to his work through Whitcomb Ministries, Inc., and Christian Workman Schools of Theology, Whitcomb has also played a key role in the founding and development of a new fellowship of churches, the Conservative Grace Brethren Churches, International. The group began in Indianapolis in September of 1993 after a split with the Fellowship of Grace Brethren Churches. Hoyt and Boyer, who are referred to by Whitcomb as the "master teachers" of the Grace Brethren movement, were still alive during the first several years of the new fellowship's history to give it theological guidance, along with Whitcomb. He currently serves as editor of the group's theological publication, *Journal of Grace*.

Now an octogenarian, Whitcomb is not resting on his laurels. He continues to travel and lecture, visiting several Bible institutes, colleges, and seminaries annually. He is still engaged regularly in preaching at churches, and reads and studies constantly. He is making new audio and videotapes, and writing syl-labi for his Christian Workman Schools of Theology course materials. He has contributed to several books in recent years, and is also updating some of his older works, attempting to bring them out in revised editions.[28] Whitcomb in-teracts with many Christian leaders and continues to be known as a scholar and Christian statesman. The horizons for Whitcomb Ministries have continued to expand, with an ever-increasing Internet presence and the start of an electronic

---

28. The Whitcombs' printed materials are now distributed by BMH Books of Winona Lake, IN. For complete information, visit www.bmhbooks.com.

newsletter.[29] Whitcomb Ministries also began to sponsor its own annual Bible conferences in the summer of 2004. Since 2006, Whitcomb has also represented Answers In Genesis as a creation speaker. In that role, he has given presentations at numerous additional creation conferences.[30]

Though he can no longer personally travel to the ends of the earth himself, Whitcomb still has a real heart for missions, as is evident by the projects that he is currently working with, foremost of which is the translation of some of his most widely used series of lectures into Mandarin Chinese (which he calls "the greatest language in the world today") for dissemination behind "the Bamboo Curtain." The Whitcombs have never received any royalties from the sale of their books in foreign languages.

Whitcomb has an international reputation as a biblical creationist. His passion, however, is that he would continue to go beyond that subject in his own ministry. "I want to be known, if for anything, as a Bible expositor," he said. "Creationism is absolutely essential, but it is not sufficient for a God-ordained teacher. I want to be balanced in my teaching of theology."

"Our ministry is not very flamboyant," his wife, Norma, said, "but we trust that it is solid for the sake of God." Norma has contributed heavily to the Whitcombs' current ministry, especially through her own writing and speaking for women and children.

Having lived through these experiences, Whitcomb's perspective is clear. "I am not my own," he stated. "I was bought with a price, and what God wants to do with my life and my experiences I would leave with Him to decide."

* * * *

I am so grateful to have had a part in recording the life experiences of Dr. John C. Whitcomb Jr., whom I met as a first-year seminary student at Faith Baptist Theological Seminary in Ankeny, Iowa, in September of 1994. He came to the school to teach a modular course on "Biblical Fundamentalism," and I was immediately impressed by Dr. Whitcomb's teaching skills, mastery of the Scriptures, and command of the classroom, not to mention his friendly demeanor and down-to-earth style. Furthermore, he seemed to have a genuine spiritual interest in every student who was in the room.

FBTS is one of the schools that Dr. Whitcomb travels to every year, and I have since studied in ten modular courses under him there — an opportunity with which I have been most blessed.

When I first met Dr. Whitcomb, I had no idea that I would one day be privileged to compile his biography, or to be involved with assisting him in his ministry. These endeavors originated when I began to interview him regarding

---

29. Visit www.whitcombministries.org and www.sermonaudio.com/whitcomb for more information.
30. For complete information on Whitcomb's work with Answers In Genesis, visit, www.answersingenesis.org/Home/Area/bios/j_whitcomb.asp.

his life's story in May of 2003. I had the urgency to complete that task because Dr. Whitcomb had been diagnosed with colon cancer the year before. Thankfully, he has since recovered from his bout with cancer, and that encounter at the Whitcombs' home has led to opportunities that I could barely dream possible.

I am so thankful to the Lord for Dr. Whitcomb — not only for his teaching, but now also for the impact that he has on me as I labor together with him. Certainly — though he would not admit it — he is most worthy of this work which is done in tribute to him.

BIBLIOGRAPHY[1]

Books

Davis, John J., and John C. Whitcomb. *Israel: From Conquest to Exile.* Winona Lake, IN: BMH Books, 1971. Combined edition printed 1989.

DeYoung, Donald B., and John C. Whitcomb. *The Moon: Its Creation, Form and Significance.* Winona Lake, IN: BMH Books, 1978 (also translated into German).

DeYoung, Don, and John C. Whitcomb. *Our Created Moon: Earth's Fascinating Neighbor.* Green Forest, AR: Master Books, 2003.

Whitcomb, John C. *The Bible and Astronomy.* Winona Lake, IN: BMH Books, 1984 (also translated into Korean).

_____. *Christ: Our Pattern and Plan.* Winona Lake, IN: BMH Books, 1976.

_____. *Daniel.* Chicago, IL: Moody Press, 1985 (also translated into French, Spanish, and Swahili).

_____. *Darius the Mede: A Study in Historical Identification.* Grand Rapids, MI: William B. Eerdmans, 1959.

_____. *Does God Want Christians to Perform Miracles Today?* Winona Lake, IN: BMH Books, 1973 (also translated into German and Arabic).

---

1. The purpose of this bibliography is to list the most significant of Dr. Whitcomb's writings and the foreign languages into which they have been translated. It is not comprehensive, as it does not contain all references to articles which he has contributed to books, journals, and magazines, or all permitted uses of his writings in works by other authors. (For links to some of these popular articles, visit www.sermonaudio. com/source_links.asp?sourceid=whitcomb.) Other areas of investigation which are not detailed here include the reviews of Dr. Whitcomb's books within the major theological journals and the references to his writings in other journal articles.

_____. *The Early Earth: An Introduction to Biblical Creationism.* rev. ed. Winona Lake, IN: BMH Books, 1986 (also translated into French, Indonesian, Italian, Japanese, Korean, Portuguese, and Spanish).

_____. *Esther: Triumph of God's Sovereignty.* Chicago, IL: Moody Press, 1979. Republished as *Esther and the Destiny of Israel.* Indianapolis, IN: Whitcomb Ministries, 2005 (also translated into Spanish).

_____. *The Origin of the Solar System: Biblical Inerrancy and the Double-Revelation Theory.* Phillipsburg, NJ: Presbyterian and Reformed Publishing Company, n.d. (also translated into Spanish).

_____. *The World That Perished: An Introduction to Biblical Catastrophism.* 3d rev. ed. Grand Rapids, MI: Baker Books, 2005 (also translated into French, German, Romanian, Russian, Serbian, and Spanish).

Whitcomb, John C., and Henry M. Morris. *The Genesis Flood: The Biblical Record and Its Scientific Implications.* Phillipsburg, NJ: Presbyterian and Reformed Publishing Company, 1961 (also translated into German, Korean, Serbian, and Spanish).

Whitcomb, John C., and Peter Masters. *The Charismatic Phenomenon.* Rev. ed. London: The Wakeman Trust, 1988.

Book Contributions

Demy, Timothy J., and John C. Whitcomb. "Witnesses, Two." In *The Popular Encyclopedia of Bible Prophecy.* Tim LaHaye and Ed Hindson, gen. eds. Eugene, OR: Harvest House Publishers, 2004, p. 401–403.

Morris, Henry, and John C. Whitcomb. "Introduction." In *Grand Canyon: A Different View.* Written and compiled by Tom Vail. Green Forest: AR: Master Books 2003, p. 4–5.

Whitcomb, John C. "Animal Sacrifices: Past and Future," "The Millennial Temple," and "The Future Roman Empire." In *Tim LaHaye Prophecy Study Bible.* James Combs, Edward Hindson, Thomas Ice, and Tim LaHaye, eds. Chattanooga, TN: AMG Publishers, 2000, p. 883, 898, and 1321.

_____. "The Genesis Flood." In *The Genesis Factor: Myths and Realities.* Ron J. Bigalke Jr., ed. Green Forest, AR: Master Books, 2008, p. 203–219.

_____. "Foreword." In *Progressive Dispensationalism: An Analysis of the Movement and Defense of Traditional Dispensationalism.* Ron J. Bigalke Jr., ed. Lanham, MD: University Press of America, Inc., 2005, p. IX, X.

_____. "Millennial Sacrifices" and "Millennial Temple." In *The Popular Encyclopedia of Bible Prophecy.* Tim LaHaye and Ed Hindson, gen. eds. Eugene, OR: Harvest House Publishers, 2004, p. 226–232.

_____. "Priorities in Presenting the Faith" and "The Two Witnesses." In *Dispensationalism Tomorrow & Beyond: A Theological Collection in Honor of Charles C. Ryrie*. Christopher Cone, gen. ed. Fort Worth, TX: Tyndale Seminary Press, 2008, p. 33–45 and 359–373.

_____. "Ezra," "Nehemiah," and "Esther." In *Wycliffe Bible Commentary*. Everett Harrison and Charles Pfeiffer, eds. Chicago, IL: Moody Press, 1990, p. 423–457.

Major Journal Articles

DeYoung, Donald B., and John C. Whitcomb. "The Origin of the Universe." *Grace Theological Journal,"* 1, no. 2, Fall 1980, p. 149–161.

Kent, Homer A., and John C. Whitcomb. "A Festschrift for Dr. Herman Arthur Hoyt." *Grace Theological Journal,"* 6, no. 2, Fall 1985, p. 167–168.

Morris, Henry M., and John C. Whitcomb Jr. "The Genesis Flood — Its Nature and Significance," Part I. *Bibliotheca Sacra* 117, no. 466, April–June 1960, p. 155–163.

_____. "The Genesis Flood — Its Nature and Significance," Part II. *Bibliotheca Sacra* 117, no. 467, July–September 1960, p. 205–213.

Whitcomb, John C. "Christ's Atonement and Animal Sacrifices in Israel." *Grace Theological Journal,"* 6, no. 2, Fall 1985, p. 201–217.

_____. "C.H. Spurgeon, Biblical Inerrancy, and Premillennialism: A Review Article." *Grace Theological Journal,"* 7, no. 2, Fall 1986, p. 229.

_____. "Contemporary Apologetics and the Christian Faith — Part I: Human Limitations in Apologetics." *Bibliotheca Sacra* 134, no. 534, April–June 1977, p. 99–106.

_____. "Contemporary Apologetics and the Christian Faith — Part II: Christian Apologetics and the Divine Solution." *Bibliotheca Sacra* 134, no. 535, July–September 1977, p. 195–202.

_____. "Contemporary Apologetics and the Christian Faith — Part III: Proof Texts for Semi-Rationalistic Apologetics." *Bibliotheca Sacra* 134, no. 536, October–December 1977, p. 291–298.

_____. "Contemporary Apologetics and the Christian Faith — Part IV: The Limitations and Values of Christian Evidences." *Bibliotheca Sacra* 135, no. 537, January–March 1978, p. 25–33.

_____. "Creation Science and Modern Biology: A Review Article." *Grace Theological Journal,"* 4, no. 1, Spring 1983, p. 109–117.

_____. "Creation Science and the Physical Universe: A Review Article." *Grace Theological Journal,"* 4, no. 2, Fall 1983, p. 289–296.

_____. "Daniel's Great Seventy-Week's Prophecy: An Exegetical Insight." *Grace Theological Journal,"* 2, no. 2, Fall 1981, p. 259–263.

_____. "The Post-Darwinian Controversies." *Grace Theological Journal,"* 2, no. 1, Spring 1981, p. 131–137.

Whitcomb, John C., and Donald B. DeYoung. "Earth's Pre-Flood Vapor Canopy: A Review Article." *Grace Theological Journal,"* 3, no. 1, Spring 1982, p. 123–132.

Whitcomb, John C., and David C. Whitcomb. "Fearfully and Wonderfully Made: A Review Article." *Grace Theological Journal,"* 2, no. 2, Fall 1981, p. 333–339.

Charts[2]

Whitcomb, John C. *Babylonian Captivity.* Winona Lake, IN: Whitcomb Ministries, 1962.

_____. *The Five Worlds of History, Science and Prophecy.* 2nd rev. ed. Winona Lake, IN: Whitcomb Ministries, 1993.

_____. *From the Creation to Abraham.* 2nd rev. ed. Winona Lake, IN: Whitcomb Ministries, 1993.

_____. *Old Testament Patriarchs and Judges.* 5th rev. ed. Winona Lake, IN: Whitcomb Ministries, 1993.

_____. *Old Testament Kings and Prophets.* 5th rev. ed. Winona Lake, IN: Whitcomb Ministries, 1993.

_____. *The Thousand-Year Reign of Christ Over the Earth.* Winona Lake, IN: Whitcomb Ministries, 1994.[3]

---

2. These famous charts were used with permission in *The MacArthur Study Bible* (Dallas, TX: Word Publishing, 1997). *The New Inductive Study Bible* (Eugene, OR: Harvest House Publishers, 2000) has adapted these charts for its use and credits Dr. Whitcomb for his Old Testament dating scheme on p. 42.

3. Three additional charts were written by Dr. Whitcomb's colleague at Grace Theological Seminary, Dr. James L. Boyer. They are: *Between the Testaments Chart* (Winona Lake, IN: BMH Books, 1968); *Chronology of the Crucifixion and the Last Week* (Winona Lake, IN: BMH Books, 1976); and *New Testament Chronological Chart* (Winona Lake, IN: BMH Books, 1968).

Affirmations and Denials Essential to a Consistent Christian (Biblical) Worldview

The following affirmations and denials reflect the almost universal consensus of the Church throughout history, until the early 19th century. Their substance, rigorously defended by many past and present scholars, is currently rejected by a large portion of the contemporary worldwide church and, sadly, by many Christian scholars involved in explaining and defending the Christian worldview. Therefore, as an addendum to the affirmations and denials of the International Council on Biblical Inerrancy and of the International Church Council,[1] the undersigned present these affirmations and denials to the Church as an essential part of the presentation of the Christian worldview to the world of the 21st century.

I. We affirm that the scientific aspects of creation are important, but are secondary in importance to the proclamation of the gospel of Jesus Christ as Sovereign, Creator, Redeemer and Judge.
We deny that the doctrines of Creator and creation can ultimately be divorced from the gospel of Jesus Christ, for the teachings of Genesis are foundational to the gospel and indeed to all biblical doctrines (directly or indirectly).

II. We affirm that the 66 books of the Bible are the written Word of God. The Bible is divinely inspired and inerrant throughout (in all the original autographs).

---

1. The "Chicago Statement on Biblical Inerrancy" of the ICBI can be read at www. bible-researcher.com/chicago1.html or in Norman L. Geisler and William E. Nix, *A General Introduction to the Bible* (Chicago, IL: Moody Press, rev. 1986), p. 181–185, and the ICBI's "Chicago Statement on Biblical Hermeneutics" can be found at www. bible-researcher.com/chicago2.html or in Earl D. Radmacher and Robert D. Preus, eds., *Hermeneutics, Inerrancy, and the Bible* (Grand Rapids, MI: Zondervan, 1994), p. 881–887. The ICC's "Forty-Two Articles of the Essentials of a Christian World View" can be found in "The Documents" section of www.churchcouncil.org.

Its assertions are factually true. It is the supreme authority, not only in all matters of faith and conduct, but in everything that it teaches.

We deny that the Bible's authority is limited to spiritual, religious, or redemptive themes and we deny the exclusion of its authority from its assertions related to such fields as history and science.

III. We affirm that the final guide to the interpretation of Scripture is Scripture itself. Scripture must be compared with Scripture to obtain the correct interpretation of a particular text, and clear Scriptures must be used to interpret ambiguous texts, not vice versa. We affirm that the special revelation of infallible and inerrant Scripture must be used to correctly interpret the general revelation of the cursed creation.

We deny that uninspired sources of truth-claims (i.e., history, archeology, science, etc.) can be used to interpret the Scriptures to mean something other than the meaning obtained by classical historical-grammatical exegesis. We further deny the view, commonly used to evade the implications or the authority of biblical teaching, that biblical truth and scientific truth must remain totally exclusive from each other and that science could never agree with the Bible.

IV. We affirm that no apparent, perceived, or claimed evidence in any field, including history, archeology, and science, can be considered valid if it contradicts the scriptural record. We also affirm that the evidence from such fields of inquiry is always subject to interpretation by fallible people who do not possess all information.

We deny that scientific "evidence" used to "prove" millions of years is objective fact and not heavily influenced by naturalistic presuppositions.

V. We affirm that the account of origins presented in Genesis is a simple but factual presentation of actual events and therefore provides a reliable framework for scientific research into the question of the origin and history of life, mankind, the earth, and the universe.

We deny that Genesis 1–11 is myth, saga, or any other type of non-historical literature. We also deny that it is a parable or prophetic vision. It therefore should be interpreted with the same care for literal accuracy as any other historical narrative sections of Scripture in, for example, Joshua, Judges, 1 and 2 Kings, the Gospels, or Acts.

VI. We affirm that the genealogies in Genesis 5 and 11 are chronological, enabling us to arrive at an approximate date of creation of the whole universe. We affirm that mankind is essentially as old as the whole creation. While some disagreement exists between young-earth creationists over whether or not these are strict, gap-less genealogies (i.e., no missing names between Adam and Noah and Noah and Abraham), we affirm that Genesis points to a date of creation between about 6,000–10,000 years ago.

We deny that millions of years of history occurred before Adam and Eve. Therefore, we deny that the geological record of strata and fossils corresponds to long geological ages before man. We also deny the big bang and any other naturalistic theory of the origin and history of the universe. We further deny that the radiometric dating methods, which are claimed to give dates of millions of years, are trustworthy and can be used to overthrow or disregard the biblical teaching on the age of the creation. We further deny that the Egyptian, Chinese, or other pagan chronologies are more reliable than the Bible's chronological statements, and we deny that those pagan chronologies can be used to overrule the careful exegesis of the relevant biblical texts regarding the age of the earth and other Old Testament events.

VII. We affirm that the days in Genesis do not correspond to geologic ages, but are six, consecutive, literal (essentially 24-hour) days of creation.

We deny that the days of creation are symbolic of long ages or that millions of years can be placed between the days or before the six days of creation.

VIII. We affirm that the various original life forms (kinds), including mankind, were made by direct, supernatural, creative acts of God. The living descendants of any of the original kinds (apart from man) may represent more than one species today, reflecting the genetic potential within a particular original created kind. Only relatively limited biological changes (due to such processes as natural selection, mutations, and other biological processes that might be discovered in the future) have occurred naturally *within* each kind since creation.

We deny that there has ever been any evolutionary change from one of the original created kinds into a different kind (e.g., fish to amphibian, reptile to mammal, reptile to bird, ape to man, or land mammal to whale, etc.).

IX. We affirm the supernatural creation of Adam from dust and the supernatural creation of Eve from Adam's rib in a very short period of time (seconds or minutes) on the sixth day of creation.

We deny that Adam was in any way made from a pre-existing hominid (or any other living creature). We further deny the existence of any creatures which looked or acted like man but which did not possess a soul. We deny also that categories of creatures such as "Neanderthal Man" and "Cro-Magnon Man" were pre- or sub-human (rather than being fully human descendants of Adam).

X. We affirm that the account of the Fall of Adam and Eve into sin is a literal historical account and that the Fall had cosmic consequences. We also affirm that both physical and spiritual death and bloodshed entered into this world subsequent to, and as a direct consequence of, man's sin. We further affirm that this historical Fall is the reason for the necessity of salvation for mankind through the redemptive work of the "Last Adam," Jesus Christ.

We deny that the account of the Fall was mythical, figurative, or otherwise largely symbolic. While certain aspects of Genesis 1–11 are typological with reference to the work of Christ, we deny that this in anyway negates or eliminates the literal historicity of the text. We deny that the judgment of God at the Fall resulted only in the spiritual death of man or only consequences for man but not for the rest of animate and inanimate creation. We therefore also deny that millions of years of death, disease, violence, and extinction occurred in the animal world before the Fall and thereby deny that those millions of years claimed by the evolutionary scientific establishment ever happened.

XI. We affirm that the great Flood described in Genesis 6–9 was an actual historic event, worldwide (global) in its extent and extremely catastrophic in its effect. As such, it produced most (but not all) of the geological record of thousands of meters of strata and fossils that we see on the earth's surface today.

We deny that Noah's Flood was limited to a localized region (e.g., the Mesopotamian valley of the Tigris and Euphrates Rivers). We also deny that the Flood was so peaceful that it left no abiding geological evidence. We further deny that the thousands of meters of sedimentary rock formations with their fossilized remains were largely produced after or before the Flood or even before Adam.

XII. We affirm that all people living and dead are descended from Adam and Eve and that as such all people equally bear the image of God, their Maker. We therefore affirm that there is only one race of human beings and that the various people groups (with their various languages, cultures, and distinctive physical characteristics, including skin color) arose as a result of God's supernatural judgment at the Tower of Babel and the subsequent dispersion of the people by families.

We deny that the so-called "races" have different origins and that any one "race" is superior to any other.

We, the undersigned, call on the Church to embrace these affirmations and denials as they are explicitly taught or implied by Holy Scripture and are consistent with the historic belief of the Church prior to the rise of old-earth ("deep time") theories in geology and astronomy in the late 18th and early 19th centuries and evolutionary theories since that time.

Signatories

Terry Mortenson, Ph.D.
Answers in Genesis

Thane H. Ury, Ph.D.
United Wesleyan Graduate
Institute, Hong Kong

William Barrick, Th.D.
The Master's Seminary

Richard Mayhue, Th.D.
The Master's Seminary

Trevor Craigen, Th.D.
The Master's Seminary

Ron Minton, Th.D.
Missionary, Ukraine

John MacArthur, D.D.
Grace Community Church

John Whitcomb, Th.D.
Whitcomb Ministries

Robert McCabe, Th.D.
Detroit Baptist Theological Seminary

James Mook, Th.D.
Capital Bible Seminary

Paul Scharf, M.Div.
Whitcomb Ministries

Travis R. Freeman, Ph.D.
Baptist College of Florida

Todd Beall, Ph.D.
Capital Bible Seminary

James Stambaugh, Ph.D.
candidate,
Capital Bible Seminary

David W. Hall, Ph.D.
Midway Presbyterian Church

Steven W. Boyd, Ph.D.
The Master's College

We invite others who are theologically trained and agree with us to add their names to this list of signatories and to do all they can to encourage Christians in their spheres of influence to embrace, teach, and defend these additional affirmations and denials. To add your name to this list of signatories, please go to **http://www.answersingenesis.org/articles/affirmations-denials-Christian-worldview** and follow the instructions in the Editor's note at the bottom of the document.

Recommended Resources

BOOKS

Austin, Steve, ed., *Grand Canyon: Monument to Catastrophe* (Santee, Ca: Institute for Creation Research, 1994). Scholarly, but understandable to students and laypeople, this book gives a thorough discussion of the canyon, considering its geology, biology, atmosphere, and early people groups residing in the canyon, which speaks of the global Flood of Noah's day. Fourteen young-earth creation scientists (7 with a Ph.D. in the relevant field) contributed to this book.

DeYoung, Don, *Thousands Not Billions* (Green Forest, AR: Master Books, 2005), summarizes in laymen's terms the technical results of the eight-year research project, Radioisotopes and the Age of the Earth (RATE). The RATE research was conducted by an international team of PhD creationist geologists, geophysicists, and physicists. It presents powerful evidence that the radiometric dating methods are not giving us reliable ages (of millions of years) for the rocks and explains why. Since radiometric dating is one of the major reasons people give for doubting the young-earth view taught in Scripture, this is a must-read resource.

Fields, Weston, *Unformed and Unfilled* (Green Forest, AR: Master Books, 1976) is the best, most thoroughly researched refutation of the gap theory ever published and was based on Fields' ThD studies at Grace Theological Seminary.

Ham, Ken, ed., *The New Answers Book, Vol. 1* (Green Forest, AR: Master Books, 2006) provides answers, in lay language, to the 27 most-asked questions regarding origins. If you learn these answers, you will be able to handle most skeptical challenges to believing in the literal historicity of Genesis 1–11.

Ham, Ken, ed., *The New Answers Book, Vol. 2* (Green Forest, AR: Master Books, 2008) provides answers to 31 additional most-asked questions regarding origins.

Kelly, Douglas, *Creation and Change* (UK: Mentor, 1999), gives a very helpful and wide-ranging defense of the literal interpretation of Genesis 1–2. Kelly is Professor of Systematic Theology at Reformed Theological Seminary in Charlotte, NC.

Morris, Henry M., *The Genesis Record* (Grand Rapids, MI: Baker Books, 1987). Though not a theologically trained biblical scholar, Henry Morris (father of the modern young-earth creationist movement) was an exceptional student of the Word. Based on Morris's extraordinary breadth of knowledge, this scientific and devotional commentary on the Book of Genesis is rich in its insights, as he defends the literal, historical accuracy of the book of beginnings.

Morris, Henry M., *Biblical Creationism* (Green Forest, AR: Master Books, 2000). It is ironic that it was a layman, not a theologian, who produced the only modern book that presents a complete survey of all the passages of Scripture that mention the creation or other themes or events recorded in the first 11 chapters of Genesis. From this thorough study flows a truly biblical creationism.

Morris, Henry M., *The Long War Against God* (Green Forest, AR: Master Books, 2000), thoroughly documents the history and impact of the creation/evolution conflict. Blending scriptural teaching with a good grasp of historical and philosophical developments, Morris shows that old-earth evolutionism is foundational to ancient and modern ethnic religions (including secular humanism) and all forms of pantheism. It is in fact a continuation of Satan's long war against God that started in the Garden of Eden at the beginning of time.

Morris, Henry M. *The Biblical Basis for Modern Science* (Green Forest, AR: Master Books, 2002), relates the teachings of the Bible in a coherent way to the findings of modern science. Loaded with empirical evidences of the veracity of the Bible, it provides a sound basis for doing and understanding science and a refutation of the notion that science is an enterprise that does not require faith.

Morris, John, *The Young Earth* (Green Forest, AR: Master Books, 2007, revised 2nd edition). This beautiful, full-color, illustrated, hardback book provides non-geologists with an excellent overview of the many lines of geological evidence for a global Flood at the time of Noah and a thousands-of-years-old earth. It includes a well-illustrated chapter on radiometric dating and a CD of PowerPoint slides suitable for teaching.

Mortenson, Terry, *The Great Turning Point: the Church's Catastrophic Mistake on Geology — After Darwin* (Green Forest, AR: Master Books, 2004). Based on Mortenson's PhD thesis, this book shows that the debate over the age of the earth is not a scientific argument primarily but is rather a worldview conflict. It highlights seven of the "scriptural geologists" who wrote against the old-earth geological theories and various Christian compromise views (gap, day-age, local Flood, etc.) that were developing during the first half of the 19th century.

Patterson, Roger, *Evolution Exposed, Vol. 1* (Hebron, KY: Answers In Genesis, 2006, 2007), shows the fallacies of biological evolution by documenting the many erroneous and misleading statements in four of the leading biology textbooks used in secular high schools in America. This is an excellent, well-organized resource for researching specific points of debate.

Patterson, Roger, *Evolution Exposed, Vol. 2* (Hebron, KY: Answers In Genesis, 2008). Following the same research-friendly format found in Volume 1, the fallacies of geological and cosmological evolution are revealed by documenting the problematic arguments in four of the leading earth science textbooks used in American public high schools.

Pipa, Joseph, and David Hall, eds., *Did God Create in Six Days?* (White Hall, WV: Tolle Lege, 2005). This is a helpful debate-format book between young-earthers and proponents of the day-age, analogical days, and framework views.

Russell, Jeffrey Burton, *Inventing the Flat Earth: Columbus and Modern Historians* (New York: Prager, 1991). Many evolutionists and old-earth creationists assert that young-earth creationists are just as scientifically mistaken as those who used to believe in a flat earth. Russell shows that except for a few oddballs, no one in the Church ever believed the earth was flat. The flat-earth myth is largely the invention of evolutionists to try to silence their critics. At the time of writing this very helpful 100-page book, Russell was Professor of History at University of California, Santa Barbara.

Sarfati, Jonathan, *Refuting Compromise: A Biblical and Scientific Refutation of Progressive Creationism (Billions of Years), As Popularized by Astronomer Hugh Ross* (Green Forest, AR: Master Books, 2004). This is a very thorough analysis of Hugh Ross's writings, showing his serious biblical, theological, historical, and scientific errors, which have had a huge impact on the Church, especially Christian leaders and seminary professors.

WEB ARTICLES
(understandable to the non-specialist, but documented
for the well-trained reader)

Lisle, Jason, "Light-travel Time: A Problem for the Big Bang," www.answersingenesis.org/creation/v25/i4/lighttravel.asp. Dr. Lisle (astrophysicist) shows that the problem of distant starlight is not only a challenge to the young-earth view but also a challenge to the evolutionary cosmologists, too. So the fact that creationists do not have a full, compelling answer on this problem cannot count against the view, since it also would count against the big-bang view as well.

Lubenow, Marvin, "The Dating Game" (appendix from his first edition of *Bones of Contention*, Baker, 2001), www.answersingenesis.org/docs2006/0816dating-game.asp. In a detailed analysis (understandable to the layman) of the dating of one particular "ape-man" fossil, Dr. Lubenow exposes how utterly untrustworthy the radiometric dating methods are.

www.answersingenesis.org/home/area/faq/geology.asp has links to many articles providing geological evidence for a young earth.

www.answersingenesis.org/home/area/faq/astronomy.asp has links to articles dealing with cosmology and the age of the universe.

www.answersingenesis.org/home/area/qa.asp contains links to many other of the most frequently asked questions regarding origins.

DVDs
(understandable for non-specialists)

About the DVD presenters: Steve Austin and Andrew Snelling both have a PhD in geology, extensive field experience, and many published technical articles; Mike Oard (MS) is a retired meteorologist with the National Weather Service in Montana and also has extensive knowledge of geology through reading and fieldwork; Jason Lisle has a PhD in astrophysics; Terry Mortenson has a PhD in history of geology.

- Geologic Evidences for Very Rapid Strata Deposition in Grand Canyon (Steve Austin)
- Mount St. Helens: Explosive Evidence for Catastrophe (Steve Austin)
- Ice Age: Only the Bible Explains It (Mike Oard)
- The Mammoth and the Ice Age (Mike Oard)
- Radioisotopes and the Age of the Earth (Steve Austin)
- Rock Strata, Fossils, and the Flood (Andrew Snelling)
- Distant Starlight: Not a Problem for a Young Universe (Jason Lisle)
- Origin of the Species: Was Darwin Right? (Terry Mortenson)
- Noah's Flood: Washing Away Millions of Years (Terry Mortenson)
- Origin of Old-Earth Geology and Christian Compromise (Terry Mortenson, 2-DVD set)

PERIODICALS

Acts and Facts is a free monthly publication of the Institute for Creation Research. Short articles inform readers about different aspects of the creation and the battle of origins in our culture. Available at www.ICR.org.

Answers Magazine is a beautiful quarterly publication produced by Answers in Genesis. It has articles for the whole family, all fully documented for the serious reader, covering creation topics but also other key subjects related to developing a biblical worldview. Available at www.AnswersInGenesis.org.

Answers Research Journal is a free, on-line, professional, peer-reviewed technical journal for the publication of interdisciplinary scientific and other relevant research from the perspective of the recent creation and the global Flood within a biblical framework. See www.AnswersInGenesis.org/arj.

ANTI-CREATIONIST RESOURCES

In addition to the creationist resources above, many secular works have been written by authors and scientists quite hostile to the young-earth view, but which include well-documented refutations of various facets of evolutionary theory. They demonstrate that the majority views in geology and cosmology are far from being proven scientific fact, and thus these works lend tacit support to the young-earth view, in spite of the authors' intentions to the contrary.

Ager, Derek, *The New Catastrophism* (Cambridge: Cambridge University Press, 1993). Ager was a world-renowned British geologist and president of the British Geological Association. He was educated (his own term was "brainwashed") to think like a uniformitarian and rule out catastrophe as an explanation of what he was looking at in the rock record. However, his life-long geological research in over 50 countries persuaded him that much of the geological record showed evidence of rapid, catastrophic deposition and lithification. This book, published posthumously, documents much of that evidence. But because Ager rejected the Bible and accepted the naturalistic, evolutionary, millions-of-years story of earth history, he could not entertain the idea that the geological evidence points toward the global, catastrophic Flood of Noah.

Gould, Stephen Jay, "The Great Scablands Debate," *Natural History*, Vol. 87:7 (Aug./Sept. 1978), p. 12–18. Gould, who was no friend of creationism, explains how and why it took over 40 years for the geological establishment to accept a catastrophic Flood as the explanation for the erosional features of the Scablands in eastern Washington. Rather than being eroded gradually over millions of years by streams, as uniformitarian dogma dictated, the observational evidence strongly supports the view that a rapidly drained lake in Montana carved the landscape in 1–2 days! The article reveals the powerful influence of the uniformitarian paradigm in blinding geologists from seeing the evidence clearly and interpreting it correctly.

Lerner, Eric J., "An Open Letter to the Scientific Community," *New Scientist* (May 22, 2004), p. 20, also on-line at www.cosmologystatement.org. Originally signed by 34 astrophysics scientists from 10 countries, the web version has now been signed by over 400 professional scientists and independent researchers from over 50 countries. They are persuaded by the scientific evidence that the big-bang theory is fatally flawed and only survives because it is protected by the scientific elite and alternative views are denied funding and a voice in the peer-reviewed journals and academic conferences. This short document is very revealing about the true nature of science, which is far less objective than we are led to believe.

Contributors to the Book

William D. Barrick (M.Div., Th.M., San Francisco Baptist Theological Seminary; Th.D., Grace Theological Seminary) is professor of Old Testament as well as director of Doctor of Theology Studies at The Master's Seminary in Sun Valley, CA. As a result of his 15 years of Bible translation ministry in Bangladesh and continued work in the United States, he has participated in the production of Bibles, New Testaments, and Bible sections in seven languages. He has also contributed to 24 books, and has authored over 100 periodical articles and book reviews. He and his wife, Barbara, have 4 married children and 14 grandchildren.

Todd Beall (Th.M. in Old Testament, Capital Bible Seminary; Ph.D. in biblical studies, The Catholic University of America) is chairman of the Department of Old Testament Literature and Exegesis, Capital Bible Seminary, where he has taught for the past 31 years. He is co-author of the *Old Testament Parsing Guide*, author of a monograph on Josephus and the Essenes, and author of various book chapters and articles on the Dead Sea Scrolls, the Essenes, Messianism, and OT Studies. He and his wife, Sharon, have 2 children and 2 grandchildren.

Steven W. Boyd (M.S., Drexel University; Th.M., Dallas Theological Seminary; Ph.D., Hebraic and Cognate studies, Hebrew Union College–Jewish Institute of Religion) is professor of Old Testament and Semitic Languages at The Master's College and a creation-science researcher, author, lecturer, and editor. He has served with the Comprehensive Aramaic Lexicon Project, and also with the RATE Group, contributing to *Radioisotopes and the Age of the Earth: Results of a Young-Earth Creationist Research Initiative* and *Thousands . . . not Billions: Challenging an Icon of Evolution — Questioning the Age of the Earth*. He is also on the research team for the Institute for Creation Research's FAST (Flood Activated Sedimentation and Tectonics) Project. He and his wife, Janette, have 1 son.

Trevor Craigen (Dip. Th. Baptist Theological College of Southern Africa; M.Div., Th.M., and Th.D., Grace Theological Seminary) ministered for 11 years in Europe before joining the faculty of The Master's Seminary as a theology professor in 1994. From 1983–1990 he was coordinator of Biblical Studies for Grace Seminary Extension in St-Albain, France. Then from 1990–1994 he was associated with Black Forest Academy in Kandern, Germany. From this base he traveled to preach and teach in several seminaries and various churches in both Eastern and Western Europe. He and his wife of 40 years, Colleen, have 2 children and 7 grandchildren.

Travis R. (Rick) Freeman (M.Div., Ph.D. in Old Testament, Southwestern Baptist Theological Seminary) is an associate professor of Old Testament at The Baptist

College of Florida, where he teaches a course each year titled "The Doctrine of Creation." Rick and his wife, Dawn, have 2 children and 2 grandchildren.

David W. Hall (M.Div., Covenant Theological Seminary; Ph.D., Whitefield Theological Seminary) has been a pastor for almost 30 years, presently serving as the senior pastor for Midway Presbyterian Church in Powder Springs, Georgia. He is also the author or editor of over 20 volumes and numerous articles. Among his works are *Did God Create in Six Days?; Savior or Servant: Putting Government in Its Place; The Genevan Reformation and the American Founding; Calvin and Political Ideas;* and *The Legacy of John Calvin.* He is married to Ann, and they have 3 grown children.

John MacArthur (M.Div., D.Litt., D.D.) is the pastor-teacher of Grace Community Church in Sun Valley, California; president of The Master's College & Seminary; and featured teacher for the Grace to You media ministry. Weekly telecasts and daily radio broadcasts of "Grace to You" are seen and heard by millions worldwide. John has also written several best-selling books, including *The MacArthur Study Bible; The Gospel According to Jesus; The New Testament Commentary* series; *Twelve Ordinary Men;* and *The Truth War.* He and his wife, Patricia, have 4 married children and 14 grandchildren.

Richard Mayhue (M.Div., Th.M., Th.D., Grace Theological Seminary) serves as the dean of The Master's Seminary (1989–present) and provost of The Master's College (2000–present). He has authored, contributed to, and/or edited more than 25 books, including *The Healing Promise; Practicing Proverbs; 1&2 Thessalonians; Unmasking Satan; Think Biblically;* and *Preaching: How to Preach Biblically.* He has been married to his wife, "B," for over 40 years, and they have 2 children and 2 grandsons.

Robert V. McCabe (M.Div., Temple Baptist Theological Seminary; Th.M. & Th.D., Old Testament Languages and Literature, Grace Theological Seminary) taught at Tennessee Temple University for four years before becoming a professor of Old Testament at Detroit Baptist Theological Seminary in 1983. Since the mid-1990s, he has developed a class on biblical creationism, conducted a number of biblical creationism seminars, has published many popular-level papers and three academic articles related to creationism in the *Detroit Baptist Seminary Journal,* where he is a regular contributor. Bob and his wife, Linda, were married in 1972 and have 3 grown children and 4 granddaughters.

Ron Minton (M.Div. and Th.M., Grace Theological Seminary; graduate work in Ancient History, Missouri State University; Th.D. in New Testament, Central Baptist Theological Seminary). He has published several articles and book reviews and has presented 50 professional seminars on "How We Got the Bible." He finished a career as a captain in the U.S. Navy Reserve Chaplain Corps, taught in seminaries in America for 20 years, and is currently a missionary in Ukraine where he has established a Bible college. Ron has been married to Nancy for 36 years. They have 2 sons and 3 grandsons.

James R. Mook (Th.M. and Th.D., historical theology, Dallas Theological Seminary) served as a pastor for four years before becoming a full-time faculty member at Capital Bible Seminary in 1991. He has chaired the Systematic Theology Department since 1999 and is the director of the Th.M. program at Capital. He has written several articles on theological and church ministry topics. He and his wife, Nancy, have been married for 23 years.

Henry Morris (1918–2006, M.S. and Ph.D. in hydraulic engineering, University of Minnesota) was the founder and long-time president of the Institute for Creation Research, which includes a graduate research school. His epic book *The Genesis Flood*, co-authored with Dr. John Whitcomb, essentially launched the modern creation movement. His other voluminous writings not only influenced the worldwide growth of creationism, but also fueled the biblical inerrancy movement, the Christian school movement, and the home school movement. A humble, godly man, he was faithfully married to Mary Louise for 66 years. Together they had 6 children, 17 grandchildren, and 9 great grandchildren.

Terry Mortenson (M.Div., Trinity Evangelical Divinity School; Ph.D., history of geology, Coventry University, England) was a missionary with Campus Crusade for Christ for 26 years (mostly in Eastern Europe) before joining Answers in Genesis in 2001 as a speaker, writer, and researcher. During the past 30 years he has lectured and debated on the subject of creation and evolution in 18 countries. He is author of numerous articles and book chapters on the subject of origins and of *The Great Turning Point: The Church's Catastrophic Mistake on Geology — Before Darwin* (Green Forest, AR: Master Books, 2004). He and his wife, Margie, have 8 children and 2 grandchildren.

Paul J. Scharf (M.A., M.Div., Faith Baptist Theological Seminary) served as a pastor of two churches for seven years and has taught the Bible on the elementary, secondary, and college levels. He has written articles on a variety of biblical themes and also has eight years of experience as a news journalist. He has assisted Dr. John Whitcomb in ministry since 2003, continues to compile Dr. Whitcomb's biography, and is an associate for Interim Ministries, Inc./Serving Other Servants International. He is married to Lynnette, and they enjoy living in rural Columbus, Wisconsin.

James Stambaugh (M.Div., Grace Theological Seminary; M.L.S., Ball State University; Ph.D. in Progress, Systematic Theology, Baptist Bible Seminary) was for nine years the library director as well as a speaker, writer, and researcher at the Institute for Creation Research. He also served for two years as director of Library Services at Washington Bible College/Capital Bible Seminary. He is author of numerous technical and popular-level articles on various topics of creation and is currently the Library Director at the Institute of World Politics. He and his wife, Page, have 4 children and 2 grandchildren.

Thane H. Ury (M.Div., Asbury Theological Seminary; Ph.D., systematic theology, Andrews University) taught in the Religion & Philosophy Department at Bethel College (Indiana) for 15 years before joining the faculty at the United Wesleyan Graduate Institute, Hong Kong, China, in 2006. He has taught theology and apologetics in Romania, Nigeria, Trinidad, and China. He and Laura have 4 children.

Subject Index

apologetics, 16, 126, 128–129, 335–336, 439, 443–444, 450, 468

assumptions, philosophical, 15, 80, 86–87, 94, 338, 427, 429, 432

Assyrian King List, 299

Atrahasis Epic, 138–139, 258

authority, 11, 17, 20–21, 25, 35, 38, 46, 84, 93, 99, 106–108, 111, 116–118, 123, 128–129, 134, 147, 161, 171, 247–248, 253, 311, 315–317, 333–334, 339–341, 345, 369–370, 419, 432–434, 453–454

Bible, 3, 5–8, 11–13, 16–21, 23, 30, 35–36, 50–51, 55, 60–61, 64–65, 73–77, 84, 90, 92–93, 96–98, 103–106, 108–111, 113, 115, 118, 123–126, 128–129, 131, 140–141, 143–144, 159, 161–162, 165, 169–171, 173–174, 179, 182, 184, 197, 201, 222, 236, 242, 248, 253, 283, 287, 291, 299–300, 308, 312, 315–316, 318, 324, 327, 329, 333–335, 343–344, 347, 366–370, 373–375, 383, 389, 397, 419, 421, 426–433, 439–441, 443–444, 446–450, 453–455, 457, 460, 462–463, 465–467

canonicity/canonical, 106, 110, 254, 325

catastrophist/catastrophism, 83–85, 94–95, 251, 413–414, 422–423, 449, 463

character, 9, 20, 106, 111–112, 118, 126, 128–129, 149, 189, 311, 374, 379, 381, 383, 387–388, 393–394, 413, 417, 419, 422, 426, 428

chiasm, 150, 255–256, 280

Christian Workman Schools of Theology, 446

Conservative Grace Brethren Churches International, 445–446

continental erosion, 277

continuity, 180–181, 229, 237–238

temporal continuity, 180–181

creation account, 11–12, 29, 34, 50, 55, 73–74, 94, 110, 132, 135–136, 138, 143–144, 146, 149, 151, 155, 173, 179, 192–194, 197, 201, 204, 207–208, 212–219, 222–226, 228, 235, 237, 239–241, 246–248, 334, 348, 351, 367, 391, 441

creation ex nihilo, 13, 53, 59

creation week, 3, 19, 70, 90, 95, 98, 156, 159, 190, 194, 197–198, 201–202, 205–207, 211–215, 219, 223–229, 231, 233, 239–242, 244–248, 318–320, 323–325, 345, 347, 354, 360–366, 382, 397

creationist, young-earth, 20–21, 48, 60, 68, 93–94, 163, 206, 316, 318, 325, 327–329, 335, 338, 342–343, 428, 432, 459, 465

creationist, old-earth, progressive, 129

Curse, 16, 354–355, 357, 367–368, 379, 384–385, 389, 394, 396–397, 402–403, 405, 415–416, 427

days, 24-hour, 29–30, 38, 50, 70, 226, 359, 412, 455

death, animal, 74, 357, 370, 377, 380, 382, 386, 391, 416–417

death, human, 38, 354, 370, 377, 397, 416–417, 430

deposition, 181, 277, 279, 462–463

discontinuity, 180–182

temporal discontinuity, 180

divine revelation, 103, 109, 111, 124, 129, 172

Early Earth, The, 79, 194, 211, 444, 449

empiricism, 111, 119–120, 209

empirical, 15, 17, 87, 106, 120–121, 168–169, 172, 460

Enuma Elish, 134–136, 189

epexegetical, 218–223

evidential, 128

evil, moral, 381, 401, 411, 428

evil, natural, 4, 55, 373, 382–383, 385, 388–389, 392–395, 397, 399, 401–403, 408–414, 420, 422–423, 428, 430–431

evil, paleonatural, 402, 411–413, 417, 420–422

extraordinary providence, 229, 239–240, 245–246

fallen mind, 106, 111, 119

Fall of man, 134, 384, 389, 405

Fellowship of Grace Brethren Churches, 444–446

Flood, 3, 5–8, 11–13, 16, 19–21, 23–24, 38, 49–51, 55, 58, 74–75, 77, 79–81, 83–85, 88–90, 94–96, 98, 100, 102, 104–105, 138–141, 144, 147–148, 158, 160, 179, 192, 204, 211, 251–252, 254–261, 263, 265–269, 272, 274–281, 283, 288, 292, 294, 296–298, 302–303, 307–309, 316, 318, 328–329, 333–335, 344–345, 347–349, 364–366, 371, 383, 401, 404–405, 408, 411–414, 419, 421, 427, 433–435, 442, 449–450, 456, 459–460, 462–463, 465, 467

Flood, chronology of, 274

Flood, geologic mechanisms, 254, 256, 260, 269, 275

Flood, prevailing phase, 268, 276–277

Flood, subsiding phase, 269, 277–278

fluidity, 283–286, 288–295, 299, 301–303, 305–308

fossilization, 279

framework hypothesis, 25, 34, 66, 157, 328

genealogy, 144, 148, 205, 283–292, 295–296, 299–302, 304–308, 312–313, 369

general revelation, 107–115, 118–120, 122–123, 125, 127–129, 247, 427, 454

generational gaps, 290, 292–293, 305–306

Genesis Flood, The, 3, 5–8, 21, 23–24, 79, 85, 102, 105, 211, 251, 329, 344, 347, 442, 449–450, 467

genre, 3, 132, 150, 153–154, 160, 163–164, 166, 168, 173–174, 184, 193, 202, 284, 290–292, 305–306

genre of Genesis 1, 150, 163, 174, 202

geological time, 199–200

Gilgamesh Epic, 138–139, 158

global tectonics, 275

gospel, 6, 20, 42, 104, 107–108, 310–311, 317–319, 334, 337, 341, 344, 350, 358–360, 366–367, 378, 426, 428, 433, 438, 440, 444, 453, 466

Grace Theological Seminary, 105, 193, 211, 251, 347, 441, 445, 459, 465–467

heavenly time, 215–216, 241, 244

hermeneutics, 12, 20, 51, 111, 122, 124, 129, 193, 208, 253, 381, 446

hermeneutical, 3, 25, 35, 51, 60, 106, 124, 131–134, 140, 144, 146–147, 149–150, 161–162, 209, 224, 246–247, 296, 303–305, 307, 402, 421, 432 historical-grammatical approach, 125

historical narrative, 138, 160, 162, 166, 178, 184, 186, 191–192, 215–219, 224, 233, 246, 454

ICBI, 16, 18, 122, 124, 315

illumination, 124–125

imperfect, 44, 65, 154, 419

inclusio, 150, 183, 189, 207, 267, 269, 280

inspiration, 20, 75, 103, 129, 134, 174, 184, 309, 329, 331, 426

integration, 128–129, 392

intelligent design, 15, 348, 429, 432–433

interpretation, literal, 54, 74, 76, 99, 161, 219, 223–226, 229, 237, 239–240, 244–245, 247–248, 285, 340–341, 459

interpretation, allegorical, 30, 50

knowledge, 8, 10, 12, 25, 27–28, 46, 57, 73, 80, 86–87, 114–115, 119–120, 122, 128–129, 164, 171, 173, 181, 199, 208, 235, 302–303, 381, 406, 425, 433, 459, 462

life, 10–12, 36, 43, 45–48, 56–57, 74, 78, 81, 84, 88, 93, 96–97, 104–106, 114, 120–122, 125, 127–128, 131, 166–167, 179, 193, 197, 199–200, 204–206, 228, 232–233, 235, 244, 255, 257, 261–263, 267–269, 275, 281, 297, 302–303, 305, 307, 315–318, 320, 345, 350, 360, 363, 368–369, 373, 375–376, 378, 380–381, 383, 385, 390, 393, 395–396, 400, 406, 408, 413, 416, 430, 437–442, 444–445, 447–448, 454–455

life spans, 297, 302–303, 305, 307

literal days, 13, 33–34, 36–38, 48, 50–51, 55, 59, 141, 150–151, 158, 160, 191, 203–204, 206, 212, 223,

226–228, 242, 246, 249, 329, 359, 427, 433

logistic regression, 175

merism, 255

merismus, 255

metaphorical approach, 387

millenary view, 39, 45

narrative literature, 217

narrative sequence, 216–217, 221–222, 231–233, 236, 238–239

naturalistic, naturalism, 7, 10, 12–13, 16, 26, 28, 50–51, 88–89, 91, 99, 123, 246, 248, 338, 427, 429, 430, 433, 454–455

nature, 3, 20–21, 27–28, 31, 40, 48, 57, 63, 65, 77, 81, 88, 91–92, 95, 105–111, 113, 115, 117–119, 122–123, 127–129, 138, 150–151, 156, 160, 179, 182, 188–189, 194, 198–199, 202, 208–209, 211–213, 215–216, 218, 223, 225, 230, 232, 235, 239–241, 244, 246, 252–253, 257, 260, 267, 271, 277, 280–281, 290, 304, 324, 344, 350, 356–358, 366, 374, 381, 384, 386–388, 390, 393, 395, 403–404, 407, 409–411, 413–417, 421–422, 425, 428–430, 433, 450, 463

neo-catastrophist, 102

nephesh, 375, 380, 382–383

Noetic environment, 389–391

non-revelatory, 128–129

null hypothesis, 175

old-earth view, 46, 83, 205, 336, 342, 359, 362, 366, 369, 393, 395

onomatopoeia, 258

ordinary providence, 59, 63, 65, 212, 228, 239–240, 246–247

orogeny, 276, 405

plants, 18, 36, 63, 66, 89, 155, 196, 219, 367, 373, 375–380, 383, 392,

396–397, 405, 408–409, 425, 427, 431, 433

pluperfect, 217–218, 220–221, 233–234, 236–239

presuppositional, 127–128, 443

preterite, 217

primeval history, 5, 133, 142, 144, 148

Princeton University, 19, 131, 438–440

rain, 230–232, 251, 257–258, 262, 264, 268–269, 276–277, 281, 350, 353, 379, 409

renewal, 24, 383–384

restoration, 349–350, 355, 368, 384, 414

resumptive repetition, 235–236, 238

Sabbath rest, 71, 214, 241, 245, 361, 383

science, 5–8, 10–13, 15, 18–20, 23, 51, 56, 73, 75–78, 80, 85–92, 94, 98, 102–103, 106, 108–109, 111, 123, 128, 141, 161, 169, 173, 185, 193, 197, 199, 209–210, 212, 247–248, 251, 329, 334–336, 344, 365, 370, 386, 389, 391, 396, 402, 411–412, 420, 423, 425–426, 428–430, 433–434, 438, 450–451, 454, 460, 463

scientifico-concept, 208–209

scriptural geologist, 99, 419

Scripture, 10–13, 16–20, 24–25, 28, 30–31, 34–35, 38, 44, 46–51, 54–55, 72, 74–75, 77, 85, 89, 93–95, 97–100, 103, 106–119, 122–129, 132, 134, 146, 159–161, 168–171, 179, 187, 194, 209, 223, 239, 244, 246–249, 253, 280, 288, 300, 302, 315–317, 320, 324, 328, 330, 333–334, 338, 343–344, 348, 374–375, 381, 383, 386, 388–391,

396–397, 403, 411, 415, 417–418, 420–421, 423, 425–428, 430–435, 441, 444, 454, 456, 459–460

sedimentation, 101, 278, 281, 465

semi-poetic style, 215, 223–224

seventh day, 28, 34, 41–43, 46–48, 64–65, 69, 71–72, 95, 138, 146, 158, 200–201, 206, 212, 214, 219, 227, 240–246, 323, 344, 359–360, 362–363, 371

sin, 120–121, 139–140, 147, 160, 201, 293–294, 317, 335, 354–358, 364, 368, 370, 374, 383–385, 389–391, 395, 397, 402–405, 407–411, 413–417, 422–423, 430, 455

67th book, 3, 105–106, 108, 110–111, 115, 129

special revelation, 106–109, 111–115, 118–120, 122–129, 159, 247, 411, 427, 454

Spirit, 11, 21–22, 47, 56, 110, 113, 122, 124, 135, 139, 166, 248, 262, 331, 355, 385, 403, 412, 435, 439

Sumerian King List, 287, 293–295, 297–298

Table of Nations, 139

temporal recapitulation, 215, 218, 220–223, 235, 237–239

theistic evolutionist, 97, 370

theodicy, 374, 382–383, 385, 388–391, 396–397, 400–401, 408, 411, 413, 418, 420–423, 431

thermodynamics, second law of, 381

Toledoth, 145, 152, 290, 295–296

topical arrangement, 213, 215–216, 235, 246

Tower of Babel, 139, 345, 456

Tree of life, 235, 368, 380–381

truth, 8, 11–13, 16–17, 21, 28, 43, 46, 70, 79–80, 85–86, 89–90, 92,

95, 100–104, 113–114, 117–118, 120–125, 127–129, 131, 140, 142–143, 149, 159, 168, 170, 173, 181, 184, 247, 252, 315, 317, 325, 329, 334, 342, 345, 347, 351, 353–354, 369, 377, 388, 394, 410, 425–427, 433–435, 454, 466

tsunami, 400

Ugaritic, 136

uniformitarian, 7, 25–26, 28, 55, 77, 83–84, 87–90, 95, 99, 101–102, 247–248, 281, 338, 429, 463

uniformitarianism, 7–8, 25, 77, 85, 131, 365, 402, 422

waw consecutive, 145, 154, 216–223, 225, 227–228, 230, 232–236, 238–239, 246

Whitcomb Ministries, Inc.,, 445–446

work-day frames, 213–214, 228

World That Perished, The, 79, 211, 444, 449

worldview, 4, 6, 10, 15, 86–89, 106, 111, 116, 125–129, 138, 141–143, 150, 168, 209, 338, 429, 433, 453, 460, 462

yôm, 69, 150, 191, 194–195, 200–207, 209, 226–228, 246, 335

young, 5–7, 13, 19, 29, 50, 79, 93–94, 99–100, 103–104, 106, 157, 159, 191–192, 292, 327, 332, 343, 347, 360–362, 387, 395, 397, 412, 415, 417, 421, 428–429, 442, 460–462

Name Index

Adam, 38, 40, 46–47, 58, 66, 76, 84, 93, 96–98, 114, 120–121, 140, 144–145, 147–148, 152, 159–160, 197, 201, 207, 209, 224, 233–234, 244–245, 248, 283–284, 286–287, 289–291, 294, 296, 302, 304, 308, 312, 316, 318, 320–321, 325, 331, 333–335, 339, 341–342, 345, 351, 354–356, 358, 364, 368–370, 374, 380–384, 389–390, 396–397, 402, 404–407, 409–410, 416, 430, 434, 454–456

Ager, Derek, 101, 429, 463

Ambrose, 35, 56, 66–67

Ames, William, 67–68

Ankerberg, John, 339–340

Archer, Gleason, , 16, 25, 98, 287, 332

Arnold, Bill, 138, 331

Atwell, James, 135, 137

Augustine, 24–26, 29, 33, 35–38, 41, 45–48, 50–51, 53, 58, 67–71, 80, 403

Austin, Steven A., 93, 278, 459, 462

Barr, James, 161, 204

Barré, Lloyd M., 254

Barrick, William D., 3, 251, 457, 465

Basil of Caesarea, 27, 30

Bauer, Hans, 271

Baumgartner, Walter, 257–258

Beveridge, William, 71

Beza (or Beze), Theodore, 59, 65, 310

Blocher, Henri, 24–25, 151, 154, 213, 215–216, 240–241, 332, 380

Boice, James, 328–329

Boyd, Steven W., 163, 216, 457, 465

Boyer, James L., 445–446

Bruce, F.F., 360–361

Buckland, William, 83–85, 89, 91, 93, 95, 412, 415–416

Buffon, Comte de, 81

Bugg, George, 412, 415–417, 419

Butler, Michael R., 226, 229–230, 239, 248

Calvin, John, 55–56, 405, 466

Cameron, Nigel, 333–334, 396–397

Cassuto, Umberto, 270

Chaffin, Eugene F., 163

Chalmers, Thomas, 94

Clarke, Adam, 76

Clement of Alexandria, 32

Cole, Henry, 103, 322, 326, 412

Collins, C. John, 92–94, 150, 153, 206–207, 238, 336–338, 343, 345

Currid, John, 137–138

Cuvier, Georges, 83–84, 89, 92, 94–95

Darwin, Charles, 9–10, 82, 84–86, 88, 96, 200, 304, 341, 425–426, 430, 460, 462, 467

Davis, John J., 156, 287, 448

Demarest, Bruce A., 330–331, 348

Dembski, William A., 389–391

Dever, William G., 253

Diodati, John, 64–65

Duncan, J. Ligon III, 219, 223

Enns, Peter, 140–141

Ephrem the Syrian, 30

Erickson, Millard J., 330

Eve, 21, 97–98, 120–122, 140, 146–148, 160, 197, 207, 209, 234, 244–245, 308, 316, 318–320, 331, 333–334, 342, 355, 357, 364, 368–369, 380–382, 390, 396, 402, 404, 406, 455–456

Faber, George Stanley, 95
Feinberg, John, 330, 395, 397
Fleming, John, 90, 95
Fouts, David M., 257
Frame, John M., 117, 228–229
Freedman, H., 263–264, 267
Fullerton, Donald B., 439, 441
Futato, Mark D., 156
Gee, Henry, 199
Geisler, Norman, 16, 20, 335–336, 339
Gill, John, 76
Godfrey, W. Robert, 150
Gordon, Cyrus H., 259
Gregory of Nazianzus, 49
Green, William H., 286, 288–289, 293, 335
Grudem, Wayne, 18–19, 331, 343, 348, 358
Gunkel, Hermann, 133–135, 153, 203
Hall, David W., 53, 157, 213, 219, 223, 225–226, 244, 247–248, 326, 332, 401, 461, 466
Hamilton, Victor, 134, 145, 150–151, 156, 203, 213–214, 231, 235, 238, 288, 293
Harris, R. Laird, 332
Hasel, Gerhard, 135, 201–203, 297–298, 307
Heidel, Alexander, 139
Henry, Carl F.H., 125–126, 208–209, 330
Henry, Matthew, 76
Hippolytus, 26, 42
Hodge, Charles, 96–97, 104, 330
Hoffmeier, James, 136
Holmes, Arthur F. 127
Holt, Roy D., 268
Horne, Thomas H., 74–76
House, Wayne, 17

Hoyt, Herman A., 441–442, 445–446, 450
Hutton, James, 82, 85, 88, 91–92
Ezra, 36, 73, 178, 290, 450
Irenaeus, 26, 41–42
Irons, Lee, 219–220, 222, 235, 237, 240–241, 247
Johnson, Phillip E., 370, 432
Jordan, James B., 291–292, 295, 302–303
Josephus, 312–313, 321, 465
Justin Martyr, 40, 49
Kaiser, Walter, 53, 146, 331, 340
Kelly, Douglas F., 334, 362–363, 459
Kent, Homer, Sr., 361–363, 441, 450
Kidner, Derrick, 150–151, 159–160, 287
Kitchen, Kenneth A., 254, 287
Kline, Meredith G., 212–213, 219–220, 222–223, 228–230, 232, 235, 237, 240–241, 246–248, 332, 343
Koehler, Ludwig, 258
Lactantius, 28–29, 43–44
Lamarck, Jean, 82–83, 92
Lambert, W.G., 135
Laplace, Pierre, 81, 89, 92
Leander, Pontus, 271
Leupold, H.C., 270, 327
Lewis, Gordon R., 330–331, 348
Longinus, 166
Luther, Martin, 53–56, 61, 64, 68, 77, 302, 307, 399, 401, 403–405, 408, 413–417, 421–423, 434
Lyell, Charles, 53–56, 77, 83, 85, 87, 90, 101
Lyell, 3, 53–56, 77, 83, 85, 87, 89–92, 95, 101, 304, 401, 423
MacArthur, John, 9, 327, 360–361, 457, 466

Malamat, Abraham, 299–301, 305, 307

Marduk, 134–136

Martyr, Peter, 62–63

Mathews, Kenneth A., 288

Mayhue, Richard L., 105, 457, 466

McCabe, Robert V., 211, 457, 466

McClain, Alva J., 441–442, 444, 446

McPhee, John, 199

McQuilken, J. Robertson, 129

Miller, Hugh, 99–100, 412, 416

Moberly, R.W.L., 271

Moo, Douglas, 353, 356

Morris, Henry M., 5, 8, 21, 23, 102–103, 105, 109, 270, 276, 327, 329–330, 339, 344, 347, 356, 359, 382, 442–443, 449–450, 459–460, 467

Mortenson, Terry, 22, 77, 79, 146, 195, 210, 315, 413, 456, 460, 462, 467

Murray, John, 353, 356, 412

Musculus, Wolfgang, 61–63

Nash, Ronald H., 15–16, 126

Niessen, Richard, 195, 296, 309–310, 313

Noll, Mark, 343–344

Northrup, Bernard E., 253

Origen, 24, 26, 29, 33–35, 41, 43, 51, 310, 403

Orr, James, 332

Packer, J.I., 427

Paul, 7, 33, 80, 102, 108, 114–115, 120–121, 124, 134, 146–148, 319–320, 324, 345, 349–358, 368, 370, 382–384, 391

Penn, Granville, 412, 419

Perkins, William, 64, 66–68

Pipa, Joseph, 159–160, 223, 242, 461

Pun, Pattle, 391–392, 402

Rahm, Urs, 186

Ramm, Bernard, 116, 331, 386

Reymond, Robert L., 329

Ridderbos, N.H., 212

Robbins, Austin, 279

Ross, Hugh, 16, 25–26, 34–35, 38, 50, 106–111, 115, 118–119, 122, 125–126, 128–129, 196–197, 332, 336, 338–340, 362, 366, 374, 461

Ross, Mark, 332

Sainte-Beuve, 166

Sarfati, Jonathan, 36, 461

Sarna, N.M., 284

Schaeffer, Francis, 334–335

Schmidt, Brian B., 254

Scott, Thomas, 75–76

Sedgwick, Adam, 84–85, 89, 93, 95

Skinner, John, 133, 138, 348

Slifkin, Nosson, 187

Smith, John Pye, 95, 99–100, 412, 416

Smith, William, 83, 92

Snelling, Andrew A., 163, 462

Speiser, E.A., 133, 257, 285, 300

Spurgeon, Charles, 96, 450

Stek, John, 149–150, 152, 154, 156, 158, 203, 332

Sternberg, Meir, 181, 184, 191

Stoner, Don, 338–339, 343

Templeton, Charles, 98, 104

Tertullian, 46, 49, 80

Theophilus of Antioch, 49, 312

Tiamat, 134–135, 190

Tsumura, David, 134, 136

Ure, Andrew, 91, 412, 417

Ursinus, Zacharias, 64

Ussher, James, 59, 62, 68–69, 71, 75, 93, 283, 289, 406

Van Till, Howard, 56, 142, 144, 150

Victorinus of Pettau, 43

Waltke, Bruce, 99, 134, 151–156, 158–161, 208, 247, 328

Walton, John, 141–142, 146, 158, 328
Warfield, Benjamin B., 77, 97, 104, 307, 332, 335
Watson, Wilfred G.E., 255
Weeks, Noel, 144, 161
Wenham, Gordon, 139, 150, 152–153, 156, 159–160, 203, 256–257, 270, 287, 292, 298, 316–317, 328, 340–341
Wenham, John, 386–387
Werner, Abraham, 82, 89, 92
Wesley, Charles, 414
Wesley, John, 55, 73–76, 399, 401, 403, 408–411, 413–417, 421–423
Westermann, Claus, 135, 153, 231, 284, 291, 299
Whitcomb, Clement Colfax, 438
Whitcomb, John C., Jr., 4-5, 8, 13, 21-23, 79, 102, 105-106, 109, 126, 131, 193-194, 196, 210-211, 226, 244, 249, 251, 253, 272, 276, 278, 326, 328-329, 334, 347, 355, 364, 437-451, 457, 467

Whitcomb, John Clement, Sr., 437
Whitcomb, Norma (Pritchett), 347, 443-445, 447
Wilson, Robert R., 253, 293, 298–301, 305, 307
Wise, Kurt P., 257
Young, Davis, 19, 29, 50, 99–100, 360–362, 428–429
Young, E. J., 157, 159, 332, 429
Young, George, 412, 415, 417
Young, Richard A., 395-397
Zacharias, Ravi, 315, 345

Scripture Index

(*) Denotes a Scripture reference occuring within a footnote.

Genesis

1 — 12, 26, 29*, 30, 30*, 33-35, 37-39, 47, 51, 65, 68, 94-96, 98-101, 131-138, 136*, 137*, 142-156, 156*, 158-162, 189, 194-198, 200-203, 206-207, 209-210, 212, 214, 215*, 218-220, 222-227, 227*, 229-230, 244*, 246, 318, 320, 334-335, 236*, 341, 348*, 354, 357-359, 359*, 363-364, 366, 368-371, 385, 389-390, 394, 397

1–2 — 18, 110, 117, 128, 137*, 138, 143*, 144, 149, 156*, 225, 246, 317*, 329, 331, 348, 459, *

1–3 — 10, 434

1–4 — 159*, 231*, 235*, 238*

1–9 — 90

1–11 — 3, 19-21, 53-54, 59, 70, 77, 79, 84, 91, 96, 100-101, 103-104, 131-134, 132*, 133*, 135*, 136*, 140, 140*, 142-149, 143*-146*, 152, 153*-154*, 161-162, 161*, 174*, 216*, 256*, 268*, 271*, 286*, 316, 318, 325, 326*, 327, 329, 331, 333, 335, 341, 345, 369-371, 401, 412, 427-428, 435, 454, 456, 459

1–15 — 135*, 140*, 143*, 145*, 151*-153*, 155*-157*, 159*, 203, 203*, 225*, 230*, 232*, 235*, 265*, 267*, 270*, 284*, 287*

1–17 — 203*, 235*, 238*

2 — 136*, 146, 148, 151, 155, 155*, 159, 160, 230*, 235, 237, 245, 333, 362

3 — 119-120, 132, 147, 152, 155, 244, 356-357, 367-368, 384, 397

4 — 179, 285, 288, 293*, 295

5 — 204-205, 285-286, 293*, 295, 369

5–9, 11 — 298

5 and 11 — 3, 18, 59, 283, 283*286-292, 295-298, 300-309, 309*-311*, 325, 326*, 333, 335, 348, 454

6–8 — 51, 147, 252

7–9 — 408

11 — 205, 285, 288, 296, 298, 308, 311, 313

12 — 144-145

12–50 — 133, 142, 144-145

19 — 147, 183

49 — 153-154, 217

1:1 — 12, 30, 30*, 57, 94, 116, 133*, 179, 189-190, 198, 217*, 218, 225, 318, 320-321, 323, 331

1:1–2 — 157*

1:1–2:3 — 3, 143*, 149-150, 152, 156*, 163-164, 165*, 166, 168, 174, 176, 179, 183-184, 187, 189, 191, 191*, 192, 196, 200-201, 207, 212, 216-218, 220, 222-227, 224*-227*, 229, 229*, 233, 237, 237*-242*, 239-242, 244-246, 248-249, 362

1:1–2:4a — 165*

1:2 — 18, 73, 94, 97*, 98, 132, 134, 136, 190, 198, 225, 239*

1:2–5 — 146*

1:3 — 60-61, 64, 97*, 214, 218

1:3-31 — 218*

1:3, 6, 9, 14, 20, 24 —
214
1:4 — 224
1:4 — 64, 239
1:5 — 58, 65, 68-69,
224, 226*, 227,
274
1:6 — 31*
1:7 — 68
1:8 — 227
1:9 — 214
1:9, 11 — 214
1:10 — 136
1:11 — 219
1–11:26 — 231*, 234*,
243*, 264*, 328*
1:14 — 97*,190, 194
1:14–15 — 220-223
1:14–19 — 190*, 219
1:14 — 113, 157, 218-
219, 221-222,
226
1:14b — 190, 190*
1:14–19 — 190*
1:15 — 221-222, 232-
238
1:16–25 — 233
1:16 — 190*, 222
1:16b — 190
1:16–17 — 186*
1:17 — 222
1:17–18 — 222
1:18–19 — 236-237
1:18 — 236, 358
1:20 — 225
1:20–21 — 380
1:21 — 189
1:21–22 — 237
1:24–25 — 237
1:24, 26 — 214
1:26 — 120, 383
1:26–28 —237
1:27 — 97*,113, 134*,

146, 189
1:29 — 113
1:29–30 — 370, 392
1:30 — 380
1:31 — 2-8, 358, 383,
401, 413, 420,
423
2:1–3 — 157*, 241-
242, 244-245,
323, 362
2:2 — 65, 146, 201,
246, 359, 359*
2:2a — 242
2:2–3 — 207-208, 229,
333, 242, 245
2:2–3....1:31 — 208
2:3 — 189, 359, 359*
2:4 — 35, 97*, 145,
151-152, 201,
217, 228-230,
230*, 335*
2:4b — 231
2:4b–6 — 231
2:4b–7 — 231
2:4–25 — 151, 217,
229, 229*, 232-
233, 236, 236*,
237, 239
2:4–3:24 — 230
2:5 — 228, 229, 229*,
230, 230*, 231*,
232, 239, 239*,
240, 240*, 246-
248
2:5–6 — 230, 232
2:5–7 — 229*
2:6 — 230, 230*
2:6–7 — 231
2:7 — 97*,159, 231-
233, 235, 237,
375*, 380
2:7a — 233
2:7–25 — 231, 236

2:7–9 — 232
2:7b–9 — 232-233,
235
2:7a — 233
2:7b–9 — 232-233,
235
2:8–9 — 235, 237
2:8 — 232-233, 235-
236, 267
2:9 — 233
2:10–14 — 232-233
2:15 —232-233, 235,
235*, 236, 238
2:15–25 — 232
2:16–25 — 233
2:17 — 120, 201
2:18 — 236
2:18–19 — 236-237
2:19 — 155, 234, 236-
238, 238*
2:19a — 236-238
2:19b — 236
2:22 — 237
2:23 — 234
2:23a — 234
2:23a–24 — 234
2:24 — 134*, 146, 234,
368
2:25— 233, 234
3:1–24 — 118
3:5 — 201
3:14 — 370
3:17–19 — 397
4:17 — 177*
4:17–18 — 284
4:25–26 — 284
4:26 — 305
5:1 — 145, 335*
5:1–18 — 148
5:1–32 — 296
5:3 — 304
5:5 — 69, 148, 192,
204, 229, 244

5:28 — 304
5:32 — 296
6:1–8 — 134*
6:3 — 121, 204
6:4 — 205
6:5–9:29 — 192
6:7 — 255
6:7, 13 — 100*
6:9 — 145
6–9 — 95, 138, 456
6:10 — 304
6:11 —204
6:12 — 243*
6:12–13 — 255
6:15 — 375
7:4 — 204, 255, 269
7:6 — 260
7:6–10 — 280
7:6, 11 — 179
7:7 — 260
7:8 — 260
7–8 — 254
7:9 — 260
7:10 — 261
7:10–23 —255
7:11 — 204, 251, 261,
    261*, 264*, 267,
    273, 275, 280-
    281
7:11b — 225*
7:11–8:14 — 272
7:11–18 — 267, 280
7:11–24 — 269
7:12 — 262, 267, 280
7:12, 17 — 269, 273
7:13 — 262, 304
7:13–16 — 274
7:14 — 262
7:15 — 262, 375*
7:16 — 262
7:17 — 263, 264*,
    268
7:17–24 — 255

7:18 — 263, 269
7:18a — 263*
7:19 — 263
7:19–20 — 256, 256*,
    264*, 280
7:19–22 — 267
7:19–8:4 — 280
7:20 — 263
7:21 — 263
7:22 — 263
7:23 — 264, 264*
7:23b — 264*
7:24 — 204, 264, 264*-
    265*, 273*, 281
8:1 — 243*, 264
8:2 — 264*, 265, 272,
    275, 281
8:3 — 252, 265, 265*,
    269, 271-272
    281
8:4 — 264*, 265, 273
8:4–5, 13–14 — 179
8:5 — 265, 272-273,
    280
8:5–12 — 265, 267,
    280
8:6 — 265, 273
8:7 — 265, 272-273
8:8 — 265, 273
8:9 — 265, 266*
8:10 — 266, 273
8:10, 12 — 158*
8:11 — 265*, 266
8:12 — 266, 273
8:13 — 266-267, 267*,
    273, 280
8:13–14 — 267, 280
8:14 — 267, 273, 280
8:15 — 304
8:21 — 243*
8:22 — 202
9:3 — 383
9:18 — 304

9:29 — 204
10:1 — 145, 304,
    335*
10:25 — 205, 291, 304,
    312
11:10 — 145, 304
11:10–26 — 285, 296
11:18 — 312
11:26 — 296
11:27 — 145
11:27–32 — 304
11:31 — 238
11:32 — 204, 296
12:1 — 238
12:1b–3 — 239
12:4 — 64
13:3 — 147
14:1 — 113, 204, 218
23:1–2 — 179
25:7 — 204
25:12 — 145
25:19 — 145
26:1 — 120, 204, 383
26:15 — 204
26:18 — 204
30:14 — 205
31:44–54 — 177-178
32:26, 32–33 — 177
35:28 — 204
35:29 — 204
36:1 — 145
37:2 — 145
47:8–9 — 204
47:13–22 — 178
48:1–18 — 217
49:2–33 — 217
49:10 — 179
50:1–23 — 217
50:3 — 202
50:24 — 182
50:25 — 182

Exodus
3–6 — 317
3:14 — 116
9:18 — 181
10:6 — 181
13:19 — 183
14:21–22 — 240
14:26 — 270
15:8a — 16
20:8–11 — 90
20:11 — 13, 242-244,
      329, 348, 350,
      367
20:8–11 — 90, 98, 159,
      194, 202, 227,
      359
20:9–10 — 243
23:12 — 383
24:18 — 202
31:12–17 — 202
31:14–17 — 227
31:15–16 — 243
31:17 — 243, 243*
33:5 — 36

Leviticus
23 — 61
11:5–6 — 186
17:11 — 375

Numbers
7 — 228
7:10 — 228, 255, 260-
      261
7:12 — 227*
7:84 — 228
11:4–34 — 177*
11:32 — 202
16:21 — 45, 36
16:31 — 262*, 268
17:8 — 155
21:26–30 — 178

Deuteronomy
32 — 390
2:9 — 183
2:10–11 — 178
2:10, 12, 20 — 182*
3:14 — 177*
4:2 — 111
12:32 — 111
14:7 — 186
16:4 — 227
18:9–14 — 143
24:1, 3 — 340
25:5–10 — 177
32:2 — 257

Joshua
4:1–9 — 172
4:1–9 — 178
4:6–7 — 172
4:18 — 270
6:25 — 178
6:26 — 180
7:25–26 — 178
7:26 — 177*
8:28 — 181
8:29 — 181
8:31 — 178
8:34 — 179
9:27 — 181
11:10 — 182*
14:6–14 — 178
14:15 — 178, 182*
15:15 — 182*
21:44 — 361
22:4 — 361
23:1 — 361
23:6 — 179
24:2 — 303*
24:26 — 179
24:32 — 183

Judges
1:10 — 178

1:10–11, 23 — 182*
1:26 — 177
3:2 — 182*
15:19 — 261*, 268

Ruth
4:7 — 177, 182*
4:8 — 177
4:18 — 179
4:18–22 — 285

1 Samuel
1:26 — 317
2:31 — 180
6:18 — 181
9:9 — 182*
27:6 — 181
30:24–25 — 177

2 Samuel
6:8 — 177*

1 Kings
2:27 — 180
6:1 — 179
8:8 — 181
9:13 — 177*
9:20–21 — 182
12:19 — 182
13:2 — 180
16:36 — 180
17:17 — 375*

2 Kings
23 — 179-180
1:17 — 180
2:22 — 181-182
6:8–12 — 172-173
7:19 — 268
8:22 — 182
14:6 — 178-179
14:7 — 177*
16:6 — 182

23:16 — 180
23:17 — 180
23:21 — 179

1 Chronicles
1–9 — 179
1:18 — 311
1:24 — 311
2:5, 9–15 — 285
4:40 — 182*
9:20 — 182*
13:11 — 177*

2 Chronicles
9:11 — 182*
17:9 — 179
20:6 — 117
20:10–12 — 183
35:12 — 178

Ezra
6:18 — 178
9:8 — 36

Nehemiah
8:1 — 178-179
13:5 — 182*
13:31 — 179

Job
14 — 257, 376-377
12:7–10 — 370
14:7–12 — 377
14:8 — 376-377
14:11 — 267*
14:19 — 257
24:8 — 257
34:14 — 117

Psalms
95 — 361
104 — 153
6:1 — 45*

8:2 — 317*
14:1 — 122
19:1–2 — 370
19:7–9, 119, 140 — 119
24:1 — 117
29:10 — 365*
32:6 — 259
36:7 — 261*
53:1 — 122
55:17 — 62
62:11 — 117
74:15* — 261*
78:15 —261*
90:4 — 39-40, 58, 366
92:1 — 40
95:7–11 — 245
95:11 — 361
97:6 — 370
104:14–16 — 383
104:18 — 186*
104:27–28 — 383
118:22 — 317*
119:18 — 124
119:89 — 117
119:130 — 124
119:142, 151, 160 — 117
121:6 — 190
148:5 — 63

Proverbs
1:7a — 171
12:10 — 383
27:13 — 257
30:26 — 186*

Ecclesiastes
1:6 — 269
3:19 — 375*
3:21 — 375*

Isaiah
4:6 — 257
11:6–8 — 384
11:9 — 268
I2:17 — 40
16:3 — 201*
19:5 — 267*
24:18 — 268
35:6 — 261*
36:1 — 179
51:10 — 261*
63:12 — 261*
65:25 — 368
66:1–2 — 435

Jeremiah
25:11–12 — 180
50:38 — 267*

Habakkuk
3:6 — 366

Daniel
2 — 42
2:4 — 43*
9:2–19 — 180
9:26 — 259
12:1 — 322*

Hosea
6:2 — 40

Amos
7:4 — 261*

Zechariah
14:4 — 268

Malachi
3:10 — 268

Matthew
1 — 287

4:1–10 — 317
4:4 — 315
4:6–7 — 317*
5:18 — 317
5:21 — 369*
5:21–22, 27–28, 33–
   34, 38–39, 43–44
   — 149*
6:26–28 — 383
6:26–30 — 401*
7:24–27 — 315
10:15 — 316
10:29–31 — 401
12:40–41 — 316
13:35 — 323
15:1–9 — 317
17:5 — 345
18:16 — 316
19:3–6 — 316
19:4 — 146, 319, 333,
   337-338, 340
19:4–6 — 134*
19:4–8 — 319
19:8 — 319, 337
19:16–19 — 316
21:12–17 — 317
22:37–39 — 316
24:14 — 320
24:21 — 321, 327*,
   337
24:35–37 — 365
24:37–38 — 147
24:37–39 — 134*,
   320
24:38–39 — 316
25:34 — 323

Mark
2:2 — 359*
7:5–13 — 317
7:8–13 — 317
8:27–16:20 — 322*
10:2 — 340

10:2–6 — 318, 328
10:3–4 — 340
10:3–9 — 316
10:5–9 — 327*
10:6 — 318-322, 325*-
   327*, 329-331,
   336-341, 345,
   356*
10:6–8 — 146, 153,
   318, 334, 345
12:14 — 317
13:19 — 320, 321*,
   322, 322*, 325*,
   326, 328, 330-
   331, 336-339,
   339*, 341, 345,
   351*, 356*
13:19–20 — 318
13:24–26 — 320
13:30–32 — 320
13:31 — 320
16:15 — 356*

Luke
11 — 338
1:2 — 320*
3:36 — 288, 311*
4:25 — 316-317
4: 25–27 — 316
6:3–4 — 317
9:8, 19 — 369*
9:25 — 321*
9:35 — 345
11:50 — 327*
11:50–51 — 316, 318,
   322-323, 325*-
   326*, 328, 338-
   341, 339*, 345
11:51 — 147
17:26–27 — 147
17:28–32 — 316
17:28–29, 32 — 147
24:25–27 — 316

24:45 — 124

John
1:1–3 — 319
1:3 — 13, 321*
1:9–10 — 323*
1:10 — 321*
3:3 — 317
3:14 — 316
3:16 — 354*
3:3 — 150, 316-317,
   319, 337
4:24 — 167
5:45–47 — 317, 345
6:25 — 320*
6:32–33, 49 — 316
6:38 — 321*
6:64 — 320*
8:31–32 — 345
8:44 — 319, 337
10:34–35 — 316
11:27 — 323*
12:24 — 377
12:47–50 — 345
12:35–36, 46
13:1 — 321*
13:3 — 321*
14:6 — 317
15:18–19 — 321*
15:27 — 320*
16:4 — 320*
16:28 — 321*
16:33 — 321*
17:5 — 321*, 323,
   323*
17:6 — 321*
17:14 — 321*
17:21 — 321*
17:24 — 323, 323*,
   337

Acts
3:21 — 113, 349, 368, 370, 384
7:2 — 238
14:15 — 350
14:15–17 — 350
17:24 — 321*, 324*
17:24–31 — 114, 350
21:16 — 369*
26:4 — 320*

Romans
1:18–20 — 102, 320, 370, 431, 433
1:18–25 — 351
1:20 — 352*, 356*
1:25 — 122, 351*, 356*
1:28 — 120
3:4 — 7
4:17 — 63, 65
5:12 — 354*-355*
5:12–14 — 147
5:12–21 — 134*
5:13 — 355
6:23 — 355*
8:1–5 — 122
8:1–22 — 355*
8:5–11 — 122
8:18–21 — 356*
8:18–23 — 354*
8:18–27 — 356*
8:19–21 — 382, 397
8:19–23 — 147*, 358*, 434
8:19–25 — 383
8:39 — 356*
10:9–13 — 109*
13:1 — 117

1 Corinthians
2:12–13 — 124
6:16 —368

11:3–12 — 355*, 368
11:8–9 — 146*
11:9 — 351*
15:17–19 — 13
15:21–22 — 368
15:22 — 147*
15:45 — 351*, 368

2 Corinthians
3:14 — 120
4:4 — 120, 122
4:6 — 146
5:17 — 356*
10:3–5 — 80
11:3 — 368
11:14 – 159*

Galatians
2:11–14 — 80
6:15 — 356*

Ephesians
1:4 — 319, 323-324
1:18–19 — 124
2:7 — 369*
2:10, 15 — 351*
3:5 — 369*
3:9 — 351*
3:21 — 369*
4:24 — 351*
4:11–12 — 125
4:17 — 120
4:18 — 120
5:31 — 368

Colossians
1:15 — 356*
1:15–20 — 384
1:16 — 351*
1:16–17 — 13, 324
1:21 — 120
1:23 — 356*
1:26 — 369*

2:4 — 120
2:8 — 80, 120
2:18 — 120
3:2 — 122
3:10 — 351*

1 Thessalonians
5:21 — 391

2 Thessalonians
1:9 — 122
2:13 — 319

1 Timothy
1:4 — 369
2:11–14 — 147, 355*
2:13–14 — 134*
4:3 — 351*
4:7 — 369
6:3–4 — 345
6:5 — 120
6:17 — 353*
6:20 — 7
6:20–21 — 9, 80

2 Timothy
1:9 — 324*
1:14 — 369
2:12–15 — 368
3:8 — 120
3:16 — 110
3:17 — 110
4:2 — 7, 12, 125
4:10 — 353*

Titus
1:2 — 324*1:14 — 369
1:15 — 120
2:12 — 353*
3:3 — 122

Philemon
4:15 — 320*

Hebrews
4 — 146, 241, 245-246,
   323, 358-361,
   364, 366, 371
1:2 — 65, 369, 369*
1:10 — 319, 323*
3:11–4:11 — 361
4:3 — 245, 323, 364
4:3–4 — 364
4:3–11 — 245, 361,
   369
4:4 — 323
4:13 — 356
9:11 — 356*
9:25–26 — 363
9:26 — 323
11:3 — 57, 59, 63,
   65, 148, 359, 361,
   369
11:3–4 — 369
11:3–7— 148
12:24 — 147*

James
3:9 — 369

1 Peter
1:10-12 — 185*
1:20 — 323-324, 337
2:3 — 356*
2:49 — 364
3:15 — 397, 400
3:18 — 364
3:18–20 — 355*, 364
3:20 — 148
4:19 — 351*

2 Peter
1:2–4 — 128
1:16 — 369

2:3 — 366
2:4–9 — 355*, 364
2:5 — 148
3:1–6 — 131
3:3–6, 7
3:3–7 — 355*
3:3–8 — 364
3:4 — 319, 356*
3:5 — 366
3:5–6 — 134*, 148
3:6 — 278
3:7 — 353*
3:8 — 39, 58, 366

1 John
1:1 — 150, 319, 337-
   338
2:7 — 125, 320*, 337
2:13–14 — 319, 337
2:15–17 — 321*
2:24 — 320*
2:27 — 125
3:8 — 319, 337
3:11 — 320*, 337

2 John
5–6 — 320*

Jude
3 — 24, 248
11 — 147*
12 — 379
14 — 355*, 369

Revelation
3:14 — 319, 356*
4:11 — 351*
10:6 — 351*
12:9 — 147*, 369
13:8 — 323, 390
14:6–7 — 367
17:8 — 323
20:2 — 369

20:2—3 — 147*
21:1–5 — 367
21:4 — 384
22:2–3 — 368
22:3 — 367, 384

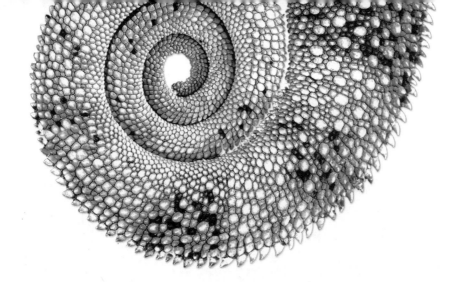

creationmuseum

www.AnswersinGenesis.org